GREAT CASES
OF
INTERPOL

GREAT CASES OF
INTERPOL

Selected
by the
Editors of
Reader's
Digest
Condensed
Books

The Reader's Digest Association·Pleasantville, New York·Cape Town·Hong Kong·London·Montreal·Sydney

The publishers gratefully acknowledge the advice and assistance of Monsieur Jean Nepote, former secretary-general of Interpol, as well as that of numerous Interpol officials in the planning and preparation of this book. The publishers, authors and researchers are equally appreciative of the cooperation provided by present and former police officers in many countries around the world, who aided their efforts in detailing the cases that are presented in these pages.

The seven cases of Interpol contained in this book are factual. Because of the unique nature of Interpol's operation and the necessity for secrecy in sensitive areas, however, the true names of some of the characters mentioned in these stories cannot be revealed, and certain facts about them have been changed. Such persons include law enforcement officers of Interpol and of various member nations, those involved in committing or abetting the crimes detailed here, as well as the actual or intended victims of those crimes. In addition, the names of several business establishments, public and private institutions and geographic locations have been altered, and some dialogue that was not recorded verbatim has been reconstructed.

CONTENTS

INTRODUCTION

CARMO reads the code word. Its meaning: "Please send all relevant information you may possess . . . about this person, in particular his criminal record, true identity and criminal activities."

So begins the Telex message, one of the thousands that will fly each year from Interpol radio transmitters outside Paris across countries and continents to police headquarters in more than one hundred and twenty-five nations around the world.

In this century crime has known no boundaries either. This was strikingly illustrated by the situation in the United States during the 1920s and 1930s. An unprecedented outburst of banditry and bank robbery was aided by the advent of fast cars that enabled criminals to rob a bank in one state and then flee to a neighboring one without being apprehended. Local police officers could not cope adequately with the situation. The answer was the development of the Federal Bureau of Investigation, whose agents were given far-reaching power to pursue and arrest fugitives wherever they might be found in the United States.

Elsewhere in the world, a similar crime situation was creating difficulties for various national police departments. What could be done about the criminal who committed a crime in one country and promptly moved on to another?

It was to handle this problem that the International Criminal Police Commission, or ICPC, was formally established in 1923. The First World War had proved something of a setback to its development, and although considerable progress was made between the wars, international police cooperation suffered another grievous blow during the Second World War. Then at a conference in Brussels in 1946 new life was breathed into the concept. Ten years later the ICPC became the International Criminal Police Organization. Because a short identifying name was needed for telegraph and cable messages, the word Interpol—a contraction of "international police"—had been adopted. It was picked up by the press and in 1956, when the present constitution was developed, it became the name by which the organization was generally known.

Still, over the years there has been one completely false image transmitted to the public by way of films and television concerning the work of the organization. That is the idea of The Man from Interpol, a freewheeling detective who moves from country to country, operating wherever he wants and making arrests from Hong Kong to London to New York. Interpol does not transcend the activities of an individual nation's police force.

In practice, each member country has what is known as a national central bureau, staffed by police officers of that country and closely tied to Interpol's General Secretariat headquarters in St. Cloud, near Paris. While the actual police work on any given case is carried out by the police of each country concerned, Interpol aids that work by acting as a clearinghouse for information, by providing technical assistance and by serving as a major communications link among the bureaus. Because Interpol cannot supersede the laws of its member countries, it must operate in certain clearly defined areas relating principally to crimes such as drug trafficking, art theft, bank robbery, counterfeiting, forgery and smuggling, and exclude areas that are ostensibly political in nature such as international terrorism.

The stories that follow are based on solid fact and diligent research. They perfectly illustrate the wide-ranging scope of Interpol's activities—from the intercontinental dragnet for a convicted murderer in *The Search for Geoffroy* to the cracking of the counterfeiting ring of *Big Charlie's Funny Money*, in which Interpol helped coordinate the efforts of the Australian, American, Swiss, British and Thai police. The seven cases related here are some of the finest examples from the hundreds Interpol has in its files, and each demonstrates the partnership between Interpol and the national police forces of its member countries.

Among the frequent messages that those countries exchange, there is often the final Interpol code word GIRID—"Thank you for your cooperation." More than just an expression of gratitude, it is time and again the final punctuation to another case successfully concluded.

Jack Higgins

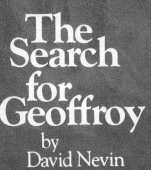

The Search for Geoffroy

by
David Nevin

PAINTINGS BY
STAN HUNTER

The day before Christmas, 1971 ... Through the front door of St. Vincent de Paul penitentiary near Montreal, Canada, stepped prisoner number 7538. He walked slowly, his hand affectionately clasping that of the shy, quietly pretty young woman he had just been given special Christmas leave to marry. Together they got into a waiting car.

Five days later Joseph Yves Geoffroy, serving a life sentence for murder, would become the subject of a worldwide manhunt. Seeking him were the police of more than a hundred nations, all members of the International Criminal Police Organization—Interpol.

In this vivid and suspenseful true account, magazine reporter and editor David Nevin traces the trails of both the hunted and the hunters to the moment of their fateful confrontation.

CHAPTER 1

THE FEDERAL PENITENTIARY in St. Vincent de Paul, across the Rivière des Prairies from Montreal proper, stands like a dark castle on an open hill, its walls a thousand feet long on each side. They are of stone, topped by a chain link fence that is topped by strands of barbed wire. Guards with sniper rifles look down on the walls from towers that soar in each corner under octagonal roofs. A railroad passes nearby and diesel horns break the icy air and remind the men inside of all the simple, wonderful, distant places waiting in the world. On the day before Christmas, 1971, the open fields around the prison were white and still. There would be more snow soon, for the sky was dirty and low. The river at the bottom of the fields was solid; one could walk to Montreal. A cold wind whispered along the walls and snapped the maple leaf of Canada that flew near a small entrance building that seemed buried in the front wall. A Christmas tree stood beside the building and a few lights winked dimly in the cold.

In the early hours of that morning, a car came to the entrance, its tires crunching packed snow. The driver stayed at the wheel, the car engine running, and a woman slipped out and opened the door of the building. She was small and slender, almost buried in her heavy coat, and her huge eyes looked strained. She entered a small anteroom and approached a tiny window. Behind it sat a single guard. Beyond him were iron doors, firmly locked.

"Your name?" The guard had a cigarette in his lips, and ashes fell.

"Carmen Parent."

"Prisoner's name?"

"Joseph Yves Geoffroy," she whispered. She gave a number.

The guard's pencil scratched on the clipboard. "Put your purse in a locker," he said, gesturing with his head to a row of small lockers to her left.

"No."

He looked up, alert, interested for the first time. He was a short, dark-haired man with sharp, knowing eyes.

"I—I'm not going in. He's coming out." Her voice was small.

"Release, you mean? On Friday? On Christmas Eve?"

"No. He has a temporary leave. Over Christmas. It lasts fifty hours."

The guard grunted. He looked as if he didn't approve of these leaves. She stood hugging her purse as he picked up the phone. Always, when visiting Geoffroy, she had been forced to leave the purse in one of the little lockers. "They're a regular pharmacy, lady," the guard had told her the first time. "Full of dope." She had winced at his grin. She didn't belong here, it wasn't her kind of place, they were not her kind of people. Not Yves's, either—and he was inside. He had been for more than a year.

The iron doors opened. Yves Geoffroy stepped through. He was thirty-eight, short, though taller than she, and he weighed two hundred pounds. But he didn't seem fat. Rather he was burly, solid, powerful. His face was round, and through the window she saw that he had trimmed his drooping mustache and that his blue eyes were nearly liquid with pleasure, though they could be chill and distant. Then, behind him, she saw Mr. Moreau. He was director of the Office of Visits and Correspondence; Geoffroy's prison work assignment was as his clerk. It was his support that had made this joyous Christmas leave possible. "Merry Christmas," he said to Geoffroy, "though I suppose that is assured, eh?" The guard looked up, surprised. Prison officials usually spoke to inmates in quite different tones.

"This is the happiest day of my life, Mr. Moreau," Geoffroy said. His voice seemed melodious. "I'm sure you know that."

"Glad I could help," Moreau said, "and good luck." He opened the door to the anteroom. "Merry Christmas," he said to Carmen.

"Carmen," Geoffroy said, taking both her hands. His big, warm voice always reassured her.

Carmen wanted to thank Moreau, but Geoffroy seemed to dominate the little anteroom. "See you in fifty hours, sir," he said, laughing, "and not one moment sooner."

Then the couple went outside, in the wind that moved the forlorn Christmas tree. The car, driven by Philip Leclerc, an old classmate of Geoffroy's, was warm. Immediately it started down the hill toward the river road; the row of slender poplars was bare and the river was all white. Geoffroy did not look at the gray walls, with their barbed wire tops and gun towers black against the metal sky.

After half a mile the car turned in at St. Vincent de Paul Church, a tall building overlooking the river, and stopped at the rear door. The trio entered the sacristy and waited for the priest to arrive. At last he appeared, fully vested for Mass, chasuble in place over his long white robe.

"Father Teterrin," he said, introducing himself. He glanced at a card in his hand. "Mademoiselle Carmen Parent?"

"Yes, Father."

"And Joseph Yves Geoffroy?"

"Yes." Geoffroy bowed slightly, smiling.

"Come. We will begin."

The priest led them from the sacristy into a tiny chapel directly behind it. It would seat about twenty-five, more than enough for the little party, which now had been joined by Geoffroy's sister; the legally required number of persons was present. The room was plain, the pews short. The stations of the cross were painted on ceramic tile neatly set in wood.

The Mass began, as always, with the liturgy; soon, after a short, impersonal homily, the priest would insert the wedding vows and complete the ceremony that would make them man and wife. Standing in the quiet room, listening to the priest, Geoffroy took Carmen's hand.

Geoffroy had been married before, to a woman named Louise Côté, and had three children. But he and Carmen had come a long way together. It was she with whom he had fallen in love as he fell out of love with Louise. Indeed, he had been with Carmen the night

Louise died. He had left Carmen at eleven o'clock and gone home and, he said, gone to bed.

It was sometime later when the trouble started in Louise's bedroom, the man and the woman struggling by the light of the flickering television set, their grunts and whimpers punctuated by the screams and shots of an ancient movie. The man slapped her hard, and when she yelled in rage and fear, he clapped a hard hand over her mouth and nose, stifling her cries until he broke her breath. She fought, kicking, her small body snapping, biting the hand that held her, but the power in his arms and shoulders was overwhelming.

Geoffroy always insisted that he had found Louise, lying dead with her false teeth snatched loose in her mouth, after some intruder had fled. Carmen believed him. The state did not, however, nor did a jury, and Geoffroy was sentenced to life imprisonment in the penitentiary from which, this morning, he had come.

But already, Carmen's hand warm in his, the prison seemed remote. The priest finished his admonitions and advices as to how the two before him should conduct their lives, and moved on to the vows that united them.

MINUTES LATER, LECLERC'S car slipped over the river and across the main island of Montreal proper, past all the simple signs of people living that were joyous to see after a year behind walls. They ran down Boulevard Pie IX, past hundreds of Montreal's typical small apartment buildings, three and four stories high, all similar and yet individual, with bright touches of stone or paint or curving iron stairs. They seemed French, and Geoffroy, French to his core, though quite bilingual, found them comfortable. The car climbed onto the Jacques-Cartier Bridge, that great old iron lacework across the St. Lawrence. Below was the big geodesic dome built for Expo 67, luminous in the snow-threatening light. Smiling, Geoffroy gestured; he and Carmen had met at the World's Fair grounds in 1968 and had often gone back there.

The car reached the suburb of Longueuil, turned onto Ste. Catherine Street, and stopped before the small brick apartment house where Carmen lived. Leclerc kissed her and shook hands with Geoffroy and drove away; they were alone.

They made love and had a good lunch which Carmen had planned carefully and a bottle of wine and made love again. Snow flurries blew outside. Late in the afternoon, as daylight faded, Geoffroy took the suitcases from the closet. While Carmen packed, putting their heaviest clothes in the two biggest cases, Geoffroy sat at her neat little desk and began to write. He drafted the letter with care, pausing for the right phrases, and then signed his name, the G in Geoffroy drawn large and looking jaunty, that of a man newly in bloom. At seven o'clock a cab with a white diamond-shaped sign on its roof appeared, and they went out. The lights of Christmas Eve glowed up and down the street through the snow gusts, but no one was about and the street was empty. "Dorval Airport," Geoffroy said.

They sped down the highway along the St. Lawrence and over the Champlain Bridge, the lights of Montreal stacked on the right; wound through interwoven freeways, and came finally to the long, massive terminal building with its square control tower on top. New snow was beginning to accumulate. "British Overseas Airways," Geoffroy said, and the car stopped at the entrance marked 4.

Carmen stepped out briskly and signaled a porter. Geoffroy opened the other door and walked quietly toward entrance 3. Carmen went into the bright lobby, with its round metallic pillars and glistening floor. A small child in snow boots and down pants was running, shrieking, to and from a tall, raffish-looking man with a beard, who laughed and flung her up and set her down again. Everyone was watching them and no one noticed Carmen as she presented two tickets at the bright blue BOAC counter.

"Yes," said the young clerk, looking at the tickets. "Two for London on BOAC flight number six hundred at ten p.m. connecting with—ah, let me see—yes, British European Airways flight seven eight two for Oslo. Return open. Right?" He was quite impersonal.

Carmen nodded and, as Geoffroy had coached her, said, "My husband is buying a paper." The clerk fixed claim checks to the five suitcases, humming to himself, and in a moment he handed back the tickets.

"There you are, and merry Christmas."

"Oh," she said, surprised at the greeting. "Thank you." But he had turned to the next in line. She walked toward the gate and saw Geoffroy ahead, blocky as the pillar he stood beside. He was reading a paper. He folded it neatly as she passed and fell in beside her.

The airport crowd was thinning late on this Christmas Eve and no one seemed to notice them as they boarded the last flight for London. The 707 was crowded. Geoffroy put Carmen on the aisle and took a middle seat beside her. He kept his coat on, the collar turned up around his face. They sat very still, and after what seemed a long time the engines started and they heard the door close. The lights outside began to move. The plane taxied slowly, snow gusts sweeping over its wings. It paused a long time at the end of the runway and then turned back toward the terminal.

"Ladies and gentlemen," the pilot's neutral voice said, "the snow is a bit of a problem and the ceiling has closed in below limits. I think it will lift, but we're going to go back to the gate for now."

"Looks as if we may get to spend the night right here," the man in the window seat said.

Geoffroy looked at him. "I hope not," he said in a slow controlled way. "I think we will leave." Something in his manner persuaded the man not to speak again; later, when Geoffroy's picture was in all the newspapers, he would recognize it and come forward.

"Yves," Carmen whispered, "do you think they've found—"

"No," he said firmly. He heard panic in her voice. Then, speaking softly, "Relax, relax. No one is looking for us. It is not as if I were a criminal, after all." Indeed, he did not feel like a felon; he felt like a tourist, with some of the self-importance of going abroad the first time. "Come on," he added eagerly. "Let's look at these brochures."

The plane was forty minutes late. They watched the gate. It was like waiting for the pain to start in the dentist's chair. But no one came aboard and no one seemed to notice them. Then the plane went booming down the runway, snow boiling over its wings, and swept up over Montreal; almost immediately the gloom closed over the city's lights. After a while Carmen got up, and when she returned, Geoffroy put her in the middle. They talked in French, which their seatmate did not understand, but he noticed that they pored over the travel folders from Norway. Carmen napped against Geoffroy's shoulder, but he sat bolt upright, still in his overcoat, eyes wide open, as dawn broke and the plane bored east toward the rising sun.

It was Christmas morning when the engines stopped at the ramp in London. This was the testing time. If anyone had seen them, or even called the apartment and found them gone and made a casual check at the airport, there would be men waiting for them here. In the finality of the dying engines, they stood and followed the other passengers into a big arrival room. An officer took their passports. He was a slender, sad-eyed man in a nondescript uniform. He glanced from the pictures to their faces and closed the books with a little snap. "Well," he said, smiling faintly. "Welcome to England."

A few minutes later they were in a cab, bowling strangely along the left side of the street, bound for the hotel where they would await the next day's flight to Oslo. Geoffroy put his arm around Carmen's shoulders and felt her body shuddering in long, silent spasms. "It's all right now," he said softly. "We're free and clear."

ON JANUARY 10, ON THE third floor of the Royal Canadian Mounted Police national headquarters in Ottawa, a stout man with glasses sat down before a shortwave radio with a Morse code key. He sent quickly, the rolling fist moving steadily, thirty-five words a minute in dots and dashes. The message flew in seconds to an antenna on the roof of a bright, glassy building that stands on a hill at St. Cloud, overlooking the lights of Paris. On the top floor an operator facing a console similar to the one in Ottawa wrote out the message as it came in. The building is the world headquarters of the International Criminal Police Organization, which is best known by its radio designation, Interpol.

The message from Ottawa had been sent in an international police code, a shorthand used for compression rather than secrecy: BOFAK GOLKA OF GEOFFROY GEGBI JOSEPH YVES EPKAL 16/7/33 MONTREAL ERBAL FOFTI GRUGU 172CM 91KG . . . To the trained eyes of the operator in Paris it said:

PLEASE INITIATE AN INVESTIGATION TO DETERMINE THE WHEREABOUTS OF GEOFFROY FIRST NAME JOSEPH YVES BORN 16/7/33 IN MONTREAL, A CANADIAN CITIZEN STANDING 172 CENTIMETERS WEIGHING 91 KILOS HEAVY BUILD BLUE EYES BROWN HAIR POSSIBLY ACCOMPANIED BY HIS WIFE FORMERLY PARENT FIRST NAME CARMEN ANDREE BORN 26/6/44 STE. BEATRIX CANADA CANADIAN PASSPORT JB 342144 ISSUED 29/6/71. . . .

The message explained the situation and ended: YOUR ASSISTANCE REQUIRED WITH A VIEW TO LOCATING THIS PERSON.

The man who received the message made a clean copy and passed it on. Before long, in a form now constituting a request from Interpol, the news of Yves Geoffroy and his new wife was flashing around the world. First the flow of words was whipped south to a pasture outside the village of St. Martin d'Abbat in rural France, eighty miles south of Paris, where a giant antenna stood against the night, and from there it was transmitted to the national police forces of more than a hundred nations. Geoffroy and Carmen were tiny figures, fleeing alone across a checkerboard world. Of course, no national police force would pursue the matter actively until there were specific indications that the wanted person was in its own country. But the first net had been cast.

In Ottawa, the radio operator, Paul Ferrar, took a copy of his message and padded down the hall to John Burris' office. Burris was chief of Canada's National Central Bureau—its link with Interpol. Most national central bureaus are arms of the central police of the nation in question. Burris also was chief of the Criminal Investigation Bureau, Royal Canadian Mounted Police.

Ferrar, a civilian member of the RCMP, walked into Burris' office. "Confirmation of your message, sir," he said, putting the copy on Burris' desk.

Burris was adding sugar to his coffee, and he continued to shake the packet, stirring the cup as he read the message. He was a solid, steady man with pale blue eyes and a neat mustache, and he had tracked many men in difficult places.

"Thank you, Paul," he said. "We're going to find this one." Ferrar noticed that the glint of dry humor often present in Burris' face was missing today. He looked cold and intractable. "It may take a while, but we're going to find this one and bring him home."

CHAPTER 2

THERE IS AN ELEMENT of the poet in all of us, but it rarely comes to the surface. Yves Geoffroy was a determinedly mundane man who met a woman who unlocked the poet in him. And that was unusual, for Carmen Parent was a plain woman—a man who met her once commented on her "consuming mousiness"—upon whom ten thousand men might have looked without poetic impulse. But in Yves Geoffroy she produced a lyrical strain that made their small passion grand and thus lifted them both in ways they had never known or understood were possible, and she could not forget that, nor could he. Yet grand passion immediately took the mundane man from his depth. Now the human tidal currents of love, hate, rage, fear and, finally, murder surged about the man who hitherto had dealt in questions of his clothes and the quality of his meals. He was a wader by temperament caught now in a channel crossing.

Geoffroy came from a good middle-class Montreal family. A brother was a physician and another was an optometrist. Geoffroy graduated from the University of Montreal with a degree in law. One classmate was Jean-Pierre Goyer, who, when life turned down for Geoffroy, would be Solicitor General of Canada, the Cabinet officer responsible for correction and law enforcement. Another classmate was Philip Leclerc, who would acquire fame in his own way.

Geoffroy chose the branch of law that dealt with business and contracts rather than trial work. He was a notary. In time he opened his own business, with offices in a northern section of Montreal, buying and selling as opportunities arose, and counseling others. He married well. Louise Côté was a member of a prominent family in Montreal and Joliette, a suburb northeast of Montreal. She was a pretty woman, with dark hair cropped short around a slender face and a pointed jaw, who never weighed much more than a hundred pounds. They built a home at Lac Noir, near Joliette and about sixty-five miles from Montreal, to which Geoffroy commuted regularly. She joined Geoffroy in a small mail-order cake-decoration and kitchen-articles business which he had opened at Lac Noir, and made herself essential. In 1963, when Geoffroy was thirty, they had their first child, Philippe, and two more little boys followed. Geoffroy was a hearty eater and gradually his weight increased to two hundred pounds; in contrast to his slender wife, he seemed even heavier. There was nothing special about Geoffroy or his life, but neither was there reason to expect anything but his steady climb toward middle-class prosperity, his net worth expanding with his girth.

Despite these favorable signs, a thread of misfortune followed Geoffroy. The businesses did not take real hold; they weren't failing, but they remained anemic. The house at Lac Noir had burned and they built another on the same property. Later Geoffroy thought the fire had changed his wife's personality, but in any event his marriage was beginning to collapse. At thirty-five, when one's mortality begins to make itself felt, Geoffroy found himself suddenly afraid. His businesses were weak, his marriage was failing—life seemed to stretch emptily toward old age. Was this really all there was?

A diary he kept in this period, which later was published in Montreal, shows how ill equipped he was to deal with such a cosmic question. His reference frame was minute and his imagination, which might have let him address the whole of life, seemed frozen. And as his unhappiness grew, his perspective shrank into ever tighter focus on himself. In time the diary became a blind lament of self-pity, an itemization of his wife's failures and demands.

Yet even through the prism of Geoffroy's attention to himself, Louise emerges as a woman trapped in a disintegrating, frightening situation. Dependent, hurt, angry, she bursts from Geoffroy's pages— drinking too much, taunting him, wanting money and clothes, denouncing him to her friends, and all at once demanding affection and love, tears flowing, begging for entry to his bed. Almost primly he notes his reaction; he finds her disgusting, he sleeps more and more often at the apartment he has set up in his Montreal office.

In this frame of mind, when he was thirty-five Geoffroy met Carmen Parent. She was twenty-four years old, a physics teacher in a public school in Longueuil. Her photographs show a certain beauty which is not apparent to most people when they meet her; perhaps the camera catches some classic bone structure, or perhaps it reaches her soul. She was small and slender, with fluffy dark hair, and there was something sad and cautious in her large, luminous eyes. Geoffroy instantly saw the beauty that usually only cameras found—and she fell in love with the finality of a stone sinking into a well. She had been educated in a convent and had considered remaining in the order. Nothing like this had ever happened to her.

Someone introduced them on the grounds of Expo 67. It was August 8, 1968. They talked for a moment, and he was suddenly taken with this slender girl, demure, quiet, her voice like a whisper, her smile warm and gentle. He could tell in an instant that she would never act out the angry scenes his wife produced. And she saw him as suave, debonair—a man of the world who projected power and assurance that was leavened by warmth and gentleness.

A flower vendor passed. On impulse Geoffroy stopped the man, gave him a dollar, and took a single rose. He held it in both hands and presented it to her, a warm, quizzical and, she thought, tender expression on his face. Might he call her?

Carmen Parent thought it the most beautiful flower she had ever seen. Its pink petals were just beginning to unfold. A water drop stood on one petal like a tear. Carmen never forgot that rose. Later, in a courtroom filled with hostile strangers, she would whisper, "He gave me a rose." It explained everything.

She took the flower. "I would like that," she said in answer to his question. After the trouble, when she was much older in pain and experience, she would say of that meeting, "We were not strangers. It was as if we knew each other well from the beginning. It was extraordinary, and when you find something like that, it is worth waiting for."

They fitted each other, he filling and demanding, she vulnerable and open and yearning to please. Almost immediately they became lovers, though both testified that throughout this period their love was platonic. Perhaps the lack of physical release heightened its emotional intensity. Geoffroy saw her constantly. There were long drives to Sorel or the Laurentians or the Eastern Townships. There were plays and concerts and dinners in quiet restaurants in Old Montreal. Once he arrived with his smoking jacket, which she took wordlessly and hung in her closet; he was enchanted.

He turned to his pen to pour out his feelings. Poetry, of course, is more feeling than form, and while Geoffroy knew nothing of form, the feeling with which he grasped at his passion flowed in an utterly genuine way. Because it was genuine, it overwhelmed her. Daily she searched her mailbox for the envelopes addressed in his strong hand. Only six weeks after they met, he sang to her:

> Because: Your doe eyes beg for tenderness and softness
> Because: Your honesty is so great and rare
> Because: Your heart is so tender and so open
> Because: You are so little in my arms . . .
> Because: Your hair is like silk on my face . . .
> Because: Your lips are so soft on mine

Because: Your youth dazzles me as the sun
Because: When you cuddle your head on my shoulder, I dare not
    move, for fear of breaking the spell
Because: In such a little body such a great soul . . .
Because: Just your presence fulfills me and charms me . . .
Because: You are my only, my last hope for happiness . . .
Because: You brought back in me feelings I thought forever dead
Because: You showed me what a woman, a real woman could be
Because: Your silences and your looks are more eloquent than the
    most beautiful speeches
And mostly because you are "what you are"
Carmen, my beautiful love, I love you!

                                                Yves

She had never heard such things; this golden moment made an impression that all that happened later could not dim. He wrote her letters of thanks: she had awakened feelings unknown since boyhood, he had never expected to know passion again—it was her gift to him. "It had to be you, my love, to be able to light this feeling in my heart, my soul, my spirit." Of his wife he simply said that things were not good between them. Carmen readily accepted this welcome news. He began a diary letter to Carmen (quite separate from his diary of Louise's failings) in which he recorded his feelings.

"I will now go for my walk outside, before going to bed. I am taking you with me; there, in the dark, I will be able to have you all to myself." He saw her often, but turned insistently to his pen. "Come, my beautiful love," he sang, "come and walk with me, hand in hand, under the gaze of the cross that shines up there on the Sugar Loaf, and whom I ask, each time that I am here, to unite us and to protect us, for I love you so." He assured her of divine support for them as a couple. "I went to the chapel at 10:45 until 12:45 to count the collections as I do every Sunday. I went to Communion this morning: for you and for me. Moreover I had two Masses sung to our intentions—I do not know if you still believe in religion, my little dove, or if, as many people your age, you threw it out, but I never ceased to believe and to trust absolutely this man-God or God-man who came 2000 years ago. With Him, I speak freely and with confidence, as to a friend, who would be with me and, as far as we are concerned, I am convinced that if we are still together, it's thanks to

Him. It is why I am asking Him to keep us together, and I feel no shame to ask it, for He can see that I tried to remain faithful to my wife, He knows her answer, the result today and the depth and quality, the honesty and the intensity of my love for you."

On New Year's Day, 1969, he wrote her a letter on which the prosecution later would dwell. He expressed his wishes for the year: "That you be happy. That we end 1969 together. That at some time during this year I become free to come and get you and make you mine forever." (He was referring, of course, he said stiffly from the witness chair, to the divorce, which he was determined to get.)

For now everything but his new love affair seemed to be failing. Louise made little effort in the mail-order business, which continued to weaken. In the new house in Lac Noir, Geoffroy and Louise engaged in bickering warfare, meticulously cited in the small entries of Geoffroy's diary. The picture of a deteriorating woman is clear. Her health was poor, her weight was down; when Geoffroy handled her she felt like a toy. She was becoming frantic. She drank too much, she lay abed seemingly to spite him, she gave him meals when she pleased and often did not bother.

She began to taunt Geoffroy: she had taken a lover. His name was Dwight, he was an Englishman, he worked for Air Canada, he was mad for her—perhaps she would decide to go to bed with him. Later her family testified that the Englishman was her invention to tantalize Geoffroy, and in his diary entries he seems to suspect that Dwight is a fantasy. But the Englishman proved useful. Geoffroy waited a few days and then "I told my wife everything was over between us and that I had been going out with a twenty-five-year-old girl for four months. It was not easy nor cheerful to say but since she told me about her Englishman . . . I jumped at the occasion to tell her. She spent the [next] week crying and above all, the madwoman, speaking to this one and that one, so that a whole crowd knows. . . ." It was the essential Geoffroy who added, "If she wants to act crazy, do silly things and walk like an elephant in a china shop, I'll help her; she does not understand that in everyone's opinion she will be more in the wrong than I because she started to go out and not me. This is always the case with people, the woman is more to blame than the man. Moreover the worst error is to start this. Instead of trying to win me back, she ends everything in trying to [be unfaithful to] me in turn; it is proof that she has always been a child and not an adult."

Tortured and torturing, they dealt each other counterblows. Her rage flickered and flashed and his built slowly. He did not let it creep into his diary. "She told me she would warn me the first time she slept with him. Poor imbecile—it won't be long when she starts seeing him regularly, she will give herself to him, like a poor little working girl." He spied on her and she on him; she refused him meals and he cut off her food allowance; she staged scenes in front of their friends and he left her demeaning notes. She came to him at night, whimpering for love, and he obliged her, or didn't, on whim. He hired a detective, who could not find her Englishman. Sometimes she seemed ready to divorce him and other times swore that he never would be free. She would strip him of his business, she would cost him a fortune. Geoffroy felt he was trapped in a pitiless purgatory. Only in the quiet, submissive Carmen did he find relief; only with her was the flight of youth not fearful.

Dr. Henri-Paul Lessard, Louise's physician, was the first to hear of her death.

Since everyone knew the state of Geoffroy's marriage, its ending was not surprising. The officials who entered the case were immediately suspicious. So was Dr. Henri-Paul Lessard, Louise's doctor. He had been treating her with vitamin shots for her loss of weight. Geoffroy thought this unnecessary and brusquely ordered Lessard to stop. So Lessard was surprised when his phone awakened him at three twenty a.m. on November 12, 1969, and Geoffroy said, "Come quickly. Something dreadful has happened. I think my wife has died of asphyxiation."

Lessard arrived in twenty minutes. Geoffroy said he was sure his wife was dead from inhaling smoke. Lessard found his patient sprawled over her bed on her back. The bed had been on fire and the window was open. Cold seeped in. Her face seemed bruised and her short hair was tangled and singed. There was a red spot on her neck, her chest was scratched, and one breast was burned.

Geoffroy told Lessard that he had returned from Montreal at one a.m. and had gone to bed. He had been using a separate bedroom for two months and so had not looked into her room. At three a.m. he got up to go to the bathroom and smelled smoke. He opened Louise's door and saw her on the floor. Her bed was on fire and the room was full of smoke. The television set was on.

The doctor studied Geoffroy's face. He thought the man quite collected. Geoffroy said he put out the fire with an extinguisher and opened the window to clear the smoke. He turned off the television set and picked up his wife and put her on the bed. Her false teeth were partly out of her mouth and he put them on the bed. He saw that Louise was not moving and he lifted her eyelid. She seemed dead. He thought smoke had killed her and called Lessard.

There was blood on the dead woman's lips and spots on the sheet. A book was open on her night table by a bottle of Valium. He would have to call the police, the doctor said, and the coroner. Really, Geoffroy asked, was that necessary? Lessard went to the phone. "Well, if it is at all possible, I would prefer that there be no autopsy," the doctor recalled Geoffroy's saying, "because of my boy Philippe. He goes to school now."

The coroner arrived with two Quebec provincial police officers from the Joliette station. The bedroom was icy, and one of the men closed the window. The family dog, a small mongrel, was tied to the back fence, alternately whimpering and howling. A woman friend of Louise's came to pick up the children. While the coroner took Louise's body to the autopsy table, the officers listened to Geoffroy's story. For the moment the assumption stood that she had died of smoke inhalation, but they were uneasy. There were those unexplained bruises, and it had been too small a fire for its smoke to have killed so quickly.

By late afternoon the autopsy report changed everything. Louise had died of asphyxiation, but there was no trace of carbon monoxide in her blood. She had been dead when the fire began. The autopsy showed massive bruises in both cheeks as well as serious lacerations around her nose and mouth.

Obviously she had been murdered, and now the hypothesis became easy. It was a crime of passion. There had been a quarrel. Louise, always voluble, began to yell, perhaps after she had been hit.

As much in fear as in rage, the man (or certainly a figure much heavier and stronger than she) seized her to stifle her cries. A big hand clamped on her face, shut off her breathing, ground thumb and forefinger into her cheeks, held her as she snapped and lunged until, quickly enough, she lost consciousness. Death would have followed immediately. Thus the police theory. Geoffroy could only hazard the idea that in such a case there must have been an intruder. The doors were rarely locked, he didn't really know his wife's habits, she had taken a lover—yes, there must have been an intruder.

But the pathologist's work continued. The blood on Louise's pillow tested group A, Rh-positive. Louise's blood type was group B. Perhaps in the moment of dying she had bitten her killer's hand. A Red Cross card in Geoffroy's wallet showed that his blood type was group A, Rh-positive. Later an officer testified that he saw cuts or scratches and a reddish substance on the index and middle fingers of Geoffroy's right hand. Geoffroy explained that he had cut his hand opening a can of beet juice.

Geoffroy was charged with murder. At the coroner's inquest, his letter to Carmen hoping to "become free to come and get you and make you mine forever" took on damning implications. Afterward Carmen leaned into the prisoner's box and whispered to Geoffroy.

Louise's sister was outraged. "I have never seen such a disgusting spectacle," she shouted.

It was a nightmare. But the courage that Geoffroy had seen in the girl's rare smile held fast. If her belief in his innocence ever wavered, she admitted it to no one. They lived together, with his youngest son, and ignored the community reaction.

Geoffroy and his lawyer had a year to prepare his defense, but if things had gone badly with Louise alive, they went much worse with Louise dead. The case against him was powerful, but there was no sign of premeditation and every indication that Louise had been killed in a burst of murderous rage. If Geoffroy had only admitted a role in her death, there were many mitigating factors that would have cushioned the final verdict. But perhaps his love affair, which lifted

At right, Geoffroy with his first wife, Louise, at a happier moment in their marriage. Above, their house in Lac Noir; the only witness to the murder—the family dog; Louise's body as the police discovered it.

him to such heights, also tripped him. An admission of guilt might have been the single thing that would have destroyed the girl from Longueuil, who in the poetry of love had allowed him a touch of immortality. Can one be both killer and poet? Does one destroy the other?

Geoffroy held to his original story, delivered in an arrogant, antagonistic manner that cost him any sympathy the jury might have held for him. Nor was an alternative theory developed as to who might have killed Louise and how the fire started. The obvious point that the fire and the murder contradicted each other was not addressed: so long as she might have died of fire, fire was plausible; when it was clear that she did not die of fire, fire became implausible. Geoffroy's defense was crumbling.

His letter to Carmen was read to the jury and she was forced to stand as an unwilling witness for the prosecution. Yes, she and Geoffroy had been in love; yes, he had hoped for a divorce; yes, they had intended to marry as soon as they could. She stepped down looking as if she had been whipped. The jury took only an hour and a half to find Geoffroy guilty. He stood stunned and silent as the judge sentenced him to life imprisonment in the penitentiary at St. Vincent de Paul. Carmen began to cry, and for a moment, before the bustle began and Geoffroy was led away, her sobs were the only sound in the quiet courtroom.

CHAPTER 3

IN EARLY NOVEMBER, 1970, Geoffroy rode in a prison van to the immense structure on the wintry hill overlooking the Rivière des Prairies. He was in handcuffs. He looked at the cold stone wall with its topping of chain link and barbed wire and the gun towers at the corners and then entered the little entrance building set in the front wall. The inner door opened and his escort delivered him and fled the stifling atmosphere. And Geoffroy, working his way through the entering process—the physical examination and job assignment and cell assignment—began to plan what must be seen as the only really creative thing in his life—his departure from this hateful place.

He settled readily enough into the routine. Carmen visited him as often as the prison allowed. The man who had been terrified by the specter of his youth vanishing down a long, empty tunnel toward old age now watched and listened and thought. It was immediately obvious that going over the walls or out in a laundry bag would not be practical for him. Geoffroy was always conscious of propriety. He was a gentleman and he became all the more conscious of this as he measured the quality of his fellow prisoners.

Christmas was approaching and some four hundred prisoners were to be granted temporary leaves of up to three days. For weeks before Christmas and afterward, this was the talk of the prison—who the lucky ones were, what they would do, and upon their return, what they had done and how they had found the world outside. The leaves—there were thirty-five thousand through the whole year in all of the Canadian Penitentiary Service—were designed for modest offenders or those nearing release. It was not likely that a man serving a life sentence for murder would be considered even for a temporary absence.

So if Geoffroy was to leave at Christmas, 1971—less than fourteen months after he entered prison—he would have to talk his way out. He decided to create a special climate.

He was a professional, which made him unusual in prison. Most prisoners are common criminals with few skills. Indeed, it usually is the lack of skill and the inability to function well on the outside that brings them inside. Geoffroy's skills fitted readily into an office, and he was assigned as a clerk in the Office of Visits and Correspondence under its genial director, Alain Moreau. The office dealt with the visitors and correspondents permitted each prisoner, and it proved to be an excellent place for Geoffroy because it considered each convict's requests and problems separately. Geoffroy set about making himself useful.

He was one of those men who respond to outside pressure by becoming nicer. He was not always so nice, but as he presented himself in prison he was very nice indeed. He adjusted quickly to the demands of prison routine. He seemed content and in harmony. He seemed to like his work and even the prison itself—well, of course, not to like the prison, but to accept it, to understand the implacable reality of the situation that required him to be there, and to harbor no ill will toward the place or toward his jailers.

For a jailer to feel that he is the agent of the prisoner's detention is to erect a barrier between them. Geoffroy took down that barrier by not seeming to feel that he was in prison. He seemed to see the officials as persons like himself, at work in the same system, albeit at a higher level than he.

There was no question of their oppressing him or of his resenting them. At the same time, he did not forget that their role was superior to his; while he was not of the common herd of prisoners, neither could he aspire to the heights of the officials, and he was respectful and obedient, not subservient, never obsequious, but very respectful. They called him by his first name and he called them sir. From their viewpoint, then, he was a capital fellow—intelligent, efficient, cooperative, smiling, harmonious, never complaining, never disgruntled. Many men resented being in prison, but Geoffroy understood that there was no purpose in resentment, that it cast an unnecessary pall on a situation that, after all, couldn't be helped. He made the officials feel comfortable.

Each evening Geoffroy went to his cell and worked on his appeal. He felt that his trial had been loaded against him and thought that a new trial would vindicate him. Half the men in any prison are working on their appeals, but with his legal background Geoffroy moved through the lawbooks and drafted his petitions with impressive assurance. Outside, Carmen and Geoffroy's old school friend Philip Leclerc collected affidavits and copies of the trial exhibits, which Geoffroy integrated into his growing file. Prison officials saw it all as commendable. The activity tended to remind them that he was a professional. It also gave him a reason for not fraternizing with other prisoners. To the extent that he associated less with other prisoners, he seemed somehow more of the class of the officials.

Geoffroy could remember very little of the night of Louise's death, which is common enough. The death rows of prisons all over the world are full of people who have wiped from their memory every trace of the terrible events that brought them there. So whatever happened that night in Lac Noir, it did not weigh on Geoffroy's conscience. As a result, his insistence that he was innocent carried the ring of truth. Most people judge another with an intuitive sense of whether the person being judged believes what he is saying. Geoffroy believed in his innocence, which explains some of Carmen's faith in him, and he managed to convey his conviction to prison officials as well.

Prison officials, of course, are familiar with the pattern of memory washed clean. And since they are not judges but enforcers of judicial orders, they don't concern themselves with guilt or innocence. Still, if you are warming to someone, it helps to have at least a doubt as to whether he has done some terrible thing. By the same token, if the prisoner is agreeable, why question his claims of innocence? That may be the only solace the poor devil has left. So the officials seemed to accept Geoffroy's claims readily, which in turn bolstered his comfort and assurance. They understood the injustice done him. They understood that he was a gentleman. Thus reassured, Geoffroy was all the more warm and cooperative.

"He was a model prisoner," one official said later. "He was a perfect gentleman." After all, his demeanor seemed to say, I am not a criminal, and this view was widely accepted. Years later policemen who had handled him would recall, "It's not as if he was a criminal, you know." In fact, he had been found guilty of the crime of murder—but he was not like the criminals with whom police and prison officials usually dealt.

Gradually his plan matured. Carmen continued to visit him and they talked at length. Geoffroy had learned to talk in a thin murmur without moving his lips—a trick that becomes natural in prisons and in politics. They worked out an understanding, for she would have to help him persuade the authorities that they should be allowed to marry.

When he was ready, he confided his overwhelming worry to the prison officials, and because they had come to see him as a likable individual, they listened. His concern was for his three little boys. They were with his two brothers, but both men had serious heart conditions and might die at any time. What would become of the boys then?

In fact, Geoffroy's brothers were caring nicely for the children and neither was at all ill, which the simplest phone call would have established. But Geoffroy had created a situation in which he was believed, and so the phone call was not made. The problem of his children was accepted at face value and became, in essence, a reason for officials doing what Geoffroy's general demeanor prompted them to do. If he and Carmen were allowed to marry, she would have the legal right to care for his children. His genial supervisor, Mr. Moreau, had come to know Carmen and was taken with her. Her visits were constant and her sincerity was evident. Her willingness to sacrifice was applauded.

On June 28, 1971, Geoffroy applied for permission to marry. The petition went to the chief of chaplaincy, Canadian Penitentiary Service. In his letter, Geoffroy said that Moreau had offered to serve as witness at the wedding if he were needed. The chaplaincy office at Ottawa was favorably inclined and asked the penitentiary to put together a report on the matter, so prison officials arranged an interview with Carmen.

The interview went very well and Carmen made a predictably good impression. Yes, she understood the implications of marrying a man who would spend years in prison. She understood that his appeals might fail and that a parole might be refused. But she loved him, and the children's future had to be seen as paramount. That much she owed him. The interviewer was touched.

The real purpose of the interview was to judge Carmen's sincerity, which was obvious, and her capacity to make an intelligent decision. In August a report endorsed the marriage and argued that while Carmen's desire to marry a man facing a life sentence was unusual, it was not abnormal. "Miss Parent seems certain of her feelings for Mr. Geoffroy and is not at all the adventurous type," it said. In other words, Carmen was not out to create a sensation. The report noted that Carmen had superior intelligence and excellent judgment and, considering everything, was remaining remarkably calm. It also stated that rejection of the marriage request might have "regrettable emotional consequences."

This same report said that both of Geoffroy's brothers "suffer from fairly serious cardiac pathology and therefore in the event of death, the children would be destitute. In this event, Miss Parent could support and take responsibility for the children, the marriage giving her the right to be their guardian." Thus the myth of the heart conditions became part of the official record.

The prison classification officer supported the marriage application, as did prison director Gerald Brennan, and on November 3, 1971, permission was granted "in view of the positive nature of the reports." This was not usual, but neither was it unusual. The wedding could take place in the prison chapel. Or they could go to a nearby church with a guard in plain clothes, get married, go to dinner with the guard along, and return to the prison. This was how it had been done in the past.

Geoffroy's next step—the crucial step—was to propose that he be given a Christmas leave and be allowed to marry then. The sentimental plan to marry thus was basic to the real question of the leave—it gave a plausible reason for the unusual request. Later, some of the milder newspaper accounts saw the matter as an issue of class, "of the snobbery and gullibility of people who think that an educated and cultivated convict is, ipso facto, trustworthy." And social class did seem to have a bearing. Prison officials saw Geoffroy as a logical recipient for a leave, even though he was neither a small offender nor nearing the end of his term. But, one gentleman to another, he seemed just the right sort of accepting, intelligent prisoner. If there was anyone who understood the futility of not returning, who understood the majesty of the law and the need for

"My dear—How I longed to hold you in my arms . . ."
began this love letter from Geoffroy to Carmen.
It was used as evidence against him at his trial.

orderly process, it was Geoffroy. His appeal was pending and he would not want to jeopardize that. And certainly his motivation in the whole matter—to give his orphaned children a mother—was entirely humane.

Decisions on leaves were made within the prison; no higher permission was needed. On November 10 Geoffroy's application went formally before a board of officials. There was an examination, but as always in such cases, there was room for discretion. Essentially, officials were free to do what they wanted. The members of the board studied the application and approved it unanimously. As one official observed later, the only real question was whether the leave should be for fifty or seventy-two hours. Opting for conservatism, they limited it to only fifty hours. Their recommendation was approved by prison director Brennan.

And so, on Christmas Eve, 1971, Geoffroy left the prison, married Carmen, and caught the night flight for London. He and Carmen stayed there one night, and the next morning they were aboard British European Airways flight 782 for Oslo. Who would ever look for them in Oslo?

CHAPTER 4

WHEN GEOFFROY DID NOT return to the prison at ten a.m. on Sunday, his absence was logged, but there was no special alarm. Perhaps weather had delayed him. A routine notice of a prisoner "unlawfully at large" went to the Quebec provincial police. Three days later, in the first mail delivery since Christmas, came a letter addressed in a bold hand to Alain Moreau. It bore Canadian stamps, but its postmark was illegible. With a certain foreboding Moreau opened it.

Longueuil, December 24, 1971

Dear Mr. Moreau:

When you read these lines you will know that I have not kept my word.

I wish to apologize most sincerely for not doing so. It was difficult for Carmen and me not to keep the promises we made to you. I am not asking you to approve what I am doing, but to try to understand that this useless fourteen months of waiting almost drove us crazy. The judge's answer to my letter [an interim motion had been rejected] decided everything. I had nothing to hope for, I had only to resign myself to more waiting, for I don't know how long. I am not guilty and I want to enjoy the last few years of youth I have left.

Thank you from the bottom of my heart for what you did for Carmen and me. You have always acted as a gentleman, and I wish I could have done the same thing.

> Best wishes,
> Yves Geoffroy

Moreau studied the letter. It seemed jaunty and elated and not nearly as respectful as the Yves Geoffroy he had come to know. "Best wishes my foot," he said.

The letter changed things. Obviously Geoffroy did not intend to return, nor expect to be caught. He was in full flight with a five-day lead and was probably beyond the province of Quebec. The provincial police turned to the Royal Canadian Mounted Police, and now a number of things happened. A Canada-wide warrant for Geoffroy's arrest was issued, and the warrant and a description of him were placed in a computer file at the Canadian Police Information Center at RCMP headquarters in Ottawa. The warrant included Carmen and explained the situation. This information also went to the National Crime Intelligence Center in Washington, D.C. It, too, put the information on computer tape, where it was available instantly on request. Since the United States has no national police, the Federal Bureau of Investigation's jurisdiction being limited and specific, the approximately forty thousand independent police forces in the United States turn first to the national center for information when they handle a suspicious stranger.

Royal Canadian Mounted Police headquarters is a cluster of buildings that once was a Catholic seminary on Alta Vista Drive, on the eastern side of Ottawa. A huge stuffed buffalo head flanked by maple leaf flags looks benignly over the entrance hall of the main building, whose third floor is dominated by the Criminal Investigation Bureau and the Interpol offices. Copies of the messages about Geoffroy's escape came to the office here of Superintendent John Burris, chief of the CIB. It was a roomy office with a plain desk and black leather armchairs. Framed police institute certificates hung on the walls. Casement windows with low sills opened onto a yard dominated by tall old trees.

In the office next door was Burris' aide, Inspector Raymond Ebert. He was a tall young man with an open, credulous face that had drawn confessions from many an unwary suspect. Burris thought he had a bright future and was grooming him.

There were ice crystals on the windowpanes, and Burris' office was cool but comfortable. He was wearing a plain tweed suit, as usual, and his gray mustache was trimmed with military precision.

Ebert entered and put a file folder on his desk. "This is a runaway from St. Vincent de Paul that may interest you," he said. Burris opened the folder and saw immediately what he meant. Yves Geoffroy had left the prison with none other than Philip Leclerc. Hastily he skimmed the file. What could those idiots at the penitentiary have been thinking of? They hold a man for murdering his wife and turn him out to marry his mistress, and then they're surprised when he doesn't come back. He shook his head.

There were several news clippings. KILLER, NEW BRIDE, OFF ON HONEYMOON. Ebert had circled in red an item in *Hansard*, the record of debates and proceedings in the House of Commons. Burris, as he would quickly protest, was just a policeman, apolitical to the core. He tried to ignore politics. In fact, however, the government for which he worked was led by Prime Minister Pierre Elliott Trudeau of the Liberal Party; the Solicitor General, Jean-Pierre Goyer, oversaw the Royal Canadian Mounted Police and thus ultimately was Burris' chief. And here, in *Hansard*, was a Conservative, Thomas M. Bell, rising during question period with a query for the Solicitor General. Might he ask, he inquired politely, if Goyer and his officials had participated in the decision to release Yves Geoffroy to get married?

Goyer answered that Geoffroy had been released under standard procedures, and Bell shot back, "May I ask the minister if he was aware that the best man at the wedding was Philip Leclerc, an old friend of the government?"

Stiffly Goyer replied, "No, I was not at all, Mr. Speaker, and I do not believe any conclusion can be drawn therefrom." Burris winced. He could smell trouble. Luckily the House was going into recess and there would be a breathing spell, but if Geoffroy were not recovered quickly, things could get hot.

"Geoffroy must be a fool," Burris said, handing the folder back to Ebert. "He writes that letter to Moreau as if he simply takes it all in his own hands—as if we haven't a thing to say about it."

In Montreal—Canada's second largest city and only half an hour by air from Ottawa—the RCMP operated from a big modern building on Dorchester Boulevard. When Burris arrived there from Ottawa that January morning, he found awaiting him a bright young corporal, Armand Fresnard, who was working the Geoffroy case with two provincial police officers. Fresnard was thirty, a muscular, quick-moving man with almost ten years on the force. He had never served outside of Quebec. He was faintly surprised to be talking to Superintendent Burris himself—it indicated that Ottawa was serious about Geoffroy—but he did not allow his aplomb to be ruffled.

"I asked Philip Leclerc to come in, sir," he said. "I thought you'd want to see him."

"Leclerc I want to see," Burris said ominously.

Leclerc looked pale and angry. He was shaken, but Burris judged his anger was genuine.

"Well, Mr. Leclerc, so you turn up again." Burris did not offer to shake hands.

"I resent that," Leclerc said crisply. "I served my time and that's all behind me."

"Right there in St. Vincent de Paul."

"In St. Vincent de Paul—but there's no reason to bring that up." Leclerc was tough and handled himself well. He was an attorney and had been a power in the federal government, serving as executive assistant to a Cabinet member until he was sentenced to two years in prison in 1967 for offering a twenty-thousand-dollar bribe. He functioned, as a newspaper later would describe it, as "a parliamentary fixer" in a celebrated case that drove the opposition party to a frenzy of attack, led to at least one Cabinet-level resignation, and shook Pierre Trudeau's administration like a stone in a can. Now, five years later, his name was still sensitive. Geoffroy, however, had not been involved in the earlier case, and both men knew Burris was on weak ground. But he had been setting the tone, and now he shifted before the other man's resentment could crystallize.

"Yes. Well, what do you know about this Geoffroy affair?"

"No more than you do."

"Then you don't know very much. You've been close to him, have you?"

"I've given him some legal assistance. I've known him for years, we went to school together, and I helped Carmen Parent collect some documents for his appeal. God knows what'll happen to that now."

"You'd known her, too?"

"Not until he was convicted. She's a nice person—plain, you know. But she certainly loved him. She talked of nothing but the marriage for months."

"And you picked them up that morning?"

"They had no car, and I was to be a witness at the wedding. Afterward I drove them home and left them there."

"You didn't see them again?"

"Of course not—it was their honeymoon."

"How were they going to get back on Sunday?"

"I don't know. She said they'd manage, and I was busy."

"No indication that he wasn't coming back, I suppose?"

Leclerc made a face. "No, none. I have problems enough without getting involved in something like this. It's damned poor use of a friend, I must say."

Standing, Burris said, "If you get any long-distance calls for advice, let us know."

"I doubt I'll be getting any calls. They've had their use of me."

Burris nodded. "Thanks for coming in," he said coolly. "We'll stay in touch." Deliberately he turned his back and looked out the window as Leclerc left.

"Do you want us to watch him?" Fresnard asked.

"No," Burris said. "Just look in on him now and then. I think he's telling the truth. It's probably just a coincidence that he's involved, but it's an unfortunate coincidence because it focuses attention on Geoffroy. It turns a simple runaway case into a potential cause célèbre."

He stood staring down at the traffic inching along Dorchester Boulevard, his thumbs hooked in his vest pockets. Fresnard waited. "All right, Corporal," Burris said at last. "You know the routine. Let's check everything out. Airlines first of all. Look at the passenger manifests for all their flights on December twenty-fourth and twenty-fifth. Bus stations. Trains. Talk to everyone on duty on those two days. Get someone to U.S. Immigration at the crossing—it's slim, but they might remember something. Check the passport office at External Affairs for both Geoffroy and the woman. Check embassies and consulates, for visas but especially for a visit from the woman. She must have made whatever arrangements were made. They got out of here somehow—see if she bought a car recently. See if Leclerc bought a car. And let's move right along on this."

Fresnard phoned two days later. "Sorry, Inspector," Fresnard said. "We've pretty much drawn a blank. There's no sign of a car involved. Parent didn't own one under her own name and none of her neighbors ever saw one. We've talked to new- and used-car dealers and there's no sign of a purchase. Checked the want ads for those two days and there's nothing on a private purchase. External Affairs issued a passport to Carmen Andrée Parent on twenty-nine June, 1971, passport number JB 342144. Nothing for Geoffroy. No visas issued, though of course no visas are needed for tourist travel abroad. No one remembers a visit to an embassy. None of the American officers at the border remember anything. The airline checks were all negative. We looked at every passenger manifest and there's no trace of either of them. Same with buses and trains. No one remembers anything.

"There are a couple of points that may mean nothing. One of Parent's neighbors thinks she used to teach school in Africa in a religious order. If that's true, she'd know her way to Africa. And Geoffroy's sister vacationed in Mexico recently."

"All right," Burris said. "Start checking banks. You don't run away without any money. Look for transfers of funds, traveler's checks, cashier's checks, anything unusual. Check the status of Parent's account."

When Burris hung up, Ebert brought him a cup of coffee and one for himself. "Maybe they didn't leave Canada?" he suggested.

"Well," Burris said, "not under their own names."

He drank the steaming coffee, turning the troublesome Mr. Geoffroy over in his mind. This was no sudden panic flight. The letter to Moreau was the thoughtful touch of a confident man. He'd planned it all damned neatly. He'd persuaded prison officials that he was all gentleman, trustworthy as a bishop. And he'd planned the outside just as neatly. No doubt the woman had handled the details, but the plan was unified—how to get out and, once out, how to disappear. The lack of tracks only meant that Geoffroy had covered them well. Burris had followed enough men to know that there are always tracks. The problem is to find them. Burris' increasing hunch was that Geoffroy and his new bride had gone abroad, but it was too early to act on the idea. And there were plenty of places in Canada where a determined and clever man could go to ground.

Burris had seen most of them, too, at one time or another, because he had served all over Canada. He was a slow-talking, steady man with a gravelly voice who rarely acted quickly and rarely made mistakes. When you talked to him, his big hands usually were folded quietly on the desk. Those hands looked as if they would be deadly steady holding a pistol, and in fact he could still squeeze down on his old regulation .38 with the four-inch barrel and blow out the black center of a target ring at fifty yards. His father had been a Mountie and so had his grandfather. It seemed to run in the family, and sometimes he wondered if his own boy would follow the tradition. But time enough for that.

He spent six months in recruit training and was posted out to a little town in Saskatchewan called Weyburn, and the sergeant had barely glanced at him. "Okay, kid," he'd said. "You take the midnight to eight." Burris had found himself the only policeman between this entire town and the forces of crime, eighteen years old, scared, not knowing what to do, not even sure of his way back to the police post. But he'd never admitted how he felt, and he learned that nothing that can happen to you is as bad as being scared that something will. With this knowledge he was all right. He was a solid man even then, and his shoulders thickened and he learned how to put a man down with one punch. He could kill a man, too, if necessary, but he counted himself deeply fortunate that it had never been necessary.

He went up through the ranks, and after he'd been in plain clothes a year, an old inspector getting ready to retire told him one day, "You know, kid, you can go places. It's not your brains, though I guess they're okay, but you're steady and you've got judgment. That's what counts. In police work, intuition follows experience and you make your own luck, but control is the thing—and my guess is you've got it." Now he was forty-two years old, running the Criminal Investigation Bureau, and had field commands behind him, and he probably would finish near the top.

The next time Fresnard reported, he had a strike. "On sixteen December Carmen Parent bought seven hundred dollars in American Express traveler's checks, one-hundred-dollar denominations, at the Banque Provinciale in Longueuil. Checks numbered X2230157 to X2230163 inclusive. Pretty well emptied her account."

This was the first of the tracks that Burris knew were there. At once the provincial police called American Express in New York City, gave the check numbers, and asked for a notification when they cleared. American Express has a huge computerized traveler's check–watching system. Its checks are cashed all over the world and come flowing in through normal banking channels for payment. The agency replaces any whose owners report them lost or stolen, and then the computer waits for those checks to appear. American Express inspectors watch for patterns that go beyond the isolated sneak thief and suggest fraud or an organized check-stealing ring. It was simple enough to add the Canadian request to the computer's list of alarm checks.

Now Burris could do what his instinct had been urging from the beginning—turn to Interpol. No one running from the police would use traveler's checks in his own country and advertise his name every time he cashed one. But changing currency abroad is different, and a careful planner would decide that traveler's checks were the most negotiable and least noticeable form for converting money. Burris was satisfied that Geoffroy had gone abroad, probably to Europe, where French was common, possibly to Africa, if the Parent woman really had taught there.

As head of the Criminal Investigation Bureau, Burris also was head of the National Central Bureau for Canada, better known as Interpol Ottawa. The national central bureau in each country is that country's link with Interpol, but the bureau itself is an agency of its own government, not of Interpol, and is responsible to its own government. Usually, as in Canada, it is part of the national police; Interpol London, for example, is in Scotland Yard, and Interpol Paris is in the Sûreté Nationale. The National Central Bureau for the United States is an independent office attached to the Justice Department and is located in the main Justice Building in Washington, D.C. The position of chief of the United States NCB rotates every two years between Justice and Treasury.

Burris drafted the message that radio operator Paul Ferrar would send in Morse code at his steady thirty-five words a minute to the roof antenna of the big building on the hill at St. Cloud, overlooking Paris. Thus the police forces of the world would be on the alert that Yves Geoffroy, of Montreal, and wife were on the run and were wanted.

THE INTERNATIONAL CRIMINAL Police Organization is unique. It is an independent world organization comparable in some ways to the United Nations, with its General Secretariat in the building at St. Cloud. It has a constitution and a governing organization and is responsible to its member nations, which sit in general assembly each year and determine its policy. The commissioner of the Royal Canadian Mounted Police had served as host for the meeting in 1971; while Yves Geoffroy was planning his departure from the penitentiary, Interpol's General Assembly held its annual meeting in Ottawa. More than a hundred and twenty-five nations belong today; at that time there were a hundred and seven members. Each member contributes to the cost of the Paris headquarters on the basis of size and ability to pay, and each agrees to abide by its rules. With the exception of Rumania and Yugoslavia, the Communist nations have elected not to join Interpol.

Interpol has a staff of about two hundred persons at St. Cloud, of whom about sixty-five are police officers assigned (and their salaries paid) by member nations. Canada has one officer there, and various federal agencies of the United States have several. These officers work cooperatively on Interpol affairs, but under the control of their own governments.

The General Secretariat of Interpol is separated into three divisions: General Administration, Research and Study, and International Police Cooperation. The last is in turn subdivided into five groups, each concentrating on certain types of cases: murder and theft, international fraud, bank frauds and forgery, drug traffic, and counterfeiting. Each subdivision gathers information and traces patterns of the ever growing international traffic in crime. They pay particular attention to those slippery individuals who specialize in operating between countries, are fluent in the language and the ways of each, and are skilled at forging documents and passports; individuals who live at great hotels as they arrange robberies, killings, frauds, narcotics sales and other profitable enterprises, and who then move on with bundles of unmarked bills destined for numbered bank accounts in Switzerland. The files at Interpol bulge with names, photographs, fingerprints and methods of operation of such people, and the agents there specialize in watching the trends that will allow them to alert this member and that to a ring of counterfeiters or a hired assassin moving in.

These officers and all national central bureaus operate under basic limitations without which an international police organization could hardly survive in this troubled world.

While Interpol adheres strictly to its nonpolitical charter, it is a kind of intelligence organization in the sense that it gathers and transmits information on criminal matters. Interpol officials have worked out a doctrine of ignoring underground or terrorist groups, which may claim a political motive—and thus immunity from Interpol. Still, Interpol stands ready to handle cases involving the same people, as individuals, once they are implicated in criminal acts such as hostage taking, bank robbery and murder. Its attention is directed clearly and unequivocally toward specific, punishable crime that happens to take an international turn.

By far its most important—and indeed, its most dramatic—function is to provide a link between police forces. There are no Interpol agents as such, nor do Interpol officers fan across the world in pursuit of suspects. Since 1972, however, a small number of "liaison officers" help to coordinate activities in specific global areas. But for the most part, the Interpol link allows nations' police forces to operate in tandem on a structured basis. They can do so only because, through Interpol, they all operate from the same ground rules. The most important of these rules is the understanding that each national central bureau operates under the laws of its own country. (When Burris received a request from Interpol Rome or Interpol Manila or Interpol Caracas, he responded as a Royal Canadian Mounted Police officer, governed by the laws of Canada as to how he would proceed.) Furthermore, no request for action may be made of a country without details of the offense, so that the responding country can be sure the situation is consistent with its laws. No request to detain a suspect may be made until a legal warrant for that person's arrest has been issued in the requesting country. (The first step in the pursuit of Geoffroy had been swearing out a warrant for his arrest.)

Thus the great role of Interpol's network is to make the police force of any member country an effective arm of any other member country's police force on a specific case. As Interpol provides the link, so the national central bureau in each country is the funnel, sending information and requests to the appropriate agency of its own police. That agency—the murder squad, for example, or the narcotics squad, or perhaps the local constable who goes to someone's door to gather a single but vital fact needed on the other side of the world—then reports back to its national central bureau, which in turn flashes the message to St. Cloud, or perhaps directly to the requesting national central bureau.

Effectively, then, all police forces become one through Interpol when they focus on a particular crime or a particular fugitive criminal. This was the coordinated force that now, with messages flashing from Paris to Rome and Melbourne and Washington and Oslo and Cairo and Rio de Janeiro, was arrayed against the still moving figures of Yves and Carmen Geoffroy.

CHAPTER 5

BRITISH EUROPEAN AIRWAYS flight 782 from London ran into savage weather over the North Sea. Both airports near Oslo closed and the pilot slipped into Göteborg, Sweden. Geoffroy and Carmen waited five hours at the airport for a bus and spent another five hours covering the two hundred miles to Oslo. It was a bad beginning.

At eleven p.m. they checked into the Fønix Hotel, a small, inconspicuous building standing on a side street just off the handsome Karl Johans Street, Oslo's main thoroughfare, overlooked at its northern end by the Royal Palace. In the hotel lobby, a couple of leather chairs stood against the wall to the left of the desk, and in the window, looking out onto the cold, icy street, was a large window box containing some small green plants huddled under two mushroom lights for warmth. One of the plants looked to Geoffroy like a palm tree.

He presented his passport at the desk and completed the necessary registration formalities. The clerk did not ask for Carmen's passport. He gave them a key and watched as the weary couple picked up their bags themselves and made for the elevator. Room 307 was a double room with minimal furnishings and two large windows. From those windows Geoffroy and Carmen looked down on the street—gray, frozen and empty.

The view from that room came to symbolize Oslo for both of them. The next morning they went out, and the cold struck them as a physical blow. They had never felt such cold. Montreal is on the 45th parallel and Oslo is on the 60th, less than seven degrees below the Arctic Circle. Norway boasts of being "the most northerly" country in the world, and they had no trouble believing it. The cold seeped through their clothes and made their faces ache and their eyes burn.

The city was quiet and they began to wonder if they were the only foreigners there. They found few English and no French, and gradually they began to feel conspicuous. They had chosen their destination blindly. Oslo had seemed the end of the earth, the last place that anyone would seek them. What they had not anticipated was that the end of the earth might be a difficult place in which to make a new start.

They hadn't really thought much about what they would do when they were free, though Geoffroy had always believed that if he could get away cleanly, Canadian authorities would be in no hurry to track him down. Part of his success in building a climate for release had been that he himself believed in it. It was a travesty that a dignified notary of good background should be in the penitentiary with common criminals, and the pleasant way that penitentiary officials treated him led him to assume that they recognized this travesty and shared his feelings. So why should they pursue him relentlessly? Oh, Moreau might be perturbed, but Geoffroy had softened any displeasure with a gracious letter, and once Moreau thought it over, he probably would feel that it was all for the best, that Geoffroy had accomplished what the authorities themselves might have liked but obviously weren't in a position to carry out. The interest in him would die, Geoffroy thought, like a passing ripple on a pond.

Now, in Oslo, he had to focus himself and begin building a new life. Money was not an immediate problem. There had been little enough left in his ruined businesses after the trial, but by liquidating everything over the last year, he had realized about six thousand dollars, most of which he carried in thousand-dollar Canadian bank notes in a money belt. Cashing them would draw attention. Still, they were his stake and he did not expect to use them until he was established. He had a bit of money for now, as did Carmen, and they would live frugally. Eventually he would work or go into business and Carmen probably could teach French. The immediate problem was to make a connection in Oslo without drawing attention. The only thing that could destroy them now would be a query about them to Montreal; even reluctant officials, if they knew where Geoffroy was, would be forced to follow.

After two days they moved from the Fønix, with a last glance at that forlorn "palm" in the lobby, to a small pension, where the landlady found them charming and a little mysterious. On impulse, Geoffroy told her he was a history professor and that Carmen was a physiotherapist. Who knew where that might lead? he told Carmen later. But it led nowhere.

Every day they went out and walked, looking, pondering this possibility and that, waiting for something to open to them so naturally that they would not have to initiate and draw attention. But nothing presented itself in the cold and quiet city, and gradually a darkness seemed to settle onto Geoffroy's spirits. This quality of internal darkness, like a slow smoldering anger, sent alarm signals through Carmen, whose bridges all lay burned behind her.

Every afternoon they went for tea to the Grand Hotel, with its clock cupola and Norwegian flags, on Karl Johans Street, the Fifth Avenue or Champs Élysées of Oslo. The steaming tea came in glasses that fitted into silver holders, and they drank slowly, watching the powerful people of the city come and go. These were the people with whom Geoffroy belonged, Carmen thought, with his neat suit and handsome mustache, but the guests seemed occupied with their own affairs and there was little chance of making a contact here. Geoffroy and Carmen nursed their tea until it was cold and did not even look at the traditional—and expensive—*koldtbord,* the lavish Norwegian "cold table" that was laid out. Then they left, and crossed the side street—Rosenkrantz—to the old Hotel Nobel Building and looked in the windows of a travel agency called Winge Reisebureau. Here hung brightly colored posters advertising sunny spots on the Mediterranean—sunny Sicily, sunny Greece, sunny Beirut. Next door, in a small windowed lobby, was a branch of the Bergens Privatbank, with just two tellers. One afternoon Carmen went in to cash a traveler's check; now she would discover if it was as easy as the advertisements said. The clerk simply handed her a pen.

He watched her sign the check, which had been issued by American Express. Because it was a quiet day, and because she was a woman, he noticed her. He usually noticed women. "Are you enjoying Oslo?" he asked in fluent English.

She hadn't expected to hear English, and looked at the clerk with positive alarm, shrinking somehow into her coat, her large eyes growing still larger, and he saw the heavy man who had been looking out the window turn and start coming toward them. There was something about the way the man moved that alarmed the clerk, and he counted out the kroner and passed them over the counter. The woman tucked the money into her purse with a tentative smile and the man took her arm.

The transaction depressed Geoffroy. The erosion of their cash emphasized the tenuousness of their position. For the burghers of the Grand Hotel were not going to speak to them, and opportunity was not going to present itself. What Geoffroy needed was a job—any job—that would let him fit quietly into Oslo society.

That night they had dinner at a good restaurant, and because it was crowded, the headwaiter asked if a young man who was alone could join them. His name was Ole Reinhardtsen; he had served with the Norwegian contingent of a United Nations force in Egypt, and had a smattering of English. He helped them order dinner and they fell into a halting conversation.

Geoffroy told the young man that he was a cook, interested in marketing a new kind of sandwich that he said was becoming popular in America. He had an idea that would make it special—but, of course, all that was in the future. For now, he had decided he should

The modern headquarters of the
International Criminal Police Organization (Interpol)
in St. Cloud, France, near Paris.

Two views of the radio and telecommunications
room on the top floor of Interpol headquarters, where
messages are transmitted to and received from
member countries worldwide.

get a job—what better way to learn Oslo's gastronomic tastes than to work with Norwegians?—and any job would do.

"Then you want Office Overload," Reinhardtsen said.

"Overload?"

"They look for people for short—for temporary—jobs. They always have openings. Not the best jobs, but maybe you"—he paused, smiled—"can get a foot in door."

Geoffroy was delighted. Why hadn't he thought of that? It was perfect. People looking for temporary help never asked questions. Why should they? The very act of seeking temporary work means you're between things. Office Overload! "Now maybe we can get going," he told Carmen.

INTERPOL HEADQUARTERS AT St. Cloud is a modern six-story building of glass and stone, its roof a tangle of antennas. It is located five miles from Notre Dame, three from the Eiffel Tower, on a quiet suburban street where only an occasional commuter train passing on the tracks below disturbs the peaceful calm. Its symbol in bronze—a world globe with a sword and the scales of justice—is set against a sheet of green marble to the right of the entranceway. There are two small elevators inside, and visitors sign in at the guard desk in the spacious entrance area. Moving from the drug-traffic section to the international fraud and counterfeiting sections, to the areas dealing with other international crimes, one finds the Spartan plainness of working police stations all over the world—two metal desks to a cubicle, plastic chairs, calendar pictures.

The heart of Interpol is the radio and telecommunications room on the top floor, which transmits to and receives from the forty giant antennas and the twenty-five transmitters spread over nearly a hundred acres of pasture at St. Martin d'Abbat. Here messages flow in and out, day and night. The room is never silent. Operators sit at four Morse code positions in a double row, their key—the bug—black-headed and angular before them, and the remote, impersonal, somehow delicate sounds of dot-dash dominate the room. Apart, behind a double glass partition that reduces their noise to a steady metallic chatter, are the Telex, Teletype and radio-telegraph machines. About half of the thousand messages a day still come through Morse code, because a majority of the poorer member countries cannot afford the more expensive equipment necessary for faster message forms. The walls are covered with maps, pins on them representing Interpol stations around the world. Interpol's languages are English, French, Spanish and Arabic, and all outgoing messages are in one of the four. Incoming messages go from the Morse positions to translators, who recast them as necessary into the Interpol code and the appropriate language. The code is merely some five thousand five-letter combinations assigned to often used phrases. "Photos and fingerprints will be sent" becomes GALKU. "His wife" becomes BONUL, and GIRID says "Thanks for your cooperation."

Burris' first message asking the world for help was handled routinely, in through the Morse positions, then to translation and out, and the message itself was general. After asking Interpol to "initiate an investigation to determine the whereabouts of Geoffroy . . . possibly accompanied by BONUL," it said:

GEOFFROY WAS SERVING LIFE IMPRISONMENT IN ST. VINCENT DE PAUL PENITENTIARY QUEBEC CANADA FOR MURDER AND WAS GRANTED LEAVE OF ABSENCE ON 24/12/71 BUT SCHEDULED TO RETURN TO THE PENITENTIARY ON 26/12/71. DURING THIS LEAVE HE MARRIED PARENT FIRST NAME CARMEN IN MONTREAL CANADA. HE HAS FAILED TO RETURN AND THERE IS AN ARREST WARRANT FOR HIM. YOUR ASSISTANCE REQUIRED WITH A VIEW TO LOCATING THIS PERSON. EBVIP [please keep us informed of any results of your investigation] END IP OTTAWA

This was the message, then, that went to Seoul and Ouagadougou and Washington and, of course, Oslo. It came in dots and dashes to Interpol Oslo's office, on the ground floor of the Norwegian Criminal Investigation Bureau building, which is about a dozen blocks from the Fønix Hotel. On January 11 a police bulletin on Geoffroy was distributed to Norway's fifty-three police districts and three hundred and eighty-eight sheriff's offices. If Geoffroy brought himself to police attention, if he got into a fight, perhaps, and was arrested, the police would connect him with the bulletin. But for the moment, despite the optimistic Canadian request to "initiate an investigation," there was no more reason to suppose that Geoffroy was in Oslo than in Ouagadougou, and the Norwegian police would not be expected to take any further action.

And back in Ottawa, John Burris understood how much more was needed. He was getting edgy. Newspapers were featuring a provincial police officer's remark, "For all we know they may be honeymooning in Mexico or some South American country," and a member of the opposition in the House of Commons was demanding a judicial inquiry. It was just talk, so far, with the House in recess, but the opposition thought it smelled a scandal in the making, and the talk would continue.

All right. Burris' bones told him Geoffroy was out of Canada. If so, he almost certainly had gone out under a different name, and that meant a passport in a different name. Canadian passport regulations had been tightened after James Earl Ray, the convicted killer of Martin Luther King, got one without trouble on his way to Europe, but one could still apply by mail. Burris called in Staff Sergeant Roger Morgan of the Immigration and Passport Division, RCMP. Morgan was a big, relaxed man, about fifty, whose easy manner belied a dogged nature.

"Look," Burris said. "Start working backward through every passport application from, say, December twentieth. Look for Geoffroy's picture on someone else's application. Work all the way back to '69, when he put out his wife, if you have to, but I want an answer. If he's got a passport, then we'll know his new name. If he hasn't, he's probably still in Canada, probably under his own name."

For that, Morgan thought, Burris deserved a salute, but probably it would tick him off. Later, as Morgan gathered his team, he said thinly, "This one's warm. The Old Man gave me a lecture on the absolutely obvious. Let's not miss anything."

Four men, each with a copy of Geoffroy's scowling prison mug shot, sat at the big table in the passport division of the Department of External Affairs. Stacks of passport applications were brought, each a single sheet with a picture glued to the lower right corner. They eliminated women and small children, ignored names, and concentrated on the remaining pictures. Presumably a man changing his identity would alter his appearance somewhat, but the picture would have to be accurate enough to satisfy customs officers.

They worked all of that day and the next, through ten thousand applications and another ten thousand. They didn't talk much and they paused only when their eyes ached from the constant comparison. "Rest when you get tired," Morgan said, "but don't let this fellow slip through us." But still the pictures seemed to blur. Late on the third day, after checking more than thirty thousand applications, a picture leaped off the page at Morgan.

"I do believe," he said quietly, "that I have won the cigar. There he is."

"About time," the man next to him said with a sigh. "And look—it's the same picture. He used his prison mug on his passport application. Now that took gall."

Geoffroy's picture was attached to an application made for one Réal Rolland Lafond, born April 25, 1934 (nine months, in fact, after Geoffroy was born), occupation administrator. The application was made September 28, 1971, three months before Geoffroy's leave began, and passport number JB 422386 had been issued by mail.

"Come on," Morgan said. "Let's run down the real owner of this name."

"Dead, I suppose," Burris said the next day.

"Yes, sir. Lafond drowned in Otter Lake on December twenty-eighth, 1959. It took ten days to recover his body. He was buried January ninth, 1960, at St. Alphonse de Rodriguez. He was the Parent woman's cousin. Vital Statistics in Quebec has issued no new certificates. Parent must have had an opportunity to get his baptismal certificate."

"Had the passport sent to her address, did she?"

"By registered mail, naturally, and she wasn't home, so the postman left a notice. She came round to the post office and signed for it. His name by her—nothing hidden."

"And the guarantor?" Canadian law demands an official signature to warrant an applicant's identity.

"Forged. A local notary who said he had never seen the application. The signature was nothing like his."

Now Burris had the key piece of information that would allow Interpol to release its most urgent notice—the red notice—calling for the immediate arrest of the individual named. Geoffroy's photographs, fingerprints and description already had gone to Paris by air; there remained only the question of the name under which he traveled: Réal Rolland Lafond.

The red notice carries the Interpol symbol in a bright red square in the upper right corner. The premier Interpol notice, it complements the radio and Telex messages, and is sent by airmail to every station. It is a printed form that includes photographs and fingerprints, and asks that the wanted person be arrested and held for extradition. There are three other notice classes—a green square calls attention to suspicious persons moving internationally, a blue one makes inquiry about suspects or missing persons, and a black one describes unidentified bodies. When the red notice reached Interpol Oslo, Geoffroy's photograph, fingerprints and alias were added to the wanted file.

Slowly the net was tightening. Interpol moves with a certain implacable deliberateness, awaiting the break that will allow the tight focus on the moving criminal that is the beginning of the end. Should Geoffroy-Lafond come to police attention, Oslo was ready to act, with full description, picture and fingerprints for identification and, most important of all, specific authority from Canada to arrest and hold for extradition. But it still had no special reason to think Geoffroy was in Oslo and therefore no reason to initiate a real search. The next step was the focusing.

That came in Ottawa when Burris' phone rang. American Express in New York was responding. "You wanted watch and notification on traveler's checks issued on December sixteenth in Montreal. Check number X2230157 for one hundred dollars Canadian just cleared our computers in New York. It was cashed by Carmen Parent at Bergens Privatbank in Oslo, Norway, on January seventh. We are maintaining the hold on the remainder of the series and will notify you when they clear."

Strike! He'd *known* they were abroad. Norway! "Thank you," Burris said. "This is crucial information."

"Glad to help. Have a good day." And he was gone in a click.

Burris grinned and reached for his pad.

Now the message went out from Interpol Ottawa again. It gave the numbers of the traveler's checks and asked Oslo:

PLEASE GIVE US ALL POSSIBLE ASSISTANCE ON THIS CASE WITH A VIEW TO LOCATING AND ARRESTING JOSEPH GEOFFROY BELIEVED TRAVELING ON CANADIAN PASSPORT JB 422386 UNDER THE NAME OF REAL LAFOND STOP BUVIT END IP OTTAWA

In Oslo, behind a glass partition at the National Central Bureau, a man with earphones sat before an orange typewriter and typed out the message as it came in.

Now it was Oslo's case.

CHAPTER 6

OFFICE OVERLOAD WAS IN a storefront. A room full of benches was empty. Behind a counter at the rear, a young man was talking to a blond girl who was seated at a typewriter. He had his back to the counter and did not turn around until Geoffroy cleared his throat loudly. Geoffroy tried to explain himself. He was Réal Lafond, Canadian, he was new here and would like temporary employment, anything would do, really, though he was trained for office management, an administrator. . . .

Eventually the young man perceived his meaning. A look of disinterest crossed his face and without any concern he said in rough English, "Oh, Mr. Lafond, there is nothing at all, no, not a thing. Come back some other day if you like, but not too soon." And he stepped into a small office behind the counter and closed the door.

The blond girl's typewriter clicked slowly and she did not look up. Geoffroy stood at the counter with his mouth drawn tight under his mustache and the darkness that alarmed Carmen in his eyes, and after a while he went outside.

The cold struck him a sharp blow and he drew his coat close. The sky was making snow. Walking would be difficult in the snow, he thought, but the pale blue trams never seemed to go where he wanted. He walked down Karl Johans Street, past the Grand Hotel, and paused as always to look in the Winge Reisebureau. There were new posters in the windows. A cut of wind staggered him. He moved on, and a few doors away he saw a stationery shop and went in and bought a map of Europe.

When he returned to the pension, Carmen was drinking tea with the obliging landlady. She saw his face and hurried after him to the bedroom. He put on a heavy sweater and sat by the window.

"I don't like the light here," he said abruptly. "It's too pale—it seems sad. It gets dark all at once, like something dying." He told her what had happened at Office Overload. "It's just not working. I feel like we're the only foreigners in the whole city. I don't think we're going to make a connection, and there's no way I can just start knocking on doors without drawing attention. It's cold today—it's going to snow, I can feel it." She saw the map of Europe that he had dropped on the bed. He stared out the window. "This must be the most boring city in the world."

So they began to talk about leaving. They locked the bedroom door and spread the map on the floor and sat with their shoulders touching, studying its shapes and colors and romantic names. It was like a ticket to light and warmth. Naturally they turned to the Mediterranean. There, thrust into the sea, was Italy, ancient, beautiful, sunny—one could hear the Pope himself say Mass. Italy would be delightful.

But practicality took hold. Italy was a poor country, exporting workers all over Europe. Since they couldn't find work for their own, they'd have little for foreigners. And then there were the men. He frowned. Italian men were pinchers. He'd heard all about it—right there on the Via Veneto, even in St. Peter's Square. No woman was safe. He shook his head.

And France. France was superb, it was their cultural spring, a feeling that runs strongly in French Canadians. But it was so obvious that surely Canadian authorities would watch for them there. But look, on across the map, over the Pyrenees and into Spain. There on the Catalonian coast of the Mediterranean lay Barcelona. He strained his memory. Barcelona. It was an ancient city, cosmopolitan, surprised by nothing. Two thousand years ago it had been a Roman outpost. It was a great seaport—there should be plenty of foreigners and there might be work. French must be common, and anyway, Spanish should be an easy transition from French. With three languages and a business and legal background, he should have some value in an international seaport, eh? And again, there was that strange sense of the man wanted but a gentleman still, identifying not with those who are pursued but with the pursuers. Spain is a strong country, he told Carmen, with a strong police force—people are safe there.

He was up and walking around the room, suddenly excited, his voice so loud Carmen was afraid the landlady would hear. Look—

Barcelona is hardly more than a hundred miles from Majorca, where the rich go to dance in the sun. "What do you say, Mrs. Geoffroy?" he cried. "Shall we go to Barcelona and dance in the sun?" Laughing, he danced easily around the room, fingers clicking imaginary castanets.

Carmen smiled. She felt good, as she always did when Geoffroy was in this mood, light and bright; the darkness passed.

INTERPOL OSLO IS A section within the Kriminalpolitisentral, the name given to the Central Office for Criminal Investigation in Norway. Its offices are on the ground floor of 3 Victoria Terrace, in a handsome four-story pile of a building of oyster-white stone with a gray lead roof. Gables and cupolas stand above its prominent Gothic windows. There is something a little forbidding about it, a quality enhanced by the fact that during the German occupation in World War II it served as Gestapo headquarters.

It was snowing when the request from Ottawa arrived. The radio operator took it to Gunnar Lund, head of the Central Office for Criminal Investigation. Lund had previously sent messages concerning this case to police authorities throughout Norway, but the report that Geoffroy's wife was cashing checks in downtown Oslo became a matter for the municipal police. Therefore, Lund contacted the head of the Oslo Criminal Investigation Department, Per Hagen, and familiarized him with the details. Hagen considered the matter carefully and nodded.

In a sense, of course, Lund was no more interested in Geoffroy than was Hagen. But he was very interested in responding correctly to an Interpol request. Soon he—quite possibly on behalf of Hagen— might be asking a national central bureau chief somewhere in the world for just this sort of help, and then the response would matter a great deal. As gracefully as possible, he pointed this out to Hagen, who agreed. "We'll move immediately," he said.

Unlike most Western nations, Norway keeps its police procedures secret, and the name of the detective assigned to the search for Geoffroy and his report remain buried in Oslo's archives. Yet it is possible to reconstruct essentially what the detective did and what he learned.

He began his rounds, wearing a plain topcoat and rubber overshoes against the dry snow. The people he encountered described him as a smallish man, wiry, of nondescript appearance, with a certain contained abrasiveness of manner. It was not so much that he was unfriendly or rough as that he seemed to expect people to be less—or worse—than they were.

Perhaps his experience had soured him. (Reinhardtsen, for example, had been a rather self-consciously bohemian sort who described himself as a commercial artist. He told readily enough what he knew of Lafond, but the detective kept circling around to how Reinhardtsen earned his living, until Reinhardtsen began to wonder if the Lafond questions were a cover for something else. Then, of course, he got angry, and the detective, still wearing an irritating half smile of doubt, left in the middle of his expostulations.)

The clerk at the Bergens Privatbank branch could not place Carmen's name, but he remembered Geoffroy's face when the detective laid the picture before him. "Oh, yes," he said, "that one could be difficult." But he knew no more.

The detective began to work the hotels in his usual manner. In each, he asked for the register and at the same time he laid the picture unobtrusively on the front desk. Had they seen this man? He paused before the fourth hotel, a place that showed a palmlike plant in its lobby window. A palm tree in Oslo! The detective shook his head and went inside.

There is a natural antagonism between police and hotelkeepers. They need each other, but their interests often are opposite. The clerk remembered the man in the picture immediately. Wordlessly he flipped open the register. Mr. and Mrs. Réal Lafond, Montreal. A passport number was noted. They had stayed only two nights. No forwarding address. Perhaps they had gone to a pension—they had asked a few questions—but no, no idea which one. The detective put the picture in his inside coat pocket and walked out.

At the pension, the fifth or sixth he visited, Mrs. Ida Jarlson remembered them well. "Of course," she said. "The professor. They were a charming couple. He seemed quite distinguished. I called the university to see if they hadn't a place for him, but they weren't at all interested. They really were rather rude. I think he was very disappointed, poor man. They made a friend, too, Reinhardtsen his name was. He's an artist, a very nice young man." Her voice trailed off and her smile faded. "But why are the police interested? Is something wrong?"

Just a routine inquiry, the detective said.

But now she wanted him to go. "Well, I know nothing more, nothing at all. They were very nice. They paid their bills. They left without saying where they were going. Called a taxi and left. They had five bags." She was standing and had her door open. "Thank you for coming."

The detective's hunch was that his quarry had left Norway. He called British European Airways. "Lafond. Yes, that's familiar. He kicked up a row of some sort about his ticket. That's it—he had a forty-five-day excursion fare from someplace in North America and he wanted a refund so he could go somewhere else. Of course, we can't do that. If you don't use the round trip, everything reverts to full fare. It's a matter of international regulations."

Where had they wanted to go?

The fussy voice paused. "Let's see. No, I don't have that. Anyway, the people at Winge smoothed it all over. They're good at working out these problems."

At the graceful old Hotel Nobel Building, of gray granite with ANNO DOM 1899 chiseled in the stone over the doorway, the detective studied the posters urging the Mediterranean on snow-weary Norwegians. He knocked snow from his boots and went in. On the second floor of the agency he found a pretty young woman whose cheerfulness—in part professional and in part growing from a delicious proposal just made by a handsome young man—managed to overcome even his dour abrasiveness. For her the detective produced a certain remote, distilled charm of his own.

Yes, she remembered them well. Lafond had been, well, a bit cranky, but she had worked it all out. The airlines really are stuffy, but there are ways around the problem. So she sent them along, happy as lambs.

And where had she sent them?

"Why, to Barcelona, via Frankfurt. SAS connecting with Iberia. They wanted a hotel and I suggested the Hotel Colón, which is excellent, four-star. I could see immediately from his face that it was a bit expensive, so I suggested its sister hotel, the Regencia Colón, which is in the street behind and really is very nice. Three-star, and it draws a lot of tourists. So I made the reservation and fixed the tickets and off they went.

"And now you're asking all these questions, so there's more to the gentleman than he told me, I suppose." She smiled brightly. "Well, I never would have known. He acted exactly like a tourist. Wasn't that clever of him?"

"Or stupid," the detective said.

Given a day and a flight number, the airline confirmed the passage of Mr. and Mrs. Lafond readily enough. Geoffroy was gone and the detective was finished. He had spent two days and the investigation had been like most, neither slower nor faster, neither more interesting nor less. He put an old kettle on a burner to heat water for his tea and sat down at the metal desk in his cubicle office and began to type his report.

THE AIRPORT AT FRANKFURT is one of the busiest in Europe, and Geoffroy and Carmen felt as if they had suddenly returned to the world. An airline clerk in a neat uniform glanced at their tickets and directed them down long corridors. The floor was of firm black rubber and the people moved silently. Geoffroy was startled to see signs for sex shops and porn stalls posted with equal prominence beside those for rest rooms, telephones and coffee shops.

He took Carmen's arm protectively, shaking his head. They found an international newsstand, but the woman attendant gazed at them blankly when they asked for Canadian papers. Geoffroy had the feeling that she had never heard of Canada. He saw a small bulletin, published in Belgium, that advertised jobs abroad: "Openings in Africa." He bought one and stuffed it in his overcoat pocket. Since they were in transit at the airport—technically they did not enter Germany—they boarded their Iberia flight without having been asked for their passports.

There was a subtle difference in ambience aboard the Spanish aircraft that Geoffroy liked. The colors were brighter, the stewardesses by chance had dark hair, the passengers were looser and louder than on the Scandinavian Airlines System plane Geoffroy and Carmen had just left. He began to feel good; she could sense his relief.

They had left Oslo in a snowstorm; they arrived in Barcelona in the sun. The Spanish immigration officer smiled as he stamped their passports, and customs waved them through. The air outside was cool, but with a promise of warmth to come, as if spring already were approaching.

The Regencia Colón is a modest building of brick and stone at Sagristans and Layetana streets, near Barcelona's ancient Gothic quarter. Its quiet entrance looks toward the rear of the grander Hotel Colón. A bellman brought in their bags, and Geoffroy was struck immediately with the lobby's warmth. It was done in the Spanish manner, creamy walls, red tile floors in intricate designs, carefully carved wood with a high polish, and a handsome staircase. Over the desk was a quote from Cervantes:

Barcelona, harbor of courtesy, shelter of foreigners, hospital of the poor, home of the brave, revenge of the oppressed and place of faithful friendship, unique in setting and beauty.

It was an excellent beginning. In their room, where the single beds were clamped together as if for lovers and the closet doors were inlaid with panels of polished wood, they changed from their heavy clothes and hurried outside. Within a couple of blocks they found their way to the Ramblas, a wide boulevard filled with open-air cafés, and then to a splendid medieval street that ran through old Barcelona to the center point, where Christopher Columbus atop his great stone pillar overlooks the harbor.

After the stillness of Oslo, there was something almost frightening about the stream of people coursing along the broad promenade, but they were swept into it immediately, anonymous and yet somehow united with the people all around them. They passed twittering birds in cages, parrots and monkeys for sale, buckets of vivid flowers stacked three-deep outside the florists' stalls. People talked and laughed and cars honked. Just off the busy thoroughfare they admired the large and noble palms surrounding the Plaza Réal. Suddenly, farther on, Geoffroy gestured. Carmen saw rising in his face some internal pleasure that was immediately infectious.

"Look," he said. "We're home." Above them she saw the street sign: CALLE DEL CARMEN. And chuckling, he put his arm around her thin shoulders and held her easily against his bulk as they walked into the warm and noisy dusk of old Barcelona.

CHAPTER 7

BURRIS HAD SOME OF the hunter in him. True, by the time he was posted to northwestern Alberta, the RCMP rarely had cause to track a fugitive, and when they did, it was by plane or car or snowmobile. But Burris could still vividly recall the tales some of the old inspectors told, stories of tracking men in the woods north of the Peace River using only a sleigh and a team of blue-eyed dogs, stories of running through the empty wilderness toward Great Slave Lake and the Arctic beyond. Sometimes the snow would come and cover all tracks, and temperatures would fall to ten and twenty below zero. If they fell to thirty or forty below, the tracker might hole up, living in the snow, dogs huddled to hold their heat. But soon enough, the quarry would be up and moving and then there would be tracks. There are always tracks when men are moving.

Burris was restless and edgy. The newspapers were biting for results as he waited for word from Oslo. There wasn't much humor in his deep-set eyes, and Inspector Ebert stayed clear of him and warned others who didn't recognize the signs. When the Interpol Oslo message came, it confirmed that Geoffroy and Carmen had been there and, as he had half suspected, that they were gone:

ACCORDING TO THE TRAVEL BUREAU WINGE REISEBYRAA OSLO THEY LEFT NORWAY BY PLANE TO BARCELONA INFORMING THAT THEY WERE DUE TO STAY AT THE HOTEL REGENCIA COLON ADDRESS SAGRISTANS 13, BARCELONA . . . END IP OSLO

He sat at his desk in the Criminal Investigation Bureau, fingering the message. The hunter and the hunted. Geoffroy was moving again, south toward Africa, probably seeing Barcelona as a logical departure point. If they reached Africa, they would be hard to find and there would be more trouble in Ottawa. They were running in the open, not trying to hide. They had made hotel reservations through a travel bureau. Burris couldn't believe such confidence— perhaps it was Geoffroy's way of doubling back. Burris' instincts were stretching toward the fleeing figure, and his shoulders moved; he realized he wanted to ready a pack and follow. Instead, smiling faintly, he prepared a message for Interpol Madrid.

The message was routed through Paris, where it was translated into Spanish. It relayed all of Oslo's information and repeated the numbers of the traveler's checks. It added: WE REQUEST AN INVESTIGATION TO EFFECT THE ARREST OF THE WANTED CONVICTED MURDERER JOSEPH GEOFFROY. It also urged a check of international arrival and departure records, travel agencies and banks.

The operator in Interpol Madrid's radio room, on the sixth floor of Madrid police headquarters, took the message immediately to the roomy, well-carpeted office of José Nieto, then chief of Spain's National Central Bureau. Nieto had already posted Ottawa's initial message and the red notice to Spain's two national security forces, the Policia Nacional and the Guardia Civil. But now Geoffroy was tied specifically to Barcelona, almost four hundred miles to the northeast. There, in the Jefatura Superior de Policia, at Via Layetana 43, Nieto's message was received and marked for attention. However, the Jefatura was humming this Sunday—there were seven hundred–odd suspicious characters caught in a police dragnet who must be examined—and the matter could not be dealt with at once.

In Ottawa, the Geoffroy affair, as the papers now called it, was embarrassing the government. This was the one development that Geoffroy could not have anticipated. Solicitor General Jean-Pierre Goyer returned from vacation to find a hailstorm of charges of "corrupt practice within the administration of law in Canada." Goyer ordered a full report and took to the House of Commons to deny the rumor that because they had gone to the same law school, he and Geoffroy were friends. There was a new outcry when someone realized that by allowing Geoffroy to marry Carmen, the state had eliminated a leading witness against him in the event the new trial he was seeking was granted.

Ducking and twisting, prison officials said that they had relied on the report of the interview with Carmen. Goyer, moving too quickly, implied that Geoffroy's departure would never have occurred without that favorable report. Immediately Gerald Brennan, the prison director who had authorized the leave, was transferred away from St. Vincent de Paul; the papers said he was fired and Goyer said it was routine. The headline on a news analysis story showed how things were going: GOYER WILL SURVIVE GEOFFROY FIASCO. Survive? Burris winced.

The issue was privilege: Was this man part of an old-club-tie network that took care of its own, even those convicted of murder? That was what brought the story of Geoffroy to debate on the floor of his nation's Parliament. There, under the vaulted arches of Tyndall limestone, the golden mace before the Speaker symbolizing the nation's authority, the solons of each party lined up on either side at oaken desks set before green velvet curtains and squabbled over the notary who had presented Carmen with a rose. It was ironic, but that did not lessen its political danger, a point that was not at all lost on that apolitical policeman John Burris.

From his seat in the row behind the Prime Minister, Goyer rose to present a report on how the Geoffroy affair had happened. He was predictably factual and bland. In passing, he mentioned Philip Leclerc. "A name of blessed memory," suddenly rumbled the old lion of the Conservatives, former Prime Minister John Diefenbaker.

When Goyer sat down, there arose from the front bench on the opposite side a rough-tongued member from western Canada named Eldon M. Woolliams, who delivered the response. After listening to "the fairy story that the minister read today," Woolliams said, he was convinced that there must be a real judicial inquiry. And, he said, Goyer "must take the responsibility. Either he had knowledge or he did not, and if he did not, his mismanagement is so grave that he should resign."

Such remarks are not unusual, but he was having sport at Goyer's expense, and that is never pleasant. Goyer sat in silence, his lips a bloodless line. Woolliams resurrected the Leclerc affair at length to appreciative cries from his side, and added, "I think the minister must be writing a new book, *A Lifer's Honeymoon*, or *How to Murder Your Wife and Marry Your Mistress*. Why wither in jail when you can go the Goyer way and inherit the murdered wife's children and be released from a dull life sentence?" As titters rose in the galleries, he cried, "I say that by corruption or incredible incompetence, he was allowed to escape."

The government still rebuffed demands for a special inquiry, but it was not clear, so long as Geoffroy remained at large, how long it could hold that position. Goyer came from the chamber looking pale and angry. A few minutes later, crossing a courtyard, he encountered Burris by chance.

"Well," he said sharply, "what do you have on the wandering Geoffroy?"

Burris' gravelly voice was calm. "We may have him located— we'll know in a day or two. We're following every lead."

"You do that," Goyer said evenly. "The sooner the better."

At Burris' level, orders do not come more directly. He went to the Interpol radio room and composed a new message for Madrid. It began, "Please indicate immediately what results you have obtained from your investigation," and added, "Arrest of Geoffroy is a matter of prime concern to this NCB."

Then Burris did something unusual. He placed an overseas call to Interpol headquarters in St. Cloud and asked for Jean Nepote, the secretary-general. Nepote was a suave, urbane man who seemed more like a diplomat than a police officer. He had served in the Sûreté Nationale of France until 1946, when he became deputy secretary-general of Interpol, rising to the post of secretary-general in 1963. Perhaps twenty-six years of buffering the police forces of more than a hundred nations had made him a diplomat. His office was on the top floor of the building, on the side that overlooked Paris. It was a big room, plainly furnished: a couple of armchairs, a coffee table, Nepote's big desk—which was always clean, always bare—a bookshelf, which held, among other things, a policeman's nightstick. His manner was always polite, but it was also straightforward and unpretentious.

The call came in late afternoon. The sun was behind the building and his window blinds were open to the view. He had the cable traffic on Geoffroy spread on his desk when Burris came on the line. Nepote read the daily traffic and he was tuned to nuances. This case, simple enough on its face, was disturbing his Canadian colleagues. He and Burris were acquainted with each other; they had worked together in arranging the General Assembly in Ottawa the year before. They chatted a moment and then Nepote said, "You are calling, perhaps, about this fellow Geoffroy?"

"Yes," Burris said. "There's a great deal of interest in him here. The concern is that he may be making for Africa. We've traced him through to Spain, you know, and he may have some African connections."

"I understand Zaire is hiring now—many kinds of jobs seem to be available, especially in the professions," Nepote answered. "If he's interested in Africa, he might be drawn there. I can put through a special message to the National Central Bureau at Kinshasa."

"Yes, that would be excellent. I'd like to make sure that all messages get full coverage in zones one and two." Interpol divides the world into zones; zone one is northern Europe, and zone two is the rest of Europe and the countries of Algeria, Tunisia and Morocco in northern Africa.

"Of course," Nepote said.

"And—well, you know, they're last heard of in Barcelona. They may still be there. I haven't heard from Madrid yet." In St. Cloud, Nepote smiled. They had reached the point. As he talked, he stacked the Geoffroy papers; his desk was neat again. Paris was fading into the dusk.

"I would be happy to ask Madrid personally to pursue the matter, John," he said. "José Nieto is an old friend. If you think that would help." He smiled again, and somehow, on the other side of the world, in the bright Canadian morning, Burris heard the smile.

"Why, yes," he said. "I'm sure that would help."

When the call ended, Nepote took a clean sheet from his drawer and unscrewed the cap on his old fountain pen. He sat watching as the lights of the city brightened, and after a while he began to write in a steady, rounded hand, the pen scratching the paper in the still room. When he was done, he closed his office, put on his topcoat, and walked around to the communications room.

"Please put priority on this," he said, and went home to dinner.

I CALL YOUR PERSONAL ATTENTION TO THE JOSEPH GEOFFROY AFFAIR MENTIONED IN RED NOTICE 56/72 A/7919 AND SEVERAL TELEGRAMS STOP IN CANADA CAPITAL IMPORTANCE IS ATTACHED TO THIS AFFAIR AND WOULD BE OBLIGED THEREFORE IF YOU WOULD UNDERTAKE MAXIMUM INVESTIGATIONS WITH A VIEW TO DISCOVERING A TRACE OF THE WANTED PERSONS ARRIVAL IN SPAIN STOP PLEASE NOTE THAT THE TRAVELERS CHECKS MENTIONED IN TELEGRAM 368/16 OTTAWA . . . ARE AMERICAN EXPRESS STOP WOULD YOU BE SO KIND AS TO INFORM ME OF MEASURES TAKEN BY SPANISH POLICE SO I CAN INFORM CANADIAN NCB STOP THANK YOU END NEPOTE

The next day another cable went out, marked ALL STATIONS, ZONES ONE AND TWO, signed with the General Secretariat's code name and ending:

CANADIAN AUTHORITIES ATTACH SPECIAL IMPORTANCE TO RAPID ARREST OF GEOFFROY STOP PLEASE GIVE ALL POSSIBLE ASSISTANCE ON THIS CASE STOP THANK YOU END GOPTI

So the messages fell upon Nieto in Madrid, and he in turn alerted the Jefatura in Barcelona. Now the Geoffroy case was placed in the hands of an interesting police inspector named Luis Serra, who headed a crack detail of Barcelona's Criminal Investigation Brigade.

Inspector Serra was forty-three and moved with the easy fluidity that comes from working out daily in a gymnasium. He was a Catalan with a reputation for warm humor combined with shrewdness. He was relaxed, as gentle as his profession allowed, a bit of a romantic in a line of work that produced hard-eyed realists. Most of his schoolmates had become businessmen, and probably he was a policeman only because as a boy, when one is most open to ideals, he had met an officer who was a grand gentleman—*un caballero.* Serra was the sort of man for whom the Spanish invented the term *simpático.*

Now he sat at the single desk in the squad room, oblivious to a peeling strip of the institutional green paint on the wall behind him, and looked at Nieto's message. He was amused. "We have here, González," he said to an assistant, "a very superior North American criminal type. He flees around the world to Barcelona and chooses a hotel that is—where? The Regencia Colón, not one hundred paces from our doorstep."

Serra turned again to the cables. The man had been convicted of murder, which meant he could be dangerous. He had been granted a leave, which meant he could be reasonable. Serra nodded thoughtfully. "Why don't you go along to the Regencia Colón and see what you can find?" he told González. Then he added, "But don't take any risks."

González nodded and stood up. He put his Cadix .38 snubnose in its leather holster on his belt, behind his hip where it was out of sight, and walked out onto Vía Layetana.

As he entered the Regencia Colón his eyes swept around the warm, gracious interior. Geoffroy was not in the lobby. González's coat was loose and he was ready if Geoffroy should step off the elevator. But none of this was evident as he approached the desk under the Cervantes quotation and placed Geoffroy's picture flat on the counter, blocking with his body the lobby's view of what he was doing. Had they seen this gentleman? he asked pleasantly. He had an easy smile, just as Serra did. The divergence of interests between hotelkeepers and police is as real in Barcelona as in Oslo, but González's technique matched his personality. He thought honey the better bait.

"Oh, yes," the clerk said. "Mr. Lafond. But he's gone."

He opened the register and found the single signature. The clerk and the cashier shook their heads; the man was gone and they knew nothing more.

IF GEOFFROY AND CARMEN had a honeymoon, it was in Barcelona. The city was almost five degrees south of Montreal's latitude and was warmed by the Mediterranean. Its color and people and sunshine soothed Geoffroy; the chill of St. Vincent de Paul was working out of his mind. The poetic impulse that Carmen inspired in him, which his trial and the year in prison had dimmed, began to return. They walked endlessly in the Gothic quarter, on ancient streets too narrow to permit automobiles. There were flower beds and benches and neat shrubbery, arches and stone stairs and mysterious blank walls, ornate windows and carved pillars and fountains and mosaic floors that hurled sprays of color. The poetry of stone and space, of light and shadow and color, warmed them and drew them together.

They would stay awhile; they should find an apartment. On impulse Geoffroy asked the advice of an elevator operator at the Regencia Colón, and that afternoon the man led them to the Apartamentos Colón, a short distance away on Vía Layetana. There a properly forbidding concierge—there would be no foolishness with her—showed them a flat on the sixth floor. It had a small bedroom, a sitting room, kitchen and bath, but it was the little balcony and the French doors that opened onto the murmur of traffic from Vía Layetana that persuaded them. They would take it, Geoffroy said, which produced the first and last smile he ever saw from this stalwart woman.

Vía Layetana was a prosaic street filled with underwriters and shipping firms. Geoffroy felt comfortable there, with the constant stream of little cars and buses and motorbikes and the sidewalks full of people. There were a variety of shops nearby—a bar and a men's shop, a drugstore and a photography shop, and one that dealt in model trains. Geoffroy liked to watch the little trains circle endlessly in the shopwindow.

The Apartamentos Colón was at Vía Layetana 42. The solid gray Jefatura Superior de Policia at Vía Layetana 43 was not directly opposite but was across and about a hundred feet up the street. Armed policemen stood before it day and night, and plainclothesmen went

in and out. Geoffroy saw no Canadian papers, and he gave little thought to what might be going on so far away. He felt at ease, and sometimes when he passed the Jefatura Superior he nodded politely to the policemen posted on the sidewalk.

The need to work was beginning to press Geoffroy. His funds were shrinking. Barcelona itself was attractive, with its great port and its busy shipping business, but first he would have to learn Spanish. And Africa was beckoning. He and Carmen sat long over meals, studying the pamphlet he had picked up in the airport at Frankfurt. It was filled with listings of jobs in Africa, particularly in Zaire.

He consulted an old map, found Kinshasa, and felt oriented when he realized this was the country once known as the Congo. They circled one job opportunity after another, debating how he might couch his applications, and eventually he wrote letters to three prospective employers.

Carmen applied for a French teacher's position in Morocco, over Geoffroy's objections. "You know how the Arabs treat women," he said. But the issue wouldn't arise, because he expected an affirmative answer from Zaire. There, he told Carmen, they would live frugally, save several thousand dollars a year, and after a few years come back to Europe to a proper life.

Restlessly he awaited the answers. His mood was changing. He began to get an uncomfortable feeling, as if he were being watched or followed. Carmen felt it, too. They joked about it a little, but it really wasn't funny. Perhaps they should go on to Zaire—surely they could find work. But the ads had seemed promising and to leave would be to miss the responses. So, nervous, the honeymoon time fading, they awaited the mail.

CHAPTER 8

WHEN LUIS SERRA DISCOVERED Geoffroy gone from the Hotel Regencia Colón, he sent immediate word to Nieto in Madrid. Spanish hotels register only the husband and so there was no mention of Carmen. Serra's message said that the wanted man had been there and gone; the search would continue. But by the time the wording went from Barcelona to Madrid to Paris to Ottawa, the message that Paul Ferrar took in Morse and put on Burris' desk said that Geoffroy had been alone at the hotel.

That hit Burris hard. He sat looking out at the fresh snow that had fallen overnight, warming his hands on a cup of coffee. If they had separated, they were running to cover, and that meant that Carmen probably was already in Africa, preparing the way. It would not be pleasant to tell Goyer that Geoffroy had slipped away again, for now the Prime Minister himself had been drawn into the clash over the honeymoon of Yves Geoffroy. Pierre Trudeau, that elegant gentleman, whose popularity was slowly waning, personally beat off new demands for a judicial inquiry. To allow an inquiry would be to agree that more than a simple runaway was involved, and it would keep the case in the headlines for weeks.

The opposition pressure did force some concessions. Against RCMP advice, the government admitted finding Geoffroy's application for a passport under an alias. A minister has to say something when under attack, but now Geoffroy might know that his cover as Réal Lafond was exposed. The name led the newspapers to the airlines and the flight to London. The man who had been their seatmate came forward and was a one-day sensation. A reporter set out for Oslo. Burris sighed. His coffee was cold. What a pain this Geoffroy was becoming.

"Corporal Fresnard is the field officer in charge," Burris told Ebert. "Call him and ask him to come up here. And tell him to pack a bag. He's going on a trip."

Four hours later, having arrived from Montreal, Fresnard sat quietly in front of Burris' desk. His suitcase stood in the corner. Nothing in his manner admitted that his situation was unusual or that he was impressed. Burris tossed him the Interpol message.

"If the Parent woman has separated, maybe they know their cover is blown. She can travel more easily than he, and he may be dug in, getting a new identity while she goes ahead and arranges a berth, probably in Zaire. So the key is to find him if he's still in Spain—or wherever he's gone—and clamp on him before he can move again. We're going to lay charges against her—false declaration in order to obtain a passport and possession of a false passport—and ask St. Cloud to put out an All Stations Alert for her traveling alone. And you'd better get over to Barcelona yourself. Accompany your provincial police colleagues and build a fire under the Spanish police— well, of course, you understand, that's delicate. You have no authority there. But I want you to let them know that this is damned urgent and that you're there to give them a hand, under their command, of course. You get started and we'll send a message through St. Cloud that you're on your way."

IN BARCELONA, LUIS SERRA sat at the single desk in his big squad room on the mezzanine floor of the Jefatura Superior de Policia. French doors opened onto a small balcony that overlooked a side street. The whole building had an airy quality, with high ceilings, and a huge stairwell around which a wide stone staircase climbed. Serra was part of the best all-purpose squad in the Criminal Investigation Brigade and his men spent much of their time on the street. The room was furnished for men who were rarely there: the desk, a horsehair sofa in the corner, a few typewriters on little tables, and several straight-backed wooden armchairs. Now González sat in one of these, cocked precariously back against the wall.

"Ah, the North Americans again," Serra said, looking at the cable on the desk. "Look, González. We're going to have to check every hotel and pension in the city, I suppose, but first let's give the staff at the Regencia Colón another going-over. Maybe the night workers remember Geoffroy."

"Here's a man who runs away from prison in Canada and goes to Oslo. Then he comes to Barcelona. He makes hotel reservations in advance. This is a man who comes here with some purpose, and he probably talks to someone, asks advice, asks directions. Chances are somebody there knows something. I'd like to make some progress on the case before the North American police get here. That's just what we need, huh, to have them come and find their man while we're sitting around propping up the walls!"

González looked up sharply and saw Serra grinning at him. He stood up, pushed the offending chair away from the wall, and folded the red notice into a coat pocket.

"*Bueno,*" he said. "I'll shake the hotel again."

González started once more with the clerks, showing the picture and waiting for recognition; tried the bellman, the bartender and the waitresses in the restaurant, and moved on to the maids. They were upstairs, and on the way he showed the picture to a man named Víctor López, who was operating the elevator.

"Certainly," López said. "A very courteous gentleman. I was of some small assistance to him."

"Oh?"

"He was interested in an apartment, and I took him to just what he wanted. Come on—I'll show you if you like."

The bellman took over the elevator, and López led González to the Apartamentos Colón.

"There," he said, pointing. "Up on the sixth floor."

"Don't point, you fool," said González.

"They're still there, I expect. I saw Lafond on the street yesterday."

"Good." González started inside.

"Mr. González," López said, stopping him. "No doubt one day I will need a little help, in getting a passport or some bit of paperwork. You understand?"

"And you shall have it, my friend," González said, clapping him on the shoulder. Then he went inside to speak to the dour concierge. She began to nod.

"They await your pleasure," González told Serra a few minutes later. "They are across the street, a hundred feet away, awaiting us like pullets in a hen house."

Serra was pleased. At that moment, on the broad staircase, Serra's secretary, Pedro, hailed him. The Canadian policemen had arrived, three of them, and were waiting in the squad room.

Serra nodded and turned to González. "Get two or three others together. We'll go now," he said. He composed himself and swept into the squad room.

"Ah, gentlemen," he said, smiling at them genially. "Welcome to Barcelona."

Fresnard stood quickly and introduced himself and the two provincial police officers from Quebec. Serra shook hands with each.

"It is a pleasure to have you here," he said. "It is a pleasure to assist you. I can assure you that all is well. Here, sit, be comfortable, have a cigarette. I will send in coffee. I have a moment of business and then we will talk. Twenty minutes, no more." He turned to the secretary. "Pedro, coffee for the gentlemen. Make them comfortable. I will return in a few minutes."

With González and three other detectives, he tripped rapidly down the broad staircase. The Cadix .38 was tucked in the small of his back, and he unbuttoned his coat. It hung loose and yet was neat, and the pistol made no bulge.

"You have them located?" he asked.

"Sixth floor, apartment B. Off the elevator and turn left. One turn in the hallway and it's the first door. The concierge says the apartment has only one door. They have not gone out today."

"All right," Serra said. His voice was much crisper than usual. "This Geoffroy was serving a life sentence for murder and he won't be happy about going back to it. He's probably armed and he's certainly dangerous. We'll use standard precautions." González nodded.

They walked separately along the sunny street and crossed at the light. Serra smiled and waved at a vendor he knew. Walking casually, he was almost past the Apartamentos Colón when he turned abruptly, pushed open the plate-glass doors, and went in. The others followed.

The concierge surged forward. "Look here—" she began.

Serra turned a cold face to her. "Silence, madame," he said. "Police. The tenant Lafond has not come down this morning?"

She shook her head.

"Very well. I have the proper authority. You are to stay here and remain quiet. Please do not use the telephone. Alberto will be here to make sure that no one uses the elevators."

He led the way onto an elevator while one of his men positioned himself so that he could see both the elevator and the interior staircase. On the sixth floor, Serra gestured toward the staircase and one of the men mounted guard on the landing.

An apartment door opened and a man looked out, startled. "Police," González said in a hard, low voice. "Go inside. Do not open your door again. Stand well clear of the door. Be quiet. Now!" The door closed quietly and there was silence.

Serra turned the corner and saw the door marked B. He had the blue-black .38 with its two-inch barrel in his hand. The doorknob was on the right.

González flattened himself against the wall to the right of the door. Serra stood well to the left: no burst of fire through the door would reach him. There was a taut, hard look on his face. He rapped on the wooden door with the pistol barrel, placed both hands around its butt, and waited. He could hear his watch ticking. There were footsteps inside and the door opened.

Carmen's hand was still on the knob when Serra stepped in smartly, his left foot against the door, weight on that foot so that the door could not be closed, pistol at the ready. "Police," he said. He saw that her face was white, bloodless.

She did not move. He noticed her huge eyes and thought she was like a deer.

Directly ahead the bathroom door opened. Geoffroy came out. He was wearing a yellow terry cloth bathrobe. Carmen heard the door open and turned her head; Serra saw her look of terror increase. She expected disaster. González took Carmen's arm, and Serra stepped toward Geoffroy.

"Police," he said in French. "Do not move. Keep your hands in sight."

And in that elongated instant something tractable, even ingratiating, appeared on Geoffroy's face. Any threat ebbed away. Serra had no way of knowing that he had just seen the quality that overpowering authority produced in Geoffroy, the quality that had allowed him to talk his way out of St. Vincent de Paul.

"What is the meaning of this?" Geoffroy demanded.

"You are under arrest, Mr. Geoffroy, on a warrant from Canada."

"Geoffroy? Ah, perhaps that explains it. There has been a mistake. My name is Réal Lafond. Permit me to show you my passport. And put away that gun, won't you? There certainly is no need for that. I am a professional man."

"Please sit down, monsieur, and we will discuss it." Serra glanced at Carmen. The color was returning to her face. "You, too, madame. Sit down, if you please." He nodded to González, who began a systematic search of the apartment.

There was a lumpy sofa covered in dark simulated leather. Geoffroy sat down and Carmen started to sit beside him, but at a gesture from Serra she took the opposite end. A look of anguish passed between the couple. Serra put his pistol back in its concealed holster.

"My passport is there on the table," Geoffroy said. It had his picture and the name Réal Lafond.

Serra's tension was passing. He rather liked the Geoffroy who now was presenting himself. He smiled pleasantly. "Very well, Mr. Lafond," he said. "Quite possibly there has been an error, and if that is the case, you will have my apologies and those of the Spanish government. But I do have a warrant that appears to be for you under the name of Joseph Yves Geoffroy, so I must ask you to accompany us to our office. It is quite near, as perhaps you know. Everything can be straightened out there. So if you will get dressed, one at a time, Mrs. Lafond first, if you please."

Carmen stood up hesitantly.

"Please, madame. If you would get ready?"

She started across the room to the bedroom door and Serra nodded to González, who followed.

"No," Geoffroy said sharply. "He cannot be in the room with my wife. That would not be right."

"No signs of weapons," González said.

Serra nodded.

"Leave the door open, Mrs. Lafond. Five minutes, no more. González, stay by the door—not in it. Allow the lady her privacy."

When Carmen was at the open bedroom door, Serra stopped her. "Mrs. Lafond," he said easily, "I trust you would not do anything foolish like produce a weapon. My colleague is right there by the door. You understand that, don't you?" The paleness came back to Carmen's face and she nodded.

While Serra stood by the bathroom door, Geoffroy shaved, the electric razor whining. Then they walked arm in arm, an unobtrusive little group, to the Jefatura Superior. Geoffroy had asked not to be manacled in the street, and as one gentleman to another, Serra obliged him.

Serra walked into the squad room first. The Canadian officers stood up. Fresnard saw that Serra seemed very pleased with himself. He had been gone twenty-eight minutes.

"Gentlemen," he said in French, "may I present a countryman of yours—Monsieur Geoffroy."

Geoffroy, behind him, said quickly, "My name is Lafond."

"Ah, Geoffroy," Corporal Fresnard said. "We're very glad to see you."

WHEN BURRIS REACHED HIS office, the phone was ringing; Fresnard was reporting. Burris phoned Goyer's office, and within ten minutes newspapermen were in his anteroom.

"Hold them off," he told Ebert, "and get Paul Ferrar down here."

A few minutes later, moving on Ferrar's steady, rolling hand, the message was off to the General Secretariat, on the hill overlook-

From the top: a police photo of Geoffroy; Carmen, as she appeared at his trial; Geoffroy and Carmen during a trial recess; a distraught Geoffroy flanked by his sister and a police officer.

ing Paris, and thence around the world. A copy reached Jean Nepote's desk and he recognized it as a reserved, businesslike thank-you.

CANCEL INTERNATIONAL RED NOTICE AS GEOFFROY AND HIS WIFE WERE TAKEN INTO CUSTODY BARCELONA SPAIN 6/3/72 END IP OTTAWA

DESPITE THEIR IMMEDIATE acquiescence to extradition, formalities delayed the return of the Geoffroys. Then on March 13 they arrived in Montreal in the custody of Canadian authorities aboard a Spanish airliner. Geoffroy was remanded at once to St. Vincent de Paul prison.

On February 19, 1973, both pleaded guilty to charges arising from Yves Geoffroy's escape.

An uncommonly penetrating judge decided that Carmen had been blinded by love, and freed her unconditionally with an expression of censure and sympathy. Yves Geoffroy received two years concurrent with his life prison term for murder.

It had lasted seventy-three days, the honeymoon, and who is to say that it had not been worth it? Later a newspaperwoman asked about that when she interviewed Carmen, who resumed her visits to Geoffroy in the penitentiary as often as she was allowed, each time placing her purse in the little locker at the gate. Carmen replied, "When we saw a chance to escape, we took it. We hoped we would have years together, but we were willing to have only weeks or months."

THE VAGABOND
REMBRANDT

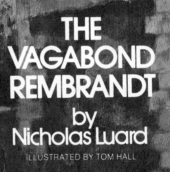

THE
VAGABOND
REMBRANDT

by
Nicholas Luard

ILLUSTRATED BY TOM HALL

Throughout his twenty-two years, Karel Whitman had done nothing that would make the world take the slightest note of him. Tall and gangly, with stringy, long hair, he seemed destined to go through life virtually anonymous. Then, early one December morning in the city of Tours, France, Whitman was to do something that would outrage that city's citizens, bewilder the police of several nations and send shock waves through the international art community.

Nicholas Luard, author of numerous spy thrillers, including *The Orion Line* and *Travelling Horseman*, here turns his considerable skills to re-creating the details of a story that had its beginnings in the shadow world of a hippie commune and ended dramatically beside a busy airport road.

Interpol's "Most Wanted" list of stolen artworks. Rembrandt, top left; van Goyen, middle right.

PROLOGUE

THE FRENCH HAVE no false modesty about their country.

To them it is and always has been *la belle France*, beautiful France, and the evidence to justify that simple but proud description is written clear on every corner of the land.

The dazzling winter snow flanks of the Alps and Pyrenees, where the midday air is as sharp and clean and cold as mountain water. The wild-flower tapestry, woven of emerald, violet, rose, and kingfisher blue, laid across the wild thyme-scented Provençal hills in spring. The rich rolling countryside of Normandy with its neat white-railed farms, the great golden wheat fields of the Beauce, starred with scarlet poppies in the high August heat. The silence of the southern plains in the fall, when leaves drift down through mist and at night woodsmoke coils up toward a harvest moon.

La belle France in every quarter and every season—and nowhere more beautiful at any time of the year than in the winding valley of the Loire River to the southwest of Paris.

It was on the banks of the Loire, during a chill December night in 1971, that an event took place which was to baffle the French police for almost a year and send shock waves throughout the entire European art establishment—shock waves that still reverberate today.

The setting was the ancient medieval town of Tours. The event was what is known in French legal parlance as a *délit*, that is to say a simple misdemeanor. Indeed the starting point of the misdemeanor could hardly have been more simple: a borrowed ladder, a gloved hand clenched around a rock, a windowpane shattering in the darkness.

Yet the story surrounding the theft which followed, for theft it proved to be, is remarkable. Reaching backward and forward in time, it contains a variety of diverse threads—the riches of the old nobility, the vain and tragic Queen Marie Antoinette, the vengeance of the French Revolution, a wandering young poet from behind the iron curtain, and a shadowy cast of underworld figures. And finally there is the shuttle that would weave all these threads together—the International Criminal Police Organization—Interpol. In 1972, a year short of its fiftieth anniversary, this unique organization, operating from a modernistic-looking building in a Paris suburb and using its computerized resources and communications network, would be instrumental in creating a fabric rich in drama and intrigue.

At the center of this fabric was the object of the crime itself. It was in the true sense of the word original. Not a bundle of bank notes, not a consignment of narcotics or a cache of contraband.

Instead, it was one of the glories of Western civilization, and as such quite literally priceless.

But let us start our story with the character who is to dominate it—the wandering poet.

CHAPTER 1

KAREL WHITMAN HAD been carefully nursing the glass of cheap red wine for twenty minutes.

Now it had come to an end. He drained the dregs, pushed the empty glass across the marble counter, and tapped its rim.

The barman glanced around. "Closed," he said in French. *"Fermé."*

Whitman frowned at him for a moment, uncomprehending. Then he rummaged in his pocket, found a one-franc piece, and held it up.

The barman shook his head. *"Fermé,"* he repeated firmly. "Finished for tonight. We're shut. *Compris?"*

He tapped his watch. Then he pointed at the clock on the far wall, which showed one a.m., and gestured at the door, miming the action of locking its bolts.

Whitman got the message. He shrugged sullenly, pushed himself away from the counter, and walked slightly unsteadily across the room. Before he reached the door he stopped. Outside, as he knew, it was bitterly cold. He buttoned up his topcoat and slipped on a pair of cheap woolen gloves.

The barman watched him leave with a mixture of distaste and contempt. He had nothing in principle against foreigners, but *les hippies,* as they were known when they first began to appear in Tours ten years earlier, they were different. Long-haired, dirty, idle, spinning out a single drink for half an hour just to get warm, putting off his regulars with their body odor—no, he couldn't stand them.

The one who'd just walked out was typical. Surly, scruffy, not speaking a word of French, keeping him up long after everyone else had gone home. Was he Dutch? German? Scandinavian? The youth might have been almost any nationality. The barman didn't know and didn't care. Through the window he could see the young man standing on the sidewalk. The barman walked over, pulled down the blind, and started locking up.

Karel Whitman lingered for a while longer outside the bar. Then he set off down the street.

Whitman was neither Dutch, German, nor Scandinavian. In spite of his curiously English-sounding surname he was in fact Czechoslovak. At the age of twenty-two he was not prepossessing.

He was tall and spare with an awkwardly made body, long stringy hair, a timid beard, and a weak, rather sulky face that nonetheless, when he smiled—which he did rarely—could manage to look impishly attractive. Yet if little else about him was remarkable, there was unmistakable intelligence in his eyes.

"It was what struck me most vividly about him," his lawyer, Maître Alain Herrault, was to recollect later. "There was something almost mystical in the way he looked at you. He had the eyes of a poet."

He was a perceptive man, M. Herrault. Although Whitman never revealed the fact to him, it was indeed as a poet that the young Czech saw himself. The conviction stemmed from the unusual circumstances of his background and upbringing.

Whitman was born in Prague on February 14, 1949. His father was by trade a plumber, with a long history of alcoholism. His mother worked as a secretary in a government bureau and had an equally long history of nervous disorders, including an attempt at suicide which resulted in her committal to a psychiatric hospital.

The turbulent and unhappy relationship between his drunken father and neurotic mother ended in divorce when Whitman was fifteen. Afterward, for reasons of convenience caused by Prague's acute housing shortage, Whitman went to live with his father, who had obtained a small apartment. Until then, despite all the difficulties and tensions of homelife, Whitman had been a model student. He obtained the Czechoslovak certificate of secondary education with excellent grades and had shown a particular aptitude for literature.

A year later the world of the exemplary young student started to come apart.

The adolescent Whitman fell deeply in love with a considerably older woman, a poet. He wanted to consummate the relationship sexually. She refused. A series of bitter quarrels took place, and late one night Whitman decided to follow his mother's example—he tried to kill himself with an overdose of sleeping pills.

The attempt was unsuccessful, but it was not to be the last.

After two months in the hospital Whitman was discharged. He returned to his studies, albeit with much less application than before. He grew his hair fashionably long, as had become the custom among his rebellious young contemporaries. And he started writing intermittently for a little avant-garde magazine, *The Wild Vine*. It was on the pages of this cheap, tattered, and irregularly produced periodical that Whitman first saw his poems in print.

Any regime is bound to respond to a gross and obvious disregard of the national mores. And to the Czechoslovak Communist government long hair and "libertine" poetry represented a challenge to the stability of the state. Whitman was ordered to have his hair cut. He declined to obey the instruction. To emphasize his refusal and to prevent the order's being executed by force, he made a second attempt to commit suicide.

That attempt was as unsuccessful as the first. He spent another month in the hospital, was discharged again, and returned to his previous life—the life of a mildly defiant, antiauthoritarian, and considerably muddleheaded student who roamed the streets and cafés of Prague with only one certain conviction. The conviction was his destiny as a poet.

By now relations between Whitman and his father had seriously deteriorated. The social alienation of the one and the ferocious drinking bouts of the other resulted in rapidly increasing conflict, at first expressed in verbal slugging matches and then in stand-up fights. Early in 1969 the outcome of one such brawl was the destruction of virtually everything in the apartment they shared.

Next day, to express both his frustration and remorse, Whitman repeated a familiar pattern of behavior—he tried to kill himself once more.

Predictably he failed. He went through the routine of hospitalization, this time for a month and a half, and returned again to the streets.

A few months later Whitman was arrested. The accusation was more serious than an affinity for long hair and poetry. He was charged with unlawful assembly in connection with a student demonstration. With no record of militancy in his past, rather the reverse, it seems likely he became involved in the demonstration by accident and not as an active participant.

Whatever the truth, the charge was a serious one. If convicted, Whitman was liable to a heavy prison sentence. Anyone who had followed his career up until then could reasonably feel entitled to predict with some certainty what he would do next—reach for the bottle of sleeping pills yet again.

As it turned out, the guess would have been wrong. Whitman chose another but, from the point of view of his Czechoslovak citizenship, equally definitive solution. He turned and ran, not just from the police but from the country of his birth.

From now on, Karel Whitman, visionary, poet, and world citizen, was going to live in countries that paid proper respect to long hair and free verse.

It has to be said that Whitman's first experiences as wandering poet and world citizen were not very encouraging. From Prague he drifted through Yugoslavia, and finally made his way to West

Germany. There he declared he was a "political refugee from the tyranny of totalitarianism." Just what reaction he expected to this grandiose description is not clear. In any event, the West German authorities treated him exactly the same as any other fugitive from the Soviet bloc, that is to say with extreme benevolence.

He was issued papers and sent to a refugee camp at Unna, an experience Whitman found thoroughly depressing. Yet even more distasteful was the advice he was given on his discharge from the camp a few weeks later. The resettlement officer handed him a list of job vacancies and suggested he find himself employment as soon as possible.

Poets write poetry. They should not be expected, in Whitman's view, to do anything as mundane as work. It was an attitude, he quickly discovered, shared by many members of his generation with which he was shortly to find himself more truly at home than at any stage in his life to date.

Since the early 1960s and then continuing into the 1970s young people had spread out in waves across both Europe and America. Beatniks, hippies, flower children, members of "the alternative society," the successive names they gave themselves—or were given by an enraged and bewildered bourgeoisie—were legion.

They repudiated both capitalism and Communism. They had no coherent philosophy, or rather they formulated endless philosophies that sometimes brought them a brief cohesion and then disintegrated. They were not necessarily lazy in the normal sense of the word, and this further baffled and irritated their parent generation; they simply did not believe in working.

"Why work, man, why? We didn't ask to be born. We didn't ask to live in your world. We're trapped here. So just let us go our own way, just let us be, okay?"

It wasn't, of course, quite as simple as that. Like it or not, to travel, to clothe oneself, even to eat required money. And money by and large could be obtained only by working. They were right. They were trapped.

Some, in frustration, turned to violence, to murderous assaults on the societies which had produced them. They became members of a variety of terrorist groups.

But the vast majority were like Karel Whitman. Whitman had a dream. The dream was out of focus. He never quite managed to see it clearly. So he did the best he could. He survived.

Survival in West Germany meant first a job laying rails for a steel producer in Essen. That lasted barely a month. From Essen Whitman drifted to Hamburg and in late 1969 found work on the docks. A few months afterward he moved on again, this time to West Berlin, which as it turned out was to become his adopted city.

By now Whitman was a fully accredited member of what we may call "the companions of the road," the youthful and footloose international community who roam all Europe as he had once roamed the streets of Prague. With their help Whitman found lodging in a Berlin commune.

Two can live as cheaply as one, so the old saw goes. But the wits and resources of two are double that of one.

One day in April, 1970, soon after Whitman's arrival in Berlin, a young French girl walked into the commune.

CHAPTER 2

ANNE-MARIE FRANK was small, fair, and pretty in a vague, unremarkable way. Her face would have been in place in any group portrait of the graduating class of '66—graduating, that is, from the very informal universities of San Francisco's Haight-Ashbury or New York's East Village, London's Chelsea or Paris' Montparnasse. Solemn, puzzled, regarding the outside world with suspicion, conscious of her apartness and at the same time vulnerable, even wistful.

Yet just as Whitman had one striking feature in an otherwise undistinguished appearance—his poet's eyes, as M. Herrault described them—so too did Anne-Marie. It was her mouth. There one can see a stubbornness, a determination, a resolution quite at variance with the rest of her physical presence.

Mlle. Anne-Marie Frank, if one studies her photograph carefully, is clearly not a young lady to be trifled with. Naïve, perhaps, and overready to trust but capable of a strong protective loyalty, of commitment and deep affection regardless of the consequences. Above all, one senses she is a practical young woman, a sharer of dreams but always with her feet firmly planted on the ground.

Yet dreamers too have to eat. Anne-Marie was determined from the start that the dreamers in her life would never go short of bread—not while it lay within her power to provide for them. The dreamer, the poet, she met that April day in Berlin was to stretch her generosity to the limit. To her credit, she never faltered.

Where did she come from, this slender but formidable young woman, and how did she find herself in Berlin in the spring of 1970?

Anne-Marie was born on September 12, 1944, in Parthenay, a small town eighty-two miles southwest of Tours, where she grew up with her two sisters in a poor but respectable family. Money was always short. France, in Anne-Marie's childhood, was only beginning to recover from the ravages on its economy—and its spirit—inflicted by Hitler's Germany.

From her earliest years Anne-Marie was taught the classic virtues of any small provincial French town: thrift, hard work, good-neighborliness, regular attendance at Mass. At school, like Whitman, she proved a model student. She gained her *bachot*—the French certificate of secondary education—and went on to study first at Poitiers and then Tours.

In 1961 her father died. The most immediate consequence of his death, apart from its emotional effects, was that Anne-Marie and her sisters had to start contributing to the family budget. The role of provider was to become very familiar to Anne-Marie in the years ahead.

Her first job was as a children's nurse. It lasted for over eighteen months. Thereafter she had a variety of occupations, each allowing her to give part of her weekly wages to her mother. Meanwhile, in the intervals between working, she continued her studies. Anne-Marie was particularly interested in the German language.

"She went to Germany every year for her summer vacation," Mme. Frank, her widowed mother, remembered. "The reason was quite simple. She wanted eventually to teach German and so she wished to learn the language as fluently as possible."

Anne-Marie wasn't the only member of her family who was drawn to Germany. For her sister Monique the country held the same attraction. To the two girls, or young women as it might now be more accurate to call them, a summer visit to Berlin, Frankfurt, Düsseldorf, or the green countryside of the Black Forest became an annual event.

In 1970, nine years after her father's death, Anne-Marie decided that if she was ever to realize her ambition of becoming a *professeur d'allemand*—a qualified teacher of the German language—she would have to spend much more time in the country than she'd previously done during her summer vacations.

"She told me she was going to live in Berlin," her mother said. "Until she left she'd always sent me a check every month, maybe only a hundred francs, but it helped. After she went to Germany for good . . ."

Mme. Frank shrugged unhappily. "She's a fine girl. Very quiet, she likes to be alone, but straightforward and sensible—she never wasted her money. I didn't get anything from her again, she didn't even write."

In fairness, Mme. Frank was to add, her daughter had never liked writing letters. Her silence as a correspondent was understandable. The termination of the monthly checks was something different, but Mme. Frank didn't know about the appearance of Karel Whitman in Anne-Marie's life.

What this respectable and hardworking young woman saw in the lanky, irresolute poet five years her junior is probably best explained by another side of her character, a side her mother knew nothing about. To Mme. Frank, Anne-Marie was a loyal and conscientious daughter. Anne-Marie's friends viewed her in a different light. They saw her as a drifter, a traveler, a fellow companion of the road.

Drifting. No other word describes so well the movements of the company to which Anne-Marie had attached herself during her voyages with Monique. Occasionally there would be some fixed destination. Venice to see the Queen of the Adriatic under snow. Istanbul before the Turkish authorities cracked down on the narcotics dealers. Katmandu because word had come through that that was where the peace and action were now to be found.

Far more often they moved on whim, on impulse, carried by tides and eddies that obeyed no natural law, that swept along in full flood, arbitrarily changed direction, doubled back, and then set off on another course. At summer's end it might be the stream of holiday-makers heading back north across Europe whose cars they'd climb aboard like rafts. The summer stream would dwindle and suddenly it would be trucks or freight cars heading south, east, and west.

Another ripple, another surge, and they would be on their way again. And it never mattered where they found themselves at journey's end. Sleeping bags, communes, bare feet, patched jeans, joints—as a way of life it clearly satisfied a need in her as deep as the need to succor and protect.

In Karel Whitman she found a person with whom she could express both those apparently contradictory aspects of her nature.

"What moved me most about it all," remarked the perceptive M. Herrault, Whitman's lawyer, "was Anne-Marie's strong affection for him. She was clearly very much in love."

Whitman no doubt in his own way loved her too. But for him Anne-Marie had an additional attraction over anything he may have felt for her mind and heart and body. The practical Anne-Marie had a job. She taught French to the children of a "musician and sculptor," as he was to describe himself, a certain Herr Klaus Leo Gormann, who also lived in Berlin.

Meanwhile, within a few weeks of their first meeting, Whitman and Anne-Marie decided to live together. The arrangement suited both sides. Anne-Marie had found her poet and the poet had found his patron. At least her earnings from Herr Gormann allowed Whitman to concentrate on his verses without being interrupted by the irksome need to carry bricks or lay rails.

Yet in spite of his newfound financial stability, the remainder of 1970 and the early months of the following year were not to prove a happy time for Whitman. Soon after he arrived at the Berlin commune he was joined by a fellow expatriate Czech, a young man he'd known in Prague who had fled Czechoslovakia a year before him.

"He was the greatest friend I ever had," Whitman was to say. "But after a while he decided he couldn't endure life in the West. So he went back to Prague. When he left I really felt like killing myself. I'd just had enough."

Whitman didn't go through the ritual of another attempted suicide, but he did have himself committed to a psychiatric hospital in Berlin. Under Czechoslovak law, hospitalization is mandatory after any suicide attempt. The West German health authorities are more flexible in their approach to potential suicide cases. It is not necessary to try to kill oneself to gain admission to a hospital, only to declare an intention of doing so. In any event, after a period of treatment Whitman was discharged. Within a month the restlessness that had become, and was to remain, such a feature of his life was tugging at him once more.

"I found life in Berlin more and more depressing," he explained. "I was so close to the border and surrounded by walls on every side. So I decided to go away for a while."

A holiday abroad. An excellent tonic for anyone suffering from acute depression. But in the case of a penniless poet, where to go and how to find the means? Once again the redoubtable Anne-Marie provided the answers.

She left for France, worked for a time, and saved up some money. Holland, so the word had been passed along the grapevine, was that year's chosen meeting point for the companions of the road. In June Anne-Marie moved to Rotterdam, where Whitman joined her. From there they traveled to The Hague and then on to Amsterdam.

It proved a pleasant enough summer and fall in Holland's lovely canalled cities, but by early winter, funds were running low. Whitman was still reluctant to return to Berlin, so Anne-Marie proposed a visit to her home country. By then her sister Monique was living in Tours; her other sister, Suzanne, was in Poitiers, sixty-five miles to the south of Tours; and besides, in France Anne-Marie could always earn enough to support them both.

So, early in December, 1971, the wandering pair set out for Tours.

CHAPTER 3

A TRIP TO TOURS is a trip back into French history. For thousands of years before the arrival of the Romans, the little wooded plain on the bank of the Loire was a well-known staging post on the trade routes that crossed ancient France. The Romans came, left their monumental imprint on the site, and departed. The Dark Ages of Europe passed and Tours emerged as a bustling, prosperous city that ranked high in importance among the country's provincial centers.

Even as recently as 1940 the town had a role, albeit a brief one, to play in world affairs. For three days, as the Wehrmacht forces advanced remorselessly across France, Tours became the seat of the national government. On June 13 Winston Churchill flew there in a final attempt to rally the demoralized nation. The attempt failed, but the locals still point with pride to a burn on an expensive desk in the *préfecture* where the great man laid his cigar in the absence of an ashtray.

Although savagely mauled by Göring's Luftwaffe, the town today, and particularly the old quarter, the heart of Tours, looks much as it must have when it came to prominence at the end of the Middle Ages. Narrow, winding streets, barely an arm's spread in width, lead down to the broad, shallow-flowing river. Houses of pale honey-colored stone with high gabled windows crowd against little shops and restaurants with gaily striped awnings. "It is difficult to eat badly in France," the citizens of the town claim. "It is impossible in Tours." It would be a bold visitor who dared to disagree.

A mellow, delightful city, then, with its steep slate roofs, its squares and chiming fountains, its carefully pruned plane trees, and the ornate ironwork balustrades on the balconies above them— ironwork that to the discerning eye hints one is heading south toward the Midi.

Even in December the weather there can be clear and crisp. More often, though, owing to the proximity of the Loire, the air is damp, dark rain clouds scud across the sky, and the wind gusts coldly through the warren of streets around the cathedral, which dominates not only the old quarter, where it is set, but the entire city. It was raining on the afternoon of December 13, 1971, when Whitman and Anne-Marie arrived in Tours.

Anne-Marie's sister Monique had taken up residence in the city a couple of months earlier. With a girl friend she had rented two rooms in a student hostel on rue Bernard Palissy, a typically narrow, but busy, shopping street close to the cathedral. Warned in advance of her sister's impending visit, Monique and her girl friend had moved into one of the two rooms, leaving the other free for Anne-Marie and Karel Whitman.

"But they only stayed one night with us," Monique said later. "I can't really remember why they left so quickly. I think they decided the room was too ugly or too dirty. Anyway, the next day they moved into a little hotel on a nearby street."

Its name was the Hotel Perugia. Outside, a neon sign flashes garishly. On the ground floor there is a drab and dimly lighted self-service restaurant with a corridor to the left that leads to the hotel proper. The corridor is puddled with dirty water, the paint on the walls is peeling, and smells of stale cooking coil through the dank stairwell. Above, the shutters are coated with grime and the tattered curtains are gray with dust.

It is not an impressive establishment, the Hotel Perugia. In fact it is what the French with characteristic bluntness call *un trou à rats,* a rat hole, and all the more incongruous against the elegance of its surroundings.

It was certainly not to the taste of our poet. "Karel couldn't stop scratching," Monique went on. "Both he and Anne-Marie were certain the room was full of fleas. So their stay there only lasted one night too. The following night they came back with us again. Next day they left Tours and went to visit Suzanne in Poitiers."

Suzanne Monteau was the only one of Mme. Frank's three daughters who was married at the time. Suzanne, however, was away. Unbeknown to her sister Anne-Marie, it seems, she had taken ill and been sent to a Paris hospital.

The poet, under the wing of his patroness, arrived at the Monteau house to find only Suzanne's husband at home. The pair spent the night with M. Monteau and returned to Tours the next morning.

"This time," Monique takes up the tale again, "they moved into another hotel. I can't remember exactly where, except it was close to the one they stayed in before. I do know that soon after they got back I left Tours. The date of my departure was December twentieth. I never saw them together again. More than a year passed before I even saw Anne-Marie."

The hotel whose whereabouts Monique couldn't remember was in the rue Émile Zola, another ancient street in the old quarter of Tours and even closer to the cathedral than the site of their previous residence.

Called the Hotel Zola, the new abode of the wandering couple was if anything sleazier than the Perugia. Another dark and damp corridor led to another gloomy, evil-smelling stairwell. Yet here the skylight overhead was so thickly smeared with dirt that at midday the sun barely penetrated to the floors below, where the door of each room carried the stern notice LOYERS PAYABLES À L'AVANCE— rentals must be paid in advance.

.It was into this grim and inhospitable rooming house that Anne-Marie and Whitman booked on December 16. The hotel manager, Karim Moonjay, remembers the couple vaguely—Anne-Marie rather better than Whitman, who, he says, was almost always out, at least during the day. It was Moonjay's habit to retire early in the evening, and after nightfall he did not give the comings and goings of his guests a second thought. As Anne-Marie and Whitman settled down in their room, they were aware that, for them, the hotel seemed to have only two virtues. It was cheap and, unlike the Perugia, it was free from fleas.

But certainly for the vast majority of the honest burghers of Tours the name of the Hotel Zola means nothing. Only if one mentions the street in which it stands is there any response.

"The rue Émile Zola? Of course! It leads toward the cathedral and our museum."

They nod, smiling, and point proudly toward the rise on which the cathedral and museum can be found. They have every reason for pride. If not quite as majestic as its sister cathedrals at Chartres and Rouen, the Cathedral of St.-Gatien is nonetheless a towering and triumphant expression of French faith and architecture during the Middle Ages.

The Musée des Beaux-Arts, housed in the former archbishop's palace opposite, is also an architectural masterpiece. But perhaps more interesting still are its contents and above all the jewel of its collection—a collection that has the unusual distinction of having been started amid the flames of a revolutionary war.

"I THOUGHT TEN THOUSAND swords must have leaped from their scabbards to avenge even a look that threatened her with insult. But the age of chivalry is gone. That of sophisters, economists and calculators, has succeeded; and the glory of Europe is extinguished for ever." These words of Edmund Burke, the fiery English orator and politician, expressed the feelings of all the ruling classes of Europe in 1792.

The tide of revolution was sweeping across France. The weak King Louis XVI and his vain and frivolous Queen Marie Antoinette, the "Austrian" as she was contemptuously known to the populace, were in prison. Tumbrels were already rattling across the cobbled streets of Paris to their grim destination at the Place de la Révolution, now the Place de la Concorde. And all across the country, in hamlet, village, and town, implacable revolutionary committees prepared to take their vengeance for the oppression of centuries against those twin targets of their hatred: the church and the nobility.

When the reviled queen finally went to the guillotine in October 1793, Tours, as did all of France, exploded in the Reign of Terror. It was a time of iron-willed men meeting by candlelight. Of racing carriages and gunfire and clashing steel. Of hammering on doors at night, of swift and summary trials, of merciless executions.

The great abbeys and châteaus of the region were ransacked and the bishops, the nobility, and their minions put to the sword. But not all was destroyed. In other countries, other societies, every trace and reminder of a hated past might well have been burned, expunged totally from memory. In France the destruction was less dramatic.

In peace, in war, in times of stability, in the turmoil of revolution, the French have always been characterized by two features that predominate over all others in the national consciousness. A passionate love of and respect for beauty and an unerring appreciation of monetary value.

So the citizens of Tours were to demonstrate even at the height of the Terror. The plunder from the surrounding estates of the *ancien régime* was neither wantonly destroyed in vengeance nor stolen for private profit. Instead, the former possessions of the dukes and prelates, their furniture, paintings, tapestries, and porcelain were carefully gathered together and installed in the archbishop's palace—expropriated by the townspeople and henceforth to be known as Tours' "principal school, library, and museum."

What better place, one might think, for the redoubtable citizens to choose as a cultural center for that section of the great Loire countryside than the seventeenth-century palace, with its triumphal arch under the cathedral's shadow, its spacious, high-ceilinged rooms, its leafy gardens full of giant elms, of shimmering ash and tulip trees and sweet-scented magnolia?

Over the century that followed, the school and library were moved to other quarters of the town. But the museum remained in the old palace. Meanwhile, its collection grew, partly by prudent acquisition and partly by bequest—from the generous gifts made by those

who loved the ancient Touraine city and who felt the noble building at its heart would provide an ideal permanent home for the
treasures they had been fortunate enough to acquire or inherit.

In January 1950 one such gift was made by Mme. Benjamin
Chaussemiche, widow of the French national architect for palaces
and gardens. Mme. Chaussemiche had many connections with the
Loire Valley and decided that the Tours museum was an excellent
choice for a painting left to her by her late husband.

The painting, executed in oils on wood, depicted the flight of
the Holy Family into Egypt to escape King Herod's massacre of
the innocents. A favorite subject for artists from the Renaissance
onward, this version is small in size—the wooden panel measures
only nine by ten inches. When it was acquired by M. Chaussemiche
it was thickly coated with layers of varnish and grime—one expert was
later to speculate that it had been hung for years above a wood fire
and that the murkiness over the paint was caused by smoke from
the burning logs below.

Yet even in the condition in which it reached the museum, something blazed through the dirt, something so powerful and assured
in the artist's treatment of the Holy Family, that the museum's
then director, M. Boris Lossky, felt sure he'd been given more than
another fine example of the Dutch seventeenth-century school—
for the painting undoubtedly belonged to that school.

It was too much to hope that the picture had actually been
painted by the greatest of all the Dutch masters, Rembrandt. But was
it not possible that it might have been the work of one of his pupils,
fired on that one occasion by the genius of his teacher?

Two years later, in 1952, Dr. Otto Benesch, the eminent art his-
torian and one of the world's leading authorities on Dutch painting,
visited the museum. With some trepidation M. Lossky showed him
his new acquisition. Dr. Benesch studied the picture and recounts
his response.

"I was faced with an entirely unknown, genuine early Rembrandt
of the highest quality, which showed the handwriting of the young
master in every stroke of the brush."

In Dr. Benesch's view even M. Lossky's wildest hopes had been
exceeded. But however authoritative Dr. Benesch's opinion, further
evidence was needed to provide conclusive proof. After consultations

between the two, M. Lossky approached the Louvre museum in Paris. The museum gave permission for its senior picture restorer, M. Jean Gabriel Goulinat, to go to Tours and personally supervise the cleaning of the panel.

The work was carried out with infinite care, and as the last layer of dirt was lifted there first emerged in the lower right-hand corner the initials R H. Rembrandt's full name was Rembrandt Harmenszoon van Rijn. R H was how he signed his paintings. The final proof was there.

Not only was the attribution complete but the painting was revealed once more in its full glory, a triumphant creation of the young genius working at the height of his powers.

Over the two decades which followed, the jewel of the Tours collection—for jewel it unquestionably was—was to travel widely. Eagerly sought after for display by the world's major museums, it was successively exhibited in Stockholm, Vienna, Montreal, Paris, and Amsterdam.

But the most extraordinary of all its travels was to start one December night in 1971, only a few months after its return from Holland—the night we first saw our young poet, huddled in his coat against the cold, wandering down a street in Tours.

CHAPTER 4

IT WAS NOW EARLY in the morning of December 22, six days since Anne-Marie and Whitman had checked into the Hotel Zola after their return from the brief trip to Poitiers. The tower clock of the cathedral had already rung one as the barman stood at the door, watching the figure of Karel Whitman slowly disappearing down the rue Émile Zola.

"Fermé," he repeated to himself, and drew the bolt.

But Whitman did not hear the sound. He was already far down the street, ambling in the direction of the Tours cathedral.

In summer the old quarter of Tours is alive until the early hours. In winter, when the chill winds cut through the winding streets and the mist drifts up from the swollen river, it is very different. By eleven o'clock most of the citizens of Tours latch their doors, turn out their lights, and retire to bed. Afterward the quarter is as silent as the cathedral tombs.

So it was that December morning when Whitman reached the Place Jeanne d'Arc, the square in front of the cathedral's imposing entrance. What impulse had brought him there he wasn't certain. Or so he was to insist later. Perhaps he'd been in search of another café that kept later hours. Perhaps he was just following his habit of nocturnal wandering. All he knew was that he suddenly found himself looking up at the cathedral towering above him, its massive spires vaguely visible against the night and mist. Lowering his eyes, he gazed around the empty square in which he stood and at the streets that branched off from it—the rue Lavoisier, the rue Jules Simon, the rue Fleury. With his rudimentary knowledge of French, Whitman wondered if rue Fleury meant the "flowery road." At any rate, it had a certain ring of poetry about it. Whitman started down the rue Fleury.

Midway, he stopped and looked around again. The lights were burning dimly in the narrow and deserted street. To his right Whitman saw the archbishop's palace; to his left, the southern face of the cathedral. That winter the stonework of the façade, ravaged by centuries of exposure to wind and rain, was being repaired. The company entrusted with the work was in the process of erecting scaffolding against the lofty buttresses. Whitman noticed that gathered next to the building were large wooden planks, along with some metal frames and support poles that would be bolted together for the scaffolding. Lying near them, almost unseen among the larger items, was a wooden ladder.

Whitman continued on to where the rue Fleury met the rue Racine. There a cold river wind struck him, making his eyes tear. He rubbed them, blinking, then turned and began retracing his steps along the rue Fleury—when again he saw the ladder.

Why Whitman did what he did in those next minutes also remains unexplained. But, on what he claimed to have been impulse, he hefted the ladder to his shoulder, carried it across the street, and set it against the wall that encircled the archbishop's palace—the palace that was now the Tours museum.

Although the rungs were slippery, he climbed the ladder quickly, agilely, and soon he was atop the wall. Abutting the wall on the courtyard side was a small hutlike structure with a metal roof. What Whitman did not know was that he was about to stand on the thin covering of the transformer that supplied electrical current to the museum. Gingerly he placed one foot down on the roof's metal surface, then the other, slowly letting it support his weight. He reached back over the wall, pulled up the ladder, swung it around, and lowered it into the courtyard. Then he jumped down.

From the courtyard Whitman studied his position. Behind him was the wall he had just scaled. Facing him was the museum, its darkened casement windows showing only dim reflections of the streetlights on the rue Fleury.

Whitman picked up the ladder again, moved with it to the museum wall, and stopped beneath a window. The window was about five yards above the ground. Still, he guessed that from the top rung of the ladder he could reach the glass.

Whitman was right. Climbing up and balancing himself precariously on the topmost rung, he placed a hand against a pane and felt its icy coldness through his glove. The window consisted of two tall hinged panels, each with twelve panes. Peering through them, Whitman saw they were secured by nothing more than a simple metal latch.

He clenched his fist and hit one of the panes hard. Nothing happened. He jabbed a second time. Still nothing. Frustrated, he descended the ladder, found a small rock, climbed again, and smashed firmly at the glass. There was a sharp splintering sound. Whitman froze as he heard the rock and shards of broken glass fall to the floor inside. Had anyone else caught the sound? A night watchman? A passerby? Whitman remained still, not breathing. The only sound he heard was the steady, distant rumble of trucks on the far side of the river.

Now Whitman put his hand through the jagged hole in the glass, slid back the latch slowly, and pushed the panels open. Then with a single thrust he was over the sill and standing in the room.

The room was almost totally dark. Whitman squinted and tried to let his eyes adjust, but all surrounding him was blackness. Then slowly, gradually, he began to make out objects on the walls. To his right and left he could now see the squarish shapes of paintings. He crossed to the wall nearest him and ran his fingers over the surfaces of several. Although he could not see the subjects, he could feel the glaze finish of hardened oil. Hurriedly he lifted one of the paintings from its hook, then grasped a second. It did not move. Feeling with his fingers at the back, Whitman found instead a secure metal bar, which held the painting to the wall. He pulled and twisted. The rod bent. Another violent twist, the rod broke, and the picture came free in his hands.

Suddenly a loud slamming sound was heard. It came from somewhere in the building, Whitman knew that. Had the broken window caused a draft that blew a door shut in another room? Or had the door been slammed by a night guard who even now was running toward the room where Whitman stood?

Panic overtook him. He fled to the window with the two pictures and clambered onto the sill. Stretching downward, reaching with his feet, he found the top rung of the ladder and descended to the courtyard. As slowly as he'd made his entry into the museum, Whitman was now a master of surefooted speed. Up the ladder to the transformer roof again, cross the roof, lower the ladder to the rue Fleury, and climb down. It was accomplished in what seemed like seconds. Once in the street, he stood a moment breathing in the damp night air. The only sound that came to him now was the sound of his own heartbeat reverberating in his ears.

Quickly Whitman replaced the ladder by the scaffolding material, slipped the two paintings under his coat, and walked toward the rue Émile Zola.

FIFTY YARDS FROM the Hotel Zola, Whitman stopped for the first time. Music and laughter echoed from a nearby discotheque. Looking down, he realized the odd figure he made with the two paintings bulging out from underneath his coat. With no one in sight, he put the paintings on the sidewalk and tried wrenching off the frames, then worked at the screws until the ornate gilded frames snapped into pieces. He dumped the splintered scraps into a butcher's refuse can, tucked the panels back under his coat, and continued rapidly to the hotel.

In his room, Whitman moved quietly so as not to wake Anne-Marie. He slid his suitcase out from underneath the bed, hid the two panels amid a jumble of laundry, and pushed the suitcase back again. Then he removed his clothes, which he found wet with per-spiration, and slipped into bed beside the sleeping girl.

A foot below the lumpy mattress, stuffed in with dirty jeans and T-shirts, were the two stolen paintings. One was a seascape by the seventeenth-century Dutch artist Jan van Goyen, a pleasing, modest picture done with considerable skill. The other was *The Flight into Egypt* by Rembrandt Harmenszoon van Rijn. Its market value in the art world, if indeed a price could be put on it, ranged upwards of one million two hundred thousand dollars.

CHAPTER 5

JACKIE JOUBERT IS A short stocky man with a round face, shrewd eyes, and thinning hair. His right arm, amputated as a result of a wound during World War II, displays a steel hook beneath the jacket sleeve of his guard's uniform.

Since 1951, exactly twenty years at the time of the theft, Joubert had been employed as one of the Tours museum's eight guards. It was Joubert who had locked the internal doors of the museum on the evening of December 21 and it was Joubert again who, making a routine check the following morning before the galleries were opened to the public, first went into the Salle Hollandaise—the Dutch Room—so called because of the school of paintings which hung there.

Even before he stepped inside, Joubert knew something was wrong. As he opened the door he felt a cold draft blowing against his face. It could come only from the room's single window—which was always closed. A moment later his gaze registered the swinging panels, the shattered pane, the rock on the floor, and the blank spaces on the wall.

Joubert realized instantly what had happened. There had been a break-in and a theft. For a moment he hesitated in indecision. He knew the matter must be reported as quickly as possible to the museum's director, he knew nothing should be touched in order to preserve possible vital clues to the robbery, and yet he was worried about the potentially damaging effects of the chill damp air—and the abrasive dust it no doubt carried—on the remaining paintings.

He raced back into the corridor and consulted one of his fellow guards. They agreed the window should be closed, but that nothing else should be touched. As the other guard remained outside, Joubert returned to the room and carefully pushed the panels shut. Then they ran, Joubert with the right arm and hook swinging at the side of his blue uniform jacket, toward the director's office.

Mme. Marie-Noëlle Pinot de Villechenon, an attractive and articulate woman in her thirties, was the French National Museums' curator assigned to the Tours collection. That morning, when Joubert and his colleague ran into her office, Mme. Pinot had held her appointment at Tours for less than a year.

Moments afterward Mme. Pinot, accompanied by a group of the museum guards, was hurrying along the corridor to the Salle Hollandaise. As she entered the room, a cold knot tightened in her stomach. Every museum curator has to live with the constant possibility of a theft. But as Mme. Pinot looked at the empty areas on the wall, her worst fears were realized. In his haste Joubert hadn't checked which paintings had been taken. Now she learned.

The fine van Goyen seascape had vanished. So had Tours' irreplaceable Rembrandt.

Five minutes later, at nine twenty, the telephone rang in Tours' main police station. The call was passed to Police Commissioner Roger Millet. Speaking crisply and calmly, Mme. Pinot told Millet what had happened. Millet immediately assembled a team of officers and went to the scene of the crime.

It took Millet and his men very little time to reconstruct in outline how the robbery had been carried out. The workmen engaged in restoring the cathedral's stonework had already noticed that their ladder had been moved during the night. An examination of the ladder's feet revealed traces of black coal dust. The museum courtyard, uniquely, is paved with a mixture of coal and soft limestone, compacted by the passage of feet over the centuries into a form of concrete. The shattered pane by the window latch told the rest of the story.

After a preliminary survey Millet hurried back to the police station. For the moment the precise details of the theft itself were secondary. The immediate priority was to take all possible measures to recover the paintings before the thieves could dispose of them.

This meant alerting a variety of individuals and organizations not only in France but throughout Europe.

During the next two hours messages containing information about the robbery were sent out to fourteen different destinations. These included the mayor's office in Tours, the local customs bureau, the national customs headquarters (it seemed probable the thieves would attempt to move the paintings outside France), the national police, the organization of French museums, and, of course, Interpol headquarters in Paris.

One of the messages was sent to the divisional commissioner of police in Orléans, seventy miles northeast of Tours and the regional capital of the area in which the city lies. In view of the gravity of the theft, the following day two experienced police officers, Inspectors Hubert Boisseau and Pierre Malahude, arrived in Tours from Orléans to assist Millet in his investigation.

By then Millet's men had been working on the case around the clock for twenty-four hours. Unquestionably conscientious in their approach to solving any crime, they had an additional incentive to crack this one. The Rembrandt was one of Tours' chief glories. The painting belonged to the whole city, to every citizen. Its theft was a cynical affront to civic pride. They wanted it back—and they wanted the culprits punished.

The problem was they had virtually nothing to go on. Further traces of coal dust had been found on the sill of the broken window. That merely confirmed what they knew already—that someone had entered the Salle Hollandaise, having crossed the courtyard below. A meticulous search was made of the surrounding area, the garden, the encircling wall, the transformer housing, the rest of the museum, even the entire length of the rue Fleury, but it yielded nothing.

There were no fingerprints, no footprints, no snagged fibers of wool or cotton. Most thorough forensic examinations produce some result. But in the case of the missing Rembrandt a complete and bewildering blank was drawn.

At the same time, of course, various other lines of inquiry were being pursued. Hotel registrations for the weeks preceding the theft were carefully scrutinized. None of the names, when fed through the police computers, showed any criminal record or even criminal associations. Discreet investigations were made into the backgrounds of the museum's employees, the laborers involved in the cathedral's restoration, and others working in the vicinity at the time.

In every case the results were the same—negative. For a month a squad of plainclothes officers even haunted the murkier bars and cafés of Tours late into the night on the off chance they might overhear some stray reference to the robbery. As an exercise it proved as fruitless as all the rest.

The paintings and the thieves (for it was assumed beyond question there were more than one) had vanished into the icy winter air.

On January 17, 1972, a frustrated Commissioner Millet wrote a formal account of the investigation—an investigation which by then had ground to a standstill. He concluded:

> It is relevant to note that for the past several months a marked increase in art thefts has been recorded. For example, on January 3, 1972, a painting was stolen from the church in Dissay-sous-Courcillon. A similar robbery took place during the night of January 6 to 7 when a number of important paintings were taken from the château of Count d'Oilliamson at Fontaine-Henry, including works by Greuze, Rubens, and Murillo.
>
> As far as the theft at Tours is concerned, we have a strong impression that the robbery was meticulously planned in advance. The thief or thieves knew exactly where they were going. The scene of the theft had been carefully reconnoitered. Once that had been done, the robbery itself presented very little difficulty. There were several paintings in the room. Only the Rembrandt and the van Goyen were taken.

Millet does not say he was up against a criminal mastermind, but he clearly, if implicitly, indicates he was confronted by a ruthlessly efficient and highly organized gang.

Had he been told then that the highly organized gang consisted only of a wandering expatriate youth, M. Millet would have been entitled to feel even more bewildered than he did.

PARIS GLISTENED IN the sunny late February morning as travelers and shoppers made their way along the streets and boulevards. To Parisians the rapidly rising temperatures brought the promise of an early spring. But in his office on the rue des Saussaies, Inspector Charles

Pontramon of the French National Police was not thinking of the weather or of spring. A cable had just come down to him from an upper floor of the same building, in which the French bureau of Interpol was housed. A senior police inspector attached to France's antitheft squad, Pontramon was a powerfully built man in his late forties, with long, graying hair and horn-rimmed glasses. He had been assigned to the Rembrandt case when the initial bulletin from Tours reached national police headquarters on the afternoon of December 22.

Throughout January he had heard nothing—but now the cable he had been hoping for was in his hands. It was addressed to the Interpol representative of the French National Police. In certain instances using the Interpol code, which substitutes often-used words and phrases, the message read:

ACCORDING TO CONFIDENTIAL INFORMATION RECEIVED BY BERLIN GATMA [police] TWO PAINTINGS APPARENTLY STOLEN DECEMBER 1971 A REMBRANDT "FLIGHT INTO EGYPT" AND VAN GOGH "SEASCAPE" ARE IN BERLIN FOR A FEW DAYS STOP PAINTINGS TO BE SOLD IN SOUTH AMERICA STOP HAVE YOU ANY INFORMATION CONCERNING SUCH OMOBA [theft] STOP IF SO PLEASE TRANSMIT END INTERPOL WIESBADEN

"For almost two months we frankly had nothing at all to go on," Pontramon says, remembering a time equally as frustrating for him as it was for Tours' Police Commissioner Millet. "All I could do here was to get my men to make the usual inquiries among our underworld contacts, and continue to hope for word of the paintings from police forces outside France. The rest was up to Tours and Orléans." There were no leads from Tours and no feedback from the Paris underworld. Pontramon had nothing to do but pace his office and give an occasional wry glance at its only decoration: a small color reproduction of another of France's masterpieces, the *Mona Lisa*.

Now, for Pontramon and the others involved in the investigation, the Interpol cable was not only the first break but also the first indication of something they'd suspected from the start—that the paintings might have been spirited out of France.

Pontramon, whose role was to coordinate and direct inquiries at the French end, rapidly reviewed the case to date. He checked with

Millet in Tours to find out if there had been any developments there, and learned the local investigation was at a standstill. The following morning he asked his colleagues in the Paris Interpol office to reply to the German message with an XD—top priority—cable.

RE THEFT REMBRANDT AND VAN GOYEN (NOT VAN GOGH) PAINTINGS STOP "FLIGHT INTO EGYPT" AND "SEASCAPE" WERE STOLEN FROM THE MUNICI- PAL MUSEUM OF TOURS NIGHT OF 21 TO 22 DECEMBER STOP PAINTINGS DISAPPEARED WITH THEIR FRAMES STOP GAKAB [photos] WILL BE SENT TO YOU STOP IF FOUND PLEASE TAKE MEASURES TO CONSERVE AND DETAIN PERSONS POSSESSING THEM STOP ADVISE URGENTLY SO THAT INTERNA- TIONAL ARREST WARRANT CAN BE ISSUED STOP IF THIS DONE FRENCH POLICE OFFICERS WILL GO TO BERLIN END IP PARIS

All Pontramon knew at that stage was that the information had been relayed to Paris from the German Interpol office in Wiesbaden. He was unaware that it came originally from his counterpart in West Berlin, Hans Deter, *Kriminalhauptkommissar* in the city's detective police force and more specifically chief of the robbery division.

A hefty, smiling man who with his graying hair and horn-rimmed glasses bears an uncanny resemblance to Pontramon, Deter was in charge of a district that ranks among the world's most difficult for a conscientious police officer to administer. As in all major cities, every form of criminal activity is to be found. But as a city divided between East and West it is also a thriving center of intrigue and espionage and a place where many police decisions can have international consequences.

That afternoon, as Deter studied the cable from Paris that Interpol had transmitted, he reflected on the strange telephone call he had received eleven days earlier, the call that had set everything in motion. Deter was used to receiving strange calls without advance warn- ing, but the one put through to his office on the morning of Febru- ary 11 was particularly intriguing.

"Hauptkommissar Deter?" the unfamiliar voice asked.

"Yes," Deter said.

"I am a member of the legal profession here in West Berlin," the man went on. "I represent a client who for certain reasons wishes for the present to remain anonymous. My client has been offered a painting by the Dutch master Rembrandt for the sum of one hundred thousand deutsche marks. There is also, so my client understands, another painting, by van Goyen, available for sale. If the sale is concluded, both paintings will go to South America. However, my client is led to believe the paintings may have been stolen in Amsterdam. He therefore wishes to know whether there is a reward for information leading to their recovery."

Deter told the caller he would investigate and asked him to telephone again.

When he put the receiver down, Deter was frowning. The story was suspicious in the extreme—to be blunt, he told a colleague, it stank. The self-styled lawyer had refused to give his name, and Deter had little doubt what lay behind the elaborate account of the anonymous client, the DM100,000, and the crude threat that the paintings were on the point of being sent to South America.

The man, perhaps with an accomplice, had either gotten wind of two stolen paintings or even had them in his possession, and was trying to get ransom money from their owner.

Yet what puzzled Deter was the man's claim to have a Rembrandt. Art thefts weren't Deter's specialty and he had no more than an average knowledge of painting—not enough to prevent his confusing van Goyen with the much more familiar van Gogh. But Rembrandt was a different matter. There could be no confusion there. Rembrandt was a household name whose works fetched millions. Ten years earlier the Metropolitan Museum of Art in New York had paid $2,300,000 for his *Aristotle Contemplating the Bust of Homer*, the largest sum ever spent on a single picture at that time and still the record price for a Rembrandt.

It seemed inconceivable to Deter that if a Rembrandt had been stolen virtually anywhere in the world he wouldn't have heard about the theft—and he'd heard nothing. Either the caller was bluffing or for some reason news of the robbery hadn't reached Deter.

With no record of it in his own files, Deter telephoned West Germany's Interpol bureau in Wiesbaden. Through a transmission glitch they too had received no information on any stolen Rembrandt, but they took the standard—and, as it proved, fortunate—precaution of double-checking with Interpol headquarters in Paris. From there they learned of the Tours theft two months earlier.

In the meantime, nothing more had been heard from the "lawyer."

But thinking back over his conversation with the caller, Deter recalled the immediate action that he took. Something in the way the story had been presented suggested the man didn't have the paintings in his possession—only that he'd heard about them.

Like any good policeman, Deter knew his "patch" inside out. If the caller had heard about two stolen paintings, the odds were that others had heard about them too—others in the twilight underworld of bars and flophouses and sleazy nightclubs, where all too often one schnapps too many led someone to boast or let something slip or even propose a job.

Deter issued instructions to his men in Berlin's plainclothes unit.

"We seem to have two hot paintings in the manor. One of them is a Rembrandt. Get out on the streets and push your sources. I want the name of the thief."

Deter's guess was right. Within a few days a name crossed his desk. It didn't register with Deter or any of the German police officers by now involved in the case, but a quick check of the Berlin files showed the man had a conviction in 1970 for petty theft. The thief was a Czech national—his name, Karel Whitman. The news resulted in the urgent query that reached Pontramon on February 22.

Then as the probing, the questioning, the listening continued, Deter learned that Whitman was reported to have a girl friend, a young Frenchwoman by the name of Anne-Marie Frank. Deter instantly cabled Interpol Paris requesting information on her.

CHAPTER 6

ON THE MORNING of December 22, at the very moment when museum guard Joubert ran into Mme. Pinot's office to report the break-in, Anne-Marie Frank and Karel Whitman were checking out of the Hotel Zola. They trudged to the outskirts of Tours and from there, using the companions' traditional method of travel, hitchhiking, they made their way to Paris.

Anne-Marie had friends in the capital, and the pair moved into an apartment on the Boulevard St.-Michel, the "Boul' Mich'" as it is affectionately known to the thousands of students who throng the quarter. Christmas passed, and soon afterward Whitman in a desultory fashion began to look for work. It was hopeless. He had no work permit, he barely spoke a word of French, his appearance was against him, and besides, the wandering poet's heart was scarcely committed to the task of finding a job.

He took to roaming the streets by day and drinking the evenings away in little Montparnasse bars and cafés. Some nights, too dizzy from the good red wine of France to find his way back to the apartment, he would even sleep out with the *clochards*—the hoboes—on the banks of the Seine beneath the icy January stars. The springtime Paris of sunsets and lovers, accordion music, and chestnut blossoms is very different from the grim city in the grip of a bitter winter.

In late January Whitman took to the road again, this time alone. By then Anne-Marie's money was virtually exhausted, he felt numb in body and spirit, an unwanted stranger in a foreign land, and he headed for the only place he could now call home—Berlin.

To reach Berlin from Paris, following the meandering route he was led on by a succession of kindly motorists, involved crossing the national boundaries of France, Belgium, Luxembourg, and Germany—all with their separate customs controls and border police.

The journey took Whitman three days. At every border post his papers were carefully examined. Several times he was questioned at length before he was allowed through. Yet not once did it occur to any of the various border officials to look inside the shabby wayfarer's single suitcase.

Had they done so, they would have found sandwiched between the dirty clothes the two paintings that had vanished from Tours.

On his arrival in Berlin, Whitman moved into a room in an apartment on Schleiermacherstrasse, a dingy street in a run-down area of the city. A week later Anne-Marie reached Berlin too. On this occasion she didn't immediately rejoin Whitman. Instead, she took up her former post of teaching French to the children of the Gormann family, having accepted their invitation to live with them.

A few days after her return, Whitman went to visit her. There for the first time he met the head of the family, Herr Klaus Leo Gormann.

At thirty-five, Gormann was dapper, educated, charming, and ambitious. He described himself as a sculptor and musician, but his money came from dealing in antiques. Antique dealing is an old

and honorable trade, yet for a few members of the profession it is something of an ambiguous term, and as with scrap-metal merchants and used-car dealers, the phrase strikes a warning chord in any policeman.

Over the weeks that followed, Whitman paid many visits to the Gormann family home, sometimes spending the night there. Undoubtedly, while Anne-Marie was teaching the children, he got to know their father well. Then one day Whitman learned that Gormann had brought back some antiques from a trip he had made to England. It gave Whitman the idea that with Gormann's help he might be able to sell the paintings.

That help was easier to come by than Whitman thought. When he broached the subject, mentioning only one painting, Gormann seemed interested. What painting was it? Gormann wondered. Whitman told him it was a seascape by van Goyen. And how had the young man gotten hold of it? the other inquired in an offhand way.

Whitman decided that, not being an art expert himself, he wouldn't be able to convince Gormann it was a genuine van Goyen unless he told the man the truth. He'd stolen it from a museum in Tours the previous December, Whitman answered. Gormann said nothing for a moment but regarded Whitman levelly. Then he smiled, amiable as always, and said that he would try to find a buyer.

A week later Gormann told Whitman there was someone who was interested in the painting. But before approaching the would-be buyer, Gormann suggested that the two men invent a cover story to explain how the painting had come into Whitman's possession.

It was finally decided that Whitman would present himself as a Sudeten German. He traveled a lot between Germany and Czechoslovakia, so the story would go, and during one of his journeys he had illegally brought the painting into Berlin. The painting supposedly belonged to an old Czech lady. Whitman had been asked to sell it because under Czech law it would go to the state when the old lady died.

Thus, having carefully rehearsed their account, Gormann and Whitman met at three thirty on an afternoon in the last week of February and proceeded to an antique shop in Bayerischestrasse.

Passersby, seeing the casually wrapped object under the arm of the young man, could hardly have guessed at what the wrapping held, its value, or the fact that it was now the subject of a unique "wanted" circular. Published by the art-theft section of Interpol and similar to those issued whenever there is an extremely important theft of art, this circular notified all Interpol national central bureaus of the continuing case of the theft of the Rembrandt and van Goyen paintings, carried descriptions and black-and-white reproductions of the works, as well as the date and place of the theft. Simultaneously the circular was sent to art magazines, museums, galleries, and antique dealers—indeed, to any organization or individual that might learn of the stolen goods.

Unfortunately, there was one such individual who did not see the circular—Herr Wilhelm Braun, antique dealer, of 49 Bayerischestrasse, Berlin.

The dealer was alone in his gallery at four p.m. when two men entered. "One was about thirty-two, tall and thin," Herr Braun recalled later. "He had short fair hair, a round face, and he was wearing a greenish jacket of some lightweight cloth. The general effect was casually smart. He opened the conversation. He said his companion wanted to sell a painting. I had the impression that the second man, who was carrying the painting, wasn't from Berlin and was somehow under the wing of the first."

According to Braun the two wanted DM18,000 for the picture. After inspecting the panel, Braun decided it had been painted in the Dutch style of the early eighteenth century and probably came from some Dutch master's studio.

At the price they were asking, Braun flatly said he wasn't interested in the painting. He ushered the pair out of the shop less than ten minutes after they walked in. The next day, again according to Braun, the younger of the two men returned alone and repeated his wish to sell the picture. This time Braun agreed with some reluctance to keep it for a couple of days to see if he could find a buyer.

The exact sequence of events between the moment the pair first entered Braun's gallery and the time when the relationship between the three of them ended is confused. What is not disputed is the outcome. Braun found a private buyer for a price of DM9,000, as it happened, although Whitman wasn't to know that. He offered Whitman DM5,000. Whitman accepted, the deal was concluded, and in gratitude Whitman gave Gormann a commission of DM500.

The same day, no doubt surprised and delighted at the result of their first collaboration, Whitman revealed to Gormann that the van Goyen wasn't all he had taken from Tours. When they returned to the Gormann household, Whitman rummaged through a pile of jeans he'd left there and produced Rembrandt's *The Flight into Egypt*.

Gormann's reaction on first seeing the masterpiece is not recorded. But he was an educated man with a taste for the arts, and it is not difficult to guess that he must have felt awed and stunned.

And then only two days later, on February 27, while Gormann was deliberating what they could do with this veritable gold mine, Whitman was arrested.

THE ARREST TOOK place in the Hotel-Pension Juno, a tawdry establishment at 74 Niebuhrstrasse in Berlin's Charlottenburg quarter. According to police records, another guest at the hotel had telephoned to complain about the noise resulting from a violent argument in a neighboring room in the early dawn hours. The same records list the cause as a dispute between Whitman and a prostitute. Within an hour of his arrest Whitman was under interrogation, not about his companion but about the missing Rembrandt.

At first Whitman denied everything.

"I've never been in Tours," he said. "Besides, even if I had been, I wouldn't remember it now. I've been mentally ill all my life as a result of a childhood accident and I've spent a considerable time in psychiatric hospitals. How could I remember anything like that?"

The interrogation went on throughout the day, and by evening Whitman's story had changed somewhat.

"Yes, it's true I had a girl friend who came from France," he agreed cautiously. "So maybe you're right after all, perhaps I did visit her in Tours."

And the Rembrandt—the police returned to the issue again and again—wasn't it true that people had heard him boasting about stealing the painting?

"Well, you know how it is." Whitman shrugged. "You hear people talking about something like that. Then a while later the subject comes up again and maybe you've had a few too many and you say you had a hand in it. But that's only because you're drunk at the time. I never had anything to do with that picture. I'm completely innocent."

Yet even while the interrogation was still in its early stages, Deter had flashed word of the development to Interpol Wiesbaden. Deter wanted to know urgently whether the French police had obtained an arrest warrant for the young Czech in connection with the Rembrandt theft. Wiesbaden relayed his query to Interpol in Paris, who replied equally promptly.

The French had no grounds whatsoever to bring charges against Karel Whitman. Observing the provision of habeas corpus—that no person may be detained for more than twenty-four hours without being charged—the West Germans, early on the morning of February 28, released Karel Whitman and he walked out of the Berlin station house a free man.

He waved gaily at the desk sergeant who saw him to the door, and winked at the upper-floor detention room where he had been questioned. Then he vanished into the tide of office workers pouring down the streets on their way to the day's work.

Cheekily confident as he appeared on his release after the statutory twenty-four hours' detention, in reality Whitman was badly and understandably shaken by what had happened. Whatever the truth about his "luck" in taking the painting in the darkness a little over two months earlier, he was certainly in no doubt now about what he had on his hands. Something that was not only immensely valuable but also very hot and, as far as he was concerned, dangerous.

As soon as he was clear of the police station and sure he was not being followed, Whitman slipped into a public telephone booth and called his new partner, Gormann. Gormann was sympathetic, concerned, and constructive in his advice.

"Don't worry," he said. "The most important thing is to find a safe hiding place for the property until we get a suitable buyer. Leave it with me to look after. Immediately I've got something arranged I'll let you know."

Without hesitation Whitman agreed. He rang off. Then he vanished into the Berlin netherworld he knew so well.

Until he heard from Gormann again, Whitman was going to keep a very low profile indeed.

WHILE ALL THIS WAS HAPPENING, the French National Police pursued their investigations of both Karel Whitman and Anne-Marie Frank. Then three weeks after Whitman went underground, Interpol in Paris answered Deter's earlier request for information about the pair. The message, relayed to Berlin via Interpol in Wiesbaden, read:

NO TRACE VISIT TO OUR AREA OF KAREL WHITMAN BORN 14 FEBRUARY 1949 PRAGUE STOP ANNE-MARIE FRANK HAS BEEN IDENTIFIED AS BORN 12 SEPTEMBER 1944 IN PARTHENAY INDRE DAUGHTER OF VICTOR (DECEASED) AND MARIE LAVALLE STOP PRESENTLY TEACHER LIVING WITH GORMANN FAMILY IN BERLIN 12 SCHILLERSTRASSE STOP ACCORDING TO MOTHER ANNE-MARIE FRANK DOES KNOW CERTAIN KAREL STOP IN LETTER DATED 13 MARCH 1972 SHE TELLS HER MOTHER THAT KAREL IS IN THE COUNTRY FOR A REST STOP ANNE-MARIE FRANK LEFT PARTHENAY IN NOVEMBER 1971 AND APPEARS TO HAVE GONE TO AMSTERDAM THEN TO GERMANY STOP GAKAB [photos] DATING FROM 1959 BUT GIVING ACCURATE IMPRESSION FOLLOW BY MAIL STOP EDBAL [for your information] PAINTINGS STOLEN TOURS MUSEUM ARE NOT INSURED AND NO REWARD PROMISED FOR RECOVERING THEM STOP PAINTING "FLIGHT INTO EGYPT" WAS INSURED FOR 600,000 FRANCS WHEN LEFT MUSEUM FOR SPECIAL EXHIBIT BUT REAL VALUE CERTAINLY FAR SUPERIOR STOP VALUE VAN GOYEN PAINTING MUCH LESS STOP PLEASE GIVE ALL RELEVANT INFORMATION AS TO CIRCUMSTANCES AND REASONS FOR ARREST KAREL WHITMAN AND SPECIFY EVIDENCE LINKING HIM TO ODGOR [theft of paintings] COMMITTED TOURS END IP PARIS

As a communication it can hardly be described as helpful to the diligent Deter, but it was the best that Pontramon's men at French National Police headquarters and Inspector Jean Gertou, from the judiciary police in Orléans and now handling the case locally, could come up with.

Still, throughout the spring, Interpol's art-theft section continued to distribute the circular on the Rembrandt and van Goyen paintings. And by May they had additional art thefts to pursue, among them the stealing of paintings by Jan Brueghel, Gainsborough, and Rubens from the Montreal Museum of Fine Arts and the disappearance of four portraits from a Swiss château. Unless recovered by year's end, these, as well as the Rembrandt, would undoubtedly be listed in Interpol's annual "The 12 Most Wanted Works of Art," a four-page circular which contained summaries of the material found in the individual notices.

The spring passed with no fresh word on either Whitman or Anne-Marie. Yet Hans Deter persisted with whatever information he had, and throughout June communications flew between Berlin and Paris via Interpol—Deter cabling the French that Anne-Marie Frank had changed her address in Berlin and querying whether the French police still had no grounds for issuing arrest warrants against her and Whitman; Paris asking if there had been any further news on the recovery of the painting itself.

To this last question, Deter sent a message to Paris through Interpol Wiesbaden unhappily replying in the negative. The trail had simply petered out. But Deter was nothing if not tenacious. Somewhere in his patch there was, or had been, one of the world's most famous paintings. He had a hunch it was still there. If it was, he was determined to find it.

He hadn't heard anything more from the anonymous lawyer or his equally anonymous client, and Deter's prime suspect, Whitman, had vanished. Whitman could be found again—Deter had no doubts about the capacity of his men to do that if required—but for what purpose?

There was no hard evidence against the feckless Czech, only underworld rumors of late night boasting in bars. Deter had pulled him in once, but Whitman had held firm, and for the moment there was no way of disproving his story. Without an arrest warrant issued in France it would be pointless to detain him again.

CHAPTER 7

THE TRUTH IS that in June Whitman left Berlin.

Our poet's wanderings were about to start again and now he had a new companion, a young married woman called Hilda Bauer. The couple went first to Holland, but there Hilda fell ill. They returned to Germany, and after Hilda had been treated in a clinic, they went to stay with her parents in the Black Forest.

Yet the urge for the road was soon on the poet again. He left

Germany once more, traveled to Italy and then on to Lake Constance, where he found a job as a waiter in a lakeside café. A month later he received word that Hilda had fully recovered. He joined her for the second time, and now the wind carried them to England.

Was there any purpose in the summer's travels? Did Whitman think that somewhere along the road one of the companions would produce a contact who might lead him to a buyer for the treasure he'd left in Gormann's care? In any event, in England, Hilda fell ill again. They hitchhiked back through the Low Countries to Germany, and there they separated. Hilda went off to rejoin her parents, while Whitman headed for Heidelberg. He rented a small room and obtained his second job of the summer, once more as a café waiter. This time he struck up acquaintance with a young man. For Whitman it was to prove a friendship with fateful consequences.

The young man was called von Arndt and by Whitman's own admission he made a strong impression on our poet. Von Arndt and Whitman adopted the practice of meeting for drinks every night after Whitman finished work at the café.

One night they went out late to a little bar in the old-town section of Heidelberg. As usual, von Arndt got completely drunk. He started rambling on about his past and all the things he'd done. He'd committed a number of thefts, he said, and been convicted several times.

One can see the two of them together in the little bar in the early hours, Whitman listening to the incoherent reminiscences of his new friend while they both poured down glass after glass of beer.

But obviously von Arndt's endless boasting got on the nerves of his young friend. Finally Whitman confronted him. If von Arndt had done all the things he'd bragged about, he ought to be able to sell a Rembrandt painting Whitman had in his possession.

Von Arndt hiccupped heartily. A Rembrandt?

Whitman backed off. He was only joking, Whitman answered his companion. He laughed and waved vaguely for *zwei Bier*.

However, von Arndt did not take the matter as a joke. A few days later he arrived in Whitman's room accompanied by another man.

Von Arndt introduced the man as Fritz. Fritz asked Whitman if he really had a Rembrandt. Whitman told him he didn't have it there, and it would take quite a time to get his hands on it again. But Fritz was obviously very interested and wanted to make a deal.

An introduction, an interested party, a deal. It sounded exactly what Whitman had been looking for ever since that night in Tours almost a year earlier. Fritz even said he'd found a buyer, a Swiss who said he knew someone who wanted it. Finally Whitman decided to telephone Gormann and find out what the situation was at his end. It was now late autumn of 1972 and Whitman hadn't seen his treasure for over half a year.

But when he called Berlin, Gormann told him he didn't have the painting any longer. Gormann added that he couldn't get hold of it for at least three weeks. Whitman guessed the man had either sold it or just didn't want him to have it. Whatever the case, since Whitman couldn't get his hands on the painting, obviously he couldn't make a deal with anyone. It was at this time that he decided to leave Heidelberg.

Why? What had happened? Ironically it was something that had less to do with the Tours Rembrandt itself than with the shadow cast of characters that was beginning to circle ever closer around the painting.

The boastful, hard-drinking von Arndt with his record of petty crime, the insistent Fritz eager to make a deal, the anonymous Swiss go-between—as a group they might have come from the fringes of crime anywhere in the world. In New York, Rome, Tokyo, in dozens of other cities, similar groups assemble like jackals to scavenge what they can. And wherever they assemble there is almost always a police informer.

So it was in Heidelberg. During the months Whitman had spent in the town a series of art thefts from local museums and churches had taken place. Word had gone out from police headquarters to the men who patrolled the streets and listened in bars: Someone's going to be talking about stolen paintings. Get his name.

Someone had indeed been talking about a stolen painting, although not one stolen in Heidelberg. The painting was a Rembrandt and the name that came back on the police grapevine was Karel Whitman.

On November 22, soon after Heidelberg police had put out a national request for his arrest, Whitman was picked up at Tempelhof airport in Berlin. He was held on suspicion of art theft in the town where he'd been living for the past few months. Commissioner Hans Deter naturally was much more interested in another art theft in which he believed the young Czech was involved, the theft of the Tours Rembrandt.

How did it come about that Whitman returned to Berlin—the one city he had excellent reasons for never visiting again?

Whitman gave no answer to the police except that he couldn't remember. But as Hans Deter later speculated, in spite of all of Whitman's protestations to the contrary, the temptation to go to Berlin, tackle Gormann face to face, and demand the painting had been too great to resist.

Meanwhile, with Whitman once more in custody, the case was rapidly heading toward a climax; the focus was now on Heidelberg and Berlin, as Interpol Wiesbaden's XD cable of November 27 spelled out:

> ODGEP [painting] PROBABLY STOLEN TOURS REMBRANDT'S "FLIGHT INTO EGYPT" HAS BEEN OFFERED FOR SALE IN HEIDELBERG STOP AT SAME TIME ERBAL FOVDO [Czechoslovak national] KAREL WHITMAN WAS ARRESTED NOV 72 IN BERLIN STOP PAINTING NOT YET RECOVERED STOP IN ORDER CONTINUE INVESTIGATIONS REQUIRE SUM OF DM5,000 TO DM6,000 FOR INFORMANT STOP WOULD MUSEUM BE WILLING TO PROVIDE THIS SUM VERY RAPIDLY AND WITHOUT ANY GUARANTEE PAINTING WILL BE RETURNED AS RESULT END IP WIESBADEN

Then suddenly, before Interpol Paris could respond, an entirely new and totally unexpected dimension was added to the case.

SOON AFTER NINE FIFTEEN a.m. on Tuesday, November 28, a buzzer sounded in one of the exhibition rooms at the Tours museum.

Mme. Pinot, the curator, was told via the internal telephone that a call for her had come through to her office on the outside line. A new display was due to open to the public that day and Mme. Pinot was busy supervising the last-minute arrangements. It was ten minutes before she was satisfied that all was in order and she was able to take the call.

Mme. Pinot returned to her office and picked up the receiver. "*Allo,*" she said. "I can only just hear you. . . ."

A woman's voice was speaking faintly through a crackle of static. Mme. Pinot started to answer, but suddenly the line went dead. Puzzled, she replaced the receiver.

The next afternoon Mme. Pinot was sitting at her desk when the telephone rang again. This time the call was relayed through the Tours central exchange in the town hall.

"Mme. Pinot? I have an important matter to discuss with you—"

It was the same woman who had called the day before, only now her voice was clear. She spoke in fluent French, although with a marked foreign accent—an accent Mme. Pinot thought was almost certainly German.

"I know a person who has access to some paintings which I believe are of considerable interest to you. There is someone in the United States prepared to pay one hundred thousand deutsche marks for the paintings. However, for sentimental reasons, my acquaintance would prefer if possible they were returned to Tours. . . ."

The anonymous caller finished by proposing a meeting at Saarbrücken in Germany to discuss the matter and said she would telephone again next morning with details.

Mme. Pinot promptly reported the call to the local police, who notified Pontramon in Paris and Inspector Gertou in Orléans. No specific mention had been made of a ransom, but the reference to DM100,000 left Mme. Pinot in little doubt as to what the woman had in mind. All other considerations aside, a ransom was out of the question. The museum's insurance policy did not cover theft, and no other funds were available.

Next morning at eight fifteen, Inspector Gertou accompanied by two other officers arrived in Mme. Pinot's office. The four sat waiting tensely. Then at nine fifteen the telephone rang again.

"Mme. Pinot?" It was the same woman's voice. "Have you considered what I said yesterday?"

"Yes."

Mme. Pinot had been carefully briefed on what she should say. She replied as instructed.

"Good," the woman continued. "I suggest we meet in the second-floor restaurant in the Saarbrücken railway station this Saturday, December second, at five p.m. So you can recognize me, I can tell you I'm thirty-five, small and brunette, and I will be wearing a yellow coat. To be absolutely certain there is no mistake, I will be carrying a copy of the French newspaper *L'Aube—*"

"*L'Aube?*" Mme. Pinot interrupted, puzzled. "I'm sorry, but I don't know any newspaper of that name. Are you perhaps thinking of *L'Aurore?*"

For a moment the woman hesitated, confused. Then she said, "Yes. I will be carrying a copy of *L'Aurore*. Until Saturday, then."

The caller rang off.

The same day—armed with an authorization to investigate in another country issued by Judge Rocheron in Tours—Inspector Gertou, representing the local police, and Charles Pontramon, from national police headquarters in Paris, flew to Germany.

It seemed the net was at last closing tight around the fugitive Rembrandt.

CHAPTER 8

ON DECEMBER 2, 1972, THE observant visitor to the railroad station at Saarbrücken, an industrial town on the French-German border, might have noticed several things that were inconsequential but unusual. An increased number of porters and cleaning personnel busied themselves about the station. In the second-floor restaurant, a few additional waiters mixed among the patrons. Curiously, also, there seemed to be more travelers than normal for a Saturday afternoon, some waiting on the station platforms, others lounging near the station's exit doors.

This same observant visitor might well have noted numerous cars parked in the forecourt of the station and near the exits to the surrounding streets. But what the visitor would not have heard were the voices of certain of these porters, cleaners, waiters, and taxi drivers—each one a police officer—reporting to Inspectors Pontramon and Gertou, positioned in an unmarked van opposite the station's main gate.

In fact, since early morning, radio-connected observation posts had been installed to link all areas inside and outside the station. "It's a great setup," Pontramon had said to Inspector Gertou. Pontramon was right. But the setting of the trap was no guarantee that the prey wouldn't detect it—or that it would spring as planned.

In the afternoon the police officers were joined by Inspector Frederick Vogel, a senior detective of the Saarbrücken police force who had been assigned to the investigation. With the two Frenchmen, Vogel settled himself in the van and reviewed the police notes on what they could expect:

"At 1700 hours a small, dark-haired woman to appear in second-floor restaurant of station seeking contact with Tours museum curator, Mme. Pinot. Woman to be wearing yellow coat and carrying copy of French newspaper *L'Aurore*. Since said contact with curator will not occur (Mme. Pinot has been instructed to remain in Tours), assume woman will eventually board train or leave station on foot. Police tail to follow, observe her actions and destination, and report. Follow-up surveillance to continue per plan. . . ."

Inspector Vogel put down the police notes and agreed with Pontramon. It was a great setup.

SEVENTEEN HUNDRED HOURS—five p.m. . . . Exactly on schedule, the express from Mainz arrived, ground to a clamorous halt, and disgorged its passengers. A woman in a yellow coat was not among them. . . .

Five twenty-three. . . . The Frankfurt–Paris limited appeared, made its accustomed stop of seven minutes, and departed. During those seven minutes, men and women mixed on the platform, some boarding the train, others heading toward the exits. Still, there was no woman in a yellow coat. . . .

Five thirty. . . . The saleslady in the newsstand of the station concourse looked up to see a woman in a brown leather coat facing her.

"*L'Aurore, s'il vous plaît*," the woman said with a marked German accent.

"*Oui. L'Aurore.*" The salesclerk nodded, reached down—and discovered to her surprise that every copy of *L'Aurore* had already been sold. The customer waited. The salesclerk apologized. The customer finally bought a copy of another newspaper and left.

Because of the delicacy of the planned operation, some of the station's staff had been given an advance briefing on what they could expect to happen. Among them was the salesclerk in the newsstand. She had been told that if something went wrong, she was to contact a police officer at once.

Confused by the woman's brown leather coat instead of the yellow one she had been watching for, and eager to notify police of the lack of copies of *L'Aurore*, the saleswoman left her stand quickly. In the middle of the concourse she was certain she saw the plainclothes policeman she had been instructed to report to. She approached the man and rattled off her story. The man listened to it gravely, nodded sympathetically—then suddenly turned, strode briskly across the station to the brown-coated woman, who had been watching the entire scene, and together the pair hurried from the station.

In the forecourt of the station, the man and woman separated quickly. By now, word had been passed to the police units outside, but the woman had already disappeared. The man remained in the forecourt a few moments, trying to determine whether he was under observation. Then he too headed off. The police followed him.

Near the station they saw the man enter a garage, get into a Volkswagen van, and drive off toward the nearby town of Kirkel. Then, like the woman—and in spite of police units tailing him—he also disappeared from sight.

"It was a great setup," Inspector Pontramon repeated to his frustrated and embarrassed German colleagues. "Only it didn't work out quite the way we planned."

IT WAS SIX FORTY, little over an hour since the railroad station fiasco, when the telephone rang at the night desk of the Saarbrücken police headquarters. The duty officer answered. For a moment he was silent, his face puzzled. He asked the caller to hold on, then transferred the call at once to Inspector Vogel. In his office, Vogel picked up the phone and muttered a weary *"Guten Abend."*

"Guten Abend, Inspector." The voice on the other end of the phone was that of a man. "I am Herr Garten," the voice continued. The name meant nothing to Vogel. "It was my wife and I who arranged the meeting at the station."

Vogel hesitated, not quite sure what to answer.

In the silence Garten added, "You and your men were at the railroad station today, *ja?"*

"*Ja,*" Vogel said cautiously.

Garten went on. "My wife made the telephone calls to Tours detailing the arrangements. However, there has been some confusion." (Some confusion. Vogel grimaced to himself.) "The rendezvous should have been at six p.m., as we knew the person we were expecting could only have arrived in Saarbrücken on the five-fifty-one train from Paris. It was my intention to call the police after the meeting and arrange to see them tomorrow, December third. I am telephoning to state that now and to fix a suitable meeting time."

Inspector Vogel countered by suggesting that in view of the importance of the matter, it would be more convenient for all parties if the meeting took place that night. Reluctantly Herr Garten agreed and suggested a parking lot about a mile from his house in Kirkel.

An hour later, a police van containing Vogel pulled up in the darkness outside a parking lot in Kirkel. Beyond the gate Vogel saw the shadowy outlines of a man smoking a cigarette. Vogel knew it must be Garten. He was right.

Garten described himself as a salesman. He claimed he'd seen the painting at a friend's house in Essen. He'd read about the theft from the Tours museum and knew the painting's history. According to his story, a group of people had something on him for reasons he couldn't explain, and they'd told him to find a buyer for it. He'd become suspicious at the station when the clerk from the newsstand asked if he were a policeman and told him what had just happened.

Garten continued. He was certain he could arrange for the recovery of the painting but said he couldn't make his contacts wait beyond December 6. He added that they would undoubtedly want DM100,000 for it, and he felt morally entitled to a percentage for his disinterested efforts in seeing the picture went back to Tours.

Vogel chuckled. "One step at a time, *mein Herr*. First you must help us obtain the picture. Without it we can discuss nothing. *Ja?*"

Garten thought a moment, then looked at Vogel and nodded. "*Ja.*"

THE FOLLOWING DAY Garten reported to Vogel that he had telephoned a friend in Berlin. He told the friend he'd at last found a buyer for the Rembrandt at the agreed price of DM100,000 and proposed a rendezvous at Tempelhof airport on Saturday, December 9, when the transaction could be completed. His friend expressed pleasure at what promised to be such a happy end to the affair and confirmed he would be at Tempelhof at the suggested time.

As soon as Vogel hung up the telephone on this call, he placed one to Detective Chief Superintendent Siegfried Rupp at West Germany's Federal Criminal Investigation Office in Wiesbaden. A specialist in art thefts, Rupp had followed the case since Deter's first message from Berlin ten months before.

The case now fell within the jurisdiction of the Saarbrücken police as well as Berlin's, so Rupp said he would gather the DM100,000 asked for and bring it to Vogel in Saarbrücken. There was too much at stake for any chances to be taken, for any shortcuts to be made. At the critical meeting at Tempelhof the buyer would have to appear genuine beyond any shadow of doubt, even to the extent of having the purchase price in cash with him.

On December 8 Superintendent Rupp, the go-between Garten, and Inspector Vogel flew to Berlin. Deter met them at the airport and the three police officers went over the arrangements for the operation next morning. The stage was set for the final scene in the yearlong drama of the vagabond Rembrandt.

CHAPTER 9

IF THE SAARBRÜCKEN railway station was swarming with police a week earlier, it was nothing compared with the stakeout at Tempelhof airport on the morning of December 9.

Armed plainclothes detectives, with photographs of Garten to aid recognition and walkie-talkies tuned to a command post, patrolled every corridor, every passenger area, every check-in point and exit. Outside, cars were stationed on every floor of the multistoried parking garages and on every feeder road that led from the airport to Berlin. The operation was under Deter's control, and after all the false leads, frustrations, and disappointments of the past eight months, he was determined that nothing go wrong. Waiting tensely with him as the hour for the rendezvous approached were Pontramon and Gertou for the French police, and Rupp on behalf of the German national authorities.

It was a chill winter evening, but Deter found himself perspiring.

Pontramon checked his watch and saw that it read five o'clock. He gave an ironic smile, thinking of that same hour one week earlier when he and the other policemen had waited outside the railroad station in Saarbrücken.

Then, almost to the minute, Garten and the Saarbrücken detective, playing the role of the prospective buyer, walked into the main hall. They hesitated. A man approached them. Instantly the news was relayed by radio to all the armed detectives in the building and the waiting cars outside. As the hidden observers watched the scene, they saw Garten make a brief introduction. Hands were quickly shaken. Then the three men hurried out of the airport and climbed into a bright yellow Volkswagen parked in an adjacent lot.

The VW left the airport with the stranger at the wheel, the detective beside him, and Garten in the back. Following it, unnoticed, were seven unmarked police cars and vans, each with a complement of armed officers. Half a mile from the airport the VW pulled to the side of the road.

The driver reached behind him and produced a slim oblong parcel wrapped in brown paper. He removed the paper and handed the object to his companion in the front seat. Vogel inspected it with a great show of care and interest. He held it up to the light, turned it on its side, examined the tiny signature at the corner, and ran his finger delicately over the thick paint.

It was a show and no more. The glory of the painting, the crowning achievement of the young Dutch genius, would have been unmistakable even to a person who had never seen its photograph before—and the detective, under Rupp's tutelage, had been studying reproductions of the work for a week.

"Very good," the detective said. "I am satisfied."

He reached into his pocket and produced a plastic bag bulging with money, which he gave the driver. "One hundred thousand deutsche marks," he said as he handed it over. "Are we agreed?"

"Correct." The driver nodded.

"Thank you."

Vogel smiled and got out of the car with the painting. Garten moved into the front seat. Vogel stepped back. Then very slowly, as if in acknowledgment of a deal successfully concluded, he raised his hat. It was a signal to the following police.

Instantly the pedestrians on the street were deafened by the sound of sirens and the shrieking of tires. Seven vehicles cordoned the VW, doors were hurled open, a wave of armed detectives surged forward, and there in the misty light of an early December evening an amazed Herr Klaus Leo Gormann, too dumbfounded to try to escape, found himself under arrest.

In his hands were the DM100,000.

AN HOUR AFTERWARD Rupp was on his way to the federal prison where Whitman was still being held on suspicion of the Heidelberg thefts. Now Rupp took up the questioning.

Whitman denied everything. He said he didn't know Gormann and had nothing to do with the theft. When Rupp told him they'd arrested Gormann and recovered the painting, Whitman said he didn't believe it.

Evening became night. Then shortly before midnight, Rupp stood up and summoned Whitman to follow him in the custody of a policeman. They were going to police headquarters to continue the questioning, Rupp said.

As the police car made its way through the streets of Berlin, Rupp suddenly stopped it. At a newsstand ahead, the driver of a delivery truck was unloading early editions of the morning papers. Given the scope of yesterday's operation and the dramatic manner of Gormann's arrest, Rupp knew the story would be featured prominently in the papers' headlines.

Rupp got out, bought several newspapers, and returned to the car. As he climbed in, Whitman looked at him, expecting him to speak. But Rupp was silent. He simply put the papers, with their bold headlines, in Whitman's lap. After reading briefly, Whitman shook his head. Then he broke down and confessed.

The flight of the Rembrandt had ended.

CHAPTER 10

FOR WHITMAN, OF COURSE, matters were far from ended. It was the cable between Interpol Wiesbaden and Interpol Paris that put the final punctuation to a year of patient police work:

AT REQUEST BERLIN CRIMINAL COURT PROSECUTOR SEEBER YOU ARE
INFORMED THAT KAREL WHITMAN BORN 14 FEB 49 PRAGUE CZECH NA-
TIONAL HAS ADMITTED THEFT PAINTING WHICH WAS SEIZED BERLIN
STOP WILL REQUEST OF BERLIN CRIMINAL COURT THAT WHITMAN BE
PLACED IN EXTRADITIONAL CUSTODY TO PREVENT HIS AVOIDING BURAN
[extradition] TO FRANCE STOP PLEASE INFORM EFRIM [examining magis-
trate] ROCHERON IN TOURS AND SEND ELFUD [arrest warrant] AND BURAN
DOCUMENTS THROUGH USUAL CHANNELS STOP GOFRI [please reply by
radio] END IP WIESBADEN

In Whitman's case extradition proceedings followed their usual
deliberate course. One year later he was handed over to the French
authorities at the Pont de L'Europe in Strasbourg. From there he
was taken to Tours to await trial. In Tours the court appointed a
local lawyer, Maître Alain Herrault, to defend him.

What most impressed M. Herrault was Anne-Marie Frank's evident
devotion to the poet. By now she was the mother of a sixteen-month-
old boy. Whitman claimed to be the father. If so, the child was almost certainly conceived in Tours during the week of the robbery.

Apart from his "poet's eyes," of Whitman himself M. Herrault
remembers less.

"I didn't find him disagreeable," M. Herrault says, "but neither
was he what I would describe as an attractive personality. He seemed
very nervous, almost to the point of being unbalanced, but certainly
not the standard criminal type. I wouldn't have classified him as an
expert even in petty crime."

Whitman finally came to trial on March 4, 1974, in Tours' massive
white neoclassical courthouse. The trial lasted barely forty-five minutes, during which Whitman's statements to Superintendent Rupp
were entered in the record—Whitman's description of the burglary
itself and even a little drawing of the museum he had made to show
how he had entered. The confession further stated that he had acted
alone, didn't know the value of the paintings he had stolen, and, in
fact, couldn't see them very well in the dark when he took them off
the wall. As for his motives, Whitman had said simply that while in
France he hadn't found a job and was tired of being financially dependent on Anne-Marie and that he had acted on the spur of the
moment after some drinks in a café in Tours.

At last the charges were read out and Whitman was asked if he wished to say anything. He merely shook his head. In his defense Herrault argued Whitman's difficult Czech background, the fact that he was a refugee living in precarious financial circumstances, and the frustration he had constantly experienced in being unable to get a job.

Before handing down sentence, the judge asked for a psychiatric report. The report scrupulously detailed Whitman's unhappy past, his suicide attempts, and his various hospitalizations, but concluded he was fully sane in the accepted sense and responsible for his actions.

In light of the report and taking into consideration the lengthy period Whitman had already spent in custody, the judge then sentenced him to two years in prison. Herrault was somewhat surprised at the leniency of the sentence—the gravity of the theft might have warranted a much longer term.

Whitman served his time in the jail at St.-Martin on the Île de Ré, three miles off La Rochelle on France's southwest coast. With remission for good behavior, he was released early and returned to West Germany in the spring of 1975.

Meanwhile, in Berlin the confession he had made to Rupp had led to the recovery of the van Goyen. Herr Braun, the dealer, was traced and reluctantly gave the name of the client to whom he had sold the painting. Outraged and protesting, the client at first denied all knowledge of the picture. But when confronted by a search warrant for his house and office, he handed the picture back. As in the case of Herr Braun, no charges were brought against him.

The elegant Herr Gormann languished in custody for several months. Then, pleading guilty to the charges brought against him, he was given a suspended sentence of six months. Regarding his future plans, he suggested that he would return to his artistic activities in the fields of music and sculpture.

Anne-Marie Frank, a sadder but perhaps wiser young woman, went back to her studies in German, pursuing her original aim of becoming a fully qualified teacher in the language.

The paintings themselves proved something of an embarrassment to Hans Deter, into whose hands they were delivered for safekeeping pending their return to France.

"I found the most any insurance company would insure them for was one million deutsche marks," he remembers, "while of course they were obviously worth infinitely more than that. In the end I went to a bank manager I know and arranged for them to be stored in his vault."

Deter was deeply relieved in April 1974 when Pontramon, accompanied by one of the Louvre's top specialists in Dutch-Flemish paintings, arrived in Berlin to collect them.

"We went to endless lengths to make sure there would be no delay or problems with French customs when the two of us flew in with one of the world's masterpieces," Pontramon says, chuckling. "We sent messages specifying our flight and everything else we could think of. As soon as we landed at Charles de Gaulle airport, we went straight to the customs office to declare we had the paintings with us. They didn't even glance at them!"

A few days later the glory of the Tours museum was back in its rightful place on the wall of the Salle Hollandaise.

EPILOGUE

Much, of course, had happened since the night of the theft almost two and a half years earlier.

Not only in France but in museums throughout Europe, indeed throughout the world, security measures were drastically overhauled and strengthened.

Yet questions remained—and still do to this day. Did Whitman really take the paintings on impulse and at random, as he claimed? Was there really no one with him that December night? Was the robbery in truth not meticulously planned in advance? Were there not accomplices and organizers, experts in art thefts who manipulated the young Czech?

All we can be certain of is that as a result of diligent police work and the cooperation Interpol makes possible between Europe's police forces, the paintings were finally recovered.

In April 1975 Hans Deter's men, in a routine report, recorded that Whitman was living in a Berlin commune. A week later he walked out into the darkness.

Our wandering poet had rejoined the companions of the road.

FOUR FROM
BUENOS AIRES

Four From Buenos Aires

by
Richard Collier

ILLUSTRATED BY BEN WOHLBERG

"The family is well" . . . "Your suit has come from the tailor" . . . "I have to pay the doctor"—all sounded innocuous enough, simple phrases exchanged in the course of telephone conversations. But to the detectives who were tapping the calls the decoded meanings of those words were sinister, for the men speaking them happened to be members of a narcotics ring smuggling heroin into New York City at an unprecedented rate. At the head of it was a short, fat man named Luis Cesar Stepenberg. "Number One" he liked to call himself—and catching him became the number one objective of scores of determined police supported by Interpol in a host of countries.

Richard Collier has published many articles and is the author of several books, including *Pay Off in Calcutta, The City That Would Not Die* and, most recently, his account of the Berlin airlift, *Bridge Across the Sky.*

PART ONE
THE SEEDS OF THE POPPY

THEY CAME DISCREETLY, each man chartering his own black-and-yellow taxi, in the early evening.

Outside the Ristorante El Sol in the quiet Buenos Aires suburb of Olivos, the fairy lights as yet stayed dark; few Porteños, as the citizens call themselves, dine before ten p.m. But the men arriving on this June evening in 1966 were coming on business, not pleasure. They were the advance guard of one of the most powerful criminal syndicates the world had ever known.

At intervals, as the doorbell pealed softly, the young maître d' scanned every caller alertly before ushering each to an inner room. From behind the closed doors he heard surprised greetings, for some of the party had not met together for a long time. Finally the group— five of them newcomers—were seated around the polished zebrawood table. A white-jacketed waiter served jiggers of *caña,* a fiery cane rum, then departed on cat feet. The visitors glanced expectantly at their host, a compact, molelike man of fifty-five wearing horn-rimmed spectacles, his hair thinning, his yellowing skin stretched tautly over sharp cheekbones.

Augusto José Ricord, alias Lucien Darguelles, alias André Cori, whose respectable business front was this restaurant, surveyed them paternally. "Gentlemen," he announced, "I have a proposition which I think will appeal to you. It could make every one of us— yes, every one of us—into millionaires."

Few among them evinced surprise. What Augusto Ricord said was taken for gospel in many criminal haunts, apart from his native Marseille. Arrested for theft and extortion at the age of sixteen, he was managing a chain of brothels by the age of twenty. When the Nazis overran France in 1940, he became an informer and bill collector for the Gestapo in Paris. Fleeing to Buenos Aires in 1947 to escape charges of armed robbery and treason, he had gone on to build up a lucrative empire of white slavery between Argentina, Brazil and Venezuela.

But prostitution was a drop in the bucket beside the proposition that Ricord now outlined to the men grouped around the table. It was one of the most far-reaching drug-trafficking syndicates ever conceived, an unchallenged heroin empire.

As always, Ricord's plans had been meticulous. During the past year he had paid several visits to Geneva, Switzerland, to confer with several Swiss suppliers, who had amassed enough capital to set up three mobile heroin laboratories. Concealed in widely scattered trailers—in central France, Germany and Belgium—the laboratories were capable of producing close to three hundred kilos of heroin a week (1 kilogram=2.2 pounds).

Some of Ricord's companions had worked closely with him, perfecting the plan. Among them was Louis Bonsignour, Ricord's nephew, a capable, thickset forty-two-year-old who posed as an export agent and used the alias of Felipe Spadaro.

The others had questions and were not slow to voice them. The first to speak was Domingo Orsini, a stocky Corsican. "Won't it be hard to find couriers you can trust?"

Ricord didn't think so. The pimps and prostitutes from his former syndicate were well versed in the arts of deception. A courier—or "mule" in the drug traffickers' argot—would be paid three thousand dollars plus expenses for each trip to Europe. There he would pick up the "Big H"—the heroin—from a "stash house" in Spain, Italy or France. On the return trip a syndicate controller—a "shotgun"—would fly the same airliner to monitor every stage of the mule's journey. It would be he, when the mule reached the United States, who would take charge of the heroin, deliver to the customers, then channel the profits into numbered Swiss bank accounts.

Michel Nicoli, his staid bookkeeper's exterior belying his criminal past, pursed his lips. "It sounds feasible," he allowed, "but where do we come in?"

Ricord inclined his head. "A good question. The syndicate will consist of five subgroups. I want five men willing to act as my subgroup heads. Each of them will appoint his own lieutenants, and the lieutenants will do the hard graft—lining up the customers, keeping them supplied, arranging the financial transfers." He paused. "At a conservative estimate, we can channel one thousand kilos of heroin into the United States per year. Each one of the subgroups will be allotted two hundred kilos. Is it a deal?"

Ricord had picked his men shrewdly. There was a general murmur of assent. They came from widely divergent backgrounds, but all had two things in common: French nationality, and a total lack of principle or regard for human life. The eldest of the newcomers was Orsini, who had fled France twenty-two years earlier and was still wanted for armed robbery. For the rest, Christian Jacques David, whose dapper good looks earned him the nickname "Le Beau Serge," had just fled France, where he had been sentenced to death *in absentia* after gunning down a police superintendent. François Rossi was another fugitive from French justice; sunburned and tough as whipcord, Rossi had graduated from a Corsican syndicate whose members were renowned for their resistance to police interrogation. André Condemine, tall and elegant, had begun his criminal life as a stickup artist, and French justice had also sentenced him to death *in absentia* as the result of some violent robberies.

It was Condemine who posed the next question. "What routes are these mules going to follow?"

Ricord was explicit. "There'll be two. One will go from Europe to Montreal, then to New York. And the other will be by way of Latin America—Europe to Buenos Aires, Rio—then on to New York."

"That's a long way round," Condemine objected.

"But maybe the shortest in the end," Ricord reminded him. "It's a route the Americans know nothing about, and that's the beauty of it. The French connection—oh, yes, they're wise to that. The Argentine connection—that they don't know about, because until tonight it's never existed."

It was the blueprint of an organization as efficient and soulless as the Nazi machine that Ricord had admired, and he now revealed to them that there was even a backup system. For years all kinds of planes, from small short-range models to cast-off World War II transport aircraft, had been flying between Miami and dirt strips carved from the bush in the jungles of Argentina, Brazil and particularly Paraguay. These pilots, known as *contrabandistas,* would give the syndicate the extra dimension it needed: its own secret airline. The way stood wide open for the Argentine connection.

The business of the meeting having been concluded, Ricord pressed a bell and ordered fresh drinks. "And now, gentlemen," he said, his eyes twinkling, "let me invite you to witness my style show."

The moment he finished speaking, a young woman entered the room. As the group relaxed beneath a whirring electric fan, she modeled a unique device that Ricord himself had perfected: beneath her skirt, to feign pregnancy, she wore a cagelike contraption, a perfect receptacle for heroin. Her act was followed by Micki Soulé, a cherubic-looking former bartender, whom the French police had vainly sought for burglary. As he stripped to the buff, a low whistle of admiration came from the spectators. Coiled tightly against his skin like a snake, extending from above his navel to his thighs, was a body harness consisting of layers of surgical tape. Beneath the tape were three plastic bags, each containing a kilo of pure heroin.

"Pretty smart contraption," one man commented, and Micki preened himself with pleasure. He had been testing Ricord's body harness for eighteen months now, carrying bags of heroin from West Germany to Puerto Rico.

Only one factor remained to be resolved: if a thousand kilos of heroin a year were going to reach the United States, a resident distributor would be needed in New York City, a man fully as ruthless and determined as any of those assembled here.

For the first time Ricord's nephew, Louis Bonsignour, broke silence. "The next time I'm in New York, it could be I'll find the guy," he volunteered. Then Bonsignour laughed. "And maybe he'll be from Argentina."

ON MARCH 22, 1967, AN air of restrained excitement pervaded the headquarters of Interpol in the modern glass-and-stone building at 26 rue Armengaud, perched on a hillside in Paris' western dormitory suburb of St. Cloud. In his seventh-floor office, overlooking the leaden waters of the Seine, the secretary-general, Jean Nepote, a trim, genial man with slightly graying crew-cut hair, was conferring urgently with the chief of the drugs section.

In some ways the case that preoccupied them was typical of all narcotics cases handled by Interpol: they had to keep abreast of the traffickers' ingenuity. For more than a year agents of the Office Centrale pour la Répression du Traffic des Stupéfiants, in liaison with the Federal Bureau of Narcotics (FBN) in the United States, had been keeping a weather eye on a known member of the Marseille mob who, with a handful of accomplices, had set up an outfit in Paris for the export of electronic equipment. They suspected the export firm might be the key link in an international drug-trafficking syndicate, and now, on this raw, overcast morning, they had proof of it. An early morning raid at Orly airport had revealed a hiding place unknown until now: in a consignment of oscilloscopes—sensitive electronic measuring devices that look a little like television sets—awaiting shipment to New York. There were six, and each contained one kilo of pure heroin.

Hence Nepote's concern, for back in December information had reached Interpol too late to prevent an earlier consignment's leaving for New York. Now bills of lading seized at the airport suggested that this morning's haul was the second part of a promised delivery. The first installment was just then reaching New York.

It was a classic case for Interpol liaison. Though the international staff wore plain clothes, made no arrests and carried no guns, they served the national central bureaus (NCBs) for member countries on five continents. On the surface the seven-story building, with its vast marbled entrance lobby and sprawling philodendron plant, closely resembled the headquarters of a prosperous multinational corporation; only the blue-and-white Interpol flag, showing the globe pierced by a giant sword, proclaimed that where international crime was concerned, theirs was a world knowing no barriers.

By midmorning, as the U.S. narcotics bureau's Paris representative, Victor Maria, was phoning his district supervisor in New York, Interpol's experts were already at work drafting a bulletin that would alert every member country about this new and ingenious ruse of the drug traffickers.

The FBN regional office in New York City lost no time in acting.

Toward dusk on March 22 a task force of agents converged on the office of the Foreign Trade Import Company, on the city's lower West Side near the financial district. The manager, Claude Mimeaux, was seized trying to make his getaway. A check on the oscilloscopes—each a bulky but compact apparatus that weighed around five kilograms—confirmed the truth of Interpol's tip-off.

In Paris an engineer had skillfully removed exactly one kilo of inner parts from each oscilloscope and had substituted, compensating for the lost weight, one kilo of heroin. So, all told, twelve oscilloscopes yielded twelve kilos (or more than twenty-six pounds) of pure heroin, with a street value of several million dollars.

At the FBN regional office, Mimeaux, glum and white-faced, agreed to cooperate, though his information was limited. Three men had been involved in the December deal: two, he thought, were of Spanish origin; the third was French, a thickset man who lived with a girl friend on East Sixty-third Street. The agents took him through files of photographs, until abruptly Mimeaux stiffened.

"That's him! That's the Frenchman!"

The face was one the agents knew well: Ricord's nephew, Louis Bonsignour, alias Felipe Spadaro, born, according to which passport he carried, in Marseille in 1922, or Algeria in 1923.

On Wednesday, April 12, following his return to New York, FBN agents closed in on Louis Bonsignour.

Early next morning, in an apartment in a quietly luxurious building on a street west of New York's Central Park, the phone rang urgently. A tall man sipping breakfast coffee stretched out a long, muscular arm to answer it. His name was Jack Grosby.

The harried voice on the phone identified the speaker as Milo and announced that at this moment Bonsignour was lodged in the Federal House of Detention in lower Manhattan, and his bail had been set at thirty-five thousand dollars. Could Grosby come over and see Milo right away?

At forty-one, the Argentine Jew Jacobo Grodnitzky, who preferred the Americanization Jack Grosby, was no stranger to trouble. Topping six feet three inches, with blond crinkly hair, and blue eyes showing behind gold-rimmed spectacles, Grosby signally failed to conform to the familiar Latin stereotype—but all his life Grosby had failed to conform. He had been sometime salesman, sometime travel agent in his native Buenos Aires; sometime dishwasher in a New Jersey restaurant; at all times a spot bettor on the races, and most recently an intermittent drug trafficker out of Puerto Rico.

From the bedroom Grosby's girl friend, Eva Santos, a striking Brazilian, called, "Who was that?"

"A friend of Bonsignour's. Seems like Louis is in trouble. I'd better get on over."

Although he moved on the fringe of the Ricord organization—at a friend's request he had even fixed up the dapper André Condemine with an apartment in this very block—Grosby was not as yet deeply involved with them. Nor was he aware, on this soft April morning, of how much he was destined to be.

As Grosby was soon to learn, money was the least of Bonsignour's problems. The thirty-five thousand dollars, stuffed inside an ordinary shopping bag, had already been delivered to a bail bondsman by Milo. What Bonsignour needed above all was a liaison man who would seek out the Ricord mob and alert them to his plight. If Grosby could see his way clear to fly to Buenos Aires, Milo went on, he would be amply reimbursed for his trouble.

The Buenos Aires meeting was destined to lay New York wide open to the Argentine connection. Within days Grosby came face to face with Ricord and those men he later recognized as the most powerful in the world of narcotics smuggling. There were Orsini, Christian David, François Rossi and Leo Santiago, an elderly bald-domed man with hooded eyes and shaggy eyebrows; the man called "El Viejo"—the old man—his skin seamed like old parchment; François Chiappe, Ricord's thick-lipped bodyguard, hovering nearby; and finally Ricord himself, like a little gray, bright-eyed mole.

At first Grosby was at a loss to understand. If money was no problem, as he had been assured, how could he be of help? Quietly Ricord explained. The bail had been raised to fifty thousand dollars at the request of U.S. prosecuting attorneys, but even with sufficient bail money, it would be necessary for someone to guarantee Bonsignour's continuing presence in the United States. This would be Grosby's role.

"Louis is a good boy," Ricord declared to Grosby. "He doesn't forget his friends."

And Rossi, smiling thinly, added, "Or his enemies."

All of them laughed then, dutifully, but there was no real mirth in that room.

Thus, ironically, the oscilloscope stratagem not only had left Bonsignour deeply indebted to Grosby but had given Ricord the New York connection he had sought. Following a tangled web of legal argument, which first forced Bonsignour to surrender his passport, then raised his bail to seventy-five thousand dollars, Grosby's presence as guarantor finally prevailed. On August 30, agreeing to stay within the boundaries of Manhattan Island, Bonsignour was freed on bail, to appear in court on October 26, 1967.

Sometime before that date he fled the country.

Ricord had spoken truly, though; despite the trade they plied, Bonsignour and those like him had their own warped code of loyalty. They did not forget a favor. In the month that followed, Grosby's sudden prosperity became more and more apparent. There were mysterious trips to Paris, Madrid and Buenos Aires, with all expenses paid. He plunged heavily at the racetrack. Sometimes he won, but not often enough to explain that growing wardrobe of tailor-made suits, or the costly gold cuff links he wore.

From this time on, few were to show a greater interest in Jack Grosby's sudden and palpable good fortune than another man whose roots were in Buenos Aires—Grosby's old friend and boyhood crony, Luis Cesar Stepenberg.

For most city dwellers, the late summer of 1967 was typical. A blue heat haze hung above the avenues from which the buildings rose like canyon walls; leaves dappled the paths that wound through Central Park.

Uptown in Spanish Harlem, by contrast, little air stirred in the streets. By day the district was a vast concrete coffin. In the evening the people sat listlessly out on the front stoops, the women in flowered housedresses, the men in short-sleeved sport shirts. There they sipped cans of beer beaded with moisture, and prayed for rain.

It was a world divorced from Park Avenue and from the harsh bright tawdry Times Square jungle. In the vegetable markets, women with scant English haggled for *toronjas*—grapefruit—and *pepinos*—cucumbers. In these tenement streets there were the *carnicerias* of the butchers, displaying trays of meat; in the small *bodegas*, the grocers hung strings of large red peppers above the cans of tamales, enchiladas and frijoles, all piled in neat pyramids. But whatever the shop, most had one thing in common: the solid galvanized steel shutters, rolled down at night to deter the stickup men.

For some latinos the edges of *el barrio*—the district—marked the boundaries of their world. Not so for Luis Stepenberg. For one thing, the three cigar stores he owned were across town on the more ethnically mixed West Side of Manhattan; the Stepenberg Cigar Store was at 2541 Broadway, another was farther north at 3555, and between them, at 3379, was the Tabaquiria Ricardo, which a partner of two years, José Colon, mostly ran. These stores were indistinguishable from similar ones in many sections of the city. Each had its running sign: STATIONERY, FILMS, PIPES, CIGARS, TOBACCO, PEPSI; the same glass display case of White Owl and Henry Clay cigars; the same miscellaneous jumble of cigarettes, newspapers, candy and paperbacks; and a sliding peephole window giving onto the street for the sale of casual items. What's more, they were small-time operations in every sense, and Luis Stepenberg knew it.

To be sure, Stepenberg had other irons in the New York fire: a used-car lot nearby, styled Export Motors; a ten percent share in the Luan Towcar Service, on upper Amsterdam Avenue east of Broadway; to say nothing of part interests in a jewelry store and a restaurant. But these, too, were fringe enterprises from which a man could wrest a fast dollar only with difficulty.

In June 1967 Luis Stepenberg had turned forty. Five feet eight inches tall, with a bulk that set the bathroom scales quivering at the two-hundred-forty-pound mark, he already looked older, and his rumpled clothes, potbelly and drooping Pancho Villa mustache enhanced that impression. Stepenberg chose to make fun of that, even using the feminine form: "La Gorda," he called himself—the fat one—but though his lips creased in a grudging smile, his blue eyes remained cold when he said it. A voracious feeder—anything from candy bars to porterhouse steaks—he secretly resented his fatness, just as he resented his tall, elegant friend Jack Grosby and Grosby's success with women.

Twelve years before, he had quit his native Buenos Aires for the United States, following in the footsteps of his father, Abraham, and his younger brother, Joseph, both of them jewelers by profession.

And on the surface he had prospered. From modest beginnings, working as a waiter in the same New Jersey restaurant where his friend Grosby had washed dishes, he had gone on to found the used-car company, employing Grosby as his first salesman. That was ten years ago, and in all those years the big time had eluded him. Stepenberg dearly wanted the big time: the fast cars, the compliant women, the fashionable nightclubs.

Many Argentine expatriates saw him as a solid citizen in the more than corporeal flesh: a notary public in the state of New York, a member of the Brazilian-American Society and the Argentine-American Chamber of Commerce. Even so, Stepenberg knew that people didn't take to him as they took to the genial Grosby. His detractors, and they were many, disliked the cutting edge his voice took on when contradicted, his readiness to despise all those who didn't aspire to "culture": Stepenberg spent long hours in the Guggenheim museum on Fifth Avenue, admiring the Chagalls and the early Picassos. They disliked his meanness: a notorious penny pincher, he shared a flat with his father on West End Avenue, now that he had separated from his wife. They doubted, rightly, his frequent boast that he was a high official of the Argentine government.

Others, meeting him in his role as notary public, secretly admired him, for Stepenberg was most expansive when lesser men brought in their problems; that was when "Number One," as he also liked to call himself, could assume his most paternalistic air. "Leave it to Number One," he would assure them.

Although he had become a U.S. citizen in 1960—retaining dual nationality—the authorities had three times had cause to investigate him. In November 1955, barely two months after he entered the United States, New York City detectives had questioned Stepenberg about an attempted extortion. But the alleged victim had recanted and the case was thrown out. Less than three years later, the Federal Bureau of Investigation drew a blank after probing a claim that Stepenberg was posing as an FBI agent. In 1962, the Immigration and Naturalization Service explored the charge that Stepenberg was shaking down immigrants in return for affidavits that he would employ them. For the third time the verdict was "Not proved."

On February 8, 1957, the immigrant visa application made by Jack Grosby at Caracas, Venezuela, had named Luis Cesar Stepenberg as the American sponsor, and now, ten years later, Stepenberg intended to make that favor pay off. As yet he only dimly suspected Grosby's newfound source of wealth, but he saw the fruits of it: the shrugged-off losses at the racetrack, the expensive suits, the nights on the town with Eva Santos.

It all spelled a way to the big time, and until he had a piece of the action, Stepenberg would give Grosby no peace day or night.

ON SATURDAY, MAY 6, 1967, while Grosby was still interceding for the grateful Bonsignour-Spadaro, Interpol, through the medium of the U.S. Customs Service, had glimpsed the first faint tip of the iceberg that the Argentine connection was fast becoming.

In the International Arrivals Building at New York's John F. Kennedy airport, the passengers from Olympic Airways flight 409, from Athens, Rome and Paris, were undergoing the routine customs inspection. Already in summer attire, officers in sky-blue short-sleeve shirts, with the distinctive shoulder patch featuring the United States eagle, were riffling expertly through passengers' baggage, scrawling the cabalistic chalk marks that spelled clearance.

One officer's eyes now focused on a corpulent middle-aged man in a creased business suit, who had opened his suitcase along with the rest. Its contents were blameless—a change of underwear, paperback whodunits, a shaving kit—but it was the man himself who compelled attention. He stood as awkwardly as a man encased in a plaster cast.

Acting on a hunch, the officer decided on a body search. His vigilance was rewarded. Beneath the man's shirt was a torso as tightly bound with surgical tape as a mummy. Under the tape were three glassine bags, each containing one kilo of pure heroin.

Minutes later two customs special agents were speeding to the airport from their lower Manhattan headquarters. Few men were better qualified for the assignment. Soft-spoken Albert W. Seeley had already spent twenty years in the New York Police Department combating organized crime. His companion, Edward T. Coyne, six years with customs, had earlier served with the Federal Bureau of Narcotics. Neither man could then realize that the investigation they were setting in motion was destined to drag on well into the 1970s.

At ten p.m., in a small bleak office at the U.S. Customs Service headquarters, they began their interrogation of a man called André Pontet. Despite an interpreter's presence, the process was long and grueling.

"Where did he get his passport?"

The interpreter translated the question, listened and then said, "From a man in Buenos Aires who promised him three thousand dollars."

"Who was the man?" Seeley asked.

"He says he doesn't know. A Frenchman—the same man who told him where to pick up the heroin in Rome."

Seeley was puzzled. Frenchman? What were Frenchmen doing in Buenos Aires?

Pontet didn't know that either. All he knew was that many Frenchmen had settled in Argentina, particularly those who had collaborated with the Nazis in wartime. Some of them were regular clients of a restaurant owned by another Frenchman.

"What's the name of the place?" But again they drew a blank. Pontet claimed total ignorance.

Seeley came to an inevitable decision. "Let's check this man's fingerprints with Interpol."

Dawn was paling in the sky as the two customs agents drove away from headquarters. Seeley was far from satisfied. For years they had been picking up drug traffickers from France, following a well-blazed trail; now, out of the blue, came a man who hailed from Argentina. But would a one-shot courier have traveled all the way from Buenos Aires to Rome, thence to New York, to deliver a few kilos of heroin? Seeley didn't think so.

In Paris, Interpol's experts studied the fingerprints sent from New York, and by late on Sunday they had identified the man: Ange Luccarotti, a Corsican hoodlum who three years earlier had shot his way out of a French jail.

"Luccarotti?" Coyne mused. "We've had that name before."

And indeed they had. In 1965 Nonce Luccarotti had been convicted for trying to smuggle a hundred kilos of heroin into the United States in a refrigerator that belonged to an army noncom returning from Europe.

"Seems like our man had a brother," Seeley reasoned.

Seeley's suspicions led him to order a neutron analysis—a laboratory test pinpointing the exact proportion of chemical agents used by a manufacturer—on every load of heroin seized in the last three years. The chemical "fingerprint" of the heroin seized from Ange Luccarotti was identical to that of a shipment from Paris seized in New York as recently as February.

In Washington, D.C., both customs officers and narcotics agents were skeptical of Seeley's theory. The major threat, they believed, still came from the infamous French connection, the laboratories controlled by Corsican gangsters which shipped the heroin direct from Marseille to New York.

Most likely Luccarotti *had* spoken the truth when he claimed to have been recruited from Buenos Aires—but Seeley's theory of a drug ring put together in that city, using couriers unknown to U.S. agents and the same European suppliers, found no favor.

Seeley bided his time. As the year progressed, he noted with quiet triumph each time the seizure of a shipment pointed up a link with Argentina. In August, agents at Port Everglades, Florida, arrested three couriers carrying twelve kilos of heroin. Each man had a tourist visa stamped in Buenos Aires. In October, another man was seized in Boston with a Buenos Aires visa. Taped to his body were three kilos of heroin. In the same month the Royal Canadian Mounted Police netted two travelers from Buenos Aires at Montreal's international airport: a man and his wife, with sixteen kilos hidden in false-bottomed luggage.

On December 5 of that year came a windfall. Interpol's National Central Bureau in Madrid reported the arrest of three suspected traffickers on the same day, including Micki Soulé, the man who had modeled the body harness for the benefit of Ricord's confederates. All of them had been taken by surprise near a bar frequented by traffickers, and two of them had had no time to dispose of their papers. Among Soulé's personal notes were the scribbled name Jack Grosby and another name and address: José Colon, 3379 Broadway, New York. Another suspect had been more painstaking—and even less security conscious. On a sketch plan of two intersecting streets, West 137th and Broadway, he had hatched in a small box marked "Tabaquiria Ricardo."

Luis Stepenberg's cigar store was now destined to feature—though still as just a tentative lead—in the files of Interpol.

ON NEW YEAR'S DAY, 1968, THE DRUGS section of Interpol did some elementary arithmetic. All told, the U.S. Customs Service, the Federal Bureau of Narcotics and the Mounties had arrested twenty-one of Ricord's couriers in the United States and Canada, all with passports that bore a Buenos Aires visa. But Americans like Seeley and Coyne felt far from triumphant. What did the seizures amount to, after all? Twenty-one petty traffickers had made their last trip for the foreseeable future. What was disturbing was that their passports revealed many previous trips. The amount of heroin found on each courier, if multiplied by all those trips, revealed a horrifying total: almost seven hundred kilos of pure heroin in eight months. ("Pure" to drug traffickers can mean eighty-five percent or better.) That represented a street value of over a hundred million dollars, but the human cost could never be measured.

Although a disturbing amount of heroin was beginning to filter in from the "Golden Triangle" spanning northeast Burma, northern Thailand and northwest Laos, most of it—about eighty percent—originated in Afyonkarahisar province in western Turkey, at the foot of the Sultan Mountains. Here in summer, just after the poppies had bloomed in a sea of soft white and purple heads and petals began to fall, farmers punctured the silken pods (or unripe fruit). The milky latex that coagulated on the shell of the pod was opium. Collected and kneaded into football-size spheres as it hardened, this Turkish opium had thousands of miles to travel: by horse, train or truck through Damascus in Syria to Beirut, Lebanon, then on by freighter to Marseille.

Often, along the way, it was converted to crude morphine or morphine base by the addition of water, lime and ammonium chloride, then by repeated heating and filtering until the milky latex had precipitated into dry gray-brown crystals. In this way five hundred kilos of opium could be reduced to fifty of morphine base.

In the trailer laboratories scattered throughout Europe, the next stage was purification—mixing the morphine with acetone, filtering and drying it. This purer form of morphine was then treated with acetic anhydride at eighty-five degrees centigrade for six hours. The balloon flasks used for this process then contained impure heroin in solution. Now for several more days the treatment continued: more filtrations, more washings, more precipitations. At length all that

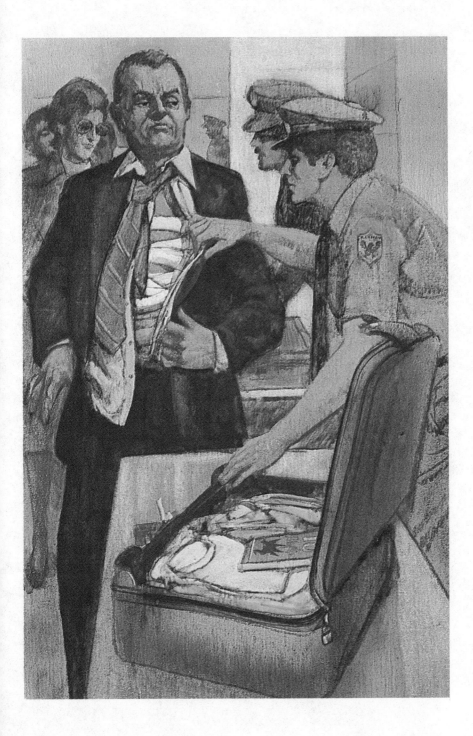

remained in the flasks was a fluffy white detergentlike powder: the finest quality heroin.

But even given the profits involved—sometimes three hundred thousand dollars a year—the chemists could work only four days each week. For the remaining three days they rested—like athletes in training—building up resistance against the noxious fumes; sleeping eight hours a night, drinking quarts of milk, bathing their hands in milk to counteract the corrosive acids.

The next problem for the traffickers was to conceal the heroin on its long journey to the United States. Whatever route it traveled, the methods were the same. Favorite hiding places with Ricord's ring were in cars: heroin stashed in false-bottomed floors or false-bottomed trunks, behind headlights or dashboards, or taped to the engine rocker arms. All along the route a freakish ingenuity was the keynote; sometimes the heroin was secreted in false-bottomed golf bags or hollowed-out melons, in leopard skins, mah-jongg tiles, or in hollowed-out ski poles. Few hit upon a method as bizarre as André Condemine's: his girl friend, who owned a fashionable Buenos Aires wig shop, sewed the heroin into the linings of wigs prior to export.

The profits escalated in transit. Enough opium to produce a kilo of heroin, worth $22 in Turkey and $350 when converted to morphine base, had upped to $3500 at the labs in Marseille and to $18,000 on the wholesale market in New York. At this stage, channeled to importers like Stepenberg, the drug was still "pure." But then the hierarchy took over: the wholesaler, who handled up to fifty kilos; the jobber, entrusted with no more than five; the street wholesaler, who broke up a kilo into bags; the addict pusher, known always as The Man, who took it from there. From the wholesaler downward many hands were employed, "cutting" or "stretching" the heroin's purity, using quinine, milk sugar, even Epsom salts. In the ghettos of the city, where the pushers heard the addicts' heart cry every day—"Daddy, lay it on me, I'm sick"—the heroin content was rarely more than six percent. One kilo had thus netted suppliers, traffickers and pushers up to $220,000.

Of all Interpol's member countries that grappled with this sickness, none was affected more acutely than the United States. Not only the U.S. Customs Service but the Federal Bureau of Narcotics and the New York Police Department were confronted with a nightmare situation; of the country's estimated three hundred and fifteen thousand addicts, nearly half, or perhaps one hundred and fifty thousand, were concentrated in the city alone. Some sought surcease from pain, oblivion, or the momentary euphoria of the sixty-second "rush," followed by the hours-long "high" of drowsy, withdrawn lethargy. "All the advantages of death without its permanence" was one addict's bitter definition.

It was a drug with many aliases—scag, smack, the Big H, horse, junk—but all its adherents dropped downward to the same agony, called "the monkey on the back": a tolerance so phenomenal that a habit could be priced at one hundred dollars or more a day.

After years of this torment, death came as a mercy to most. Depending on the complications, a physician would then certify death as due to endocarditis, tetanus or serum hepatitis. Laymen might have recorded a simpler verdict: willful homicide.

BY THE EARLY summer of 1968 Stepenberg had achieved his piece of the action. A year earlier, when he had first broached the idea to Grosby directly, the big man had coolly brushed his insinuation aside. But Stepenberg persisted. By dint of veiled innuendos, covert threats and hints as to Grosby's ingratitude, he slowly won himself a toehold in his friend's newfound world, gradually wheedling introductions, first to André Condemine, then to Michel Nicoli. So Number One was now in a unique position to become Ricord's top distributor in New York.

All later evidence suggested that Grosby accepted this without rancor. Not long after Bonsignour had skipped bail, Grosby met him in several European haunts used by traffickers, and Ricord's nephew had come up with a cast-iron offer to repay Grosby's favor: the entire Marseille connection. Ricord, he said, would even finance the purchase of a small boat to smuggle two hundred kilos of heroin into the United States at one time.

Grosby demurred. Affable and easygoing, his inclination was to dabble on the sidelines, concerning himself with financial transfers. Where heroin was concerned, he would limit himself to smaller quantities, twelve-kilo deliveries at most. "The bigger the deal, the bigger the risk, right? That's not for me" was the way he put it to Stepenberg on one visit to the Tabaquiria Ricardo.

Stepenberg made no answer at the time, but he didn't agree. He had watched with envy the change wrought on Grosby's life-style by these small-time transactions, but he wanted more than that: he wanted only the biggest of big deals. He was out to become not only New York's biggest importer but the biggest importer in the United States.

As YET THE risks were minimal. Back in February, Seeley and Coyne had set down their thoughts on paper for the commissioner of customs in Washington, D.C. These were the results of months of painstaking needle-in-a-haystack tracing—the names of mules and shotguns that cropped up with dubious frequency on the same airline passenger manifests, slips of paper found on arrested couriers that spotlighted addresses like Stepenberg's—and everything pointed to a giant conspiracy with the United States as its target.

"It is our belief," Seeley concluded, "that these people [in Buenos Aires] are part of what could be one of the largest, most influential and best financed international heroin-smuggling organizations uncovered in recent years. We believe that this organization is responsible for between fifty and seventy-five percent of all heroin smuggled into the United States."

Still, the Federal Bureau of Narcotics, as highly trained as their men were, had just eight hundred and fifty agents to police the entire United States. In New York, only fifteen customs men covered the drug beat at airports and along the waterfront. Literally thousands of additional agents would be needed to stem the flood tide of heroin. "This," one customs agent complained angrily, "is like being a blind goalie in a hockey game."

THE NEWLY FLEDGED Stepenberg-Grosby drug ring stood in good stead with Ricord. On March 21 Michel Nicoli flew into New York City from Montevideo, Uruguay. He was awaiting forty kilos of heroin from San Antonio, Texas, which had already traveled by freighter from Italy to the Gulf of Mexico. Neither his serious bookkeeper's mien—nor a passport with a forged name—lulled the suspicions of passport control at Kennedy International airport; they booked him for the possession of false documents.

At once the Ricord organization moved to the rescue. Within a month a bail bondsman had arrived with the now obligatory fifty thousand dollars. Nicoli then made for the Manhattan apartment of Florencio Gonzalez, an ailing sixty-year-old Argentinian who served as one of Ricord's New York agents. There he found a familiar figure lounging on a sofa—the broadly grinning Jack Grosby.

"Don't worry," Grosby reassured him. "Marcello"—the undercover name for François Rossi—"has fixed everything."

Within the hour a courier had arrived with another false passport. "We'll have you back in Buenos Aires in time for breakfast," said Grosby breezily.

A past master at currying favor with the powerful, Stepenberg was not to be outdone when his turn came, some weeks later. On May 20 the dapper André Condemine called him at the Tabaquiria Ricardo: a Ricord agent had been held for questioning. It was Stepenberg who put up the bail this time; Grosby was not the only man to whom Ricord would remain indebted.

The ambitious Stepenberg was looking far ahead. In the garish bars and nightclubs of the upper West Side he built up a reliable network of six to eight regular customers, each of whom undertook to distribute between twenty and sixty kilos of heroin every six weeks. Among his favorites was Henry Wood, already known to the police as a major narcotics violator. Since Ricord was, by a later estimate, shipping a hundred kilos of heroin a month into the United States, Stepenberg had already cornered the lion's share of the action.

At the same time Seeley and Coyne, like their colleagues in the narcotics bureau, had reached an impasse. The business card of the Ristorante El Sol, Buenos Aires, had been found in the billfold of more than one courier. In a four-page intelligence report on French criminals linked to a prostitution ring, a document that had come from the Argentine federal police, they chanced on the restaurant's name again, as the "property of the international French delinquent Augusto José Ricord." But though the Interpol folder on Ricord confirmed his vicious past, no evidence had linked him with organized crime since 1963.

In June 1968 his name cropped up once more—this time at the New York City headquarters of the Federal Bureau of Narcotics. An anonymous letter, posted in Brussels on June 2, was asking for hard cash. The writer promised:

In return I can offer:

1. Several gangs that import drugs into the United States and that are established in various countries of Europe and South America.

2. The buyers in the United States.

3. The names of the associates of . . . Ricord-Cori. . . .

"For this," he added superfluously, "they will give me a bullet in the head."

Liaison had to be established without delay. Each Monday and Tuesday, for the next two weeks, an advertisement would appear in the columns of the Brussels paper *Le Soir*. The phrasing was innocuous: "Cats for sale. Call _____" The narcotics agents, if interested, were to phone and establish their identities.

All that summer and autumn the agents stayed close to the disgruntled Latin-American courier who claimed the syndicate had cheated him, questioning the man, annotating and sifting the details he provided. By degrees a cat's cradle of interwoven names, dates and addresses began to take shape. Yet much of the evidence was inferential. Ricord had to be the leader of the syndicate and Stepenberg his primary United States importer—but there was nothing to link the small fish, already in the net, with the barracudas.

At this moment, in the late summer of 1968, two things happened simultaneously. The Argentine police, angered by a bank robbery staged by a French-speaking gunman, cracked down on prominent French criminals. Promptly Ricord dropped from sight. At the same time, seizures of heroin at U.S. ports of entry dwindled to a trickle, as though, suddenly and inexplicably, the organization had canceled its courier flights across the North Atlantic.

One suggestion was that the ring had taken their profits while the going was good, but Al Seeley of customs disagreed. "Nobody making that much money can quit while he's ahead. It's like gambling."

At the same time informers had word that the shipments were being stepped up, and this was true. Combining as a team, Rossi and Nicoli had shipped thirty kilos of heroin into Miami by late that summer, following with a hundred kilos through San Antonio. The consignee was Luis Stepenberg, yet neither the narcotics bureau nor customs had had a trace of the shipments. It took both time and a lucky break for them to understand why.

SOMETIME AROUND JULY 9 TWO MEN met for the first time in the coffee shop at O'Hare International Airport, Chicago. They had one thing in common: the French language. Although both had been recruited in Geneva to carry shipments of heroin to Grosby in New York, there was otherwise no meeting of minds between Joseph Villeda, a young Frenchman born in Morocco, who was stocky, coarse and illiterate, and Willie Wouters, a Belgian restaurant proprietor.

A balding, dignified man, Wouters seemed an unlikely choice for a drug trafficker. Few customs officers would have suspected the courtly Wouters—a man fluent in six languages, whose horn-rimmed spectacles gave him the air of a banker—of trafficking in narcotics.

Alone and depressed, grieving over the death of his beloved wife, Wouters had ultimately proved suggestible. A frequent visitor at his restaurant had cajoled him. "How about it, Willie? We need some gold smuggled into the United States. And we've got a foolproof way—inside the airplane. You could clean up a lot of money."

Wouters smiled disbelievingly. "Don't the police know all the places to look in an airplane?"

"Not this place. It's a brand-new one. Wait until you hear."

From June 24 on, Wouters had made several trips before he realized that he was smuggling a commodity far more precious than gold. Yet the pay was good, three thousand dollars per trip, and all for delivering six to twelve kilos to Jack Grosby, whom he met in the lobby of the Belmont-Plaza Hotel, at East Forty-ninth Street and Lexington Avenue in New York City.

Now, sipping coffee at O'Hare, Wouters eyed his new fellow courier with disfavor. Villeda was brash and likely, he thought, to run needless risks—unlike himself, a man of extreme caution.

"So okay," Villeda said. "They sent me over here to work under you, right? And any money I get I turn over to you. That the way you've heard it?"

Wouters nodded. From his inner breast pocket he extracted a folded sketch. "This is a plan of the interior of a 707. Take it with you, memorize it, then burn it. It shows you exactly where you will find the merchandise. I will tell you what flights to take when the time comes. Call me every other day at the Belmont-Plaza in New York. I am registered there as Mr. Victor."

Both men paused as a waitress refilled their cups. Then Villeda, peeking covertly at the plan, said, "Something here I don't quite understand. You mean this stuff is hidden in the john?"

Dropping his voice to an undertone, Wouters explained. Soon after World War II, smugglers of watches had hit on the technique of secreting their cargoes inside men's socks, tucked behind the panels of airplane lavatories. In January 1968 this technique had been adapted for a new and deadlier cargo—heroin.

"They're all TWA planes," Wouters elaborated. "Let's say the mule boards a particular flight in Frankfurt, Germany. He is not subjected to any search—why should he be? The first stop is London, Heathrow. Between Frankfurt and London all he has to do is stash the merchandise behind the towel-disposal unit in the rest room. At London he leaves the plane. If they search him, why worry? He is clean."

"So nobody is keeping an eye on the junk all the way from London to New York?"

Wouters shrugged. "Why should they? It is safe. Let's say again that this plane comes in at Washington, D.C.—Dulles airport. But it could be New York or Boston. Here's where you get on, because now it becomes a domestic flight, with stops—sometimes St. Louis and Denver, sometimes Chicago. During the flight you"—he smiled faintly—"obey the needs of nature. You retrieve the . . . merchandise. But again you are a domestic passenger. The customs will not concern themselves with you."

Villeda's broad face creased in a grin.

"Sounds like a pushover, Willie boy," he said, and the older man winced visibly. "We have no problems."

Wouters wasn't so sure, and in the days that followed, his uncertainty increased. By now he had done six trips, and instinct warned him—correctly—that all was not plain sailing. Alerted by the disgruntled informer in Brussels, customs and narcotics agents were stepping up their vigilance.

Within days of this meeting, all his misgivings regarding Villeda had redoubled. On his next flight to O'Hare, Wouters was convinced he was under surveillance; he made no trip to the lavatory. But, to his alarm, he had no sooner cleared the arrivals area than Villeda hastened up.

"Did you get the stuff?"

"No! I think they're watching this flight . . . they're watching us. I didn't go near it."

Villeda was incredulous. "What? Now, Willie, you're just a coward. Let me handle this thing."

Before Wouters could stop him, Villeda had barged back through the arrivals gate and down the walkway to the plane. He explained volubly to all who tried to bar his way that he was an arriving passenger who had forgotten his spectacles. He managed to bluff his way into the lavatory and retrieve the heroin, but from this moment on he was a marked man.

Then, on July 27, the courier boarding flight 709 at Frankfurt got careless. At four forty-five p.m. local time, when the plane arrived at Washington's Dulles airport, a cleaner who was emptying the towel-disposal unit found a glassine bag containing half a kilo of a white crystalline powder glinting among the crumpled paper towels. Suspicious, he called in a customs agent. One sniff and a taste of the substance—sourer than cider vinegar and as bitter as quinine on the tongue—confirmed the hunch.

"That's junk, all right," the agent confirmed. "Now, where there's half a kilo, there's gotta be more."

And there was. Secreted inside the lavatory wall, customs officers found eleven more half-kilo glassine bags of heroin. Prudently they left them where they were, hastily replacing the opened twelfth with another. The trap was now set to snap shut. About six p.m., when flight 709 took off for St. Louis, Denver and San Francisco, customs agent George Festa had taken a strategic seat near the rear doorway of the plane.

An hour later flight 709 reached St. Louis. As the last passengers deplaned, Festa carefully checked the lavatory. The glassine bags remained, intact.

Soon the passengers for the next leg of the flight began to file aboard. As they took their seats, Festa noticed a slightly built, soberly dressed man settle in the smoking section near the lavatory. The pilot jockeyed the aircraft onto the runway, the sound of the jet engines continuing their steady whine, and the voice of the TWA hostess crackled over the intercom. "Good evening, ladies and gentlemen. Welcome aboard TWA's flight 709 for Denver, Colorado."

The plane was bouncing along the runway now; soon it was

airborne, and the "no smoking" lights snapped off. From the corner of his eye Festa watched the man seated near the lavatory fumble for a cigarette. It was the first of several that Wouters, a chain smoker, would light throughout this trip.

By degrees the passengers shrugged off jackets, fiddled with the airflow vents, leafed through newspapers. About twenty minutes before the plane was due to land in Denver, Wouters struggled from his seat and, with a muttered pardon to his seatmate, headed for the rest room in back. He was, Festa noted, tightly clutching his briefcase. Somewhere in the recesses of the agent's mind a warning bell rang. Why would a man take his briefcase to the lavatory?

The "engaged" light had snapped on over the rest-room door.

Thirty-three thousand feet above the Kansas plains, Wouters was crouched in the small cubicle, his hand extended gingerly into the narrow slot of the towel-disposal unit. He was feeling for a paper clip bent into an S hook and fastened to the inside of the panel. Attached to the hook was a hanging string linking a dozen men's socks filled with half-kilo glassine bags of heroin—what U.S. customs and narcotics agents call a "narcotic sausage." A moment's probing, then, as deftly as an angler landing a fish, Wouters had retrieved the packages, stuffing them into his briefcase.

As he returned to his seat, a man who had been waiting patiently in the aisle entered the lavatory. And even as Wouters settled to light a fresh cigarette, Festa's groping fingers established that the heroin was gone.

Finally, toward nine p.m., flight 709 touched down in Denver. Along with a knot of other passengers, Wouters disembarked. Now, before his connecting flight, he needed a night's sleep. At a discreet distance Festa tailed him through the echoing concourse. After Wouters had approached the United Airlines reservations counter, a covert inquiry established that Wouters was booked on flight 178, nonstop to New York, at four fifty p.m. next day.

Festa called customs headquarters in New York, then booked himself seat space on the same plane. He, too, could use a night's sleep.

THE ARREST OF Willie Wouters at Kennedy airport by special agents Edward Coyne and Mortimer Benjamin the following evening set off an explosive chain of events through the drug-trafficking world.

The actual procedure was undramatic. Wouters, seeming tired, almost resigned, from the first proved courteous and cooperative. On his own initiative he took Coyne to the Belmont-Plaza Hotel and requested the key for Mr. Victor's room. There he passed over to the agent forty-four thousand-dollar bills. He confessed freely that on the ten trips he had made, Jack Grosby had passed him eighty-five hundred dollars per kilo, but after expenses and middleman fees, he netted three thousand dollars a trip.

In the idiom of the narcotics traffickers, Wouters had agreed to "flip"—to tell everything. This readiness of many of those remotely connected with Ricord to flip when faced with long prison terms was ultimately to prove of vital help to Interpol.

Before midnight on this day, Villeda and Grosby were under arrest. The charge: a conspiracy to smuggle a quantity of heroin into the United States.

Grosby, from the first, maintained a philosophic front: any man who worked with the Ricord organization expected to be sprung from jail. What astonished him was the man offering to stand bail for him: the penny-pinching Stepenberg.

But Luis Stepenberg knew a choice investment when he saw one. At first he was appalled that Grosby's bail had been set at one hundred thousand dollars, but when Grosby's lawyer was successful in having it reduced to fifty thousand, Stepenberg set to work. It took him close to a month to obtain the money: checks payable to himself totaling thirty thousand dollars, plus ten thousand transferred from his account with a Swiss bank, and the final check for ten thousand from Louis Bonsignour's account in a Barcelona bank. By gathering Grosby's bail money and involving Ricord's nephew in the transaction, Stepenberg cleverly ensured that Ricord would learn of this act of generosity.

At the courtroom hearing, customs agent Coyne had protested vigorously against the reduction of the original bail; the previous pattern of Latin-American couriers made it plain that Grosby would abscond. Not surprisingly, Coyne was right. On September 5 Grosby pulled out for Brazil, following the example of Stepenberg's partner, José Colon, who had fled to Buenos Aires on July 29.

Now the third man from Buenos Aires stepped into the picture: Eduardo Poeta, who had arrived in New York only eighteen months previously. Nicknamed "El Rubio"—the blond one—Poeta was a florid, preoccupied man with the drooping, discontented mouth of a compulsive worrier, who until now had worked as manager of Stepenberg's store at 3555 Broadway. The customers were mostly Spanish speaking, which was fortunate; in a year and a half, Poeta had mastered scarcely a word of English.

Around the first week in September, he was later to recall, Stepenberg approached him in some trepidation and motioned him to the store's back room. "Eduardo, listen—will you do me a favor?"

Poeta was puzzled. It was rarely that Stepenberg could bring himself to ask anyone for a favor.

"Sure, Luis. What is it?"

"Your apartment . . . Could I move in with you for a day or two?"

The younger man's puzzlement grew. His modest apartment on West 137th Street hardly matched up to the solid middle-class comfort of the West End Avenue apartment where Stepenberg lived with his father. But he answered, "I guess so. What's the problem?"

"It's Jack Grosby. He's skipped bail, like José. And maybe—you know—people might be around asking some questions."

"Police?"

"Maybe police, maybe agents. I don't know." Quite suddenly he said, "Jack and José, they were both into junk. Did you know that?"

Poeta was startled. "No, I didn't." The truth dawned on him. "But you did. Is that what you're trying to tell me?"

Stepenberg smiled secretively. "Yes, Eduardo. That's what I'm trying to tell you. How about you? Would you like a piece of the action? You could take over José's place."

The thought of profits to come was enough to dispel Poeta's anxiety. He agreed without hesitation.

"Grosby will be all right," Stepenberg assured him. "He'll still be working with us." No one knew that better than Stepenberg; it was he who had procured from a shady travel agent a faked passport for Grosby and then spirited him to Rio de Janeiro.

"Now we'll be three from Buenos Aires," he rallied Poeta. "You can't lick us Porteños."

Though Stepenberg was unaware of it, the trail to his door was growing warmer. On September 6, one day after Grosby had jumped bail, a bugged conversation in the Federal House of Detention in Manhattan had reached Seeley and Coyne. One man in custody was lamenting that at the time of his arrest he had been carrying the telephone number of his contact man in the city. The agents were not slow to note that the man's address book bore the notation: "Export Motors, 545 West 136th Street, N.Y. Tel: AU 1-1667." Appended to this were three words: "Ask for Luis."

At about this time the Federal Bureau of Narcotics and another government agency were being merged into the Bureau of Narcotics and Dangerous Drugs (BNDD). In the lower Manhattan office of BNDD, the file on Luis Stepenberg continued to grow. On July 26 special agent Peter Scrocca was touring the upper West Side with a newly recruited informer who had worked with both Grosby and Bonsignour. Pointing to the façade of Export Motors, the informer told Scrocca proudly, "My heroin connection owns that joint."

Scrocca noted the statement in his report but was uncertain whether to believe it. The evidence against Stepenberg was no more than inferential. The worst that could be said of him was that he was none too particular in his choice of associates.

Even so, it might have been prudent to lie low, but Stepenberg was thirsting for action. Jack Grosby owed him for two favors now. First, the sponsorship into the United States; second, the bail. And who stood in better with Ricord and the other big-timers than Grosby? Stepenberg was ready to collect.

TOWARD MIDNIGHT ON November 27, five men were engaged in a noisy celebration at a nightclub in Geneva. With his high-domed forehead and rumpled hair, the host, fifty-nine-year-old Philippe Moulon, most closely resembled a university professor. The former director of a Swiss bank that had failed under suspicious circumstances, Moulon was known by the jet set as a man who lived it up in Geneva's nightclubs nine nights out of ten. His guests were Jack Grosby and Luis Stepenberg and two French traffickers.

It was a club much favored by Spanish expatriates and tired businessmen, and tonight fully a hundred of them were clustered around the dance hall on the upper story, where a floor show was in progress. As they watched, chorus girls in the broad-brimmed black hats and boleros of Argentine gauchos were prancing through a number.

In the throbbing half-light, Stepenberg knew a deep satisfaction; a small pulse working in his cheek showed how excited he was. He had prevailed on Grosby to effect this introduction, and now he had found Moulon far from dismayed that the towel-disposal method had been blown. He was, he boasted, on the point of perfecting something new. The front would be a legitimate business, with its own warehouse in Whitestone, Queens, not very far from New York City's airports.

Stepenberg was too wise to press for details. What mattered was that he had arranged to buy from Moulon, at seventy-five hundred dollars per kilo, heroin that he would sell at between twelve and thirteen thousand dollars. Soon he would be rich. He would have couriers of his own, his own stash houses.

"Hey, *garçon*, bring more champagne! No, no, I insist—this is on La Gorda, eh?"

With the passage of time, Number One was growing greedy and incautious. Number One was riding for a fall.

PART TWO

THE BITTER HARVEST

IN THE TERRACE restaurant of the Hotel Copacabana, Rio de Janeiro, Luis Stepenberg hailed a bootblack. It was late afternoon in the second week of December, 1968; there were few people about. Sugar Loaf Mountain was veiled in haze; the last sunbathers were furling their candy-striped umbrellas and drifting away from the white sand beach. Thick foam came creaming in their wake, powered by the booming gray Atlantic rollers.

"*Boa tarde*, Senhor Luis." Cosme Sandin, the bootblack, an undersize twenty-two-year-old, had known Stepenberg for four years now. Though the fat man used the hotel for socializing on his periodic visits, he was not in fact a guest; he rented his own apartment nearby. Cosme found him a good customer and a liberal tipper.

Smearing the polish with his index finger, Cosme bent to his task, buffing steadily with a soft cloth.

"You want to get rich?" Stepenberg asked him suddenly.

Cosme looked at him wonderingly. With Senhor Luis, you never knew whether he was kidding or not. But he answered, "Who doesn't, Senhor Luis? What do I have to do?"

Stepenberg grinned. Few things pleased him more than toying with the expectations of others.

"Oh, not much. Just come to New York and carry suitcases."

Cosme's eyes widened. "Suitcases? What do I have to do—be a bellhop?"

Stepenberg chuckled. "Bellhop, eh? That's good, *menino*. No, there's a little more to it than that."

Cosme didn't have to think too hard. A product of the slums, he earned all of thirty dollars a month. At twenty-two, he was too old to be called *"menino"*—little boy. He'd take that from Senhor Luis but from few others. Yet the irony was that he had never known a childhood. He had always been alone and fighting for himself.

It crossed his mind that Stepenberg wanted him as a live-in house-boy, but the fat man disillusioned him. If Cosme did take up the offer and come to New York, he would never even meet Stepenberg. Nor must he ever try to contact him. Another man, whom he'd meet in time, would give him his instructions and pay his daily expenses.

"Tell me more about the suitcases," Cosme temporized.

Stepenberg minced no words. "It's going to be dangerous, I'll tell you that."

Cosme grinned, a twisted grin. So what else was scratching for your living at thirty dollars a month if it wasn't dangerous?

But when the fat man had tipped him and shambled away, Cosme had cause to wonder. Had Stepenberg been serious? Was he really going to get rich? Within the week, though, Cosme had proof that Stepenberg was in earnest. Cosme was to leave in four days' time for New York. Stepenberg had arranged for his passport, along with a tourist visa renewable every six months for four years.

"We'll see you to the airport," Stepenberg promised, "but after that, remember—no more contact."

Cosme was almost too excited to speak. "Anything you say, Senhor Luis. I'll earn my money, you'll see."

"Just do what you're told, *menino*," Stepenberg said gruffly, "and you'll be all right."

On the night of December 20 the main hall of Rio's Galeao International Airport was colorful as always. The vast tiled lobby was a scene of tearful partings and tearful greetings; families exchanged hugs and embraces, weeping and laughing. On the observation floor above them, white handkerchiefs fluttered like moths in the tropical night, hailing newly arrived relatives.

It was all bewildering to Cosme. Puzzling, too, was the fact that the taxi which had picked him up contained not only Stepenberg but Jack Grosby, Eva Santos and another girl whose name he never knew. En route to the airport it had been like a family party, with everyone laughing and joking and telling him how he'd soon be rich.

"Take a look, *menino*," Stepenberg said as the five of them clustered in a little knot near the Varig baggage check-in. "See that guy over there by the newsstand? He'll be on your flight—but he won't contact you until you get to New York. From then on you'll be working for *him*."

Cosme stared. He saw a small, cocky pouter pigeon of a man leafing through a newspaper. He was in his mid-thirties, with bulging eyes and heavy sideburns.

"Just do what he tells you, *menino*," Stepenberg counseled. "He'll look after you good."

VARIG FLIGHT 854 DRONED through the night toward New York. In a seat in the economy section the man who was to look after Cosme, Jimmy Cohen, courted sleep in vain. The strangeness of all that had happened in the past week had left his brain in a whirl.

As recently as December 12, when he had signed off from his last voyage, Cohen had worked intermittently as a second chef on the SS *Independence*, cruising to the Mediterranean, Japan, even Russia. The fourth man from Buenos Aires to enter the Stepenberg ring, and the one who would inadvertently bring it toppling, he had known Stepenberg and Grosby when they had all worked in the same New Jersey restaurant. After that he had run into them occasionally at the Argentina Consulate General on West Fifty-sixth Street in Manhattan.

Cohen had heard that La Gorda was doing well, but just how well he had never realized until a few days back. Out of the blue a cable to his apartment on West Forty-fifth Street had summoned him to Rio for a meeting with Stepenberg. A business project that might interest him was in the offing.

In Stepenberg's roomy apartment overlooking Copacabana Beach, the fat man had lost no time in getting down to business.

"You want to make some money?" he asked Cohen appraisingly. "Fast money?"

A shrewd picker of hirelings, Stepenberg had gauged his man accurately, just as he had Poeta and José Colon. None of these three men was the kind to look beyond the profit motive to plumb the true horror and misery of addiction to Big H. Addicts were men and women beyond their understanding, faceless, shadowy figures whose habit was incomprehensible.

"Where is this junk?" was all Cohen asked when Stepenberg had outlined the proposition. "And where do I have to shift it?"

"In New York. All you have to do is move suitcases in New York from one house to another. That's all. Pick them up in one place, deliver them in another place."

Cohen's next questions accurately betrayed his total lack of scruples. "How many suitcases do I get to handle a month? And how many kilos to a suitcase?" Already he was concerned with nothing more than a calculation of his profits, profits which in the course of time were to escalate to a thousand, even two thousand dollars a kilo.

Stepenberg's answer to his first question was vague but on the second explicit. Each suitcase would contain fifteen to twenty kilos.

Cohen did some rapid arithmetic. So each suitcase might net him at least fifteen thousand dollars—the equivalent of almost two years' pay on the SS *Independence*. He, like Poeta, wanted in.

Just as he had cautioned Cosme Sandin, Stepenberg did not minimize the risks. "It's a dangerous business. Someday you may get arrested. But if you do, you have to be patient. Maybe you're in jail sixty days, ninety days, till the thing cools down. If that happens, you don't speak with anybody. There'll be a lawyer sent to you and he's going to take care of you." Then Stepenberg mentioned Cosme Sandin. "You can use this guy, too, to help you move the suitcases. That way there's less risk."

Cohen was wary. "So who's going to take care of *his* expenses?"

Stepenberg chuckled; he liked a man to watch the pennies. "I'll take care of that when I see you at Galeao."

Then had followed more bewildering instructions. When Cohen returned to New York he was to rent a house. Plainly Stepenberg had given this matter much thought, for he described the building he wanted as accurately as if reading from a blueprint. It had to be in Queens, New York's biggest borough, which took in not only Kennedy and La Guardia airports and nearly two hundred miles of waterfront but also unending rows of small and ugly houses. It must be a one-family house, with a yard and an attached garage.

"That," Stepenberg summed up, "is where you'll pick up the junk."

Cohen had scratched his head. "You want me to go live there?" he asked, then recoiled at the violence of the fat man's reaction.

"Definitely not! Get that right out of your head! That's where the Frenchmen stay when they bring in the heroin. Never, never go to that house until you've had instructions first."

"Okay, Luis," said Cohen pacifically. "Just trying to get things clear in my mind, right? So never go there until I get instructions from you."

"Maybe not from me," said Stepenberg mysteriously. "Tomorrow at the airport I'll give you an address. When you get to New York you go there and a man will be expecting you. Now, when you've rented that house, you give him a set of keys. And never go there until he tells you first."

Cohen had been bright enough to see that Stepenberg was protecting himself through a series of switches. In the true tradition of the Ricord mob, each man would have only a narrow circuit of contacts. Thus nobody could gain more than limited knowledge of the overall operation.

At Galeao airport on the night just past, Stepenberg had crossed the lobby to greet him at the newsstand. "Don't talk with him now," Stepenberg cautioned, "but that's your man."

Cohen's first impression of Cosme Sandin had been unfavorable. He's just a kid, he thought, taking in the young man's stray-dog air as he clutched his cheap fiber suitcase.

By way of farewell Stepenberg pressed on Cohen two flat white envelopes, neither of which bore an address. One, unsealed, contained two thousand dollars; this was for his and Sandin's expenses when they reached New York. The other, firmly sealed, was to be delivered to the Tabaquiria Ricardo, where Poeta—El Rubio—would be expecting him.

All through the flight Cosme was in a daze. Never in his life had he boarded a plane; a kindly stewardess even had to help him fasten his seat belt. Jimmy Cohen, sitting four rows ahead of him, hadn't spared him a glance.

At dawn on December 21, when the passengers deplaned at Kennedy, Cosme stepped shivering into the alien world of a New York winter. Only when he had passed uneventfully through the customs area did the little ship's cook appear beside him. "I'm Jimmy," Cohen said. "We'll share a taxi."

Like any new recruit eager to make good, Cosme was avid for instructions. But, once in the cab, Cohen had few instructions to give him. He explained that Cosme was to stay at a YMCA hotel in midtown Manhattan. This, Cosme learned by degrees, was where young men looking for cheap but respectable lodgings set down tentative roots on their first trip to New York.

"Just wait now," was all Cohen would tell him. "You're going to come and work for us. Just wait."

After the squalor of home, the fifteen-story red brick hotel seemed to Cosme like a chilly but palatial mansion. As Cohen bustled him toward the reception-information desk, his eyes took in the clean white tile floor, the store that sold candy and newspapers, the elevators supervised by a uniformed guard whose desk bore a sign: NO ONE BEYOND THE FIRST FLOOR WITHOUT A KEY. At the desk, Cohen busily took charge of everything, signing Cosme in for one week. As an afterthought, having paid the young man's lodging, he slipped him four five-dollar bills.

"Now that's got to last a bit," he warned him. "But I'll call you tomorrow. In fact, I'll call you every day. And next week, after Christmas, I'll be down again to pay the bill."

For the time being, Cosme was content. As the days passed he explored the wonders of the neighborhood: Macy's department store, the Empire State Building and, along Park Avenue, the Christmas trees decked out with glittering white bulbs. In the evenings there was always color television in the Y's second-floor lounge.

Though Cosme sensed this new life might soon begin to pall, he told himself, with the optimism of a youngster who had nothing to lose, Soon I'll get rich carrying suitcases for Senhor Luis.

Meanwhile, on December 22 Cohen had journeyed uptown to

the Tabaquiria Ricardo and handed the sealed envelope to Poeta.

"Luis called me to say you'd be stopping by," Poeta acknowledged. "You know what you have to do?"

Cohen knew. After the new year arrived, he took time out from the small stereo business that he had run as a sideline in his apartment for three years now. He began to haunt the offices of real estate agents.

Little by little the Stepenberg empire was taking shape.

EARLY IN FEBRUARY, 1969, Cohen had a stroke of luck. An agent sent him to look over a house at 68-19 Dartmouth Street, Forest Hills, Queens, near the West Side Tennis Club. Cohen took his time surveying it, both inside and out, and it seemed to fit all Stepenberg's specifications. It was in a residential neighborhood, the ground floor faced with red brick, the top two stories with white, peeling stucco. It ran the whole width of the front yard, with an entrance to the far left. Though the front lawn was no more than a bed of shrubbery twenty-one feet wide by twelve feet deep, bordering on the street, wide modern windows across the front of the lower two levels of the house would give any resident courier a vantage viewpoint of both street and sidewalk.

In this area not all the houses had attached garages, but 68-19 did, and it opened on an alley at the back. That clinched it, Cohen thought. A wooden extension jutted out almost fifteen feet from the second floor, over the garage. The owner was an engineer away on assignment in Rio, so the house was for rent furnished, with linen and cutlery provided.

Cohen used most of the money that Stepenberg had given him for two months' rent and a thousand-dollar refundable security deposit on the furniture. Although he rented the house in his own name, caution led him to get the telephone hooked up for another name altogether: Julio Silverberg, a waiter he had known in New York. The transaction was completed on February 9, and Cohen took a duplicate set of keys to Poeta. But as the days wore on, no word came from Stepenberg, and Cohen grew restive. It was two months since he had signed off from the *Independence,* and what with living expenses and keeping Cosme Sandin in pocket money, his funds were growing short.

Unknown to the Stepenberg ring, the U.S. Customs Service, with vital help from Interpol, was one jump ahead of them.

Even before Stepenberg and Grosby had met Moulon in Geneva in November 1968, a European informer had alerted Seeley and Coyne that Moulon had a new venture in hand. The former banker, he warned, had invested in an expensive canning machine. At the same time Moulon and his associates set up an export firm in the Mediterranean port of Málaga, on the coast of southern Spain.

From this base they had made contact with a food manufacturer eight hundred miles northwest in the Atlantic port of Vigo, whose specialty was shipping canned Spanish paella and Basque codfish stew to an importer in New York. The man saw no reason to doubt their story: to launch a large-scale promotion of his products in New York's supermarkets, they needed samples, plus labels and empty cans.

The operation was now relatively simple. Codfish stew came in cans four inches across and three inches deep, and these were packed twenty-four to a cardboard case. Spanish paella came in larger cans, holding five hundred and fifty grams of food, six inches across and two inches deep; a case held no more than twelve of these cans.

The empty cans were filled with heroin. Then, once Moulon's machine had sealed them, some of the labels were marked with yellow paint, some with green, others with red and black. In this way the receiver in New York could identify the quantity of heroin and the specific customer as well as the specific price.

But who was Moulon's receiver? Combing the customs files in New York, Seeley and Coyne found that a new importer—the Panamanian Chemical and Food Products Company—had recently begun importing Spanish foodstuffs. The importers, two French nationals, Christian Serge Hysohion and Charles Darge, had rented premises in Whitestone, Queens. Their first two shipments, made direct from Vigo, had contained no heroin; they were sent solely to establish the New York customs routine. The third, a shipment of olive oil in cans, did contain ten kilos of heroin, though Seeley didn't learn this until later.

As yet there was nothing to tie Stepenberg in with this ingenious operation; the actual customers were not known. Yet all later evidence pointed to his involvement. In December, Poeta was subsequently to reveal, he was given both the address of the company and instructions to pick up a quantity of heroin. Thus, around December 18, Poeta had gone to the Whitestone warehouse and received ten kilos of heroin from an unknown Frenchman. He paid seventy-five hundred dollars and sold it for thirteen thousand five hundred.

And more was on the way, as Seeley was later to learn. On December 10 the Swedish freighter SS *Ragunda* had sailed from Málaga. Stowed in her holds were more than seven hundred cases of Basque codfish stew.

On December 20 the stevedores went out on strike; involved were twenty-two thousand dockworkers, with a logjam of more than two hundred ships. The port of New York was at a standstill and would be so for eight weeks. In January 1969 negotiations between the maritime authorities and the International Longshoremen's Association broke down.

Seeley and Coyne seized their chance. Armed with a portable X-ray machine, they boarded the *Ragunda* in mid-harbor from a customs launch. It was to be a time-consuming search, but the dock strike had bought them time. Out of almost seventeen thousand cans of fish, which, if any, contained heroin? The odds were weighted heavily against them, for out of seven hundred and two cases no more than six had been utilized to conceal twenty-eight kilos of heroin.

Taking their time, Seeley and Coyne fell to examining the cardboard cases. Even in the cramped, dimly lighted holds, one fact became apparent.

"You see what I see?" Coyne asked suddenly. "Somebody's been busy with a screwdriver."

It was true. At intervals, the sides of a cardboard case were marked with a series of punctures and indentations.

"They've been smart," Seeley allowed, "but not quite smart enough. Notice the stencils?"

The consignee firm had been registered as a trade abbreviation: Panamanian Chemical and Food Products Company was reduced to PCH FD Products for labeling purposes, and on the six cases that bore the marks of the screwdriver, the loop of the initial P had been blacked out. Thus the importer, Hysohion, could readily single out the cases he sought by looking for the partly obliterated P.

"Let's get that machine into action," Seeley said.

One by one the cans were unloaded from the suspect cases and passed before the X-ray machine. Dark outlines resembling two fingers now became apparent. Seeley called for a can opener, and as the lid peeled back, fluffy white powder came spurting out.

The mystery of the dark shadows was now explained. To make up the difference in the weight of the cans containing the heroin, Moulon's experts had inserted two small lead weights.

The cases of fish stew were ultimately unloaded on the dockside early in March. One case, containing seven kilos, had been deliberately kept aside to cause a discrepancy; once Hysohion discovered the contents did not tally, he would be certain to contact Moulon in Geneva. But on the night of Friday, March 7, the rest of the shipment left the pier, to be dogged all the way to Whitestone by undercover agents.

In the sixteen days since the *Ragunda* had arrived, U.S. customs had been busy. The Whitestone warehouse was now the focus of attention for the agents. Twice Seeley and Coyne had flown to Washington to seek authorization from Department of Justice officials for a wiretap.

The authorization was granted none too soon. On March 8 Hysohion was repeatedly in touch with Geneva, querying the discrepancy, and note was taken of the numbers he called, for urgent circulation by Interpol. From a discreet distance, the Whitestone warehouse became subject to twenty-four-hour surveillance. This did not go unremarked by local residents. Twice on that day suspicious callers phoned the neighborhood precinct to query the number of unfamiliar cars parked in the surrounding streets. The agents were causing more unease locally than the traffickers.

On this day, too, a Moulon courier arrived from Geneva. His role was to carry back to Europe the money from the sale of the drug. Plainly suspecting a stakeout, the courier set out on a walking tour of the neighborhood, scanning every parked truck and automobile. Several times agents had to dive headlong for the floor, pulling coats over their heads.

Early the following morning, customs agents moved in. Hysohion, who had spent a busy weekend opening cans of fish stew, was spotted leaving the warehouse along with the courier. At this time of day the quiet tree-lined street seemed devoid of life. Both men were walking fast, heads down against the wind, in search of a taxi. Abruptly the dark sidewalks came alive with knots of running men.

A familiar cry halted the two traffickers. "Hold it! Police!"

They found Hysohion was equipped with a large leather satchel stuffed with twenty-one kilos of heroin. The men's destination was said to be Grand Central Station, where they planned to hide the satchel in a public locker.

The arrests were destined to have worldwide repercussions. At Interpol headquarters, red corner tabs, signifying "immediate arrest," were placed on the dossiers of no fewer than fifteen men— Philippe Moulon and fourteen other foreign nationals—whose names were sent to Interpol NCBs in Bern, Madrid, Paris and Rome. One day later, a second freighter, the SS *Grundsunda*, was searched as she unloaded, and twenty-eight kilos of heroin were recovered intact from four hundred cases of paella.

Six of the men would ultimately be convicted. Moulon, due to failing health, received only six years and six months. Hysohion and the courier were each sentenced to thirty years and were sent to the U.S. Penitentiary in Atlanta, Georgia.

One loophole out of many had been plugged. But as yet the men at the hub of the traffic remained obstinately free.

DID THE ARREST of Moulon and so many of his recently acquired associates trouble Luis Stepenberg? On March 12, shortly after the crackdown, Jimmy Cohen would have sworn that the fat man hadn't a care in the world.

One day earlier, a call to his apartment had set Cohen hastily packing an overnight bag. It had been Stepenberg, speaking long-distance from Buenos Aires, and he sounded incisive. "Get on down here. I want to give you some instructions."

Cohen needed no second bidding. He had already paid the March installment of rent for the house on Dartmouth Street, and the money Stepenberg had given him was almost exhausted. Catching the first plane to Buenos Aires, he went straight from the airport to a fashionable hotel near the Plaza San Martin.

As he entered Stepenberg's suite, Cohen was relieved to find Jack Grosby present, his long legs coiled over an armchair. Somehow the atmosphere was always more relaxed when Grosby was around.

"All right," said Stepenberg briskly. "We've got a brand-new method of transportation, and pretty soon you're going to find yourself a customer."

Cohen was relieved. This was it, then, the key briefing he had long awaited. "How am I going to do that, Luis?"

"You aren't," Grosby said with evident relish. "We've already found him for you."

"Okay, so where do I meet him? Here?"

"Uh-uh. Back in New York City. His name is Felix Martinez. And he's interested in buying large quantities. We've checked him out and he's a good man. You can do business with him."

Stepenberg took over the briefing. "Now you may go looking for other customers, but never sell any horse to anybody before you check with me or Eduardo. Make sure, too, they want to buy in big quantities—twenty to thirty kilos a month. And sell at thirteen thousand five hundred dollars a kilo—no credit!"

On much of the higher-level organization Cohen was kept completely in the dark. He was unaware that Grosby had become the lieutenant of Christian David or that Stepenberg saw his source of supply as triply assured, since he was about to do business not only with David but also with André Condemine and François Rossi.

But on certain points Stepenberg was more specific. Cohen was curious as to where the heroin was coming from, and Stepenberg told him: primarily from Marseille.

"How?" Cohen ventured to ask.

"Mostly by car. Say someone rents or maybe buys a car. He has it shipped to Canada. The horse is somewhere inside that car. So then Eduardo goes over the border and drives the car back."

"Suppose he has a run-in with the law?"

Stepenberg and Grosby exchanged glances. Then Grosby said, "You're going to have to learn a new language, Jimmy. In the first place, when you talk on the phone, from now on you speak Spanish."

"Well, that's no problem."

"There's more to it than that. We've worked out a kind of a code to make it harder for the police if they're using a wiretap. Here's an example. If you ring Eduardo and you have problems, you say, 'The family is sick.'"

"The family is sick?"

"That's right. On account of the police is like a sickness. But if it's all okay, 'The family is well.' "

Cohen was concentrating hard. He did not know it yet, but he was learning a lesson that would one day be of vital import to the forces arrayed against Stepenberg.

Grosby continued with his crash course. "Incidentally, you don't use a telephone. It's a 'tube' or a 'pipe,' got it? And you never talk about horse or junk, or anything like that. A kilo of heroin is a 'suit'—so if you tell a customer his suit is ready or his suit has come from the tailor's, they know to come and pick the stuff up."

It was no easy lesson for Cohen to master. Over the months Stepenberg and Grosby seemed to have evolved bizarre figures of speech to cover any and every eventuality. A "cane" was a police officer tailing you. A "doctor" was a lawyer you should call in case "the family got sick." "Con Edison" meant not Consolidated Edison, the power company for the New York area, but ten kilos of heroin. There was even a complex system of word inversion, dating back to their boyhood in Buenos Aires. In this way, Grosby, whose nickname was "El Lungo"—the tall one—became "El Golun," and the Spanish for house, *casa*, became instead *"saca."*

Finally Stepenberg returned to the question of cash payments. "Tell Martinez you want to be paid in fifty- or hundred-dollar bills. That way the money travels to Switzerland easy. If you have big bills, you can get up to four hundred thousand dollars in an attaché case. Just imagine trying to carry that in *small* bills!"

"If he pays me in small bills, what do I do?"

"Then go to a bank. Have them make change. But don't use the same bank too often. Be smart."

To Cohen, who had learned a whole new glossary in one afternoon, there seemed to be only one final question. "How do I get to meet this Martinez?"

Grosby grinned. "That's easy. All you have to do when you get back to New York is to go to the movies."

IN THE DARKNESS of the Coliseum movie theater on upper Broadway, Jimmy Cohen fidgeted uneasily. It was close to nine p.m. on Friday, April 25, more than six weeks since his meeting with Stepenberg and Grosby, and this was the third time that he had occupied a shabby tip-up seat in this old, baroquely ornate movie palace. Each time he had sat here for two hours at a stretch—from seven to nine p.m., as Grosby had specified—awaiting an approach from Felix Martinez.

Lee Marvin in *Hell in the Pacific* had been succeeded by Rod Steiger in *The Sergeant,* and now he was sitting fretfully through a movie called *The Big Bounce.* As instructed, he sat in the very front row, a carton of Pall Mall cigarettes perched on his knees as an identification symbol.

Although the luminous dial of his watch showed nine, nobody had come. In a mood of black frustration, Cohen quit the theater.

Riding the subway downtown to Times Square, he felt angry and cheated. The wealth that Stepenberg had promised him seemed as elusive as ever. It was almost as if the fat man and Grosby were playing some malicious game of cat and mouse with him, for he had obeyed all their instructions to the letter. Go at the appointed hour on April 15, 20 and 25, he had been told, and keep going every five days until Martinez shows. Now he must wait five more days, and he was finding the suspense unbearable. This was perhaps what Stepenberg had anticipated, knowing that the longer Cohen was kept waiting, the more eager he would be to start.

On the evening of April 30 Cohen was once more paying his entrance fee at the Coliseum ticket office. Above his head a sign one story high proclaimed: A BULLET FOR THE GENERAL. Blurbs read, "Looting, Killing, Loving—Everything in Sight!" Shouldering through dusty velvet curtains, Cohen sat numbly in the front row clutching his cigarette carton, expecting nothing more than fresh disappointment.

Suddenly a man who seemed to come from nowhere eased himself gently into the seat beside him.

His voice was a whisper in the darkness. "I am Felix. Do you have a Pall Mall cigarette?"

Relief flooded through Cohen like a shot of neat liquor. "Man," he said, "I thought you'd never show. You hungry? Come on, let's go eat."

Cohen picked a place he often frequented when in funds: the Press Box Restaurant, a steak house on East Forty-fifth Street. They made their way past a long mahogany bar dimly lighted from behind dark red glass, settled in a booth with red leather seats and ordered cocktails.

Over steaks Martinez revealed himself as the complete professional, easy and relaxed. Cohen learned that he lived in Elmhurst, Queens, and that for him this whole business was just a sideline—"kinda like moonlighting." By day he worked in a business owned by his brother.

Martinez glanced at Cohen appraisingly.

"You ever handled suits before?"

Then, when Cohen shook his head: "Well, you gotta know what you're handling. That way nobody is going to two-time you."

Martinez didn't add that he knew so well what he was handling that in 1965 he had copped five years, later reduced to three, for narcotics trafficking. Nor did he reveal that his own specialty was smuggling in cocaine concealed in crates of bananas.

But plainly he took an expert's pride in knowing every trick of the trade. He never peddled heroin, he explained, in what Cohen took to be a friendly warning, without first testing it. First he smelled it; you could develop a perfumer's nose for the purity of heroin. "And by the smell I know how good it can be, it's good or it's no good." If Martinez was suspicious that it had been cut before reaching him, he took a little in a teaspoon, added a few drops of water and heated it gently over a naked flame. If the purity was high, then so too was the melting point; if it had been cut, the melting point was low. It was as simple as that.

The meal concluded, Cohen trudged back to his apartment well satisfied. To date the slowness of the operation had irked him, and on top of that there was the daily chore of phoning Cosme Sandin at the YMCA and keeping him sweet. No doubt about it, the kid was becoming a pain, with his always asking, "When do I get to carry the suitcases?"

But Cohen's contentment was short-lived. May dragged by and there was no word from Stepenberg. Thus, with no merchandise to offer, Cohen was in no position to make further contacts with Martinez. Why, he wondered angrily, was Stepenberg waiting?

All later evidence suggested that the shake-up following the arrests of Moulon, Hysohion and the others had temporarily held up supplies. Not until Thursday, June 5, did the phone in Cohen's apartment ring abruptly. It was Poeta.

Speaking distinctly, he said, "You have to go to the *saca*. In the front room on the first floor there is a piano. Next to the piano, on the right, you'll find a shopping bag. There is a suit in it. That's your start in the business."

Cohen replied, *"Muchas gracias, compadre,"* then hung up.

A seven-minute walk took him down Eighth Avenue to the subway at Forty-second Street. From there he boarded a train to Forest Hills. Emerging onto Queens Boulevard, he hesitated. It was a hot day; for a moment he was tempted to take a cab. But Poeta had warned him against taxis; drivers could remember faces. To take a bus meant a half-hour wait. He would walk it.

It was a route he came to know well: down Seventy-first Avenue, then under the Long Island Rail Road bridge, turning right onto the long, winding stretch of Burns Street. On Burns he passed the big bubble designed for indoor tennis, then the outdoor courts of the West Side Tennis Club. At Dartmouth Street he turned right; on the right-hand side, three fourths of the way down a long block, stood the stash house.

Understandably Cohen was nervous. It was the first time Poeta had allowed him near the house since he had signed the lease; he had the sense of being an intruder. The front door seemed to creak very loudly as he opened it; the hallway felt airless and unlived in. Yet somewhere, surely, there was a faint whiff of coarse French tobacco? The Frenchmen of whom Stepenberg had spoken had been here, and not very long ago.

Irrationally Cohen felt his spine crawling. His heart was racing with the excitement and the exertion of the walk. Tentatively he called, "Hello," but there was no response.

On tiptoe he entered the first-floor front room. Sure enough, there was a piano, untouched for months past and filmed with dust. Propped against a chair on the right was the shopping bag, containing two small glassine bags. That was a suit, or a kilo of heroin: the first thousand-dollar profit for Jimmy Cohen.

Breathing hard, he stuffed the glassine bags into his trousers pocket. As he left, the front door seemed to echo behind him and he quickened his step, glad to be gone. From the courts of the tennis club, the reverberating thump of balls against racket strings followed him as he headed back toward the subway station.

The beauty of the system—from Stepenberg's viewpoint—as yet escaped Cohen. In this eerie rendezvous in the silent house, only Jimmy Cohen, the buyer, could have been apprehended if narcotics agents had been waiting to make a pinch. There was nothing to connect Stepenberg with a rented house on Dartmouth Street.

By early evening Cohen was back in his own apartment; he at once called Martinez. "The suit is here. So long," was all he said.

Martinez arrived within the hour. He brought with him a girl he did not introduce, who took the heroin and stuffed it into her purse. As Martinez paid him thirteen thousand five hundred dollars, Cohen, anxious to cement further deals, launched into a sales talk.

"This is the best quality junk ever in the market. We've started with a small quantity, but later we'll have more. . . ."

Martinez nodded abstractedly; five minutes later he and the girl departed.

Cohen listened intently to the sound of their footsteps dying away down the stairs; in that apartment house the sound of a lavatory flushing could be heard clearly from the first to the sixteenth floor. Then he reached for the phone again, to call the cigar store at 3379 Broadway. In a moment Poeta answered. "Tabaquiria Ricardo."

"Everything is all right," Cohen told him, recalling the code that Grosby had taught him. "The family is very well. If you're coming to visit me, I have something for you."

"Very good," Poeta replied. "I am coming to see you."

The call established a pattern that scarcely varied one iota over the months that followed. At nine p.m. a curt knock announced Poeta's arrival. Cohen, anxious for further commissions, was careful to stress: "That Felix Martinez, he's a very happy fella. He's interested in buying more—if I get more."

Poeta nodded noncommittally as Cohen counted out twelve thousand five hundred dollars in hundreds and fifties, retaining a thousand for himself.

"Stick around," Poeta said. "You'll be hearing from us."

In the days following, Cohen was not alone in his elation. The Argentine connection was establishing fresh routes and sources of supply, and Stepenberg was in great good humor. To Jimmy Cohen's surprise, he found himself invited to lunch at the Press Box. With Stepenberg at the table were Grosby's girl friend, Eva Santos, and a Brazilian girl called Laura. It was a social occasion, with no business discussed, and Stepenberg dominated the proceedings. He took pride in his gargantuan appetite. "Number One must have a porterhouse, *verdad?* And a double order of French fries!" He aired his superior knowledge of the famous correspondents who had frequented the bar in its heyday, whose portraits lined the walls.

After they left the restaurant, they strolled over to Fifth Avenue and headed downtown. Stepenberg asked the girls to walk ahead.

"And Eva, don't go buying up Altman's. You spend all his money, that Jack will hold *me* responsible."

To Cohen he said quietly, "How was your first sale with Felix Martinez?"

Cohen was jubilant. "Okay. More than okay."

"*Muy bien.*" Stepenberg nodded approvingly. "Do you have any other customers in mind?"

As yet Cohen hadn't, but the impression that Poeta was restricting the quantity he handled was never far from his mind.

"Luis, Felix Martinez looks to me a very good customer. He's interested in buying large quantities. He pays cash. He wants more, but Eduardo don't give me more. He only gives me one kilo."

Stepenberg was judicious. "Well, maybe next month you'll get more. You know how this business is. It's better not to have too much business but to be one hundred percent sure."

His face darkened. All his life there had been struggle, and so much more lay ahead. This was the year—though Cohen did not suspect it—when Stepenberg was reporting a gross income of less than six thousand dollars and depositing more than a million in three bank accounts. Most men would have felt secure in this knowledge, but not Stepenberg; things could so easily go awry.

Almost as if he had a premonition, he warned Cohen, "Remember, never talk to anybody about this business. If something happens to you, never mention my name—definitely never mention my name. You don't know anybody."

Then, seeing Cohen grow dejected, he boasted, as much to reassure himself as the other man, "And don't worry—in a couple of months I'll be *the* big distributor of heroin."

Cohen reminded him gently, "Well, I went to work over six months ago, but all I've sold is one kilo."

Stepenberg's expression grew suddenly beatific. The doubts had vanished as swiftly as they had descended. Ahead he saw only more power, more profit: Number One on the pinnacle of a white and glittering mountain of heroin.

"Don't worry," he told Cohen again. "Little by little you are going to have more and more and more."

IN THE LAST ten days of June, 1969, the death toll from drugs soared astonishingly. On an average weekend in New York five heroin fatalities might be recorded, but during the weekend of June 28–29 twenty-eight persons died, an increase of almost five hundred percent. They were found on rooftops and in basements throughout the slums of the city, sprawled on fire escapes and in blind alleys, in hallways and in abandoned buildings, collapsed with their legs twisted beneath them. Some still had the needles protruding from their arms. The victims ranged in age from fifteen to thirty-five, and all had two features in common: the dark sick-looking skin that circled their eyes and the tangled stretch of brownish-red puncture marks, blurred together until they resembled a healed burn, that marked their forearms.

Were uncommonly pure and therefore more potent bags being peddled by an addict pusher anxious to enlarge his clientele by offering quality merchandise? As June ended, the chief medical examiner of New York City had to confess he did not know.

TO THE NARCOTICS agents, the evidence against Stepenberg was still tenuous at best. There were the scribbled notes found on two of the couriers who had been arrested in Madrid, the bugged conversation between the prisoners in the Federal House of Detention, and the fact that Stepenberg had stood bail for Grosby and another Ricord agent. Yet Stepenberg—if it was Stepenberg—was masterminding as much as forty kilos a month. The problem was to prove it.

In August, one attempt to incriminate him came to nothing. Eugene Kremen, a Puerto Rican headwaiter and convicted narcotics trafficker, now an *agent provocateur*, had known Stepenberg for eight years. Prompted by BNDD officers, Kremen later testified, he

called at the small wooden shack on the fat man's used-car lot on upper Broadway. With the air of a man requesting a trifling favor, Kremen asked to buy two kilos of heroin.

"I need to make some money, Luis," he apologized.

Stepenberg shook all over with silent laughter. "Look," he said, "I'm Number One—the number one heroin dealer in New York. I don't deal in one or two, and I don't deal with you in any case. You're very hot."

The crestfallen Kremen had to report back to the BNDD, "He don't want to make no deal."

It took more than an amateurish attempt such as this to rattle Stepenberg's nerves.

Poeta, by contrast, was a man who started at shadows. That summer the volume of traffic was so constant he hired an assistant, Emilio Cordero, whose front was as a clerk at the cigar store at 3555 Broadway. Soon after this, Stepenberg gave Poeta a parking-garage receipt and instructed him to pick up a car and take it to Cordero's apartment nearby. From four suitcases lodged in the trunk, the two took a hundred kilos of heroin, but Poeta adjudged the purity of thirty-three kilos to be substandard. So the panicky Poeta washed this entire quantity down Cordero's kitchen sink.

This contravened Ricord's cardinal rule: if an importer was dissatisfied with a shipment, he must hold on to it until one of Ricord's agents flew in to confirm that it was faulty. Poeta's hasty act came close to severing Stepenberg's prized Argentine connection.

Poeta's wary demeanor did not escape the bulging eyes of Jimmy Cohen. Anxious to ensure that liaison continued smoothly, Cohen arranged a meeting between Poeta and Felix Martinez in a restaurant near the George Washington Bridge.

"If anything should happen to me," Cohen told Martinez, "this is the man you get in touch with."

But Poeta only sat there, unwilling to utter one word for fear he would incriminate himself. He was jumpy, too, about the house on Dartmouth Street, convinced that the BNDD had it staked out. Since his first trip in June, Cohen had made two more journeys there— once in July to retrieve two kilos of heroin from behind a kitchen blender, and once in August to find two more kilos wrapped in foil in a bedroom drawer. But when Cohen sought permission to drop by and forward the absent owner's mail, Poeta was morbidly reluctant to grant it.

Cohen protested. "Eduardo, a lot of mail is piling up for the guy. We don't want him asking any questions."

Poeta vacillated. "Well, you can't go today. Go tomorrow morning. But call me at the store beforehand, around ten."

Cohen guessed accurately the reason for Poeta's trepidation: if he should run into those mysterious French couriers, he might at a later stage be able to identify them. He knew they were still using the house at regular intervals; on his last trip he had seen copies of *Paris Match* and *Sélection du Reader's Digest* stacked on the bedside table.

BUT AS THE narcotics agents were ultimately to realize, the final downfall of the Stepenberg empire would be caused by disaffection from within.

The most bewildered of all the fat man's acolytes was Cosme Sandin. On August 12, almost eight months after he entered the United States, the bootblack was excited to receive a call from Stepenberg himself.

"You got to go to Europe, *menino*," Stepenberg announced, "and bring a suitcase back to America."

Just as instructed, Cosme loitered outside the Argentina Consulate General. His rendezvous was not with Stepenberg but with another Argentinian, Carlos Rojas, the controller for Stepenberg's European sources. Cosme's instructions were to buy a ticket from New York to Lisbon, then to Paris and back to New York, from TAP, the Portuguese airline. In Lisbon he must check in at a hotel and inform Rojas of his whereabouts. Before they parted, Rojas handed Cosme his passage money and a thousand dollars for expenses.

Cosme did precisely what he was told. On August 14 he checked in at a small pension in the center of Lisbon and sent Rojas an airmail letter. But six weeks passed without acknowledgment and now Cosme was worried. Had his letter gone astray? When Rojas finally surfaced, around September 25, he offered no explanation for the long delay.

"You'll get the suitcase in Paris, kid," was all he said. "Fix yourself a reservation for tomorrow."

So Cosme moved on to Paris, this time to a quiet Left Bank hotel, and duly awaited events. Three days passed before Rojas once again showed up. "There's nothing for you to take." He shrugged. "You got to get back to New York."

On September 30, when Cosme cleared customs at Kennedy International, he was still carrying nobody's suitcase but his own.

The likely explanation is that Stepenberg had slipped up. Always eager to surround himself with yes-men, totally dependent on him for patronage, he overlooked the fact that his European sources might have decided views on whom they would trust as couriers. Whoever surveyed Cosme, unbeknown to him, during his time in Europe, saw at a glance that the bootblack was a pushover for a customs checkup: his appearance, which was both bewildered and furtive, would be certain to arouse suspicion.

Thus that autumn was a season rife with discontent. Felix Martinez was complaining bitterly that Cohen had cut his last delivery of heroin, a charge that Cohen stoutly denied. Much against his will, Poeta was forced to agree to a rendezvous with Martinez at the Dartmouth Street house and to submit apologies. He explained shamefacedly that the heroin was part of a consignment already on offer and that the addict pusher had got caught.

"If you could do us a favor and get rid of it just this once," Poeta told Martinez, "we'd really be obligated."

Cohen, too, was growing restless. Like most wholesalers, he was becoming increasingly avid for a bigger share of the profits.

In vain Poeta reassured him. "I think very soon you'll get a large amount of junk."

But the quantities didn't increase, and Cohen's dissatisfaction grew. In mid-October he made direct contact with Stepenberg at a hole-in-the-wall radio shop on the Avenue of the Americas. They talked against a background of soundlessly flickering TV sets, and Stepenberg gave him scant satisfaction.

"Next month is election time," he reminded Cohen. "There'll be a lot of policemen around, so the tailors have gone on vacation. No suits."

Now for the first time Cohen broached the name of a likely customer: Frank Hughes, a Puerto Rican cook whom he had known on the SS *Independence*. Stepenberg was cautious.

"You know him very well? How well do you know him?"

"How can you know a person better than on a ship? You work together, sleep together. . . ."

"Okay," said Stepenberg reluctantly. "We'll see."

Meanwhile, Cohen took time out to solve another problem: settling Cosme Sandin in a job. Since his return from Paris the young man had been more importunate than ever, and Cohen, on his own initiative, fixed him up as a kitchen hand for sixty dollars a week at a New Jersey restaurant. By now Cosme had found himself a live-in girl friend and quit the YMCA for a seedy walk-up apartment on West Forty-sixth Street. With unwarranted optimism, Cohen hoped he'd heard the last of him.

But Cohen himself was still discontented, and this was to prove his undoing. To be sure, in December he made two trips to Dartmouth Street and, unknown to either Stepenberg or Poeta, had raised Felix Martinez' price by five hundred dollars per kilo, pocketing the difference. Sometime in that month also he met up with the cook Frank Hughes at the National Maritime Union building in Manhattan, a white tile edifice pierced with portholes. Part social club and part hiring hall for working seamen, it was a rendezvous where they could talk undisturbed.

He asked Hughes the question that had marred the lives of thousands of addicts. "You want to make some fast money?"

"I'm interested," said Hughes evenly.

Hughes was tough; at fifty-six he had already spent time in prison after three jail convictions—two for narcotics, one for robbery—and he wasn't afraid to face a fourth if the price was right.

Cohen's problem now was how to pry more heroin out of Poeta.

Quite suddenly, on a raw December morning, it seemed this problem was solved. The phone rang in Cohen's apartment and he recognized the voice of Jack Grosby, speaking from Geneva.

"I've been hearing a lot about you from La Gorda and El Rubio," Grosby said affably. "They're very happy about the way you're handling the business. Now, do you think you can handle a big load? Can you handle thirty suits?"

Cohen was beside himself. *Thirty kilos of heroin* . . . At last the promised wealth no longer seemed illusory. Without hesitation he answered, "I've got people who want to buy."

He was certain that Martinez would continue to pay the increased price and that Hughes would take up any surplus quantity.

"You want it all together?" Grosby queried. "Or ten suits at a time?"

Caution at least prompted Cohen to settle for spaced-out deliveries of ten kilos. He asked, "How's it coming in?"

"With the horses," said Grosby obscurely before he hung up.

Cohen was not then aware that for some time heroin had been secreted in the sides and floors of portable stalls used to import race-horses from Latin America. He knew only that thirty kilos was the nicest Christmas present he had ever had.

But Jimmy Cohen had now bitten off more than he could chew.

DESPITE THE WEALTH he was amassing—and rumor now had it that he had acquired a five-hundred-acre cattle ranch in Argentina—the year ended badly for Stepenberg. Early in December he had been summoned to Rio de Janeiro for a stormy meeting with Ricord's muscular group chief, François Rossi. In a scene that he would long remember, Stepenberg was forced to apologize abjectly for the spoiled heroin that Poeta had washed down the kitchen sink. For this shipment Stepenberg had made no payment, and Rossi was cold and implacable.

"Men have been killed for less," he told Stepenberg. "You try that again and don't think we won't cut you up for bait."

From now on Number One would be forced to pay between one thousand and two thousand dollars more per kilo on all future shipments, to allow Rossi to recoup part of his loss.

That was around December 6, the day that customs agents at Kennedy International found more than six kilos of pure heroin in two false-bottomed half-gallon Argentine wine jugs. The first direct link with Latin America had been established.

THE U.S. COMMISSIONER of customs, Myles J. Ambrose, was a determined man at the outset of 1970. In a stepped-up blitz designed to smash Stepenberg and his kind once and for all, he had called for far-reaching changes. Two years earlier, the service had employed only three hundred special agents; now the newly announced program called for three hundred and seventy-eight additional inspectors, three hundred and seven investigators, and an eight-and-three-quarter-million-dollar supplemental appropriation to combat the narcotics traffickers.

What had prompted this expansion was the realization that narcotics, once the scourge of the black slums, was now a problem affecting all levels of society—above all, the white middle class. The deaths of heroin users who had barely approached puberty in the high schools of affluent neighborhoods cried out for vigorous government action.

"Heroin was something grown on another planet, beyond fearing," the father of one teenage addict had written, but now all middle America was to know this dread.

It was a fear that inspired a new cooperation between such rival agencies as the New York Police Department and the BNDD. Until now narcotics investigation in New York City had been the prerogative of the elite eighty-strong Special Investigations Unit (SIU), men of the NYPD strong in city expertise but lacking in both up-to-date equipment and funds. The men of the BNDD, though strong in material resources, were deficient in local knowledge. So four SIU men—detectives Richard Bell, Mario Martinez and Douglas Reid and Patrolman Luis Martinez—were assigned as a team to work on a tentative basis with the BNDD.

With the establishment of this unit, designed to crack the trafficking system, Jimmy Cohen's life as a wholesaler was now numbered in weeks. Ironically for Stepenberg, Cohen was the man on whom the unit agreed as a test case, though he was by no means the biggest trafficker on the streets of New York.

The reasons were twofold. Cohen's apartment building was a known hotbed of Latin-American traffickers. Equally, Cohen's stereo business raised questions: it was known that he imported radios, tape recorders and cassettes from Argentina, storing them in a bonded warehouse. No evidence ever suggested that he used this means to import either heroin or cocaine, but after the oscilloscope seizure of 1967, all electronic equipment was suspect.

Cohen remained unaware. On the evening of January 3, 1970, Poeta called personally at his apartment. "The big time is coming for you!" he exclaimed, adding, "You say many times you want a big load. Now is the time to prove you can sell it."

Once again, Poeta indicated, Cohen was to set out for Dartmouth Street. And once again, as if enacting the ritual of a macabre treasure hunt, the cache for the heroin had been switched. Cohen found ten kilos inside a bedroom closet, lodged in a steamer trunk.

But now, for the first time, Cohen began to encounter sales resistance. Almost twelve days passed before he made his first sale to Frank Hughes, and the man confessed to a cash-flow problem. Against Stepenberg's instructions—and his own better judgment—Cohen was obliged to give Hughes credit while he peddled half a kilo at a time, paying off a few days later at the punitive price of sixteen thousand dollars a kilo.

"That's top-grade horse," Hughes said. "I tested it and it's for real. I get some hard narcotics users, old hands, to shoot it. If they get a high, then I know it's good." This revelation of a man so debased that he virtually maintained a stable of addicts to test his heroin was somehow symbolic of the world that Stepenberg had created around him.

On this same day, January 15, another contact called Cohen to establish a liaison. Unknown to him, this contact had turned informer, and beside him in the pay phone booth was Detective Richard Bell. In accordance with police procedure, Bell had to verify that this was Cohen's phone number before a judge would authorize a wiretap.

At midnight, as arranged, Bell's informer called on Cohen. Bell himself had earlier gained access to the West Forty-fifth Street building and was on a stakeout, observing Cohen's apartment from the stairwell above the landing. Here he stayed until one thirty a.m. on January 16. He heard lavatories flush noisily in the night, and the mingled smells of a run-down apartment building assailed his nostrils: ammonia and disinfectant, old linoleum and old beds. He watched three men, apart from his own informer, come and go furtively. One was a man then unknown to him, a worried-looking man glancing nervously over his shoulder: Eduardo Poeta.

On February 4—one day after Cohen returned to Dartmouth Street for a further ten kilos—a wiretap was installed on his apartment phone.

Now the expertise of the SIU made itself felt. Detectives like Mario Martinez could assert with certainty that the mentions of "Maria" in Cohen's telephone calls were references to cocaine, while "Antonio" meant heroin.

Meanwhile, Cohen was in possession of more drugs than anyone wanted to buy. Perhaps irked by his cavalier treatment in the past, Felix Martinez had found another supplier and was out of the running. That left Frank Hughes, who could afford only half a kilo at a time.

Alarmed at the realization that he had eight and a half kilos of surplus heroin—seventeen glassine bags in all—Cohen moved them to the top of a wardrobe in his girl friend's apartment in Elmhurst. Only half a kilo remained at his apartment, to meet the needs of Frank Hughes.

On the evening of February 12, watching agents saw Hughes enter Cohen's apartment building. They bided their time until he exited, heading for a nearby parking lot. At once Richard Bell and another detective moved swiftly to intercept him. Moving with the well-drilled precision of a commando unit, three others, headed by special agent Domenick Mingione of the BNDD, mounted to Cohen's apartment.

The rumor had spread that Cohen was a "tough guy" who was most likely armed; thus the police took no chances. Quietly inserting a latchkey they had obtained, they eased the door open. It gave an inch and then resisted; Cohen had put on the chain.

All three acted as one then; they drew back and charged. From inside the room came a wild yell of fear, but they charged again. The chain ripped from the doorframe and they tumbled in.

They saw Jimmy Cohen, shaking with fear at the far side of the room and staring with revulsion at the damp dark stain spreading across his left thigh. Their tough guy had wet his pants.

On that February night, when the thermometer stood at freezing point, Jimmy Cohen's morale touched rock bottom. Even so, native caution told him that he had better cooperate to a degree. He saw little other choice.

When the three men hustled him into the street, Cohen had almost at once proposed a trade-off. He would take them to his girl friend's apartment, provided that she would not be involved. It was agreed that while Cohen waited in the car with special agent Mingione, two other officers would enter the apartment and retrieve the heroin. Almost at once Mingione had begun to try to gain Cohen's confidence.

"Jimmy, we'll do all we can to protect you, but we'd like to know a little bit about the people you're getting your stuff from. Like, you know, your sources in South America."

Cynical and bitter, Cohen had flared back. "Yeah, I'm gonna get myself killed. Big deal."

But Mingione was an old hand at this. Sooner or later most suspects agreed to cooperate. The two sat huddled in the car, awaiting the return of the others; at intervals cars went secretly by with a sigh of tires and a sudden small flare of headlights.

"Jimmy, you know, just give me a name or two. . . . If these people you're dealing with are of interest to us, those names by themselves may be sufficient for us to go to bat for you."

Perhaps thinking it was safe, since the big man was in Geneva, Cohen muttered, "Jack Grosby."

Mingione fought to contain his excitement. He said with elaborate casualness, "Grosby? Wasn't that the guy who jumped bail in the fall of '68? Let me see, who put up that bail?"

"Luis Stepenberg."

Number One had said, "Definitely never mention my name." But the secret was out.

The rest of that night passed like a surreal dream. At the Elmhurst precinct house, where Cohen was fingerprinted and photographed, there was a constant coming and going of agents. The little man sat alone in a corner, sullen and shaken, while detectives busied themselves listing the serial numbers on the eight thousand dollars that Frank Hughes had paid him. Detective Douglas Reid was already en route to Dartmouth Street, following an admission by Cohen, but he found no couriers, only dusty furniture and French magazines.

In the BNDD laboratory, Detective Reid and a colleague waited patiently. The bureau's chemist was concluding an analysis of the heroin found in the apartment of Cohen's girl friend.

"Almost like an Ivory commercial," said the chemist at length. "Ninety-eight and seven tenths percent pure."

The two detectives exchanged glances. There were enough counts against Cohen to make sentences that could total life.

So the softening-up process continued. On February 14, in an oak-paneled courtroom in Queens, Cohen was arraigned and his bail set at two hundred and fifty thousand dollars. Thereafter, though held in a separate cell, he was rarely alone. Sometimes Reid sat with him, at other times Mingione or Bell. But if the company varied, the topic of conversation never did.

"We could put you in and toss the keys away, Jimmy. But you can give us maybe five for one. That would mean something to this office."

Or, "We want cooperation, Jimmy. We've been after you for a long time. Now we have you. How about it?"

Okay, so they wanted him to be a songbird, Cohen knew that. In the long hours of the night, when he got to thinking hard, he knew he faced sentences that would add up to life. It was Reid who first suggested the idea of a voluntary phone tap, and Cohen resisted fiercely. But then he thought again, for Reid added, "What difference would it make? We had you tapped even before the pinch, only you didn't know it." So the pigs knew all about him anyway. What had he to lose?

Then there was the question of his bail. If he cooperated, they said, it could be scaled down overnight to only fifteen thousand dollars, and soon he might be free.

At other times the questions concerned his income. All right, in 1969 he had been out of work, but he had sold heroin, hadn't he? Had he included those profits on his tax return? No? Then he might face prosecution for filing a false income tax return.

Day and night the process continued, and the agents were not displeased. Jimmy Cohen, narcotics wholesaler, was being transformed into Secret Confidential Informant (SCI) 0-0016.

Afterward, the fifteen days he spent in the detention center in the back of the Queens courthouse seemed to Cohen the longest he had ever endured. By now he knew that the agents had him where they wanted him. His sole hope of a pardon was to agree to a telephone tap and to tell everything he knew. The decision was more crucial than he could then know. Both federal prosecutors assigned to the case now saw him as the key figure through whom they could trap Stepenberg, Grosby and Poeta.

First, though, Cohen faced a problem the police could not solve for him. Who was going to come up with his bail—even at only fifteen thousand dollars?

Unknown to Cohen, a ludicrous comedy of errors was at that moment being played to its conclusion. On the night of the Cohen arrest, Felix Martinez had also been taken into custody, but the police found no evidence more damning than Epsom salts, a cutting agent. Set free, Martinez had undergone a change of heart over his old friend Jimmy. Anxious to help, he called on Poeta at the cigar store, but El Rubio was dumbfounded at the sight of him.

"Not here," he hissed. "Come to my car."

But even the sanctuary of his Chevrolet was not safe enough for Poeta. To Martinez' mystification, he drove downtown to Columbus Avenue, where he parked the car between Ninety-sixth and Ninety-seventh streets. Then Poeta and Martinez hastened on foot toward Central Park and walked south on Central Park West. Not far from the Hayden Planetarium, Poeta pulled Martinez into the doorway of a tall building.

"Jimmy's in trouble," Martinez expostulated, but Poeta, trembling from head to foot, was plainly going to be of no help at all.

"We have to wait sixty days to give him any kind of help," he insisted. "Don't come to the cigar store anymore."

Martinez was shocked. He and Cohen had had their differences, but he saw this as no way to treat a partner in crime. Loyal to a fault, he went out and sold a kilo and a half of cocaine for fifteen thousand dollars and stood bail for Cohen himself.

LATE IN THE afternoon on February 28, Cohen and a select coterie of agents under Victor Maria, now a group supervisor of the BNDD in New York, met in an anonymous brown-draped motel room on Queens Boulevard. The debriefing was scheduled to last fully seven hours, and one agent after another took up the questioning. Slowly a jigsawlike pattern began to take shape: the traffickers' elaborate code, their meeting places, their pseudonyms.

"We're going to use you," Maria told Cohen frankly, "to find out what comes and goes, and how."

The first stage was to install Cohen in a new apartment. The location was a plausible one for a man of modest means: a high-rise apartment house, part of a gigantic housing development in the center of Queens. It was an elaborate complex of red and yellow-tan brick buildings, some of them surrounding central courts with swimming pools and playgrounds.

The three-bedroom apartment occupied by Cohen, and on occasion by his girl friend and her three children, also included a living room and kitchen and had a balcony. It differed from all the others in two essentials: not only was the telephone bugged, but a listening device had been installed in the living room to monitor face-to-face conversations. And to make doubly sure that nothing escaped them, this new anti-Stepenberg unit had rented apartment 15E, next door to Cohen.

In this new abode Jimmy Cohen was now preparing to live a lie, to adopt a whole new persona. He was to be the little man suffering a cruel injustice; yet a man, it must be conceded, who had not stooped to finger a pal. Only by stubbornly maintaining this front could he hope to induce the wily Stepenberg to do business with him again.

At eleven a.m. on April 11 the phone rang in the West Side Manhattan apartment of Stepenberg's father. The slothful Luis Stepenberg, who normally slept late, awoke to hear the voice of Jimmy Cohen, and an indignant Jimmy Cohen at that.

At first Detective Mario Martinez, who was monitoring the call, was puzzled. Cohen seemed to be accusing Stepenberg of introducing him to a girl who had given him a venereal infection. It was a moment before the detective saw the significance of the words in the drug traffickers' code: the contact with Felix Martinez had resulted in Cohen's arrest.

"She's the one who got me contagious," Cohen insisted, "and I got sick over it. If you want, you can ask the doctor."

Stepenberg was cautious. "Well, this is not the time to think about this thing. You have to rest. In a couple of months you're going to be able to work again, to be fine."

Cohen's voice took on a note of urgency. "Yes, but in the meantime I need bread. I have to pay the doctor."

"Listen," said Stepenberg coldly, "you're talking to me as if I was in the middle of this business of yours."

"But you can give me a hand," Cohen pleaded.

"We're in this world to help one another," Stepenberg agreed sententiously.

"Because of me nobody got contagious," Cohen reminded him. "Now I'm asking for some help."

Stepenberg's voice was silky. "My dear friend, do you have the idea that you're going to put the blame on somebody?"

"Well . . ."

The command came back like a whiplash. "Forget it!"

But Cohen kept talking, a rambling self-pitying monologue, until Stepenberg asked abruptly, "Where do you live now? What part? Don't tell me anything else."

"In Queens. Do you want to write down the pipe?"

"No, no, no, forget the pipe. If we meet, it would be better in public. How are you from the back?"

Cohen strained his memory. What was the code when an agent was tailing you? A cane, that was it—a cane.

"First I walked with two canes at my back," he replied, "then with one. Now, I give thanks to God, I don't have a cane."

It was Stepenberg who suggested the actual time and place for a meeting: that afternoon, outside the Radio City Music Hall, in midtown Manhattan.

"Always look behind you, please," Stepenberg cautioned. "Watch your back. Because you are a little confident. And if you see the fat one, keep walking behind him."

In Central Park the pigeons were strutting pompously, like old men lost in thought, and office workers basked on the benches in the sunshine, finishing the last of their sandwiches from brown paper bags. The occupants of a green Hornet SST sedan barely spared them a glance. Detective Richard Bell was keeping an eye on the early afternoon traffic as he drove. In the rear, Detective Douglas Reid was doubled up on the floor. He was accomplishing the difficult task of changing from civilian clothes into the uniform of a New York patrolman. They exchanged a small wry joke about Reid's speedy reversion to pounding a beat if he fell down on this afternoon's surveillance of Luis Stepenberg.

At two forty p.m. Reid slipped from the car and took up a position near the Radio City Music Hall. Ten minutes later he watched

Stepenberg arrive and then kill time studying the stills outside the theater. On the stroke of three Cohen sauntered into view.

On the surface, two New Yorkers were meeting like hundreds of others, and no one would have spared them a glance. The one distinction was that no effusive greetings or handshakes were exchanged. At the sight of Cohen, Stepenberg only nodded curtly and walked north on the Avenue of the Americas. Dutifully Cohen followed.

Taking his time, Reid strolled after them, twirling his nightstick absently. Stepenberg headed east on Fifty-first Street, and at Madison Avenue he entered a Schrafft's restaurant, taking a seat near the long plate-glass window, from which he could see St. Patrick's Cathedral. Cohen took a seat at the same table. It was quiet now, after the lunchtime rush, as Stepenberg ordered coffee.

Outside on Fifty-first Street, Detective Reid took up a stance beside the window. Cohen, he noted, was doing most of the talking: a man airing his legitimate sense of grievance.

"You have to rest now," Stepenberg was telling Cohen. "You have to be very careful with everything. You are very hot."

Cohen pressed him. "Listen, Luis, I have to go to the hospital. I need some money and I don't have any money."

Stepenberg grimaced. "How come you don't have any money? I figured out how much heroin you've sold, how much you've lost or spent. I think you're supposed to have the money."

From the street Reid watched Stepenberg grab for a paper napkin. Taking a pencil from his pocket, the fat man began scribbling, absorbed in calculations. "You should have ten or fifteen thousand dollars left," he concluded.

"It's not true," said Cohen miserably. "I don't have it."

"How long did the authorities question you?" Stepenberg asked.

"I was interrogated all night," Cohen said truthfully. "But you see, nobody got arrested. I don't mention your name. They ask me a lot of questions about where I get the heroin from, and I tell them a seaman from Italy gave it to me."

But soon, he reminded Stepenberg, he would have to go to court again. The lawyer Stepenberg had retained for him would need another three thousand dollars. "I don't want to take one penny from nobody," Cohen maintained. "But now I don't have that money. Please do me that favor, call the lawyer and explain to him."

"Okay," said Stepenberg finally. "A telephone call will be made. But please don't call my father's house anymore." He got up. Time was precious and he was wasting it. As an afterthought, Reid noted, he took up the disfigured paper napkin and stuffed it into the left-hand pocket of his jacket.

Cohen made a last desperate attempt. "I have to start working again and make some money—to get well," he hinted.

Stepenberg ruled out any such hope. "Put that out of your mind. And never call anybody. You want to make everyone sick?"

As Cohen tried to win back Stepenberg's trust, Cosme Sandin came back into his life. Despite the money he was now earning, the bootblack remained fretful. He hadn't come so far to wash dishes. When was he going to get rich carrying suitcases? As the agents who monitored his solicitations were later to calculate, Cosme phoned Cohen sixty-eight times and called at his Queens apartment on thirty-five separate occasions.

Despite himself, Cohen felt sorry for the young man, without a family and with few friends in New York. More often than not, when Cosme phoned he weakened and suggested, "Come over to dinner." After the meal they sometimes watched television, but as April passed into May they most often sat out on the balcony, talking desultorily, usually in Spanish, only occasionally using Portuguese. Each balcony served two apartments, but a yellow plastic folding divider six feet high afforded some privacy between neighbors. Cosme never suspected that the occupant of apartment 15E was Patrolman Luis Martinez, whose knowledge of Spanish enabled him to monitor fifteen of those balcony conversations, sitting two and a half feet away.

And nobody suspected Cohen of being on intimate terms with the Feds, since on at least six occasions the agents gave him money to purchase cocaine from Felix Martinez and others. Each time Cohen passed the stuff on to the agents.

By now the narcotics agents realized that to trap Stepenberg through Cohen would be a long and tortuous process. There were both the telephone tap and a bug, or listening device, in Cohen's apartment, but often the voices of children in the playground below blurred his conversations. At other times the agents found themselves concerned with trivia; one fifteen-minute transcript of a telephone call turned out to be Cohen's weekly grocery order.

One alternative solution was to bug Stepenberg's own phone. Sometime in April he had quit his father's apartment and moved to more opulent quarters: a white brick apartment building called the Dorchester Towers, just north of the Lincoln Center cultural complex. Plainly Stepenberg, or Cesar Berg, as he was known here, was moving up in the world; this building, with its shrub-lined driveway, fountain and carpeted lobby, was a world away from the faded grandeur of West End Avenue.

On May 7 a wiretap was duly authorized on the telephone in apartment 420 at the Dorchester Towers, but seemingly in vain. Though day succeeded day, the phone rang on unanswered.

At the time of the wiretap, Stepenberg was more than thirty-five hundred miles from New York City. Late in April he had checked in at one of his favorite luxury hotels, the Melia Madrid on the Calle Princesa, Madrid. In the muted hush of the hotel's bar, with its discreet taped music and deep mustard-yellow leather armchairs, he met early in May with André Condemine and an associate.

The men brought welcome news. Ricord had put together an entirely new drug ring in Asunción, Paraguay, where massive bribes to high government officials promised almost total immunity from arrest. An army general even rented his *estancia*—ranch—as a landing strip for nonscheduled cargo aircraft for twenty thousand dollars per trip.

The heroin was still traveling a long and tortuous road—by freighter from the mobile laboratories of Europe to Buenos Aires or Montevideo, thence by fleets of automobiles, light airplanes and river barges twelve hundred miles inland to Paraguay. But once in Asunción there were no more problems; even customs officers helped unload the heroin and transport it to safe houses—including Ricord's restaurant and motel, the Paris Niza.

At this point the *contrabandistas* would take over—daredevil pilots, adept at flying small planes from narrow dirt strips in the mountains. (Since the journey was all of six thousand miles, Ricord's men had been active in buying cooperation in Panama, vital as a refueling center.) Some pilots were so skilled they could zoom across the border at two hundred feet above ground level, then climb steeply to eight thousand feet; on a radar screen this would suggest that they had just taken off from a nearby commercial field. Their ultimate destination was Florida, with its checkerboard of two hundred and sixty airfields and landing strips. From Florida the heroin would be brought to New York by mules who rode the long-distance buses, free from all customs interference.

Stepenberg returned to New York well pleased. He looked forward to the late summer of 1970 as a golden and limitless harvest.

Jimmy Cohen knew nothing of this, but by May 13 he was a desperate man. Stepenberg had categorically forbidden him to call, but nobody had called Cohen in the meantime, so somehow a contact must be made. The prospect of a life sentence was only in abeyance; the agents had made that plain. On this Wednesday he again called Stepenberg senior's house; the fat man's move to the Dorchester Towers was unknown to him. But by chance Luis was paying his father a visit.

"It's a long time I don't hear from you," Cohen said with assumed cordiality. "What happened? I'd like to see you."

Stepenberg was not forthcoming. "What about?"

"You know I can cook," Cohen said, "and I can start working in any restaurant."

Stepenberg took his point: the little man was begging for work. How much he now trusted Cohen has never emerged, but the thought may well have crossed his mind that if the flow of heroin from its new Paraguayan conduit were to be unceasing, he would need wholesalers. He agreed to a meeting as before, outside the Radio City Music Hall, the following morning.

Now the agents encountered Cohen's stubborn streak. Despite all persuasion, he resolutely refused to wear a "wire"—a hidden microphone—to record the conversation. Stepenberg, he maintained, had the cautious habit of scrutinizing the knots of other men's neckties to see if they were equipped with a mike.

Yet somehow the rendezvous must be recorded. At ten a.m., when the two men met, the BNDD's James Guy, on a first-floor balcony of a bank across the avenue, covertly snapped the action with a camera. From another nearby building Detective Douglas Reid did the same. Camera shutters were clicking unheard as Stepenberg, in a rumpled gray suit and open-necked yellow shirt, made for a restaurant in the Radio City complex, with Cohen following.

As they sipped coffee, Cohen sensed with relief that Stepenberg was already nearer to accepting him.

"Are you still in touch with your people, the people you sold to before?" was one of his first questions.

Cohen intimated that he was. He had Hughes, Martinez and another client, a figment of his imagination, a wealthy Italian.

"Well, you keep in touch with them," Stepenberg told him. "I think very soon we will receive another big load and you'll get something to work on."

Typically, although he was salting away millions, Stepenberg was furious that Cohen had never visited the real estate agent to recover the thousand-dollar deposit on the Dartmouth Street house.

Cohen saw a way to turn this to his own advantage. "After I was arrested and got out, I never went near that house. I never mentioned that house to nobody."

Stepenberg seemed partly mollified. "Telephone your customers and see if they're still interested in buying. Then tell Eduardo, but tell him the truth—not like before. Be sure how many of these people can buy. Don't say you want to buy fifty kilos if you can only buy twenty."

But Stepenberg was taking no chances. Cohen was to note down the number of the nearest pay phone booth to his apartment; the fat man was convinced, and rightly, that Cohen's phone was tapped.

The next contact—at eleven a.m. on May 15, outside the Argentina Consulate General—was so fleeting that Detective Richard Bell, crouching in a vacant loft above a restaurant opposite, barely had time to set his small movie camera in motion. Promptly on the hour, a green Chevrolet pulled up outside the consulate, and from the driver's seat Poeta beckoned curtly.

As he climbed in beside Poeta, Cohen lied: "Okay, I can handle ten kilos very easily because I've got a new customer. He could buy in one shot, cash—big bills."

For answer Poeta gave him further instructions. Cohen must meet Stepenberg at two p.m. that day at Chock Full O'Nuts, at

Broadway and 116th Street, a fast-food place patronized by students and professors from Columbia University. This was it, Cohen thought. Once more he would be part of the privileged circle.

He was doomed to disappointment. On Broadway, outside the restaurant that afternoon, he was greeted again by Poeta in his Chevrolet. Poeta gestured to Cohen to get in and, still fearful of a tail, drove to Riverside Drive and 113th Street before parking the car.

The precaution was fruitless. Agent James Guy had already filmed the Broadway meeting from an office across the street, and having tailed the Chevrolet, another agent had a movie camera whirring busily for the prosecution at 113th Street.

"Luis is busy right now," Poeta was explaining. "He couldn't make it. But soon the heroin will be coming in. We'll call you." Stepenberg, he added, still wanted the number of the pay phone booth nearest to Cohen's apartment, and this Cohen gave him.

On this same day Poeta had received a cable from Carlos Rojas in Buenos Aires indicating a delay in the shipment. Despite this setback, the Stepenberg ring's uneasy relationship with Cohen continued. Though they had no immediate need of him, the garbled phone calls and furtive meetings went on—as if only by making daily contact with him could they assuage their latent fears.

On May 19, for instance, Cohen's apartment phone rang. Answering it, he recognized Stepenberg's voice, pretending to have dialed a wrong number. This was the prearranged signal for Cohen to go to a booth on Queens Boulevard; there, five minutes later, the phone was ringing. Again it was Stepenberg, telling Cohen to meet Poeta at the same Chock Full O'Nuts at two p.m. on May 20.

The uneasy farce continued: the same elaborate trip to Riverside Drive to evade detection, the same agents filming the conspirators at either end. Inexplicably, since the shipment was delayed, Poeta now seemed pathologically certain that Cohen was being tailed.

"I'm positively sure nobody is following me," Cohen reiterated.

Poeta looked dispirited. "You don't have to be so sure," he cautioned. "You be careful."

Nonetheless he insisted that Cohen meet him next morning, this time at a pizzeria on upper Broadway. They sat in the back room and wrangled inconclusively; once more Poeta counseled caution, and Cohen was clever enough to feign anger.

"Well, Eduardo," he said finally, "is the heroin here or not?"
Poeta shook his head. "Not yet. Soon begin to come."

"Every day you tell me the same thing," Cohen exploded. "What is the reason? We meet together, talk together. Somebody follows me and sees me talking with you—with no reason. Every time I've seen you, you've told me the heroin is coming, but I don't see it. *When?* My people are getting tired."

In a quieter vein he pressed Poeta: How was it coming? But Poeta genuinely didn't know. If from Buenos Aires, then in racehorse stalls; if from Canada, then by car.

About this time Stepenberg received an evening phone call from an unidentified male. The fat man's reaction tallied with no code that Cohen or anybody else had ever heard: "The Peruvian has one now and is looking at it. It is going for seventy-six carat."

As THE HOT June days dragged by, Cohen and the agents in apartment 15E waited vainly for Stepenberg's next move. All the evidence had suggested that Stepenberg did need Cohen and was prepared to trust him. But now Cohen's phone stayed silent.

Not until Saturday, June 13, a still and breathless day, did the tap on the Dorchester Towers apartment pay off. For the first time Stepenberg was relaxing his guard sufficiently to risk calling Cohen from home. The fat man was suffering from summer flu—"I'm all screwed up with this crappy cold"—which gave an excuse to revert to the medical code. And here was the first positive evidence that the heroin was coming.

Detective Richard Bell, who was monitoring the call, heard Stepenberg say, "I know you've been waiting—that's why I called you."

When Cohen asked, "Do you think it could be next week?" Stepenberg seemed hopeful.

"I think so, because I just spoke to some people," he said.

By the following Monday Stepenberg had recovered enough to investigate other methods of importation, seeking out an old contact and exploring one more likely pipeline for the channeling of heroin. But it was not destined for fulfillment. Time was running out for Luis Stepenberg.

On Saturday, June 20, the agents intercepted a second call from Stepenberg to Cohen. The conversation left no doubt that the shipment whose delay had been announced in Rojas' cable was now in transit. This time Stepenberg was talking in soccer metaphors—a clever move, since Brazil was contesting the World Cup against Italy the following day.

"Will it be before the soccer game?" Cohen asked. Stepenberg was uncertain. "What do you think for July—the first week of July?" Cohen pressed him. Stepenberg thought that more likely.

Around-the-clock surveillance of the Stepenberg ring was now put in motion. On June 26 an observation post was set up in a third-floor window of a public school, overlooking the Tabaquiria Ricardo from a distance of two blocks. The agents were equipped with movie cameras with telescopic lenses, special telephone sets and two-way radios, waxed packets of sandwiches, thermoses and, above all, good binoculars.

At nine a.m. on Saturday, June 27, Stepenberg's phone rang. The transatlantic operator announced that a Mr. Meniska was calling from Switzerland, and simultaneously both Stepenberg and Detective Mario Martinez heard the voice of Jack Grosby.

Much of the ensuing conversation was gibberish, even to Jimmy Cohen later, but one phrase of Grosby's had Detective Martinez instantly alerted.

"I'm going ahead with Edison," Grosby said. "From now on I'll settle for what they'll give me."

Con Edison, Martinez remembered, ten kilos of heroin. Jimmy Cohen had done his homework well, memorizing all the phrases Number One had taught him: the doctors, the canes, Con Edison; and in turn he had taught the narcotics agents.

"The way things are right now, they couldn't be better," Stepenberg assured Grosby, which meant the heroin was due.

Others, apart from the agents, were keeping tabs on Stepenberg. That evening, as always on a Saturday, he was at the Caborro-Jeno, a nightclub whose plastic orange marquee and glaring neon lights dominated the sidewalk between 144th and 145th streets, on the east side of Broadway. It was Stepenberg's long-standing habit to reserve a table here every weekend. Relaxed with friends that evening, he was annoyed to see Cosme Sandin making a determined way through the press of dancers.

If Stepenberg suspected this was Cohen's doing, he was right. "If you want to see Luis," the badgered Cohen had finally told Cosme, "go to the Caborro-Jeno." With a meaningful nod, Stepenberg signaled the former bootblack to await him at the bar.

Cosme lost no time in coming to the point. "Senhor Luis," he told Stepenberg, "I am in America for one year and a half. I didn't have no work. I don't make no money, you know. I need to do something to make money to go back to my country."

Cosme was so indignant that he never noticed that the man on the next bar stool, studiously giving him his back, was listening intently. Nor did he know that the man was Jimmy Cohen's neighbor, Luis Martinez.

They spoke in a mixture of Spanish and Portuguese, but above the pulsing rhythm of a mambo the undercover policeman could distinguish Stepenberg's reply.

"I can do nothing for you now. But when I come by a big load, you'll get plenty of work. Then you'll make money and go back."

Other informers had warned of that "big load," and it had the agents worried. Some sources claimed that it would touch an all-time high of two hundred kilos, five times the amount seized when the notorious French connection was broken. Word also had it that the port of entry would be Miami; from there it would travel to New York by bus.

"It spread a lot of fear in our minds," one agent still recalls, "because we knew the dollar value of two hundred kilos. We knew what lengths they would go to to protect that. And we knew that we would not have an easy time taking it. But we were going to take it, no question in our minds."

No one, in fact, could discount the chances of a bloody and spectacular shoot-out, for with such a sum at stake more than one mule would be armed. Nor would the couriers hesitate to gun down any man bold enough to intercept them.

It was significant that Carlos Rojas had suddenly returned to New York; he and Stepenberg and Poeta were being dogged from street to street. Fully a dozen agents were now involved in this deadly game of hide-and-seek, and all of them, incongruously, were driving brand-new green Hornet SST sedans. As each man's relief took over, the agent ostensibly off duty caught up on his paperwork: a flurry of forms and reports, tapped out on battered typewriters.

The following is a detailed analysis of surveillance activities covering the period June 20 to July 20, 1970:

A confidential informant records that Poeta held a conference this afternoon about 4 p.m. with an unidentified Latin male. The male questioned Poeta as to whether any of his people had been seized. . . . Poeta replied that his people were safe and that soon he would be back in business. . . .

11 p.m., Sunday June 28. Stepenberg, Poeta and Cordero proceeded from 137th Street to Greenwich Village area in Cordero's vehicle, a 1968 green Chevrolet with a black vinyl top, New York license number YV7331. The three spent approximately two hours in El Gaucho Restaurant at 102 McDougall Street.

"What kept us on the street from April to almost September," special agent James Guy of the BNDD was later to clarify, "was that we anticipated getting them dirty. Eventually we would get them with the drugs." Nor was there any doubt that when the heroin reached New York the agents would achieve precisely this. In anticipation of this haul, evidence had been presented to the grand jury, and on July 2 a formal thirty-six-count charge against Stepenberg, Grosby and Poeta was submitted to the Eastern District Court of New York. Soon the details were telexed to Interpol.

Count one was typical of them all: "The Grand Jury charges: In or about June 1969, within the Eastern District of New York, the defendant LUIS STEPENBERG, the defendant JACOBO GRODNTZSKY, also known as JACK GROSBY, and the defendant EDUARDO POETA did fraudulently and knowingly import and bring into the United States approximately one (1) kilogram of heroin, a narcotic drug, contrary to law. . . ."

It was the truth, both as the law understood it and as the law must phrase it, but the dry, precise wording would have sounded strange to the junkies on the street. They lived in another world and spoke another language: "Daddy, lay it on me, I'm sick."

TOWARD EIGHT P.M. on the same day, the action peaked abruptly. Agents tailing Poeta reported his Chevrolet had crossed the Triborough Bridge, heading for La Guardia Airport. In the passenger seat was his young assistant, Emilio Cordero. At La Guardia the two men parted company. Cordero, who was carrying an at-

taché case but had no ticket or reservation, went on standby at National Airlines for a flight to Miami. Poeta drove back to the city. The Dorchester Towers wiretap confirmed that Poeta had no sooner returned to his apartment than Stepenberg called to check that Cordero had reached La Guardia. Clearly this was to be a crucial flight.

At nine p.m. Cordero boarded a flight for Miami. No less than three narcotics agents—Richard Bell, the NYPD detective, and group supervisor Jerry Carey and special agent James Guy of the BNDD—boarded the plane in his wake. They, too, were on standby, unwilling to draw attention to themselves by pulling rank at the ticket counter. Simultaneously the BNDD in New York alerted its regional office in Miami that they were on their way, stressing the need for double, even triple surveillance.

As Cordero passed through the Miami arrivals gate soon after midnight, special agent Guy was close behind him. He nodded surreptitiously to the regional special agents, Henry Spence and Carlo Harrison, indicating the slim young Argentinian ahead of him. Dressed in a light tan jacket, dark blue shirt open at the collar and bright blue striped trousers, Cordero was not an easy man to miss. But he melted into the throng, and the local agents followed, only to lose him among the crowds. For two harassed days and nights Guy and the others combed the airport and every hotel within miles, but without results. On July 4, sorely disappointed, they returned to New York.

Further surveillance yielded only dead ends. Sunday, July 5, produced nothing more spectacular than Poeta suffering a flat tire driving home from Greenwich Village. In a talk Poeta had with Stepenberg an important phone call was mentioned, to be made at midnight, but shortly before that the fat man took a drive, returning a few minutes later. Evidently he had made that call from a public pipe.

The previous evening, as usual, he had relaxed at the Caborro-Jeno, once more to be bearded by the persistent Cosme Sandin. This time Luis Martinez, the undercover policeman who had become almost a fixture at the bar, heard Stepenberg say, "Stay with Jimmy Cohen. A big load is coming and there'll be plenty of work for you."

Throughout Monday, July 6, Poeta and Stepenberg were insep-
arable. From a restaurant on Seventy-third Street, where Stepenberg made a phone call, they moved on to the restaurant at the
Central Park Zoo. From there they walked to Fifty-seventh Street
and Broadway, where Stepenberg entered an office building to chat
with a man who wore a brown jacket and pants. Soon they left the
lobby and joined Poeta. After they had walked back to Poeta's car,
he first dropped Stepenberg off at the Dorchester Towers, then
drove the unknown man for another furtive conference on Riverside
Drive.

There was no doubt about it; the big load was on the move—from
André Condemine, it was rumored. All the shabby jackals of the
ghetto—the jobbers, the street wholesalers and the addict pushers—
were gathering for their share of the pickings.

On the evening of July 7 Stepenberg, in his sporty maroon
Toronado, license number YF9792, headed out on the Shore Park-
way with Poeta in the passenger seat. The two-way radios crackled
into life: Yankee Foxtrot 9792 was en route to Kennedy International. At eight fifty p.m., when Poeta, dressed in a black Banlon
shirt and black slacks and carrying a black attaché case, went
aboard a National Airlines plane bound for Miami, two BNDD
agents and Detective Mario Martinez went with him. Now, they
were determined, there were going to be no slipups.

And now, deservedly, they had better luck. When Poeta reached
Miami International very early on the morning of July 8, he headed
straight for a phone booth and dialed several numbers in succession.
At two a.m. the agents knew they were nearing the end of the trail.
On the arrivals ramp they saw Poeta exchanging warm handshakes
with both Carlos Rojas and the missing Cordero.

All three men then entered a rented Chevrolet with Florida
license plates and drove to an all-night diner. By three a.m. Poeta
was back at the airport, trying without success to secure a return
flight to New York. Half an hour later he gave up, checking into a
room at the Airport International Hotel under the alias of Eduardo
Arroyo.

Meantime the Miami BNDD agents, in another stroke of bad
luck, had lost track of Cordero once more. Although they had
traced him to the Columbus Hotel, his car was parked in a garage

elsewhere. Curiously, a check revealed that Cordero had previously rented a car on July 6, three days after the agents had first lost sight of him. When he returned it, exactly a day later, it had been driven one hundred and twenty-three miles.

Thus Cordero might have been collecting heroin at any point approximately sixty miles from Miami. To prospect that terrain would call for more resources than the BNDD could command.

In Miami and New York, watchful eyes now followed every move that Poeta made. By the afternoon of July 8, he had returned to New York and taken a cab to his apartment. Four hours later he picked up Stepenberg at the Dorchester Towers, and the two men drove to the Port Authority Bus Terminal, the city's main terminal for both long-distance and commuter bus travel.

Here an apparently innocuous bystander leafing through a telephone directory saw Stepenberg dial Greyhound bus information, checking schedules. Evidently no bus was due that night, and both men left the terminal.

The watching and the waiting continued.

At seven fifteen p.m. on July 9 Poeta received a phone call that jolted him into action. An unknown voice announced, "Lilo [Cordero] is not here, and someone is waiting to see him."

At once Poeta ran to his car and drove to the cigar store at 3555 Broadway. He gave hasty instructions to three unknown males, whom the agents suspected to be stash men. Shortly before ten p.m. he was back in the lower level of the bus terminal, perched on a bench under the harsh fluorescent lighting. Among the milling crowds, the diesel fumes and the incomprehensible crackle of the public-address system he looked alien and ill at ease.

At intervals in the crowd, six pairs of eyes were watching him. The agents had gathered in strength and all of them were armed, anticipating trouble. One of them, James Guy, could at least congratulate himself that his cover was impeccable. To his surprise—and gratification—Poeta actually approached him, inquiring in broken English, "Miami? *El autobús, por favor?*"

"I'm waiting for the same bus myself," Guy replied courteously.

At ten o'clock the large and crowded coach bearing the sign of the greyhound pulled into the terminal. Now, as the weary passengers began alighting, the agents drew back. Poeta must be given every leeway to make contact with Cordero. But as Poeta scanned the tanned faces of the returning holidaymakers, the agents saw his alarm and perplexity growing. He moved closer to the coach, examining each face with frantic intensity. But none of them belonged to Cordero.

Events then moved swiftly. As the last passenger disembarked, Poeta ran to a pay phone. Momentarily a crush of bodies blocked off the agents' field of vision. It was impossible to tell whether or not he had made a call. When they sighted him again, Poeta was emerging from the booth. As he hurried from the terminal, one agent reported with fine understatement, "He seemed nervous."

Every agent except one—a young and inexperienced member of the department—followed Poeta.

At the time, the decision to follow him seemed logical. James Guy thought it likely that an alternative plan existed, one of which they knew nothing. If Poeta had established telephone contact, perhaps he had learned that the big load was coming in by plane. But by eleven p.m., after driving uptown in a desultory way, tailed by five men, Poeta returned to his apartment.

What neither Poeta nor the agents realized was that the scheduled service was overloaded; the ten-o'clock arrival represented only half the passengers traveling that schedule from Miami. Forty-five minutes later a second bus crawled into the terminal, and from it stepped not only Cordero with four suitcases but at least six women couriers, each of whom claimed two suitcases from the baggage compartment. In their wake came Stepenberg's top customer, the notorious Henry Wood, who had ridden shotgun on the fifty kilos earmarked for him, flanked by several armed men.

Not one of these faces was remotely familiar to the tyro agent who had remained behind. As he lingered on, uncertain as to whom he was supposed to tail, a small convoy of taxis was bearing two hundred kilos of heroin unscathed up Eighth Avenue.

Stepenberg had not been remotely concerned; he knew his organization was good. While Poeta was darting around the terminal, and then leaving it, the fat man was enjoying one of his cultural evenings; in the New York State Theater of Lincoln Center he was watching a ballet performance. It was after midnight when Stepenberg arrived home.

At seven minutes after one a.m. on July 10, agents logged a call to Stepenberg's apartment. They recognized Poeta's voice.

"Happy birthday," was all he said before disconnecting.

When this news came to special agent James Guy, he knew ruefully that the unit had more work to do. Months ago Jimmy Cohen had taught them the significance of that phrase. It meant not only that the heroin had arrived; it had already been distributed. All hopes of surpassing the French connection snatch of eight years ago had eluded them.

On the face of it, the Argentine connection had scored a consummate victory, but Poeta, for one, was far from reassured. The incident at the bus terminal had rattled him badly, and as the morning of July 10 wore on, uneasy instinct told him that all too many unknown men were loitering in the vicinity of the cigar store. To test his suspicions he drove north on Broadway, then swung his Chevrolet hard right into a car wash at 155th Street and Amsterdam Avenue. Now he knew that it was more than coincidence: at least three brand-new Hornet SST sedans, all in the same shade of green, were cruising at strategic points near the car wash.

His nerve near to cracking, Poeta gunned the car back toward the cigar store. A glance in the rearview mirror confirmed his fears: steadily the green sedans were keeping pace. At the Tabaquiria Ricardo he parked the car hastily, then dived into the store's back room and snatched up the phone. His hand was sweating on the receiver, and as Stepenberg answered, Poeta blurted out, "Listen carefully. Desist."

"Eh?" said Stepenberg, uncomprehending.

"There's a tail," Poeta told him.

"No kidding," Stepenberg said incredulously.

"There's a tail, like in the books," Poeta almost screamed at him. "A double, triple tail was coming at me."

Stepenberg was decisive. "Then hold—kill the telephone."

Did Stepenberg sense that his time was drawing near? On Sunday, July 12, he gave no sign of it. While Poeta sped his Chevrolet toward the Catskill Mountains, north and west of the city, Stepenberg was again steeping himself in culture. At midmorning he took a girl friend to the Guggenheim museum to look at some modern art; from there they moved down Fifth Avenue to the Metropolitan

Museum of Art. Four hours later, after browsing among Egyptian antiquities and Flemish old masters, they returned to Stepenberg's apartment. That evening they were once more on the town, watching a film in a Third Avenue movie house.

Around ten p.m., having dropped the girl at her home in the Bronx, Stepenberg set out alone for the Caborro-Jeno nightclub. He left his maroon Toronado parked on Broadway.

Detective Douglas Reid, keeping watch from behind the wheel of his own car, fought against fatigue. Since March, scarcely any man on the team had been home for more than five weekends, and then never for more than eight hours at a time. The strain was beginning to tell.

But at least it was a relief to know that the decision had been taken; heroin or no heroin, the team was going to go ahead and round up the entire Stepenberg ring. To spend another six months amassing yet more evidence, in the hope of seizing a load of narcotics, might only result in letting the key men slip through the dragnet. Both U.S. attorneys assigned to the case were agreed on that. They would rely on Cohen's testimony, the wiretaps, the months of intensive surveillance, to make their case stand up.

Midnight passed, but there was still no sign of Stepenberg. One a.m. . . . two a.m. . . . The lights of the Caborro-Jeno dimmed and the iron shutters came down. Now uptown Broadway was given over to the night people: a little old lady rummaging in a garbage can, a wino shambling unsteadily along the sidewalk, a prostitute prowling in search of a "trick."

Reid watched doggedly on, but no one approached Stepenberg's car, even after dawn, when the sanitation trucks lumbered past. Sometime after eight a.m. on Monday, July 13, a tow truck, inscribed LUAN TOWCAR SERVICE—a Stepenberg enterprise—arrived with two men. The man accompanying the driver entered the Toronado with a key and drove it to a nearby service station, where the tow-car company was located.

Number One had dropped from sight.

THEREAFTER, FOR THE space of days, the investigation was shrouded in mystery. Late on Monday, Stepenberg's Toronado was returned to the garage at the Dorchester Towers by an employee of the tow-car company. The keys were left in the ignition and the windows were rolled down.

But where *was* Stepenberg? Where was Poeta? Their telephones rang unanswered, and at all the haunts they frequented the agents drew a blank.

On July 17 an informer passed the confidential word that Stepenberg was still in the United States. He had called his father, telling him not to worry, since he was resting in the Catskills. Confirmation checks at La Guardia and Kennedy International gave no clue as to whether he had left the country.

ON JULY 15, FORTY-EIGHT hours after Stepenberg vanished without trace, another search was under way: the search for Jack Grosby. In his fourth-floor office at the U.S. embassy annex in Paris, the head of the BNDD's regional office, a thoughtful man named John T. Cusack, had a problem: he believed he knew Grosby's whereabouts—on foreign soil—but that was where Cusack was powerless to track him. As always in the past, he turned to Interpol.

Thus, on July 15 an operator in the seventh-floor communications room passed Cusack's urgent message to Madrid in the code that Interpol had used as far back as the 1920s:

TO: INTERPOL PARIS SECGEN [secretary-general] FOR INTERPOL MADRID FOR MATO REBOREDO NARCOTICS BRIGADE STOP INFORMATION FROM BNDD NEW YORK REVEALS GROSBY GEGAD [first name] JACK ALIAS GRODNITZKY GEGAD JACOBO IS PRESENTLY AT CENTRO PRINCESA HOTEL MADRID STOP . . . REQUEST PRESENCE GROSBY AT ABOVE HOTEL BE VERIFIED AND DISCREET SURVEILLANCE BE INSTITUTED TO ENSURE PROPER MONITORING OF GROSBY MOVEMENTS STOP GROSBY IS FESDO [wanted] ON AN ARREST WARRANT FOR VIOLATION OF FOKUL [U.S.A.] NARCOTICS LAWS STOP ARREST AND BURAN [extradition] PROCEEDINGS WILL BE REQUESTED SHOULD GROSBY TRAVEL THROUGH COUNTRY HAVING BURAN TREATY WITH FOKUL FOR NARCOTICS OFFENSES END BNDD EMB PARIS

For six days thereafter the files on Grosby in Paris and Madrid bore a green corner tab, signifying "keep under surveillance." And this is what Reboredo's men were doing. On July 21 they replied by letter with a detailed breakdown of Grosby's movements. Much of it was negative; Grosby was indeed at the Hotel Centro Princesa, an apartment house attached to Stepenberg's favorite Hotel Melia Madrid, where he had been registered under his own name since July 3. In this time he had made two local calls and one to a Geneva number. "The requested discreet surveillance," the letter ended, "will be continued."

In New York, meanwhile, group supervisor Victor Maria of the BNDD had had a brain wave. If a rumor that reached him was true, Stepenberg was shortly due to meet up with Grosby in Switzerland. To check out this rumor, BNDD agents once more called in Jimmy Cohen. Cohen was instructed to write a letter reestablishing contact, hinting that he had lined up some interested customers. He delivered this by hand to Abraham Stepenberg's jewelry store at 2541 Broadway.

On the morning of August 4 Luis Stepenberg's younger brother, Joseph, en route to his own store in the diamond district on West Forty-seventh Street, stopped by to chat with his father. The main topic was the mounting heat; it would be ninety-one degrees Fahrenheit in the city before the day was out. As they parted, Abraham gave Joseph two letters to mail, and Joseph placed them in a large white envelope and took it to his shop. Later he asked one of his young employees to take it to the post office at Rockefeller Center.

The young man glanced twice at the address, shrugged, then tossed the envelope into a slot. It was not an easy address for an American to remember:

L.C.S.
Case Postale [post-office box] 45
1224 Chêne Bougeries
Geneva, Switzerland

Neither Abraham nor Joseph realized that they had unwittingly brought Interpol one step closer to Luis. On his business trips abroad Luis used a chain of forwarding addresses; this was just one more with which they had long been familiar. But to agents of the BNDD and U.S. customs, who had already intercepted the letter in the sorting room at the post office, it meant much more. It suggested a Geneva rendezvous was imminent.

The suggestion was swiftly confirmed. At thirteen fifteen hours

Greenwich mean time—to which the clocks of all Interpol national central bureaus are synchronized—Interpol Madrid cabled the Bern NCB via Paris headquarters:

> CONCERNING TELEGRAM JULY 15, 1970, NO. 4472, RELATIVE TO JACK GROSBY STOP THE CHIEF OF THE SPECIAL NARCOTICS BRIGADE ADVISES THAT SUBJECT LEFT ON IBERIA FLIGHT 284 FOR GENEVA SWITZERLAND YESTERDAY AUGUST 3, 1970, AT 15:30 HOURS

Although Grosby's arrest in Madrid had not been specifically requested, Cusack saw it was time for urgent action. In an XD—top priority—cable to Interpol Paris for onward transmission to Bern and Madrid, he summarized the details, adding:

> WHEN SUBJECT IS LOCATED FINAL ARREST AND EXTRADITION PROCEEDINGS WILL BE REQUESTED THROUGH U.S. STATE DEPT AMERICAN EMBASSY BERN STOP PLS ADVISE RESULTS THIS INVESTIGATION STOP

By now the wires were humming. In Interpol's communications room, where a twenty-four-hour shift system saw the lights burning all through the night, the air resounded with the clatter of teleprinters and the mosquito-shrill whine of Morse code; since not all member countries were linked to the teleprinter circuit, radio transmitters could beam the message to twenty national central bureaus simultaneously.

It was a case that Secretary-General Jean Nepote was following with more than passing interest. Narcotics trafficking to him was "a crime that could affect the whole stability of modern life," and in his time he had followed the route of the Golden Triangle, snapping pictures to be used in audiovisual training by police forces around the world.

In New York City, the BNDD was also working overtime. On August 5 another XD cable was routed through Interpol, giving all relevant details on Stepenberg:

> TO: INTERPOL PARIS SECGEN FOR INTERPOL SWITZERLAND STOP LUIS CESAR STEPENBERG BORN 28 JUNE 1927 ARGENTINA 5 FEET 8 INS. TALL 250 LBS. BLUE EYES BROWN HAIR STOCKY BUILD POTBELLY CASUAL OR SLOPPY DRESSER PREFERS MUSTACHE BUT RECENTLY SHAVED STOP NATURALIZA-

TION NUMBER 8198829 STOP BELIEVED TO BE TRAVELING ON AN ARGEN-
TINE PASSPORT USING HIS TRUE NAME AND PASSES HIMSELF OFF AS AR-
GENTINE OFFICIAL STOP STEPENBERG IS KNOWN TO HAVE SECRET ACCOUNT
AT THE BANCO DE PARIS Y LOS PAISES BAJOS GENEVA WHERE HE REPRE-
SENTS HIMSELF AS AN ARGENTINE OFFICIAL STOP STEPENBERG HAS PREVI-
OUSLY BEEN KNOWN TO USE THE UNION BANK OF SWITZERLAND AT GENEVA

Now a puzzling factor arose. On August 11 Jimmy Cohen, sweltering in his apartment, had a telephone call from Stepenberg's lawyer. Though the attorney's message was guarded, Cohen was left in no doubt that Stepenberg had taken possession of the letter routed to post-office box 45.

Had Stepenberg already reached Geneva? If so, he had come and gone with bewildering speed; the Swiss police had had no trace of him. For seven days agents had maintained a discreet vigil on the small one-story post office located in front of the local primary school at 147 Route de Chêne, three kilometers from central Geneva on the road to the French border. But the post-office boxes were located outside, and thus accessible day or night.

There was an alternative explanation. The officers on watch knew that the post-office box had been rented by Irmgard Böhmer, a blond Zurich-born secretary who lived in a nearby apartment complex. Checking the Geneva telephone number that Grosby had called from Madrid, they came up with the same name: Fraulein Böhmer.

They had waited diligently for Stepenberg, but they netted Grosby instead.

At ten a.m. on August 18 two officers thumbed the doorbell of Irmgard Böhmer's first-floor apartment. The woman, speaking French with a strong Swiss-German accent, led them to the living room. "Grosby," one officer recalls, "seemed surprised, but people are always surprised under these circumstances." Offering no re-sistance, he buttoned his jacket and quietly followed the officers to the waiting car.

Stepenberg's whereabouts, meanwhile, remained an enigma to Interpol.

But only for the space of hours. That same day, confidential in-formation passed to Cusack prompted another XD cable through Interpol to Inspector Mato Reboredo in Madrid. In part it read:

BNDD PARIS LEARNED THAT U.S. FUGITIVE LUIS CESAR STEPENBERG IS
PRESENTLY RESIDING AT THE HOTEL MELIA MADRID STOP STEPENBERG
IS U.S. CITIZEN AND HAS U.S. PASSPORT K1574069 ISSUED 23 MARCH
1970 AT NEW YORK STOP WAS INDICTED IN U.S. COURT FOR THE EAST-
ERN DISTRICT OF NEW YORK . . . OFFENSES RELATING TO UNLAWFUL
IMPORTATION OF HEROIN PURSUANT TO CONSPIRACY . . . WHEN SUB-
JECT IS LOCATED FORMAL ARREST AND EXTRADITION WILL BE REQUESTED
STOP PLS ADVISE WHETHER EXTRADITION OR EXPULSION THIS INSTANCE
POSSIBLE BETWEEN SPAIN AND U.S.

Interpol was now, as was often the case, involved in a delicate
point of protocol. The extradition treaty between the United
States and Spain was at that time imprecise as to whether narcotics
trafficking was an extraditable offense. Playing for time, the Spanish
police replied through Interpol Paris:

TO PROCEED WITH PREVENTIVE ARREST WITH VIEW TO EXTRADITION WE
MUST HAVE BRIEF RÉSUMÉ OF THE CRIME FOR WHICH HE IS WANTED
AND INDICATION THAT EXTRADITION WILL BE REQUESTED THROUGH DIPLO-
MATIC CHANNELS

This additional delay, Cusack feared, might give Stepenberg time
to disappear for good. On August 22 he sent an immediate—and
sharp—reply through Interpol Paris:

XD INTERPOL MADRID ATTN MR MATO REBOREDO STOP WOULD APPRECI-
ATE BEING INFORMED YOUR EFFORTS LOCATE STEPENBERG LUIS CESAR AND
IF ACTION CAN BE TAKEN RETURN HIM FOKUL [U.S.A.] FOR PROSECUTION
ON NARCOTICS TRAFFICKING CHARGES

Meanwhile, two agents who had been in the battle from the beginning had arrived in Geneva. Edward Coyne of the U.S. customs
and James Guy of the BNDD had been authorized by the Swiss
police to interview Jack Grosby. The interview had a curious aura
of old home week as Grosby, without rancor, recognized Coyne as
one of the officers who had arrested him on July 28, 1968.

"Long time no see, Mr. Coyne," he greeted him. "Did you get
the letter I wrote you before I left the States? No? Well, I was real
sorry to leave the way I did. The syndicate talked me into it.
They've made me something of an international hero."

Although he refused to name names, Grosby was frank in many other respects. Since fleeing the United States he had traveled to Russia, Japan, Czechoslovakia, Argentina, Brazil, Hong Kong, England, Spain, Portugal, Switzerland and Uruguay. He claimed that most of his involvement in the drug traffic consisted of transferring money to Switzerland for deposit in secret accounts. For this service his commission had been five percent, and in the intervening two years he had netted seventy thousand dollars.

This represented the handling of some one and a half million dollars, but even so, Guy and Coyne were skeptical. "It is the consensus of agents Guy and Coyne and the Swiss police that Grosby minimized the amounts of heroin his organization handled, the frequency of the shipments smuggled into the United States and the money he has made from his participation," concluded one section of Guy's report.

When Stepenberg's name cropped up, Grosby was cagey. "He's not in Geneva," he said blithely. "He's planning to meet a girl friend in Madrid. They're going for ten days' vacation in Venice."

On August 23 this intelligence became abruptly out of date. With some relief Interpol's NCB in Madrid reported that the fat man and a girl were quitting Spanish soil for French. This was welcome news to Cusack, for there was a far greater chance that the French police would cooperate on the arrest. With twenty thousand heroin addicts in Marseille alone, the French now faced a problem similar to that in the United States.

The sixth XD cable since the hunt began went from Cusack to Interpol's Paris NCB on August 23. It warned that Stepenberg and the girl would arrive in Nice on Air France's flight 580 at seven p.m. that day. Five days later they were scheduled to depart for Frankfurt; from there they would go on to Berlin the same day.

Cusack's cable wound up:

YOU ARE REQUESTED ARREST STEPENBERG UPON ENTRY FRENCH TERRITORY PURSUANT ARTICLE IV OF 1909 U.S./FRENCH EXTRADITION TREATY STOP FORMAL EXTRADITION PROCEEDINGS WILL BE TRANSMITTED BY U.S. DEPARTMENT OF STATE THROUGH U.S. EMBASSY PARIS WITHIN FORTY DAYS AS PROVIDED BY PAR. 5 OF ARTICLE IV STOP . . . PAR. 16 OF ARTICLE XL WHICH WAS ADDED BY 1929 SUPPLEMENTARY EXTRADITION CONVENTION AMPLY COVERS OFFENSE FOR WHICH STEPENBERG CHARGED STOP

As Stepenberg and the girl cleared passport control at Nice–Côte d'Azur airport that evening, the surprise was total. While the pair headed for the baggage-claim area, two soberly dressed plainclothesmen unobtrusively fell into step beside them.

One said, "Monsieur Stepenberg? We are *police judiciaire*. I must ask you to come with us."

Outside, a police car was waiting. As Stepenberg and the girl climbed in, they were introduced formally to two BNDD agents from Cusack's staff who had flown down from Paris to assist in the arrest. At Nice police headquarters, one of the agents informed them officially that they were under arrest by French authorities for violating U.S. narcotics laws and that proceedings were under way for extradition to the United States. But after a brief interrogation, the girl, who was entirely unconnected with the case, was released. Stepenberg, sullen and uncommunicative, refused all comment until he had seen a lawyer.

But next day Stepenberg was far from reticent. Again Interpol liaison had ensured that Guy and Coyne, who had flown on from Geneva, could meet the man they sought face to face.

They began guilelessly: Stepenberg could waive extradition and return to the United States immediately if he agreed to assist the government in its current investigations.

Stepenberg was scornful. What kind of evidence did they think they had that would stand up in a courtroom? A good trial lawyer would tie them into knots.

As they talked, Guy casually let drop some names. Jack Grosby— well, they had him already. Jimmy Cohen—he had been singing for a long time now. Frank Hughes—he, too, was under protective custody and cooperating. Guy let drop some phrases, too. "Will it be before the soccer game?" . . . "I'm going ahead with Edison." . . . "A big load is coming and there'll be plenty of work for you." Finally the ace in the hole: "Happy birthday."

Stepenberg had grown thoughtful, a proud man whose armor had been penetrated. "I can tell you have been listening to me for a long period of time," he conceded.

Guy and Coyne thought they saw their chance. Why not waive extradition, they asked Stepenberg, and return with them to the States and cooperate?

Stepenberg's face grew thunderous, and now for the first time they saw him as he was. For months he had been no more than a shadow figure: a fat man glimpsed briefly on a dusty sidewalk through a camera's viewfinder, a disembodied voice echoing on a telephone wire. But at last they had come face to face with the real Stepenberg: a man whose ambitions had swollen to megalomaniac proportions, who now saw himself as beyond any law.

"I will never be extradited," he told them. "I will never be brought to trial, never be sentenced. I shall renounce my U.S. affiliation and return to Argentina. And let me tell you this—if I stand in a courtroom in front of Jimmy Cohen or anybody, I will strike such fear into them that they will never open their mouths against me for fear of my retribution."

"Think it over," was all Guy said. "We'll be back in a day or so."

THE TWO AGENTS stayed on for two more days in the languid heat of the Côte d'Azur, and the delay was providential. Word came from police headquarters that Stepenberg "had no interest in seeing them again," so on August 27 Guy and Coyne flew to Madrid. Their mission was routine: to thank the Spanish police for their assistance and to discuss the ramifications of the Stepenberg ring throughout Spain. Almost by chance it cropped up that the one defendant remaining at large was Eduardo Poeta.

If Poeta was in Europe, no one was aware of it, but on the off chance, routine bulletins were sent to the Madrid international airport and to the Hotel Melia. Within the hour there was news. Poeta, as agitated as ever, had just checked in at the hotel, asking for Luis Stepenberg. Before he had even seen his room he asked to pay the bill; it might be that he would have to leave in a hurry.

Again the vexing question of protocol arose. Guy and Coyne were promised that Poeta could be kept under surveillance—but if he was to be arrested and detained for extradition to the United States, a proper request would have to come through Interpol.

It was now a hectic race against time, for Poeta was poised for flight. On the night of August 27 Cusack telephoned urgently to agent Guy in Madrid, relaying a verbal request, and Spain's narcotics police acted on it. At midnight Poeta and a woman friend were arrested at the Aerolineas Argentinas baggage counter in the

Madrid airport. The third man from Buenos Aires was planning to return to that city.

On August 28 Cusack's formal petition through Interpol arrived. The next day the Spanish police replied:

TO: INTERPOL PARIS SECGEN FOR BNDD U.S. EMBASSY PARIS STOP EGVID [reference your cable] 5761 DATE 28 AUGUST 70 CONCERNED POETA GEGAD EDUARDO JOSÉ STOP EDBAL [you are informed] THAT ABOVE MENTIONED HAS BEEN ARRESTED ON 28 AUGUST 70 IN MADRID STOP PLS CONFIRM THAT EXTRADITION WILL BE DEMANDED STOP TRANSMIT URGENTLY THROUGH DIPLOMATIC CHANNELS

One day earlier, at eleven a.m., Guy and Coyne had confronted Poeta in the presence of several Spanish officers, with a third secretary from the U.S. embassy standing in as interpreter. In a dusty room above Madrid's central square, the Puerta del Sol, they explained to Poeta the charges against him, offering him the same options as they had offered Stepenberg.

At first Poeta played it tough. "I know nothing about these charges," he asserted, "and in any case I have important friends who will help me."

"You mean like Luis Stepenberg? Like Jack Grosby?" Guy challenged him. "Oh, we have them, too."

Watching, they saw Poeta's face grow blank with despair. He knew the party was over.

THE TRIAL OF Stepenberg, Grosby and Poeta opened in Brooklyn on February 9, 1971, in New York's Eastern District Court, housed in the Federal Building near the Brooklyn Bridge. It was a bleak day, only five degrees above freezing. In the chill, high-ceilinged, black-and-gray marble lobby, the footsteps of the witnesses sounded hollow. The chamber was quiet and austere, lined with oak paneling and lighted by modernistic fixtures. Behind the judge's bench a mural rising the full height of the wall depicted the goddess of justice, flanked by the American flag and a grave, intelligent eagle. At the prosecutor's table sat the U.S. attorneys. At the defense counsel table were Stepenberg, in a rumpled gray suit, and Poeta, flanked by their respective lawyers.

Grosby was being tried *in absentia;* he was still in Geneva, fighting extradition, a procedure complicated by the unexpected appearance of a woman who claimed to be his wife demanding that his funds—more than a hundred thousand dollars, blocked in two Swiss banks—be handed over to her.

Stepenberg also had fought extradition for three months—notably on the grounds that the treaty between the United States and France did not authorize extradition on twenty-six of the thirty-six counts against him.

All these motions being denied, he was returned from Nice on December 7, accompanied by special agent James Guy. His bail was set at one and a half million dollars, the highest ever fixed for an individual in a criminal case, but the fat man was undeterred.

"I shall never be sentenced," he told Guy defiantly on the flight back. "Even *you* will never dare testify against me; nor will anyone else."

From the beginning he was proved wrong. There was a multiplicity of people willing to testify against Stepenberg, men emerging from the underworld twilight to tarnish the reputable front he had so sedulously maintained. Frank Hughes took the stand and, to the palpable disgust of the jurors, talked freely of his stable of hardened addicts. Felix Martinez was there, too, to relate his methods of testing heroin and to speak of his time behind bars as a trafficker. Even Cosme Sandin took a day off from washing dishes to tell of how Senhor Luis had lured him to New York with a spurious promise of wealth. To the end, Cosme's main grievance seemed to be that he never got to carry the suitcases.

As the prosecution's star witness, Jimmy Cohen was in the limelight for two and a half days. Through much of that time Poeta's attorney sought valiantly to cast doubts on both Cohen's testimony and his character: "He swaggered up to the stand . . . and he kept walking . . . as if he was the boy that had outwitted everybody." Cohen, the lawyer contended, had said he wanted to clear his conscience, but "this fellow never had any conscience at all. This is just a couple of words he put together. Probably learned them from some source and thought it was an apt answer to give to a lawyer."

But there was no denying the tortuous chain of evidence—the wiretaps, the telltale photos, and the strange argot of the traffickers, with its canes, pipes and doctors—and the government prosecutor punched that message home.

"James Cohen told us that the doctors could mean a lawyer and a cane the police. And who told James Cohen about the doctors and the canes? Number One, Luis Stepenberg."

No doubt about it, the prosecutor allowed, Cohen was inconsistent at times. But then he pointed to a government exhibit—the heroin that had been seized at the Queens apartment of Cohen's girl friend—and said, "Was he ever inconsistent about that white garbage which is in evidence? Was he ever inconsistent about the money he paid to Number One? Not once."

With each day's evidence Stepenberg seemed to see the writing on the wall. "You could see the man debilitating through that trial," James Guy was to recall. "He was being destroyed."

As the trial proceeded, Interpol flashes around the world were helping to round up the others involved, even though it would be a long and arduous process. The battle was beginning for the custody of Augusto Ricord, a battle carried to the highest possible level when the U.S. government, putting pressure on Paraguay, suspended five million dollars in credit lines to that country, as well as all military aid, stiffened by a threat to suspend eleven million in direct U.S. aid. From that moment on, the Paraguayans saw Ricord as expendable. Extradited to the United States in September 1972, he was tried and convicted and was remanded to the Federal Penitentiary in Atlanta, Georgia, under a twenty-year sentence.

Almost all the lieutenants who had convened at the Ristorante El Sol on that June evening in 1966 met the same fate. Michel Nicoli, Christian David and Domingo Orsini, seized in locations as far apart as Senegal and Brazil, also got twenty years. Louis Bonsignour, Ricord's nephew, was last heard of incarcerated on the West Indian island of Guadeloupe, an overseas department of France. François Rossi, after fighting extradition from Spain for two and a half years, appeared in a Brooklyn court with bail set at five million dollars. In May 1976 he, too, drew a twenty-year sentence. Only the dapper André Condemine did not join them. Suspected of knowing too many of the organization's secrets, he became a victim of gang justice; jammed inside a metal trunk, with a bullet in his head and another in his chest, he was dragged from the Seine in July 1973, alongside the Quai Carnot, Paris. It was an appropriate last resting place, just below Interpol headquarters.

At five twenty p.m. on February 26, 1971, twelve jurors in New York's Eastern District Court found Stepenberg and Poeta guilty on fifteen counts of violating narcotics laws, involving the smuggling of over ten million dollars' worth of heroin into the United States. Two of the men from Buenos Aires got off lightly: Poeta, sentenced to a jail term and a stiff fine, cooperated with the authorities and was released. Grosby, returned from Switzerland in June 1971 in exchange for an Israeli jewel robber, netted only a hundred-thousand-dollar fine; he, too, cooperated. He changed his name, as Poeta and Jimmy Cohen had done, and vanished into limbo; none of them has ever been heard of again.

Stepenberg made good his boast. "I will never be sentenced," he had announced repeatedly, and his prediction came true. On March 11, while still awaiting a jail term that most agents thought would be sixty years, he succumbed to a heart attack in the Federal House of Detention. He was found dead in his cell.

The judge who had presided at his trial even paid him a kind of reluctant tribute. "The man was right," he told the assembled court. "We were not able to sentence him. The sentencing was taken out of our hands by somebody who probably has a much warmer sentence waiting for him in the beyond."

To the very end, then, it had been Stepenberg who called the shots. Number One would have liked that.

ULIA · IP OTTAWA · IP BRAZZAVILLE · IP MAN
NBERRA · IP STOCKHOLM · IP LIMA · IP WIESB
IP WASHINGTON · IP CAIRO · IP LISBON · I
PAL · IP CARACAS · IP LONDON · IP MEXICO
NACO · IP WELLINGTON · IP VIENNA · IP
BRUSSELS · IP ATHENS · IP JAKARTA · IP
IP HELSINKI · IP DUBLIN · IP NASSAU ·
IP BEIRUT · IP SINGAPORE · IP BELGRAD
RIS · IP ACCRA · IP ISLAMABAD · IP REYKJAVIK
IP TUNIS · IP COPENHAGEN · IP KINSHASA ·

INTERPOL: FROM CRIME TO CAPTURE

P OSLO · IP KINGSTON · IP ANKARA · IP
HAREST · IP TUNIS · IP RABAT · IP PORT LOU
US · IP NEW DELHI · IP GUATEMALA CIT
GALPA · IP QUITO · IP BRIDGETOWN · IP
PORT-AU-PRINCE · IP GIBRALTAR · IP BO
IP SANTIAGO · IP JERUSALEM · IP SALISI
IP TAIPEI · IP NAURU · IP KATMANDU · IF
AO · IP LAGOS · IP RANGOON · IP SANTIA
VADUZ · IP TRIPOLI · IP LUXEMBOURG
EO · IP AMMAN · IP TANANARIVE · IP NE
IP ROME · IP TRINIDAD · IP LUSAKA ·
ADDIS ABABA · IP BAHRAIN · IP MANAC
IP KHARTOUM · IP BAGHDAD · IP PARA
CITY · IP NEW DELHI · IP DAMASCUS
GUATEMALA CITY · IP BAGHDAD · IP WA
RABAT · IP MONROVIA · IP PARIS · IP SAN
REYKJAVIK · IP MANILA · IP BUENOS AIRES
OTTAWA · IP BRAZZAVILLE · IP MANIL
BERRA · IP STOCKHOLM · IP LIMA · IP WIESB

The crime committed may be counterfeiting, theft, drug trafficking, murder or one of a dozen others, but whenever the dimensions of that crime are international, Interpol, through its vast communications network, can signal an immediate alert to the police forces of its member countries around the world. . . .

SEE....**ANALYSIS PROVIDED**..

Interpol's Research and Study Division is equipped to provide up-to-date information on scientific matters dealing with worldwide criminal activity, as well as the results of technical analyses gathered from crime laboratories in a variety of countries. . . .

Magnification of United States currency shows clear, connected lines of genuine bill (left); irregular, broken lines of counterfeit (right).

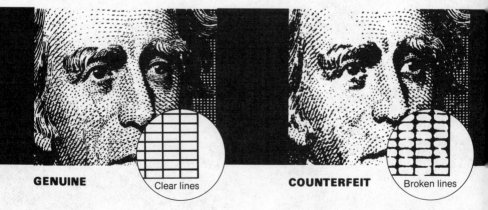

GENUINE   Clear lines   **COUNTERFEIT**   Broken lines

Below, photomicrographic study of a signature. Bottom left, a ballistics test reveals cartridge markings. Bottom right, a specialist photographs a pistol and shells.

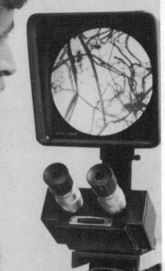

PARIS

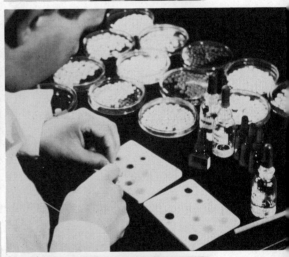

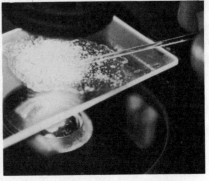

Above, top, fiber content of paper currency seen under microscope. Middle and bottom, laboratory analyses of narcotic substances.

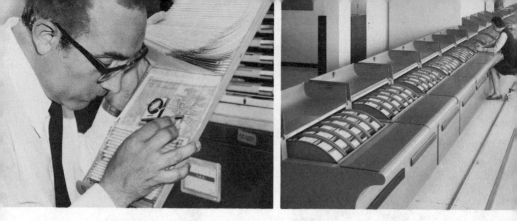

IP OTTAWA CONFIRMS WHEREABOU

.... PURSUIT OF SUSPECT .... CONTINUES

As the search for a fleeing criminal goes on, Interpol can gather information on him from its voluminous files, which contain the names, descriptions, photographs and fingerprints of almost three quarters of a million criminals, and transmit it instantly by telegraph, radio and in some cases phototelegraphy to the national police forces involved. . . .

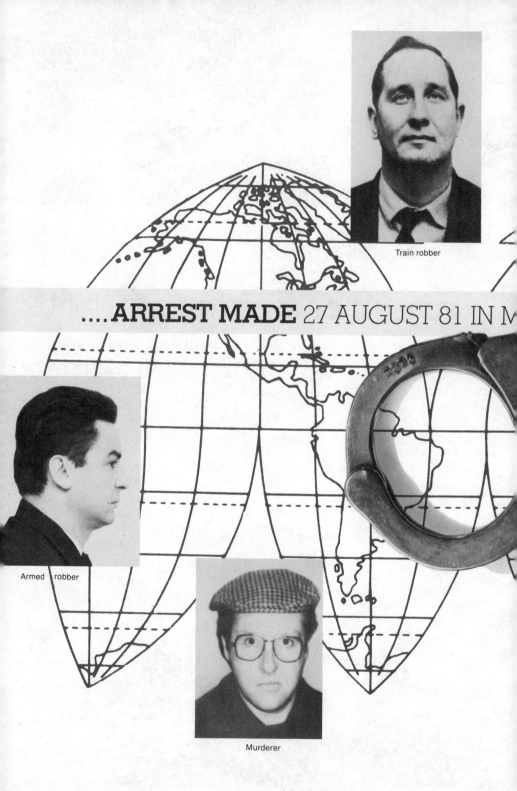

Train robber

....**ARREST MADE** 27 AUGUST 81 IN M

Armed robber

Murderer

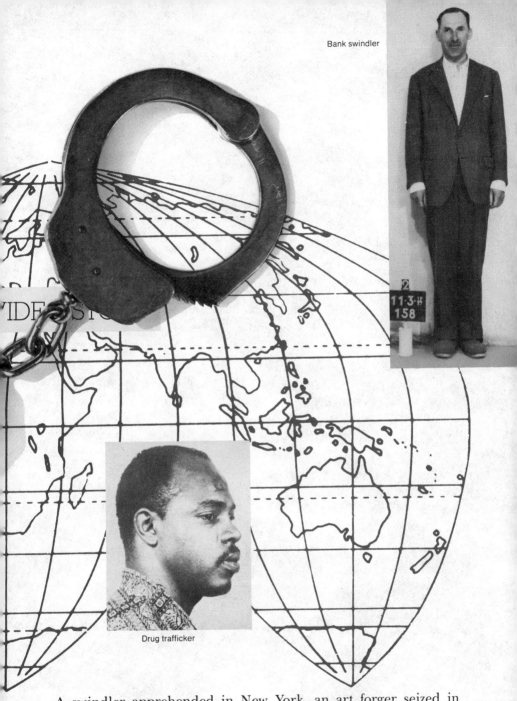

Bank swidler

Drug trafficker

A swindler apprehended in New York, an art forger seized in Rome, a drug smuggler detained in Tokyo—continually Interpol central headquarters receives messages from the police of member countries acknowledging the completion of another case in which Interpol has made an important contribution.

THE BALDAU
TOUCH

THE BALDAU TOUCH

by
Clive Egleton

ILLUSTRATED BY RICK McCOLLUM

Wherever he traveled, Peter Michael Baldau
always stayed in the best hotels. He loved fine wine,
good food, beautiful women and luxurious living.
Most of all he loved money. Given a talent for glib talk,
a vivid imagination and skill as an actor of sorts, he
developed his own method for acquiring wealth.
Before long "the Baldau touch" resulted in a string
of perplexed victims bilked out of fortunes and made
its ingenious creator infamous throughout Europe.
Moreover, he seemed to lead a charmed life,
and neither Interpol nor the police of several
nations knew who the notorious Baldau might
choose to touch next.

Clive Egleton is the author of numerous mysteries
and television plays. His novel *Seven Days to a Killing*
was the basis for the movie *The Black Windmill*.

CHAPTER 1

Nurse Régine smiled. Peter Baldau smiled back and, anticipating the inevitable request, obediently opened his mouth. Deftly slipping the thermometer under his tongue, she reached for his hand, and then, with eyes downcast at the tiny gold watch on her slender wrist, she took his pulse.

"I hear you're leaving us this morning," she murmured presently.

Baldau nodded. After trying various treatments over a period of two months, the doctors had finally succeeded in curing his facial paralysis. Of course, if he'd wanted, it could have taken them much longer, but certain developments in the last few days had made it imperative for him to leave Munich in a hurry, so he'd effected a miraculous recovery.

"We shall miss you, Herr Baldau." Régine removed the thermometer from his mouth and held it up to the light. "Ninety-eight point six," she announced. "Quite normal."

"I must be getting old." Baldau shook his head and put on a mournful expression. "A pretty girl like you holds my hand, and my temperature remains normal?"

Régine smiled and moved toward the door. She was plain, and he was making fun of her, but she didn't mind. With his zest for life and great charm, it was impossible not to like him.

"Don't go yet, Régine. I have a small going-away present for you." Baldau leaned over, opened the bedside cabinet and, reaching inside, produced a bottle of champagne. "Dom Pérignon," he said. "Only the best is good enough for you."

"It's very kind of you, but you'll get me into trouble."

"Ah, yes—your superior. I was forgetting her." Baldau clucked his tongue. "Tell you what. I'll leave it with the porter, and then you can pick it up when you go off duty."

Régine demurred with another smile. Even after their brief acquaintance, experience had taught her that once Peter Baldau made up his mind, he wouldn't take no for an answer. Thanking him profusely, she edged out of the room and closed the door behind her. The champagne would go unclaimed.

As her footsteps faded away down the corridor, Baldau flung the bedcovers aside and got out of bed. Time was running on, and there were certain people he had to see before leaving Munich; people like Horst Steinhardt, the director of a bogus finance and trust company, and Charly Begovich, who owed him money on the emerald deal they had started back in March. Baldau ran an electric shaver over his face, stripped off his silk pajamas, washed and hurriedly changed into an expensively cut checked suit.

Ten minutes later, having packed the rest of his belongings in a suitcase he intended to collect later, Baldau strolled out of the front entrance of the Rechts der Isar Clinic and down the walk. Turning left at the street, he made his way to the cabstand in Einsteinstrasse, not in the least perturbed by the fact that, as of that moment, he was practically flat broke. After all, there was enough loose change in his pocket for the fare into town, and once he'd met up with Steinhardt and Begovich, Baldau knew he would have money to burn.

THE SPATEN BREWERY was near the headquarters of the Bavarian Criminal Investigation Office on Maillingerstrasse, and the sickly sweet aroma of fermenting wort pervaded Wilhelm Wöbking's office. Much as he found the smell nauseating, closing the windows was not a practical solution when the temperature was already in the eighties and likely to go higher as the morning wore on. Despite a faint breeze, the heat was still oppressive and enervating to the point where it required a supreme effort to concentrate on the report from the Swiss police that Chief Commissioner Helmut Bauer and Detective Sergeant Karl Dietrich had submitted to him. As public prosecutor for the First Judicial District, Wöbking had dealt with any number of fraud cases. But from what he'd read, it looked as though this particular swindle could be the biggest and the most complicated affair ever to land on his desk.

"This operation involves at least nine million marks." Wöbking looked up from the file and gazed at the two police officers. "I'm amazed that anyone could be so gullible as to part with such a large sum of money. I'm even more astounded that a man like Peter Baldau possessed the know-how to pull it off."

"I agree it seems way out of his league," said Bauer. "Until now, we've always regarded him as a small-time crook. Of course, it's true Baldau does have three previous convictions for fraud, but the amounts involved were relatively small."

"He's a born swindler, sir," Dietrich said quietly. "He's smooth, charming, quick-witted and very, very plausible. The stage lost a good actor when he turned to crime."

"What makes you say that, Sergeant?" asked Wöbking.

"I've been looking into his background, sir. Believe me, he's quite a character."

Wöbking picked up a pad and pencil from the corner of his desk. "The background first," he said. "Then we'll get to the foreground."

Dietrich took his cue from there. The son of a textile buyer, Peter Baldau was born in Danzig on November 2, 1938, he explained. Six years later, mother and son fled to the West ahead of the advancing Red Army and made their way to Hannover, where eventually the family was reunited when the father, Walter Baldau, was released from a prisoner-of-war camp after the war. Baldau senior, a hardworking and thrifty man, soon joined the Karstadt chain stores as a salesman. He gradually won promotions in the company, and the family was obliged to move from Hannover to Hamburg and then on to Recklinghausen, near Dortmund, where Walter Baldau had been made branch manager. As a result, Peter's education was frequently interrupted, first at elementary school and then at junior high. When he finally left school at the age of sixteen, his father obtained a sales apprenticeship for him with the Karstadt branch at Herne.

"He was a good salesman," said Dietrich, "eloquent, convincing and very persuasive; in fact, just the kind of young man the Becker car agency, a local new-car dealership, was looking for. One of their hiring agents spotted Baldau, and shortly after, he left Karstadt's for Becker's. He was paid twenty-five hundred marks a month and within a short time was earning between fifteen hundred and two thousand extra in commissions on his sales. This was only a few hundred marks short of what his father was paid, but it wasn't good enough for Peter. Unlike the senior Baldau, he was a big spender and lived beyond his means. To supplement his income, he began dealing on the side."

Even though Volkswagen was setting new production records, demand was still exceeding supply in the late 1950s, especially in America. With an eye to the main chance, a trait that was destined to become his predominant characteristic, Baldau saw a way to corner a small slice of the used-car market. Having obtained a personal loan from a finance house, he persuaded a customer to sell his Volkswagen to him instead of trading it in as part of a deal for a new car at Becker's. With his contacts in the trade, it was then a comparatively simple matter to arrange a paint job and have the car reconditioned before exporting it to an American dealer at a handsome profit. It was a transaction he was to repeat over and over again.

"You could describe the process as a sort of black market," Dietrich added, "but there was nothing illegal about it. However, once Becker's discovered what he was up to, they fired Baldau on the spot. Shortly after his dismissal, he had his first brush with the law and, at the age of twenty, was sentenced to seven months' imprisonment for serious traffic offenses."

The short imprisonment failed to teach Peter Baldau a lesson, and over the next two years there followed a whole series of convictions for other traffic offenses. In between jail sentences, he continued to dabble in the used-car market, but the pickings weren't fat enough for him and he began to defraud the original owners. At that stage in his career, Baldau's methods were clumsy, and between March 1961 and October 1966 he was tried and convicted on three separate occasions for fraud.

"He was learning the ropes." Dietrich paused to wipe his damp forehead with a large handkerchief before continuing. "The swindles he perpetrated were all on a small scale, and the heaviest sentence he received was in Hamburg, where the judge gave him two years and seven months. When he was released from prison in 1968, he came to Munich, intending to make a fresh start with some money his father had given him. Within a few weeks he fell in with a clique of smooth operators who frequented the Café Luitpold in Amiraplatz. These men, all of whom appeared to be very well off, referred to themselves as The Gallery."

"The Gallery?" Wöbking asked him.

"A nickname that aptly describes their activities," Bauer offered. "They sold pictures and jewelry to people who wanted to invest in objects of real value. We have no hard evidence to prove it, but the precious stones and the pictures were usually worth only a fraction of what the clients paid."

Wöbking raised his eyebrows in disbelief. "Why didn't they complain to the police?"

"Well, some people don't like to admit that they've been fooled." Bauer smiled knowingly. "And there are others who are in no position to complain; people who have been cheating on their taxes. Anyway, it was through The Gallery that Baldau was introduced to the Swiss industrialist Ernst Oetiker."

Wöbking glanced at the file on his desk. "From whom he is alleged to have swindled the sum of nine million marks."

"So it would appear," said Bauer.

"I still think it incredible that a multimillionaire like Oetiker could be taken in by a petty crook like Baldau."

"Well, it seems Oetiker was prepared to entrust large sums of money to other people for the purpose of investing in schemes to make him even richer. He was sixty-eight when Baldau first met him. I think the man was ripe for plucking, and as Sergeant Dietrich has already pointed out, Baldau can be very plausible."

Wöbking was inclined to agree. Although the investigation was far from complete, there was sufficient evidence in the report from the Swiss police to support that contention. Baldau had set out to win Oetiker's friendship and trust, giving him expensive cigars and other gifts, including some gold coins, which, though counterfeit, had aroused the interest of the industrialist. Oetiker became even more intrigued when the con man announced that he knew how and where to obtain gold ingots at thirty percent below the market price. As proof of his contention, Baldau purchased a small quantity of gold from a reputable source and then sold it at a loss to Oetiker. Having thus whetted the old man's appetite, Baldau casually mentioned that he could purchase a much greater quantity but lacked the necessary funds.

Confident that he was dealing with an honest man, Oetiker advanced him a large sum of money. After failing to deliver the gold on time, Baldau explained that the dealer had let him down by selling the ingots to a third party, but had promised to set matters right within a few days.

That sort of con trick was an old and familiar one, but Baldau played it, with minor variations, time and again during the next three and a half years. The amount of gold to be delivered was gradually increased, and always there were new reasons why Oetiker had to pay in advance. Baldau was nothing if not inventive. On one occasion he told the industrialist that the consignment was part of some Nazi loot that had been deposited in Africa, while in another instance he claimed that the gold had come from Arabia. However, from time to time, small quantities of gold actually were delivered, a ploy that maintained Oetiker's misguided trust. This trust had been further reinforced by a number of formal contracts drawn up by various lawyers. And so Oetiker continued to part with cash, checks and bills of exchange.

"Then Baldau must have duped some of the lawyers as well," Bauer said, voicing his thoughts aloud.

"Just as he probably duped the prison authorities at Stadelheim," said Wöbking. "I'm willing to bet his facial paralysis was self-induced."

In 1970 Baldau had been convicted for a sex offense involving pornographic material shown to a minor. Sentenced to two years' imprisonment, he automatically filed an appeal, which the court finally rejected on November 10, 1971. But Baldau hadn't bothered to await the outcome of his appeal. Long before the appellate court rejected it, he started traveling, making what amounted to a grand tour of Western Europe, which lasted until December 22, 1972. Then, acting on a tip that he was back in town, the Munich police arrested him in a beer hall on Arnulfstrasse. Baldau was now undergoing treatment in the Rechts der Isar Clinic, because under German law a jail term for a conviction of this sort could be interrupted to enable a prisoner to receive outside medical treatment.

"I think we may have let a big fish jump back into the water," Wöbking said ruefully.

"I agree," said Bauer. "That's why we'd like to see him back inside."

Wöbking cleared his throat. "This new case is still diffuse and incomplete. So I'm going to issue a warrant committing Baldau back to prison forthwith."

"Good," said Bauer. "I'll have two of my men pick him up at the clinic."

BALDAU PAID OFF the cab outside the clinic, gave the driver a handsome tip and then headed toward the building to collect his personal belongings. He had every reason to feel on top of the world; the business lunch with Horst Steinhardt and Charly Begovich had been very successful. His final share of the emerald deal had amounted to sixteen thousand marks, and while this was not exactly a fortune, it would certainly tide him over until the next transaction came along. Of even greater satisfaction to him was the fact that his friends had arranged for him to leave Munich.

Kristin Kohler would be going with Baldau, and that too was good news. Kristin Kohler was an ideal accomplice; an attractive brunette, vivacious and clever, she was the kind of girl he liked to be seen with.

As he was starting up the walk to the front doors, Baldau glanced briefly at the street. There, several cars away, he saw a small gray BMW. Nothing made it any more conspicuous than the other empty cars parked on the street, but he had seen cars like it before, and he thought instinctively: Bavarian police.

Suddenly the clinic doors swung open and a young couple appeared, the man pausing to hold one door aside for Baldau. But Baldau hesitated, stopped and shook his head. "Oh, thank you"—he smiled—"but I won't be going in." The puzzled couple watched as Baldau turned abruptly and walked off.

THERE WAS NO NEED for Sergeant Dietrich to tell him what had happened. One look at the down-in-the-mouth expression on the tall blond detective's face and Chief Commissioner Bauer sensed that the fish had indeed jumped back into the water. "Let me guess," he said. "Baldau gave us the slip."

Dietrich nodded glumly. "It looks like it, sir. Sergeant Zwick telephoned from the clinic a few minutes ago to say that he still hasn't returned for his personal belongings."

"And he left there this morning to go for a stroll?"

"Yes, sir. At least, that's what the porter told Zwick."

Bauer glanced at his wristwatch. "It's now five thirty, Sergeant. That's one hell of a long stroll."

"It most definitely is." Dietrich took a paper from his clipboard and placed it on the chief commissioner's desk. "I'd like to send this as a Telex to Wiesbaden."

Wiesbaden was the headquarters of the West German Bundeskriminalamt (BKA)—the Federal Criminal Investigation Office. Sharing offices with the BKA in the low rectangular buildings set in the wooded hills above the spa town of Wiesbaden was one of the largest national central bureaus in Europe.

Headed by Jürgen Jeschke, the Interpol bureau had seven police officers, thirty translators and a clerical staff of twelve, all of whom had at their disposal an efficient communications system capable of handling with ease the forty thousand messages a year that flowed in and out of the headquarters.

The message that Dietrich had drafted was brief and to the point. It read:

Request that red notice be issued in respect to Peter Michael Baldau. Description: age—thirty-four; height—six feet three; weight—one sixty-five pounds. Color of hair—brown. Color of eyes—gray-green. Visible distinguishing marks—scar on upper lip. Subject escaped from Rechts der Isar Clinic, Munich, on 7 June 1973 while still having six hundred and fifteen days of current sentence to serve.

Dietrich reached for his pen and added "Urgent" at the top of the draft.

The Telex was received by Interpol Wiesbaden at 1740 hours. By that time Peter Baldau and Kristin Kohler were already north of Heidelberg and heading toward the Netherlands in a white Mercedes.

CHAPTER 2

THE URGENT REQUEST to Interpol on June 7, 1973, had been followed by another on July 10, when the Bavarian Criminal Investigation Office was tipped off that Baldau was in London, staying at the Churchill Hotel in Portman Square. This request (like the previous one and others that would be made in the following months) was circulated around Europe by Interpol as a red notice—the equivalent of an international arrest warrant—with an XD prefix to indicate top priority. Both messages, however, drew a blank, except for Interpol London's reply that Baldau had indeed been registered at the Churchill but had already checked out. Nonetheless, Wilhelm Wöbking had the satisfaction of knowing his suspicion about the Baldau case had been more than borne out by events. It had rapidly become evident that Ernst Oetiker was not the only person to have been taken for a ride. There were other victims who had been equally gullible and only too anxious to entrust their money to Peter Baldau in the naïve belief that he would make them rich.

The ramifications stemming from this discovery were so complex that Helmut Bauer found it necessary to form a special commission of senior officers to pursue the various lines of inquiry. However, the addition of Chief Commissioner Lars Liebermann and Commissioners Walter Keller, Heinrich Hauptmann and Otto Faber to the team in no way altered things as far as Sergeants Dietrich and Zwick were concerned. For them, life went on much the same as before—they continued to do most of the legwork.

By the end of July the whole of one wall in Dietrich's tiny office was taken up by a montage of photographs, which only went to prove, said Zwick, that Baldau had had a harem in tow. The pinups, all of which had appeared in the glossy magazines that reported the goings-on in high society, were enlargements of candid shots taken in various Munich night spots over the years. Baldau in 1968, looking very self-conscious, with a glass in his right hand and an arm around a blonde in a low-cut dress that sought to contain her breasts as she sat on his lap and leaned against him, smiling into the camera. Baldau three years later with another blonde, but looking much more sophisticated in a suit with velvet trim on the collar.

Different girls, different occasions: a brunette wearing a headband and gazing up at him in openmouthed admiration while delicately holding a long cigarette holder between forefinger and thumb. Baldau in a checked jacket, his plaid tie loosened and shirt collar undone, leaning across a table to kiss a blonde whose hair is swept back from her face. Baldau again that night, being kissed on the cheek by a girl with long dark hair falling below her shoulders. Baldau in the same checked jacket, but this time wearing a black turtleneck sweater under it, kissing a girl with an urchin haircut and huge earrings that swing against her slender neck. Baldau in earnest conversation with yet another girl, one dressed in a low-cut velvet bodice and a tight miniskirt, a spray of artificial flowers in her raven hair and a faraway expression in her eyes.

From the moment the photographs had appeared on the wall, Dietrich's office had become a popular meeting place. Unlike most of his visitors, however, the man who called to see him this morning was not the least bit interested in the picture gallery. His name was Wilhelm Humml, and he had been conned into parting with a great deal of money, or so he claimed.

"I'm only a small businessman, Sergeant. I own a tobacco kiosk here in Munich, and ninety-four thousand marks is a fortune to me." Humml blinked his eyes. "I'm ashamed to say that I even borrowed twenty-eight thousand marks from a friend."

"Perhaps it would be best if you started at the beginning," Dietrich suggested kindly.

"Well, there was this fellow Stendal, who dealt in precious stones. I met him through Herr Steinhardt and another gentleman called Begovich, both of whom used to buy their cigars from me; they always asked for the most expensive brands." Humml managed a rueful smile. "We used to talk about this and that, and they would ask me how I was doing."

"And so you told them about your finances?"

"You mean my little nest egg?" said Humml. "Well, at the time, I didn't see any harm in mentioning that, Sergeant. After all, both of them were extremely well heeled. I should know; I saw the contents of their wallets often enough."

"I see. And when did you meet Stendal?"

"On March nineteenth. That would be about two weeks after I'd

told Herr Begovich that the money I had on deposit in the bank was earning very little interest, and that I was thinking of investing some of it elsewhere. Herr Steinhardt then said he knew a man who could put me on to something good."

The four of them—Humml, Steinhardt, Stendal and Begovich—met for lunch; Steinhardt had chosen a smart restaurant in town that very much impressed the kiosk owner. Over coffee, Stendal produced some emeralds that he intended to sell at a handsome profit to a client who was anxious to buy them. There was, however, a slight hitch. Stendal had the gems on approval from a third party and was still negotiating with the bank for the rest of the money he'd need to pay for them. The interest rate they proposed to charge him was preposterously high, which was why he was prepared to cut Humml in on the deal. By investing the sum of forty-six thousand marks—the better part of his nest egg—Humml could secure a profit of six thousand marks within a matter of a few days.

"Stendal showed me a certificate from a reputable jeweler in Augsburg, so I thought the emeralds were genuine. After drawing the money out of my account, I was allowed to keep them as a surety."

Dietrich looked up from the notes he was taking. "What did you do with the gems?" he asked.

"I deposited them in the bank for safekeeping."

"And then what happened?"

"I was introduced to Herr Peter Baldau, who was undergoing treatment in the Rechts der Isar Clinic. Stendal told me he was a wealthy businessman, and I believed him. I mean, you could tell Baldau was rich just by his appearance and manner. I thought he was going to buy the stones for himself, but it turned out that Baldau wanted me and Stendal to become his partners in a much larger deal. Apparently he already had a quantity of gems, which together with the emeralds we possessed were just what his client was looking for. He led me to understand that if I went in with him, I could expect to make a much higher profit on my money than Stendal had indicated. Of course, I would have to put up another twenty thousand marks." Humml sucked on his teeth. "I was a bit dubious about that, since it was almost all I had left, but when Baldau suggested we arrange for a lawyer to draw up a formal contract, that sort of clinched it for me."

Humml didn't know any lawyers, but Dietrich wasn't surprised to hear that Baldau did. On May 11 they met an attorney, Dr. Fischau, and signed a contract he had drawn up. A few days later the con man said that in addition to the twenty thousand marks—and the emeralds—he needed another thirty thousand marks in order to complete the deal.

"It was all very complicated, Sergeant." Humml sighed. "I told Herr Baldau that all my savings were gone, and he said why didn't I raise the money elsewhere?"

Dietrich could imagine how Humml must have felt. The tobacconist had already invested sixty-six thousand, he no longer had the emeralds, and the contract he'd signed covered only the last payment of twenty thousand marks.

"I suppose I must have looked a bit shaken by that suggestion, because Baldau then offered to give me a mortgage deed on a piece of land worth a hundred and sixty thousand marks. He said that would more than cover me, and that Dr. Fischau would handle the necessary transaction on his behalf."

"And on the strength of that assurance, you asked your friend to lend you the money?"

Humml nodded. "She transferred twenty-eight thousand marks to my account, which was all she could afford. This was less than Baldau had asked for, but he didn't quibble about it, and on May twenty-first Dr. Fischau accompanied me to the bank, and I drew it all out."

Humml believed that the deal would now go ahead, but as the days went by with no word from Baldau, he became increasingly worried. Finally, in desperation, he went to the clinic to have it out with him. "They told me that Baldau had left on June seventh. Nobody seemed to know where he had gone, but one of the porters hinted that the police were looking for him. That's why I came to see you, Sergeant."

Dietrich smiled sympathetically. "Have you seen Steinhardt, Stendal or Begovich recently?" he asked.

Humml shook his head.

"Do you know where they live?"

"No. I only wish I did," Humml said in a voice that was little more than a whisper.

"All right, let's try another tack," said Dietrich. "Can you describe them to me?"

Humml was a little vague about Stendal, but he was on much firmer ground regarding the other two. Steinhardt, he said, was in his late forties or early fifties and had darkish brown curly hair that was receding from his forehead. His face was craggy, and there were two parallel creases on the right side of his mouth that were very noticeable whenever he smiled. Charly Begovich resembled Baldau, though he appeared much younger. He was very good-looking and had dark hair and long sideburns. Always stylishly dressed, he reminded Humml of a mischievous schoolboy.

"You couldn't help liking him, Sergeant. He and Baldau are two of a kind."

"I can believe that," said Dietrich.

"Do you think there's any chance I'll get my money back?"

Dietrich doubted it. Certainly Humml could say good-by to the first payment of forty-six thousand marks. Without the emeralds, which were probably worth next to nothing anyway, there was no proof of fraud. It was just his word against Stendal's, Steinhardt's and Begovich's that any money had changed hands.

"This mortgage deed," he said. "Is it still in your possession?"

"Yes. I can go and fetch it if you like."

"I'd be grateful if you would." Dietrich stood up. "In the meantime, I'll arrange to have your statement typed, so that it's ready for your signature when you return."

Although he was prepared to bet that the mortgage deed was a forgery, Dietrich thought it best not to say so. The truth would come out sooner or later, and for the moment Humml had enough worries on his mind. Urging him to bring the deed as quickly as he could, the detective escorted the man out of the building and then left the statement with the typing pool.

Eventually, when Dietrich returned to his office, he found that he had another visitor, Sergeant Zwick.

"What brings you here?" he said. "As if I didn't know."

"I've been looking at your portrait gallery, Karl. And I don't see Kristin Kohler among the talent on view."

"Kristin Kohler?" Dietrich shook his head. "The name doesn't ring a bell."

"According to my informant, she's Baldau's latest girl friend."
Zwick grinned. "He says they're in Italy, staying at the Hotel Moresco on the island of Ischia."

"Does Interpol know this?"

"They do now. I sent them a Telex five minutes ago."

"That makes it three in a row," said Dietrich. "Wiesbaden is going to love us."

KRISTIN KOHLER HAD to admit that life was never dull with Peter Baldau. It was just as well that she liked traveling, because since leaving Munich they'd never stayed long enough in one place for her to become bored with the surroundings. In a few short weeks they had been to the Netherlands, England and Italy, and now they were in London again, staying at the Cumberland Hotel.

New places, new faces. Fritz Seifert had been a new face as far as she was concerned, but not to Peter. He and Fritz had worked together before; that much had become very clear over lunch in the Grill Room and during the business discussion in their suite afterward. Much of their talk had been way over her head, and quickly losing interest, she'd picked up a magazine and wandered into the bedroom. About an hour later Peter had called her back to sign a number of papers, which he'd then handed over to Seifert. Now, long after Fritz Seifert had departed, she was still waiting to hear why her signature had been required and just why she'd had to forge a man's name.

"I think you owe me an explanation," Kristin said presently.

"What about?" Baldau propped himself up on one elbow and stared at her from the sofa, where he was lying stretched out.

"Those papers you asked me to sign."

"Ah, yes—the securities." Baldau smiled and sat up. "Well, if you come over here, I'll tell you all about them."

Kristin shrugged. There were times when Peter could be very exasperating, but she did as he asked. Leaving her chair, she walked across the room, kicked off her high-heeled shoes and sat down on the sofa beside him. "All right," she said. "I'm listening."

"What do you want to know?"

"Who is Dr. Samuel Dickinson?"

"I haven't the faintest idea," said Baldau. "Dickinson is just a name I picked out of the telephone directory and liked the sound of. I also thought it was the kind of name you'd expect to see on a batch of American securities. I made him a doctor because that always impresses the sort of people we do business with. If Fritz plays his cards right, he could make a small fortune with those papers. They're worth more than two hundred thousand marks."

"Two hundred thousand!" Kristin shook her head in disbelief. "And you gave them to Seifert? I don't understand you, Peter."

"It's really very simple. Fritz asked me to help him raise some funds, and since I owed him a favor, I gave him the bonds I'd obtained from John Bormaster. You remember John?"

Kristin nodded. She wouldn't forget that man in a hurry. Born in Czechoslovakia, he had changed his name from Jan Borgmeister to John Bormaster when he became a naturalized American. At five feet six, he was a good nine inches shorter than Peter and was very thickset, with a large double chin that folded over his shirt collar. She also recalled that he had brown eyes and that his brown hair had retreated a long way from his forehead. He saw himself as one of the jet set and claimed to be fluent in Czech, Hungarian, Yiddish, French, German and Spanish, but for all his expensive, made-to-order suits, Kristin thought Bormaster was just another fat man who perspired a great deal.

"Anyway, I don't see what you're so worried about," said Baldau. "Fritz will give me a share of the proceeds."

"How can you be sure of that?" she asked.

"Because we're partners. Together with Charly Begovich and John Bormaster, he helped me to put one over on Florian Brucker."

"Who's he?"

"A master butcher and owner of a retail store in Villingen. He's also a manufacturer and a very rich man. If there's one thing I've learned about the rich, it's that they always want more. So when I heard that Brucker was interested in gold, I phoned him on the pretext of ordering some Christmas food baskets. This was in September of 1972, and because my appeal had been rejected and the police were looking for me in Germany, I asked Charly and Fritz to handle the preliminary negotiations while I stayed in Rome."

On his instructions, Begovich and Seifert had arranged to meet Florian Brucker at the Sheraton Hotel in Munich, where, over drinks, they explained to him just how it was possible to buy a large quantity of gold at a bargain price. The gold, Begovich said, had been received by a consortium of European arms dealers who had sold weapons and ammunition to dissident groups in the Congo, Namibia, Angola and Mozambique. As a man of the world, Herr Brucker would appreciate that such a large-scale operation would have been impossible without the connivance of senior officials in the customs departments of Italy, France, Switzerland and West Germany. Naturally, Charly Begovich explained, these civil servants expected to be rewarded for their cooperation, but gold was of no use to them. They could scarcely deposit the ingots in a bank, and if they tried to sell the bars to a dealer, they would soon find themselves in trouble. Hence it was necessary to convert the bullion into paper currency in a way that would not upset the equilibrium of the market. Begovich and Seifert then produced several genuine ingots, which they claimed to have purchased from Peter Baldau, a reputable financier based in Rome, whom the consortium had asked to act as intermediary. If Brucker was interested in acquiring some of the gold, he would have to go to Rome to sign a contract, drawn up by the lawyer of his choice.

"I knew that would do the trick," said Baldau. "Once Florian Brucker learned that his own attorney would be allowed to draw up the necessary papers, he couldn't get to Rome fast enough. After preliminary discussions at my apartment, Brucker introduced me to his lawyer and economic adviser, a man called Nussbaum, whom Brucker knew from previous business in Rome. I gathered that Nussbaum had conducted a number of transactions for him in the past, and it soon became obvious that Florian had a lot of faith in his judgment. Nussbaum inserted all kinds of stipulations into the contract, but none of his conditions bothered me one bit. At the end of the day Brucker had agreed to pay me one hundred and ninety thousand deutsche marks for fifty kilograms of gold, and my only problem was how to separate him from his money without delivering a single ingot."

In due course, Florian Brucker was informed that the money would have to be paid in advance. Of course, it was accepted that Herr Brucker would be reluctant to part with such a large sum of money unless he received some tangible asset in return. The asset

Baldau had in mind was a collection of emeralds whose value he alleged was far in excess of a hundred and ninety thousand marks.

"In fact," he continued, "the gems were of no intrinsic value, but Brucker was not to know that. I picked the largest bank in Rome and arranged for Fritz and Charly to bring him there one afternoon so he could examine the stones for himself. Although I managed to create the impression that the four bags of emeralds had been kept in a large safe-deposit box in the vault, the man who really stole the show was John Bormaster. You should have seen the way he passed himself off as an expert employee of the bank. I swear, he almost convinced me the emeralds were genuine by the time he finished examining them. Not only did John confirm that the stones were worth far more than a hundred and ninety thousand marks, but he also offered to buy the whole lot on behalf of the bank. Right on cue, Charly then said he would like to participate in the gold deal and was prepared to advance a similar amount of money."

The transaction was completed the next day in Nussbaum's office, Brucker handing over one hundred and ninety thousand marks in cash in exchange for two bags of worthless emeralds. With an absolute poker face, Begovich then gave Baldau sixty thousand marks plus a check for his share of the emeralds.

Baldau laughed. "The check would have bounced higher than a rubber ball, and I tore it up after we left the office. I also gave the sixty thousand back to Charly, because I figured he'd earned it. It was all a bit of a joke really. Charly didn't have a bean to his name, and I'd given him the sixty thousand in the first place so he could participate in the deal."

"And the other two men?" Kristin said quietly. "What did they get out of it?"

"Fritz and John got twenty thousand apiece, fifteen thousand went to the man who'd supplied the emeralds and I kept the rest." Baldau laughed again.

"It's just a game to you, isn't it?" Kristin said.

A game? Baldau frowned. It wasn't a game when two men broke into your apartment and roughed you up because you wanted out. It wasn't a game when you were attacked a second time and stabbed in the thigh with a spike to persuade you to think again.

"A game?" he echoed. "You don't know the half of it."

CHAPTER 3

F. J. HALDER, THE MANAGER in charge of loans and securities at the Commerzbank branch in Frankfurt, was in his early thirties but looked older. Everything about him was conservative, from his neat hairstyle and rimless glasses to the dark gray suit and knitted tie he was wearing. Standing aside respectfully while Commissioner Hauptmann shook Halder's hand, Sergeant Dietrich saw him as a typical banker, a man who was cool and efficient and no doubt very discreet. It was also apparent that Halder had an orderly mind. You could tell that from the state of his desk. Everything was in its place: the blotter exactly in the center, directly behind the penholder, the filing trays positioned within easy reach, the "in" to his left, the "pending" and "out" on the right. Beyond the farthest tray, a single rosebud, not yet opened, stood erect in a small crystal vase.

Hauptmann said, "It's good of you to see us on such short notice."

"Not at all, Commissioner." Halder waved a well-manicured hand toward the two tubular steel chairs that sat side by side in front of his desk. "I'm only too glad to be of assistance to the police."

"Good. Well, perhaps you'd like to take a look at this photograph and tell us if it's the same man who came to see you on Friday, August twenty-fourth?" Hauptmann extracted a print from the envelope he was carrying, placed it on the manager's desk and then sat down, crossing his feet at the ankles.

"Yes, that's definitely Fritz Seifert," Halder said instantly, "but it's hardly a flattering likeness."

"Mug shots rarely are. This one was taken some years ago by the Swiss police."

"He has a criminal record, then?"

"He's served a term of imprisonment," Hauptmann said, his voice noncommittal.

Halder glanced at the photograph again. "I see that his full name is Fritz Rudolf Seifert."

"Yes. I daresay Seifert would have preferred to use an alias, but I imagine you asked for proof of identity."

Halder nodded. "I certainly did, Commissioner. Nobody can walk into the Commerzbank and obtain a loan just like that. We have to know whom we are dealing with. However, I must admit that Seifert did come within a whisker of fooling me."

The appointment had been made on the telephone, Seifert calling Halder from the Hotel Hessischer Hof in Frankfurt. The matter that Seifert wanted to discuss was of a confidential nature, but he'd led Halder to believe he was in the retail electrical trade and was thinking of opening a local branch.

"He was a great name-dropper, Commissioner. Even as we shook hands, he told me that he was a close friend of Ernst Oetiker, the Swiss industrialist. No doubt this was intended to impress me, as were the other names Seifert reeled off. I must have looked a bit skeptical, because all of a sudden Seifert opened his briefcase and produced a number of invoices and a real estate brochure. The invoices indicated he had a thriving business, while the brochure contained details of a desirable property in the center of town, which he wished to acquire. During our conversation Seifert intimated he would be opening an account with the Commerzbank, provided we would be prepared to extend him a loan of some two hundred and twenty thousand marks. Without committing the bank in any way, I then asked him what sort of collateral he had in mind."

It transpired that Seifert possessed a number of American bonds worth well in excess of two hundred thousand deutsche marks. The securities, nineteen in all, had been issued by Pan American Airways, IBM, Anaconda and Pizza Hut.

"That more than covered the loan he was asking for, didn't it?" Dietrich said.

"Yes, it did, but I had no reason to be suspicious of Seifert at that stage. All securities fluctuate in value, according to the state of the market, and as a businessman, Seifert would know that we would take this factor into account when he offered them as collateral."

"So what did make you suspicious, Herr Halder?"

"The bonds. Oh, they were genuine all right, but when I examined them more closely, I saw that they had all been endorsed by a Dr. Samuel Dickinson. As you might suppose, this aroused my curiosity, and I thought it advisable to ask a number of pertinent questions. Among other things, I wanted to know how the bonds came to be in his possession."

Seifert told him that Dr. Dickinson was an American businessman whom he'd met in London through a mutual acquaintance. Dickinson was convinced that nothing the United States government did would ease the pressure on the dollar, so he was keen to invest some of his money abroad, particularly in Germany. Since Seifert was seeking to expand his business, the two men had readily agreed to form a partnership.

"At least, that was the story Seifert gave me." Halder smiled fleetingly. "And it sounded totally convincing. What I mean is that I could understand Dickinson's anxiety about the American economy. The Americans have an alarming trade deficit, and their domestic inflation is at an all-time high. Anyway, up to that point, Seifert seemed a pretty good risk from the bank's point of view, but when I asked to see a copy of the agreement he must have signed with Dr. Dickinson, I could tell from his blank expression that no such document existed."

Seifert had tried to talk his way out of it. Their lawyers were still drawing up the necessary papers, he said, but if it would set Herr Halder's mind at ease, he would telephone Dr. Dickinson, who was staying at the Cumberland Hotel in London, and ask him to confirm that they had formed a partnership.

"I said that a letter from Dr. Dickinson would certainly help expedite matters," Halder continued. "In the meantime, I would ask my superiors to approve the loan in principle. Naturally they would want to see the bonds, and I assumed there would be no objection if I retained them for the time being. I could see Seifert didn't like the idea, but he could hardly refuse my request."

Promising to give Seifert a definite answer by the following Monday, Halder then ran a check on the bonds. Within a matter of hours he discovered that the Pan Am securities had been stolen on November 29, 1972, from a home in Long Island City, New York. Once that piece of information came to light, he wasn't surprised to learn that the rest of the bonds also had been stolen from various addresses in and around New York City. Guessing that Seifert was unlikely to return to the bank on Monday as they'd arranged, he immediately got in touch with the police.

"I presume you know the rest?" said Halder.

Hauptmann nodded. Although the local police had acted quickly, Seifert had checked out of the Hessischer Hof before they arrived.

The commissioner and Sergeant Dietrich were here now because the Frankfurt police automatically had sent an urgent message to Wiesbaden, and Interpol had advised Helmut Bauer, knowing that Fritz Seifert was one of Baldau's associates.

"Is there anything else I can tell you, Commissioner?" Halder inquired politely.

"I don't think so." Hauptmann stood up and shook hands with Halder. "Thank you for being so helpful."

Dietrich thanked him too and then followed the commissioner out to the street. Their car was parked by the entrance, baking under the heat from the sun. Already sweating in the oppressive weather, Dietrich unlocked the door for Hauptmann, then walked around the BMW and got in behind the wheel. As he'd expected, the interior was like the inside of a furnace.

"I wish this car had air conditioning," he grumbled.

"You'll cool off once we get moving on the autobahn." Hauptmann wound his window down and angled one of the air vents in the dashboard toward him. "Mind you, we'll have to stop off at police headquarters first so I can send a Telex to Wiesbaden. You know something, Sergeant?" He turned to Dietrich, smiling. "I have a hunch that Dr. Samuel Dickinson is none other than our old friend Peter Baldau. In fact, I'd be willing to stake my pension that we'll find he's the one staying at the Cumberland Hotel in London. Seifert made a real slip when he dropped that. Trying to raise a loan on those securities was another mistake."

"That's putting it mildly." Dietrich glanced into the rearview mirror and then pulled out from the curb. "Seifert must have known they were stolen."

"Exactly," said Hauptmann. "Baldau must be losing his touch if he seriously believed they could get away with a stunt like that."

FROM THE WATERFRONT at Como, Baldau could just make out the Villa d'Este at Cernobbio. The Villa d'Este had a reputation for being one of the most luxurious hotels in Europe, a haven for the rich, beautiful people of the international jet set and a landmark for the pleasure boats that cruised up and down Lake Como. The Villa d'Este was Baldau's kind of place—elegant, fashionable and very exclusive. He wished there were more hotels like it, with its narrow private road, the armed guard at the gate and the spacious forecourt in front of the main entrance. The imposing lobby, the restaurants, the terrace and the lido—they were all part of a very private world inhabited by the wealthy and successful, whom he both envied and admired.

Baldau walked on past the marina filled with pleasure craft and turned into the park, the Villa d'Este gradually disappearing from view behind the trees. The wealthy and successful: Why should he admire their kind when many of them were no better than he and just as crooked? Some were so gullible, too, that fleecing them was like stealing pennies from blind men. Ernst Oetiker fell into that category.

Baldau sat down on a bench facing the lake. He ought not be contemptuous of Ernst; after all, he was a steady source of income. Still, the family was watching him with increasing suspicion. When they'd met yesterday, Oetiker's brother-in-law, Dr. Zuber, had been there to hold the old man's hand. Just what Zuber had made of their conversation was anybody's guess, but Baldau imagined that Ernst must have had a difficult time back in Switzerland explaining to Zuber why Baldau, his friend and business associate, was using an assumed name at the hotel where he was staying. No doubt the industrialist had also been hard pressed to explain the significance of the two checks he'd been asked to endorse.

Oetiker had made the journey to Como at Baldau's request, perhaps half believing the story that he really did want to settle up with him. At any rate, Ernst had listened attentively to what he'd had to say and the two checks had certainly impressed him. Supposedly issued by the Canadian Imperial Bank of Commerce, Montreal, and drawn on the Hong Kong–Shanghai Bankers Corporation in favor of Peter Baldau, they totaled more than six hundred thousand marks. Baldau also convinced Oetiker that he would furnish shares worth an additional two and a half million marks, so the old man had meekly handed over forty thousand Swiss francs against delivery of the checks. Any notion that Oetiker would be allowed to keep them after they'd been endorsed had been swiftly dispelled. "The checks will have to be channeled through a central clearing bank," Baldau had told him glibly, but had added that naturally the money would be transferred to Oetiker's account within a day or two. He had then sent him on his way empty-handed and somewhat poorer.

From the look in his eye, it had been apparent that Dr. Zuber suspected his brother-in-law had seen the last of the two checks, and of course he was right. They had been forged by John Bormaster with all the skill of a master craftsman, but Baldau was only too aware that if they fell into the wrong hands, those two scraps of paper could put him away for years.

A shadow fell across Baldau's feet, and looking up, he saw Kristin standing beside him. "Oh, hello," he said casually. "I thought you were going to have your hair done."

"I was," she said, "but in the end, I decided it was too hot to sit under a dryer." Kristin sat down beside him and stretched out her legs. "Why didn't you tell me where you were going? I've been looking for you everywhere."

"Did you go to the bank?" he asked, neatly sidestepping Kristin's accusation.

"Yes." Opening her handbag, she showed him a wad of notes tucked inside her passport. "I changed five thousand."

Baldau fingered the heat rash that had developed under his chin. "Fritz Seifert called me on the telephone after you'd left the hotel," he said idly. "He suggested it could be to our mutual advantage if I met a man called Rudolf Huber."

"I hope you told him what to do with his suggestion," Kristin said tersely. "I wonder he had the nerve to contact you after that fiasco with the Commerzbank in Frankfurt."

"That wasn't entirely his fault."

"Like hell it wasn't," Kristin said. "He lied to you, Peter. Fritz didn't have a client; that was just an excuse to get his hands on those bonds."

She didn't know what she was talking about, Baldau told her. If anyone had lied, it was Marcus Vogt, the financial consultant who'd convinced Fritz that he had lined up a client for him; Vogt may have misled him deliberately. Some years back, he had been the victim of a swindle engineered by Charly Begovich and Fritz Seifert, and despite the fact that since then he had participated in several fraudulent deals with Seifert and had been compensated for his losses, it was conceivable that Vogt had decided to settle an old score.

"Fritz is all right," Baldau added. "He warned us in good time, didn't he? Besides, he's put me in touch with quite a number of wealthy people in the past."

"And just what does that mean?" Kristin asked.

"It means I'm thinking of going to Paris," said Baldau. "I have a feeling that Rudolf Huber can put a lot of money our way."

CHAPTER 4

RUDOLF HUBER WAS a business manager, financial adviser and fund raiser all rolled into one. Based in Switzerland, he was also the general agent for Dr. Rosa Müller, whose ambitious plans to establish a foundation and build a clinic to care for the old and the sick were still very much on the drawing board. From the thumbnail sketch Fritz Seifert had given him before they met for lunch, Baldau knew that Rosa Müller had implicit faith in Huber, believing him to be a shrewd judge of character. Thanks to Seifert, who had softened him up, Huber had come to Paris under the illusion that Baldau, a financial broker with an international reputation, might be prepared to help him finance the Müller foundation.

In keeping with his new role, Baldau had changed his name to Peter Kohler and had checked into the Hotel Lotti in the rue de Castiglione just off the Place Vendôme. The hotel had impressed Huber, and lunch at Delmonico's in the Avenue de l'Opéra had helped put him in a very receptive mood. Biding his time, Baldau waited until they were having coffee and brandy before he attempted to sound Huber out.

"Fritz tells me you and Dr. Müller are hoping to build some sort of clinic for the sick and elderly." Baldau smiled sympathetically. "I'm sure that's a most worthy project."

"We think so, Herr Kohler," Huber said cautiously. "Unfortunately it appears not everybody agrees with us."

"I did hear rumors you're finding it difficult to raise a loan."

Huber snorted. "That's putting it mildly. Every bank we've approached has put obstacles in our way. I suppose they feel the clinic will not be a sound investment."

"Because you don't have sufficient collateral?" Baldau suggested.

"Far from it. Dr. Müller owns the plot of land on which the clinic is to be built."

"Then I don't see why you have a problem. I should think any bank would regard the lady as a good risk."

"It was the conditions they wanted to impose, Peter." Seifert contrived to appear indignant. "Dr. Müller found them quite unacceptable. Isn't that so, Rudolf?"

Huber nodded. "Rosa felt that if she accepted their conditions for a loan, she would virtually surrender control of the foundation."

"You mean the banks were insisting the clinic be run on commercial lines?" Baldau reached for his glass of brandy. "I wouldn't say that was an unreasonable demand."

"I don't think you've fully understood the purpose of the foundation," Huber said loftily. "You see, Rosa plans to charge her patients according to their means. Naturally it is not her intention to run the place at a loss, but no one who is sick or too elderly and infirm to look after themselves will be turned away simply because they can't afford the terms."

"That's a very laudable sentiment, but it's hardly likely to attract many investors." Baldau pursed his lips. "In your shoes, I'd advise Dr. Müller to swallow her pride and accept the bank's conditions."

"Now just a minute, Peter." Seifert jabbed the air with his cigar as if it were a pointer. "What's this talk of going to the bank again? I persuaded Rudolf to come to Paris because I understood you might be prepared to assist him."

"I'm trying to," Baldau said patiently.

"With advice?" Seifert looked disgusted. "Rudolf can get plenty of that back home in Switzerland."

"I think Herr Kohler wants to suggest that the money market is not a charitable institution." Huber smiled wryly. "The trouble is we can't afford to have a millstone around our necks."

Baldau studied him thoughtfully. Their conversation so far was not unlike a game of poker, but with one subtle difference. Huber might think he was holding his cards close to his chest, but he'd already disclosed his hand. If there had been the slightest chance of raising the money from some other source, he would never have come to Paris. Huber had also unwittingly confirmed that Seifert had discovered another wealthy victim.

"It won't be easy to float a loan," Baldau said amiably. "As I said before, your foundation is not an attractive investment." He finished the rest of his brandy and placed the glass to one side. "However, I think I know a way to get around the problem."

"You do?"

The eager tone of his voice was all the proof Baldau needed of Huber's willingness to clutch at any straw.

"It just so happens that I have some shares in Mercedes, Volkswagen and Siemens on which I could raise eight hundred thousand marks," Baldau said. "That's about a million Swiss francs at the current rate of exchange."

"I must say that's very generous of you, Herr Kohler, but how do we raise the rest of the money? We'll need more than that."

"It's a matter of confidence," Baldau said airily. "Once my contacts in the business world learn that I have put one million francs into your clinic, I've no doubt they'll be only too anxious to come in on the deal."

"You see," Seifert said triumphantly. "I told you Peter wouldn't let us down."

"Of course, you do realize that raising the loan will entail a small bank charge?"

"That's understood." Huber nodded. "Dr. Müller and I wouldn't expect you to be out of pocket in this matter."

"Yes, indeed." Seifert clucked his tongue. "Can you give us an estimate, Peter?"

"Oh, I should think the bank will charge me about ten thousand Swiss francs."

Seifert turned to Huber. "What do you say, Rudolf?"

"Well, of course I shall have to consult my client, but I'm sure she won't object."

"Good," said Baldau. "Now, if we're going to float a loan, I think Dr. Müller ought to be present at our next meeting, otherwise we'll waste a lot of time." Reaching inside his jacket, he produced a slim pocket diary. The pages for September and October were completely blank, but Huber would never have guessed that from the way Baldau acted. "I see I'm due in Amsterdam on October fifth, so it will have to be before then. I can manage Monday, the first. How does that suit you?"

"I'm free, but I can't vouch for Dr. Müller. However, I'm sure she will cancel any appointments she may have."

"How about you, Fritz?"

"Monday is all right with me," said Seifert.

"That's settled, then," said Baldau. "Shall we say two thirty at the Hotel Lotti?"

He would have to tell Kristin to make herself scarce that afternoon. She was fun to have around, but there was a distinct possibility that Dr. Müller might think her just a shade too glamorous to be the wife of a high-powered financier. In Baldau's considerable experience with women, they were usually very good at sizing one another up, and he couldn't afford to take any chances.

BY THE END OF September, the Baldau investigation had become a tedious and frustrating business for the seven police officers of the special commission. Tedious because each new fraud case that came to light was virtually a repeat performance of the one before; frustrating because their quarry always seemed to be one jump ahead of them. Wöbking and Bauer sometimes wondered if the circumstances would ever change.

"Up to now, there has been no lack of information concerning his movements, Herr Wöbking." Despite all the setbacks and disappointments, Bauer managed a philosophical smile for the public prosecutor. "Unfortunately either the tip has been way out of date by the time we've received it, or else it has been shown to be wholly false. For example, on September seventh we were told that he had been seen in Marbella and was thought to be staying at the Hotel Melia Don Pepe, but when the Spanish police checked it out, they drew a complete blank, which is hardly surprising considering that he was back in London around then."

"That's news to me," said Wöbking.

"We've only just heard about it ourselves. Apparently Oetiker has been seeing Baldau on and off since he walked out of the Rechts der Isar Clinic. They met in Como and then again at Heathrow airport on September fifth, when Oetiker was accompanied by his lawyer, Gross. As you might guess, Baldau was up to his old tricks, but for once he was out of luck. Gross wouldn't allow Oetiker to part with any of his money."

According to the deposition Gross had made to the Swiss authorities, Baldau had tried to offer his client shares in the American Baptist Foundation, which he claimed were worth more than two and a half million marks. Although these shares represented only a fraction of what he owed his old friend, Baldau wanted him to know that he was in the process of buying back certain bills of exchange, amounting to nine hundred and ten thousand marks, which Ernst had given him at one time or another in the distant past. He was purchasing them at a knockdown price, but he needed another hundred thousand in order to clinch the deal.

"That was enough for Gross," said Bauer. "He told Baldau exactly what he could do with the shares. But what's really important to us is the fact that the Oetiker family is taking steps to have the old man placed under the guardianship of the law. He won't be allowed to sign checks or issue bills of exchange, and that's bad news for Baldau; it means he's lost his main source of income."

Wöbking was not impressed with that news. He thought it wouldn't be long before Baldau found another victim, since he had a small army of talent scouts working for him; men like Karl-Heinz Branig, an office manager in a Swiss finance and loan company, who had passed Oetiker's bills of exchange through the firm, and Peter Jonas, an art dealer who had sold a number of forged masterpieces to the industrialist before he introduced him to Baldau. And then there were Horst Steinhardt and Charly Begovich.

"How many accomplices do you suppose he has?" Wöbking said, voicing his thoughts aloud.

"Twenty-five according to our latest count." Bauer grimaced. "And that's not including what I call the one-time helpers."

The one-time helpers were former victims who introduced well-heeled acquaintances to the con man in the hope of recouping some of their losses. It was through one of these people that Baldau had met Egon Swoboda, a stamp dealer from Winterthur, Switzerland. Swoboda had traveled to Munich on June 14, 1972, and, after being wined and dined, had been shown the usual specimen gold ingots, which on this occasion had been furnished by Karl-Heinz Branig. The following day Swoboda had gone to Steinhardt's office at the fraudulent finance and trust company, where he had signed a contract to buy two hundred kilograms of gold.

Swoboda had then been whisked off to the Deutsche Bank to cash a certified check for two hundred thousand marks before being driven out to the airport, ostensibly to see the initial consignment of one hundred kilograms loaded onto one of the regular flights to Zurich. Karl-Heinz Branig had joined Baldau and Swoboda at the bank and had accompanied them to the airport. When they arrived, the two men persuaded Swoboda to leave the envelope containing the money in the car. Baldau had taken Swoboda into the terminal, had purchased a ticket for him and had then managed to lose him in the freight area.

Branig and Steinhardt were still at liberty, because following his arrest at the Munich beer hall in December 1972, Baldau had repaid Swoboda in full. As the police were beginning to discover, he often reimbursed one victim at the expense of another in order to stave off the threat of prosecution.

"Twenty-five known accomplices." Bauer struck the palm of his left hand with a clenched fist. "If only we had enough evidence to charge either Branig or Steinhardt, it would put the heat on the others. But right now we're just marking time."

"If we keep plugging away, we're bound to get a break sooner or later."

"We can certainly use one," Bauer said grimly.

BALDAU WAS CERTAIN that Rosa Müller would be no match for him. He'd already fooled Rudolf Huber, and if her general agent was convinced that he was an important financial broker, it stood to reason the good lady doctor would also believe it. Over drinks in his hotel suite, Baldau spoke of the inflationary effects of a too liberal money supply and was rewarded with a blank look of incomprehension. The longer he dwelt on the subjects of macroeconomics and microeconomics, the clearer it became that she had no idea what he was talking about. Huber was nodding sagely, but it was evident that he was equally mystified.

"Well now," Baldau said briskly, "let's get down to business. I presume Herr Huber has told you all about the shares I'm prepared to place at your disposal?"

"Yes. I must say it's very kind of you to go to so much trouble on my behalf." Looking somewhat flustered, Dr. Müller opened her handbag and produced a checkbook. "I understand that the bank charge will be ten thousand francs."

"Actually that's too much." Baldau smiled. "I learned from the bank that the exact charge will be nine thousand six hundred. But there's really no hurry for your check."

It was the sprat to catch a mackerel. Before he was through with her, Dr. Müller would lose a small fortune.

"When we met the other day, Peter, you said something about floating a loan." Fritz Seifert leaned forward to stub out his cigarette in the ashtray on the occasional table between them. "I wonder if you've given the matter any further thought?"

"I've spoken to one or two speculators." Baldau frowned. "Unfortunately they weren't interested."

"It's just as you thought, then." Seifert turned to Huber. "If you remember, Rudolf, Herr Kohler did warn us that the clinic was unlikely to be an attractive investment."

"Yes, he did." Huber cleared his throat. "Nevertheless, it's a great disappointment. To be frank, I don't know where we go from here."

It was going better than Baldau had dared hope. Although Seifert had steered the conversation in a prearranged direction, it was Huber who had provided him with the opening he needed.

"Well, cheer up," Baldau said. "Apart from the shares, I can let you have another two million Swiss francs in cash."

"Why, that's marvelous!" Dr. Müller clapped her hands and beamed. "You've solved all my problems, Herr Kohler."

Baldau stared up at the ceiling, unable to meet her excited gaze for fear he would burst out laughing. He had solved all her problems, had he? Well, that was pretty rich. If only she knew—they were just beginning!

"That's the good news," he said smoothly. "Now for the bad. Much as it goes against the grain, I'm afraid I shall have to charge you interest on the shares. I think you'll agree that's only fair."

"And precisely what is the rate?" Huber asked quietly.

"As Fritz may have told you," Baldau said, "I play the stock market. The way things are, I could expect to make upwards of twenty percent this year."

"Twenty percent?" Huber gaped at him. "That's a bit steep, isn't it?"

"So I consider a hundred and ninety-two thousand francs a modest charge." Baldau shrugged. "However, if you think I'm being unreasonable, you're free to look elsewhere for a loan."

"Oh, come on, Peter, you know damn well Dr. Müller can't do that." Seifert glared at him, his eyes narrowing in feigned anger. "If I'd known you were going to drive such a hard bargain, I would never have recommended you to Rudolf."

"I don't think you quite understand the arrangement I have in mind." Baldau explained that the shares would be made available to Dr. Müller for a period of one year, with the option of a three-month extension. "In all honesty, Fritz, I don't think your friends will get a fairer deal from anybody else."

"Indeed not," admitted Seifert. "It's a very generous offer."

"Of course, you do understand that the hundred and ninety-two thousand will have to be paid in advance, don't you?" Baldau turned to Rosa Müller with an engaging smile.

"Yes—yes, I can see you'll need some sort of security." Her eyes were glazed, and it was obvious to Baldau that she was thoroughly confused.

"Can we have time to consider your proposition, Herr Kohler?" Huber stroked his chin and looked solemn. "There's a lot to be said in favor of your scheme, but I think we should weigh all the pros and cons before we decide."

"I think you're wise. Why don't we leave everything in abeyance until I return from Amsterdam?" Baldau consulted his pocket diary. "Unless anything crops up, I should be back in Paris on October twelfth. Will that be too soon for you?"

Huber moistened his lips. "Oh, I don't think we need that long," he said.

"Well, if that's the case," said Baldau, "may I suggest we meet again on Wednesday? In the meantime, I'll make arrangements to have those shares that we talked about—they're worth eight hundred thousand deutsche marks, you remember—available for you on October fifteenth."

Will you walk into my parlour? said the spider to the fly; and since she trusted him, Baldau knew Dr. Müller would do just that. When they met on October 3, he would persuade her to make out checks totaling six hundred thousand francs, on the ground that the bank had asked him for additional collateral before it would sanction the loan. He would also suggest that Huber should receive fifty thousand in the way of expenses. If friend Rudolf did have any misgivings about the deal, a substantial fee would undoubtedly allay his fears. Not for the first time, Baldau reckoned he'd missed his vocation; he should have been a psychologist.

CHAPTER 5

UNABLE TO FIND a parking place near the U-bahn—subway—station in Marienplatz, Sergeant Zwick finally left his car in Sparkassenstrasse and doubled back through the pouring rain. He had been looking forward to a quiet evening at home, but just as he was about to leave the office Max had telephoned, hinting it would be worth his while if they met at the usual place for a quiet talk, and would seven thirty be all right? From a personal standpoint, he thought Max could not have picked a more inconvenient time, but when a reliable informer asked for a meet, you didn't quibble about things like that.

At the U-bahn station, Zwick bought a ticket to Kieferngarten and went down to the platform, where Max was standing at the far end. A small, dapper-looking man, he was wearing a trilby with a feather in the hatband and carrying an umbrella. One of Munich's more successful petty crooks, Max had tried his hand at everything from pimping to obtaining money under false pretenses. As was their usual practice, both men ignored one another until the train drew into the station. Then they got into the same car. Even so, Max waited until they were two stops down the line from Marienplatz before he moved close to Zwick.

"I didn't like the look of him," he said in a low voice.

"Who?" asked Zwick.

"The guy who got out at Odeonsplatz. I thought he might be tailing you."

"You've got too vivid an imagination, Max—that's your trouble."

"Yes? Well, in my line of business you can't be too careful. Some people I know wouldn't think twice about breaking an arm or a leg. They didn't hesitate to give Baldau a going-over."

"When was this?" Zwick asked sharply.

"Oh, a couple of years back, when he was living in the Bogen-hausen district. They broke into the basement of his apartment building, switched off the electricity and then picked the lock on his door. It seems Baldau was still half asleep when they stormed into the bedroom and started to beat him up."

The attack on Baldau was news to Zwick, but the information was out of date, and it wouldn't help them trace him. If that was the best Max had to offer, he wished he'd gone on home.

"Listen," Zwick said irritably, "I've got better things to do than listen to ancient history. If you've got something to tell me, then tell me; otherwise, I'm getting off at the next station."

Max glanced around, his birdlike eyes darting nervously from one passenger to another. "The word is that Baldau has found himself a new gold mine," he muttered out of the corner of his mouth. "Some Swiss lady doctor who wants to build a clinic. I hear he's conducting the deal from Paris."

"Do we know where in Paris?"

"No, but you can bet he's staying at a luxury-class hotel."

Zwick wasn't sure how many luxury- and first-class hotels there were in Paris, but he supposed there couldn't be fewer than forty. On that basis, he thought, it would take the French police roughly ten days to check them out.

"I also hear that he's changed his name to Kohler."

"How very original of him," Zwick said acidly. "Kohler happens to be the surname of his latest girl friend."

"And good-looking she is too." Max described her contours with his hands and grinned. "One thing you can say for Peter, he always takes the pick of the bunch."

Zwick ignored the comment. Maybe Baldau hadn't been very original, but Kohler was not exactly an uncommon name, and that meant the French police would still have to visit every likely hotel, showing Baldau's photograph to the staff.

"Do you have anything else for me?" Zwick asked.

"Not at the moment. I'll be in touch if I hear anything."

"Right."

Max rose. "I'll get off at the next station, okay?"

"You do that," said Zwick.

IF ANYONE HAD ASKED BALDAU to describe Gustav Schlagmeir in a few words, jovial and distinguished were the two adjectives that would have most readily sprung to mind. With his chubby face and silver hair, Schlagmeir was the prototype of everyone's favorite uncle, the kind of warmhearted person who is instantly liked and trusted. It was because Baldau had such a high opinion of his talents that Schlagmeir was in London now, dining with him at Au Jardin des Gourmets in Greek Street.

"Why the five-star treatment, Peter?" Schlagmeir wiped his mouth on a napkin. "Or isn't this an opportune moment to ask?"

Baldau looked around the restaurant. The theater crowd had departed, and except for a young couple at the next table, they had the place pretty much to themselves.

"I shouldn't worry about those two," said Schlagmeir. "They're only interested in each other. Besides, I doubt if they can understand German. The English have a difficult enough time mastering their own complicated language."

"There's such a thing as being discreet," Baldau said in a low voice. He lifted the bottle of wine out of the ice bucket and refilled their glasses. "I need your help, Gustav."

"I didn't think you'd dragged me all the way from Munich just for the pleasure of my company," Schlagmeir said amiably. "Who is the pigeon this time?"

"Emil Huber."

"Dr. Müller's agent? I was under the impression that you'd already taken him to the cleaners."

"This is a different Huber."

"How confusing! Sometimes I find it difficult to keep up with you, Peter."

"That's understandable," Baldau said with a smile. "I'm a busy little bee."

"What does this Emil Huber do for a living?"

"He owns half a dozen companies in and around Frauenfeld and Zurich. He's also in debt up to his eyeballs."

"And he came to you for help?" Schlagmeir said, laughing.

"You haven't heard the best part of the joke yet. Fritz Seifert and I were recommended to him by Vitold Graz. Remember him?"

"I certainly do."

Vitold Graz was a victim of one of their early swindles and had been conned out of thirty thousand marks. Like a good many others, Graz had come to the conclusion that in order to recoup any of his losses, he'd better find Baldau another client to fleece.

"Well," said Baldau, "Graz told Huber I was on the board of an international finance company, and that if he wanted to raise a million francs on some mortgage bonds, I was the man to see."

Two free airline tickets for him and his wife finally persuaded Emil Huber that it would be worth his while to come to London on November 14. Fritz Seifert met the Hubers at Heathrow in a rented Rolls-Royce. As part of the red-carpet treatment, Seifert had booked them into a plush hotel within easy walking distance of the Athenaeum Court in Mayfair, where Baldau was staying under the name of Peter Kohler.

"Huber saw me the following morning," Baldau continued. "I examined his mortgage bonds as if they were gilt-edged securities. Eventually I said I was in a position to lend him two and a half million francs for a period of three years at seven and a half percent per annum. However, there were certain conditions. The money had been placed at my disposal by a certain Dr. Lempertz, a plastic surgeon whose clinics in France and West Germany had made him a multimillionaire, and it was my duty to safeguard his interests. I therefore asked Huber for two hundred and seventy-five thousand Swiss francs in advance."

The news that he was to pay an advance came as a blow to Emil Huber. He didn't see how he could raise anything like two hundred and seventy-five thousand francs. Close to despair, he caught the next flight back to Zurich.

"I immediately got in touch with Vitold Graz and told him to go to work on Huber," Baldau explained to Schlagmeir. "It occurred to me that our friend might be able to arrange a substantial overdraft with some obliging bank on the strength of the loan I'd promised him."

At his wit's end, Huber listened to Graz and, acting on his advice, approached the Amexco Bank in Basel. After some discussion, the bank agreed to lend him the two hundred and seventy-five thousand francs he'd asked for. However, there was one awkward proviso: Huber would not be allowed to withdraw any of the money until the loan he'd obtained from Herr Kohler had been transferred from London to Basel.

"It was the classic Catch-22 situation," said Baldau, "one that brought Huber hotfooting it to London with Vitold Graz and a guy called Haenger. I wasn't particularly happy about the way things were going either. Huber had got a loan, but it was conditional on his receiving two and a half million from me."

"Which you didn't have," Schlagmeir prompted.

"Of course I didn't. But we had to keep Huber dangling while I figured out some way to get our hands on the money. Thanks to Graz, who telephoned me the day before they left Zurich for London, I had time to organize a holding operation."

Anticipating that Huber wouldn't be satisfied unless he was given some proof the money was available, Baldau decided to call in John Bormaster. The part Bormaster was asked to play was a familiar one. When they had taken Florian Brucker for a ride with the worthless collection of emeralds, John had passed himself off as a bank employee. On this occasion, Baldau thought it would be more appropriate if he were introduced as a director of Barclays Bank.

"I chose the branch in St. James's Street," Baldau elaborated, "because it was so close to many of London's exclusive clubs, and I reckoned this would impress Emil. At the hotel, as soon as Huber demanded to see the money, I telephoned John, pretended I was speaking to his secretary and then, after a suitable pause, asked to see him at the bank. When we arrived, John was waiting for us in the main hall, and after greeting me profusely, he confirmed that Barclays had credited my account with the sterling equivalent of two and a half million Swiss francs. Unfortunately his word wasn't good enough for Haenger."

Determined to protect Huber's interests, Haenger insisted that Bormaster produce a bank statement so they could see the figures for themselves. The more Bormaster prevaricated, the more incensed and heated Haenger became, with the result that Baldau was forced to call the whole thing off.

"I could have cheerfully throttled the creep." Baldau scowled. "But, as it happens, Haenger did me a favor."

Huber returned to Switzerland that same afternoon. His financial problems in no way diminished, despite his friend's intervention, he clung obstinately to the belief that Herr Kohler would help him, provided he raised the cash advance. So he went to the Investment Bank in St. Gall.

"And would you believe it?" said Baldau. "They actually granted him a loan of two hundred and fifty thousand Swiss francs without attaching any conditions. Furthermore, this quarter of a million has now been transferred to a joint account that Fritz Seifert and I have opened with the head office of the Swiss Bank Corporation in Gresham Street."

"And where do I fit into the picture?" asked Schlagmeir.

"Huber is coming to London again on Monday, November twenty-sixth. I'd like you to put in an appearance as the celebrated Dr. Lempertz just to reassure him that the loan of two and a half million we promised him is okay."

"All right, Peter. How much do I get?"

"Six thousand."

"Pounds?"

"Francs," said Baldau.

"You've got to be joking." Schlagmeir threw his napkin down on the table and pushed his chair back. "I came here expecting to receive a slice of the cake, and you have the nerve to offer me a few crumbs. If that's the best you can do, forget it."

"Hear me out, Gustav—there's more to come." Baldau smiled knowingly. "The quarter of a million we've already got from Huber is merely the icing on the cake. To change the metaphor, I think Huber's looking for that pot of gold at the end of the rainbow, and no scheme is too preposterous for him. I can dream up one outlandish deal after another, and he'll buy it every time."

"Then you'd better think up a fresh story immediately."

Mulling it over, Baldau came to the conclusion that Schlagmeir was right. The present yarn was wearing a little thin, but up to now he'd only looked upon Huber as a short-term investment.

"We could double the loan to five million and draw up a formal contract," he suggested tentatively.

"That's one possibility, but we need a carrot, Peter. I can let you have some bills of exchange that are allegedly worth a cool two million deutsche marks."

"I like the word allegedly. I presume they're forgeries?"

"Let's say they wouldn't stand up under close examination. However, if Huber showed them to his friends, there's no doubt the bills would inspire a good deal of confidence. Moreover, there's a chance a small bank would extend him a loan."

Baldau's face lit up. Schlagmeir was erring on the side of caution. The smaller banks had a reputation for taking risks that the established houses wouldn't entertain for a minute.

"You know something, Gustav," he said happily. "I think you've just hit the jackpot."

"I'll drink to that," said Schlagmeir, and raised his glass.

CHAPTER 6

DESPITE THE FACT that Emil Huber had yet to receive any money from Herr Peter Kohler, he still had complete faith in him. Just as Baldau had prophesied, no deal was too preposterous for Huber to buy.

When the original loan he'd been promised didn't come through, Huber eagerly swallowed the story that Herr Kohler and Dr. Lempertz were now ready to lend him five million Swiss francs for a period of three years. The loan was to be paid in two installments: one million francs on January 8, 1974, the balance on January 28. The stipulation that he would be required to pay an advance fee didn't bother Huber one bit. With a written confirmation of the new loan from Kohler and Lempertz in his possession, Huber had returned to Switzerland on Monday, December 10, convinced that he would not find it difficult to raise the additional advance they'd demanded.

His euphoria had been partially dispelled by the Swiss Bank Corporation when the manager of the branch in Wil, from whom he'd hoped to obtain the loan, asked for a bank guarantee or some other surety. That little bombshell had been enough to send Huber scurrying back to London to see Herr Kohler. Responding to Huber's frantic telephone call, Baldau arranged for Fritz Seifert to pick him up at the airport in the rented Rolls-Royce and bring him straight to Chalfont House in Chesham Place, Belgravia.

As soon as they met, Baldau could tell at a glance that Huber was impressed by Peter Kohler's new luxury apartment; it was additional proof that Kohler was an extremely wealthy man.

"I trust you had a good flight?" Baldau said politely.

Huber nodded. "I can see why you moved out of the hotel," he said. "I imagine this place is much more private."

"Well, it was never my intention to stay at the Athenaeum Court permanently. I heard this apartment was coming on the market, so I grabbed it. One needs a base in London." Baldau waved him to a chair. "Now what can I get you to drink? Gin? Whiskey?"

Huber glanced at his wristwatch and frowned. "It's a little early in the day for me, but I could do with a small whiskey and soda." He smiled feebly. "Just to warm the blood."

And steady your nerves, Baldau thought. "How about you, Fritz?"

"I'd like the same," said Seifert.

"This bank manager in Wil is being remarkably stuffy," Baldau said casually. "Isn't our written confirmation good enough for him?"

Huber accepted the whiskey and soda. "He said it wasn't a realizable asset, that he couldn't give me the loan I needed unless he was satisfied the bank was adequately covered."

"Ah, bankers," Baldau said briskly as he sat down. "Well, we are more flexible than the banks. I looked into your affairs and decided you were a good risk. However, as I've said many times before, it's my duty to protect Dr. Lempertz's interests. After all, he is the man who is providing the lion's share of the loan."

The downcast expression on Huber's face showed that he'd understood the inference. No advance, no five-million-franc loan. "If you gentlemen could just give me some positive guarantee for the bank," he pleaded.

Seifert rubbed his jaw and glanced at Baldau. "What do you think, Peter?"

"I've got an idea." Baldau left his chair and walked over to the writing desk. Unlocking the top drawer, he produced a bundle of documents tied together with red ribbon. "I can make these bills of exchange available until December nineteenth. They're good for two million deutsche marks."

"December nineteenth," Huber repeated dully. "But that's next Wednesday."

"Quite." Baldau smiled. "I realize this doesn't give you much time, Emil, but your tiresome bank manager will undoubtedly furnish you with a loan on the strength of these papers."

Allegedly issued by a certain Georg Weinberg, the details on the bills of exchange had been copied from bona fide orders accepted by a wealthy commodity broker. Naturally the bank would check the credit rating of the broker, but until such time as the bills were presented to him for payment, no one would know that they were forgeries.

"What if the manager wants to retain them?" Huber asked.

"Then you refer him to me, and I'll explain that they're a temporary surety." Baldau glanced at his wristwatch and frowned at Seifert. "Isn't it about time you were leaving, Fritz?"

Seifert snapped his fingers. "Thanks for reminding me." He smiled apologetically at Huber. "I've got an appointment with one of the directors of Lombard's Merchant Bank at eleven thirty."

"I must be going too." Huber stood up. "I'm very grateful for all you've done, Herr Kohler," he mumbled. "You've taken a great weight off my mind. I was feeling pretty desperate when I flew into London this morning."

"My dear fellow, I'm only too glad to have been of some help." Baldau placed a restraining hand on his arm. "But there's no need for you to rush off unless you've got a plane to catch."

"Well, actually I don't know the time of the next flight to Zurich."

"No problem," said Baldau. "I'll check with Swissair before I drive you out to the airport."

"In that case, you'd better take the Rolls, Peter." Seifert placed a bunch of keys on the writing desk. "Can I count on seeing you at three o'clock?" he asked.

"Indeed you can. We certainly need to go over the Whitfield contract with a fine-tooth comb."

Asking Huber to excuse him, Baldau accompanied Seifert into the hall, leaving the door ajar so that Emil could overhear their conversation. He returned to the living room two minutes later. "I'm sorry about that," he said, "but the Whitfield contract is worth eleven million pounds to my group."

"I seem to have caught you at a busy time," Huber said.

"I'm never too busy to see you. As a matter of fact, I wanted to have a word with you in private." Gently but firmly, Baldau steered

Huber toward an armchair. "You see, I'm not too happy about the loan we've arranged for you. Naturally I couldn't say this in front of my partner, but I don't think you're getting a fair deal. Given your present circumstances, I believe it's wrong to ask for the whole advance at once."

"Well, I can't pretend that it won't be a considerable burden," Huber admitted reluctantly.

"Quite," said Baldau. "That's why I wondered if you would be interested in an alternative proposition."

The alternative proposition that Baldau had in mind was comparatively simple to explain. In what was purely a private arrangement, he was in the process of acquiring shares in the Swiss Bank Corporation from a sixty-two-year-old widow. These shares would be used as collateral to raise seven hundred and fifty thousand francs, which could be placed at Huber's disposal before Christmas, provided he could manage the rest of the purchase price.

"How much do you need?" Huber asked cautiously.

"A mere twenty-five thousand francs." Baldau retrieved Huber's glass, walked over to the sideboard and refilled it from the crystal whiskey decanter. "I could easily raise it on those bills of exchange I've lent you, but that would take time, and the widow has another prospective buyer in the wings."

"I think Haenger might be prepared to lend me the money," Huber said slowly.

Baldau nodded. He thought it was the least Haenger could do after the scene he'd brought about at Barclays Bank.

"And then there's my friend Dr. Studer. He knows a man named Georges Pillonel who has his own bank."

Georges Pillonel, the owner of a private bank. Baldau smiled. It was getting better all the time.

IF HALF THE POPULATION of Munich were out on the streets ambling from one department store to the next, Sergeant Zwick reckoned the other fifty percent were riding around in their cars intent on seeing the neon lights and Christmas decorations. With the TV commercials reminding everybody that there were only so many shopping days left, he supposed this was to be expected, but it made for one big snarl-up. Crawling through the Bahnhofplatz, he just beat the light at the next intersection and, to a chorus of angry blasts, cut across the path of the oncoming traffic into Schillerstrasse. The Drei Löwen was on the right-hand side of the road. Cruising slowly past the hotel, Zwick sounded the horn twice and then pulled to the curb directly opposite its private parking lot. Seconds later a small figure wearing a dark overcoat and a cossack-style hat with ear-muffs appeared from a shop doorway and scrambled into the BMW.

"You're late," Max panted. "You said you'd be here by seven."

"So I'm ten minutes late." Zwick shifted into gear and pulled out from the curb. "Is that so terrible?"

"I don't like hanging around in shop doorways at this time of night. It makes me feel conspicuous."

"It's your clothes," said Zwick. "You look as though you've just stepped off the plane from Moscow."

"Are you trying to be funny?" Max wriggled about, sinking down in the seat until his head was below the level of the window. "Let me tell you something. You don't know these people like I do."

"What people?"

"Baldau's friends, that's who. Listen, this BMW may not have a flashing blue light on the roof, but don't kid yourself that they don't have the registration number of every unmarked car belonging to the special commission. We can't be too careful."

It was as he'd suspected: Max was allowing his imagination to run riot again. Zwick turned into Fraunhoferstrasse and headed toward the river.

"Ever heard of Gustav Schlagmeir?" Max asked presently.

Zwick shook his head. "I can't say the name rings a bell."

"I've never met him, but he's said to be a financial broker, the kind that's about as straight as a corkscrew. He's also on very friendly terms with Baldau."

Zwick turned left beyond the Reichenbach bridge and went up Eduard-Schmid-Strasse on the right bank of the Isar. "Do you have any idea where I can find Schlagmeir?"

"You could try London," said Max. "He went there about a week ago to see about some business deal."

"With Baldau?"

"That's the betting on the street."

Zwick frowned. It wasn't much of a lead to go on, but Max had his ear to the ground, and his information was usually reliable. He had been right about Paris; the French police had traced Baldau to the Hotel Lotti, where he had stayed from September 26 to October 3, and again three weeks later from October 20 to October 22. In what was rapidly becoming an old and all too familiar story, Interpol Paris had added that Baldau and Kristin Kohler had checked out of the hotel without leaving a forwarding address.

"I wonder if he's still using her surname."

"What?"

"Nothing," said Zwick. "I'm just thinking aloud. Where would you like me to drop you off?"

"You can put me down at the National Museum," said Max. "I'll catch a bus from there."

Zwick agreed and then lapsed into silence, turning over in his mind the Telex he would send to Interpol Wiesbaden. Trying to net Baldau in London would be like looking for a particular fish in a large lake, and Zwick wished it were possible to give Scotland Yard a clearer indication of the con man's whereabouts. He reckoned the odds were stacked against them enough as it was, with Baldau apparently possessing a sixth sense that warned him when it was time to move on.

THE ALARM FINALLY roused Baldau, and rolling over onto his left side, he reached out, groping for the clock on the bedside table so he could stop the discordant jangle.

"What's the time?" Kristin mumbled sleepily.

"Three forty-five."

"It's the middle of the night!"

"What are you complaining about?" Baldau yawned. "You're not the one who has to get up."

Still yawning, he crawled out of bed and staggered into the bathroom. He thought it was just about the most ungodly hour to be up and about, but with more than half a million francs at stake, one had to make sacrifices.

The benefactor was Georges Pillonel, the private banker from Estavayer le Lac, in the French-speaking area of Switzerland. In a last desperate bid to stave off the threat of bankruptcy, Huber had approached Pillonel for a short-term loan, showing him all the documents he had accumulated. It was doubtful if these scraps of paper had impressed the banker, but Haenger and Dr. Studer, who'd accompanied Huber to provide moral support, had spoken up for him, with the result that Georges Pillonel had been persuaded to contact Herr Kohler.

That had been his first big mistake. After telephone conversations with Baldau and Seifert, Pillonel was satisfied that the London-based financial group was sound. His second mistake was even bigger. Convinced that by furnishing Huber with a short-term loan he could make a quick and profitable return on his money, Pillonel had withdrawn more than five hundred thousand francs from his bank and traveled to London.

The sum involved represented the balance of the advance owed on the loan to Huber, which Baldau had now increased from two and a half million to seven million francs. Before the meeting on January 14, Baldau had wondered if Emil Huber had told Pillonel the whole story. If he had, it seemed incredible that the banker would be prepared to trust them, when they had failed to advance his client a single franc of the various loans they'd promised him. After Baldau had met Pillonel and had introduced him to John Bormaster, he came to the conclusion that Pillonel was just as gullible as the next man. Of course, it had to be said that with his smooth line of talk, Bormaster could have sold a color television set to a blind man.

"As a director of Barclays Bank," Bormaster had said, "I can assure you, Monsieur Pillonel, that the economic outlook for this country is extremely bleak. The Arab-Israeli war has sent the price of oil skyrocketing, the British government has lost control of the money supply, and with inflation already rampant, the miners are now going on strike. With the pound under severe pressure, the Bank of England has had to take remedial action to halt its downward slide."

As described by John Bormaster, the remedial action included cash deposits from the High Street banks, higher interest rates and the imposition of much tougher foreign-exchange controls. Overseas investment was not precluded, but the transfer of sterling in the form of personal loans was forbidden. Therefore, much as Herr Kohler and Dr. Lempertz would like to honor their agreement with

Huber, it was impossible for them to transfer the sterling equivalent of seven million francs to Zurich.

"Cash is a different matter," Bormaster had added half jokingly. "One could move cash abroad in a suitcase, provided one knew the right customs officer."

Baldau had then produced a suitcase stuffed to the brim with bundles of twenty-pound notes wrapped in cellophane, each packet bearing a wrapper stamped by the Bank of England. The money, he alleged, was part of the haul from the Great Train Robbery of 1963; a certain insurance company had passed it on to his financial group for disposal. Any doubts that Pillonel might have entertained were removed by Bormaster, who confirmed everything Baldau said. The currency was being offered below the official rate of exchange because Herr Kohler had received instructions that the money was to be unloaded on whatever terms he could get. Seeing an opportunity, Pillonel had then offered Baldau five hundred and seventy thousand francs for the sample suitcase and two others that were in his possession, containing an equally impressive amount of currency.

Baldau dried his face with a hand towel. Five hundred and seventy thousand francs might seem like a small fortune, but after John Bormaster and Fritz Seifert had received their shares, he would be left with just over two hundred thousand. Out of that he would have to give Gustav Schlagmeir a sizable reward and pay for the plane he'd hired to take Pillonel back to Switzerland.

Leaving the bathroom, Baldau returned to the bedroom, stripped off his pajamas and changed into a dark single-breasted suit before rousing Kristin once more. "Come on, wake up," he said urgently. "John Bormaster will be here shortly."

"So what?" Kristin cupped her mouth, stifling a yawn.

"So let's hear what you're going to do while I'm away."

Kristin sighed. They had gone over that time and time again. "Don't worry," she mumbled. "I'll have packed everything by the time you return."

"And then?" he prompted.

"We part company. I go to Munich, find a printer who's willing to counterfeit a batch of debentures and then I join you at the Hotel Bristol in Genoa."

"What else?"

"I've got a new name," she said. "I'm now Mrs. Rudolf Baur."

"Good girl." Baldau patted her on the shoulder and left the room. Bormaster arrived ten minutes later with the three suitcases in the trunk of the Rolls-Royce. His only worry was that Pillonel might ask to inspect one of the packets. That would really put the cat among the pigeons, because only the top and bottom notes were genuine; the rest were simply blank sheets of paper cut to the right size.

"He won't get the chance," said Baldau. "I'll just allow him a glimpse of the money, and then I'll bundle him into the car. When we arrive at the airport, you'll keep him talking while I go into the terminal building to make sure our friendly customs officer is on duty."

"And what do you know?" said Bormaster. "He's out sick."

"Right," said Baldau. "The pilot will then say it's time they were going, and I'll suggest you bring the suitcases over on the British European Airways flight to Zurich this afternoon."

"Do you really think Pillonel is going to hand over his five hundred and seventy thousand francs on that assurance?"

"I'm certain of it," said Baldau. "You see, he trusts us. Now, unless you've got any other questions, I think it's time we picked him up at his hotel. After all, we don't want to keep the dear man waiting, do we?"

CHAPTER 7

BALDAU HAD SEEN better forgeries. In fact, the eight percent mortgage debentures of the Bayerische Vereinsbank that Kristin Kohler had brought back from Munich were downright amateurish. Considering that the printer had taken the better part of three months to produce them, they were hardly an example of the craftsmanship synonymous with the German economic miracle.

"Look at them." Baldau scowled at the pile of debentures on their bed. "Twenty-five hundred worthless scraps of paper."

"Well, of course they're worthless," Kristin said brightly. "They've been counterfeited."

"And a sloppy piece of work they are too. There's no embossed stamp, no handwritten control signature, and they all have the same serial number." Baldau scooped the debentures together and stuffed them into a suitcase. "God knows how we are going to unload that junk," he said morosely.

"It's not my fault," Kristin protested. "You should have told me exactly what you wanted. I don't know the first thing about debentures. Besides, the printer was reluctant to do them until I pretended they were meant as props for a TV film."

"I'm not blaming you," he said wearily.

Kristin picked up a certificate that had fallen off the bed and waved it at him. "I did my best, but apparently that's not good enough for you. Sometimes I wonder why I bother."

"All right," he snapped. "You want an apology? You can have one; it's all my fault. Now just shut up and let me think."

No matter how poor their quality, the debentures would have to be unloaded somehow. Three months of high living in the best places had made a large hole in the money he'd swindled out of Georges Pillonel, and with funds running low, he needed to find another affluent victim, and fast. Fortunately there was no shortage of talent scouts; he reckoned that either Karl-Heinz Branig or Marcus Vogt could line up somebody for him. Both men were well qualified, but of the two, Marcus Vogt certainly owed him a favor. After the way he'd let Fritz Seifert down in the Frankfurt bank scheme, it was about time Marcus made amends. Peter would telephone him, then, but not from the extension in the bedroom.

"Amuse yourself," said Baldau. "I won't be long."

"Where are you going, Peter?" Kristin asked.

"The name is Rudolf," he said coldly. "How many more times do I have to tell you?"

Baldau left the hotel bedroom, went down to the lobby and entered one of the phone booths. Although he would still need the assistance of an operator to obtain the number he wanted, he thought it was safer to use a pay phone rather than go through the hotel switchboard. For one thing, it was unlikely that the international operator would remember placing a call to Munich, and secondly, there would be no record of it on his hotel bill. A few minutes after giving the operator the number, he was put through to Herr Vogt.

Baldau said, "Hello, Marcus. It's me—Rudolf Baur."

"Who?"

"Rudolf Baur. Don't tell me you can't recognize my voice?"

After what seemed an eternity, Vogt caught on to the fact that his old acquaintance was using yet another alias. "Rudolf." His voice rose in feigned pleasure. "Well, this is a pleasant surprise. Where are you phoning from?"

"Genoa," said Baldau. "I'm here on business. As a matter of fact, that's why I want to have a word with you."

Vogt laughed. "I might have guessed this wasn't a social call."

"Oh, I don't know about that, Marcus. I've always maintained that business and pleasure go hand in hand. Now, it so happens that I can offer you a profitable deal on some mortgage debentures issued by the Bayerische Vereinsbank."

"How many have you got?" Vogt asked him tersely.

"Twenty-five hundred. They're worth about five hundred deutsche marks each."

"And you'd like me to find a buyer for them?"

"That thought had crossed my mind. Naturally I'll make it worth your while, even though you do owe me a favor."

"What happened in Frankfurt wasn't entirely my fault," Vogt said defensively. "Fritz was too impatient; he should have waited until I found him another buyer."

It sounded like the preamble to a long-winded explanation. Determined to cut it short, Baldau said that there had probably been faults on both sides, and then returned to the subject of the mortgage debentures. "The securities originally belonged to Ernst Oetiker. He gave them to me after I had carried out a number of transactions on his behalf. You can offer them for sale at their face value."

"Right. I presume I'm allowed to mention Oetiker's name to the prospective client?"

"You may," said Baldau.

"Good. His name is bound to carry a lot of weight."

That was the whole idea. Since the debentures were linked to the Swiss industrialist, no one would suspect that they were anything but blue-chip securities.

"Well, with any luck, I should have a prospective buyer within the next week or so. Where can I reach you?" Vogt asked.

"I think it's best if I call you," said Baldau.

"All right. Let's make it next Monday. Incidentally, I'll need a specimen debenture to show the client."

"I'll send you one by special delivery." Baldau cleared his throat. "About next week, when's the best time to call?"

"It would be easier for me if you phoned in the evening, say between five and six."

Baldau said that was fine by him and then hung up.

AFTER THE LONG, hard winter, spring had finally come to Munich, but the change of seasons scarcely filled Sergeant Dietrich and the other officers of the special commission with joy. In nine months, every tip, every lead they'd received concerning Peter Baldau had got them nowhere, and while this latest anonymous phone call was tantalizingly different, Dietrich thought it would pose all kinds of problems for Interpol.

As Chief Commissioner Lars Liebermann read the hastily scribbled message, it was evident from the frown on his forehead that he shared Dietrich's opinion. A stocky, somewhat introverted man of forty, Lars Liebermann was Helmut Bauer's deputy and the officer responsible for coordinating the activities of the special commission in Bauer's absence.

"These Munich telephone numbers that Baldau is supposed to have called on April third and fifth," said Liebermann. "Have you traced the subscribers?"

"Yes, sir. Both 59-45-53 and 59-45-16 belong to business firms. As far as we know, they're thoroughly legitimate."

"And the informant had no idea where Baldau was calling from?"

"No. He just said it was an international call. He also stated that Baldau is expected to telephone 59-45-53 again on Monday—April eighth. Not that I feel we can place too much reliance on any of the dates he quoted."

"Did you get the impression it might be a hoax, Sergeant?"

"No, sir. The information may be vague, but I think it's genuine. In fact, I'd say this tip was at least as reliable as some of the stuff we've been getting."

Early in February one informer had reported that Baldau was known to have stayed at the Palace and Excelsior hotels in Milan and the Ambassador Hotel in Turin. By the end of that month the search had switched to Torremolinos, in Spain, but nothing had come of that lead either. The only accurate information had come earlier, on January 18, from Interpol London in a cable to Wiesbaden: Scotland Yard had learned that the con man had stayed at the Athenaeum Court until November 22, then moved to Chalfont House. A man answering the description of Fritz Seifert had also been observed driving a rented Rolls-Royce, but as a result of further inquiries, the English authorities had reason to believe that both suspect and car had left the country on or about January 16. Although Baldau had vacated his apartment in Chalfont House that same Wednesday, the police suspected he was still in London.

On the strength of that information, Helmut Bauer had flown to London armed with an arrest warrant, which he'd presented to the British National Central Bureau at Scotland Yard. Unfortunately it had proved a fruitless journey. Fritz Seifert had dropped out of sight, but there had been any number of reports that Baldau had been seen elsewhere—reports that had sent Dietrich and other officers of the special commission scurrying to Switzerland, Italy, Austria and France. As recently as Wednesday, April 3, Wiesbaden had cabled the national central bureaus of Spain and Portugal that, according to various informers, Baldau was supposed to be in Palma, Barcelona, Madrid or Lisbon.

"It would be a help if we knew roughly what time Baldau was going to place his call on April eighth." Liebermann pointed an accusing finger at the telephone on his desk. "If he comes through during office hours, monitoring those two telephone numbers in Munich is unlikely to get us very far. I mean, he could be using another alias for all we know."

"And it's also possible that our informant has given us a couple of wrong numbers," said Dietrich.

"There's only one answer, Sergeant. We'll have to ask Wiesbaden to organize a massive surveillance operation."

Liebermann began to draft a message to Interpol that would be labeled XD and would be repeated to the national central bureaus of Austria, France, Italy, Portugal, Spain and Switzerland. Before the day was out, telephone operators in Vienna, Innsbruck, Salzburg, Paris, Bordeaux, Lyons, Nice, Nancy, Strasbourg, Rome, Bologna,

Bolzano, Florence, Genoa, Milan, Pisa, Trieste, Turin, Venice, Verona, Lisbon, Madrid, Basel, Bern and Zurich would be alerted to monitor all international calls to Munich.

BALDAU SUPPOSED THAT if ever worst came to worst, he could always write a travelogue, although it was doubtful whether Salzburg needed any publicity from him after the way Julie Andrews had given the city a newfound eminence. There wasn't a guidebook to be had that didn't contain a reference to *The Sound of Music*, with the result that a lot of tourists were left wondering whether the movie or Mozart was the more famous. However, unlike the tourists, Baldau found the house on the Getreidegasse where Mozart was born, the Hohensalzburg fortress, the cathedral in the Domplatz and the Neptune fountain of scant interest. His motives for visiting the city were entirely different. When you were a fugitive, you couldn't afford to stay too long in one place, and with northern Italy in danger of becoming a little too hot for comfort, he'd thought it advisable to move on. Salzburg had appealed to him because it was just over the border from West Germany, and he thought the police would most likely reason it was the last place he'd choose for a refuge. Also Munich was less than ninety miles away, so it was much easier to keep in touch with Vogt.

The close proximity had removed the necessity for holding long conversations in veiled speech on the telephone; he had only to suggest that they meet for lunch, and Vogt would drive down the autobahn to meet him at a prearranged rendezvous. Today, however, the pattern was different: instead of driving to Salzburg, Vogt was coming in on the Austrian Airlines flight from Frankfurt, accompanied by the client he had lined up. And Baldau was waiting at the airport to meet them.

The client was Joachim Wegner, a businessman whom Vogt had first met some years back. Vogt had been legitimate in those days, and until now all the transactions he'd conducted with Wegner had been perfectly legal. As a well-modulated voice announced the arrival of the Austrian Airlines flight, Baldau was acutely conscious of how little he'd been told about the businessman.

The more he thought about it, the more Wegner seemed a complete stranger. It made Baldau increasingly uneasy. But he assumed that Vogt would certainly have smoothed the way with Wegner. In their parlance, "smoothing the way" meant Wegner had been shown the genuine debenture that had served as the model for the counterfeits. Once he could see the businessman was interested, Marcus had used all his considerable eloquence to persuade him to meet Baldau in Salzburg.

The uneasy feeling that his associate had picked the wrong man was confirmed the instant they met at the airport. Wegner's firm handshake, his businesslike manner, the way he appeared to take charge as they walked toward the parking lot suggested that he had a shrewd head on his shoulders and was a man to be reckoned with.

"I thought we'd talk things over at the Café Fürst," Baldau said tentatively.

"Anything you say." Wegner got into the back of the Mercedes with Vogt. "For my part, I would have preferred to hold a business discussion in your office."

Baldau could see they were going to have a sticky time with Joachim Wegner. He drove out of the parking lot, then followed the airport exit signs and, turning right on the Innsbrucker Bundesstrasse, headed into town.

"I expect Marcus has already told you that the debentures originally belonged to Ernst Oetiker?"

"He has," Wegner said brusquely. "And you've deposited most of them with the Swiss Bank Corporation in Lucerne?"

"That's right."

"If it's not an impertinent question, why are you selling these blue-chip securities at their face value?"

"I need the cash to close a lucrative property deal," Baldau said glibly.

"But surely any bank would consider those securities ample collateral to advance you a loan."

Baldau tightened his grip on the steering wheel. He didn't care for this adroit line of reasoning.

"I don't like the interest they charge," he said. "I don't see why the banks should grow fat off me."

Wegner grunted, apparently unimpressed by his answer. "I've only seen one debenture," he observed in an ominous voice. "Do you have any others to show me?"

"Yes, indeed." At a traffic light, Baldau reached for his briefcase beside him and, opening it, produced a sheaf of papers. "I think you'll find this handful enough to go over," he said, trying to remain jovial.

Wegner examined the debentures, shuffling them with about as much enthusiasm as a bridge player suddenly discovering that he'd been dealt a worthless hand. Watching him in the rearview mirror, Baldau noted the thoughtful expression in his eyes as he handed the securities to Vogt, and feared the worst. For once, his usual sangfroid deserted him, and he couldn't think of a thing to say. Vogt did his best to draw Wegner out of his shell, but meeting with no response, he too lapsed into silence. By the time they arrived at the Café Fürst the atmosphere had become noticeably strained, but any hope that the businessman would mellow over coffee and brandy was rudely shattered the moment Vogt mentioned the debentures.

"I think they're forgeries," Wegner said bluntly.

"Forgeries? I've never heard such a ridiculous suggestion." Baldau tried hard to smile, but the end result was a sickly grimace. "They belonged to Ernst Oetiker."

"I don't care who they belonged to—they're forgeries. They have the same serial number, the embossed stamps are missing and there's no signature."

"My dear Joachim," Vogt said reassuringly, "I'm sure those debentures are perfectly all right."

"If it will set your mind at rest, I can always get them authenticated." Baldau pushed his chair back. "It won't take me a minute; there's a bank just around the corner from here."

Wegner glanced from one man to the other. "I don't want to put you gentlemen to any unnecessary trouble. . . ."

"It's no trouble."

Baldau rose to his feet, caught Vogt's eye and, with an imperceptible nod, signaled that he wanted to have a few words with him in private. In spite of efforts to smooth things over, the deal was busted, and if they didn't watch it, Wegner was going to make a lot of trouble for them. Boiling with anger, Baldau somehow managed to keep his temper until they were outside.

"You idiot," he snapped at Vogt. "Of all the fish in the sea, you have to land a shark. What the hell made you choose Joachim

Wegner? He's so sharp, he could head the International Monetary Fund. As soon as he set his eyes on those debentures, he knew they were fakes."

"Are you telling me they were counterfeited?" Vogt said incredulously.

"I didn't pick them off the trees."

"I thought they were stolen property."

"Well, you were wrong, that's all I can say." Baldau moved on a few paces and then stopped. "I'm going to destroy them."

"No, don't do that, Peter. I can find another buyer for them."

"You'd better," said Baldau. "I'm running out of money, and you know what'll happen if the police catch up with me."

"Yes, I do. The rest of us will go down with you."

Right, they would. Baldau would talk his head off if it would get him a lighter sentence. "I'm glad you know where we stand," he said. "Now, what do we do about Wegner?"

"We tell him that according to the local bank it's quite possible for the debentures to have the same serial number, and it's not unusual for the control signature to be printed. Then you'll say that you will go to the Swiss Bank Corporation in Lucerne this afternoon and instruct them to forward twenty of the securities to him so he can inspect them at his leisure. And that's the last Wegner will hear of us."

"All right," said Baldau. "Let's get it over with." Retracing his steps to the café, he pushed the door open and went inside, a confident smile on his lips, disappointment in his heart.

CHAPTER 8

THE MASSIVE SURVEILLANCE operation on April 8 had drawn a complete blank, and a repeat performance two days later had met with the same result. In Wöbking's opinion, these latest failures, though disappointing, were not entirely unexpected. Since it had been necessary to cast such a wide net, embracing twenty-five major cities in six different countries, there had never been more than a slim hope that somewhere a switchboard operator would intercept Baldau's telephone call to Munich. Then, too, it was a pity they hadn't known that Baldau was calling himself Rudolf Baur. Such information had only come to light on April 11, and like all the other tips to date, it had been received too late. Too late also was Interpol Rome's report of April 22 that a Rudolf Baur had checked out of the Hotel Bristol in Genoa on April 3.

"I get the feeling that we're running around in ever decreasing circles." Helmut Bauer uncapped his fountain pen and described a circle on his scratch pad as if to illustrate the point. "I suppose our luck is bound to change one day. At least, that's what I keep telling myself, but I find it hard to believe."

"Perhaps it's time we should ask the public to assist us," Wöbking suggested.

"You mean through the newspapers?"

"Well, they could certainly help. But I was really thinking of that crime program they show on television."

" 'File XY Unsolved'?" said Bauer.

"Yes. It's shown nationwide once a month. The next program will go out on Friday, May tenth."

"File XY Unsolved" was said to be extremely popular. Since the program was also beamed at Austria and Switzerland, Baldau's photograph would be seen by millions of viewers.

"Of course, there's always the risk that Baldau will see the program," said Wöbking.

"Even if he does, I don't think we'll be any the worse off. We're not exactly breathing down his neck, are we?"

"Well, it would seem that we're not having much success with conventional methods," Wöbking observed in a mild voice.

KRISTIN KOHLER HAD returned to the hotel bedroom, poured herself a drink and then settled down in front of the television. It wasn't her favorite way of spending an evening, but with Peter out somewhere on business she had nothing better to do. So far the evening had been one long yawn, and it wasn't likely to improve, because Friday night was hardly the high spot of the week for watching television. In her opinion, the programs were all uniformly dull, as if the planners had worked on the assumption that most people would be out on the town enjoying themselves and there was no need to provide much in the way of entertainment. Even the commercials seemed to lack any spark of originality, and she sat there in front of the screen, besotted with boredom.

The advertisements came to an end, the news followed, and suddenly Kristin was no longer bored; suddenly she found herself staring at a very familiar face and the caption, "File XY Unsolved."

"Peter!" Her voice sounded a long way off as she spoke his name aloud.

The glass trembled in her hand, and her body felt as if it were paralyzed from the waist down. Her mind in a whirl, she heard the program host explain just why the police were anxious to trace Peter Michael Baldau, alias Peter Kohler, alias Rudolf Baur.

Rudolf Baur: the name spurred her into action, and springing from the chair, she pressed the on-off switch, plunging the screen into darkness. Her heart still pounding, she raised the glass to her lips; slowly her brain registered the fact that the glass was empty, and glancing down, Kristin saw a large stain on her dress where she had spilled the drink. Mumbling a string of expletives under her breath, she walked over to the small refrigerator and found a miniature bottle of Courvoisier. With a savage twist, she broke the seal, unscrewed the cap and poured the brandy into her glass. Downing it in one swallow, she felt a warm glow in her stomach, which gradually spread to the rest of her body. Within a few minutes the brandy had steadied her nerves to the point where she was able to think more calmly about their situation.

Clearly they would have to leave Salzburg as soon as Peter returned from his business meeting. No matter what the staff might think, they simply couldn't afford to spend another night in the hotel. Leaving the empty glass on top of the refrigerator, Kristin fetched their suitcases from the luggage rack and dumped them on the bed. It wasn't the first time that she'd had to pack in a hurry, but the way things were, she thought it could well be the last. Methodically she went through the bureau, emptying the drawers of handkerchiefs, shirts, socks, vests, pajamas, tights, bras, slips, panties and her nightgowns, before turning her attention to the closet. Removing the clothes from their hangers, she carefully folded the suits and dresses, packing his things in one suitcase, hers in the other. Then she went into the bathroom and cleared out the hamper, stuffing the soiled garments into a laundry bag supplied by the hotel.

That done, she changed into a clean slip and dress and sat down at the dressing table.

She was still putting the finishing touches to her makeup when Baldau returned. "Don't," she warned.

"Don't what?"

"Make any jokes," said Kristin. "I saw the smile on your lips when you noticed the suitcases."

Baldau flopped into a chair. "Do you mind telling me what's going on?" he asked quietly.

"You've just been featured on television."

" 'File XY Unsolved,' I presume?" Baldau said in an offhand way. "I suppose that was bound to happen sooner or later."

"Well, don't just sit there. We've got to get out of here."

Kristin was right, of course. They would have to leave Austria, and fast. But where to go? Since the program was also beamed to Switzerland, there was no safe refuge there. Italy? Interpol had made things pretty hot for him in Genoa, Milan and Turin, but there was something to be said in favor of doubling back on his tracks.

"Did you hear what I said, Peter?"

"I'm not deaf," Baldau shot back. "I'm going to make a phone call, but not from this room."

"A phone call?" Her voice rose in disbelief. "You must be out of your mind."

"I'm in the middle of a deal, and I'm not about to walk away from that when we're short of money."

"Money!" Kristin swung around to face him, her eyes narrowed in anger. "Is that all you can think of at a time like this?"

"Use your head," Baldau said coldly. "We're not going to get very far without it."

He left the room and went downstairs to the lobby. He wasn't sure he would find Vogt at home, but it was worth a try. Turning left outside the hotel, he walked to the end of the street and entered a phone booth on the corner. More in hope than expectation, he tried Vogt's home number and got lucky.

Vogt said, "I was expecting you to call, Rudolf. It seems you've become very popular all of a sudden."

"Yes—fame at last." Baldau laughed nervously. "Actually I'm thinking of taking a holiday—pressure of work and all that."

"You could certainly do with a break right now. Have you made any plans yet?"

"I thought I might go to Italy—to Riva, on Lake Garda. Trouble is I'm right in the middle of a business deal."

"How very awkward. Is there anything I can do?"

"Yes, but I don't want to go into details over the phone. Could you meet me in Riva tomorrow or the next day?"

"Riva? That's one hell of a journey!"

"What are you talking about? It's autobahn nearly all the way."

After a long pause Vogt said, "Tomorrow is out, but I'm free on the twelfth. Where will you be staying in Riva?"

"At the best hotel," said Baldau. "Where else?" Vogt was still chuckling as Baldau hung up.

One problem had been solved, but another remained. As he walked back to the hotel, Baldau racked his brains for a convincing reason why they had to check out at such short notice. Urgent business in Paris? The explanation might seem a little thin, but the hotel desk clerk would believe it. Like most of the staff, she thought he was a high-powered financier.

By the time he was face to face with the woman at the desk, the story had acquired a number of embellishments to make it seem more authentic, but in fact Baldau needn't have bothered. No one, least of all the clerk, was sufficiently curious to ask him why he and his wife were leaving in such a hurry.

THEY SAT SIDE BY side at a small table on the terrace, two gentlemen of leisure admiring the view across Lake Garda after lunching in the hotel restaurant.

"You know something?" said Vogt. "This is the life for me."

"And me," said Baldau. "Do you feel like another brandy before we get down to business?"

"I think not." Vogt stretched both arms above his head and yawned. "One more and I might drop off to sleep."

"I knew we shouldn't have had that second bottle of wine."

"Well, we did. So if you've got something to tell me, you'd better get it off your chest while I'm still awake."

Baldau turned to Vogt and asked, "Does the name Gassner mean anything to you?"

Frederick Gassner was a land speculator from Linz, Austria, who had got himself into a fine mess over a large property deal. Extended beyond his means and faced with a cash-flow problem, he had been searching around for a quick and easy way to raise a lot of money.

"Gassner believed I could either help him with a profitable gold deal or else sell his wretched land to an English group I was supposed to represent." Baldau sighed. "Gassner was a big disappointment to me. I only got thirty thousand deutsche marks out of him before he caught on to the fact that I was taking him for a ride."

"End of story," said Vogt.

"Wrong. Gassner admired my style and intimated he'd like to work with me. I said that maybe we could try our luck with a small bank, and did he know anybody in that line."

Gassner most certainly did. He had once been employed as a cashier by the Volksbank in Reichenhall and by the Schellenberg and Berchtesgaden branches of the Raiffeisenbank. The victim he had in mind was a man called Wrede, who was manager of the branch office of the Raiffeisenbank at Piding, with whom he was on friendly terms.

"There's nothing like dropping your friends in the mire," Vogt said cheerfully.

"It happens all the time in pyramid selling," Baldau said, airing his homespun philosophy. "Some housewife signs up with a mail-order company to make herself a bit of pin money and then discovers that she is going to be well and truly out of pocket unless she can rustle up four or five other clients. Next thing you know, she's roped in her best friends. Anyway, at my suggestion, Gassner told Wrede that I represented a group of English businessmen who were keen to invest sixty to ninety thousand pounds in deutsche marks as a hedge against inflation. The bank would do very nicely on the currency exchange, and Gassner could personally vouch for my integrity, because I'd already handled a deal on his behalf involving seven hundred and ten thousand U.S. dollars. The upshot is that Gassner has arranged for me to meet Wrede at the Gasthaus Röhrnwirt in Salzburg at noon tomorrow."

"And you'd like me to keep the appointment instead?" Vogt asked.

"No. It's essential I put in an appearance."

"You must be mad. So far as the Austrian police are concerned, you're public enemy number one."

"I enjoy living dangerously," Baldau answered with great cheer. "Mind you, I shall go in disguise."

"What are you going to do?" Vogt scoffed. "Wear a wig?"

"Something like that."

"Hair dye?"

"Perhaps. Maybe a beard would do it."

"Peter, you go too far. One of these days you'll take too many chances."

"You're wrong. I'll take just enough." Baldau leaned back in his chair, enjoying the view of Lake Garda once more. "I figure out all the angles and plan ahead. That's why you're here."

The meeting on Monday would be no more than an exploratory discussion, since Wrede would obviously have to obtain the approval of the bank's head office before he could go ahead with the deal. This Wrede could do on the telephone, and an agreement in principle having been reached, the transaction would then be completed a few days later.

"I'll tell Wrede the sterling is deposited with a notary public in Rome and arrange to meet him again on May sixteenth at his office in Piding. You and Gassner will keep the appointment for me."

"What's my cover story?" asked Vogt.

"I thought you could be the kind of man who has a finger in every pie—a sort of property consultant with connections in the import-export line of business. For good measure, Gassner will tell Wrede that you're the son of a senior provincial judge."

"I like that." Vogt laughed. "It makes me sound respectable."

"Don't let it go to your head, Marcus. I don't want you to change character overnight. With your help, I propose to secure an advance payment of sixty thousand marks from Wrede."

"That's in keeping with your usual style." Vogt pursed his lips. "All the same, our banker friend isn't likely to part with any cash unless we can give him something in return."

"How about a few baubles?"

"What constitutes a few?"

"Enough emeralds to convince Wrede that his bank is well covered. Something in excess of a hundred thousand marks' worth. I don't care what price you put on the gems, but don't round it off. An odd number always seems more reassuring."

"One hundred and three thousand nine hundred and fifty-five deutsche marks." Vogt smiled. "How does that grab you?"

"I'm filled with admiration," Baldau said dryly. "Let's hope it grabs Wrede as well."

CHAPTER 9

IN VOGT'S OPINION, Wrede's office was an indication of his status. The size of the room, the functional steel desk and chairs and the thin green carpet were visible signs that the manager had a long way to go before he reached the top of the ladder. However, since they had just met and Gassner was doing most of the talking, Vogt was as yet unable to judge whether Wrede was on the way up or had reached his ceiling.

"You had no desire to follow in your father's footsteps?"

Vogt looked up, suddenly aware that Wrede's question was directed at him and not Gassner. "Oh, no," he said. "Somehow I could never see myself as a judge. The law is an honorable profession, but it's far too dull for my liking."

"And commerce isn't?"

"Not when you have someone like Herr Rudolf Baur for a partner," Vogt said, trying to keep a straight face.

"Ah, yes, Herr Baur. I'm sorry he was unavoidably detained." Wrede rested both arms on the desk and leaned forward, his worried frown signaling that he was about to touch on a delicate matter. "I hope his absence has nothing to do with the transaction we discussed on Monday?"

Vogt had been wondering how he could ask for a lump sum in advance, and now Wrede had presented him with an opening.

"I'm afraid it has," he said gravely. "From what Herr Baur told me on the telephone this morning, it would seem that our English clients are having second thoughts."

Wrede stared at him. "I don't understand." The sentence came out in a whisper, and instinctively he cleared his throat. "What are they having second thoughts about?"

"A lot of money is at stake, and there's a growing feeling among the group that perhaps they should deal with a larger bank. I gather the Commerzbank has been mentioned."

The color drained from Wrede's face. One of the biggest transactions he'd ever handled looked as though it were about to slip through his fingers, and he could just imagine how his superiors would react if that should happen.

"You know what the trouble is?" said Gassner. "The Raiffeisenbank is not too well known outside Germany."

"We can provide as good a service as any other bank," Wrede said vigorously.

"But they don't know that, do they, Marcus?"

"There's no reason why they should," said Vogt. "Until now, they've never had any occasion to use the Raiffeisenbank."

Without bothering to explain to Wrede why Baldau had chosen to do business with his bank in the first place, Vogt launched into a far-ranging economic survey. With a recession expected, he said, and the dollar still weak, the industrial nations would look to West Germany and Japan to stave off the worst effects of the slump. In this connection, there were already strong indications that the deutsche mark was about to be revalued once more. Since the pound was losing ground against all the major European currencies, Herr Baur's English clients stood to gain both ways. However, speed was essential if they were to take full advantage of the monetary situation.

"You've got to go out and win their confidence," Gassner said, chipping in at exactly the right moment.

"How am I going to do that?" Wrede asked.

"I don't know. Perhaps you should offer to make a down payment in advance."

"A down payment?"

"Why not?" said Gassner. "It need only be a gesture. I should think something in the region of sixty thousand marks would be appropriate."

"I've never heard of such an arrangement," Wrede spluttered. "Not in all the years I've been with the Raiffeisenbank."

"This is all rather embarrassing for me," said Gassner. "It was on my recommendation that Herr Baur approached you in the first place. I told him you were thoroughly reliable and efficient. I said that you were definitely on the way up and were highly thought of by your superiors."

Although a little flattery never did any harm, Wrede appeared unmoved by the compliment.

"I'm not very happy with the idea," he murmured. "I mean, what guarantee does the bank have in this matter?"

"It would seem we have reached an impasse." Gassner glanced at his companion. "Unless, of course, you can think of a way around this problem, Marcus?" he added innocently.

Vogt could have dived to the briefcase at his feet and produced the emeralds then and there, but that would have been the hallmark of an amateur. A professional kept the victim on tenterhooks until he judged the moment ripe to make his pitch. Somewhat reluctantly, as if he were doing Wrede a great favor, Vogt indicated it might be possible to arrange some sort of temporary cover for the Raiffeisenbank. He had a collection of emeralds that could be made available, even though it would be thoroughly inconvenient for him.

"They were intended as collateral to finance another deal." Opening the briefcase, he produced five small bags of emeralds and placed them on the desk, together with a jeweler's certificate. "As you'll see, Herr Wrede, they are worth one hundred and three thousand nine hundred and fifty-five marks."

"Yes, indeed." Wrede opened each bag in turn and examined the stones. "Unfortunately I'm no expert on emeralds."

"No, but the jeweler who signed this certificate certainly is," Vogt said coldly.

"Quite, quite," Wrede acknowledged, and hastily scooped the gems into their leather pouches. "Herr Baur had arranged to meet me at the Gasthaus Röhrnwirt again tonight. I presume he will be able to keep the appointment?"

"I see no reason why he shouldn't," said Vogt.

Wrede would get to see Peter all right, but not at the Gasthaus Röhrnwirt. Too many Austrian policemen were on the lookout for Baldau to risk that. Before the day was over, Wrede would have to be told that the venue had been changed to Vipiteno. Right now, however, it would be inappropriate to break the news to him that a one-hundred-and-forty-mile drive to Italy lay ahead of him; right now Vogt's first priority was to push the deal through.

"About the emeralds," he said. "I must have a decision."

The decision went the way Vogt had expected. In the naïve belief that the bank was adequately protected, Wrede decided to hand over the sum of twenty thousand eight hundred marks without further ado. The fact that he proposed to retain the remaining thirty-nine thousand two hundred until he saw Herr Baur that evening in no way bothered the other two men. They knew he was no match for Peter Baldau.

SIX DAYS AFTER the "File XY Unsolved" program was shown on television, the Munich police were still sifting the information that had come in as a result of their appeal for help. Although in some ways the response from the public had been gratifying, most of the tips they'd received could be classed as too little and too late.

Once it became generally known that Baldau was traveling under the name of Rudolf Baur, Interpol Vienna informed Wiesbaden that he and Kristin Kohler had been traced to a hotel in Innsbruck, where they'd spent three weeks leading a life of luxury at a cost of thirty thousand Austrian schillings, half of which had gone for telephone calls. The hotel staff had also volunteered the information that the couple had gone to London, where it was said they intended to stay at the Churchill Hotel. Since Baldau was known to have stayed at the Churchill back in July 1973, Chief Commissioner Helmut Bauer, along with the other officers working on the case, suspected that he had deliberately put out that piece of information in order to throw them off the scent. The story that Baldau had grown a beard and a mustache to disguise his appearance could be another red herring, but nobody was prepared to take that chance. When the next "File XY Unsolved" program went out on Friday, June 7, Baldau's face would acquire a set of whiskers.

VOGT THOUGHT THE next twenty minutes or so were going to be very interesting. Wrede couldn't understand why they'd had to go to Vipiteno and had repeatedly said as much throughout the two-and-a-half-hour journey. He'd only agreed to the change of venue because he'd been assured by both Gassner and Vogt that Herr Baur would meet them there with the money. The trip had passed mostly in silence, but when they finally arrived, good old Peter had been delighted to see them. Bubbling over with good humor, he'd conducted them to a bar, across the street from the marketplace, where the waiters had practically fallen over themselves to make his guests welcome. Although Vogt was prepared to concede that no actor could have started his performance on a higher note, he wondered how Peter was going to carry it off. Wrede was no fool; sooner or later he was bound to smell a rat.

Baldau said, "I see you've brought the money with you."

Vogt held his breath. Suddenly and without any prior warning, they had reached the critical point. What staggered him more than anything else was the fact that Baldau could approach so tricky a situation with such apparent cheerfulness.

"But of course." Wrede hugged his briefcase close to his side. "Have you?"

Baldau merely raised his eyebrows, a gesture that suggested he considered the question entirely irrelevant. "My English clients were becoming a little restive." A warm smile appeared, and his eyes sparkled. "Now, thanks to you, I can set their minds at rest. I don't mind telling you, they weren't at all happy about doing business with the Raiffeisenbank."

"They weren't?" Wrede said in a small faraway voice.

"No. As a matter of fact, none of them had ever heard of you. However, once I hand over the advance payment, they will be only too willing to complete their side of the bargain."

"I'm not sure I follow you." Wrede looked at Baldau uncertainly, then at Gassner and then back to Baldau. "Are you implying that you don't have the money with you?"

"That was never the arrangement," Baldau said calmly.

"But I was definitely told you would." Wrede turned to Gassner. "Isn't that so?" he demanded.

Gassner swallowed and looked to Baldau for help.

"Obviously there has been a misunderstanding," said Baldau, "although I can't think how it came about. I mean, you didn't seriously believe that my clients would hand over forty thousand pounds in exchange for sixty thousand marks, when we agreed the going rate would be five to one?"

"Forty thousand pounds?" Wrede said hoarsely. "When we met on Monday you said they wanted to convert ninety thousand."

"That was three days ago," said Baldau. "They've changed their minds since then, as I explained to Marcus when we spoke on the telephone this afternoon."

It was a fastball, one that would have left most people dazed, but Vogt picked it up effortlessly, as if he'd had forewarning it was coming his way.

"I'm afraid I'm the one who's misled Herr Wrede," he said diffidently. "The line was so bad this afternoon that I got only the gist of your message, Rudolf."

"The Italians really ought to do something about their damn telephone system, but I don't suppose they will." Baldau changed tone and became philosophical. "However, no harm has been done, and I'm sure the Raiffeisenbank won't be too displeased. It's not every day that one of their smaller branches attracts such a large account. You must be their blue-eyed boy, Herr Wrede." He smiled and then added, "Long may it continue."

Wrede glanced at the briefcase resting against his side. Sixty thousand marks was a small fortune to him, but there was such a thing as being too cautious, and he knew there would be hell to pay if the deal fell through at the last moment.

"Could you clarify the position regarding the emeralds?" he asked hesitantly.

"What emeralds?" said Baldau.

"The ones Herr Vogt gave me as a temporary surety. I'm holding just over a hundred thousand marks' worth."

"Then what are you worried about? Your bank is more than adequately protected."

"It isn't that simple, Rudolf," said Vogt. "I told Herr Wrede that the stones were needed to finance another deal."

"In other words, he's supposed to return them forthwith?"

"That's about the size of it," Vogt agreed.

"You'll have to think again, Marcus. Those emeralds will remain where they are until this transaction has been completed."

"If you say so, Rudolf."

"I do." Baldau turned to Wrede. "That should make you feel happier," he said.

It certainly did. The last nagging doubt had been quieted, and Wrede no longer had any inhibitions about parting with his precious briefcase, although passing it under the table to Herr Baur did strike him as an undignified way of doing business.

"Another glass of wine?" Baldau lifted the bottle from the ice bucket, saw that only a few drops remained and made a face. "We seem to have run dry, but never mind, we can soon put that right." He started to raise a hand, as if to catch the headwaiter's eye, and then lowered it rapidly. "I'm being very inconsiderate," he said. "Time's running on, and with a long drive in front of you, I daresay you'd like to be making tracks."

Wrede nodded. The last thing he wanted was to outlast his welcome, and since their business was finished, it seemed only good manners to take the hint and go.

"Well, it is getting rather late," he said lamely.

"It certainly is," said Vogt.

"I wonder if you would mind staying on, Marcus?" Baldau said quickly. "There's another business matter I'd like to discuss with you. Gassner can run Herr Wrede home."

Gassner looked up, said that it would be a pleasure and asked Vogt for the keys to his car. At the same time, Baldau signaled the headwaiter to bring him the bill and, in keeping with his reputation for being a big spender, pressed a ten-thousand-lira note into his hand, which ensured they were shown off the premises with all the deference accorded visiting royalty.

Once outside, Baldau shook hands with Wrede and, with a non-chalant assurance that the briefcase would be returned in the morning, waved good-by.

"My car's over there, Marcus," he said, pointing to a Fiat saloon.

"Very nice," said Vogt.

"Don't get the wrong idea; I hired it for the week."

"Are you trying to make a point?"

"I'm not made of money, that's what I'm saying." Baldau unlocked the car doors and tossed the briefcase into the back. "By the way," he said, "how much is in there?"

"Thirty-nine thousand two hundred. I've got the balance of the sixty thousand at home."

"All right, you hang on to that. I'll give Gassner some of my share." Baldau got in behind the wheel and waited for Vogt to join him. "You know something?" he said presently. "If we play our cards right, we should be able to take Wrede for another hundred and forty thousand marks."

"Why put a limit on it?"

Baldau told him it was necessary to maintain credibility. The sum of forty thousand pounds had been bandied about, and they'd agreed the rate of exchange should be five marks to the pound. Since Wrede had already made an advance payment of sixty thousand marks, it would be logical to press him for the balance.

"Naturally you and Gassner will have to soften him up, and it might be a good idea if I were to rent an office in Rome."

"Assuming I can persuade Wrede to come to Rome," said Vogt, "what happens then?"

"I do my usual vanishing trick with the money," Baldau answered. "You know—in one door and out the other."

"As long as you don't try the same stunt on me."

"Don't worry, Marcus, I'll do right by you."

"How right is right?"

"I thought another forty thousand marks might be a fair split."

"I don't want to appear greedy, but it doesn't seem all that generous an offer to me." Vogt snapped his fingers. "I tell you what—I won't quibble about my share if you give me Wrede after you've finished with him."

"Agreed," said Baldau. "Now we'd better see if we can find you a room for the night."

CHAPTER 10

OBSERVING WREDE AS he was being questioned by Commissioner Walter Keller, Sergeant Dietrich thought that if ever a man had aged in a matter of a few weeks, it was the manager of the Piding branch of the Raiffeisenbank. There was a dazed, almost haunted look about Wrede, as if he still didn't fully comprehend what had happened to him.

"You know what the really awful thing is?" Wrede licked his lips. "I thought Gassner was my friend, and I trusted him. It was he who introduced me to Rudolf Baur—or rather, Peter Baldau."

"I understand." Keller was genuinely sorry for the man, but he had a job to do. "Now, let's see if I've got the facts straight," he said, not unkindly. "Gassner and Vogt accompanied you to Vipiteno on May sixteenth, where you handed over the rest of the sixty thousand marks to Baldau, believing you would receive forty thousand pounds in return for this down payment. When he failed to keep his side of the bargain, you were not unduly alarmed, because you believed the emeralds were genuine and the bank was therefore adequately protected. Is that correct?"

"Yes." Wrede swallowed nervously. "I was also assured the transaction would be completed within the next twenty-four hours."

"So what happened then?"

Nothing, and that was the whole trouble. The money didn't come through, but Wrede had seen both Gassner and Vogt more times than he cared to remember. Hardly a day went by without one or the other dropping into the bank to assure him that the deal would be completed shortly.

"This went on for about ten days," Wrede continued, "and take it from me, they told a very convincing story. On reflection, I realize now that I wanted to believe them, and you can imagine my relief when they informed me that the English group was now ready to proceed with the transaction."

There had been no revaluation, and the currency was to be exchanged at the rate of five marks to one pound, in accordance with the existing agreement. After taking the down payment into account, the amount outstanding from the bank was therefore one hundred and forty thousand deutsche marks. Since the emeralds would then represent only a little more than half the total outlay, Wrede thought it advisable to consult his superiors before he went ahead with the deal.

"I told them about the collateral I was holding, and they gave me the green light. I passed this on to Vogt and Gassner, and they informed me later that a meeting had been arranged in Rome for May thirtieth. I asked them why they had chosen that date, because I had told them I had a previous business engagement."

Unmoved by his protests, Vogt said flatly that it was a case of then or never. If this previous appointment was so vital, why couldn't Wrede send one of his cashiers to Rome instead? After all, what was so complicated about the currency exchange that he had to be present?

Acting on the principle that two heads were better than one, Wrede decided that two of his cashiers should go to Rome. Calling Rieger and Tait into his office, he gave them explicit instructions that on no account were they to hand over the money before Herr Baur delivered the sum of forty thousand pounds.

"They left for Rome on Wednesday, May twenty-ninth, with Gassner in tow. The following morning he introduced them to Baur at his office on the Via Veneto."

What happened then was a reenactment of one of the oldest ploys in the game. Ably assisted by Gassner, Baldau informed the two astonished cashiers that they had committed a serious offense by importing foreign currency into Italy without prior clearance. If they were caught, the penalties would be severe. A heavy fine was the least they could expect to receive; it was conceivable that they would also be sentenced to a term of imprisonment. However, there was a chance that they could get away with it, since the sterling was deposited at a nearby bank. According to Baldau, the head cashier there would not report the offense because he was a close friend, but it would be a different story if anybody else approached him with the German currency. Rieger and Tait could come to the bank, but they would have to stay outside with Gassner while Baldau made the exchange. They could join him inside when Gassner gave the word.

"That was the last they saw of Baldau." Wrede scowled. "There were a lot of people about, and Gassner claimed that he lost sight of him in the crowd."

Wrede was dismayed when he heard what had happened in Rome. Gassner pretended to be equally concerned. He said he would make it his business to put things right, because obviously there had been a misunderstanding of some kind. It could be that Baldau's friend, the head cashier, had been absent that day. For all that it was a flimsy excuse, Wrede seized on it like a drowning man clutching at a straw. When Baldau summoned him to Rome on June 8, Wrede went willingly, in the naïve belief that at long last he would receive the money owed to his bank.

"It was a wasted journey. Baldau gave me the same old excuses, and I returned home empty-handed. Much later I began to have this awful feeling that the emeralds were probably worthless."

"I don't suppose it's any consolation, but you're not the only one to be taken in by those men."

Keller turned to Dietrich. "Are there any questions you'd like to ask Herr Wrede, Sergeant?"

"Only one," said Dietrich. "Apart from Baldau, who else did you meet in Rome?"

"His secretary," said Wrede. "Fräulein Krista Franke."

Dietrich produced a snapshot and handed it to him. "Would this be the woman?" he asked.

"That's her all right. Who is she?"

"Her real name is Kristin Kohler."

"She struck me as being such a nice girl." Wrede shook his head. "Obviously Baldau had rehearsed her. She seemed to know an awful lot about debentures and bills of exchange."

Keller said, "Thank you, Herr Wrede, you've been most helpful. Now, if we could see Herr Rieger?"

"Yes—yes, of course." Wrede pushed his chair back and stood up. His shoulders bowed, he slowly walked out of his office, a man seemingly old before his time.

FROM THEIR APARTMENT on the seafront at Villeneuve-Loubet, Baldau could see the whole sweep of the Baie des Anges. The view was magnificent, though just how much longer they could afford to stay on the Riviera was open to question. Of the two hundred thousand deutsche marks he'd swindled from the Raiffeisenbank, just under half had gone to Vogt and Gassner, and the rest had simply melted away. Naturally there had been quite a few expenses—his office on the Via Veneto and various business lunches—but it was difficult to know where most of the money had gone. Easy come, easy go had always been his motto, but lately things had been going none too well for him.

His whole network of talent scouts was collapsing. Some of his helpers had already been arrested, and with Charly Begovich, Fritz Seifert, John Bormaster, Karl-Heinz Branig, Gustav Schlagmeir and Marcus Vogt on the run, he could feel the net closing around him. Things were going from bad to worse.

If you didn't have any friends who were prepared to hide you from the police, you had to keep moving, and that cost money. Because he was low on funds, it was vital he put one over on Hans Birzele, a German businessman from Rottach-Egern.

"Zero hour minus twenty." Baldau turned away from the window and smiled at Kristin. "Time I was leaving."

"What?"

"To meet Hans Birzele at the airport. His flight is due in at eleven thirty."

"I wish you would stop talking in riddles." Kristin swung her feet off the bed and sat up. "Do you want me to come with you?"

Baldau wasn't sure. Kristin hadn't been a lot of help when she had sat in on their previous meeting on September 11. Birzele was a hardnose, and although Kristin had turned on the allure, he had refused to pay money in advance. The businessman had also been adamant that he was not prepared to pay Baldau two hundred thousand deutsche marks for his services in securing a loan of three and a half million French francs. Mere feminine charms were unlikely to make Birzele change his mind, and Kristin's presence might even be counterproductive.

"I think you'd better stay here," said Baldau.

"I see. What do you plan to do about lunch?"

"I thought I'd take him to the Hotel Négresco in Nice."

"Lucky you."

Baldau could tell from her tone of voice that she was more than a little annoyed with him. He extracted five hundred francs from his wallet and pressed the notes into her hand.

"Here," he said. "Go out and buy yourself a new dress."

"Are you trying to bribe me, Peter?"

"No, of course I'm not."

"Then why the new dress?"

"Because with any luck we'll soon have something to celebrate."

Luck was the operative word, and he would need a lot of it to get anything out of Hans Birzele. Hiding his lack of confidence behind a jaunty smile, Baldau left the apartment and drove out to the airport.

BIRZELE WAS NOT IN a talkative mood. He'd said very little to Baldau on the way to Nice; two large Scotches on the rocks in the cocktail bar had failed to loosen his tongue, and he was still uncommunicative when they sat down to lunch in the Négresco. By the time the straw-berries and cream arrived, Baldau was getting a little desperate.

"Well," he demanded, "what do you think of my proposition?"

Birzele looked up, a spoonful of strawberries halfway to his mouth. "Not much," he grunted, and went on eating.

"Listen," said Baldau, "I've already reduced my fee by half."

"A hundred thousand marks is still a lot for your services."

"But look what you're getting for it."

"That's just it. I'm not getting a damn pfennig." Birzele polished off the rest of the strawberries and pushed his plate aside. "You'll get your fee when I see the money."

"And that's your last word on the subject?"

"It certainly is. Anyway, if raising this loan in Paris is supposed to be so easy, I don't see what you're worried about."

Baldau denied that he was worried and even managed to sound convincing. Just how he could now take Birzele for a ride was far from clear, but he wasn't about to give up yet. Maybe he could open a bank account in Birzele's name and forge the balance? That would be difficult, but not impossible.

"We'll need to meet in Paris if this loan is to go through quickly," he said. "How about next Thursday, the twenty-sixth—say ten thirty at the Hilton hotel?"

Birzele said the Hilton was all right with him and then withdrew into his shell again, with the result that their conversation became more and more sporadic. Baldau finally signaled the headwaiter to bring him the bill. An expensive lunch was part of the softening-up process, which usually paid a handsome dividend, but he had a nasty feeling that this was going to be one of those occasions where he ended up heavily out of pocket. That depressing thought stayed with Baldau all the way to the airport and back to the apartment in Villeneuve-Loubet, by which time he was in a thoroughly grim mood. His mood would have been even blacker if, like Birzele at the airport, he had bought a copy of the newspaper *Nice-Matin* and seen the photo of the "fugitive swindler"—Peter Baldau.

ONE OF THE MORE useless statistics concerning the Baldau investiga-tion was the fact that in fifteen months it had generated enough cables to fill three loose-leaf notebooks, each about four inches thick.

But now, as Helmut Bauer reached for the telephone, he had a feeling that the long, often frustrating manhunt was drawing to a close. Flashing the operator, he asked for Interpol Wiesbaden, his eyes still fixed on the hastily scribbled message that Sergeant Zwick had taken down a few minutes ago. Barely able to contain his excitement, he heard the operator say that she was putting him through to Herr Werther, who had just returned from doing a two-year stint with Interpol headquarters at St. Cloud.

Werther said, "Good morning. What can I do for you?"

"You can make me a very happy man," said Bauer. "We've just heard that Peter Baldau will be meeting one of his clients at the Hilton hotel in Paris at ten thirty this morning."

"Ten thirty?" Werther clucked his tongue. "That won't give the French police much time to get organized."

"No, I don't suppose it will."

"Tell you what," said Werther. "I'll call Michel Jean at Interpol Paris and ask him if I can deal direct with the Office Central pour la Répression du Banditisme."

"The what?" said Bauer.

"The bandit squad. Their headquarters is in the rue du Faubourg St. Honoré. Among other things, they're responsible for all criminal cases with foreign ramifications. I'd say that puts Baldau firmly in their court."

"Look," said Bauer. "I don't want to seem pessimistic, but are you sure you can bypass the usual channels?"

"I'm certain of it," said Werther. "You see, Michel Jean, chief of the French National Central Bureau, is a close friend, and I know Jean Bellemin-Noël of the bandit squad. I don't want you to get the idea that Baldau is as good as in the bag, but if anybody can catch him, those people will."

"I'll keep my fingers crossed and hope you're right," said Bauer.

FROM THE MOMENT Jean Bellemin-Noël called him into his office and broke the news that he was to be in charge of the Baldau operation, Detective Michel Cordier knew it was going to be a race against time. All the members of the bandit squad were used to working at a fast tempo, but Cordier had barely an hour in which to brief and deploy his team, and that was cutting things just a bit fine. With this in mind, he chose three of his most experienced officers, Pierre Noël, Henri Serdat and Jean Mercadier, plus a driver.

The amount of information they had to go on was not exactly overwhelming, because all the previous inquiries from Wiesbaden had been handled by the Paris police, and a photograph of their quarry was not readily available. All Cordier could tell his men was that they were looking for a tall German with a scar on his upper lip, who was either staying at the Hilton hotel or was about to meet someone there. The wanted man was also thought to be armed and dangerous.

Michel Cordier reckoned that three officers were sufficient to effect the arrest, provided they were in the right place at the right time. However, it would be a vastly different story if Baldau either failed to keep his appointment or suspected that the police were waiting for him. The con man appeared to possess an uncanny sixth sense; it had enabled him to stay at large for fifteen months despite the fact that every police force in Western Europe had been on the lookout for him. If Baldau eluded them today, there was a very real possibility that what was intended as a small operation could develop into a large-scale manhunt. Thus it seemed only sensible to have a support man remain behind in the office. Detailing Henri Serdat for this task, Cordier and the rest of his team left the headquarters building and made their way across town to the Hilton hotel in the Avenue de Suffren.

They took the fastest route, and turning into the Avenue Franklin D. Roosevelt, they drove around the Rond Point des Champs-Élysées, down the Avenue Montaigne and across the Alma Bridge. Speeding along the Quai Branly in front of the Eiffel Tower, they turned left into the Avenue de Suffren. On Cordier's instructions, the driver of their Simca 1100 pulled to the curb some fifty yards up the road from the Hilton. Leaving Noël to watch the street, Cordier and Mercadier then went into the hotel.

Where Baldau was concerned, nothing was ever simple or straightforward, and Cordier wasn't surprised to learn from the hotel clerk that no one answering his description was staying at the Hilton. Posting Mercadier inside the lobby, Cordier returned to the street for a hurried consultation with Noël. There was little they could do except make themselves as inconspicuous as possible while they waited to see if Baldau turned up for his appointment. Their chances of successfully merging into the background in that broad, treelined avenue near the Eiffel Tower and the Champ de Mars park were pretty slim, and they could only hope that for once Baldau's sixth sense would desert him.

The appointed time came and went. Another hour ticked by, each minute seeming like an eternity. Watching Noël out of the corner of his eye, Cordier wondered if any of the passersby suspected that the muscular young man in the short leather jacket was a police officer; wondered, too, what they made of him, a forty-nine-year-old man who had nothing better to do than hang about on the street. Did his steel-rimmed glasses make him look sinister? Did they think he was waiting to keep an assignation with some young woman? Could they see the beads of perspiration on his face, the telltale bulge of the .357 Magnum? One thing was certain; with the sun now blazing down from a cloudless sky, he looked pretty foolish in a gabardine topcoat.

Cordier glanced at his wristwatch, saw that it was almost noon and decided to get rid of the topcoat; it was obvious Baldau wasn't going to show up. As he started toward the car, Cordier froze in mid stride, scarcely able to believe his eyes.

Baldau had suddenly appeared from nowhere and was standing outside the hotel gazing at the entrance, seemingly of two minds whether to go inside or not. As Cordier signaled Noël to close in on him, Baldau abruptly turned away and moved off toward the Seine, his leisurely pace suggesting that he didn't feel himself to be in any danger. Taking slightly longer strides than their quarry, the two detectives overtook Baldau, and then, acting in unison, they drew their side arms and whirled around to face him.

Cordier said, "Police—don't move."

The con man stared at them, his mouth open, the color gone from his face. Shocked and unnerved, he could only mumble, "I'm Baldau, I'm Baldau," and then the Simca was alongside them, and Noël started to clamp a handcuff on his wrist.

"Make it snappy," said Cordier. "We don't want a crowd here."

"I hate to tell you this," said Noël, "but we've got a problem. His wrist is too big for the handcuff."

Even Baldau saw the funny side of that.

THE HUNT FOR PETER BALDAU ENDED at noon on Thursday, September 26, 1974, but almost two and a half years passed before he was brought to trial in Germany. At the time of his arrest Baldau had in his possession a forged passport in the name of Christian Henkel, and for this he was sentenced by the French courts to six months' imprisonment.

Extradited to West Germany in October 1975, he spent the next nine months being questioned by Helmut Bauer and the officers of the special commission, during which time he obligingly named close to sixty accomplices. His girl friend Kristin Kohler was equally cooperative, and in consideration of this, her sentence of two years' imprisonment was suspended.

At his trial in Munich, on February 15, 1977, Baldau was charged with fourteen offenses of fraud, two offenses of attempted fraud, one of receiving stolen securities and one of procuring forged bonds. The indictment ran almost to a full-length novel, but Baldau saved the state a lot of time and money by pleading guilty to every charge, although the prosecution dropped five full charges and part of a sixth. Charges against Fritz Seifert and Marcus Vogt in these latter cases were also dismissed. Much to the surprise of the prosecution, Baldau disclosed a number of other offenses that were not included in the indictment. But as he said to Wilhelm Wöbking, "We don't want to quarrel about a few unimportant details, do we?"

Before passing sentence, the judge asked Baldau what he planned to do with his life when he was released. After giving the matter some thought, Baldau said that as he obviously had a talent for raising money, it ought to be possible for him to use this financial bent without being confronted afterward by an indictment of a hundred and fifty-six pages.

The judge appeared to believe this was wishful thinking and sentenced him to eleven years' imprisonment.

THE BIKINI
MURDERS

THE
BIKINI
MURDERS

by
Noel Barber

ILLUSTRATED BY DENNIS LUZAK

"May I introduce myself. My name is
Alain Gautier." The voice was soft, almost
hypnotic; the speaker strikingly handsome and
intelligent. And from Bangkok to Katmandu,
from Hong Kong to New Delhi, the adventurous
young tourists he met were dazzled by his charms.

But behind the smiling face and proffered
hospitality lay a web of mystery—a mystery that
may never be solved. Only one fact remains certain.
Many of those travelers he befriended were never
seen alive again.

Noel Barber, journalist and author of such books
as *The Black Hole of Calcutta* and *The Fall of
Shanghai*, has lived and worked in Southeast Asia.
Here he follows the trail of Alain Gautier, a trail
that was as convoluted as a cobra's path and—to
Interpol and the police of more than thirteen
nations—just as deadly.

CHAPTER 1

BANGKOK IS A MEETING place of past and present, a frenetic city of almost five million people, where the bewildered visitor, still adjusting to the magic of the East, can be part of today's events that swirl all around him, yet turn his head and be transported into yesterday.

With an almost mystical force, the past breathes fresh life at every corner. The screeching of brakes as the phalanx of cars tears along Rama IV Road may assail the ears day and night, but it is the gentle, silent crocodile of saffron-robed Buddhist monks, heads shaven, that touches and ennobles the spirit. The coachloads of peering tourists, setting off each morning before the heat of the day presses down like a blanket, may explore the concrete jungle of a throbbing capital; but it is the splash of a single oar, the throb of a small tug making its way along the mighty Chao Phraya River into the klongs—the canals—toward a floating market, that gently ask you never to forget that this is a river city. And even in the city itself, with its buildings dedicated to mammon—skyscraper banks, hotels, office blocks—it is not the towering spire of the Dusit Thani Hotel that haunts the memory but the exquisite pointed spire of some ancient wat—a temple dedicated to the more durable Lord Buddha.

This is Bangkok, heart of a country of forty-six million people, where the past still'rules the present; where, an hour's drive beyond the airless city, blue waters lap white beaches framed in palms swaying in a precious whisper of wind; where tranquil canals bisect the flat, green, terraced rice paddies; where the elephant still hauls great loads of teak in a country that has never been conquered, never been a vassal state—the only one in Southeast Asia to have successfully guarded its independence against all covetous plunderers.

Of course, every city has more than one face. In Bangkok, hawkers cajole the unsuspecting; shoddy shops offer gimcrack souvenirs; brilliantly lit windows blaze with gold and gems to tempt the unwary; and to many the excitement of the city has always been its garish bars, its girlie shows, its massage parlors, with barely concealed promises of experiences never to be tasted nearer home, and inevitably its assurance of easy-to-obtain drugs. By 1975 Bangkok had become an almost obligatory stop on the hippie trail, especially since it offered not only five-star hotels but a quota of seedy, cheap establishments where friendships blossomed easily among young and often solitary travelers doing Asia on a shoestring.

Alain Gautier was no hippie—far from it; as a dealer in precious stones he liked to cut a dash, yet he was so intrigued by Bangkok that soon after visiting it in July 1975 he decided to stay. He sent for his Canadian girl friend, Suzanne Ponchet, and on September 6 they moved into a furnished apartment.

He was thirty-one and had been born in Saigon. "But I'm French, of course," he told his friends, "and we moved to Paris when I was fourteen."

He made new friends easily—particularly among women, who found his dark, glossy hair above black eyes, his olive skin, his high cheekbones and his white teeth fascinating; and when he was on the beach, they admired the rippling muscles of his magnificent body. Though he was only five feet seven inches tall, he was a dashing figure of a man, with only one flaw—several of his fingers had been broken practicing karate. But in a curious way those fingers held an almost magnetic extra attraction.

When you first met him, it was not only his appearance that intrigued you but the feeling that here was a man of the world, for Alain had his beautiful suits tailored for him in Paris in classic style. His shirts had monogrammed pockets. Around his neck he wore a thin gold chain, and on his wrist a chunky, rectangular, yellow-gold Omega de Ville watch on a gold bracelet. His lighter was a Dupont; so was his pen. The tinted glasses that he occasionally wore were by Bronzini. He drove a dark blue Toyota, and drove it well—well and fast.

It all seemed to go with the engaging personality of an intelligent man who spoke half a dozen languages, was a generous spender, something of a gourmet, who, in short, had a way about him—a combination of Gallic charm and brooding good looks hinting at mysterious hidden depths; a generous nature, an easygoing life-style that immediately made you feel at home in his company, particularly if you were one of the increasing number of tourists who by 1975 were exploring the Far East for the first time in their lives. He knew the East like the back of his hand, and had an easy familiarity with all the places you had just visited or were about to visit, for he and Suzanne jetted casually from one Oriental capital to another.

If there were some who doubted that Alain and Suzanne were really married—for sometimes he passed her off as his wife—well, what about it? This was the Orient, where anything could happen, where a new world waited to be explored by people who found, at some chance meeting, a man who asked for nothing, but out of the kindness of his heart offered to show you around; who could talk to you in your own language and whose offers of hospitality were if anything almost embarrassing. For after the first drink Alain would often invite a newfound friend home to his apartment, or rather apartments, in Kanit House, in the heart of the diplomatic quarter of Bangkok.

Kanit House was located at the corner of Sala Daeng Road and Sala Daeng 1 Lane. The Dusit Thani Hotel was a block away. More than a dozen embassies crowded the neighboring streets, and though the five-story building itself tended to be rather run down and needed a lick of paint, Kanit House was pleasant enough to attract lower-echelon embassy staff who were working their way up. It had privacy. It was built in three wings, which enfolded a beautiful pool, shielded by leafy trees and edged with tropical plants, and a kind of patio dotted with long chairs and mattresses on which the tenants could sunbathe.

Here, with typical dash, Alain had rented not one apartment, not two, but three—two adjoining fifth-floor apartments, numbers 503 and 504, the latter overlooking the tree-shaded pool below, together with a third apartment, number 103, which he kept for his frequent guests.

Suzanne had once been a medical orderly, was not exactly pretty but at thirty had a slightly pinched, haunting look—an effect accentuated by her waiflike figure and long legs. Her blue eyes, beneath severely plucked eyebrows, were hard to see behind large, gold-rimmed tinted glasses. Certainly she adored Alain; Alain and her fluffy white Samoyed puppy, Frankie. The dog had been bought for her by Alain at Bangkok's Sunday Market, and it was taken out for its daily morning walk by their factotum—a sort of man Friday, an easygoing Indian called Rajesh Khosla. Cheerfully doing anything he was asked—shopping, driving, secretarial work, traveling with Alain and Suzanne on business trips—Raj, as he was called, was generally regarded as one of the family.

And a very happy "family" it was. Everyone in Kanit House knew "the Gautiers." When the gem business was not particularly brisk, Alain and Suzanne spent part of the day by the pool, often together with their fellow tenants.

"It could be a lot worse!" Alain once said as he turned, laughing, to a neighbor they both particularly liked—a delightful, dark-haired French girl in her early twenties called Nadine Gires, whose husband, Rémi, was a chef at the prestigious Oriental Hotel.

Lonely when her husband was working all hours, Nadine frequently went to the pool, and she, Suzanne and Alain found it agreeable to be able to speak French to one another. Often when Nadine's husband was working late—he was responsible for the hotel's French restaurant—Suzanne would phone Madame Gires in apartment 307A, and Nadine would pop in for a drink and a chat.

Everyone liked Alain, many for his generosity. One of the cleaners at Kanit House remembered gratefully: "He was a good tipper; everyone wanted to clean his apartment."

And one of the managers recalled the parties and the stream of new young friends who seemed to visit the apartment. "Alain often asked me to his parties. They were wonderful. He was so generous, he would invite young tourists. He hardly knew some of them, but he enjoyed being hospitable."

Then the manager echoed the words of almost everyone who knew Alain Gautier: "He was a man with many friends."

CHAPTER 2

THEY NEVER MET, of course, and yet they all shared one thing in common—all five of them, three girls and two men: they epitomized the cheerful maxim of youth that you can be poor but happy. They were not starving or destitute, and they were happy with life as they found it—sleeping in dingy hotels, snatching meals in busy eating houses, buzzing with talk, grabbing each experience as they moved around a new and exciting world.

In fact, nothing seemed to trouble Mary Jane McLachlan, a pretty eighteen-year-old American student from San Pedro, California, who arrived in Bangkok on October 13, 1975. She had little luggage—only a holdall, and a capacious handbag that she could sling over her shoulder—and she had been given the address of a cheap hotel by a friend she had met before arriving.

In its day the Malaysia Hotel had been a home away from home for thousands of American troops on duty in Southeast Asia who had spent their brief leaves there. It was a big white building, looking more like an apartment house, really, than a hotel, but by now the paint was flaking off the woodwork, and the modest gardens that separated the building from the alleys and lanes with their shops and stalls were untended. Still, for a few dollars a night it offered a clean bedroom with air conditioning. Best of all, the Malaysia boasted a pool, hidden from the roadway, and a big open lobby filled with chairs and tables where "everyone" on the hippie trail seemed to meet up sooner or later.

Mary Jane had decided to stop for only a few days at the Malaysia on her way to Nepal, for she had become vaguely intrigued by the study of Buddhism; indeed she told some casual acquaintances in the hotel that she was thinking of becoming a Buddhist nun.

She was soon the center of a cheerful group of travelers in the big lobby, swapping stories, retelling experiences. Because she had a pert sense of humor and was an attractive five-foot-three-inch blonde, she was easily remembered by many of the people there—particularly by several young men, who cast appraising eyes at a new and pretty face and weighed the chances of a quick romantic encounter.

Most of the conversation, however, was soon monopolized by one man, Rajesh Khosla, who often visited the Malaysia for, as he put it, "a change of scene." Raj looked at the smiling, youthful face and said, "Aren't you a bit young to be traveling alone?"

Mary Jane laughed. "I'm interested in Buddhism," she said. "I want to learn more about it. I'm not afraid. Why should I be? Buddhism is a creed of peace."

She showed Raj a small book on Buddhism, which had been printed in Canada. On the flyleaf he read the name: Mary Jane.

"Is that your name?"

She nodded.

"A pretty name," he said. "But watch your step, Mary Jane. Especially in a place like Bangkok."

"I've managed to stay alive so far!" She laughed and shook her mop of blond hair.

Raj bought a round of drinks and told Mary Jane a little about himself. "I was born in Delhi, where my father is a wealthy businessman," he explained, "but I got fed up and came here to enjoy life."

Raj was the right age to strike up a friendship with a lonely girl of eighteen—just twenty-one. He was slender, with a dark complexion, short curly hair and a pencil-thin mustache.

"I'm working now," he added, "for a noted dealer in precious stones. He's called Alain Gautier. You'd love him. He's throwing a party tonight, and I can invite anyone I like. Care to come?"

Perhaps Raj saw her hesitate—after all, he had warned her against the dangers of Bangkok—for he added with a laugh, "Don't worry. This is a very respectable party, and Alain's girl friend is going to be there. I've got his car outside."

Mary Jane didn't need much persuading. She was alone in Bangkok, in search of she knew not what, but certainly not an early night on her own. Though she had told everyone in the lobby that she had come to the Far East because she was intrigued by Buddhism, she had also made it clear that any half-formed religious convictions would not stand in the way of having a good time.

They walked out to the parking lot and Raj opened the door of Alain's snappy blue Toyota, explaining that he borrowed it whenever he liked. "I'm like a member of the family," he said as they turned left into the wide Rama IV Road, then left again into Sala Daeng 1 Lane, and then right into Sala Daeng Road.

A high wall surrounded the grounds of the five-story Kanit House, shielding it from curious passersby. Raj drove the Toyota through the main gate, past the pool, and drew up under the covered parking lot in the corner. They walked across to the entrance of the left-hand wing and took the elevator up to the fifth floor. Raj opened the door to apartment 504 with his own key, and Mary Jane stepped into a different world.

The walls of the large living room were painted a soft aqua, and a gentle light emanated from a hanging lamp over the bar. A dozen guests lounged on deep, comfortable sofas and armchairs grouped around a rectangular coffee table. Stereo music blared from speakers, and a TV flickered in a corner, though its sound had been turned down. Next to the TV was a heavy safe, where presumably Gautier kept the precious jewels that were his stock-in-trade.

Gautier, immaculately dressed in a well-cut suit with a monogrammed shirt, came forward to greet Mary Jane. "I'm so glad Raj brought you." He took her to the drinks table and filled her glass. Suzanne came to introduce herself and explained, "We have the next apartment as well; it's useful when we have friends staying."

One door led to a balcony—a spacious, agreeable and private balcony with tables and deck chairs. It ran the length of the apartment, and as Mary Jane looked over the railings the pool flickered five stories below, inviting, the water seeming to change color from greens to blues while she stared down.

It didn't take the other guests long to notice that Gautier was immediately attracted to Mary Jane—perhaps because she was uninhibited and after a few drinks and giggles was telling the guests grouped around Gautier more than a few details of her sexual experiences along the hippie trail. Any worries that Mary Jane might have entertained about Suzanne were quickly dispelled by Gautier. "She's very understanding"—he smiled—"and so are you."

When Alain and Mary Jane danced cheek to cheek, and she caught Suzanne's eye, the other smiled. Suzanne didn't seem to mind, even when they returned to the large sofa and, later, with the lights turned down, started necking.

Gautier turned to one guest and told him, "She's a fun girl—I like her. I'm going to take her to Pattaya."

Gautier asked Mary Jane about her plans. Was she going to relax by the beach? What! She had never been to Pattaya, the beach resort that Thais like to call the Waikiki of the East? Mary Jane had another drink, then another.

"Like to go to the beach tomorrow?" Gautier asked her.

Starry-eyed and excited, Mary Jane nodded and whispered, "I'd love to!"

The next morning after an early breakfast Gautier picked her up at the Malaysia in his Toyota. In a few minutes they were on the Sukhumvit Highway, which opened up into a fine new expressway along which they could cover the eighty-five miles to Pattaya in just over an hour.

Soon they were by the coast, and it was entrancing—blue waters studded with coral islands, quiet waves lapping sun-soaked beaches, and behind the gently waving palms the hills sloping away, covered with riotously growing tropical vegetation. Pattaya was a paradise, but a paradise with every modern convenience—five-star hotels, tennis courts, saunas, glass-bottomed boats through which you could watch the hundreds of vivid darting fish on the coral reef.

Three miles south of the point where the road had branched off for Pattaya, Alain swung the car right, onto a smaller, tarred road leading to some bungalows perched on an isolated beach. Half a mile away they could see the original village, little more than a collection of fishermen's huts, around which this resort was being built.

"It's even more beautiful than Pattaya," Alain told her. "It's absolutely unspoiled. Not one single hotel. And you know what it's called? Sea Gull Village. It's a pretty name, isn't it?"

The beach was so dazzling and white it hurt the eyes, and even though this was the rainy season, they were lucky, for the skies were blue and the sun so hot that Mary Jane hurriedly changed in the back of the car, pulling off her jeans and shirt and wriggling into a minuscule patterned bikini.

As she undressed, a small book fell on the ground, and Alain picked it up. It was Mary Jane's book on Buddhism. "It'll be safe in the car," he assured her, and tossed it into the back seat with her clothes. "We'll read it together tonight." He laughed. "That is if we have time for Buddhism!"

The invitation from a wealthy, dashing man of the world cannot have been lost on Mary Jane. And no doubt she much preferred the delights of Pattaya to the meager comforts of the Malaysia Hotel. With an invitation like that, there was no need to return to Bangkok. She didn't.

ALAIN GAUTIER WAS not only a generous extrovert who gave wonderful parties; he was that rare individual, a dealer in precious gems who could be trusted to find you a bargain in an area where swindlers and con men waited at every corner, and indeed in many shops, to offer unwary tourists rubies and sapphires that had no more value than the ground glass from which they were made.

"He was a real expert in the gem market," said one man who knew him, "and he never diddled anyone. I told him he was cutting his prices too much, but he shrugged and said that if he liked people, he didn't want to make money out of them. I got the impression that he enjoyed helping tourists, and that his money really came from much bigger deals about which I knew nothing. After all, he was always traveling all over the East."

Gautier's reputation for honesty was no doubt the main reason why in late November an American friend introduced him to Yusuf Bilgin, a Turkish musician of sorts from a wealthy Istanbul family.

Yusuf, who had opted out of the dull routine life of his family in Istanbul, wore his long black hair waved in gypsy fashion and boasted a luxurious mustache. He spoke correct but halting French and English, and since he was looking for gems, he soon visited Gautier at Kanit House. He met and liked Suzanne and also Rajesh. Bilgin bought stones and rings from Gautier for which he paid sixteen hundred dollars. He was delighted when an independent expert told him he had made a terrific bargain, and Bilgin told Gautier afterward that he wanted to buy more.

"If you really mean that," Gautier suggested, "let's drive out together to the famous gem mines at Chanthaburi." This was the area southeast of Bangkok where the finest precious stones were to be found. Gautier said that he had excellent connections there, he bought stones from the mines himself, and if you took an expert with you, there were bargains waiting to be picked up. Bilgin was delighted with the idea, and Gautier then suggested, "As it's a long drive, let's make it a family party. Suzanne can come along and so can Raj—he can take turns at driving."

Everything was arranged. At the last moment Gautier commented to Bilgin that it would be foolish to waste money on his hotel bedroom. "Why don't you check out and leave your luggage in our apartment?" he said. "It'll save you hotel bills, anyway."

It seemed a good idea, but Bilgin hesitated for a moment because he had already asked his French girl friend, Yvonne Desbois, to come and join him for a holiday. He had suggested that she stay at the expensive President Hotel, in the heart of the Rajprasong shopping area. Why he asked her to stay at a different hotel from his is a puzzle, but he had told her to phone him when she arrived. Now he had to let her know where to reach him, in case she got there before he returned from the mines.

"Yes, of course I'd love to leave my luggage in your apartment," he told Gautier. And the last thing Bilgin did before checking out of the hotel was to telephone the President Hotel and leave a message for Yvonne, telling her that he would be away for a few days. He left Gautier's telephone number so that she could contact him there or at least find out where he was. Then he checked out late at night and set off for Kanit House. Gautier had decided that because of the long drive they would start in the cool of the night; well in advance of departure time Bilgin arrived, wearing a black shirt patterned with yellow stars and carrying his one piece of luggage, a canvas travel bag. He left it in apartment 504.

At the last minute, after a quick meal and a drink in the apartment, there was almost a hitch. Bilgin began to feel terribly ill. He could hardly reach the bathroom before vomiting. He was dizzy. Gautier was all concern. Perhaps it was something he had eaten—or drunk—before he arrived, or even in the apartment?

For a short time it was touch and go whether they could leave. But Bilgin was tough, and he was also anxious to buy more stones. When Gautier said that all the appointments had been made in Chanthaburi, Bilgin pulled himself together and said that he felt sure that the attack of nausea would pass.

Gently Gautier and Raj helped Bilgin out the front door of the apartment and almost dragged him along the corridor and into the elevator. They had some difficulty getting him into the car, for he could hardly keep his legs steady. Worse, he seemed to be in an incoherent stupor; even so, the quartet finally set off, with Bilgin in the back seat. They took the same highway along which Alain and Mary Jane had made their trip to Pattaya.

The plan was to drive past Pattaya and then make straight for Chanthaburi, but according to Gautier, Bilgin—who began to feel better as they drove along—suddenly remembered that he had friends near Pattaya. "We're in no hurry," suggested Bilgin. "Let's call in and see them!" Gautier hesitated, for, as he told friends later, he had a suspicion, nothing more, that maybe Bilgin was involved in drug trafficking. Gautier hated anyone connected with drugs. But he was a pleasant host, and he gave way to Bilgin's suggestion. Not far from the spur leading from the highway to Pattaya, Gautier turned left and took a pretty road, lined with trees and shrubs and tapioca plants, which led to the exclusive Siam Country Club and its golf course.

There Bilgin met his friends and, according to Gautier, abruptly changed his mind and decided not to go to Chanthaburi but to stay with his friends in Pattaya. Alain acquiesced and he, Suzanne and Raj returned to Bangkok without him.

YVONNE DESBOIS, A PRETTY twenty-four-year-old French girl who was a dressmaker by profession, had been staying on the Spanish Mediterranean island of Formentera when she received Bilgin's invitation. She jumped at the offer and flew straight to Bangkok early in December, booking into the President Hotel as arranged, though she was not rich enough to afford it. Still, the boy friend was paying!

As soon as she had settled in her hotel and received Bilgin's message, Yvonne rang Gautier.

"But he's not here," said Gautier. "Bilgin decided to stay with some friends in Pattaya. Didn't he tell you?" They were both speaking French, and perhaps Gautier sensed Yvonne's disappointment. She had flown all this way from Europe, only to find herself alone in Bangkok.

"And I don't have much money," she told Gautier. "It was Yusuf's idea to stay in this hotel. I can't afford it. When do you think he'll be back?"

Gautier said that he had no idea. Nor did he have a telephone number where Bilgin could be reached, though he did know the address of his friends. "But there's no problem," he comforted her.

"It's only a little more than an hour's drive to Pattaya. Would you like me to take you there to meet Yusuf?"

If Yvonne demurred, if she said that she mustn't really put him to all that trouble, she probably in her heart wanted to go—no doubt because Gautier himself extolled the delights of Pattaya. In the end she accepted. Looking very pretty in a purple flowered dress, she checked out of the hotel and went to Kanit House. Soon they were off along Sukhumvit Highway.

The next day Gautier returned alone, having presumably found Bilgin's friends and left Yvonne there to enjoy the delights of Thailand's Waikiki Beach.

ALAIN GAUTIER HAD a passion for names—names that he enjoyed using himself, not in Bangkok, where he was the highly respected Monsieur Gautier, but on his innumerable trips abroad. In early December, on a visit to Hong Kong, he decided to forget Gautier for a while, and so he checked in at the luxurious Hyatt Regency Hotel in Kowloon, across the bay from the island, as Alain Dupuis.

And it was in Kowloon that on December 6, 1975, Alain met a Dutch couple, Franciscus Bintarang, known as Frans, and Wilhelmina Jansen, nicknamed Mina. Frans was a twenty-nine-year-old chemist and Mina a twenty-five-year-old secretary. In Amsterdam they lived together in apartment 3E at 250 Oosterparkstraat.

Frans was the son of a Dutch mother and an Indonesian father. He had long, dark curly hair draped over his shoulders, a drooping mustache and a small triangular beard. He wore round spectacles. Mina was an attractive girl with long, straight blond hair framing an almost childlike face. Each was about five feet four inches tall.

They had been traveling together for ten months, making a grand tour of the East, and had already visited India, Nepal, Indonesia and Malaysia. Each week Mina wrote detailed accounts of their adventures to her parents and her sister, and Frans kept a diary. Now they were in Hong Kong, planning to leave on December 10 for Bangkok and then make a visit to Chiang Mai, a center of Thai handicrafts, carved teak, lacquer ware and silk.

In Kowloon they stayed at a cheap but comfortable pension-type hotel in a seventeen-story building, of which the first three floors consisted of an arcade of shops. They had found the hotel in a book called *Asia on the Cheap*, and for only six dollars a night they had an air-conditioned room and a private bathroom.

On the evening of December 6 Frans was sitting in the hotel's TV lounge, watching a film, which he found rather boring, when he fell into conversation with a Frenchman who said that he dealt in precious stones. He bought sapphires and rubies that were mined in Thailand, he said, and sold them in Hong Kong. In Hong Kong he bought diamonds, which he sold in Thailand. When Frans said that he and his girl friend, Mina, were traveling to Bangkok in a few days and then hoped to visit Chiang Mai, the Frenchman, who introduced himself as Alain Dupuis, offered to drive them there and also to take them to visit the Thai mining area. "If you feel like going," he said, "I'll show you round with pleasure."

Alain was not staying at the same hotel as the Dutch couple. "I'm at the Hyatt Regency," he said, "but I popped in here for a change of scene. Why don't you both come to the Regency? I'll show you some stones, and then, if you feel like it, we can make arrangements for a trip when you come to Thailand. How about a drink before lunch tomorrow?"

Frans and Mina arrived at the Hyatt Regency late the following morning, and were so visibly impressed by Alain's room that Mina wrote home describing the wall-to-wall carpeting, the color television, the bedroom refrigerator with ice cubes, and most of all a push-button bar dispenser of miniatures—whiskey, gin, vodka and cognac—as well as Coke, soda and ginger ale.

"You don't even have to put any money in," Alain explained. "Someone comes round every morning and checks the stock, and then what you've drunk goes onto your bill at the end of your stay. It's clever, isn't it?"

He offered them whiskey from the dispenser and after a drink or two showed them some of his stones, explaining to Frans how they should be judged. "Sapphires," he said, "should be deep blue and have a sparkle, that is if they're of any value." They had another drink, and then Alain suggested, "Please, why don't you stay and have lunch with me?"

Mina politely refused. The hotel was so obviously expensive that she felt it would be unfair to land a comparative stranger with a bill for lunch that would cost a small fortune.

"Well, I might be stopping by your hotel this evening," said Alain. "If so, I hope to see you."

He did stop by—and suggested that Frans and Mina should come and have a drink with him in the bar of the Hyatt Regency. He was very persuasive and very charming, and they went. Finally, after a few more drinks, Alain insisted that they should dine with him. They agreed. After dinner the conversation turned again to precious gems, and Mina admitted rather shyly that she *was* interested in acquiring a stone that could be set in a ring.

"Frans has half promised me one," she said.

"If it's the right price!" Frans said, laughing.

"Come up to my room again," said Alain, "and I'll show you my collection of stones and a ring that I carry round as a sample setting. I have my rings made for me by a Chinese in Bangkok."

It was a beauty, no doubt about it, a ring of eighteen karat white gold with fourteen tiny diamonds, and in the center a light greenish blue sapphire. Alain told Mina she could have the ring with any stone of her choice from his collection.

"I prefer a dark blue sapphire," said Mina, "since you said they're the ones of value."

Frans asked about prices. Using a phrase that sounds a little odd in English, Alain promised that he would let them have a ring at "a friendship price." It was a literal translation of the well-known French phrase *un prix d'ami.*

In fact, Alain offered them the ring without a stone at factory price—a mere twenty-eight dollars. With the dark blue sapphire, which was the best in the collection that he had shown them, it would cost a hundred and forty dollars. On the other hand, if Mina liked the blue-green sapphire, she could have it for forty dollars.

Mina looked at Frans appealingly. "Don't you agree that the dark blue is the only one, really—it's so perfect?"

Frans nodded. "You're right, and I think it's a bargain." He turned to his newfound friend and said, "We'll take it!"

A delighted Mina hugged Frans and told him jokingly, "I'll regard it as an early Christmas present!"

Alain also was delighted. "Not because of the money," he explained as he skillfully changed the stones in the ring, "but because you really have got a super bargain, and I like to see people happy."

To round off the evening Alain took them to a nightclub in his hotel, where they danced to a wonderful band—"far better than those in the usual discos," said Mina. She was alarmed, though, when she saw that the drinks were costing about five dollars each.

"You must let me stand a round," Frans said as he offered to pick up the bill. Alain, however, grabbed it, almost insulted. "Of course not," he said, adding, "Just send me a souvenir from Holland."

As Frans and Mina prepared to return to their hotel, Alain invited them to stay with him and his wife in their apartment in Bangkok. "I can promise you a super French meal," he said, "because I've got a French friend staying with me who's a wonderful cook—in fact, he's a chef—and he'll cook a meal for all of us."

Mina protested that Alain's wife would hardly welcome any more guests, but Alain pooh-poohed the idea. "She would be delighted," he assured them.

The Dutch couple didn't commit themselves to staying, though they did say they would be pleased to accept the invitation to dinner. Mina could not help thinking that by the time Alain had finished lavishing all this hospitality on them, they would be getting the ring for virtually nothing! It was three in the morning by the time they returned to their own modest hotel.

Later the same morning Alain phoned to say that he had to leave for Bangkok suddenly. He just wanted to check when they would be arriving. Frans told him their plane would be landing in Bangkok at two thirty a.m. on December 11.

"I'll send my male secretary to meet you," Alain promised them, at which Mina jokingly said to Frans that she was sure the unfortunate man would much prefer to sleep at that hour of the night.

Not until Alain had hung up did they both wonder if they would ever see him again. And not until that moment did it occur to Frans and Mina to wonder if Alain might be a swindler. Was their beautiful sapphire really worth the money they had paid for it? To them a fortune! Hurriedly they dressed and set off on a tour of jeweler's shops, examining all the sapphire and diamond rings they could see, comparing prices, comparing quality. To Mina's relief, every ring that resembled hers seemed to cost twice as much as the amount Alain had asked. There was no doubt about it—Alain was honest.

Mina went back to the hotel and wrote letters home, mostly about her new ring. "It is so beautiful that I immediately wanted to write to you," she said.

They only had a few days more in Hong Kong, and they didn't do much. Frans bought himself some new spectacles, because his old ones were falling apart, and they visited the archaeological department of the Museum of History. They had one meal at the Holiday Inn, in a delicatessen there, which reminded them both of Dutch food. The weather was miserable, though as a slight compensation Nathan Road, which cuts its way through Kowloon, looked wonderful with its blaze of Christmas decorations.

Still, they were ready to go—and excited when at eleven p.m. on December 10 they boarded Air Siam's flight 903 to Bangkok.

"I wonder if Alain will send his secretary to meet us," Mina asked Frans. Both were doubtful and had already decided to stay at the Malaysia Hotel in Bangkok. Their doubts increased when there were no messages awaiting them on their arrival at two thirty in the morning at Don Muang, Thailand's international airport, fifteen miles north of the capital. They were granted tourist visas entitling them to stay for thirty days, and on the immigration cards, where they had to fill out their proposed address, Frans and Mina both wrote "Malaysia Hotel." Then they went outside into the cool night air—and straight into the arms of Alain!

"I always keep my word," Alain said, laughing. "I thought I'd come and fetch you myself." They explained they had told the police they were going to stay at the Malaysia Hotel, but Alain told them not to worry about it, and he would not hear of their going to the hotel. "Suzanne is expecting you," he said as he ordered the porter to put their bags in his blue Toyota, "and you're going to stay with us at Kanit House."

As they drove from the airport Alain explained how he had rented three apartments at Kanit House, two of them adjoining. He and Suzanne slept in 504, which had two bedrooms. He told Frans and Mina to make themselves at home in apartment 503. He had three other guests staying as well, two of them in the smaller apartment, 103, and the third in the second bedroom in his own apartment, 504. The other guests were French, and one of them, Dominique Renelleau, a twenty-four-year-old Frenchman who worked in a bank in France, was far from well. He had met Alain and Suzanne in

Chiang Mai the previous September and had been taken ill shortly afterward, so they had offered him a bed at Kanit House until he recovered. Alain had told him not to worry, and had even put Renelleau's passport, checks and money in his own safe as a precaution.

Every time Renelleau seemed to be on the way to recovering and made tentative plans to leave, he suffered a relapse. "He's an old friend, and I'm very worried about him," Alain confessed to the Dutch couple. "He spends most of his time in bed and he's lost twenty-two pounds in three months."

The other two guests were old acquaintances who had served together in the Paris police. One was Jean-Jacques Philippe and the other was Yannick Malgorn, now a cook, who was the French chef Alain had mentioned to Frans in Kowloon.

Both these Frenchmen had met Alain at the Blue Fox bar near the Malaysia Hotel. Later they went with him to Pattaya, where Malgorn and Philippe became violently ill. Worse, both then lost their passports and money. Malgorn was full of gratitude to Alain for helping them, and when he recovered from his illness, he tried to repay him by doing a little secretarial work when necessary.

Frans and Mina had planned to spend time window-shopping or exploring the river or visiting Buddhist temples, but they both became unaccountably ill. At times they were suddenly so weak— even on that first night—that they fell out of bed. Then they would start to feel better. Meanwhile Alain suggested they would recover if they could only change the heavy heat of the city for a little country air, and he made plans for them to visit the mines and Chiang Mai. He would, he insisted, drive them there himself.

All was ready for the departure on the night of December 15 when Frans and Mina became even more violently ill. They were attacked by dysentery together with a terrifying nausea. Both were doubtful they could make the trip. Yet they felt that Alain was right about their needing some country air, and so with a little help they got out of bed and dressed. Alain warned Mina to wrap up against the cool night air, so she wore her favorite sweater, an orange one with green and yellow stripes at the neck, cuffs and waist.

Then Alain woke Raj, who on this particular night was sharing the second bedroom in apartment 504 with Yannick Malgorn. Indeed Malgorn also woke up as Alain entered the room to arouse

Raj, and a few minutes later Malgorn could see through the open door Alain and Raj helping the Dutch couple out of apartment 503 and half carrying them toward the elevator.

The four roared off in the Toyota. This time Alain went in a northerly direction along the famous road known in those days simply as the Superhighway. (In 1977 it was renamed the Vipavadi Rangsit Highway after a Thai princess who was shot dead by Communist insurgents while traveling in a helicopter.)

For thirty miles Alain drove along the well-built road until it split, the left fork heading due north, the right heading northeast. Alain took the right-hand fork until he passed the Wat Kudee Prasit, a Buddhist temple incorporating a school for children of local farmers, which was built on stilts as a protection against floods. The temple stands a quarter of a mile away from the highway on a dusty track lined on one side by pine trees.

A little farther on, Alain stopped the car. Frans and Mina, it seems, were feeling so ill that something had to be done.

Shortly afterward Alain turned the car around, and he and Raj returned to Bangkok.

How STRANGE THE way fate draws people with similar characteristics into the same kind of web. All five people—Mary Jane McLachlan, Yusuf Bilgin, Yvonne Desbois, Frans Bintarang and Mina Jansen—shared their God-given optimism: a happy-go-lucky attitude toward life. They enjoyed meeting people—strangers like Alain—for they were not the kind to harbor suspicions.

Yet if each of the five shared similar traits in life, they shared, too, similar moments in death. For after meeting Alain, and falling victim to his charms, none of them was ever seen alive again.

CHAPTER 3

THERE IS NO MOMENT more magical than the fleeting glimpse of dawn in the tropics, before the heat batters out the dampness of the earth, when a breeze rustles the casuarina trees or sighs among the fronds of the palms edging the sea, and the countryside seems poised in still beauty before the onslaught of the sun.

It was still cool at six a.m. on October 18 when a group of Thai fishermen emerged sleepily from their huts and made for their boats on the beach near Sea Gull Village, a few miles from Pattaya.

Two of them eased their fifteen-foot boat across the silver sand, leaving a deep furrow before they slid it into the water. The oarsman, Chid Changwan, dexterously steered the boat with its single oar while his colleague eased out the long net, its top edge kept on the surface of the water by plastic floats. Each dawn when the weather was fine they went through the same routine, the patient floating of the net as they rowed out, until they were far enough from the beach to make a U-turn and come back to where the other fishermen waited to haul in the net with, they hoped, the catch.

About twenty yards out from the beach Chid saw something floating in the water. He leaned over the gunwale, preparing to grab what at first he thought was a floating coconut, which might foul the net. But it wasn't a coconut; it was larger—far larger. Carefully he steered the boat toward it. Within a few feet of bumping against it, he realized he was peering down at a body—the body of a girl, floating face downward, a white-skinned girl in a patterned bikini.

Instinct, superstition, fear—all made Chid terrified of touching the body. Telling his fellow fisherman to keep the boat steady, he grabbed a length of rope that was lying in the bottom and made a loop at one end.

Carefully, and still without touching the body, Chid managed to loop the rope around the neck of the corpse. Shouting to the fishermen on the shore, he told them to send for the village leader and then turned the boat back toward the beach. The loop tightened around the girl's neck, and he was able to tow the corpse carefully to shore. Once it was on the beach, less squeamish hands pulled the body just clear of the water. Already one of the fishermen had gone to fetch the *puyaiban*—the village headman.

In Thailand a *muban*—village—is the smallest unit of local government, consisting, ideally, of two hundred inhabitants. They elect their *puyaiban*, who is responsible for maintaining law and order, keeping records and leading the village in any emergency. His duties are not arduous, but for them the Thai government pays him a small annual stipend.

As soon as the headman heard the news he went off to notify the

Pattaya police. At eight thirty a.m. the first police officers reached the beach. From a superficial examination the investigating officer, Lieutenant Chai Boriwat, judged the girl to be about eighteen years old, five feet three or four inches tall. He could discover no signs of injury other than a small cut on the right side of the neck, and this, he surmised, had been caused by the rope that Chid the fisherman had used. There was water in the girl's lungs, her nails were blue, and it seemed clear that she had drowned while swimming.

Chid Changwan caught no fish that day, for he spent most of the time answering questions at the local police station. There was little he could tell the police. There was no suspicion of foul play.

On the other hand, this was the body of a white girl, and that, Lieutenant Chai knew, could lead to complications and difficulties in establishing her identity, especially since there were no signs of any clothing on the beach, and the bikini bore no clue to its origin or the name of the girl. With great presence of mind, Lieutenant Chai took pictures of the corpse with an Instamatic camera.

Then, because the girl was obviously a foreigner, Lieutenant Chai sent a copy of the photograph to the Bangkok *Post*, Thailand's leading English daily newspaper. Graeme Stanton, its energetic managing editor, printed it on page one with an appeal to readers for any information about her. Despite the headline, GIRL STILL UNIDENTIFIED, no one came forward. Stanton could not know it at the time, but much later he was to print another, longer article involving not only this death but a string of others, which were to become known as the Bikini Murders.

The girl was buried at Sawang Boriboon Cemetery, not far from where her body had been found. The undertaker placed the body in a plastic bag before interment, and this proved to be fortunate, for many months afterward it would have to be exhumed.

SIX WEEKS LATER, on November 29, when the rainy season had given way to cooler weather and the temperature was pleasantly mild, Tuan Janmak, a peasant who owned a house along the road leading from the Sukhumvit Highway to the Siam Country Club, decided to make an early start to the day's work. By four thirty a.m. he was fetching hay to feed his cattle. To prevent theft during the night, Tuan kept his animals in a pen not far from the road. He got the hay he needed, and then, as he was feeding his cattle, he saw the flames of a small fire less than a mile away. Though he was curious, he did not bother to investigate. It was still dark, and it might easily be a neighbor burning grass or hay. But after he had attended to his animals, his curiosity returned. Dawn had broken by then, and he walked down a small path that led from the line of six coconut trees at the edge of his little plot of land toward the place where he had seen the flames.

Suddenly he stopped, transfixed. The middle of the pathway was barred—by the charred body of a man, his contorted limbs in their death throes in a begging position, as though he had in the last moments of life been supplicating for mercy.

Tuan ran back to the house, awakening everyone in the area with his cries: "Someone call the police, someone call the police!" Before long a car rounded the corner and a police lieutenant arrived to investigate the strange case of the burned and begging corpse. Carefully he examined the horrifying sight, black and charred, in the middle of the pathway. The man seemed to be about twenty-one years old and was rather short in build—not more than five feet three inches tall. Most of his clothing had been burned off his body, yet the lieutenant was able to see the remnants of blue underpants, and a black shirt with a pattern of yellow stars on it. The man's feet were bare, and the lieutenant surmised that he had been killed somewhere else and dumped at this lonely spot.

This, he felt, might account for the horrifying begging position of the corpse. The man could have been trussed up before being thrown out of the car. If there had been a car, that is. The path was certainly wide enough for someone to drive a car along it, but the grass-covered ground was hard and the police officer could find no trace of tire marks.

Soon the entire local community was watching the gruesome scene and offering advice. The lieutenant, however, thought the man was probably a Thai—and that didn't merit much of a fuss. Though the policeman was new to the area, he was aware that Pattaya attracted a large number of drifters, many of whom had formerly worked at American bases in Thailand. When they got into trouble, even died, they were difficult to trace, and the murder of one man would hardly make the headlines of a newspaper. So the case was soon relegated to the archives of other unsolved local crimes.

The body was buried in the Sawang Boriboon Cemetery, not far from that of the unknown girl, which nobody had claimed. The man's body was also put in a plastic bag before it was interred.

Two WEEKS LATER, on December 14, a local peasant was walking to work about five miles south of Pattaya, not far from the Sukhumvit Highway. Where the road branches off for Pattaya, there are several reddish tracks leading toward the sea, mostly constructed of red laterite rock and covering a large area of waste ground, rather like rambling veins. The peasant was walking along one known locally as the Hardsai Tong, or Golden Sands Beach Road. It is rarely used, even by fishermen, who prefer a better road that runs parallel to it nearly two hundred and fifty yards away.

It is an area in strange contrast to the lushness of the tropical vegetation behind the beaches. Here only a few stunted plants and a small row of ten-foot trees line the Golden Sands Beach Road, with a freshwater ditch running alongside. In summer the ditch is dry, but by December it held a foot of water.

Without warning, the peasant came across the body of a white girl lying half in, half out of the ditch. The face was distorted. The upper part of the body, above water, was covered with a terrifying mask that never stopped moving—a swarm of giant red ants, each one about half an inch long. One of the curses of Thai country life, these ants inflict agonizing stings upon their victims.

The peasant dashed to the home of the deputy headman, who contacted the police. The area was just outside the jurisdiction of the Bang Lamung police, so the case was handled by the Sattahip district police.

The girl was wearing red bikini panties, and a purple flowered dress bunched up to the waist. There were bruise marks around her neck and, though this was not apparent at first, there appeared to be hypodermic needle marks on her left arm. Because of the bruises, the Sattahip police believed that perhaps she had been strangled to death. The girl was unknown; there had been no notification of any missing white girl in her age group, but because of the suspicious circumstances of her death, the body was sent to the Police Hospital in Bangkok for a postmortem.

Two days later, at about half past two, an ice-cream vendor was riding his motorcycle along the road not far from the Wat Kudee Prasit, the Buddhist temple and school for farmers' children. There is a white marker a mile past the temple, embellished with a black *garuda*, the mythical bird of enormous strength that is the symbol of the land over all Thailand. Also on the marker are the distances: BANGKOK 56 KM, WANG NOI 9 KM. As the ice-cream vendor droned along, he could see the land with its rice fields intersected by irrigation canals. He had more time to look about than the motorists who were speeding past him on the pride of Thailand's highway system. And it was perhaps because of this that he noticed the two bodies sprawled on the embankment below the road.

He rode as fast as he could to the nearest police station, which was in Wang Noi village.

Within the hour the police arrived. They found the faces and the upper parts of both corpses almost incinerated by fire. One body was that of a man who seemed to be about twenty years old. Clinging to the burned flesh there remained fragments of a dark gray or black sweater and blue jeans. In a pocket of the jeans was a scrap of paper that had somehow missed the ravages of the flames. It was a bill from Delicatessen Corner, Holiday Inn, Kowloon, and it was dated December 9. The other body was that of a blond girl of nineteen or so in an orange sweater. Traces of green and yellow stripes around the neck, the cuffs and the waist had also escaped the fire. Underneath it she was wearing a yellow bra. Both the man and the woman were about five feet six inches tall.

Nobody had the faintest idea who they were. The bodies were also taken to the Police Hospital at Bangkok, where a postmortem revealed that the man had been strangled and the girl had been struck on the head with some blunt instrument. Then the pathologist added another horrifying conclusion. The couple had still been alive, though unconscious, when gasoline had been poured over them and they had been set ablaze.

At first, identification seemed impossible, but then one of the police remembered meeting two Australian tourists who had been staying at Ayutthaya, the ancient capital of Thailand, which lies at the northern fork of the Superhighway. At the time they had talked about a visit they had made to Wang Noi and about the wonderful time they had spent talking to the children in the Buddhist temple complex.

The Australian couple seemed to have disappeared, and so—though the identification could not be positive—the two pitiful burned bodies were tentatively identified as two Australian tourists. Police were fairly certain they had been murdered.

CHAPTER 4

FOR WEEKS NOTHING happened. Despite press publicity, the New Year passed with nobody coming forward to identify photos of the five corpses. There seemed to be no leads of any kind.

None of the clothing on the bodies bore any clues to identification, unless one counted the solitary fact, which was published in one Thai-language newspaper, that the "Australian" girl had been wearing a yellow bra made in Holland.

Yet there was a lead, one that was ignored by the Thai police, perhaps because it was not a police tip, not an underworld squeal, but came in the form of a memorandum from Mr. John Howard, the British consul in Bangkok.

Consular personnel the world over—and certainly the British in Bangkok—knew that any day, out of the blue, they could receive a desperate telephone call telling them that one of their nationals had landed in trouble. Drugs alone presented a never ending problem in the East, and so most foreign diplomats had their unofficial network of friends and contacts, who kept them abreast of the latest rumors and gave them all the information they could. When any particularly ugly rumors bore the stamp of truth, the British and other consuls would make their findings available to the Thai police.

Some contacts were the kinds of people that are spawned in every big city—men and women who haunt bars, chat with the owners of girlie houses, know the drug scene—and who had, over the years, proved invaluable as sources of information in a country where hippies of all nationalities, many almost penniless, arrived in search of drugs or even just to escape from homes and dull lives. These wanderers included their quota of British subjects. And John Howard was not alone among consular officials in believing that it was best to be forewarned and forearmed. Though the gruesome murders had nothing to do with the British, the five bodies had not after all been identified, so it was possible that one or more might turn out to be British. Consequently all casual information, gossip or rumor, was automatically sifted in the consulate, collated and filed for future reference.

A series of the most improbable coincidences—the sort that no author would dare to employ in a work of fiction—now led the British to point the finger of suspicion toward Kanit House.

First, John Howard was an ex-newspaperman who was accustomed to appraising all information, official or otherwise. And when he did learn something, he was used to taking action. Second, his wife was French and their daughter, Charlaine, who was in her twenties and spoke four languages, worked for a Swiss businessman named Antoine Lemaire, who also had a French wife. Consequently the Lemaires and the Howards would occasionally dine together. And third, the Lemaires were good friends of another French couple—none other than Nadine Gires and her husband, Rémi, a chef at the Oriental Hotel, who lived in Kanit House. Thus it was that the British, who had no real interest in the five dead bodies, became seriously involved.

On the evening of December 22 Nadine and Rémi Gires had returned to Kanit House from a four-day holiday in Hua Hin. After unpacking and relaxing for a while, they decided to visit their friends on the fifth floor. There they found Dominique Renelleau and Yannick Malgorn alone and completely unnerved. Alain, Suzanne and Raj had left for Nepal several days earlier, and the third Frenchman, Jean-Jacques Philippe, was in Malaysia getting a new Thai visa.

"Alain is a murderer and a thief," blurted Yannick, and he went on to tell a terrifying story to the shocked Nadine and Rémi. He brought out a Bangkok *Post* article which described the death of a young Australian couple. "They weren't Australian," said Yannick. "They were Dutch. And they were here at Kanit House with Gautier." Then he and Dominique showed the Gires a rubber gas hose still reeking of gasoline, hypodermic needles, postcards written by the Dutch couple but never sent, Mina's brown leather bag and Frans's new transistor radio. Malgorn, who had been entrusted with the key and the combination to Gautier's safe, opened it and brought out a dozen stolen passports, mostly French, traveler's checks and wallets.

The next day Rémi insisted that his wife go to stay with the Lemaires, and there Nadine broke down and told the story. The Lemaires told John Howard.

Meticulously the British consul went through the statements of Nadine Gires. The consulate also checked with the Australians, who flatly denied that any of their nationals had been murdered.

On January 7, 1976, the British consul sent an *aide-mémoire* on the subject to the director general of the Thai police force in Bangkok. It was marked "Confidential," and the unproved allegations were, of course, covered by diplomatic immunity. It was a damning document, telling all, including Frans Bintarang's address in Holland. It also included the name of Alain Gautier.

The memo landed on the desk of the director's adjutant, who was told to investigate. What he did—if anything—is not known. He certainly did not contact the Dutch embassy, which, in view of the fact that a Dutch national was involved, was among the first steps he should have taken.

The most charitable view of the man's lamentable lack of action is that his desk was probably cluttered every morning with reports from foreign sources and that it was impossible to deal with them all in a city where drugs, illicit sex and murders form part of everyday life. He had probably never even heard of the missing people. And, too, in a country proud of its independence, he might—only might— have wondered what business it was of the British to dabble in the lives and deaths of people not under their jurisdiction.

Whatever the reason, the adjutant did nothing. Had he just picked up the telephone and asked for the Dutch embassy, everything might have been different.

But he didn't. And, of course, the British were powerless to take any action in a foreign country. They could do only what they had done—as a matter of diplomatic courtesy, pass on the information they had received.

ABOUT TWO WEEKS later, on Friday, January 23, an official of the Ministry of Foreign Affairs in Amsterdam was sitting at his desk thinking of the weekend ahead when a clerk told him that a Mr. Van

Kan had arrived at the inquiry desk to see if anyone could help him trace a missing relative.

"Show him in," said the official with a sigh. Nine out of ten distraught relatives entertained fears that on investigation proved groundless.

Mr. Van Kan *looked* worried, and he came straight to the point. He was concerned about the safety of his wife's sister, Wilhelmina Jansen, and her boy friend Franciscus Bintarang.

"Where do you think they are?" asked the official.

"They *should* be in Thailand," said Van Kan, "or at least they should have been in Thailand, though they might have moved on by now. They left Holland eleven months ago." He gave the exact date, February 8, 1975. "They're on a round-the-world tour. Mina wrote regularly until December 8. That was the date on the last letter, though the postmark was the eleventh. Mina—that's her nickname—said they were just about to leave Hong Kong for Bangkok. Since then we haven't heard a word from them."

He paused, then added, "What we really can't understand is that Mina ignored her mother's birthday on January 18 and her sister's three days later. She'd never do a thing like that."

The official asked the usual questions. Were they short of money? No, they were traveling on the cheap, but they had funds. Was it possible they had had a row—even split up? Never, never. They adored each other.

"Well," suggested the official, "the only thing I can advise you to do is write to the Dutch embassy in Bangkok." He scribbled down the Wireless Road address on a piece of paper. "I'm sure they'll do everything they can to help."

Van Kan did just that. Two days later, in a long letter, he outlined what had happened, his doubts, his fears, and posted it to Bangkok. On February 8 it arrived on the desk of a third secretary called Herman Knippenberg, an attractive, intense man in his thirties, with keen eyes below thick dark hair. He spoke fluent English and lived in a lovely home not far from the Dutch embassy, with his beautiful wife, Angela, and their dachshund, Nestor.

In character Knippenberg just happened to be the opposite of the adjutant in the Thai police force. Herman had the determination of a terrier who, having grabbed hold of a slipper, refused to let it go and worried it, fought its problems, until there was nothing left for anyone else to do. "It must be heredity," Herman would often reflect. "Our family crest reads, 'Strong and persistent.'"

Now Knippenberg studied the facts that Mina's brother-in-law had sent him: names, ages, address, occupations. In the photographs that Van Kan had sent with his letter, Frans looked a bit of a hippie; apart from the long hair over his shoulders and his round glasses, the drooping mustache and the rather ridiculous triangular beard were not exactly prepossessing. Mina, with her blond hair, looked much more attractive, thought Knippenberg.

Van Kan had also sent copies of Mina's last letters, mentioning their meeting with the "hospitable Frenchman" who had invited them to stay in Bangkok. The letters, however, did not give the man's name and there was no reason for Knippenberg to connect this routine inquiry with the much publicized deaths of the "Australians." But he was well aware that the identification of the couple was tentative, and he remembered that when their bodies had been found, it was reported that the woman had been wearing a yellow bra made in Holland.

Seeking more information, Knippenberg contacted the Australian embassy, and like John Howard, he learned that no Australian nationals had been murdered. Then Knippenberg got in touch with Commissioner Toorenaar, head of the Amsterdam Homicide Department, and informed him that two Dutch citizens, Wilhelmina Jansen and Franciscus Bintarang, might have been murdered in Thailand. Toorenaar took charge of inquiries at his end. Within a few hours he had traced the two different dentists who had treated Frans and Mina in Holland, obtained the necessary dental records and sent them off to Bangkok.

On March 3 Knippenberg met with the chief dental surgeon of the Bangkok Adventist Hospital, Dr. Antje Twijnstra, and Colonel Paitoon Limrat, who had carried out the postmortems on the bodies. Together they compared charts and X rays with the teeth in the heads of the victims, working with dental mirrors under double-strength lights. Mina's record showed that a bicuspid of the left upper jaw had been extracted when she was younger and a molar had moved toward the front to take up the space. The mouth of the dead girl showed the same formation, and the fillings also matched. Frans's records showed that two fillings in front teeth matched the victim's exactly.

Thus Knippenberg was convinced that two of his fellow Dutchmen had been murdered. But by whom? All he knew was the chilling nature of the murders. One of the victims, as the postmortems showed, had been strangled, the other had been bludgeoned with something hard. Added to this was the terrifying knowledge that the murderer was a sadistic monster who had doused the unconscious bodies with gasoline and set fire to them while they were still alive.

How on earth could he hope to trace this fiend? There seemed no real reason even to link Frans and Mina's chance meeting with the stranger in Kowloon to such a violent end in Bangkok. True, the stranger had invited them to stay with him, but had they accepted his offer, and if so, where had they gone? In Bangkok, a city of some four and a half million people, where no questions are asked, it was like looking for a needle in a haystack. What a pity, Knippenberg told a friend, that Mina had not mentioned the elegant Frenchman's name. It would at least have been a place to start.

CHAPTER 5

WITHIN A FEW DAYS, however, the elegant Frenchman's name no longer eluded Herman Knippenberg. Through a mutual acquaintance he learned of the extraordinary story Nadine Gires had told the Lemaires. An excited Knippenberg immediately phoned Madame Gires and asked her if she could spare the time to meet him. He explained the subject he wanted to discuss, and Nadine offered to come to his office. She talked for three consecutive days, telling everything she knew. It was a terrifying story. She was able to give Knippenberg many details of Gautier's life-style, of Suzanne Ponchet, his mistress, and of Rajesh Khosla. She remembered that Gautier said he had stayed at the Sheraton Bangkok Hotel when he had first arrived in Bangkok, before moving into Kanit House on September 6, when she had first met him. She felt that he was given to boasting. "He boasted of having smuggled cars into India early in his life," she remembered. He was inordinately proud of his narrow-waisted body. He even kept a photograph of himself in the nude in the apartment. Though she had liked him at first, and had been intrigued by the way in which he acquired friends with ease, Madame Gires soon began to realize that having acquired friends, Gautier had to dominate them.

She told Knippenberg details about Gautier's sex life in Bangkok before Suzanne arrived, when Gautier had been extremely friendly with a stunning twenty-six-year-old Thai called Naree Soontra, who worked in a jewelry boutique in the same building as the Indra Regent Hotel. After Suzanne had joined Gautier in Bangkok, she became savagely jealous of Naree—and Naree became very ill. She complained of nausea and dysentery and had to visit a French doctor.

Gautier also had another local girl whose name was Dara Permpong. She had worked until the end of December as a waitress in a coffee shop at the same Indra Regent Hotel, but she had left because she wanted more time to study. Suzanne was even more jealous of her than she had been of Naree.

As to Suzanne herself, Madame Gires was able to pinpoint one intriguing fact. "She calls herself Suzanne Ponchet," said Nadine, "but I've noticed that letters she receives from Canada are addressed to Catherine Ponchet." Madame Gires understood that she'd been a nurse. "She's a funny one. She can hardly bear to be parted from the white Samoyed puppy Gautier bought for her."

Madame Gires looked on Rajesh Khosla as a servant. "They leave him to pay cabdrivers, they send him out to buy cigarettes, but he seems perfectly happy with his role," she said.

It was only now that Knippenberg learned about the trio of Frenchmen who had been staying at Kanit House just around the time when the Dutch couple were expected to arrive from Hong Kong. Madame Gires had met them all. "I was in and out of the apartment all the time, and poor Monsieur Renelleau was very, very ill."

"Can you tell me anything about the night the Dutch arrived?" asked Knippenberg.

Yes, she could, for on that night, while Frans and Mina must have been flying from Hong Kong, Nadine and her husband, Rémi, were actually in Gautier's apartment, and he told them that he was going to Don Muang airport to meet two friends. She had gone home to bed by the time they arrived. She remembers that later the Dutch couple became violently ill, apparently suffering from acute dysentery. It was Yannick Malgorn who, during the night of December 15, had awakened and seen Gautier and Raj leave the apartment half carrying the Dutch couple with them.

"Did Malgorn tell you that?" asked Knippenberg.

"Yes," she replied, "and Malgorn told me something else. He and Renelleau were awake when Gautier and Raj returned the following morning—without the Dutch couple." Malgorn had told her that Gautier's shoes and trousers were spattered with mud.

Gautier's French visitors began to feel frightened; especially when two days after the disappearance of the Dutch couple, and after demands by Renelleau for more information, Gautier made a partial confession to Malgorn and Renelleau. As Malgorn told Madame Gires later, Gautier admitted that Bintarang's postal money orders had enabled him to get hold of some American dollars. When Malgorn asked what he had done with the Dutch couple, Gautier told him, "Don't worry about them. After what I did to them, they will be in the hospital for six months, and they won't be able to remember what happened."

On that same morning—December 17—Renelleau had asked for his passport back. Gautier had given it to him, apologizing for the fact that he had cashed some of Renelleau's traveler's checks. He promised to repay him later.

Malgorn told Madame Gires that the next day Gautier, Suzanne and Raj left for Don Muang airport. Renelleau and Malgorn drove them, and once there, Gautier bought tickets for Katmandu, the capital of Nepal, on the slopes of the Himalayas. He told Malgorn that he was going to make the best deal of his career, but asked him to tell everyone he had gone to Hong Kong.

While they were waiting for the boarding gate to open, someone bought a copy of the Bangkok *Post* and read aloud to the others the first story about the murders beside the Superhighway. The headline ran: AUSTRALIAN COUPLE KILLED AND BURNT. The aircraft was now ready for boarding, and with a wave of the hand from Gautier, he, Suzanne and Raj boarded the plane. Malgorn and Renelleau couldn't have been more glad to see them go.

But when they were back at Kanit House, they were panic-stricken. For four days they sat around the apartment not knowing what to do.

Their first thought was to get away—and fast. But neither of them had any money. Only the third Frenchman, Philippe, had enough to buy plane tickets for all three of them, and he had gone to Penang, in Malaysia, to renew his visa.

"When we returned from our short vacation in Hua Hin on December 22," Nadine told Knippenberg, "we found the two men in a state of shock. Both were convinced they had been lodging with murderers. And that evening, while Gautier was abroad, Dominique and Yannick showed us a whole series of exhibits. There was a rubber gas tube, still reeking of gasoline. I saw two hypodermic syringes. In a drawer there was a pair of white rubber surgical gloves. In an attaché case Gautier even kept a false mustache. I saw the Dutchman's transistor radio and the Dutch girl's brown leather handbag. In a drawer were some postcards written by the Dutch couple but never posted." Malgorn also pointed out some jewelry and articles that he said were owned by the Turk who had disappeared. Then Malgorn, who had the key and knew the combination, opened the safe. "Inside," Madame Gires remembered, "there were several stolen passports."

Knippenberg was intrigued by the fate of the three Frenchmen. "What happened to them?" he asked Madame Gires.

"They knew that Gautier was expected back from Nepal the next day—and they were terrified. Malgorn told me they were convinced that they would be murdered if they stayed any longer."

Luckily Philippe came back from Penang the next day, before Gautier and the others returned, and the three Frenchmen booked seats on the first available plane to France. Malgorn made one last gesture of revenge before leaving Kanit House. He changed the combination of Gautier's safe, and then at Don Muang airport he threw the key to the safe into a wastebasket.

According to Madame Gires, when Gautier and Raj returned to Kanit House they were furious to find that the guests had left.

"They telephoned me right away," she said, "to ask if I knew anything about what had happened. I went straight upstairs. Gautier had been unpacking—or checking the contents of cupboards and drawers—because articles were strewn about the room. I noticed two Dutch money orders bearing the name of Franciscus Bintarang. I also noticed a diary the Dutchman had kept."

Madame Gires remembered that Gautier was "obviously ruffled" that his French friends had departed so suddenly. He was also furious at not being able to open the safe, but next day he flew back to Nepal, leaving Raj to deal with the problem. Raj sent for two Thai workmen, who arrived with a large toolbox, but Madame Gires didn't know if they were able to open the safe, because that same day Raj also left for Nepal.

Madame Gires informed Knippenberg of the *aide-mémoire* sent by the British consul, John Howard, to the Thai police, and she also mentioned that she had managed to "borrow" the Dutchman's diary, which she had handed over to Howard. On March 9 Knippenberg met with John Howard and reviewed the confidential document and Frans's diary. Though Mina had never mentioned the name of the dashing stranger they met in Kowloon, Frans had done so. He was, according to the diary, a man called Alain Dupuis.

To Knippenberg there could be no doubt that Dupuis and Gautier were the same man.

AT ABOUT THIS TIME Knippenberg was presented with a long and detailed statement made to the Australian police by Russell Lapthorne, an Australian, and his Indonesian wife, Vera. The real significance of the statement was to come out a little later, but at this stage it provided a fascinating picture of two murderers at work, of their methods, of the manner in which they preyed on unsuspecting tourists and gained their confidence.

The Lapthornes lived in Moorabbin, a suburb of Melbourne, Victoria, and in August and September 1975 they were on holiday in Thailand. Russell was twenty-four and Vera was three years older. They had stayed in the Crown Hotel in Bangkok, and on September 1 they went to spend the day at the beach at Pattaya.

At about half past one they were sitting on the beach buying coconuts from which to drink when a French couple also approached the coconut vendor. The couple had bicycles, and Lapthorne noticed that the woman was carrying a white Samoyed puppy, which she called Frankie. The four began to talk together. The man spoke good English, though with a marked French accent, and introduced himself as Jean Belmont. The girl, whose English was less fluent, was called Suzanne.

They were well dressed, seemed to be educated, and volunteered the information that they came from Paris and had been staying at the Tropicana Hotel in Pattaya for four days but were not very keen on the area. They said they intended to visit Singapore, Bali, Hong Kong and the Philippines. They seemed rather doubtful about what route to travel, and Lapthorne was delighted to offer suggestions.

"Why not go to Singapore via Penang?" he said. "And by train rather than by air?"

Belmont seemed to think it a capital idea. "Let's go to my hotel room and talk it over," he said. "We could have a beer."

They did so, and talked more about their travel plans. "We're supposed to leave Bangkok in a couple of days' time—on Wednesday," said Lapthorne. "We want to visit Hua Hin, which is about a hundred miles southwest of Bangkok." In fact, Hua Hin is immediately across the bay from Pattaya, but to reach it you have to return to Bangkok and then go south again.

"Could we come with you?" Belmont asked.

"Why not?" The Lapthornes had no objections.

The only problem, as Belmont pointed out, was that the Lapthornes were in Pattaya only for the day and were returning to Bangkok later the same afternoon, while he was going to spend another day with Suzanne at the beach. "Perhaps," he asked Lapthorne, "you'd be kind enough to buy train tickets for us as well as for yourselves, and then we'll meet in Bangkok on Tuesday night."

He gave Lapthorne two hundred bahts—about ten dollars—which was the price of two train tickets, then suggested to him, "Why don't you telephone me at the Imperial Hotel in Bangkok? That's where we'll stay on Tuesday night. Then you can tell me the train time, and we'll arrange a meeting place."

At eight o'clock on Tuesday evening Lapthorne did ring the Imperial Hotel, but no Jean Belmont was registered. At seven o'clock the following morning Belmont called Lapthorne.

"Suzanne and I didn't get away from Pattaya until midnight," he explained. The four agreed to meet at Hualampong Station at eleven o'clock. All went according to plan, and the two couples traveled together to Hua Hin. Lapthorne noticed that the Belmonts carried very little luggage.

They registered for two nights at the Railway Hotel, and were allotted adjacent rooms. They planned to leave on Friday evening for Hat Yai, in southern Thailand.

Once they had settled in, unpacked and looked around, the four of them went for a walk on the beach. Lapthorne noticed that Belmont and Suzanne were not in a very good mood. They had not enjoyed the train trip, they said, and were disappointed by the hotel and the beach.

Back at the hotel they sat on their verandas. These had a splendid view of the sea, and the dividing partition between them had been pulled back, making one long and comfortable veranda. Belmont was more cheerful now, and he ordered four milk shakes from the coffee shop. Lapthorne remembered later that he didn't see the milk shakes arrive, as the waiter left them at Belmont's door. However, they all drank them.

That evening they walked around the little town and picked out a restaurant on the street between the hotel and the station. Belmont insisted on paying for dinner, though once again he seemed to be in a bad mood. He didn't like the food, and he was impatient, almost rude, with the waitress. On the way back to the hotel they came across a few stalls and started to bargain for a basket for Frankie, the Samoyed puppy. Once again Lapthorne thought that Belmont was rude and rough in his approach to the local people. In the end they didn't buy the basket.

That night the Lapthornes were taken violently ill with diarrhea and nausea. They both assumed it had been caused by the food they had eaten—either on the train or at the restaurant.

On Thursday morning the four of them met for breakfast, though understandably neither of the Lapthornes was very hungry. They sat on the beach while Belmont and Suzanne ate fresh crabs.

Later the Lapthornes went with Suzanne to the railway station, where they bought four advance sleeper tickets to Hat Yai for Friday night. When Lapthorne asked where Belmont was, Suzanne replied, "I think he's gone off to buy some milk."

Back at the hotel, Lapthorne and Vera sat in deck chairs on their veranda. Belmont and Suzanne retired to their room to shower. About three 'oclock they brought out four glasses of chocolate milk together with a bowl of milk for the dog. Vera drank only part of her glass and went to rest on her bed, feeling dizzy. She remembered later that she thought the milk had a bitter taste. Lapthorne drank all his milk, and the last thing he remembers that afternoon is reading a book, *Oil Politics*, and vaguely seeing Belmont and Suzanne standing on the veranda.

It was five a.m. on Saturday before Lapthorne woke up, and he was not in his room. He and Vera had been taken to the Hua Hin health center. The assistant manager of the hotel, who had been expecting them to check out in order to catch the sleeper train, had come around midnight to their room to see what had happened. Vera was on the bed, unconscious. Russell Lapthorne was on the floor. They were rushed to the health center, where doctors immediately used stomach pumps. One doctor later said they both appeared to have had a heavy sedative.

At four o'clock Saturday morning, before Lapthorne woke up, Vera—who had not drunk the entire glass of milk and so was not as badly poisoned—asked to return to the hotel. She went straight to their room, which looked as though it had been stripped by a tornado. Their American Express traveler's checks, for four hundred and thirty U.S. dollars, were gone. So was cash totaling eight hundred Singapore dollars and fifteen hundred bahts. Their passports had been stolen—Lapthorne's Australian one and her Indonesian one— together with their marriage and health certificates and their driver's licenses. In fact, all their identity papers were missing. Their valuables were gone too—a movie camera, a diamond ring and a gold chain—though Vera's gold pendant and rings, which, significantly, did not indicate the number of karats, had been left. The book, *Oil Politics*, had been taken.

Vera noticed immediately that the glasses out of which they had drunk the milk had been carefully washed. A dog's toy ball and batteries from a cassette recorder had been left behind.

It never entered her head that the Belmonts were the thieves. Indeed her first instinct was to turn to the Belmonts for help. She ran to the next room and knocked on the door. It was opened immediately—by a complete stranger. Vera ran down the hotel stairs and found the porter.

"Where are Mr. Belmont and his wife?" she asked.

The porter looked at her blankly and said, "They booked out to catch the sleeper."

Vera returned to the health center and told her husband what had happened. At about eight a.m. the two left the health center and went to the police station. No one there could speak English, and they were told to come back at ten o'clock. This they did, and were able to tell their story to an English-speaking police officer, though he did not seem particularly interested.

A Thai businessman who happened to be at the police station gave the Lapthornes some money, and later they sold their Instamatic pocket camera to the hotel manager to pay for the rooms. The Belmonts presumably had not bothered to take the camera because it was not worth much.

Later that day the police took a statement from the Lapthornes through an interpreter, but it was written down in Thai, and they were not sure what it said; nor did they have time to worry about such details, because that evening Lapthorne became so ill that he had to return to the health center for treatment. Vera took the first bus she could to Bangkok, and there, terribly distraught, she notified his parents in Australia, who contacted an Australian member of Parliament, who notified the Australian embassy in Bangkok.

Lapthorne was able to travel to Bangkok soon afterward, and the couple were given new passports and visas. Both felt they had recovered, but a week later Lapthorne became ill again and had to be admitted to the St. Louis Hospital in Bangkok, where he stayed for two weeks, suffering from high fever and abdominal pain.

The Lapthornes had not bothered with the statement the police had taken through an interpreter, but back in Australia they found it had been condensed in translation, and in parts was wildly inaccurate. Among many errors, it said they had taken some medicine that had had a poisonous effect. They had not taken any medicine. They had been poisoned.

The statement also referred to Belmont as Bremman. It was when they read this that they decided to make a new statement to the Australian police, and it was this that had now come to rest on the desk of Herman Knippenberg.

To Knippenberg the Lapthornes' experience bore all the hallmarks of the murders in Thailand. However, one thing was missing from the statement: a detailed and foolproof identification of the villains.

Knippenberg sent photographs of Gautier, Suzanne and even the Samoyed to the Australian embassy in Bangkok, where officials immediately forwarded them to police in Melbourne. The Lapthornes took one look at them and formally identified them as Jean Belmont, Suzanne and Frankie.

As HE PONDERED OVER everything he had learned so far, Knippenberg was interrupted by an unexpected call from Graeme Stanton, the managing editor of the Bangkok *Post*. He asked Stanton to come and have a drink with him so that he could tell the editor all that had happened. Stanton obviously had been intrigued by the strange murders of the "Australian" couple, to say nothing of the girl in the bikini and the others who had so mysteriously died. But though he had publicized the murders in the *Post*, any suggestions that the police should take more action had been ignored. It was as though there was a conspiracy of silence, a wall of indifference to the fate of these foreigners that nothing could break down.

Stanton went to see Knippenberg. This was the first of many, many meetings they had together, and a strong friendship ensued. Stanton remembers "the evenings we spent drinking Scotch and talking, because poor Herman knew so much and could find no one to take any real action against the murderers of foreigners who had been so wickedly killed in Bangkok."

Knippenberg, however, was convinced he knew who had murdered Mina and Frans and the others. He had collected some one hundred and seventy pages of documentation and he was determined to make someone pay attention to it. But all this, remember, was in March 1976. Gautier had flown into Nepal the previous December. What had happened during the intervening time?

CHAPTER 6

THE TRAVELING ANTICS of the Kanit House trio that winter—and however bloodstained the motives, antics is the only word—might have been expressly arranged to show how easy it is for anyone with brazen effrontery to make a fool of the law. Sometimes together, sometimes separately, changing identities from day to day—once with

Suzanne even traveling on a man's passport—they flew across the face of the East. At times they could hardly remember what to call each other, for with stolen passports they switched identities so swiftly that they sometimes forgot who they were.

It would be months before a precise picture of what happened during this period would emerge, but eventually the sinister tableau would begin to take shape. And in the heart of it there always seemed to be the smiling face of a dashing, generous young man.

THE KINGDOM OF NEPAL is known for many things—its brave Gurkha soldiers, its mountains such as Everest and Kanchenjunga. The capital, Katmandu, with its Hindu and Buddhist temples and royal palaces, stands over four thousand feet high in a valley, and on a clear day Everest is visible. There is a regular nonstop air service between Bangkok and Katmandu, and the threesome took advantage of it on December 18, Gautier and Suzanne traveling on the passports of Frans Bintarang and Mina Jansen, with crudely substituted photographs of themselves stuck into the Dutch passports. They used these names when they booked into the five-star Soaltee Oberoi Hotel.

Gautier and Suzanne were not interested in sight-seeing; they were looking for the foreigners who are drawn to Katmandu—tourists with whom they always found it easy to strike up casual friendships—students, hippies, drifters. Katmandu was a haven for dropouts from every corner of the world. In 1975 there were nearly two thousand of them, many attracted by the ease with which they could obtain drugs.

LSD and hashish were plentiful. Heroin was available in increasing quantities. Drug addicts, hippies, peddlers—all seemed to congregate around Katmandu's "Freak Street" and the lanes branching behind it, where in dim and dirty cafés they could get a pill or a fix.

Among the hundreds staying in cheap hotels on Freak Street were Henri Gilbert, a thirty-year-old Canadian student, and his girl friend, Sally Dalton, a twenty-nine-year-old American. They were sitting in the lobby of their modest hotel when they fell into conversation with a charming man who said he had just flown up from Bangkok.

"My name is Alain Gautier," he introduced himself. "I specialize in transactions involving precious stones."

Neither Gilbert nor Dalton wrote letters home, so apart from the testimony of the few eyewitnesses in the hotel, the details of what happened will always remain sketchy. But on December 21, three days after Gautier's arrival, Gilbert went walking into the beautiful hills with their narrow footpaths that snaked along the sides of the mountains outside the city. He never returned. When Sally became worried, she set off to search for him, thinking perhaps that he had been taken ill. She never returned either.

Later that same day, hikers taking the paths along the edge of the mountainside stumbled on the badly burned body of Henri Gilbert. Two days later the burned body of Sally Dalton was discovered. Gilbert had been strangled. According to one report, Sally had been stabbed. Both had been soaked in gasoline and incinerated. Sally's face was unrecognizable, and girl friends from the hotel who were called in to identify the body could do so only by her earrings.

By the afternoon of December 24, Gautier and Suzanne had not only flown back to Bangkok, they had actually returned to Nepal. On the flight to Bangkok, Gautier used Gilbert's passport. Suzanne used her own passport to enter Thailand. No one in the immigration department noticed that it bore no exit stamp from Thailand, for, of course, she had left Bangkok as Mina Jansen. Nor did it bear an exit stamp from Nepal, so she must have used one passport to leave Katmandu and another to reenter Thailand.

Curiously neither of them seemed to face any problems at the various airport immigration desks during their crazy flights across the East. True, they invariably took the precaution of presenting themselves before officials during their busiest periods, but all the same, immigration officers time after time failed to notice the crude way in which the two had altered passports, stuck in photographs and sometimes finished off visas or stamps with a ball-point pen.

When Gautier returned to Bangkok from Katmandu, he was (as Madame Gires had told Knippenberg) annoyed by the way that his French guests had fled so abruptly. No doubt he was worried in case they might talk. So he decided to leave again after spending only one night in the apartment. Incredibly he returned to Katmandu; even more incredibly he again used the murdered man Gilbert's passport when leaving Bangkok.

Raj, who had stayed an extra day in Bangkok to try and open the locked safe, flew to join Gautier and Suzanne in Katmandu. He left

Bangkok using a Turkish passport in the name of Yusuf Bilgin, with a forged Nepalese visa.

A few days later, after Gautier had left Katmandu, the police found in the trunk of a Datsun, rented in the name of Bintarang, a pair of jeans, metal-framed dark glasses and a nylon bag, all of which belonged to Gilbert. In Sally Dalton's hotel room they had found a diary in which she had written the name Alain Gautier.

On December 27 Gautier, Suzanne and Raj drove across the border into India at the frontier town of Birganj, presumably in another rented car. Daunting formalities are usually involved in taking cars into India, but somehow they managed it, Gautier and Suzanne remaining in the car while Raj took their passports to the immigration office. One of the immigration officers noticed that Raj had a bandage on one hand, partially concealing a burn.

Once in India, they abandoned the car—and their identities. By the time they booked into a hotel on Park Street in Calcutta, Gautier and Suzanne had become Monsieur and Madame Ponent, a French couple, as their passports clearly testified.

In Calcutta they fell into conversation with a thirty-four-year-old Israeli, Sol Levi. "I've been working in Iran as a crane driver to make some money," he told them. "I've always been interested in India and thought I'd make a trip here before I head for home."

They were having a few drinks together when Levi revealed that he was on his way to Varanasi, the holy city on the left bank of the Ganges. "But we're on our way to Varanasi too," exclaimed Gautier, much to the surprise of Suzanne and Raj. "Why don't we travel together?"

Arriving in Varanasi by train, the four went immediately to a hotel close to the station. Gautier suggested that to save money Raj and Levi could share a double room. "Suits me," said Levi. "I've worked like hell in Iran and saved five thousand dollars. I want to keep every cent of it I can until I get home." So they booked two double rooms.

In the middle of the night Raj got up without waking the Israeli. So did Gautier and Suzanne. All three left, and by dawn they were many miles away. At seven thirty a.m. a porter brought morning tea to Levi's room, knocked repeatedly and, when there was no reply, carefully pushed the door open. With a scream he dropped the tray and rushed out into the corridor, wailing for help. The manager arrived to find the drugged and strangled body of Sol Levi. The five thousand dollars for which he had worked so hard were gone.

The trio moved on to New Delhi and booked in at the Lodhi Hotel, where Gautier registered as Sol Levi, nonchalantly tossing his passport on the reception desk to prove it.

By January 6, 1976, the three of them had reached Goa, the former Portuguese enclave, and there they met three French engineers—all in their early twenties—who were heading for Colombo in Sri Lanka in a Ford van equipped with bunk beds.

"That's a coincidence," said Gautier. "The three of us are making for Colombo as well. Why don't we join forces and share the expenses? It'll not only save us a lot of money, but we'll see much more of the countryside than if we went by plane."

Everyone seemed delighted, and one of the Frenchmen, whose name was Eric Damour, suggested that they drive southward in slow stages and enjoy themselves, stopping in villages where there were beach houses that could be rented by the night.

They set off, with Bertrand Tell, another of the Frenchmen, at the wheel. It was January 9. On the first day they covered one hundred and twenty miles, reaching the small beach resort of Amaldi. They rented a bungalow for the night, and Raj was sent off to buy crabs and chickens, which he started to cook on the beach after lighting a bonfire. They were all in great spirits, especially after Gautier mixed them cocktails of whiskey, vodka and orange juice. He served them by the flickering flames of the fire—after which the three Frenchmen knew nothing until they regained consciousness thirty-six hours later in an Indian hospital.

Once the men were unconscious, Alain and Raj threw them into the van. Then the trio, with Raj driving, hastily cleared the campsite. The night was dark, the road narrow, and they had gone but a few miles before Raj failed to swerve in time to avoid an approaching bullock cart. A group of villagers, hearing the sound of the accident, came running up. Gautier, Raj and Suzanne fled.

The three French engineers had yielded a good haul—twenty-six hundred dollars in traveler's checks, six hundred dollars in cash, together with still and movie cameras worth another three thousand dollars—plus three invaluable passports. Suzanne and Alain left India from Madras, with Gautier flying to Bangkok in mid-January as Eric Damour. It took some time for Raj to link up with them later. This time Alain did not return to Kanit House. Instead he booked in at the twenty-three-story Dusit Thani Hotel, not far from his apartment. Four days later he switched passports for a few moments, using that of Bertrand Tell's to cash traveler's checks at the Bank of Canton, also near Kanit House.

For some reason Suzanne had flown from India to Singapore, so Gautier, once again using Eric Damour's passport, flew to meet her there. On January 25 she flew to Hong Kong, while he returned briefly to Bangkok. But after five days he flew to Hong Kong to join Suzanne. She had been staying at the YWCA, but when Gautier arrived they moved into the Sheraton.

Suzanne reminded Alain that they had been together for exactly six months. They celebrated the occasion by traveling to Macao for the night, though it does not seem to have been a successful trip. In the diary that Suzanne kept fitfully, she wrote the following morning, January 31, "Bad evening. I was tired but I didn't sleep."

Two days later, back in Hong Kong, they met Peter Frederick Clark, an American teacher, born in Java, who was on a round-the-world trip. Gautier introduced himself as Eric Damour, and he and Suzanne invited Clark to have dinner with them at the Sheraton.

After dinner the three decided to visit a nightclub district nearby. Before leaving, "Eric" suggested they all go upstairs to his hotel room for sweaters, because the night air was chilly. Once in the room, Eric and Suzanne excused themselves to get ready to go out, and Clark switched on the television.

Three days later, February 5, Peter Clark woke up on the floor of the hotel room. He was completely alone. Though extremely dizzy, he managed to stumble out of the room and summon help. Later, when he had recovered sufficiently to return to his own hotel, he found all his possessions gone—his passport, traveler's checks and credit cards.

On the same day that Clark awoke from his long sleep, Gautier and Suzanne flew back to Singapore. They stayed only one night and then flew to Hat Yai, in the south of Thailand near the frontier with Malaysia. By this time they had become so contemptuous of passport checks and immigration controls that Suzanne actually traveled on a man's passport—Eric Damour's—to which she had affixed her own photograph.

Unexpectedly Rajesh Khosla reappeared to greet them when they finally returned to Bangkok. No one knows where he had been since the trio split up in India. But here he was again, the faithful servant, ready and anxious to do anything they wanted, and with him was a new arrival in the apartment, a balding, thirty-year-old French salesman called Alfred Colin.

CHAPTER 7

BY THE BEGINNING of March an exasperated Herman Knippenberg felt that he had enough material to back up his conviction that he knew the identities of the murderers of his compatriots, and he decided to act.

First he circulated copies of his evidence to the American, British, Canadian, French and Nepalese embassies. Then on Wednesday, March 10, he telephoned Major General Rak Thamrongrak, the commander of Bangkok's Crime Suppression Squad, an elite force dealing only with serious crime, which the Thais like to think is their equivalent of Britain's Scotland Yard. Knippenberg asked Rak to take immediate action against Gautier and his apartment mates—and Rak did, after a fashion. He instructed Colonel Pravit Ruangkarn and his deputy, Captain Sura Chuvasna, to visit Knippenberg at the Dutch embassy.

Knippenberg was waiting for them with all the evidence ready—and was furious to discover that neither officer had any inkling of what he was talking about. Apologetically Colonel Pravit explained that they had been handed the murder file only a short while before setting out for the Dutch embassy. They had had no time to study it.

Patiently the Dutch diplomat gave them an exhaustive briefing. He showed them photographs of the suspects taken surreptitiously by Madame Gires. Knippenberg also provided sketches of the two fifth-floor apartments at Kanit House. Colonel Pravit appeared to be impressed and agreed that the police should stage a raid at six o'clock the following morning.

Knippenberg asked if he could accompany the police on the raid. "I can't be sure yet," said Pravit. "Will you please call me at seven thirty this evening and I will give you an answer then."

Promptly at half past seven Knippenberg telephoned the headquarters of the Crime Suppression Squad. To his astonishment he was told, "The raid has been postponed."

"But why?" he asked.

"It's to safeguard the security of witnesses," was the astonishing reply.

Even on the following morning the Thai police had not decided the exact time when the raid was going to take place. Knippenberg was pondering on the sloppiness of the police force when Nadine Gires arrived suddenly at the Dutch embassy.

"I'm in a hurry," she said, "but I thought I ought to warn you that Alain and Suzanne seem to be planning to leave town."

"Today?" asked Knippenberg.

"I don't think so. They don't seem to be in a desperate hurry, but they are certainly packing their bags."

Knippenberg asked her, "Do you think there's time for you to take a few more photographs of them before they leave?"

"I'll try," promised Nadine.

Armed with these new facts, Knippenberg telephoned General Rak Thamrongrak and pressed for immediate action.

Rak finally promised him in the affirmative. "The raid will take place this afternoon."

The police, Rak explained, would go to the apartment ostensibly searching for drugs, but they would be instructed to keep their eyes open for any possessions of the murdered Dutch couple, such as stolen passports or any other evidence.

At four thirty p.m. a police squad with drawn guns burst into apartments 503 and 504 at Kanit House, taking the suspects by surprise. The first brusque request by the police was "Your passports, please!"

Suzanne rummaged in her bag and produced a Canadian passport. It bore the name of Catherine Nicole Ponchet. This appeared to be in order. The Indian produced an Indian passport. It bore his real name, Rajesh Khosla. Without a flicker of apprehension, Gautier produced an American passport. It bore the name of Peter Frederick

Clark. It seemed, from a cursory inspection, to be in order. The three suspects were, however, bundled into a corner while the police made a search—of sorts—of the two apartments. Then Gautier, Suzanne and Raj were taken to Crime Suppression Squad headquarters for further questioning.

At seven thirty that evening an anxious Knippenberg telephoned Colonel Pravit. "Tell me what's happened," he said. "What was the result of the raid? Did you find everything?"

Hardly able to believe his ears, Knippenberg listened as Pravit calmly told him that "nothing of interest" had been found.

"There must be a mistake," cried Knippenberg. "Can I have permission to go to the apartment and see for myself?"

"I'm sorry, that's impossible," said Pravit. "However, we still have to open the safe. The people in the apartment told the police the key was missing, so we took the safe to headquarters and we've arranged for a locksmith to open it tomorrow in the presence of the three suspects."

"Well," said the baffled Knippenberg, sighing, "at least we've got them safely behind bars."

"Actually we've allowed them to go back to their apartment," said Pravit. The Thai policeman must have heard Knippenberg's cry of astonishment, for he added hastily, as though to excuse the action, "Of course, we have retained their passports."

Knippenberg might have wondered if any of them would ever see the Kanit House trio again, but in any event he telephoned the United States embassy and told them about the American passport in the name of Clark, which Gautier was using.

Rather to Knippenberg's surprise, the three suspects dutifully reported back to police headquarters the next morning, Friday, March 12. There the safe was opened, and nothing incriminating was found inside it.

But now American agents had arrived at police headquarters to offer their assistance to the police. To lend credence to the overt reason for the raid—which ostensibly was to search for drugs—the Americans came from the U.S. Drug Enforcement Agency. When they inspected the passport of Peter Clark, they were immediately suspicious. The physical description of the owner had been changed and the photograph had been inserted incorrectly. Within a few days the Americans would discover from their consul in Hong Kong that the real Clark had reported the theft of his passport there in February.

Added to all this, "Clark" was evasive when answering the questions put by the American drug enforcement officers. One asked him the town of his birth in Iowa. Gautier, who presumably had failed to memorize the details on the passport, gave the name of a street instead of the name of the town.

"We'd like you to hold these people until we can check with Washington about this passport," the Americans told the Thai police.

The Americans also asked permission to borrow the passport, but the Thai police refused on the ground that it was required as evidence. They did however promise, verbally, to hold the three in custody. It was a promise quickly broken. Later that same day the Dutch and American officials were stunned and outraged to learn that the three suspects had been released. They protested, but in vain. "The police claimed that when they raided the apartment they found nothing of interest," said one diplomat bitterly, "but it was all there waiting to be found."

According to one rumor, the trio just walked out of police headquarters when they were left in a room without a guard. But there was a more sinister rumor—that a lot of money had passed hands, that Gautier had bribed someone with three hundred thousand bahts (nearly fifteen thousand dollars).

There was a third possibility: that the police felt they did not have sufficient evidence to hold the three people. But this could hardly be true, because the police had made a return visit to the apartment in Kanit House, and this time they had found an assortment of drugs and medicines, together with some hypodermic syringes. They had also found a book on Buddhism with the name Mary Jane on the flyleaf. They found a French passport in the name of Eric Damour, though it bore the picture of a woman who looked like Suzanne.

Nadine Gires had, of course, heard all about the raid and the subsequent arrest of her "friends." She had fully expected them to be kept in custody—at least for a while—but later that evening she saw lights burning in the fifth-floor apartment. She was so surprised that she telephoned to see who was there.

Raj answered and suggested, "Come up and have a drink."

She went up to apartment 504. Raj told her more details of the raid. Knowing nothing of the information that Nadine had supplied to Knippenberg, he said, "I'm sure it was the result of a complaint made by a customer who had bought some diamonds."

Madame Gires asked where Gautier and Suzanne were.

"They came to the apartment early," said Raj, "and collected gems worth about thirty thousand dollars."

About midnight, when Nadine had returned to her own apartment, she heard a car drawing up outside the front door of the wing in which they all lived. A door of the car banged, as though someone had gotten out, but she noticed that the engine had been left running. Peeping out the window, she saw Gautier and Suzanne running toward the entrance. Suzanne was carrying a suitcase and a large brown paper bag. But it was late and Nadine fell asleep, so she never did see any of them leave.

The next morning, Saturday, Raj telephoned her and asked her to come upstairs. While he was busy in apartment 504, Madame Gires took a quick look around 503. She saw some car insurance papers, issued in Barcelona to a man called Yusuf Bilgin. Another folder contained three passport pictures of Bilgin. To Nadine the police search seemed to have been utterly ineffective. As soon as she could get away, she took the pictures to Knippenberg, and he contacted the Turkish embassy.

On Sunday afternoon Gautier telephoned Madame Gires from Malaysia. "I'll ring you again in a few days," he said, "so you can tell me if you have any news of Raj. Dara"—his Thai girl friend—"is looking after Frankie." Gautier's last words to Nadine Gires were, "Will you please keep an eye on our apartment?"

Madame Gires was never able to do that, for the next morning, Monday, the police finally decided to stop anyone entering or leaving either of the two apartments. The management of Kanit House was ordered to station civilian guards outside the entrances.

On Wednesday, March 17, Raj demanded his passport back from the police. Doubtless to his surprise he got it without any trouble, and as soon as he had it, he went to the U.S. embassy and volunteered a statement, telling them everything he knew about the passport of Peter Clark. Then Rajesh disappeared from Bangkok. He also disappeared from the story. He has never been seen since.

GAUTIER AND SUZANNE HAD GOT clean away to Malaysia using a rented car and were laying plans to travel to Europe.

Gradually, however, the evidence against Gautier began to pile up. A few days after the police raid on Kanit House, Knippenberg learned from the Dutch police that Renelleau and Philippe, who had fled the apartment, had volunteered statements to the Dutch embassy in Paris. They were able to expand considerably on the information that Madame Gires had given to Knippenberg.

Then the body of the bikini-clad girl was exhumed and finally identified in Washington as that of Mary Jane McLachlan. Once the identity of the girl was known, it was not difficult to reconstruct some of her last movements in Bangkok before her death, including her visit to Kanit House.

The second victim was traced through the photographs that Madame Gires had found in the apartment, which Knippenberg had handed to the Turkish embassy. He was identified as Yusuf Bilgin by his father, who had traveled to Bangkok to identify the exhumed body; he fainted when he saw its charred and decomposed state.

The third body, which had been found in a ditch, was identified later and quite by chance through a man who was to become intimately involved with all the murders, Lieutenant Colonel Sompol Suthimai, chief of the Interpol section of the Thai police. A Mr. Barry worked at a United Nations agency in Bangkok with Colonel Sompol's French wife, Nicole. Barry asked Nicole if she could quietly ask her husband to try and trace a French girl called Yvonne Desbois. Mutual friends in France had written to say that she had disappeared and they were becoming worried about her.

As it happened, Barry knew the girl. Indeed, he told Nicole that he had once saved Yvonne from forced prostitution in the Middle East.

Sompol invited Barry to his office to look over Interpol picture files of unidentified bodies.

"That's the one!" Barry immediately recognized Yvonne from one of the photographs. He was taken straight to the Police Hospital, and there he formally identified the body. One thing puzzled Mr. Barry. He knew Yvonne Desbois's background well enough to tell Colonel Sompol that she certainly did not have the sort of money needed to stay in the luxury President Hotel. Why would a part-time dressmaker, a girl who once nearly became a prostitute, suddenly arrive in Bangkok to find rooms already reserved for her in a posh hotel like the President?

Sompol made some discreet inquiries. First of all, he established that the rooms for Yvonne had not been booked by anyone staying in the hotel but by someone calling from outside. It immediately occurred to him that she might have been invited to Bangkok by a man who didn't want their liaison to be made public; perhaps he was a married man, staying in an apartment or another hotel. The poor girl, of course, would never be able to enlighten him, and as for the man, well, he could be anyone. Still, it was a puzzle. He sent a team of highly specialized detectives to the President Hotel to find out everything they could about the mysterious Yvonne Desbois.

At first they drew a blank. She had signed no bills for meals; she did not seem to be remembered at all. But then, when they had almost given up hope, one detective tracked down a telephone operator who had been manning the hotel switchboard part of the time during Yvonne Desbois's brief stay. Desbois had made only one telephone call, but this operator had noted the number. It was that of Gautier's apartment.

After further investigation, Sompol was finally able to piece together the connection between Bilgin and Yvonne. Sompol reasoned that Bilgin, known to Interpol as a drug dealer, had suggested that Yvonne come to Bangkok to collect narcotics that he was buying, then fly with them to Europe. Bilgin had made arrangements for her to stay at the President Hotel. But it wasn't until later that Sompol was able to connect Yvonne's death and Bilgin's with the string of murders occurring throughout Asia.

CHAPTER 8

KNIPPENBERG'S PATIENCE WAS exhausted. He felt that largely through his efforts and those of his colleagues all the necessary evidence had been assembled, not only about the murders of Frans and Mina—those, of course, were his main concern as a Dutch official—but about other murders in Thailand. He had handed the ball to the police, who had dropped it and let it roll away.

Night after night Graeme Stanton of the Bangkok *Post* visited the Knippenberg home, drinking Scotch with Herman as the Dutchman tried to plan his next move.

"I could see a hell of a fine story for the *Post*," Stanton remembers. "I sat on it for weeks—dying to print it but afraid of the laws of libel."

After all, none of the Kanit House trio had been charged, the evidence was largely circumstantial, and what was to prevent any of them from suing? Until this time, although the individual murders had been reported separately, no link had been suggested between them. The names of Alain Gautier and Suzanne Ponchet were unknown to the public.

On the night of May 7 Stanton and Knippenberg discussed the possibility of blowing everything wide open with front-page publicity. At first they hesitated. Since the suspects were out of the country, they would not be in a position to take legal action. But what if they returned to Bangkok? And then, too, Knippenberg did not want to alarm them and jeopardize their eventual arrest. Nevertheless, after talking long into the night, a weary Knippenberg finally stated flatly, "We're at a virtual standstill, Graeme. Let's print it."

"Right you are!" cried the cheerful Stanton. "We'll have a go!"

Stanton put together a dossier, assembled his photographs and broke the story on Saturday, May 8.

Across the front page the *Post* splashed the headline:

THE WEB OF DEATH
MORE BODIES LINKED TO MURDER RIDDLE

There were photographs of Frans, Mina, Mary Jane and Yvonne, as well as a large picture of Gautier and Suzanne, whom the *Post* described as his mistress. The story traced the gruesome murders and told in detail how these four people had visited Alain Gautier in Kanit House. Within a few days the story was picked up by the Thai newspaper *Siang Puang Chon*—voice of the people.

ONE MAN, ON vacation with his wife in Chiang Mai, read the story with mounting interest. He was Lieutenant Colonel Sompol Suthimai of Thai Interpol, the same man who had investigated the death of Yvonne Desbois. A dedicated officer with a reputation for honesty and devotion to duty, Sompol realized immediately the story's implications for Interpol. He broke off his vacation at once and began the return trip to Bangkok.

Arriving at police headquarters, on Rama I Road, Colonel Sompol discovered that the widespread attention given to the newspaper accounts had generated a flurry of activity. On his desk Sompol found a formal memorandum from the director general of police ordering him to set up a special committee to investigate the case. Armed with this, Sompol at once began enlisting the resources of Interpol. In the next few days more than fifty messages traveled from his office to Interpol headquarters in St. Cloud and to Interpol bureaus in many countries and cities—among them Nepal, India, Pakistan, Malaysia, Singapore, Hong Kong, Holland, Israel, Greece, Turkey, Spain, West Germany, Switzerland and France.

At the same time Sompol was given the name of a foreign diplomat who, he was told matter-of-factly, had "expressed an interest in the case." The man was Herman Knippenberg. He called him at once and they made arrangements to meet.

When Sompol arrived at the Dutch embassy, on Wireless Road, he was escorted to Knippenberg's office, a small but comfortable room with a picture of Queen Juliana on the wall. Knippenberg greeted Sompol warmly and the two shook hands. They spoke in English, and as Knippenberg related the details of his own investigation, supporting them with photographs and sketches, Sompol listened and made notes. When the interview concluded, Sompol returned to police headquarters. Alone in his own office, he put a piece of paper in his typewriter and began to draft a new message to Interpol. Its request was clear: provide as much specific information as possible on the tenants of apartments 503 and 504, Kanit House.

It was a painstaking task. The French police suggested to Interpol that Gautier might be a man known to them as Charles Grolier or Grotier. The information was processed through Interpol's central files at St. Cloud, but neither name proved to be Gautier's real one.

On the other hand, Interpol Ottawa came up with a fairly complete picture of Suzanne Ponchet. As Madame Gires had insisted, her real given name was not Suzanne but Catherine, and she had a younger sister, Claire. Suzanne was a convent-educated girl, born in

Lévis, Quebec, a small factory town of sawmills and foundries, separated from Quebec City by the St. Lawrence River, only two miles wide at this point.

She had worked as a medical secretary, and it was then that she met an elderly and wealthy man called Pierre Levant. They became engaged. Levant took her on a trip to India in April 1975—and there she met Gautier. Apparently she switched her favors quickly. Indeed some accounts suggested that Levant, returning to his hotel room unexpectedly, found his fiancée and Gautier together. Whatever happened, Levant returned to Canada. Gautier, according to the police reports, was at that time on the point of moving to Bangkok, and Suzanne went home to Canada, presumably in the hope of asking forgiveness and becoming reunited with her wealthy fiancé. Then Gautier had second thoughts. He wrote begging Suzanne to join him in the Far East, and she needed no urging, especially as Gautier sent her air tickets and pocket money. She caught the first plane she could to Bangkok. The couple stayed in the small Nana Hotel for a night or two, then they moved to the Malaysia, where they met Rajesh. From there they later moved to Kanit House.

Meanwhile, more messages received by way of Interpol were rapidly building a dossier on the suspects' movements since they bolted from Bangkok. They had gone from Penang to Kuala Lumpur, Singapore, Bombay, New Delhi, Karachi, Geneva, then to Germany—where Gautier had made a trip to sell gems—and to France, where they stayed with their newfound friend Alfred Colin at his house twenty-five miles outside Paris.

On May 14 Interpol headquarters at St. Cloud sent a message to Thailand, Canada, Holland, Nepal and Spain. Based on information obtained by the Canadian police, it said that Suzanne had contacted her family in Canada by letter from Geneva in April and had told them that she was going on to Barcelona. In view of everything that had happened, the Canadian authorities had formally canceled her passport, but this did not seem to have stopped her traveling, because later in April she telephoned her home in Canada from Spain, saying that she was on the move again but would leave a forwarding address with Gautier's mother in Marseille.

That address never reached Canada, though, in fact, Gautier, Suzanne and Colin did drive down to the south of France. Interpol did not know at that time—because they did not know Gautier's real identity—that the three of them dropped in on Gautier's Vietnamese-born mother, who had married a man called Monteaux. Monteaux was now in an institution, and she was living alone in a small red-tiled villa stuck like a stamp on the hillside of a little village on the outskirts of Marseille.

Simone (her French baptismal name) must have been a beauty when she was young. Even now, at fifty-three, she was quick and bright. She dressed in slacks, and she drove her little French car around the countryside and into Marseille.

Gautier's mother was astounded when the three of them turned up. She found Suzanne "very pretty, but frightened and nervous. She was wild about my son, though," Simone insisted. But the visit of a few days wasn't really a success. Gautier's mother intensely disliked Colin. "He was a terrible man," she said. "He had frightful table manners and was very impolite. I hated to see my son in such company."

And, too, she several times found her son rummaging through family papers, some of which he stole, as she discovered later. After the three had left, she received a phone call from a woman who said that Simone's son, using the name of Monteaux, had swindled her out of a considerable sum of money.

Soon, via Interpol, Colonel Sompol heard that Gautier, Suzanne and Colin were in Pakistan.

Interpol now asked Nepal to supply details of the murders that had taken place there in December. Another Interpol message asked Thailand and Holland if they were making any formal charges that might be brought against the Kanit House trio. Yet another Interpol message from St. Cloud—this time on May 19—went to the police of France, Thailand, Holland and Spain, giving more biographical details of Suzanne. Once again Interpol asked Thailand whether a formal arrest warrant had been issued.

This time—and at long last—the Thai police were moved into action, and warrants for the arrest of Gautier, Suzanne and Rajesh Khosla were issued. They were charged with conspiring to murder, using forged passports and receiving stolen goods.

On May 24 Interpol circulated a message to France, Canada, the United States, Spain, Holland, India, Turkey, Switzerland, Hong

Kong, Indonesia, Malaysia, Australia and Singapore. "Arrest the suspects on sight," it asked, "and inform Thai Interpol."

As Interpol put out its worldwide appeal for the arrest of the three from Kanit House, one major question still remained unanswered: Just who was Alain Gautier?

COLONEL SOMPOL HAD always been dubious about Gautier's "French" ancestry, and during the laborious process of building up details of the case, he had wondered more than once whether Gautier's dark skin was due perhaps to Indian or Pakistani parentage.

When he learned that Gautier had made for Pakistan, Sompol decided to ask Interpol to warn Pakistan of his suspicions, and also to warn India that Gautier might be heading their way. Instinct told him that many criminals—particularly those given to boasting, to megalomania—find it almost impossible not to return from time to time to their homeland.

And so, on Colonel Sompol's suggestion, St. Cloud warned Pakistan and India and sent the police in both countries a set of Gautier's fingerprints. It was to prove a fortuitous step.

CHAPTER 9

LOUIS CHABRIER WAS a good-looking twenty-eight-year-old Frenchman who arrived in India as a tourist in June 1976 ready and eager to taste anything which that exotic country could offer him. Like most Frenchmen he had a roving eye for a pretty girl, and so when he checked in at the Ranjit Hotel in New Delhi, his arms were wide open—ready not only to embrace the spectacle of India but any pretty girls who happened to come his way.

At first he did not have much luck. But the day he was leaving, an opportunity presented itself. He had checked out of his room and was in the lobby, killing time before leaving to catch a train out of Old Delhi, when a suave, charming stranger introduced himself in French. Delighted to meet a fellow countryman, Chabrier agreed to join the stranger and his friends—three women and a man—for dinner at a nearby restaurant. His excitement increased when the stranger discreetly hinted that, if Chabrier so wished, one of the ladies in the group could be persuaded to spend the night with him.

The stranger was Alain Gautier, back again in India, with Suzanne, Alfred Colin and two new friends, Margaret Wilson, an English girl age twenty-two, and a twenty-six-year-old Australian nurse named Diana Johnson. Gautier was driving a flashy Citroën, and the gang was making a habit of meeting Air France planes, picking out likely victims and, by waiting at the airport bus terminal or taxi stand, discovering where they were staying. Once a person was marked as a potential victim by Gautier, the trap for him could be baited, set and sprung.

That evening at the restaurant, Chabrier enjoyed a delicious chicken curry. And later, when Margaret Wilson agreed to let him come up to her room, Chabrier decided to postpone his departure. By the time he got to Margaret's room, however, Chabrier was already feeling groggy and nauseated.

As dawn broke over the crenellated towers of Delhi's Red Fort, Gautier and his friends were speeding away from the city. Maids passing Margaret's room for the next two days respected the DO NOT DISTURB sign hung on the door. On the third day, however, after having telephoned the room repeatedly from the reception desk and having received no reply, several of the hotel staff unlocked the door and entered.

They found Chabrier's nude body slumped near the balcony of the room. Though he was rushed to a hospital for treatment, he died twenty-four hours later.

The case was handed to Assistant Commissioner Narinder Nath Tuli of the Delhi police crime branch. Through Interpol, Tuli discovered that Gautier had "worked" before in Delhi, under the name of Pierre Boucher. Boucher's fingerprints matched those of Gautier—whoever Gautier was.

The Boucher crime had happened in 1971. Assistant Commissioner Tuli looked up the details of the case, which had caused a great deal of excitement at the time. According to the records, on the night of October 31, 1971, Boucher and two Frenchmen had visited the Ashoka Hotel, a five-star government-run hotel, and had made for the room occupied by an American dancer called Zoey Ames, who was performing in the hotel.

Boucher had posed as a casino owner from Macao interested in booking her act. Once in the room, however, he pulled a revolver and threatened to kill her unless she remained silent while he and his accomplices endeavored to drill a hole through the floor of her room into a jewelry shop situated directly below.

It was an incredible caper, and, of course, they were never able to make a hole through the hotel-room floor, though they tried for three days. When Boucher realized that he would never succeed, he forced the dancer to telephone the jeweler's shop and ask for a member of the staff to bring an assortment of jewelry to her room, so she could choose a present for her mother, who would be visiting India soon. A short while later a salesman arrived laden with necklaces, bracelets and rings. Boucher and one of his accomplices hid in the bathroom; the other sat next to Miss Ames, the revolver hidden under his coat. As Boucher had instructed, Miss Ames declared that the jewels the salesman had brought weren't good enough for her mother, so the salesman went back downstairs for more expensive items. When he returned with a new selection, the owner of the shop accompanied him.

Minutes later Boucher emerged from the bathroom. The dancer and the two men from the shop were bound and drugged. Boucher took not only the jewels but also the key to the store, which the owner had in his pocket. He waited until the shop closed for the day and then he ransacked it. After that, Boucher and his accomplices bolted straight for Palam Airport.

They booked one-way passage to Tehran, convinced that no suspicion could fall on them once they were airborne. But Boucher was unaware that the drug he had used to knock out the jeweler and his assistant was not strong enough. It had worn off before Boucher and his friends had reached the airport, and the victims had been able to call out for help. At the same time, a guard patrolling the hotel lobby had seen the open door of the jewelry shop and had summoned the police. Before long, Miss Ames and the two bound men were discovered.

As Boucher strolled nonchalantly toward the departure customs lounge, he was staggered to catch a glimpse of the jeweler standing behind a couple of police officers, obviously looking for him. Quickly Boucher told the customs officer that he had to go to the toilet, and asked the officer to look after his bag for him. He never returned to claim it. He and his accomplices slipped out without the loot, hired a taxi to take them to the train station, and there caught a train to Bombay. From Bombay Boucher flew to Tehran.

This was not the end of the dossier. Boucher and two new accomplices, both Iranians, returned to Bombay on November 13, but the police had been tipped off and the three were arrested as they stepped into the street from the entrance hall of the Taj Mahal Hotel. Among them they had several forged passports, two revolvers and three toy pistols.

They were taken to Delhi and clapped in jail to await court proceedings. But Boucher complained of feeling ill. Appendicitis was diagnosed, and he was taken to Willingdon Hospital for an emergency operation. His French wife, Françoise, flew down from Bombay to see him.

During the period of recuperation Boucher was always heavily guarded, the police keeping close to him even when he visited the bathroom. But one night he persuaded them to shut off the lights in his room. "The nurse suggested I try to sleep tonight without taking a sedative," he told the guards. "If you shut off the lights for a little while, I might succeed." The guards complied but not before chaining Boucher's right ankle to the bed frame. However, as they were chaining his ankle, Boucher managed to slip his right hand, hidden under the blanket, into the loop as well. While Françoise kept the guards distracted by chatting with them, Boucher pulled his hand out. The chain was now loose, and with a little effort Boucher was able to extricate his foot. He escaped through a window—in his striped pajamas.

Boucher managed to reach the Delhi railway station, still dressed in the striped pajamas of a hospital patient but with a coat over them. Unluckily for him, the policeman who had been sent to watch the railway station happened to have guarded him at one time in the hospital. He spotted Boucher buying a ticket at the counter and arrested him.

Even so, Boucher got away again. He was released on bail for medical reasons, but jumped bail and disappeared. "Wanted" posters were printed and distributed—and eventually forgotten.

Now the old photographs were brought out by the police and shown to hoteliers all over India. They might have been of Boucher or Gautier, but none looked like the new Gautier, who had by this time grown a heavy beard. Even when Gautier and the gang drugged three French tourists in the Delhi YMCA and got away with three thousand dollars in traveler's checks together with clothes and cameras, which they sold in Delhi, the police were unable to make a positive identification.

Finally Gautier overreached himself. All the evidence compiled by Interpol indicated that he usually worked according to a pattern. First he would drug an unsuspecting tourist with some potion that took a couple of hours to work, and wait until the tourist returned to his room, as he would do after complaining of feeling ill. Gautier would then go to the victim and find him unconscious, at which time it was an easy matter to rob him.

But now Gautier was no longer content to drug his victims singly or in couples. With an incredible contempt for the law—or an incredible belief that he was smarter than the law and could never be caught—Gautier decided to try a mass drugging.

WHAT HAPPENED NEXT could only be the product of a man so drunk with belief in his own infallibility that the thin thread separating audacity from stupidity, effrontery from carelessness, even a kind of sanity—however twisted—from madness, suddenly snapped.

Gautier had discovered that sixty-two French tourists staying at the Vikram Hotel in New Delhi were arranging to make a conducted tour to Agra to see the Taj Mahal. Together with Colin, Suzanne and the two other girls, Gautier set about charming—and being helpful to—his "fellow tourists" from France.

He spoke not only perfect French but Hindi as well, and this together with his engaging manners—enhanced by the presence of his French-Canadian wife—made "Charles," as he now called himself, a firm favorite with many of the tourist group, particularly those ladies of a certain age, to whom he was doubly attentive. When Charles heard that Madame Dupont, a widow from Toulon making her first trip to India, was intent on buying a ruby ring, he insisted on getting his Citroën out of the Vikram parking lot and taking her to a jeweler he knew.

"He's a friend of mine," Charles assured her, "and you'll get the bargain of your life, I promise you."

It *was* a bargain. When Madame Dupont had chosen her ring, Charles started haggling with the shopkeeper while she looked on in amazement. "In the end," she remembered later, "I felt almost sorry for the man who was selling the jewelry. He can't have made any profit at all."

When Charles had finally reduced the price by more than half the original demand, he gallantly put the ring on Madame Dupont's finger and told her, with his infectious little laugh, "And if you ever want to sell it, madame, I'll buy it for twice what you paid." (Madame Dupont discovered much later in France that it was worth three times what she had paid for it.)

It was the same with all the others, many of whom were in India for the first time, and slightly overwhelmed by their surroundings—the waiters in their white uniforms suddenly sidling up silently, the ornate furniture, the magnificence of New Delhi, the smells and crowds and beggars that infested Chandni Chauk, or Silver Street, the market stalls filled with gold and silver filigree work, shawls, saris, carpets. Always Charles was there at the elbow of a bewildered traveler in need of a friend, ordering tea with a snap of his fingers, sending for the manager if someone wanted an extra pillow on his or her bed. Long before the tour set off for Agra, *"cher* Charles" was treated as one of them. In fact, most believed that he was a paid-up member of the tour party.

The cavalcade set off for the Taj Mahal, Gautier—or Charles—driving his Citroën. As they waited to be guided around the exquisite building, Charles warned several of the tourists to beware of drinking the local water. "It's often polluted and can be very dangerous. If you have to drink, stick to bottled stuff," he said, adding in French, *"Hélas,* no Perrier or Evian here!"

The outing was a great success, thanks to Charles. Once again he helped several tourists to buy jewelry from the small shops—very often tourist traps—that clutter the streets of Agra and the approaches to the Taj Mahal. So when everyone returned to the Vikram tired but happy, ready for a shower and a good dinner, it seemed the most natural thing in the world for Charles to join them at their tables in the dining room.

Just as they were sitting down for the evening meal, as the waiters were actually placing some of the water carafes on the tables, Charles

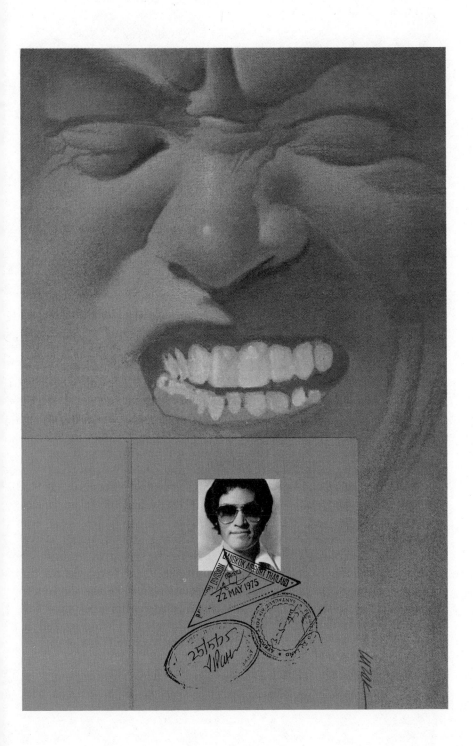

warned the French tourists once more of the perils of drinking local water. "In fact"—he lifted up a black leather bag—"I've got some pills in here that I always take as a precaution. Anybody want one?"

There were cries from every corner of the room. "*Merci*, Charles!" cried Madame Dupont, holding out her hand gratefully. "Please," cried another, "I'd like one." "*Une bonne idée!*" cried a third. In all, twenty-two of the group popped the pills into their mouths, then gulped them down.

Presumably Gautier intended to watch carefully those who had taken the pills, so that he and the girls could safely visit the victims in their rooms after they had become unconscious. But it didn't happen like that. Something went horribly wrong.

The first screams of agony tore through the hot air of the dining room before dinner was over. As heads turned in horror in the direction of the sound, an elderly man at the far end of the room crashed forward onto the plates in front of him, clawing frenziedly at the snowy tablecloth, scattering knives and forks, smashing two glasses in his agony.

More screams came from the nearby lounge—this time from diners who had just left the tables. One woman fell to the ground, clawing the carpet in her spasms of agony. A porter rushed to her aid, trying to help her to a sofa. In her convulsions she bit him so hard that she almost severed his thumb.

The piercing screams, as though coming from captives on the rack or wheel, later reminded one old Frenchman who had not taken a pill of the time he had been tortured by the Nazis in Dachau. "It was a nightmare," he said, "indescribable. Nobody had the faintest idea what was happening."

Not one of those who had taken a pill was able to reach his or her room. During the brief period before the clang of ambulance bells and the sirens of police cars announced that help was on the way, the most awful factor was the frenzied refusal of the victims to allow anyone to help them. Every attempt to render assistance was rewarded with flailing arms as men and women, who looked as though they had been stricken with madness, vomited on the carpets and chairs, writhed on the ground, mouths frothing, only the whites of their rolling eyes showing, their arms and legs fighting some invisible but excruciating pain.

One man stood aloof—the helpful Frenchman, Charles. But only for a few minutes, for suddenly one waiter pointed at him and shouted, "He's the one! I saw him hand the pills round!"

Within seconds a dozen jabbering members of the hotel staff had pounced on Gautier. They had seen him distributing the pills—and it was obvious that the pills must be the cause of the violent illness. Several waiters tried to pinion him, only to be confronted by irate French tourists.

"Leave that man alone!" one infuriated Frenchman bellowed. "He's one of us!"

Another Frenchman even struggled with the waiters to free Gautier. "You must be crazy," he shouted. "He couldn't have done it. Charles is our friend."

Luckily the ambulances started to arrive. Those tourists who were still squirming with agony received swift jabs of sedatives, and then they were taken to the All India Institute of Medical Sciences. Thanks to the unexpected swift reaction to the pills, doctors using stomach pumps were able to save everyone's life.

The very first police car to arrive contained Assistant Commissioner Tuli, who had been resolutely on Gautier's trail since the Chabrier murder. Now Tuli personally arrested Gautier. In the chaos Colin and the girls managed to escape, but they were rounded up within twenty-four hours.

Suzanne, Diana Johnson and Alfred Colin were picked up in two different hotels. Margaret Wilson was arrested in a well-known Delhi discotheque. The four confessed to their roles in Charles's crimes and made statements.

But Charles insisted that he was innocent. "I am a respectable businessman," he fumed at Tuli, "and my country will not take a light view of this matter, let me assure you." Tuli, however, compared Charles's fingerprints with those of Boucher, the clumsy jewel thief of 1971—they matched. They also matched the set sent to Delhi at the suggestion of Thai Interpol's Colonel Sompol. Tuli asked Charles to lift up his shirt and lower his trousers: the long appendicitis scar on his stomach was revealed. Charles refused to say anything about it.

For ten days, though the Delhi police tried every method they could think of, he sat almost completely mute. On the tenth day he broke. "Hats off to you!" he told Tuli. "I never dreamed that I would be caught by the Indian police."

Many miles away in Bangkok the telephone rang at the home of Angela and Herman Knippenberg. For them, months of anxious waiting had ended. Alain Gautier had finally been apprehended.

CHAPTER 10

THE TIME HAS now come to use Gautier's real name, Charles Gurmukh Sobhraj, and to try to see what twists of character, fate, environment flawed the life of a man who was described by one French newspaper as having "the face of an angel." His life is, in fact, an open book, though a book in which many pages have been torn or defaced.

Charles was born in Saigon in 1944, while Indochina was still under the Japanese occupation during World War II. His mother was a beautiful Vietnamese who, at the age of twenty-one, fell in love with a rich and dashing Indian textile merchant from Bombay called Hotchand Bhawnani Sobhraj. She met him when she was working as a cashier in a Japanese-owned textile firm. The two fell madly in love, though they never married. Nonetheless, Simone—the name she would later take—became Sobhraj's concubine and moved into his house, where Charles was born on April 6, 1944.

"It was wartime and there was a great deal of bombing," Simone remembers now, "but life was still very gay in Saigon, and while I lived with Charles's father, I lived like a princess. We had many servants, a cook and someone to care for my baby son. I brought him up as a Catholic and had him baptized Charles. Later he took his first Communion and confirmation."

According to Simone, Sobhraj—like her son later—was an incurable chaser of women. In the end, when Charles was around five years old, Simone's lover went to Bombay, and when he returned to Saigon, he was accompanied by a legitimate wife.

"What could I do?" Simone asks now. "By then I was pregnant again, but I left Sobhraj and married René Monteaux, a noncommissioned officer in the French army. He was a wonderful man. He even recognized Charles's sister, who was born with the name Monteaux." When Monteaux was moved—on army orders—Simone went along with him, but she did not take Charles. His father wanted to keep him.

In 1952, as the fighting increased in Indochina—it was only two years before the defeat of the French at Dien Bien Phu—Monteaux and his wife returned to France. Charles, who was now eight, went with them, together with his sister. Several years later Monteaux bought a modest villa near Marseille, with an eye to vacations and eventual retirement. But most of the time was spent around Paris.

No one can tell whether Charles had previously felt abandoned by his beautiful mother, or for that matter whether he had got along with his Indian stepmother. He was fond of his stepfather, Monteaux, but the two had vastly different personalities and Charles may have felt somewhat of an outsider. Certainly life in France was a brutal change of life-style for Charles, as it had been for his mother.

"I know his father had spoiled him," Simone remembers. "He had everything he wanted when he lived in Saigon. But with us it was different. We were always fairly poor." Financial difficulties increased over the years as Simone and Monteaux had more children. Soon they were a family of seven, and the salary of a French NCO has never been very large.

Though the transition to France must have been a riches-to-rags story for Charles, he did seem at first to fall in love with France, certainly with Paris. Still, it was a time when the French capital was undergoing dramatic changes. The empire was collapsing. Not only had France suffered a resounding defeat in Indochina in 1954, but that same year war broke out in Algeria. Refugees from both places began crowding the streets of the most beautiful capital in the world. It was an exciting city, but there did not seem to be a place in it for Charles. In a way, Paris renounced him. Perhaps his dark skin worked against him at a time when people in France were getting more and more worried about racial tensions. And, of course, it could not have been easy for him to become settled, since his stepfather was still a working soldier, which meant changes of schools and other sudden movements for Charles. It did not take him long to drift into petty crime.

Even Simone admits that Charles finally became miserable in France. He missed his real father, and twice when the family were down at their holiday villa outside Marseille, Charles tried to stow away on a ship headed for Vietnam. Finally Charles's father agreed that Charles should return to him in Saigon, and he did so. He was about eighteen when he returned to Vietnam in the early 1960s, at a time marked by a resurgence of the conflict between Communists and non-Communists, and by an increase in American military involvement. How did corrupt, gay Saigon affect the handsome young man who had no roots, no real country, no culture? It was here that he certainly started to go really wrong. And apparently it wasn't long before relations between father and son began to turn sour.

When the break finally came, Charles wrote to his mother begging for enough money for a boat ticket to Marseille. She sent the money but said it was all she could let him have. Back in France, with only a temporary residence permit and no regular work, Charles soon launched into a series of petty crimes. Arrested in Grasse in 1963, he was sentenced to six months in prison for car theft, driving without a license and carrying an illegal firearm. He served this term without incident but resumed his illegal activities once he was set free. Barely a year after the conviction in Grasse he was arrested again, and this time the judge in a Paris court was particularly severe. For more thefts, using false papers and license plates, Charles landed a three-year term in Poissy Central Prison.

Then it looked as though his luck might take a turn for the better, for it was in the Poissy jail that Charles made a new friend. He was a volunteer prison visitor called Xavier Sailly. From a well-to-do French family, Sailly found himself drawn—with a mixture of pity, sympathy and fascination—to the frail but intense Charles.

It was Sailly who took care of all the formalities that made Charles a legal French citizen.

It was also through Sailly that Charles met and fell in love with a beautiful brunette French girl called Françoise Gilet, the daughter of a retired civil engineer who, after many years in Morocco, had returned with his wife and only daughter and settled in the village of Sceaux, about nine miles from Paris.

"Françoise was always attracted to foreigners," Monsieur Gilet remembers. "The two met at a party, and I do admit that Charles was handsome and had a lot of charm. She fell head over heels in love with him. It was love at first sight."

But Françoise's father took an instant dislike to Sobhraj. "I was heartbroken when my daughter went to live with him in a studio apartment in St. Germain," he said. "Françoise worked for a notary public, and Charles did odd jobs—I never really knew quite what. They never seemed to have much money."

Monsieur Gilet wasn't the only one deeply suspicious of Sobhraj. Charles's Indian father came to see Gilet on one occasion, and as Gilet remembers, "Sobhraj's father seemed a nice, decent man. When he came to see me, he was in despair over his son. He was disgusted and had thrown him out."

Even before Sobhraj and Françoise were married, things started to go wrong. "Sobhraj would literally hypnotize my daughter and get her to steal things," said Gilet. "She would never have done such a thing if she had been in her right mind.

"Once," Gilet added, "they stole a car and drove up to Deauville, where Sobhraj liked to gamble in the casino." On that trip Françoise's father received a phone call from a hospital in Evreux saying that his daughter had been hurt in a bad automobile crash. He knew the couple didn't own a car. When Gilet reached the hospital to find Françoise badly cut up, he told her, "This is the last straw! I'm taking you home with me."

Françoise refused to go; she said she was going to stay with Sobhraj, and finally the two decided to get married.

Françoise's father was violently opposed to the marriage, but there was nothing he could do. So, with as much good grace as possible, he gave the daughter he loved a big wedding. A wedding photograph which he has kept shows a slender, short-haired Sobhraj smiling and holding the hand of Françoise, who looked beautiful in white silk trousers and a white tunic, her hair pulled back and fastened with a sprig of jasmine, looking for all the world like a princess being married to an Indian prince.

The bliss soon wore off the marriage. Charles had left bad checks all over Paris, and the police were beginning to catch up with him, though a first indictment in November 1970 came to nothing. By this time Françoise was pregnant, and there were more bad checks; but before a second indictment, dated April 1971, caught up with Sobhraj, they had headed for Bombay, where their baby girl was born and named Asha, the Hindi word for hope.

In India Charles stole, forged, used more false identification papers, and was finally arrested in November 1971 following the robbery of the jewelry shop in the Ashoka Hotel in Delhi. After a rather spectacular escape from Willingdon Hospital and subsequent cat-and-mouse contests with the police, Charles—or Pierre Boucher, as he then called himself—ended up in prison once again.

In despair, but still in love with Charles and reluctant to leave him, Françoise persuaded an English girl to take Asha to her parents in France. "The English girl carted that poor baby all over Europe," says Françoise's father. "She reached Sceaux via Moscow and London. Both of them were filthy when they arrived on our doorstep. The girl didn't speak a word of French. Asha was covered with lice."

Back in India, Charles didn't stay in prison for long. He was released on bail for medical reasons and immediately fled with Françoise to Afghanistan. There, more misdemeanors landed them both in a Kabul jail.

Françoise's father remembers, "I moved heaven and earth and spent a fortune of three million old francs (about six thousand dollars) to get Françoise out. On top of everything else, it was Sobhraj who escaped from prison, leaving his wife—my daughter—behind. I kept on working through diplomatic channels to try to get Françoise out. Months went by. At least we had the baby with us during that time—but then Sobhraj did the most despicable thing of all."

While his wife languished in jail, Sobhraj returned to France on a stolen passport and cold-bloodedly set out to kidnap the baby. One day (in late summer, 1972) he called his mother-in-law in Sceaux to say that Françoise had left prison in Kabul and was back in France. She was very ill but wanted to see her mother and the baby. Could Madame Gilet bring the baby into Paris, to the Hilton Hotel? Excitedly Madame Gilet bundled up Asha and drove to Paris. When she arrived at the Hilton, Sobhraj, who was dressed to kill, led her up to his luxurious hotel room and sat the poor woman down with the baby on her lap. Françoise, he said, was in the bathroom and would be out in a moment.

"Meanwhile, *m'amie*," Sobhraj said, using an affectionate term, "please have some coffee."

"Don't call me *m'amie*," retorted Madame Gilet. "I don't want to have anything to do with you. I'm only here for Françoise, and

I'm not thirsty." Sobhraj insisted, and finally Madame Gilet took a sip. She said it tasted terrible and refused to drink any more.

"One sip was all it took," said Monsieur Gilet. "The coffee was drugged, and my wife passed out like a light. Hours later I got a phone call from the Hilton. I thought it was a joke and hung up. But they called again to say that my wife was at the hotel and very sick. A doctor told me that if she'd drunk the entire cup she would have died. Sobhraj had registered at the Hilton under the name of a Brazilian. But, of course, he was gone—vanished—taking the baby with him. He must have carried Asha out of the country in a suitcase, because he didn't have any papers for her. I had kept all the papers."

A little over a month later police caught up with Sobhraj and recovered Asha at Tehran airport. Gilet managed to arrange for her to be brought back to France by an airline stewardess.

Subsequently Sobhraj was sentenced in Tehran to a year's imprisonment for theft, forgery and using altered passports.

"You can imagine what we went through," Monsieur Gilet remembers. "Finally Françoise got out of prison, but altogether we had looked after Asha for about one and a half years. Thank God that my daughter met an American, who fell in love with her, and now they are happily married and are living in America."

THAT IS THE STORY of Charles Sobhraj, alias Alain Gautier, a megalomaniac to whom the trappings of material success—clothes, cars, a life of luxury—were essential; and so essential that he never cared how he acquired them.

POSTSCRIPT

A TRIAL CONCERNING the death of Louis Chabrier dragged on for months. When it was over, in August 1978, the Delhi Sessions Court sentenced Sobhraj to seven years of rigorous imprisonment for "culpable homicide not amounting to murder, administering drugs and for robbery." The two girls, Margaret Wilson and Diana Johnson, turned state's evidence and were discharged. Catherine Ponchet and Alfred Colin were given "the benefit of the doubt" and acquitted.

But Sobhraj appealed to the High Court, which overturned the verdict against him and acquitted him. It was discovered that Louis Chabrier had been a drug addict, and the doctor who examined him could not determine whether he'd died of the drug Sobhraj had given him or one he had injected into himself.

In a separate case Sobhraj was found guilty of robbing the jewelry shop at the Ashoka Hotel, and was sentenced to five years in prison. In two other cases he received prison terms for escaping from Willingdon Hospital and for drugging the French tourists at the Vikram Hotel and was immediately remanded to Delhi's Tihar Central Jail.

Colonel Sompol is hopeful that eventually Sobhraj will face trial in Bangkok. He and Major General Anant Dejrangsi, commander of the Thai Immigration Division, flew to India to try to negotiate eventual extradition to Thailand, and though there is no formal extradition pact between the countries, the Indians at that time indicated that they would be prepared to hand over Sobhraj.

On the other hand, there is always the possibility that the Thai police will never take custody of Charles Sobhraj. As Xavier Sailly, the friend who, in effect, adopted Sobhraj at one stage, said recently, "It doesn't seem to have occurred to anyone that Charles will probably refuse extradition. He is spending his time in prison studying all the legal aspects of the case."

Sailly added, "If he can claim Indian nationality through his father, he counts on the fact that the Indians will refuse to extradite him to Thailand and other requesting countries."

THE DIAMOND
WIZARD

The Diamond Wizard

by

Polly Toynbee

ILLUSTRATED BY MITCHELL HOOKS

The man seemed to have as many brilliant facets to him as the diamonds he stole. SIMONETTI, LUIS read his name on an Interpol file. But was that his real name? What was his true nationality? And, most important, where would he strike next? The police forces of four continents were stymied, while with each new theft he added to his reputation as one of the world's master jewel thieves.

But one policeman, Marcel Sicot, the recently appointed head of Interpol, knew that sometime, somewhere, the man would make a mistake that would lead ultimately to his capture. And Sicot was certain that one day he himself would have the pleasure of seeing this elusive quarry behind bars.

Novelist and journalist Polly Toynbee traces the extraordinary—and notorious—career of the man whose wizardry with diamonds became legendary.

CHAPTER 1

THROUGH HIS OFFICE window Marcel Sicot surveyed the threatening gray clouds over Paris and reflected that they looked as gloomy as he felt. He had been in his post since June 1951, about a year. The title sounded imposing—secretary-general of the International Criminal Police Commission, Interpol. But there was nothing imposing about Sicot's cramped office. To take this new job he had given up his post as a director and inspector general of the Sûreté Nationale, the French national police. Sometimes he wondered if he had made a mistake.

The door was open a crack, and by tipping back in his chair Sicot could see down the narrow corridor outside. He contemplated the ten equally small offices that had been allocated to Interpol by the Ministry of the Interior, and he wondered if he would ever get the whole operation off the ground. Here they were, situated in the Porte Maillot district, miles from the center of Paris, in these modest quarters. Being a man of taste and refinement, Sicot found this temporary building, thrown up in a hurry after the war, somewhat less than one might have hoped for. The partitions appeared to be made of cardboard, and he suspected if someone sneezed violently, the whole pack of cards might come tumbling down.

How was he to build up a filing system in this place? They possessed only three filing cabinets. Out there was a whole world of criminality, and all he had on record were some ten thousand sets of fingerprints. In theory, the organization sounded impressive. It had thirty-five member countries from around the world. But, in fact, it had these tiny offices and a desperately overworked staff. Finances were tight, to say the least. How could anyone take them seriously when they had to send all their messages by ordinary mail?

Marcel Sicot had had many moments of dour reflection like this lately, for he was an unusual policeman. He was a man of vision, not a plodding, methodical, step-by-step sort of man. He hadn't acquired the weary uninquisitiveness that old policemen often display, an air of having seen it all already. His small sensitive features and mild brown eyes seemed to be constantly musing, assessing, weighing probabilities. He was known among his colleagues as an intellectual—an attribute that might not necessarily speed the way to promotion in the American or British police forces but was regarded here in France as a treasured quality in any occupation.

On this particular morning he had been projected into a mood of pessimism by statistical confirmation that there was one kind of international crime on the rapid increase. It was exactly the sort of crime that Interpol had been brought into being to deal with. But had he the resources to catch up with its unique kind of criminal, who flitted around the world, stealing enormous sums and then vanishing into thin air?

Sicot picked up a slightly worn index card that had lain in the unsolved crime box since October 1947, nearly five years. The card told the story, all too briefly, of the first of these crimes to be reported to Interpol. It was a theft by substitution, a fraud of highly specialized cunning, which could be carried out only by a professional criminal of extraordinary skill.

The substitution thief is the true magician among thieves. He is as artful and deceptive as a master sleight-of-hand man. He approaches a dealer in gems, gold or money with an offer to buy or sell. In the course of the transaction the thief discreetly substitutes fake items for the real goods to be bought or sold. Sometimes, if the thief poses as a buyer, the payment for such goods proves ultimately to be only worthless paper. In all cases, great knowledge is required by the thief of the subtleties of the markets and of the habits of the men who make their living in them, as well as great feats of legerdemain, to carry off such deceptions successfully.

This first reported substitution theft described on the card had been pulled off in Zurich by a man calling himself Wyeber—a false name, Sicot assumed.

Sicot shifted in his creaking desk chair and sighed quietly. Since this card had been filed, substitution thefts had proliferated all over the world. Were they the work of an organized gang? Or could they possibly be the work of just one man? Could one man move so fast around the world as these reports would indicate?

There was a growing consistency in reports of the thief's physical appearance—nothing you could exactly identify, no tattoos, scars or obvious peculiarities. Still, these reports all generally described him as a man of about thirty-five, short but well built, with wavy brown hair and a trim mustache. He was said to wear horn-rimmed glasses of that slightly unusual kind with rims only around the top half of each lens. He was a charmer, the reports acknowledged, a man of refinement, an educated man. He appeared to speak fluent Spanish, Hungarian, Hebrew, Russian, German and Yiddish. Could the reports possibly refer to one man?

The most striking element in these substitution thefts was the sheer nerve with which they were carried out. Fashionably dressed, with a look of intelligence and uprightness, the thief would captivate his victim with his manners and erudition. He would charm his mark into a frame of mind where suspicion was unthinkable—and then he would vanish, taking with him pocketfuls of jewels.

Marcel Sicot rubbed the long bridge of his nose with his fingertips and for a moment closed his eyes in silent meditation. He tried to picture his thief hopping from continent to continent, picking off his prey as surely and as beautifully as a kingfisher darts down into the river and spears his fish, a single perfect swoop, brilliantly executed in one swift flash of color. One day, Sicot thought, I shall catch that kingfisher. Let him try his hypnotic charm on me!

Suddenly Sicot spun his chair around and gave two sharp thumps on the thin partition wall behind him. In a moment his secretary stood at the door, a harassed woman who did the job of several secretaries. "Don't look at me so balefully," he said to her with a smile. She was trying to pin up a strand or two of hair, but she smiled back wanly. "I'm going to ask the Sûreté Nationale for three good men," he continued. "It will take a team to catch this bird."

He started to dictate a memorandum to the chief of police, laying down with meticulous precision the facts of the case, subtly emphasizing that these crimes had occurred in France as well as elsewhere and it was therefore not an unreasonable burden upon the French taxpayer to ask for the loan of three police specialists. As he dictated, his secretary smiled to herself. Marcel Sicot's memorandums were noted for a certain distinction. His was not the prose of the policeman giving evidence in court. With delicacy he complimented the chief on the excellence of his men. Without gross flattery he suggested that the chief was a man of insight who truly comprehended the importance in this modern age of international cooperation.

Thus it was that in a matter of days three keen and bright-eyed detectives arrived outside Marcel Sicot's door—Raymond Brigandat, Roger Haffa and Maurice Renault. There was hardly room for them all to squeeze into his office. They leaned, broad shoulder to broad shoulder, against the wall, none of them wishing to occupy the one vacant chair.

"Detective Brigandat? Detective Haffa? Detective Renault?" Sicot addressed the three men formally. Each nodded in response. "I know you men are well aware of the type of crime known as theft by substitution. I gather you, Renault, are something of an expert on the subject. But, though this crime is on the increase, we have yet to catch any of the criminals involved. Working together, perhaps we shall. Let's review what we know.

"The substitution thief," he began his summary, "is a highly professional criminal. He deals almost exclusively in loose diamonds, though he may also deal in money, mounted jewels, gold or other precious metals. To understand how he operates, you must understand the working of the international diamond markets.

"The diamond markets are controlled almost entirely by Orthodox Jews, and only by passing himself off as part of this curious world of diamonds can the substitution thief succeed in defrauding his victims so brilliantly. For in this market there are no legally binding contracts, no receipts. It operates entirely on trust, a kind of trust that is easily abused by the cunning man. Millions are exchanged between dealers on a simple handshake and the benediction *mit mazel und broche*—with luck and blessing—a Yiddish phrase that has now become standard even among non-Jewish dealers.

"There are two reasons for the informality of the diamond markets. In the first place, the diamonds themselves have no fixed value. With gold you simply weigh the metal and check the current fixed price. Ah! But a diamond may be differently valued by different dealers. Its beauty is in the eye of the beholder. Each dealer may see different qualities in the same diamond. This introduces a psychological element into all dealings in these stones. The mood of the dealer and his estimate of the man he is buying from are surprisingly important parts of the transaction.

"In the second place, the diamond business is a secret world, often hidden from the tax collectors and also from the police. The deals are usually conducted in cash, or exchanges of one kind or another, and it is extremely difficult for the tax man to keep up with them. Thus, to a small, unscrupulous fringe, honesty is relative in this world, even as the value of the commodity is relative. This element increases the extent to which the dealer must rely upon his instinct and his intuition concerning a seller's or buyer's trustworthiness.

"In dealing with such men the substitution thief can claim, with some reason, that he is stealing only from thieves, and they get no more than they deserve. The more unorthodox the method of sealing a bargain, the more certain the thief is that his victim is also dishonest. And for this reason, you can be certain that the thefts that have been reported are but a fraction of the total number. Ten times the number of frauds of this kind are being committed, but they never come to light. Most victimized dealers are loath to discuss the situation with the police. It is also against their sense of pride to admit that they have been bilked and gulled at their very own game."

As he spoke, Marcel Sicot recollected his own recent investigations in the diamond markets of Paris. They had been a revelation to him. He had enjoyed watching the extraordinary and incomprehensible transactions, hearing the curious language and feeling the mystique of the fascinating gems. Now he paused and studied the three detectives before him. They were each taking notes in their regulation books with great speed and efficiency. He suspected they would become as absorbed in this new world as he himself had. Could anyone watch those transactions without being stirred by some ancient primeval excitement? Diamonds are powerful, almost magical jewels, and the dealers, with their earlocks and their black robes of the ghetto, seemed like priests of an arcane cult.

He waited until the three of them had caught up with their note-taking. Then he cleared his throat and began to discourse upon the nature of the crime itself. The three men looked even more interested. What they had heard seemed vague and academic to their trained minds. Crime was what they wanted to know about.

"The crime," he said, "takes place at the moment that the bargain is actually sealed. Once the stones have been examined and a price has been set, the next ritual is 'making a seal.' According to this practice, the stones to be sold are placed on a double sheet of diamond paper—the slightly waxed and shiny paper that heightens the sparkle of the stones. The paper is folded in a special way, several times, and the weight of the stones, in carats, is marked in one corner. This folded package is then slid inside an envelope and folded again. The sum that has been agreed upon is marked on the envelope, and the envelope is then initialed by both parties and sealed with wax. It sounds like a straightforward and foolproof method.

"But the thief is not only an impressive con man who can persuade any dealer of his unquestionable good faith; he is also a conjurer who could earn his living just as well on the stage. He can spirit away objects before your very eyes, the speed of his fingers defying the imagination. Sitting there, within inches of his victim, he can snatch away thousands of dollars' worth of diamonds without the other being any the wiser. And this is how it is done.

"The thief attends the meeting with his victim, having already decided exactly which stones he intends to pretend to buy or sell. In his pocket he carries a signed and sealed envelope identical to the one he knows will be made up during his meeting with the dealer. If he is pretending to sell, he will have fake diamonds in the package; if he is intending to buy, he will have fake money. At the crucial stage of making the seal he substitutes his own package for the one prepared on the table and pockets the genuine seal.

"In this way he sells fake diamonds for real money, or he buys real diamonds with fake money. His victim will not discover the fraud for perhaps a day, since he is bound not to open the envelope until he next sees the thief. For the thief will cunningly have said that he has more diamonds, or more money, at home, and that he wishes to add to the deal tomorrow. Officially, then, the deal has not yet been concluded, and the envelope must not be opened. It is only when the thief fails to turn up at the next meeting that the victim may become suspicious and open the envelope. '*Oy!* . . . *Mon Dieu!* . . . *Mein Gott!*' In whatever language, all over the world, it is happening all the time," said Marcel Sicot.

The three detectives smiled at each other and rested their pens from their busy note-taking. Sicot smiled also, with a hint of satisfaction. He felt as if he too were a master magician, one who had just conjured up a picture of a perfect crime.

"Well," he continued, "that is the general background. All that remains is for me to outline for you the workings of this great and powerful organization you have been assigned to, with its wonderful facilities and limitless resources." Sicot allowed himself a wry grimace. The three men were not sure whether he was being sarcastic or not, and playing it safe, they did not allow themselves to smile in return.

The International Criminal Police Commission, he explained, had been founded in 1923 in Vienna, with twenty member countries. Membership grew to thirty-four countries, but by 1942, when the Nazis took all the files away to Berlin, the organization had ceased to exist.

"If the Gestapo hoped to find a gold mine of political information, they were disappointed," he added. "All they found were files on common-law crimes—but that experience gave rise to the rules forbidding the organization to handle political crimes."

In 1946, Sicot continued, the International Criminal Police Commission was set up again, here in Paris, and Interpol was registered then as the telegraphic address. "Here," he said, making a sweeping gesture with his hand, "as you see, gentlemen, we have the privilege of occupying these lavish premises, in this charming postwar temporary building of such outstanding architectural elegance." This time they dared laugh, as there was no mistaking his meaning.

He then produced the worn index card and handed it to them to examine. WYEBER, it said, in red capital letters; IDENTITY UNKNOWN. And it outlined the brief facts of the substitution theft in Zurich back in October 1947. He explained to them that this was the first substitution theft to have been reported. Whoever it was had never used that alias again, or at least not in any reported case. But different names in different places had turned up since then in similar crimes. Was a gang at work? Or was it possible that one man could have been responsible for all of them? No fingerprint had yet been found. So far he, or they, had left not a clue.

"The work of a gang?" Marcel Sicot paused for emphasis. "Perhaps," he said. "But I feel in my bones that we are dealing with the work of one single man. You will note that the reports we have received from his victims have a surprising consistency about them. We are told he is brilliant and charming, a great Talmudic scholar, who makes many of his best contacts among diamond dealers through the synagogue. His Hebrew is said to be of the purest and best. His charm and his gentleness are always extolled. Now, I ask you, can there be a whole gang of gentleman Talmudic scholars of ineffable charm who are also prestidigitators of the greatest skill, diamond experts, and criminal to the bottom of their hearts? Is it reasonable?"

Detective Renault cleared his throat. "If you'll excuse me, is it likely that one man could speak so many languages, each one well enough to fool people into thinking he comes from their own country? Is it likely one man could move with such speed around the world? And the sums of money involved are enormous. Surely a wise thief would steal and spend, and only steal again when he needed more money. This fellow seems to spend all his time stealing and none at all spending, except for air travel—"

"You mention travel, Renault. That is a key word in this case. Travel. So you shall. So shall all of you." Sicot looked at each man in turn and concluded softly, "I want the travels—and the crimes— of our thief or our gang of thieves stopped."

The following week Renault was dispatched to London, Zurich and Vienna to investigate more thoroughly the police documents relating to substitution thefts reported from those cities. The reports Sicot had in hand were brief, and he wanted everything examined in detail. Perhaps a clue had been overlooked. Detectives Brigandat and Haffa were sent off into the little streets and narrow passageways of lower Montmartre, where most of the Paris diamond business is conducted. They were to find out in much greater detail everything they could about the operation of the diamond trade. For instance, how skilled must a man be to learn to deal effectively in these gems?

How long would it take a man to master the business, as these criminals appeared to have? How closed was the society of diamond merchants, if such criminals could worm their way into it without causing suspicion? What must it be about these criminals that made them seem like bona fide dealers? There was no end to the questions that needed answering.

For those answers, there was nothing Marcel Sicot could do except wait—wait for reports from his men or for reports of new crimes, each one, perhaps, bearing some vital clue. Sicot kept his mind open to the possibility that a worldwide gang of supercriminals had sprung up spontaneously. But deep in his heart he harbored the notion of one man, a man he intended one day to meet.

CHAPTER 2

THE MAN SICOT WAS seeking with such single-minded determination had some idea his incredible luck could not hold up forever. His name is Berl Farcas, or at least that is the name that history has settled upon him. In the course of his life he has had more names than even he can remember, but now, while he sits in prison, he answers to that name, though it is not the one he was born with. The facts of his life also are uncertain. According to the man himself, they are as follows:

He was born Bela Weinberger, in Satu-Mare in northern Rumania. The town lies on the banks of the Somes River in a broad fertile plain, and today has a population of about eighty thousand. It is mainly a textile-manufacturing center, as it was back in 1917, when he was born.

His father, Abraham Weider, was a wealthy textile merchant who dealt not only in the wools and cottons of the region but also in silks from Lyons and the East, georgettes and taffetas. His mother was Drezel Weinberger. She was married to his father only under rabbinic law, so Bela and his twelve brothers and sisters were known by their mother's surname and not their father's.

Satu-Mare was a small place in those days, but it was a famous center for Orthodox Judaism. It was nearby that the modern sect of Hasidim was founded in the eighteenth century. Like the earlier

Hasidic Jews, members of this newer sect were devoted to strict observance of the ritual law, but they added mysticism and ecstatic worship to their rigid Orthodoxy.

Bela Weinberger's parents were also Orthodox, but not Hasidic. Still, his was a rigid upbringing, with many aspects of life governed by rules. He was an exceptionally bright small boy but not a very happy one, and he kicked hard against the traces.

He was sent to the local *heder*—the Jewish school—and at thirteen, after his bar mitzvah, he was enrolled in the yeshiva—the academy for study of the Talmud. This institution provided a most remarkable kind of education, requiring almost incredible feats of memory and of reasoning. It demanded the learning not only of the Talmud itself but of hundreds of books, tracts and commentaries on it. Being an excellent scholar, sharp of mind and memory, Bela was soon regarded as a learned man and could have become a rabbi.

Despite his success in that world, he harbored deeply rebellious thoughts. He did not always obey the laws he had learned to discourse on so well. He sometimes ran away on the Sabbath to play football, and once, when he was playing with some non-Jewish children, a small moment of revelation came to him. One of the children gave him a ham sandwich. He took it, and hiding behind the goalpost, he ate the sandwich, tiny bit by tiny bit, pausing between each mouthful to see if the sky would fall in upon him. He became increasingly disillusioned, and began to read books that were utterly forbidden by the strictest Hasidim; Bela read *Oliver Twist*, Spinoza, Socrates and Aristotle, studying them secretly under his bedclothes, as if they were pornography.

Placed as he was in a peculiar crossroads of Central Europe, he was brought up speaking several languages at once. Yiddish was his first language. Rumanian and Hungarian came a close second. His Yiddish made learning German easy. His Rumanian was at least a good start for the learning of Italian and Spanish. Later, during the war, he picked up Russian, Czech and Polish as well. He learned Arabic later in his life, when he went to night school in Israel. Oddly enough, French was one of his last languages. His English is not entirely fluent, but passable.

He studied religion in a detached way, loving it with a special fascination but always apparently observing it from outside. He came to mock Orthodox Judaism, like a naughty boy rebelling against something he still felt around him. "For instance," he would say, "on the Sabbath you can't move a finger even to pick a plum off a tree. But imagine you are passing a plum tree and you are tall and the tree has a low branch. Nothing in rabbinic law prevents you from jumping up and eating the plum off the branch."

All that irreverence and rebellion couldn't stand the straitjacket of yeshiva life. The young men were forbidden frivolous pursuits—no football, no swimming in the river, no coffeehouses. They wore their skullcaps, and Bela pictured himself in later years growing long earlocks and a beard. All his secret reading had made the restrictions seem to him grotesque and burdensome. He wanted to leave; he wanted an occupation and some money he could call his own. When he apprenticed himself to a dental technician to learn how to make bridges and false teeth, both his father and the rabbi were sorely disappointed. But the break with family tradition and the family business brought him a measure of independence.

Though he was paid little, he saved enough money to travel, and on a trip to Bucharest he managed to conduct several successful textile deals through a wholesaler friend of his father's. This was his first taste of dealing, bartering, haggling, buying and selling at a profit. It thrilled him and he was delighted with the money he earned. But he took most of it home to his mother or gave it away to friends. That was a pattern Bela followed all his life. Although several fortunes were to pass through his fingers later, he did not care what became of the money. He never wanted grand cars, yachts or villas. Nor did he care to save or invest for a comfortable retirement. He simply handed money out all over the place.

Everyone he met remembers him as a generous man. The truth was that he didn't care. There was something about this reckless giving that implied he would just as easily have given away his life. Then in the horror of the next few years he was to show that he had a greater instinct for survival than most men.

It was April 1943 when twenty-eight freight trains, packed to near suffocation, transported the thirteen thousand Jews of Satu-Mare to concentration camps. Bela's large family was separated.

When their freight train was unloaded at Auschwitz, all the Jews were stripped naked and made to stand in rows. As each came to the front of the line, his or her possessions were examined for money or jewels. The men at the desks looked over the Jews' bodies and said, *"Gesund"*—healthy—for those who looked as if they could work. Then they shouted out, *"Rechts,"* which meant the healthy were to stand with the group on the right. If the Jew looked too ill, too old or too young to work, the order *"Links"* was bellowed out, and the person would join the group to the left. Everyone on the left was marched to the gas chambers.

Bela came to the front of his line, was pronounced *gesund* and sent to the *rechts* group. In the work detail he found himself with a number of Hungarian men. They were kept at Auschwitz for a short while and were then moved from one work camp to another, often without knowing exactly where they were. Surviving as best he could from one hour to the next, Bela came to understand that those who dwelt on the past and speculated on the future and the horror of their existence were the ones who despaired, the first to die. He became absorbed in all the details of staying alive.

When it comes to a matter of simple survival, there is little a man won't do, he told himself. Values, morals and standards are the luxuries of men with full stomachs. There was no trust or loyalty between men degraded to the condition of dogs. Even a lifetime of deep moral and religious teaching was no protection against the ravages of starvation. Bela adapted himself to the business of surviving, and he never lost that way of looking at the world.

He was already an efficient salesman, taught by his father, and he had a good head for trade. But in the camps he mastered quite different skills. In particular, there were two Polish stage magicians who told him all the secrets of their trade. He learned how to deceive the eye, how to hide even quite large objects behind the hand or up the sleeve. He learned how to carry on a normal conversation with six pebbles hidden in his mouth. He learned the art of substitution, how to distract his victim for a moment at the crucial stage of the trick. Now it was all for a scrap of margarine, a crust of bread, a used end of soap, but the same techniques were later used to fill his pockets with hundreds of thousands in cash or jewels.

In the work camps there was contact with the outside world, and there were opportunities for bribery or smuggling things in and out past the guards. Bela became an artist at hustling. Somehow he got hold of a watch, which he managed to sell more than ten times for food, using sleight of hand, substitution or the simple trick of stealing it back within moments of having bartered it. He collected small pieces of metal until he could work them into a lump that had the same weight and feel as a watch. He would show a real watch to a guard, to barter it for cigarettes or food. At the last moment, wrapping the watch in a cloth, he would substitute the lump of metal.

Wherever he was sent, Bela became renowned for his cunning and his ability to create situations that made his wretched companions laugh. Once he acquired a watch with no inner works. He caught a fly and put it inside just before selling the watch; the buzzing fooled the prospective buyer long enough for Bela to make off with the food he had bargained for.

In the spring of 1945 Bela was liberated by the Americans from a camp near Munich, and he started at once back to Satu-Mare, hitchhiking and bribing and begging his way. When he got there, he found the family house had been burned down. He waited in Satu-Mare month after month for the survivors of his huge family to come home. Often he camped in what was left of the house, peopling it in his mind with all those children. He refused hospitality from neighbors who took pity on him. Sometimes he opened the door of the great textile warehouse, which was still intact, and walked between the rows of fabrics, fingering them as he thought about his father.

In the six months that he waited, only a few hundred of the thirteen thousand Jews who had been taken away in cattle cars came back to Satu-Mare. When they did, Bela hardly recognized them: men younger than himself now gray and aged; women once bright and spirited now moving slowly, silently along the street. Then he learned that a sister, Rosalie, had also survived. Day after day, he scanned the faces of those who returned, hoping to catch a glimpse of her. At last it was reported that acquaintances had made arrangements for her to emigrate to the United States.

Bela was offered the opportunity to emigrate too. He refused. He would stay in Satu-Mare, he said, and await others of his family who might be alive and might return. But no one appeared. Bit by bit, he sold the stock of his father's warehouse and lived off the proceeds while he waited with fading hope.

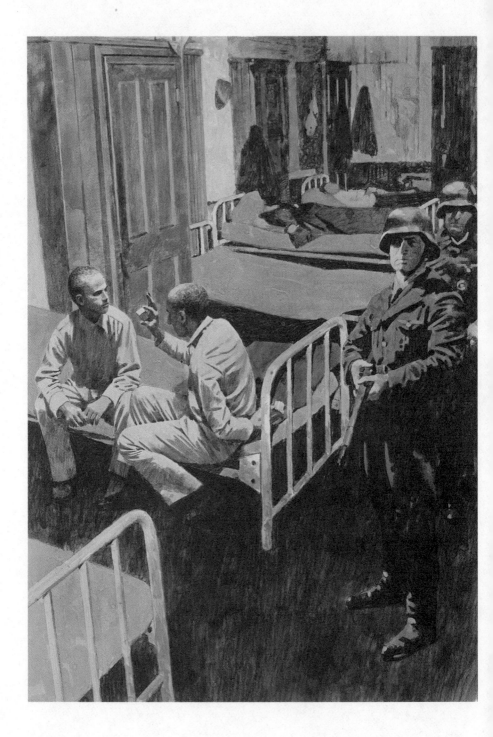

CHAPTER 3

NOTHING CONSOLED BELA. He hated Satu-Mare now. He felt rootless, nationless. There was no reason why he should make for one part of the world rather than another. Some might call that absolute freedom, others absolute despair.

So Bela set off through Central Europe, aimless and without plans or hopes for his future. But he found that part of the world still in a state of turmoil and confusion; troops came and went, while refugees struggled to get into or out of their homelands.

His name stopped meaning anything to him. What did it matter what he was called, since he had no family to derive a name from? There were times when he changed names so rapidly that it almost seemed as if he had forgotten who he was.

It was dusk when Bela reached Budapest, tired and starved, with only a little money in his pocket. He had crossed borders without trouble. By now, acquiring papers and charming and cheating his way through border posts was so easy, he hardly thought more about doing it than other people might think about displaying their passports. A man who had been able to cheat his way through Auschwitz, defrauding and deceiving Nazi guards and officers, found it child's play to get past groups of confused soldiers and disordered government officials.

On this particular evening dark was falling fast as Bela turned a corner and saw, on the other side of the road, a misty lighted café window. He quickened his step until he stood outside it, and he peered through the glass. He could see a group of men in Russian army uniforms, their enormous greatcoats draped carelessly across the backs of their chairs. Several half-empty bottles of vodka stood on the table, and a basket of black bread was nearby, casually unattended. These men had plenty of food. Put that basket down for a moment in any town for a hundred miles around and a thousand hungry hands would grab at it.

Bela glanced at his reflection in the window, straightened his collar, pulled out his old comb, which had half its teeth missing, and ran it through his hair. Then he did something he hadn't done for a long while. He fixed his face, almost as if a cosmetic surgeon had set to work upon it. He lifted his whole expression; the ends of his mouth turned up, his thin pursed lips with their distressed tautness relaxed. His eyes started to sparkle; his feet itched with a kind of bounce that made him want to walk on air. He breathed deep, and each breath seemed to inflate his tired, half-broken body with new life and energy. When he stepped brightly across the doorway of the café, anyone who had seen him drag himself listlessly along the street five minutes ago would scarcely have recognized him as the same man.

"Vashe zdorovye!" he said boldly as he approached the soldiers' table. He extended his hand and shook each man's hand firmly, smiling with confidence. "At last, fellow Russians in this godforsaken town!" His tone was friendly, not too bluff, but full of a calm and cheerful self-confidence.

The soldiers smiled and said *Zdorovye* back to him. They were already quite drunk. One of them moved his chair to make room and indicated to Bela that he should pull a chair up to the table.

Bela could see there was one sergeant, who seemed a little more drunk than the rest, and the others were corporals. He addressed himself to the sergeant. "Where are you from, Comrade?" he asked, in order to be sure of not being caught out himself.

"A long way, friend," said the sergeant, staring gloomily into his half-empty glass. "Vladivostok. Ever been there?"

Bela said he had never had the pleasure, but by all accounts it was a fine place. He asked the other five where they came from and then announced that he himself—Piotr Simonovitch—was from the Georgian Republic, secure in the knowledge that none of them lived within a thousand miles of there.

As Bela spoke, he reached into his pocket and felt around for the few coins he had. Then he slipped his hand into the pocket of the greatcoat that was draped over the chair next to his. Nothing. So he tried the coat on the other side, and his fingers closed upon a fine roll of notes. He wouldn't make the mistake of taking them all; he simply peeled off the top ten, hoping they were in big denominations. Transferring the notes to his own inside jacket pocket, he kept up a nostalgic patter about the beauty of his homeland. Then he thumped the table and ostentatiously rose to his feet. "Service!" he shouted with a sharp authoritarian tone.

When the waitress hurried up to the table, he ordered another bottle of vodka and whatever food her grubby little kitchen could provide. The Russians smiled in approval.

The soldiers, Bela rapidly perceived, were tired and bored. They had been away from home too long. Now the war was over, they'd had enough. There was a great deal of information Bela wanted from them, but he took things slowly. Before they could start asking questions, he began to talk about himself.

"I'm an interpreter," he said. "But what have I to interpret? Nothing. No one wants to talk to these morons here anyway, and I have lost my detachment. They sent me to take some reports downcountry, and when I came back to Budapest today, they'd gone. Sent home. And here I am, stuck, like a fool, with no order papers, no travel warrant and no senior officer. What's a man to do but drink?" He poured more vodka all around but gave himself little.

The sergeant stirred. "Interpreter, eh? What do you speak?"

Bela smiled. "You name it, I speak it, even Hungarian, if you want to try me." He began to gabble at them, sliding from language to language as if he were merely changing key on a piano.

"Okay, okay!" said the sergeant, lifting his hands to his ears. "I believe you! Look, we can give you some work. Don't worry about the formalities, I can see to that side of it. We'll call it a transfer. Who's to know in this place where the authorization came from? I wouldn't even know who to ask."

Bela looked only moderately interested and shrugged his shoulders. "Makes no difference to me. Give me valid authority and I'm yours. What do you want me for anyway?"

The sergeant yawned, and Bela wondered whether he would complete the negotiation before he fell asleep. "Want? Oh, yes. Had a lot of trouble with the natives and their lingo. Filthy lot, babbling away at you and pretending not to understand what they're supposed to do. I'm fed up with it." He yawned again. Bela poured more drinks, but faked knocking one back down his own gullet.

"Quartermaster, provisions, you know," a young corporal with a shaved head said to Bela. "We're in charge of the supplies for the garrison here. We hand out rations, if we've got them, to people with proper signed authority to have them, if they've got it." He guffawed and slapped his thigh.

If they'd been less drunk, the Russians might have noticed the flash of joy that crossed Bela's face. How was it possible that he had fallen on such luck? Here was a chance for him to make his fortune, not once but a hundred times over. These thickheaded muzhiks wouldn't know if they were coming or going by the time he got to work on their storerooms. A starving population for hundreds of miles in every direction—and he had here at his disposal the very things people would trade their greatest treasures for.

The sergeant nodded and held up his thumbs. "That's what we are, shopkeepers, not soldiers at all."

Then the crop-eared corporal began to sing. At first he hummed, and the others started to join in. It was one of those slow, lugubrious songs of the steppes. Oddly enough, Bela knew the tune well, but he knew the words only in Yiddish. He hummed along with the others until he had picked up the Russian choruses. Then he sang in a fine tenor voice. They all swayed from side to side with the rhythm of the soporific dirge, until the sergeant's head rolled onto his arms on the table and he fell asleep.

THE NEXT MORNING BELA presented himself at the soldiers' billet. It was an enormous and grand house, the former property of a count who had retreated with his family to his country estate. Massive chandeliers wrapped in dust sheets swung precariously from ceilings made unsafe by bomb damage. If the sergeant, rubbing his blood-shot eyes, could not remember precisely who Bela was, Bela didn't give him the chance to forget.

"Piotr Simonovitch reporting for duty, Comrade Sergeant," he said in a firm but cheerful voice. "Official interpreter to the divisional quartermaster, Budapest section."

That very first morning he was sent down to the storerooms to translate some written Hungarian, and to speak to a group of merchants in the town who were trying to do business with the quartermaster. When he stepped inside the two well-guarded warehouses, he found tobacco, gasoline, wheat and boots—all of which were the hardest currency in the region—and his eyes glittered with pleasure.

In no time he established his own ways and means of extracting what he wanted from the depot. He carried a large briefcase wherever he went, full of papers, but at times full of other things. Sometimes he could steal a large amount of tobacco; other times he could supply himself with the correct documentation to carry off a whole cartload of wheat. It was almost too easy to be fun.

He would usually take his supplies to Vienna, where he found the richest pickings. It gave him particular pleasure to take jewelry from the Viennese, since he suspected, often correctly, that a great deal of that jewelry had originally belonged to Jews who had thrust their valuables into neighbors' hands for safekeeping even as they were marched away to concentration camps. After the war, when the Jews never returned and people were starving, the Austrians felt no compunction about selling or bartering away the jewels for food. And Bela felt no compunction about relieving them of these ill-gotten gains in any way he could.

In a hungry population, word circulates quickly about anyone who might have food to sell. Bela's name was on many lips. Simonovitch could provide, and occasionally he did, just often enough to keep this valuable reputation. But often he didn't.

One morning, for instance, he was accosted at a street corner in the smart district of Vienna by an enormously fat Austrian *Frau*. She puffed up behind him and touched his arm. He turned to look at her. Her dyed blond braids, wound around her head, had slipped a little and looked like a jaunty, unbecoming hat. She pulled a diamond from her pocket and offered to exchange it for eight kilos of meat.

Bela took the diamond and held it for a moment. Then he put his jeweler's loupe to his eye and examined the stone carefully. In all probability, he thought, it had belonged to a Jew, for whom loose diamonds were common currency. "Two and a half carats," he said, turning the stone in his hand. "A nice little diamond. I'll bring you five kilos of meat." The woman agreed, and he said he would be back at the same street corner the next day.

Having memorized the particulars of the stone, he hurried away to find a paste one that would match it almost exactly. The next day he came back to the street corner with the paste stone in his pocket, but no meat. "I'm not so sure about that diamond, when I think about it," he said. "Maybe it's not worth five kilos. The meat price on the black market doubled yesterday, and I want another look to see what it's really worth."

He took the stone from her, fixed his loupe again and, even under her wary and eager gaze, substituted his paste stone for her diamond.

He gave the paste one to her, saying he'd be back in the same place that afternoon with the meat. The stone, he said, was fine. He reached in his pocket and gave her a small pouch of tobacco. "As a sign of my good faith," he said, dazzling her with one of his most endearing smiles. He turned and stepped off down the street, swinging his arms and humming to himself, the woman's diamond safely in his pocket, never to return to that street corner again.

In the months that followed, Bela swept through Vienna like an avenging angel, then began bartering and stealing his way through all the surrounding towns and villages. His pockets were filled with gold and jewels, but diamonds were his specialty. He loved them above all things. Diamonds had almost become his birthright.

And so it was that Bela Weinberger gained the experience that was to make him one of the world's most skillful jewel thieves. He didn't lack a single qualification for reaching the top of his profession. He had the speed and cunning of a magician, with feats of legerdemain to his credit that could not be bettered. He had the brilliant intelligence and the subtlety to assess with deadly accuracy the weaknesses and strengths of his potential victims. He had daring and panache. He had the charm and the flexibility of an actor. Life in the camps had taught him many things that would serve him well in his newfound profession. It had also taught him that values are relative. In the end there is only survival.

His Viennese career finally ran its full course. By this time his credibility had run thin. Enough people had had their fingers burned in dealings with him for them to be extremely wary. He looked about for new fields of adventure.

In 1948 Argentina was looking to Europe for laborers. So Bela changed his name to Willy Kratzer and emigrated. He stayed awhile in Argentina, but he couldn't settle down, and he began to travel across Latin America.

About this time he met the man who would be his lifelong accomplice, Hersz Chazan. Chazan was a specialist in forged checks; he and Bela, with his substitution expertise, made a formidable team. They started to travel all over the world. Chazan, like Bela, was quite an actor. He enjoyed dressing up in ridiculous disguises, but sometimes he used merely a monocle or some impressive decoration to achieve an effect.

On one occasion they went to India together. In Bombay they managed to gain audience with a maharaja. Bela and Hersz were both small men who lived by their wits and not their brawn, so they were more than a little disconcerted when they were led into the maharaja's presence and found him attended by five of the largest, toughest bodyguards they had ever seen. But Bela's nerves had been forged of steel in the concentration camps. He was not afraid any longer of physical dangers.

The maharaja listened to them and agreed to buy some diamonds. The negotiation was long, formal and ritualistic, but the very pomposity and complication of the process made Bela's job all the easier. At the last moment he substituted glass for the diamonds he was selling. Then, taking the money, he and Chazan backed humbly out of the maharaja's presence and left the country on the first boat they could find.

Back in Argentina, Bela set up a practice as a dental technician, but under the guise of this respectable occupation he began to smuggle gold on a large scale. He also carried out at least six diamond thefts by substitution, taking about twelve thousand dollars in all. He had, of course, mastered Spanish in a few months.

But he never learned to settle in one place. With or without Chazan, he kept moving. They traveled to Australia for a little diamond thieving, then went on to Hong Kong. It was Chazan's idea to visit South Africa to see if they couldn't get hold of some diamonds at the source. Bela thought the idea was idiotic, but also fun. So they both arrived in Kimberley; neither of them knew anything about diamond mining.

Bela could hardly restrain his laughter when Chazan appeared wearing a Legion of Honor medal and posing as a diplomat. Chazan then tried to persuade some of the miners to bring diamonds out of the mine for him. He lectured them at length about ingenious techniques for secreting diamonds in peculiar parts of the body so as to make them undetectable. The miners listened politely to him until one of them quietly pointed out that none of this was any use. They were all x-rayed carefully every time they came up from the mine, as anyone with any knowledge about diamond mines should know very well indeed. Chazan withdrew somewhat abashed from this enterprise and went to his hotel room to sulk.

Meanwhile Bela decided that they ought not waste their South African trip, and he took himself down to the diamond market, where a group of Jews could be found, as usual, dealing in the stones. Using all his customary tactics, calling first at the synagogue, Bela pulled off a large substitution theft and came away with diamonds worth more than sixteen thousand dollars. It was some of these that were found in his possession when he was finally arrested.

Bela did not worry much about getting caught. He lived as if he were still in the camps, surviving day by day from one escapade to the next. His life had no overall plan or shape. He gave away the money as soon as he got it. Large sums he sent to needy families in Israel and elsewhere. He enjoyed giving money and cared nothing for saving.

He developed a taste for casinos around the world. But he took to gambling almost as if it were a way of disposing quickly of large and inconvenient sums, so that he could resume the real business of his life, stealing. He liked luxury, staying in the best hotels, eating in the grandest restaurants. His clothes were of the best, and his taste in travel was expensive. Some of his crimes can hardly have made him much profit, after the air fares and the hotel bills.

It was his rootlessness that made him so hard to capture. But this also made him the perfect criminal for Interpol to focus attention upon. After the war, when Interpol was just getting off the ground, here was a quarry that gave the organization its best possible *raison d'être*. If they had wanted to invent a criminal who would help build up international cooperation on a grand scale, Bela Weinberger was their man.

CHAPTER 4

BY THE TIME MARCEL Sicot received the massive dossiers from his three detectives, several additional daring diamond thefts had been reported from different parts of the world. After reading all that they had discovered in their investigations, he felt he knew everything he could know about the world of diamond merchants and about the way this thief operated.

Sicot now felt justified in following his original hunch about the

man he was seeking, whose fingerprints were all over the crimes—
but alas, only metaphorically speaking. One actual fingerprint might
tell the whole story, but so far not one of the thefts had revealed so
obvious a clue.

The man might use several different accomplices, but nothing yet
had been found out about them either. It was only a matter of time,
Sicot thought. The day must come, this year, next year, when the
man or an accomplice would make some small error. Even a tiny
mistake could lead them to him. And Marcel Sicot had not the
slightest doubt that in the end they would catch him.

Imagine Sicot's delight when in July 1952 there came a major
breakthrough. Detective Haffa appeared at his office.

"Another case," Haffa said, full of excitement. "Exactly the same
method, same two fellows, by the sound of it!"

"Where this time?" the secretary-general asked.

"Mexico," Haffa said. "But this is different. This time his accomplice has left us a beautiful set of prints!"

Sicot sat bolt upright in his chair. "Prints!" he said.

Haffa hurried on with his story. "Two men went into the jewelry
shop in a small town in Baja California, and they sought to purchase numerous items. The accomplice gave his name to the jeweler
as something fancy. Here it is," he said, reading from a sheet of
paper in his hand. "Ridiculous! Fabian Blas-Chandé y Rossano he
called himself. Before he departed he left a lovely right-hander on
the side of the glass counter. The police picked it up right away, and
they've sent us a copy to see if it means anything to us. They're
working on the prints now, down in the fingerprint files."

Sicot rushed down to the file room. Half the staff of Interpol
seemed to be there to help, pulling out the cards of every criminal
they had listed who was known to have a record for fraud, swindling
or anything to do with jewels.

Several hours later they were all still at it. Matching up fingerprints was a slow and laborious process; they had to work carefully
with the magnifying glass, looking for points of similarity in the
whorls of lines on the fingers and thumbs.

Finally they found their man. A cry went up all around the room,
and the fingerprint expert triumphantly handed the card to Sicot.
He picked up the file on the man and read out his name, "Chazan!"

as if it were a magic word. "Hersz Chazan," he repeated to his three detectives.

He then withdrew to his office, beckoning to the three to follow him. Once inside, with the men perched uncomfortably wherever they could, Sicot opened up the file and began to read it aloud.

Chazan's first reported crime had been in 1949. He had succeeded, not particularly adeptly, in swindling a Lisbon jeweler out of diamonds worth twenty thousand dollars. From all reports, it looked as if he had been lucky to get away with it. He had on that occasion used the same name, Chandé, and left a fine set of prints.

He wasn't caught until he was arrested for a minor swindle in Israel that same year. There he was going under the name Pedro Cambo, but once they got his fingerprints and sent them to Interpol, it was discovered he was the same man who had called himself Chandé in Lisbon.

The Israelis gave him a short prison term, and they discovered his real name was Hersz Chazan. Since then the man had dropped out of sight, and unless he had committed other crimes that no one had bothered to report to Interpol, he had kept out of trouble.

But here he was again, and now he might lead Interpol to the man they were hunting. Did he work often with him, or had this been a single assignment? In any case, an alert would be sent out for anyone calling himself Chazan, Chandé or Cambo.

Now that Interpol had the name, description, photograph and fingerprints of the man who might well be their thief's chief accomplice, surely it would be only a matter of time before police in some town somewhere in the world picked him up. But the swindles were beginning to get out of hand. They had accelerated to the rate of a major theft a month. This master thief seemed to Sicot and his men to be flying in the face of reason. Why was he apparently provoking Interpol, defying them to catch him? To commit so many major crimes in such rapid succession was sheer impudence; but perhaps, with luck, impudence would lead to imprudence.

In September 1952 two men answering the description of Chazan and his master relieved a jeweler in Geneva of Swiss francs worth two thousand dollars. When Sicot read the details, he had no doubt that the man who had called himself Goldberg was the criminal he was seeking.

The report described how Moshe Gross, a salesman who spoke only Yiddish, went into his local synagogue in Geneva after work one evening. After he had prayed for a while he was approached by a man who said he was a stranger in these parts, and they fell into conversation. Gross was a small, nervous, rather wizened-looking man, a Hasidic Jew, who wore long earlocks and a broad-brimmed black hat. A synagogue seemed such a safe place to meet someone, he said later, plaintively wailing that once this last sanctuary of trust had been breached, there was nowhere to turn in the world.

Goldberg had said he came from Khust in Carpathian Ruthenia, now part of the Ukraine. He and Gross had many mutual friends from that part of the world, and they exchanged memories of the days when they had both lived there. Gross was charmed by him and, hearing that he knew no one in Geneva, immediately invited him home for dinner.

Over a delicious meal, exquisitely prepared by Gross's wife, the two men talked on for a long while. Gross could see that Goldberg, though not Hasidic himself, had spent much time with Hasidim and seemed to know every ritual and convention of their life. Sometimes it was so difficult to invite people to one's house, Gross said, even Jews, if they did not understand the importance of small gestures, symbols and rules.

It was only when the meal was over that Gross mentioned his business, in the most offhand way. He said that he had watches and fine Swiss embroideries to sell. He brought some out and they mused over them together, enjoying the quality of the items and turning them over in their hands with pleasure.

Goldberg praised Gross for his excellent goods, but said alas, he was not interested for himself. But he thought a friend of his might be pleased to buy. His friend, he said, was called Horowitz, and he would be arriving in Geneva tomorrow. If Gross would like, he'd bring Horowitz around to have a look at his goods. Gross said he would be delighted.

Conversation moved on after that. Finally Goldberg told Gross that he had just had a great piece of good fortune. He had been carrying a large amount of money in U.S. dollars around and had lost it, but suddenly it had been returned to him, just when he had given up hope of ever seeing the money again. According to tradition, he would now like to give a portion of it to some good cause, to show gratitude for his good luck.

"I'm so sorry to trouble you with this request," Goldberg said to Gross. "But I have learned my lesson once and I am very much afraid of having this money stolen or of losing it a second time. I'm staying in a small hotel, and, you know how it is, you can't trust a soul these days. So, as I shall be returning here tomorrow, I wonder if I may leave the money here with you for safekeeping?" Gross said it would be no trouble at all.

Afterward Gross said he had never before met a stranger who could be so absolutely trusting. The money was real, and Goldberg handed it over without even asking for a receipt or checking the exact sum. Gross did indeed feel honored to be so well liked and trusted by this new friend, and his confidence was won over completely. This was one of Bela's favorite tricks. He would utterly disarm his victims by entrusting them with objects of great value. He did not make the common mistake of thieves who assume everyone else is as crooked as themselves.

The next morning Goldberg returned, bringing his friend Horowitz, as promised. Horowitz said he would like to buy the watches Gross showed him, but he also wanted to sell three loose diamonds and two diamond rings.

"I'm afraid I am not really a diamond man," Gross said apologetically. "I couldn't possibly tell you the value of those stones. But I will gladly go to a friend of mine for an estimate."

Goldberg and Horowitz said that would be fine, and they left the diamonds with Gross, promising to return later. Gross took the stones to his friend, who gave their value as somewhere around twelve thousand dollars.

When the three men met again at Gross's apartment, Horowitz said the price sounded reasonable, but he'd like just a little time to think it over. Gross smiled. "But of course. In our world we never rush things. Take it easy; that way you make no mistakes and you don't die young of a heart attack."

Goldberg clapped Gross on the back and said he was a wise man. Horowitz said, "Look, I'd like to do a bit of shopping while I'm out. Would it be possible for you to advance me a little money on the diamonds? Of course, I'll leave you the diamonds and a check as collateral. I know it's ridiculous, but I'm short of cash." Gross said that would be no trouble at all, so Horowitz made out a check for two thousand dollars, and Gross gave him the money in Swiss francs.

"I hope I will see you gentlemen at dinner again tonight," Gross said. "I would be most pleased if you would dine with me."

Goldberg thanked him profusely and added, "But we shall meet in the synagogue this evening before that, shall we not?"

Gross shook both men by the hand. "Of course. I will see you in the synagogue, and you will come back here afterward. Meanwhile, one can never be too careful, and I will put the diamonds and the check in this vase here, by the wall in the dining room." Goldberg and Horowitz watched carefully as he put the valuables away. "I have your money in there too," Gross said. "So just tell me when you want it." Goldberg and Horowitz stood close to the vase for a moment or two, and then Goldberg said something that made them all laugh. Later Gross forgot what it was, but it is doubtful that he would still think it was a good joke.

Goldberg and Horowitz set off on their shopping expedition. Gross worked for another couple of hours, and then washed himself carefully for the evening service and set off for the synagogue. He prayed and then waited there for his two new friends to come. At first he just thought they were late, but then he began to feel a little nervous. He waited until eight thirty before he panicked. He ran home so fast that all his neighbors stared at him in amazement; he wasn't the sort of man to run like that, and his curled earlocks went bouncing and flying out behind him. When he got the apartment door open, he rushed to the vase and found that the money and diamonds were gone. The crime had been committed in that brief moment of distraction when Goldberg had made that joke. The bank check was, of course, worthless.

Only a month later, in October, Sicot received a report from Scotland Yard of a theft in Leeds, England, of diamonds worth six hundred pounds. Chazan and his master had been there. But how had they managed to pass through yet another country, despite Interpol's repeated warning notices?

It was shortly after the Leeds incident that Firmin Franssen, then commissioner-general of Belgian police and later president of Interpol, received a crucial tip. Someone in Antwerp warned him that two notorious diamond thieves were on their way to Belgium. Antwerp is one of the most important diamond centers in the world, where colossal sums of money change hands daily. The Belgian police provide Antwerp with special surveillance and protection.

The whisper was that a man named Chandé was one of the thieves. With him was a man called Simonetti. The same source gave a good description of this Simonetti—a small dapper man with horn-rimmed glasses, well educated, well spoken. It matched the man Interpol was hunting. As for Chandé, the Belgian police already had him in their files from Interpol warning notices, with photograph, fingerprints and description. The underworld tipster said that these two men had committed crimes in Mexico and New York, among other places.

On hearing that the thieves were heading for Antwerp, Franssen wrote at once to J. Edgar Hoover, director of the Federal Bureau of Investigation in Washington, D.C., enclosing a picture of Chandé and a description of Simonetti. At the time the FBI had the best single-print files of any large police organization, and given the earlier crimes in Mexico and New York City, Franssen hoped that Hoover might be able to provide some additional information.

On December 23 Hoover replied to Franssen, describing in detail the Mexican and New York crimes but also noting that "our files do not contain any fingerprints" on the man the Belgians knew as Simonetti. Still, even if the FBI had forwarded such prints to the Belgian commissioner-general, it would have been too late. For by then the diamond wizard, as some at Interpol were now calling him, had performed still another feat of wizardry.

CHAPTER 5

ON DECEMBER 10, WHEN Bela had arrived in Antwerp, the weather had been bitter—a chilly, gray, damp day. He knew the town well, especially the diamond center. The four or five city blocks that comprise the Beurs voor Diamanthandel and the Diamant Club he knew like the back of his hand. Far from the romantic old port, a long way from the gingerbread façades and the old palaces, there was nothing to stir the heart or excite the eye about this dreary quarter of the town. But Bela's face was radiant and his step was light and quick as he came down the Pelikaanstraat, where most of the diamond dealers congregated.

There are around fifteen thousand diamond polishers, cutters and dealers in that small district, and they handle forty percent of the world's diamonds. The better dealers have rooms that face north, as they find the attenuated light heightens the brilliance of the stones. But from the outside there is nothing to be seen. The nondescript buildings, dark with soot, tell nothing of their dazzling contents to the outside world.

Bela did not approach any of the diamond dealers but went straight to the big synagogue, which was bustling at this hour. Strangers arriving in town were likely to get a warm welcome from their fellowmen, and it was not long before Bela had insinuated himself into a deep Talmudic discussion that was in progress in one corner of the synagogue. He introduced himself as Benjamin Rabinowitz. Welcomed into the group, at first he sat silently, listening to the others. He listened for the tone and mood of the conversation, and found that it was not being conducted at a very high level. With great tact and humility he began to inject his own thoughts into the discussion, and soon the others began to listen closely to his words. It was some time since they had heard such erudition. The leading men in the group were deeply impressed, and told the police so later when they were asked for their evidence. Aaron Klaus said, "He was a very religious man and a great Talmudic scholar." Josef Mendel recalled that Rabinowitz had discoursed brilliantly, and also that he wore a gold ring. Mendel said that from the way the man spoke Yiddish he could tell Rabinowitz was Hungarian, from near the Rumanian border.

After the discussion in the synagogue, Bela had talked with Pincus Rubin, the cantor. They spoke Hungarian to one another and discovered they were from the same region. They began to exchange stories and names, and Pincus Rubin invited Bela home for tea.

Over tea they talked a great deal about everything that had befallen mutual friends and acquaintances since the war. It was only after an hour or two that Bela said casually, "By the way, I happen to have a few stones and a little jewelry I'd like to sell. Can you introduce me to some trustworthy man?"

Rubin cast an eye over the stones Bela displayed in his hand, and he smiled. "Of course," he said. He suggested several names, explained where the men could be found and even supplied his own card to be shown to them as an introduction.

Bela went back to the synagogue later, hoping to find one or two of these people. His fame had already spread among Pincus Rubin's friends. All the same, Bela politely explained to Ephraim Silberstein that his friend Rubin had mentioned his name, and he drew the introduction card out of his pocket. Silberstein was not a suspicious man and he had no reason to be wary of this distinguished scholar here in the synagogue.

Bela explained that he had two diamonds to sell, and also that he wished to buy a necklace for his wife. Silberstein was a stocky man in his mid-fifties, with what Bela detected as a solid, complacent look in his eye.

"I have heard about you already," Silberstein said with a smile. "A fine Talmudic mind, they say. It would be an honor to do business with you. Perhaps you will also honor me by coming around to my house, which is a minute or two away from the synagogue?"

Bela said indeed he himself would be honored. They set out into the street and headed toward Lange Kievitstraat across the railway lines. They passed two Hasidim, walking bowed forward braced against the wind, thin and gaunt in their black coats. Suddenly the wind lifted one of their broad-brimmed black hats and sent it scuttling across the street. With a few nimble steps Bela caught up with the hat and handed it back to the Hasid. Bela and Silberstein smiled at one another. Bela had a way of establishing trust and intimacy with another person in a remarkably short time. He would never have caught so many wary men in his trap had he not had the skill to lull them into a false sense of security.

They reached number 5 Lange Kievitstraat and Silberstein led the way up a narrow, dimly lit staircase to the second floor. In the half-light he reached for his key and let them both into a small apartment, filled with objects of all kinds. The ancestral paintings on the walls caught Bela's eye first, and then he noticed a great deal of porcelain and glass in somewhat garish colors.

Silberstein, Bela correctly surmised, was not in the big time. He was a small diamond merchant, dealing mainly on commission from bigger dealers. Bela rarely approached the leading dealers themselves, and looking around at the dingy, overdecorated little apartment, he knew he had reached exactly the right milieu.

Silberstein offered him some sherry, which Bela accepted graciously. It was clear Silberstein felt he had a real gentleman in his house, a man above his own station in life. Once they were seated with their sherry glasses before them, they began to talk, in the way such business is always conducted, beginning with subjects far from the matter in hand. It is an elaborate ritual, but an integral part of the practice of buying and selling diamonds. They spoke of the weather, they spoke of the sherry, they spoke of the state of the world, and Bela described his own imaginary business as a textile merchant in Holland.

Finally Bela produced his two diamonds from his pocket and handed them to Silberstein for his perusal. The man fixed his jeweler's loupe in his eye to inspect them thoroughly. He hummed to himself faintly under his breath, as if nothing in the world made him happier than peering into the crystalline heart of a diamond. "Ah, you know how it is with values, actual prices," Silberstein said, shaking his head and shrugging. "Every diamond is unique. Each has a different formation and different flaws." He spoke as if Bela were a man with no knowledge of diamonds, and Bela encouraged him to think so.

"Really?" Bela said. "I thought they were measured in carats and had a standard value." His eyes radiated innocence.

Silberstein shook his head again. "Carats, yes, but values, that's more difficult. I'd estimate that this brilliant here is about two-point-six-five carats. That one is less, perhaps two-point-two-four carats. I'll have to take them down to the Beurs to get you a proper price. They'll be able to tell me far more accurately. Now, you were looking for a necklace for your wife? I'll tell you what, I'll bring one back with me."

Bela said that would be wonderful.

"And I may take these with me?" Silberstein asked, pointing to the stones on the table.

"By all means," Bela replied, with one of his sincere smiles. "How else can you ascertain their value?"

Silberstein blushed at having implied that they were not entirely trusting friends. "I only meant to say," he stammered, "some men are not so trusting these days."

Bela smiled again, patted Silberstein comfortingly on the shoulder and said, "If religious men like us can't trust one another, my friend, then who can?"

They left the apartment together, and Bela promised to return next afternoon at two. He mentioned that he might have a business associate with him, and Silberstein said he would be delighted to meet him. They shook hands and parted in the street.

Silberstein went to his friends and learned that the two stones together were worth about a quarter of a million Belgian francs, about five thousand dollars at that time. As he had known when he first saw the stones, they were really beyond the range of diamonds he usually dealt with, which was why he had been uncertain as to what price to name.

But he had a keen eye for jewelry. And he guessed that this man Rabinowitz was a discriminating gentleman who would not like anything too showy or vulgar for his wife. He selected a necklace of outstanding beauty. It consisted of a hundred small and medium-size diamonds mounted in delicately worked platinum. All the stones were brilliants, which means they were cut with many facets and with flat tabletops on their upper surface, and therefore were especially pure, as any flaws are made more visible in this style. He took the necklace from a dealer friend on a commission basis. If Rabinowitz bought it, he stood to make a decent ten percent, or perhaps more, out of the sale.

When Bela came back the next afternoon, a little after two o'clock, Silberstein was already there. His wife, Esther, was in the small kitchen just off the dining room with the housemaid, Rosa; they were preparing soup together. Bela had brought his friend, whom he introduced as Mr. Blas. Esther at once bustled about and brought the men glasses of tea and sherry, which she placed on the dining-room table.

The men carried on a long conversation of a polite and friendly kind, almost formal, but leading inexorably to the moment when Silberstein reached in his pocket and brought out first Bela's own diamonds and then slowly, with a smile, a small package.

Silberstein placed the stones and the package on the table and, with a little professional showmanship, unwrapped the necklace and let it sit there for a moment while the two others stared at it in fascination. Clusters of diamonds have a quality that draws the eye, and while the necklace rested there on the table, no one in the room could stop gazing at it. Esther, from the kitchen doorway, stopped to admire it. Rosa, standing just behind her, stared too at the glittering stones.

Bela bent forward, gently picked up the necklace and took it to the window. He let it swing and twist in the light. "Ah, it is most beautiful!" he said at last, and Silberstein gave a little sigh of satisfaction. "What do you think? Would Rebecca like this?" Bela asked of his accomplice.

"Who can tell with women?" Mr. Blas said. "You bring them a hat and they say they want a coat. You bring them a coat and they say they want shoes."

Silberstein laughed—a little too vigorously, as if he feared this Mr. Blas might persuade his friend not to buy the necklace after all. Bela was still dangling the necklace in the air, mesmerized as it caught the light and sent out prismatic rainbows across the opposite wall, as if he had never seen diamonds before in his life.

"Surely any woman would be delighted to own such a thing of beauty?" Bela said more insistently to his accomplice.

Mr. Blas shrugged. "I'm not sure, my friend, what made you fix on a necklace. When have you ever seen Rebecca wear a necklace of any kind? She wears brooches, surely?"

Bela's face fell. "True, she does wear brooches on all her dresses, and perhaps she would find this a little flamboyant. Yes, my friend, I'm afraid you're right." He turned to Silberstein with a rueful smile. "My dear Silberstein," he said. "I do apologize most sincerely for putting you to this inconvenience, but is it possible that you might have a brooch to show us instead? A brooch as beautiful as the necklace?"

Silberstein sighed a little but said, "Why, yes, of course. You are making a big investment and it would be wise to make sure you choose what the lady would like best." It was easy to see that he was more than a little put out. However, he got to his feet and said he had some fine brooches in his office, and he would hurry along and collect them if the gentlemen would care to wait.

Bela rose to his feet at once and apologized again for putting him to so much trouble, with such warmth and sincerity that Silberstein's heart was melted and he felt willing to do anything for this kind friend. He started to wrap the necklace to take it away with him. Bela looked at it longingly and said, "Oh, leave it here for us to gaze at a little longer. It is such a work of art!" Silberstein was gratified that his taste in having selected the necklace was in no doubt, and he left it on the table.

To allay suspicion, Bela then said, "But perhaps we should come with you to keep you company? What do you say, Blas?"

Blas yawned and said he was a little tired.

"Very well, we will wait for you here," Bela went on, and patted Silberstein on the shoulder in a friendly fashion.

Silberstein was secretly relieved that Rabinowitz was not going to accompany him back to the diamond merchant. He did not particularly want this man to see that he was only a humble commission agent and did not have a large stock of jewelry of his own, so he hastened to leave. He bent down to pick up the two diamonds on the table, and he tucked them into his wallet.

But as Silberstein was about to leave the apartment, Bela stepped forward and said, "My good man, why carry about valuables more often than you have to? Aren't there enough pickpockets and thieves in the streets these days to make one think twice about what one carries about in one's pockets?"

Since the diamonds were still Bela's, Silberstein could hardly refuse, and he stepped back into the room and put them on the table with the necklace. Then he hurried away.

Once he had gone, Esther apologized to the two men in her dining room and said she had work to do. When she retreated to the kitchen, Bela jumped up and followed her. He leaned against the doorway and talked to her about his textile business in Holland, and he sought her advice about brooches and necklaces. Then Blas stood up and asked if he might use the bathroom; he knew that in such apartments it could be reached only by passing through the kitchen. Bela went and sat down again at the dining-room table, where the diamonds and the necklace were.

When Blas came back he dawdled in the small cramped kitchen and hung about in the doorway, effectively blocking Esther's view of the dining room for the crucial seconds it took for Bela to slip the jewels into his pocket. Then Bela stood up and sauntered over to the kitchen doorway, leaning across Blas to say casually, "I think your husband will be a little while finding what we are looking for, so I thought perhaps I would take the opportunity to go out and do a little shopping. You know how it is, when I come back from a trip, the children run up to me shouting and tugging at me. Do they say, 'Daddy, Daddy, we missed you'? No, I'm afraid they say, 'Daddy, Daddy, what have you brought us?'"

Esther smiled and dried her hands on her apron, and Bela shook her hand firmly, saying they would not be gone long. The two gentlemen put on their coats, which had been hanging over a chair, and let themselves out of the apartment, while Esther returned to the vegetables in the sink.

Later Esther said that she felt a little uncomfortable at the time. She thought her husband might be cross at her for having let them go, but how could she keep them there? It never occurred to her that they were thieves, but she feared they might have changed their minds about buying any jewelry at all, and her husband would be angry at having wasted his time.

It was only a quarter of an hour later when poor Silberstein came puffing and panting up the stairs. Sweat stood on his brow, and at the apartment door he stopped to take out a handkerchief and wipe his face. He had been running—that is, he had waddled as fast as his short round frame would allow—and he had visited three diamond merchants. This time he had chosen several suitable brooches, one of which he was sure Mr. Rabinowitz would select.

When he threw open the front door and saw that the visitors had gone, his heart fluttered and pounded so violently he could scarcely speak. "Esther!" he croaked. "Esther! Where are they? Where is the necklace? Esther! Esther!" Silberstein sank into a chair and put his head on the table, on the spot where the necklace and the diamonds had been.

Esther was rendered speechless with horror when she understood what she had allowed to happen. But then she shook her husband violently, grabbed Rosa by the wrist and ran for the coatrack in the hall. "The police! Quick, the police!" They all tore out of the house and down the street.

CHAPTER 6

AT THE LOCAL POLICE station, the officers were well acquainted with the peculiarities of the diamond trade. They were also on the alert, having received the news that some kind of diamond theft was to be expected. Then the Silbersteins and their timid-looking housemaid burst into the station, blurting out, "Stolen! Gone!" Several officers questioned Silberstein closely and learned the broad outline of the case. The police chief suspected at once that this might be the handiwork of the master thief Interpol was chasing.

"Tell me, Mr. Silberstein," one of the policemen said quietly. "Did the two men touch anything when they were in your house?"

"Yes, yes!" said Esther, understanding at once. "I gave them tea in a glass, and also sherry, and they drank! They must both have touched their glasses and the table." She got more excited as she remembered. "And the chairs, and the doors. Oh, they touched everything, I'm sure of it!"

"Did they wear gloves?" asked the same policeman.

"Gloves? Indoors? Of course not," Esther retorted. "Would guests of mine drink tea wearing gloves?" The policemen smiled.

The police chief decided not to waste a moment. The chief technician of the police laboratory was sent for, and the Silbersteins led him and a flotilla of other policemen back to their apartment. Silberstein kept muttering, "I trusted that man. I really trusted him! So scholarly, so polite, I don't understand it. My friends in the synagogue . . . I had confidence. . . ." The police chief tried to assure him that if this thief really was the man Interpol was hunting, then he could swindle anyone out of anything.

They reached the apartment, and Silberstein fumbled with his keys, his hands trembling with emotion. As he stepped inside, the voice of the police chief called out sharply, "Don't touch anything! Absolutely nothing!" Then the chief technician came into the middle of the room and set down his heavy brown satchel and his large bag full of photographic equipment. The Silbersteins pointed out all the places where they thought the two men must have put their hands. The technician followed them around, sprinkling aluminum bronze powder. When fingerprints emerged, he photographed them. But his greatest finds were on the glasses that the two men had drunk from. One glass was half full, and the technician carefully emptied out its contents. He neatly wrapped the glasses up and tucked them away in his satchel. He was humming to himself with satisfaction, certain that he had some very good prints. Finally he packed everything, nodded to everyone in the room, said a jaunty good-by and departed.

It was later that evening that the technician came up with his prints, a nearly perfect set. It was this set, fixed upon a glass of tea, that sealed Bela's fate.

When the fingerprint photographs were ready, they were rapidly sent on to Marcel Sicot at Interpol. Of course, Mr. Blas was readily identified as Chazan. And because he had communicated with the FBI on an earlier occasion, the Belgian commissioner-general of police wrote once more to J. Edgar Hoover and sent the fingerprints of Chazan and Rabinowitz. The commissioner-general also inquired if this Rabinowitz could be the Simonetti about whom the Belgians had sought information previously.

A letter from J. Edgar Hoover himself corroborated the fact that one man was Fabian Blas-Chandé y Rossano, with many aliases, whose real name was probably Chazan. The other man, Hoover said, was almost certainly a Luis Simonetti, who possessed a passport in that name, had entered the United States on a visa granted in that name, but whose real name was thought to be Weider. He also used many aliases, one especially—Shapiro. But because of his passport, he was filed as Simonetti.

The two crimes for which he was wanted made familiar reading by now. In Mexico, calling himself Shapiro, he had approached a jeweler who sold on commission, like Silberstein, and he had selected rings, loose stones, platinum earrings and watches worth six thousand dollars. He gave the man a check for eight thousand five hundred dollars, saying he would return the next day to choose some more rings. He never went back, and the check turned out to be worthless.

In New York, calling himself Weider, he went into a jeweler's shop with Chandé, wanting to sell six diamonds valued at six thousand dollars. The jeweler agreed to buy them, but had only four thousand in cash. Weider and Chandé agreed to leave the diamonds with the jeweler and to return when he had obtained the other two thousand dollars. So the diamonds were sealed in the customary manner in diamond paper in a marked envelope. Weider then asked for a cigarette, and in the moment it took for the jeweler to fetch one from a back room, Weider and Chandé left, taking with them the four thousand dollars and leaving the envelope. But, of course, when the jeweler opened the envelope he found the diamonds had been exchanged for glass.

Hoover enclosed photographs of both men and their fingerprints, which had been taken at the American embassy in Mexico at a time when they had made their applications for visas, before the American police had gotten hold of the fact that this Weider-Shapiro man was traveling with a passport in the name of Simonetti. They had let him slip through their fingers. The Belgian police passed the information at once to Interpol, together with the two sets of prints taken from the Silbersteins' tea glasses.

Sicot was overjoyed. Out came the magnifying glasses and the fine metal pointers. It did not take him and his team long to reach the happy conclusion that Simonetti was their man, and that he was still working with his old accomplice, Chazan. If they ever set foot in France, they'd be caught, without a doubt.

Bela could not have realized how close upon his heels his pursuers were now, or he would surely have kept well away from France. But perhaps he enjoyed playing with fire, for he hopped in and out of France and committed two other spectacular crimes, under the very nose of Interpol, without being caught.

After Sicot had made his triumphant identification of Simonetti, he waited for a report, from passport control on some border, about a man of that name attempting to gain entry. It was only a couple of weeks later that Sicot received word, not that Simonetti had been captured at the border but that he had been and gone.

First he had been in Nice. At least, a man corresponding perfectly to his description was reported in Nice. Calling himself Basel Horowitz, the man arrived at a pawnbroker's with a dazzling necklace of diamonds, which sounded identical to the one stolen from Silberstein. Against this the man had borrowed one million francs. But, of course, when the pawnbroker came to examine the necklace again the next day, he found he had an exact replica of the one the man had originally shown him, except that all the diamonds were glass.

Sicot was angry that the man had managed to enter the country unnoticed, and even more outraged when, a few days later, a man called Steimer reported a theft of six hundred thousand francs' worth of diamonds in Paris itself. There was no doubt, from the description that Steimer gave of the man who stole the jewels, that it was Simonetti again.

How many different passports did this criminal carry, Sicot wondered; surely he could not have passed through the border as Simonetti. Sicot felt quite powerless now. He must wait for some piece of luck, or some fatal error on the part of the master thief.

The next report came by radio from Pretoria, South Africa, on March 19, 1953. The day before, two men, answering exactly the descriptions of Simonetti and Chazan, had made off with diamonds valued in Kimberley at fifty-five hundred pounds. Sicot sent top-priority messages flashing around the world. Rumors and reported sightings flashed back to him. But it was on the island of Mauritius that the law finally caught up with Chazan, when the Mauritian police arrested him in the capital, Port Louis. They had missed Simonetti, but the news that he was certainly heading for Europe was sent out. Under Sicot's directions, airports all over Europe were alerted.

Sicot hardly left his office for two whole days. He now had the feeling that it might be only a matter of hours before they laid hands on their man. All the underworld contacts that Interpol and the French police could summon were pumped for information. All eyes and ears were open. It seemed that the diamond thief didn't realize yet that his Simonetti passport had been traced, for he had used it recently; with luck, he might use it again.

But time passed and there was no word of Simonetti. He had gone underground again. Perhaps the arrest of his accomplice had shocked him out of attempting further crimes for the time being. Sicot feared that he might disappear for a long time.

Sicot had almost given up hope.

IT WAS ONLY DAYS later, while he was lying asleep at five thirty on Sunday morning, March 29, that the telephone rang. It was Detective Haffa on the line, sounding breathless. "We've got something at last, sir!" he said. "He's here in Paris. We've just heard. Brigandat and I were out last night rustling up a few of our less attractive contacts in the diamond district. Well, one little pigeon came home to roost. He said he'd heard our man had just come into town. We're down at police headquarters now—looking through the hotel registration cards to see if he has registered in any of the hotels under any of the aliases we recognize."

Sicot was into his clothes in less than a minute, and he charged out of the house. At this early hour the streets were deserted. He leaped into his car and tore out to his office in Porte Maillot, his tires squealing as he took the curves without losing speed. As head of Interpol, he, of course, had no direct jurisdiction on the local level. That was a job for the French police, but no one could deny him his very special interest in this case, and he wanted to be among the first to know when the catch was made. His man was here, somewhere in the city, lying asleep in some hotel room. Maybe he was an early riser. Maybe he'd slip through their fingers yet again, this evasive, slippery phantom of a thief. Every hotel Sicot passed he stared at, half expecting that dapper little man with the mustache and the elegant clothes to be creeping away even now.

In those days there was a system in France whereby anyone staying in a hotel had to fill out a police form. People had to show the hotel their identity cards or, if they were foreigners, their passports. Each night the hotel had to send in all its registration forms to the police. In this way the police could rapidly locate anyone, provided, of course, that they knew what passport or what identity-card name the person was traveling with.

What Sicot feared most, as he came pounding up the stairs to his office, was that their man would have acquired for himself a passport under some alias that Interpol had not yet come across. The police could not very easily check every single person who had stayed in a Paris hotel that night.

Entering his office, Sicot found the telephone ringing. He grabbed up the receiver and heard Brigandat's voice. "It's him!" Brigandat shouted. "The idiot has gone and registered in the hotel as Simonetti! He's using that old passport!"

"Where is he staying?" Sicot asked.

"At the Hotel St. Germain, of all places—right out in the limelight. Only three blocks from the Luxembourg Gardens. We've had the place under surveillance since six."

Brigandat, Haffa and Renault had gone down to the hotel with the first detachment of police. Worried that some accomplice or some hotel porter might tip Simonetti off, they were reluctant to approach the desk and ask if Mr. Simonetti definitely was inside. In the end, Brigandat decided to risk it, and was much relieved and gratified by the news that the gentleman was still in his room. The detectives deployed their men at the corners of the streets and at the back, where the rear door led into an alleyway, and they positioned one on the roof to watch a couple of skylights.

Marcel Sicot paced his office, waiting for news. A colleague brought him some hot croissants and a steaming cup of coffee, which calmed his nerves a little. His great fear was that if they let the diamond thief escape this time, he would know never to use the Simonetti name or passport again. It might take them a long time to catch up with a new name and identity.

After phoning Sicot from the hotel, Brigandat had gone outside to rejoin the other men, whom he found increasingly restless. He returned to the hotel and confronted the desk clerk. "Are you sure he is really in that room?" he demanded.

The clerk said she was sure. The key to Mr. Simonetti's room was not on the board. What more could she do?

"Call the manager," Brigandat said brusquely.

The manager came, a little bleary-eyed, since he was not on duty and had been sleeping late. "Why did you not tell me that there was a drama going on out here?" he asked his desk clerk crossly. "Now, sir, what can we do for you? You are interested in one of our guests? A foreign gentleman?"

Brigandat said they were indeed extremely interested in Mr. Simonetti. Could the manager assure him that the man was in fact on the premises? The manager nodded his head, flicked his fingers at the clerk and asked her to summon the chambermaid from the second floor, where Simonetti's room was.

The maid came downstairs nervously. When she understood that the police wanted to talk to her, she turned white with terror, imagining something had been stolen from her floor and she was being falsely accused. It took time to calm her and explain the situation.

"The man in room 101," Brigandat said, as encouragingly as he could. "Have you seen him?"

The chambermaid still looked petrified. "I've taken nothing from room 101. I'm not a thief!" she protested.

Brigandat touched her hand in an avuncular fashion. "I know. You're a good girl. But you can help us, if only you could tell us about the man in room 101. He is not a good man. He is a thief."

"Oh!" she said, suddenly understanding. "A thief! He couldn't be. He's such a charming gentleman, polite and most generous. He gave me a big tip when I brought him a glass of tea this morning."

The glass of tea pleased Brigandat, and he patted her hand again. It was, after all, a glass of tea that had first given them Simonetti's fingerprints. "So you've seen him this morning? He is in his room?" Brigandat persisted. The chambermaid said she was almost certain he was, but he could have left without her noticing while she had been doing one of the other rooms on the floor. She agreed to go upstairs and see if she could find any sign of him.

She came back a few minutes later to report that Mr. Simonetti's very smart pair of soft crocodile shoes were still standing outside, where the bootblack had put them after cleaning them this morning. Brigandat thanked her profusely and warned her not to give the game away. He withdrew to where Haffa and Renault were standing watchfully outside, and he told them the good news.

All the same, Brigandat and the other two detectives were getting nervous again when Simonetti had still not appeared at noon. Could he have gotten wind of the trap awaiting him? Had he escaped despite all their precautions? They were so full of fantasies about the wondrous skills of this man that they began to discuss the possibility that he might have slid past them in disguise. What about the middle-aged lady in the head scarf, had they really noticed her face? What of the old man with crutches?

The weather was cold and bright, the March wind cutting through to the bones—lovely to look at but cruel to stand about in. The men had all been out there for more than six hours, blowing on their fingers and trying to look as if they had some legitimate reason to be hanging about on street corners, when anyone could see they were blue with cold.

But then, at twelve thirty precisely, a small neat man stepped lightly out into the air, an elegant black fedora on his head. In the buttonhole of his obviously expensive suit was a perfect red carnation, and on his feet were a pair of newly polished crocodile shoes. Renault, who saw him first, breathed deeply. He knew at once that this was Simonetti. This was the man whose description he had read so many times. He was not dressed as a woman or a cripple. He was dressed, quite perfectly, as himself, and for a moment Renault caught a whiff of a most delicate and expensive scent.

Simonetti appeared to hesitate; then he set off with a light springy step, heading briskly down the street toward rue Bonaparte. He suspected nothing. Renault gestured to Haffa. Renault, on his rubber soles, came up on Simonetti's right, and Haffa moved in on the left.

Plainclothesmen along both sides of the street were bristling with readiness to give chase if Simonetti took to his heels. Detectives Haffa and Renault moved forward with such smoothness that Simonetti hardly glanced to either side until, all at once, they each grabbed one of his arms.

"Monsieur Simonetti?" said Haffa.

"Yes? What can I do for you gentlemen?" Bela answered, giving each of them a slightly perplexed look.

"You are under arrest," said Renault. A car drew up beside them with a squealing of brakes. Brigandat was sitting in the front seat next to the police driver.

"It's Simonetti," Haffa said as he opened the rear door.

"Yes," Brigandat said. "Monsieur Simonetti, we're most glad to make your acquaintance after so long."

Bela smiled one of his most radiant smiles and tipped his hat politely to him, yet without a hint of subservience. *"Enchanté,"* he said, and stepped inside the car. Haffa and Renault sat on either side of him in the back seat. The car accelerated into traffic, then turned and sped rapidly toward the Seine in the direction of the Préfecture de Police.

As soon as he could get to a phone, Detective Brigandat dialed Sicot. "It's all over, sir," he said. "We've got our man, and it *is* Simonetti."

According to protocol, Sicot would get his hands on Simonetti for questioning only after the French police had thoroughly investigated the crimes he had committed on French soil. Sicot sighed wearily to himself. What he wanted was a couple of days alone with Simonetti in his office, just a couple of days to find out who he was and how he had pulled off so many astoundingly successful thefts. And what had become of all that money?

CHAPTER 7

PERHAPS IF SICOT had known then how incredibly difficult Simonetti was to interrogate, he wouldn't have wanted the job to fall to him. The baffled Paris police began to tear out their hair in frustration. Every time Bela gave them a name, that alias collapsed, and then he would give them another, and that too would turn out to be false. Who was this man? The only fact they could attach to him without a shadow of doubt was that he was the one who had committed the Silberstein theft in Antwerp.

As had been suspected, the Simonetti passport was a fake. Bela then said his name was Vargas, and produced a Bolivian passport to prove it. At first they thought this passport was authentic, but it too turned out to be fraudulent.

Under the French legal system the police do a certain amount of investigation once a suspect has been arrested, but the bulk of the case is prepared by a *juge d'instruction*—an examining magistrate. The poor magistrate who interrogated Bela prior to the trial was driven to distraction by his evasive tactics.

He claimed to be a Bela Vargas, born in 1918 in Milan. But there was no record in Milan of such a man. Then he said he was Bela Vargas, born in 1917 in Ödenburg, Austria. The Austrians had no record of that either. But then Ödenburg was now Sopron, part of Hungary, and there was no way of checking the town's old records. Bela claimed he had changed his name to Simonetti because his mother had married a man of that name in 1922. They checked again with police in La Paz, Bolivia, to see if the Simonetti identity might not after all be the real one. It was not. Then Bela admitted that he had bought the Bolivian passport from a man named Rodriguez, a gold smuggler.

At various points in his career Bela had signed himself in hotel

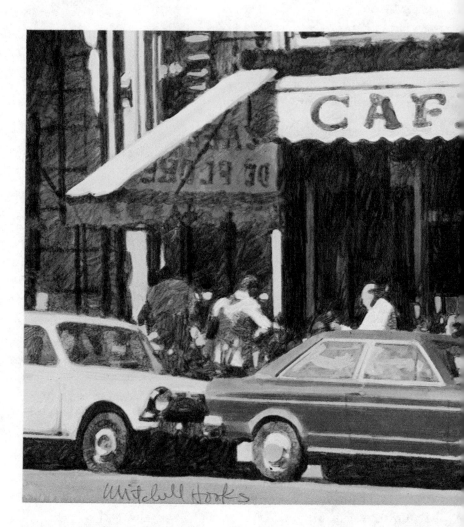

registers as Farkas, and the police held on to this identity with grim
determination. But they had misread the name and had him listed
as Farcas. Interpol's main record on him even now gives his name as
Berl Farcas.

Eventually, after ten months of interrogation, in which Bela used
his great abilities to send police all around the world scurrying after
misinformation, the examining magistrate gave up and decided to
try him under the name of Luis Simonetti, although he and the
police knew it was not Bela's own. When Bela came to trial, the
judge leaned over toward him and asked, "Quite frankly, Monsieur

Simonetti, Vargas, Farcas or who knows, do *you,* do even *you* know your own name?"

With a big smile Bela replied brightly, "If I told you my real name, if I told you my name was Eisenhower, or Jacobsen, or O'Reilly, would *you* believe me?"

To be on the safe side, Interpol filed him, cross-indexed many times, under as many names as they had a record of—Vargas, Farcas, Horowitz, Rabinowitz, Simonetti, Weider, Weinberger, Shapiro, Goldberg and the rest.

The name problem would be abandoned at the trial. But during the months of police investigation and interrogation that preceded the trial, Bela had more tricks up his sleeve. He used his languages as a weapon of confusion. First he demanded a Yiddish interpreter. Then he demanded a Spanish interpreter.

His next tactic was not to deny that he had committed some crimes of the type of which he stood accused but to protest vigorously that he had not stolen from those particular jewelers at those particular times. He said, for example, that he had never used the alias of Wyeber and that he'd had nothing to do with that first substitution theft reported to Interpol—the 1947 theft of gold and diamonds from a Zurich dealer. Then he would confess to some other crime in some out-of-the-way place, and the police would be sent chasing after information on the theft, only to discover that it had never taken place. Bela's inventiveness and cunning were unlimited. He knew that the police would have to investigate, and he sent them chasing after myths and phantasms of his own ingenious imagination. Each story had some convincing element that lent it credibility, and they fell for his tricks every time.

There were moments when his interrogators had to admit they enjoyed listening to Bela. His jokes made them laugh, his charm made them smile, his epigrams, his elegant turns of phrase made it impossible not to listen to him with pleasure. Sometimes they were exasperated, but often they were delighted. He was so different from the usual kind of criminal they dealt with.

The evidence the police found in Bela's hotel room was certainly incriminating, but he tried hard to explain it away. There were the packages of diamonds, with the carat weight marked in the corners of the envelopes—each containing a diamond of great value. There were a man's diamond ring with a large stone, gold cuff links with yellow diamonds, a diamond tiepin, a gold watch, fake passports and identity cards to match. Then there were a package of fake white diamonds and another of fake yellow diamonds. There were envelopes and special diamond paper, the kind used in the sealing of diamonds during a deal. There were packets of paper cut to the size of U.S. currency. There was a roll of toilet tissue shaped like a wad of paper money. There were elastic bands and Scotch tape and two jeweler's loupes. In other words, there in his hotel room were all the tools of his trade.

Bela, of course, invented long and funny stories about each item. When it came to the roll of toilet paper disguised as paper money, he tossed his hands in the air and said, "Gentlemen, it has never been used for anything other than the purpose for which it was intended." When he was asked to identify the hotel registration card, which indicated that he had been in Paris earlier that year and thus could indeed have perpetrated the Steimer theft, he turned the card over in his hands, brought it close to his eyes and shook his head. "Now it certainly looks like my handwriting, but I'm not at all sure that is my signature. I'm afraid only an expert in handwriting would be able to ascertain it for you with any degree of accuracy." Everyone laughed. It was absurd.

Detective Renault checked through everything in the hotel room. He examined every article of clothing with the minutest care. But he missed one important item. The crocodile shoes that Bela had been wearing the morning he was arrested had hollow heels, but they couldn't be opened except by a shoemaker. Inside them was a quantity of valuable diamonds, and these never fell into the hands of the police. When full, the shoes were heavy to wear. They fitted both Bela and Chazan, and the men would take turns wearing them. During Bela's time in prison the precious shoes were kept for him by the police, along with his suitcases, and later he managed to arrange to have these possessions collected by a friend. The stones would be waiting for him when he came out.

The most dramatic parts of the investigation were those when Bela was brought face to face with some of the people from whom he had stolen. Bela remained impassive while Silberstein retold his story. The expression on Bela's face implied detachment, as if he had never heard the story before but found it most interesting.

Confronting him, Silberstein blushed and stammered. He told his tale back to front and inside out, flushing with anger and hurt pride every time he looked at the man held for trial, whom he had taken for such a fine and scholarly gentleman. When Silberstein was asked if Bela was the man who had called himself Rabinowitz, he nodded his head vigorously. "Of course! Just let him dare look me in the eye and deny that he came to my house as my honored guest, and stole a beautiful necklace from me!"

Bela looked across the room at him and shook his head sorrowfully, as if he regretted the poor fellow's sad delusions. "My man," he said. "I am most loath to disabuse you, but I am afraid you are mistaken. I have never seen you before in my life. I am sure you are anxious to lay hands on the scoundrel who took such cruel advantage of you, but alas, you see, I am not he." There were some stifled giggles in the room as Silberstein blew himself up with indignation until he looked as if he would burst.

Moshe Gross was brought in a few weeks later, and he took his turn to describe how he had been duped in Geneva the year before. He told his story, and tears of anger stood in his eyes when he described his looking in the vase and finding it empty. Bela looked at him, again with a detachment that was unnerving. Everyone in the interrogation room knew it was Bela who had stolen from Gross. But such was Bela's extraordinary power to persuade anyone of anything that many began to wonder when they saw Bela looking at Gross as if he were a total stranger. "I'm afraid I don't know Mr. Gross," he said. "He really has made a mistake. I have never used the alias Goldberg, and whatever he says, I am not his man. He thinks it is me just because I am here being interrogated, which is, of course, quite understandable." Gross was led away shaking his head in disbelief at such perfidy.

Finally Bela's examiners called a halt to his charades. No credence was given to anything he said. The trial, when it came, would stand on the evidence of witnesses who identified him.

But at last Sicot at Interpol was allowed to question this *criminel extraordinaire* himself. Sicot had waited impatiently for a long time, observing and receiving reports on the progress of the case. The Americans had asked if he could give them more information, as they were still deciding whether or not to apply for extradition so that they could try Simonetti, once the French had finished with him. Sicot sent them a long report, explaining what a slippery fish Simonetti was. "Only limited credit should be given to the declarations of the accused. These should be subject to extreme caution, since they appear to constitute the major tactic of his defense. He goes so far as to deny crimes in which his participation seems certain," Sicot wrote.

Even though Sicot knew that he would probably get a lot of lies from Simonetti, he thought he might also get useful insights into the world of diamond theft. His curiosity was very great. He wanted to talk with the man and assess him for himself. When you hunt down a man over a period of more than a year and he continually eludes your grasp, you build up a strong impression of your prey. Perhaps you even identify with him a little.

There was a hum of anticipation in the Interpol offices that morning. Sicot had commandeered a larger office, and he brought in the top men of the theft division to listen to Simonetti. Of course, the three detectives—Haffa, Renault and Brigandat—were there.

It was an event that people in Interpol still remember. Bela was their star criminal. His exploits were truly international, and his case gave the struggling, reconstituted organization a sense of renewed purpose. He would never have been caught without Interpol, of this Sicot had not a doubt. It was Interpol that had collated the different aliases and the fingerprints and had finally brought them together to build a picture of a single master criminal. Without the information from Antwerp and America, supplemented by reports from Geneva and South Africa, the Paris police could never have laid hands on him.

Bela understood this well. As he was led into that room and introduced to Sicot, he immediately realized that this was the man chiefly responsible for his arrest. Surveying the room, he recognized Haffa and Renault, who had each taken him by the arm that morning as he stepped out of the hotel. Brigandat was also there, and Bela bowed to all four men and smiled. He knew he was their prize possession and that in a perverse way they were almost proud of him. The greater his skill and dexterity, the greater their honor in having caught him.

All the policemen, even many witnesses against him, had noted with surprise how little resentment Bela showed. He did not sink into a sullen state of self-pity. He did not abuse or berate his captors. He remained polite, friendly and charming, and on this bright June day he stepped into the Interpol office not as a convicted criminal but as an eminent lecturer with a worldwide reputation in the art of swindling.

He raised his hat to them, the same elegant fedora, then he gave it to the Paris policeman who was escorting him. He took off his coat and handed that also to the surprised gendarme.

Sicot could not suppress the smile that rose to his lips, and he indicated the empty chair that was ready for Bela in the middle of the group. Bela sat down, carefully pinching the crisp creases in his trousers. Sicot wondered vaguely how the man had remained so elegant after nearly a year in police custody, but then he remembered, with another hint of a smile, that this man could get anyone to do anything for him, and realized someone somewhere had been persuaded to press his trousers for this visit.

"Now, what can I do for you gentlemen?" Bela asked, seizing the initiative, which he never lost during the whole meeting.

Sicot, the only one to question Bela, simply asked, "How did you do it? You chose some of the most canny dealers in the world, people accustomed to pushing a very hard bargain. How did you get away with it? You weren't stealing from little old ladies and innocent housewives, but from men who watch each other like hawks."

Sicot knew his man. No other question could so well have aroused Bela's pride, and from then on he held forth. "That was my great strength," Bela said. "It was easy for me from my first meeting with a man to judge if he would go along with me. I offered diamonds or dollars or gold at a price far below the going rate. Or, if I let him mention the price, I could tell how honest he was by the price he suggested. Now, if he wanted to buy from me because I was offering diamonds cheap, he must have known quite well that the diamonds were not honestly acquired. At the very least he must have known I was avoiding taxes, dealing illegally and trying to move money around the world on the black market. The underworld in diamonds and gold is full of men conducting shady transactions. If the price was too low, I knew my man was dishonest. If the price he suggested was the going rate, I knew he was honest and I abandoned the attempt on him."

Bela explained that this was not out of scruple, but out of caution. While he stole from men who did not want their affairs looked into too carefully, he was relatively safe from the police. When such men did go to the police, they never told the true story, he said, which often complicated police investigations. Usually they didn't report the crime for a couple of days, by which time he was at the other end of the world with a different passport.

How, Sicot asked gently, did he identify these men, in a town he didn't know? Since he met them in the synagogue, how could he know these apparently religious men were crooks?

"Ah," Bela said, with another smile. *"You* would not know. *You* could not possibly ever know. You are not a Jew, and even most Jews would not know. Within the community of Hasidim there is a small group of unscrupulous men. They act deeply religious. But they are evil men who hide under a pious exterior. And they are powerful. They protect each other, and they conduct their business in every diamond quarter of every town in the world—yes, even out there in that little scrap heap of a village in Mexico." Everyone smiled at this first overt reference to a particular crime.

"I know them. Where I come from, my town, you might almost call it the birthplace of these men." Sicot tried to get him to elaborate about his town, but since Bela had not revealed his true identity and was still being held for trial as Luis Simonetti, he would not be drawn out further on this.

"These Hasidim are not reasonable men," Bela went on, for the first time displaying anger. "I am not saying that I was justified in stealing from them," he added. "But at least while I steal I do not pretend to myself that I am holier than other men, as they do."

Bela paused. "This is not the time or place for boasting, but if you want to know where a lot of my money has gone, it went to Israel. I sent it to families arriving there who needed money to help them settle. If you steal from these men, what better place to send it?" Later Sicot was to receive letters and information that gave credence to this claim of Bela's. Rabbis in New York and other places, especially Israel, pleaded for mercy for him on the grounds of his goodness and generosity.

Bela seemed to feel uneasy at having given so much of himself away. "Well, certainly most Hasidim are good and honest. I do not mean to attack them all. These others are just a small group." He coughed a hard little dry cough and appeared to make an effort to turn himself back into a calm and composed charmer.

"Now," he said, in another tone of voice, "I will show you how it was done." He reached across a desk and took some stationery and envelopes, together with some pages from a memo pad that were the size and shape of franc notes. From the desk he also took a handful of paper clips, explaining that they would represent the gems.

"The most important part of my technique involves having a preliminary conversation, in which I find out the lay of the land. I can estimate what price we will agree on, and I can see what kind of envelopes the man uses. Then when I return I have already made up my package, so." He demonstrated folding the paper clips into the stationery and envelope, in the traditional manner.

"Now, sir," he said to the gendarme who was his official escort. "I noticed you have a very fine wristwatch. Let us conduct a little bargain, and I will buy it from you." Everyone in the room waited eagerly to see what would happen. The gendarme rather reluctantly folded back the cuff of his left sleeve, and then he gasped. There was no watch.

Bela laughed and reached inside his pocket. "Ah, I'm so sorry. I quite forgot. I removed it on the way here, thinking I might need it for a little demonstration. Allow me." He pulled out the watch, and the gendarme blushed with indignation.

"Let us agree upon a sum. Say five hundred francs?" The gendarme nodded. For demonstration purposes, Bela borrowed five hundred francs from one of the detectives present. He sealed the money inside one of the envelopes while those in the room watched every movement with rapt attention. He put the watch into another envelope, and with a pencil he wrote the agreed sum in a corner. "Now, there is one important thing you should realize. Usually I would have met this gentleman before and we would more or less have agreed on a sum for the watch. Though, of course, I *have* had the pleasure of meeting him, I'm afraid on the way here we did not make a deal concerning the price of his watch." Everyone laughed except the discomfited gendarme, who was beginning to hate all this attention. Bela pointed at him and said kindly, "I assure you he is a most honest policeman. You have my testimonial for that!" And again everyone laughed, no one more than Bela.

Bela gave the gendarme the envelope with the money in it, pocketed the watch and shook hands with the man, saying, *"Mit mazel und broche,"* in the traditional manner. Then Bela stood up and walked toward the door. "Now I make my departure." He reached for his hat and coat and waved a breezy *au revoir*. For a moment Sicot rose to his feet, as if he thought Bela was going to slip away. But Bela turned back and said casually, "Just check how much money you have in that envelope, will you?" The gendarme opened it up, and of course there was nothing in it but a bundle of pages from the memo pad. There was a gasp from around the room.

"You see, gentlemen, it's easy!" Bela exclaimed triumphantly. "While you were laughing at the embarrassment of our good friend here, I exchanged the envelope you saw me seal for another I had in my pocket, and you never saw me do it."

There was a knock on the door. Two inspectors had arrived to help escort Bela back to prison. Sicot politely thanked Bela for his most helpful information. Bela handed back the borrowed francs to the detective and the envelope with the watch to the gendarme. Then the officer snapped a handcuff on Bela's right wrist for the trip across Paris and clipped the other cuff onto his own left wrist, stuffing the envelope Bela had just given him into his pocket.

Managing to make light of his captivity, Bela reached out his free hand and shook hands with Sicot, Brigandat, Haffa and Renault, and as he departed, he tipped his hat to them, again with his free hand. Then he was led away down the long corridor by his escort, and the four men watching him go felt a moment of loss. They had enjoyed his company.

Sicot would have liked to talk to him longer, though he doubted if he would ever get any usable information from him. The man was no informer. He had refused to mention Chazan or any other accomplice. But he was a gifted entertainer.

Just before Bela reached the end of the passage he turned around and spoke so they could all hear. "My dear friend," he said, addressing the gendarme who was sharing his handcuffs. "You are trusting by nature. You have not even looked inside the envelope I gave you." The gendarme fumbled about until he got the envelope open with his free hand. There inside, instead of his watch, was a small flat paperweight from the desk. Everyone laughed again.

VERY LITTLE LAUGHTER followed. On February 1, 1954, Bela was sentenced in a French court to three years in prison, with a substantial fine to pay. On appeal, the sentence was reduced to thirty months' imprisonment and the amount of the fine was lowered.

Once he had served his French sentence, other countries wanted to get their hands on him. He was extradited first to Belgium, where he served a sentence of three years' imprisonment and paid a fine of three hundred Belgian francs for the Silberstein theft. He was then extradited to Switzerland. In all, he served seven years in prison. The authorities in Great Britain, South Africa, the United States and other countries where he had committed crimes decided after that not to apply for extradition, and he was not tried in those countries.

It was not, alas, the end of his criminal life, but his spirit did seem broken. For six years he lived quietly in Israel. He became respectable there; he even had himself photographed with government officials. He smiles at those photographs now, for he soon returned to thievery. He didn't go back to the big time, but to an endless succession of petty crimes, and he was often caught. He has spent time in prisons all over the world since then.

Finally, on August 11, 1980, he was back before a French judge, having perpetrated yet another diamond theft in a small jewelry shop in Paris' ancient Marais quarter. Although Bela continued to deny his guilt—or at least the gravity of his action—he was sentenced to two years in prison and was remanded to France's huge central prison-city at Fleury-Mérogis.

Interpol has brushed up against him frequently since his original capture. He is in prison under the name of Berl Farcas, and that is the official identity that Interpol has settled on him.

He claims now that he has become a naturalized Uruguayan citizen. Age and many years of prison life have taken some of the jauntiness and self-confidence out of him. But as before he will serve his time in prison and walk free again. Interpol knows this, and today, years after his first downfall, Berl Farcas continues to be featured on one of its green notices. It is circulated to Interpol's member countries, warning them to be on the lookout for him after he is finally released. But it admits: "Identity uncertain. Nationality unknown."

BIG CHARLIE'S
FUNNY MONEY

BIG CHARLIE'S FUNNY MONEY

BY
EDWARD KEYES

ILLUSTRATED BY CHUCK HAMRICK

The small brick building in a dreary working-class suburb of Melbourne, Australia, attracted scant attention from its neighbors. Its blank façade revealed no clues to the activity inside. But activity there was. For behind the building's locked doors a printing press was busily at work, day after day, week after week, producing nearly twelve million dollars in American twenty-dollar bills.

The search for those bills would take a group of determined Australian police officers across three continents and lead them ultimately to a wealthy and extremely fat man known as Big Charlie. More important, their efforts, aided by Interpol, would result in the largest seizure of counterfeit U.S. currency to that date.

Edward Keyes is the author of numerous magazine articles and several books, among them *The Michigan Murders* and, with Robin Moore, the best-selling thriller *The French Connection*.

CHAPTER 1

THE SATURDAY BETWEEN Christmas and the New Year was crackling bright in Zurich, and the marvelous old Helvetian town had a festive air about it. Its spotless downtown streets streamed with cheerful, unhurried shoppers, and the picturesque quays along the Limmat River were alive with curio seekers. Strollers enjoyed the panorama of Alps looming in misty splendor out of the distant southern end of the Lake of Zurich. It was a fine day to be in Switzerland's largest city, this twenty-ninth of December, 1973.

Many who thronged the streets were foreign visitors, skiers coming and going, or simply holiday travelers. Unexceptional among these were two casually but neatly dressed gentlemen who, on this lovely afternoon, browsed in PKZ, a large men's apparel store on the fashionable Bahnhofstrasse. The men, who sounded and looked British, eventually selected a pair of pigskin gloves and a T-shirt. They paid for their purchases with two crisp American twenty-dollar bills. Then, taking the change in Swiss francs, they went on their leisurely way.

It was not an especially notable transaction; U.S. dollars, one of the world's soundest currencies, were gladly accepted for exchange. But within moments after the two customers had left the store, the PKZ cashier was uneasy. Gustav Huber, thirty-seven, had handled money long enough to have developed a reliable instinct for incongruity. He looked about and caught the eye of the store manager across the floor. Walter Meier, graying and distinguished, made his way over to the desk.

Huber indicated the pair of twenty-dollar bills. "I think," he said quietly, "there is something not right here." His young apprentice, Robert Sulger, stood by wide-eyed.

"What is it?" asked Meier, at the same time nodding with a smile to a passing customer.

"I'm not quite sure. The feel of these notes. And something about the two men who just left—Britishers, I think."

Meier fingered the notes. Frowning, he told Huber, "Take them to the bank at once."

Swiss banks were open this last Saturday of December for year-end bookkeeping. Huber left his desk in Sulger's charge and hurried to the Schweizerische Volksbank a few doors away. When he returned minutes later, his jaw was set.

"Well?" demanded Meier.

Huber, shaking his head, handed the manager the two twenties. They were pocked with tiny perforations—the standard bank cancellation branding them as counterfeits.

Meier sniffed. "Britishers, you say? Do you remember them? Could you recognize them?" He glanced sharply at young Sulger, who flushed and nodded.

"You showed no suspicion?" Meier asked Huber.

"Well, it was not until they were almost outside—" the cashier began. "No, not to them."

Meier gazed thoughtfully toward the store's entrance. "Perhaps they *could* still be nearby," he mused. "If they feel secure . . ."

He addressed his two employees. "Go look for them. One to the right, the other left on Bahnhofstrasse. If you don't find them within a few blocks of the store, give it up. It's too slim a chance to spend all day on it. But if either of you does happen upon them, I want no personal heroics! Just keep them in sight and telephone me. I will handle it then."

As Huber and Sulger went out, Walter Meier walked back to his office and dialed Zurich police headquarters. The son of a veteran police official, Meier knew many men there. Now he reached an old friend, Kurt Glanzmann, a sergeant in the Currency Squad. Glanzmann said he would come to PKZ as soon as possible.

Outside, Robert Sulger threaded his way along the crowded sidewalk, his eyes darting this way and that. He was agitated. Just a short time in his position and already witness to a swindle! Several hundred yards along the avenue, he slowed in hopelessness. It was a charade. Those two would have vanished like steam by now. He might as well go back—

Sulger froze with a gasp. There they were!

The two Britons had paused a moment at an entrance to the Jelmoli department store. Then they went inside. Heart pounding, Sulger followed.

The pair ambled about the main floor, browsing as they had done at PKZ. At last they stopped at one counter; approached by a female clerk, they began chatting amiably with her.

Drawing in a deep breath, Sulger—Meier's order having flown his mind—went up to them. "Many pardons, gentlemen," he said tremulously in German (he understood some English but did not yet speak it). "If I might have a moment . . . ?"

The foreigners regarded the newcomer blandly. One was quite good-looking, with thick, combed dark hair, perhaps thirty years of age; his companion, who wore an obvious brown toupee, appeared some years older, with more weathered skin and a wearier expression. They were of about the same medium height and fair coloring. The younger turned to the saleswoman with a smile of embarrassment. "What does he want?" he asked her.

She spoke to Sulger in German, and haltingly he answered her. Her face darkened, and when she looked back to the customers her eyes were questioning. "He is from the PKZ store," she said in accented English. "He says there is some . . . difficulty about the money you paid for items purchased there. He asks you to return with him to see about it."

The men glanced at one another in evident surprise. The older said, "What kind of difficulty?"

"I don't know. An irregularity, he says." The woman studied them. "Perhaps it's merely that you did not pay enough or were overcharged."

They all looked at Sulger. He smiled with what he hoped was assurance, praying that his excitement did not betray him.

The two men stepped aside and conversed in rapid murmurs. The younger one appeared upset, but the other shook his head with insistence. Turning back, the older man said, "Of course. We'll see to it at once. We don't wish to leave any ill feeling in your beautiful city." But his smile was dour. The clerk translated for Sulger; he grinned in relief and gave the men an awkward little bow.

Walking back to PKZ, the two Britons chattered together in English without any attempt to keep their voices low. Sulger recognized only an occasional word. "Dollars" the young Swiss of course knew, and "American" and, he thought, "Singapore." He perceived that the older one dominated.

No sooner had they stepped through the automatic sliding glass doors of the PKZ store than they were confronted by a quartet of grim-looking men. Gustav Huber declared to Walter Meier, "Yes, these are the ones."

Immediately two burly individuals, who wore leather greatcoats and flanked the cashier and the manager, stepped forward. "I am Sergeant Glanzmann, Zurich police," announced one. "I'm afraid you must answer some questions."

The foreigners were dumbfounded. Finally the younger exclaimed, "How *stupid* we are!" and glared at his companion. The other's face had sagged, but he said nothing.

As Glanzmann and his partner led the two out of the store, Meier went to Sulger and warmly shook his hand. The young apprentice beamed. His heart had still not slowed its hammering.

AT POLICE HEADQUARTERS the suspects identified themselves as Alan Wray, age forty, who said he was a business manager, and Roger Gilbert, thirty, a clothing manufacturer. They had left their passports at their hotel, the Chesa Rustica, but explained that they were British nationals and had lived in Australia for some years. Old friends, they had flown together from Melbourne on a combined business and pleasure trip that would take them through much of Europe; Zurich, where they had arrived only the day before, was their first stop.

As soon as Sergeant Glanzmann had dispatched two officers to the men's hotel to retrieve their passports, he produced the bogus twenty-dollar bills and asked the suspects where they had got them.

Wray, the elder, spoke for both. He said that they were astonished.

Neither had departed from Melbourne with any American currency. Their Qantas flight had made a stop at Singapore, however, and in buying souvenirs they had received American bills as change—but they'd thought nothing of it. At Rome, where they'd changed from Qantas to Swissair, they probably had used some of the American dollars for purchases—Gilbert had bought a Dunhill cigarette lighter, for one item—and no doubt had disposed of the few remaining bills in Zurich. Wray was sure they had no others and suggested that they empty their pockets to prove it. The possibility that they'd been passing illegal money had never occurred to them, he said. They were mortified.

Their story was not implausible; many an international traveler, Glanzmann knew, was gulled in like manner. He tried to pin down just where in the Singapore airport they had acquired the American bills, but neither could recollect. Still, Glanzmann's impression was that they seemed sincere in both their embarrassment and their eagerness to cooperate.

At that moment the sergeant's men returned and asked to speak with Glanzmann outside his office. They'd brought back with them something more than two passports. At the Chesa Rustica, a modest, quaint riverside inn on Limmatquai, having picked up the passports, the officers had made a routine check of the suspects' room, number 52. It seemed in order, containing only several pieces of luggage, a few items of clothing hung in a closet and some toilet articles on a dresser.

But when they were examining the luggage, they opened one overnight bag and were startled to discover it packed with cash—neat stacks, snugly bound by rubber bands, of U.S. twenty-dollar bills! A second small bag was also crammed with cash. The officers hadn't stopped to count it all, but they estimated the total number of bank notes to be in the thousands!

The sergeant marched back into his office with the two cases and sprung them open on his desk before Wray and Gilbert. The two stared dumbly at the evidence, then at the silently accusing policeman. Gilbert slumped down in his chair. Wray sat rigid, lips clamped. Glanzmann knew he had a case.

How big a case it was to become, however, not even this veteran lawman could yet quite appreciate.

IT WAS BY FAR THE MOST extraordinary haul in recent years for the Zurich police. The number of counterfeit twenty-dollar bills confiscated, including several recovered from local shops, counted out to 5004—a total face value of $100,080 in U.S. currency. Because passing the notes violated Swiss law, prosecution of the malefactors would rest in local hands; nevertheless, there were obvious international ramifications, and the Zurich authorities alerted the federal police in Bern, the capital, for action by the Swiss Interpol section.

The case came to the attention of Boris Wüthrich, chief of the Swiss Central Office for the Repression of Counterfeiting, a specialist for more than thirty years in that field and a senior Swiss Interpol representative. Glanzmann had sent specimens of the fake notes to Wüthrich, who in turn forwarded them to Interpol's central headquarters at St. Cloud, just outside Paris, for expert analysis. There, in a modern seven-story office building of the unprepossessing sort common to any suburban professional center, Interpol maintains— among its voluminous dossiers of international crime—the world's most comprehensive files on counterfeit currencies. The new forgeries would be examined minutely and catalogued, and then cautionary advisories would be circulated to banks and monetary exchanges everywhere.

Wüthrich next put through a personal telephone call to Paris, to an attaché at the American embassy named Frank Leyva, with whom he had worked many times previously, to their mutual advantage. Frank Leyva was in fact a special agent of the U.S. Secret Service, in charge of its operations in Europe, the Middle East and Africa. In 1973 the Secret Service was not only the worldwide police arm of the U.S. Treasury Department, which would have natural interest in any counterfeit U.S. currency, but also the official American representative of Interpol.

Leyva dispatched an agent to Zurich to observe interrogations of the two suspects being held there, while he himself went to St. Cloud to assist in analysis of the sample forgeries. These twenty-dollar bills were not remarkably deceptive: under magnification, a number of defects were detected in design, coloring, lettering and printing. Only the paper stock came close to approximating the genuine, yet here, too, the notes were betrayed by a somewhat artificial texture, and chemical tests indicated that the stock had been treated with some alien substance. Still, the Interpol experts knew that the public tended not to be critical, especially of low-denomination notes. (In American currency, twenty-dollar bills seemed to be the favorite of counterfeiters for just that reason.) Extensive dissemination of these forgeries in an unsuspecting world's currency markets could have generated a host of problems, and not only for the United States. They were lucky to have stumbled upon this scheme early on.

But were they really early? The fraud could have been operating unnoticed for any length of time. It was most important to see what information could be extracted from the pair in custody in Zurich, where Secret Service Special Agent Douglas Chalfant sat in on the separate interviews conducted by the Swiss police. Alan Wray, confronted with the incontrovertible fact of possession of more than one hundred thousand dollars in counterfeit twenties, first expanded upon his earlier story.

Wray admitted having knowingly carried the notes with him from Melbourne. But he insisted that until the moment of arrest, neither he nor his companion had had the slightest clue that they were not genuine. He did concede to having been party to another kind of fraud, however. He'd thought he was transporting authentic American currency out of Australia for a friend there who wanted to sidestep that country's strict exchange regulations. This person, he said, having learned of Wray's imminent trip to Europe, had offered him five thousand dollars upon safe delivery of the suitcase full of cash to a contact in Leeds, England.

"Who is this friend?" a detective asked.

"Well . . . actually he's not a friend of *mine*," Wray backtracked. "He's rather an acquaintance, a friend of a friend. His name is Robert. Bob. That's all I know him by."

"You barely know him?" one of his interrogators repeated incredulously. "All right, who is *your* friend?"

Wray shook his head. "He has nothing to do with this. He is perfectly respectable, and I will not bring him into it needlessly."

"Did he put you together with this Robert?"

"Yes. At some point, I suppose. But not in connection with this."

"Then how—"

"I was in a restaurant one evening, a place I go to quite often, a cabaret . . . and Robert came over to me at the bar. I remembered him slightly from my other friend, and he brought up the trip I would soon be off on, which I assumed he must have heard about from the other fellow. Then, after a drink or two, he began to talk about this idea...."

Wray went on to describe Robert as either American or Canadian, judging by his manner of speech; perhaps forty years of age, just under six feet in height, slim, with a thin beaklike nose and, he thought, a dark toupee.

"And what of the Leeds end?" he was asked.

"All I was told was, when I got to Leeds I was to leave word at a hotel there, the Merrion."

The officers were dubious. "Why," one asked him impatiently, "would you have stuck your neck into a serious criminal offense for someone you hardly knew?"

Wray shrugged. "All I could think of was the five thousand dollars I was to get. I could use it. And it did seem easy enough—just carrying an extra suitcase. I switched my first stop from Rome to Zurich, because Robert told me the customs are easier here." He pursed his lips. "Naturally, one never dreams things will turn out like *this!*"

"It likely wouldn't have turned out like this if you hadn't dipped into the cash," a detective noted. "Dishonor among thieves, eh?"

Wray smiled forlornly. "Poor judgment, no doubt. Perhaps even a touch of greed. But I didn't think of it as stealing. After all, five thousand of it would be mine anyway."

"What about Gilbert—he was in on the scheme, of course?"

"Well, Roger knew what I was up to, but he wasn't part of the deal—though I'd planned to cut him a share of my payoff. The first time he saw the money was after we got here, at the hotel. He assumed it was genuine, as I did."

Roger Gilbert, questioned next, appeared the more frightened of the two. He was also rather more voluble than Wray.

It was true, he said, that he'd first seen the twenty-dollar notes only following their arrival in Zurich. It was then, too, that he'd learned of Wray's arrangement with someone named Bob; previously he'd had no knowledge of such a person. And then, though incredulous and unnerved, he'd believed Wray when he said the money was genuine, because after all, Wray had promised to pay him as his aide on this trip.

It had all begun for him, Gilbert claimed, when a restaurant he'd operated in Melbourne had gone bankrupt, leaving him deep in personal debt. Wray, an old friend, knew of his situation and shortly proposed that he accompany him on a European trip for several weeks. It was primarily business, Wray said, but they would be able to sightsee and have a lot of fun as well. If he could scrape together the air fare, Wray would take care of all his other expenses and even arrange, if all went well, to pay him between five hundred and one thousand Australian dollars a week!

"What kind of business did Wray say he was going on?" asked a detective.

"He never did tell me, really," replied Gilbert. "He'd only say it was like sales of some kind, and that he'd fill me in completely once we'd got to Europe."

"So off you went with him half-cocked. Didn't you wonder if this wasn't all just a bit too pat?"

"I did wonder some. I'd known Alan long enough"—he licked his lips nervously—"but I didn't want to think of anything. I was being hounded by creditors, and I was desperate for a way out, and . . . this just seemed a godsend."

They left Melbourne on December 27 aboard a Qantas flight to Rome. There was a stop at Singapore en route, but Wray and Gilbert had remained in the transit lounge. After switching at Rome to Swissair, they landed in Zurich at about noon on Friday, the twenty-eighth. Through some mix-up their checked luggage had been left in Rome, but they were advised that it would follow on the next Swissair flight and be delivered to them at their hotel.

When their errant luggage finally arrived late that afternoon, Gilbert went on, Wray, who had been dozing, immediately jumped up and unlocked one of the bags. He laughed and cried, "Here now, have a squint at this!"

"My eyes fair bugged out," related Gilbert. "The bag was crammed with cash—American twenty-dollar bills! 'Good Lord!' I said. 'Where did that come from? Is it real?'

"Alan said, 'What do *you* think, chum?' Then he told me—for the first time—this tale about his arrangement with a chap named Bob, about getting the money to England and being paid five thousand. After a day or two in Zurich, he said, we would buy ourselves an auto and set out—for Italy, perhaps, or Germany, anywhere we chose. There was no hurry in delivering the money, he said. He made it sound a lark."

"But you still didn't know what business you were on?" Gilbert was asked.

"Well, I guess I thought, This must be the business."

"Then how did you think your expenses were to be paid, and Wray's? And from where was he to get the money to pay you? You weren't to use the cash that Wray had agreed to deliver, were you? Or had Wray suggested that he'd already deducted his five-thousand-dollar commission?"

"No . . . I don't know." Gilbert fidgeted. "I *didn't* think."

"The fact is," one of his interrogators pressed, "the very next day you did try to spend some of that presumed American currency. Didn't that worry you at all?"

Gilbert nodded. "I didn't think we ought . . . so soon. But Alan was so chipper about it. We had some shopping to do, and he said it wouldn't hurt just to take a few of the notes and— Well, you know what happened then." He sat morosely chewing at his lips, eyes staring off dully, so defeated-looking that his interrogators could not resist sympathy for him.

Hardly had this interview been concluded when one of the prison guards brought to the investigating detectives an intercepted message from Alan Wray to his compatriot; Wray had tried to bribe the guard to smuggle it to Gilbert, whose cell was in another wing. From a recent magazine Wray had torn a glossy page advertising High & Dry gin. In a cramped hand he had scrawled a summary of their predicament over all the available white space, with pointed reminders to Gilbert of what Wray characterized as the true facts.

I have told them that you knew nothing about the deal until I told you 2 weeks before we left & that I would be paid 5000 on delivery in Leeds. That neither of us knew that the money was forged. The first time you saw the money was in Zurich. . . .

I never really told you all the details, just the basics and I would tell you all when we were in Zurich, even then I did not tell you all. All this is to remind you of the facts as they happened. Both you and I know that we did not know the money was forged, but the police do not know this & I told you so many stories that you are most probably mixed up and do not know what to say, so just remember that you must forget all the stories I told you, & that the above is the truth. The thing I am most sorry about is that I did not keep to my bargain with Bob, he told me not to spend any of the money in the suitcase . . . that is what you get for being greedy . . . but of course we had no idea the money was no good. . . .

I am not guilty about telling them about Bob as he should have told me the money was no good, although if he had, I would not have taken it for anything, I did a stupid thing but neither of us are criminals. I wish I had never met Bob at all, but the $5000 was what made me do it. . . . One of us could so easily have got away from the young salesman who asked us to come back to see the police, & disposed of the money, if we had known the money was forged. . . . I only hope the authorities can see the sense in that simple fact. Just tell them the truth Roger. . . . I hope all goes well for us both. I can never forgive myself for involving you. Keep your chin up.

Despite the one discrepancy revealed between the pair's separate accounts, concerning when Gilbert knew of the money and of Wray's deal with Bob, neither the content nor tenor of the note added much to the investigators' knowledge of the true nature of this caper. It was possible that Wray had expected this "confidential" communication to be intercepted, hoping that his stated ingenuousness would thus be affirmed for the police. If so, he could be marked less ingenuous than canny. Still, from the surface facts obtained so far, these two men appeared to have been but cat's-paws in someone else's dangerous game of chance—somewhat loose in their ethics but nonetheless gullible, unwitting pawns. And clumsy. It was mystifying why, with stakes so high, the person or persons behind the counterfeiting scheme had entrusted its execution to such apparent bunglers.

On January 10, 1974, the U.S. Secret Service bureau in Paris cabled to Interpol in Canberra, the capital of Australia. The message summarized the circumstances of the arrests in Zurich and the prisoners' own accounts, with briefs of what had been learned meanwhile of Wray's and Gilbert's personal backgrounds.

ALAN WRAY IS A WHITE BRITISH MALE, BORN 6/12/33 AT LEEDS, EN-GLAND. HE IS 5′ 9″, HAS GREEN EYES, BROWN HAIR AND IS BALDING, WEARS A TOUPEE. HIS RESIDENCE IS 384 TOORAK ROAD, MELBOURNE, AUSTRALIA.

HE CARRIES BRITISH PASSPORT C 546290, ISSUED 1/30/68 AT JOHANNES-
BURG. HE IS A SALESMAN. SCOTLAND YARD HAS A RECORD OF ONE CON-
VICTION, IN 1957 FOR THEFT. THE SUBJECT DEPARTED ENGLAND FOR
AUSTRALIA IN 1960.

ROGER FRANCIS GILBERT IS A WHITE BRITISH MALE, BORN AT SHEERNESS,
KENT, ENGLAND, ON 5/6/43. HE IS 5′ 8½″, HAS HAZEL EYES AND BROWN
HAIR. HE RESIDES AT 9 MATILDA ROAD, MOORABBIN, MELBOURNE, AUS-
TRALIA. HE CARRIES BRITISH PASSPORT D 465194, ISSUED 11/20/64 IN
CANBERRA. HE LAST WORKED AS A NIGHTCLUB MANAGER.

The cable also said that Wray had lived for a time in South Africa, that his passport showed considerable travel and that he'd visited the United States in December 1972 and held a valid U.S. multiple-entry visa. It concluded with a request that Interpol Canberra initiate investigations in Melbourne and communicate the results as soon as possible.

CHAPTER 2

THE REPLY A WEEK later, from Interpol Canberra, was disillusioning. All indications were that Alan Wray and Roger Gilbert were anything but pawns, much less unwitting innocents.

In March 1967, at age twenty-three, Gilbert had deserted the Australian army after two years of a six-year enlistment and had fled to South Africa. He'd returned in November 1969, military charges against him having been suspended, and he established a men's clothing manufacturing business, which prospered modestly. Eventually he'd grown ambitious and also opened a small café in Melbourne. This folded after five months of heavy losses, and shortly Gilbert's neglected clothing business collapsed as well under the burden of his debts.

Since May of 1973 he'd been ducking creditors, a number of whom had court actions pending against him. His last known employment, from October until near the end of December—when he'd dropped out of sight—had been as manager of The Distillery, a nightclub located in a Melbourne hotel.

Alan Wray's reputation was as a would-be wheeler-dealer who'd had more downs than ups. Like Gilbert, Wray had left Australia for South Africa early in 1967. The police of the state of Victoria had no updated information on his whereabouts.

IT APPEARED NOW, Interpol Canberra conjectured, that Wray and Gilbert might be involved in what could be a major conspiracy, which had come to the attention of the Victoria state police some months earlier but which investigators there so far had been unable to pin down.

The first tantalizing whiff of it had surfaced in late October of 1973, when a Victoria detective received a call that a large quantity of new counterfeit U.S. currency would soon be available in the Melbourne area. Because this information involved a possible currency offense—a federal matter—it was passed on to the Commonwealth police. But investigation had turned up nothing to substantiate the tip until a month later, when another Victoria police officer got a new line on the matter from an underworld informer.

Detective Senior Sergeant Austin ("Aussie") Trewhitt, a ranking member of the Breaking Squad—a specialist squad within the Victoria Criminal Investigation Bureau (CIB), which investigates major breaking and entering crimes—was approached by the proprietor of an illegal gambling den that was often the target of police raids. Dennis King, whose baccarat club was located in a rundown area of St. Kilda, the bayside resort south of Melbourne, told Trewhitt that a man unknown to him, who'd been referred by one of his customers, had recently made him an unusual proposition; the man said he had access to a substantial source of counterfeit U.S. dollars, and would offer a percentage of the face value if King undertook to handle distribution. The man—described by King as probably in his thirties, a bit mod, clean-cut, dark and glib—had taken a bundle of fresh-looking notes from a suitcase, apparently all U.S. twenties. He told King that this batch, amounting to twenty thousand dollars, was available immediately; up to a million dollars more could be delivered within twenty-four hours.

King had asked for a few days to think it over. He had then decided to tell the police, hoping they might in return lay off raiding his club for a while.

Sergeant Trewhitt—a dour, no-nonsense, twenty-five-year police veteran—was used to dealing with men of King's sort. He had a certain contempt for them, but there were times when such "traders" could be useful, even indispensable, to police.

"You don't have the man's name?" he had asked King.

"No. But I should be able to get it."

Trewhitt had agreed that King was to get the identity of the mystery man if he could; then he was to string the fellow along, but without commitment, gathering as much additional information as possible for Trewhitt. If it got to a point where King had to give a definite yes or no to the man's offer, of course he was expected to bow out.

A week later King got back to Trewhitt. He'd learned the man's name but nothing more about what he was up to. The fellow had not contacted him again. Maybe he'd been scared off. His name was John Singer.

Trewhitt was elated—now he was sure they were on to something. For he knew about John Maxwell Singer, sometime black sheep of a fairly prominent Melbourne family. At thirty-three, John Singer considered himself an operator; he dallied in some of the city's more questionable circles, from sharp to shady, and had intermittently drawn the attention of the police. Just recently, on a tip from an informer, the Breaking Squad had surprised Singer in possession of a large quantity of stolen jade, part of a theft of jewelry worth more than fifty thousand dollars. Singer was the receiver, not the actual thief; but the CIB used their knowledge of him gained in this first felony arrest to enlist his help as an informer in fingering his accomplice as well as in recovering the rest of the loot. Singer walked away from it on low bail, with the intimation that court proceedings might be postponed indefinitely . . . if he stayed "a good boy."

All this had taken place only weeks before Singer's apparent participation in a counterfeiting operation. Now Trewhitt was tempted to put Singer straight to the wall, but thought better of it. He preferred not to compromise his informer King quite so soon; and he felt that more might be learned by keeping Singer discreetly under surveillance.

But, well into December, Singer had still not betrayed any evidence of occupation with illegal currency. Not that he hadn't kept himself and his observers busy. He'd attended to several of his legitimate enterprises, including a small plant that manufactured sheepskin products, the cultivation of shellfish beds up north, and some real estate holdings shared with his father. He was ever on the go, and it could not always be determined whether his pursuits were business or pleasure.

John Singer affected an elaborately indifferent appearance wherever he went, wearing tailored jeans and heeled boots, colorful sport shirts and neck beads, hair carefully styled in the insouciant windblown fashion. And where he went spanned the extremes of urban life, from Melbourne's posh hotels and clubs and elegant office buildings to seedy bars and tenements in mean factory neighborhoods. He was seen to associate with people of social and financial influence and with some individuals the police regarded as hoodlums. But nothing overtly illegal transpired that could impel the police to move in.

Perhaps Singer sensed he was being watched and was careful not to tip his hand; or possibly whatever he was into was either delayed or just wasn't going to happen. For that matter, the information the police had got might have been wrong in the first place. (Singer never *had* followed up his reported proposition to Dennis King.) In any case, in the press of other police matters, late in December the surveillance on Singer had been withdrawn.

One morning in mid-January, 1974, Aussie Trewhitt was sitting at his desk in police headquarters on Russell Street in Melbourne, sipping coffee and chatting with a Breaking Squad associate, Detective Sergeant Rex Hornbuckle. It was Hornbuckle who had arrested John Singer earlier, in the jade theft. Hornbuckle was also the officer to whom the tip had first come, back in October, of an imminent flood of counterfeit U.S. money in the Melbourne area. Now Trewhitt had just been notified by the Australian Interpol office of the arrest in Zurich of two Australians with more than a hundred thousand dollars in forged U.S. currency.

"It would have been tidy if we could have put Singer together with those two," Trewhitt said, sighing. "But—" He was stopped by a curious expression on Hornbuckle's face. "What is it, Rex? Do you know something?"

"I was just remembering," Hornbuckle replied. "A month or so ago I got a peep from one of my pigeons—the same one who'd given me Singer in the jade business, interestingly—who'd heard that a couple of couriers were soon to head off to Europe with a sizable load of counterfeits. That was all he could give me—and there was no mention of Singer, by the way. I thought it over at the time, and I was afraid the information might be a plant, a setup—we take the bait and make a fuss, and before you know it, my contact's a goner. So"—he tapped his head with a finger—"I just filed it."

"Two men, was it?" asked Trewhitt, interested.

"That was the word. When did the two turn up in Zurich?"

"Just after Christmas."

"That about fits," said Hornbuckle. "Do we have the identities of the two in Switzerland?"

"We do." Trewhitt glanced at a sheet on his desk. "An Alan Wray and a Roger Gilbert. Both of Melbourne. Ring any bells?"

"No, but we can find out if they fit with Singer quick enough."

"Let's get cracking, then," declared Trewhitt.

Investigating Singer's activities in late December, Trewhitt and Hornbuckle soon learned that he had driven two men to the Melbourne airport on December 27 and had seen them off on a Qantas flight. An inquiry to Qantas produced immediate results. The names of the two Zurich suspects were on the passenger manifest of the December 27 flight to Rome. The Australian Interpol office was apprised of the discovered connection.

Detectives then checked out the residences of the two. At Alan Wray's address, a South Melbourne apartment building, neighbors said he lived alone and came and went unobtrusively, and few in fact were aware that he'd been away of late; none knew quite what he did for a livelihood.

The address given for Roger Gilbert in suburban Moorabbin was his parents' home, but he hadn't lived there for some time; he'd been sharing an apartment with another fellow in South Yarra, Mr. and Mrs. Gilbert told the police. The fellow's name: John Singer.

The Gilberts, a middle-aged couple of modest circumstances, were stunned and distressed to learn of their son's arrest. Why, they'd only just received a cheery New Year's card from him from Zurich (postmarked December 31—two days after he and Wray had been jailed). They were rather surprised, too, that he was with Alan Wray. They knew Alan quite well—Roger and he were old friends. But Roger had never mentioned to them that it was Alan he was going to Europe with! He had told them that he'd gotten a fine opportunity to represent some "business syndicate" in Europe. He didn't say who they were or what they did, only that they were paying his way and providing a handsome salary to boot, and that he might be gone three or four months.

The arrangement had sounded just marvelous to his parents, who'd been worried about the extended strain he'd been under, what with his businesses failing and so many debts. A well-deserved shift of fortune, they'd thought, for he had always been such a loving, hardworking and devoted son.

Had Roger acted in any way peculiarly in recent months or weeks? Had his behavior patterns changed?

"No . . ." said Mr. Gilbert after a moment. "Of course, since Roger's had his own place we haven't seen that much of him. There *was* one thing, though, about this trip of his that struck us as, well"—he glanced at his wife for affirmation—"a little odd, perhaps. We were so pleased for him that we were all for giving him a grand do at the airport on leaving. But Roger wouldn't hear of it. Said he'd be too busy with last-minute things and so forth. He was rather insistent, in fact, about our *not* seeing him off."

Now the cooperating Commonwealth and Victoria forces took stock of what had been garnered to date. First, in October 1973 they had had an unsubstantiated tip that large amounts of counterfeit U.S. currency would soon surface in and around Melbourne. A month later, a credible informer claimed to have been shown a quantity of fake U.S. twenty-dollar notes by an individual interested in having them distributed. That individual, identified as John Singer, is known to have diverse interests, some notorious. Then, another month later, by way of information from Interpol, had come the news that two men, both residents of Melbourne, had been discovered in Switzerland in possession of a number of forged U.S. twenty-dollar notes. On the heels of this, they had learned that both these men had been close associates of the prime suspect on the Australian side, John Singer! Meanwhile, Singer has given no further indication of activity in the counterfeit market; nor, so far as is known, have any bogus twenties been passed in Australia.

So, where did it all stand? Was the $100,080 seized in Switzerland actually all of it? Was the promise by Singer to King of up to a million dollars no more than braggadocio, or a con, or overestimation? Whichever, it had to be assumed that Singer had other confederates. No such operation was ever a one-man show. Aside from Wray and Gilbert as active principals, there must be the profiteers who would have helped finance production, the agents counted upon for distribution and, not least, the artisans who actually designed and printed the forgeries. All these had yet to be found.

But which way should the police move next? Confronting Singer head-on, without evidence, could bury the entire business for good. It was felt wiser, for now, to put him back on his long leash and watch him.

That left the only other known parties to the conspiracy: Wray and Gilbert. However deeply they might actually be involved, it seemed inarguable that either or both had to know something more about the workings of the scheme than they'd so far admitted.

In Zurich the Swiss police worked on Gilbert first.

"We are disappointed, Mr. Gilbert," one began, "to have found you rather, ah . . . less candid, shall we say . . . than your friend Mr. Wray."

Gilbert looked perplexed. "I don't follow."

"Too bad." The officer shook his head gravely. "We had almost been convinced that *you* really had little or no part in this criminal affair—"

"Wait!" Gilbert started. "What are you saying? I didn't know about the money—until the last."

"That's not what Alan Wray says. He says you knew about it from the start—*all* of it—that they were counterfeits, everything."

"Alan told you that? He—" Gilbert choked off, mouth agape.

"*He* was in it all the time, of course. And the information we've now got from Melbourne seems to confirm that you were as well."

"What information?" Gilbert's eyes narrowed, sudden perspiration glistening on his flushed face.

"Certain associations of yours with the plotters of this scheme. Highly incriminating . . ."

"But I never . . . !"

"However," the policeman went on earnestly, "there still may be a way out for you. You do seem a decent chap"—he riffled through a sheaf of papers in his hand—"never in any serious trouble before. Perhaps you were an unwilling participant to all this, found yourself on the horns of a dilemma, so to speak, and had little choice but to go along out of fear of retaliation should you back out, or, once realizing how deep you *were* in it, fear of exposure."

Gilbert opened his mouth to speak but only gulped.

"We can understand your predicament, you know," another officer interjected assuringly, "in either case. Happens all too often, sad to say, a normally law-abiding individual getting himself caught up in something sinister that he can't control. When that happens, and we feel the person to be basically the right sort—just a victim of unfortunate circumstances—we want to offer him every chance to set things right. You do get my meaning? The only way to establish, reestablish, your true good intent is to be open with us now and tell us all you know of this matter. We can promise you the court will take it into vital account." The detective paused, his gaze unblinking upon the prisoner.

Gilbert, staring as though mesmerized, croaked, "I—I—" He swallowed hard and wet his lips. "I had no part in it, I swear," he managed at last in a strained voice. "I—I didn't find out the money was counterfeit until we arrived here—"

"Come off it!" shot one of his inquisitors. "Wray says you knew all about it weeks before you left Melbourne."

Gilbert's knuckles whitened as he gripped the arms of his chair. "All right. I did know of his carrying American currency out of Australia. I was nervous enough over that. But counterfeit—no! You must believe me!"

The policemen eyed him in silence a moment. "Now then," one said wearily. "Tell us your version."

"Well . . . I do realize now that he must have known all along. The night our bags arrived at the hotel, when he opened the suitcase and showed me the notes, he said, 'Look real enough, don't they?' I was startled. I said, 'Aren't they?' And he laughed. 'For all we need care. I'm told they're near foolproof,' he said. 'Who?' I said. 'Who told you? Where did you get them?' He told me, 'That's nothing for you to concern yourself with. All we have to know is how to spend the bloomin' stuff!' That's when I got really scared. But by then, what could I do?"

"Did he brief you," asked a detective, "on how and where the notes were to be disposed of?"

"Yes," said Gilbert huskily. "He said we would get a car—he had some genuine cash for such things, he said—and leisurely tour the Continent, cashing the American notes along the way and collecting legitimate currencies as change—francs, lire, marks, whatever. We were to use the dollars only on small, inconspicuous purchases and minimum living expenses, so as to collect the maximum amount of negotiable currencies. We could exchange the fakes anywhere except at banks; he was quite emphatic about that. Finally, if all went well, we would end up in London. Alan would then deduct his five thousand dollars from the proceeds and give me a commission of ten percent on however much I'd cashed."

"What was to be done with the balance of the proceeds?"

"I never did know. I had an inkling that from London we were to return here, to Switzerland. . . . But what the arrangement was next, I have no idea."

"Open a bank account, probably," mused another detective. "Or deposit the collection into an existing one. You're saying you have no knowledge of who Wray was in this with, who the two of you were working for?"

"None. I swear to you! I didn't want to know. I was too frightened as it was."

"Yet you didn't say no. You went right ahead with it."

"I—I didn't know what to do. I pleaded with Alan that involvement in this sort of thing was insane, dangerous; we could both go to prison for years. But he kept telling me how safe it really was, that if we kept our wits, there was practically no way to be caught. American twenties, he said, were everywhere as acceptable as gold. And of course he reminded me again and again about my debt situation at home . . . how by taking this one small chance I could resolve all my difficulties and make a fresh start. I was confused. . . ."

"Tell us about John Singer," one of the questioners said abruptly.

"John . . . ?" Gilbert's surprise looked unfeigned. "He's a friend. We'd been flatting together in Melbourne. Why?"

"How long have you known him?"

"Oh, four or five months. Alan introduced us."

"You've known Singer that period of time and shared a flat with him. Then you must have some knowledge of his activities, business affairs, associations?"

"Some, I suppose. We weren't really close chums." He mentioned a few of Singer's legitimate enterprises, which the police already knew about. Then, "John did speak about some deal he had brewing out of the country, in the Far East, I believe—Thailand?"

"What sort of deal?"

"I'm not really sure. Something about surplus war matériel or some such. But why?"

"How would you characterize Wray's relationship with Singer?"

"Why, just friendly, so far as I know."

"No business dealings?"

"Possibly. I'm not aware of any." Gilbert looked about at them searchingly. "See here, why all these questions about John? Are you implying that he is somehow involved in all this?" The consternation in his voice and on his face appeared real.

"It's more than implication. Singer *is* in it, and he's told the Melbourne police that you and Wray are in it with him." The lie was spoken matter-of-factly.

Gilbert gaped at them in spontaneous amazement. *"John told you?"* His expression changed from shock to horror. "I can't believe this is happening. It's a nightmare!" Tears welled in his eyes and his shoulders began to heave, and he slumped in his chair in abject despair. "I swear to God, I have nothing more to do with this!" he said, before yielding to racking sobs.

His questioners studied him glumly and flicked wry glances at one another. It dawned on them that perhaps Gilbert really had no key information to give. He might in fact have been little more than a pawn in this game, and a hapless one at that.

They decided to try their luck with Alan Wray. All things considered, there was little question now but that Wray, the stronger, knew more about the plot than did Gilbert.

Wray was composed, stolid, as he faced them in the same interrogation room. First he was asked to go over his earlier account of how he came to be in possession of the forged notes, and in a flat, resigned manner he repeated the story of Robert and the scheme to smuggle real American currency out of Australia and deliver it to a hotel in Leeds.

"That's really just a lot of smoke, isn't it?" one of them challenged him. "That business about a mysterious connection at Leeds?"

"I only know that's what I was told," replied Wray evenly.

The policeman scanned an official-looking sheet of correspondence. "We have an Interpol report from Scotland Yard. They've investigated in and about Leeds and the Merrion Hotel, and have been unable to turn up the slightest corroboration for such a planned liaison there. Actually"—he smiled wryly—"the only connection between yourself and Leeds would seem to be that it is your own place of origin."

Wray smiled back. "I spent my youth there, yes. It seemed an interesting coincidence. I was rather looking forward to seeing the old homestead again."

"If you insist . . ." The detective glanced at a note pad. "As to the currency, nonetheless, we now know you were fully aware before leaving Australia that these notes were forgeries. It was not your mission to deliver them intact to England or any other place, but in fact to distribute them over the European continent and fraudulently collect negotiable currencies in return. Isn't that so?"

"No," answered Wray.

"Your friend Roger Gilbert will testify otherwise—has done so, in fact."

Wray shrugged without change of expression. "Roger is a frightened boy. He's vulnerable to fairy tales."

"You think so? And what of John Singer—would you say the same of him?"

Wray gave a slight, involuntary start.

The detective pressed on. "Oh yes, we know about Singer and your association with him."

"Singer's a friend of mine, yes. And of Roger's."

"But a better one of yours, correct? He's been doing some talking, and unhappily for you, he's drawn you into it."

Wray remained stony, unwavering. "Into what?"

"The counterfeiting scheme. Says you're his courier."

Wray snorted. "What rot!"

"Interestingly enough, Mr. Singer does not implicate Gilbert, only yourself," the officer bluffed. "Which seems to confirm what Gilbert himself insists—that he was an unwitting dupe, used by you to further this conspiracy. We believe him, and taking this into account along with his cooperativeness, I'm sure the court will be most lenient toward him when you both come to trial."

"Cheers for Roger," sneered Wray. "I'm sorry I can't produce as gripping a story."

"But you can, Mr. Wray—that is, there's every chance for you to help yourself almost as well by accommodating to reality. Essentially, the scheme has been aborted, with you caught out front. And as it stands now, *you* will take the full brunt of the consequences. That's neither fair nor profitable, is it? Surely you and Singer are not the only ones involved. If you can see the situation in this light, you will realize that the only way to better your own position—"

"Is to tell you all I know about the whole operation," cut in Wray tartly.

"Precisely."

"I've *told* you all I know."

"Oh, come now, Mr. Wray!"

"I stand on that. And now the present interview is over. I'll answer no more questions out of presence of counsel."

All further attempts to cajole or intimidate him were unavailing; Alan Wray remained adamant. Finally, weary and frustrated, his inquisitors had him returned to his cell, where, showing no sign of stress, he stretched out on his cot, hands clasped behind his head, and dropped off to sleep.

CHAPTER 3

DURING THE NEXT two weeks, the last weeks of January, 1974, the counterfeiting investigation bogged down on all fronts. Messages and continually updated reports flew back and forth between Interpol sections in Canberra, Bern, Paris, Washington and London. But little new information was unearthed. In Melbourne, John Singer continued to keep a low profile; in Zurich, the prisoners either had no more to tell or were refusing to say any more. No other American twenties of the new forged series had surfaced, and the international police units still had no idea how deep the conspiracy went or how widespread it might be.

Perhaps most impatient with the impasse were the two police detectives most intimately concerned with the case, Aussie Trewhitt and Rex Hornbuckle of the Victoria Breaking Squad. Trewhitt had been having Singer watched for close to two months, with frustration largely the result. Trewhitt's years of experience and his finely tempered instinct assured him that Singer was into something big; it was only a matter of waiting him out. Yet Singer was no common street hoodlum; it might just be that he was shrewd and collected enough to have written off the caper by now as too far blown. If so, then the cat-and-mouse strategy was a washout. Trewhitt was beginning to wrestle with himself over what else to do. He couldn't very well devote the rest of his career to Singer and the counterfeit American twenties; there was more than enough other police business. If something didn't break soon . . .

"We could put more pressure on Singer," offered Hornbuckle. It was Thursday, January 31, and the two veteran detectives were hunched over Trewhitt's desk.

Trewhitt squinted at Hornbuckle and said, "You'd want to do the honors, I expect?"

"Makes sense, don't you think? I landed on him last time; I'd be the logical one to pop back and haunt him."

So Hornbuckle discreetly arranged a meeting with Singer for the next day. Singer chose the place: by the lake at Albert Park, on the southernmost outskirts of Melbourne. He would be alone.

Albert Park, about two and a half miles south of the center city, is a huge recreational oasis amid deluxe apartment buildings, fashionable restaurants and motels. It contains a golf course and cricket grounds, and on the lake there are a small boating club and public rowing facilities.

It was a warm, glary summer's day, and Hornbuckle found Singer lounging in the shade of a large tree on the lakeshore, within view of the boat sheds. He was wearing sandals and a checked shirt over flared trousers. From behind opaque reflector sunglasses he peered at Hornbuckle. "Seems I've had quite a bit of company from you recently," he said. "What are you on to? I've no more jade to hand over."

"I know, John. No, it's not jewelry this time."

"What, then?"

Hornbuckle paused, eyeing him. "Currency," he said at last.

Singer's brows shot up over the rims of his glasses. "Would you please tell me what you're talking about?"

"You tell me," Hornbuckle said. "What do you know of a recent issue of counterfeit American twenty-dollar notes?"

Singer's tan could not hide a sudden flush. "Me? Why should *I* know anything about it?"

"Because you were hawking a batch of them a couple of months ago—trying to set up a pipeline abroad."

"Who told you such a thing?" protested Singer.

"Now, do you tell me all *your* little secrets?" chided Hornbuckle. "Well?"

Singer chewed his lip a moment, then sighed deeply. "There were some around. Somebody asked me to make a few inquiries. . . ."

"Who?"

"I don't want to cause any trouble. The person I'm referring to was not in it himself, you see. He was just doing a favor for a third party, acting as middleman, and he asked my help because he knew I had certain . . . contacts. All I did—"

"All you did was display a quantity of American twenties, which you said were new counterfeits, to a certain person and suggest to him that a great many more could be supplied from where those came from. Now the question is where did they come from—and who was the supplier."

Singer shook his head vigorously. "Whoever told you that is a liar! I never handled any counterfeit notes—too risky for my taste. All I did do was ask around. I've no idea about the source."

"Well, what was the outcome of your inquiries?"

"Negative. Nobody was interested. So I sent the word back, and then . . ." He shrugged.

"Was that the end of it?"

"So far as I was concerned."

"Really! You know nothing more, have heard nothing more, about disposition of these counterfeits?"

Singer hesitated, the clicking of his brain all but audible, before replying, "No, not lately."

Hornbuckle changed the subject. "You know two men named Alan Wray and Roger Gilbert?"

Again Singer flushed. "Yes, they're friends."

"Gilbert shares a flat with you, doesn't he?"

"Yes . . . well, he did."

"You mean you've split up?"

"Not exactly. Roger's . . . away right now."

"In Europe, isn't he?"

"He was going there, yes."

"With Alan Wray?"

"I—I believe so."

"In fact, you saw them off in late December, didn't you?"

Singer showed surprise. "This is beginning to stink of police harassment, spying on—"

"You saw them off," snapped Hornbuckle. "Have you heard from either since?"

"No."

"Are you aware they were arrested in Switzerland?"

Singer tensed but did not appear startled. "I suspected they'd run afoul of some difficulty or other. I'd heard that coppers were inquiring after them."

"Can you guess what difficulty they ran afoul of?"

"I can't imagine," answered Singer. "Neither Alan nor Roger are notorious criminal types."

"You can't imagine! I think you bloody well can," Hornbuckle said. "They were caught with a suitcase full of counterfeit American twenty-dollar notes. Don't you think that's a striking coincidence? In November, you admit, you played the agent for an issuance of American twenties hot off the press; then in December two of your friends flew off to Europe with a consignment of the same notes. And who personally chaperoned them to the airport to see they got off safely? You."

Singer fumbled to light a cigarette. "None of that proves anything," he said defensively.

"Doesn't it?" retorted Hornbuckle. "That's not what they say."

"*They* say?" Now Singer was startled.

"Wray and Gilbert. They've told the Swiss police you put them up to it."

"Oh, that's ridiculous! Who would believe that?"

"A judge and jury might. Everything considered—including your, shall we say, questionable history—I think we've the makings of a fair case here."

Singer fidgeted uncomfortably, as though struggling inwardly to quell mounting turmoil. He did not speak for several moments, puffing on his cigarette and squinting out over the lake. Then he exhaled with distaste and turned to Hornbuckle. "What do you want from me?"

"Why, it's plain enough, isn't it?" Hornbuckle said. "I want to know all about this counterfeiting setup."

"Well, first off, I don't know all about it. I've heard some about it, here and there. I knew—I learned that Alan Wray was into something chancy. When he gave me an idea what it was, I tried to tell him to give it up, that he was mucking about in deep and treacherous waters. But he was set on having a go. . . . I tried to the last, even as far as the airport." He shook his head disappointedly.

"Did all you could, eh?" commented Hornbuckle, eyes crinkling. "And, of course, you would have no part of it?"

"I told you. Too hot for me."

"Yes. Then do you know who Wray was in it with, or for?"

"Like I also told you, I didn't ever find that out."

"How'd Wray get into it?"

"I don't really know."

"What about Gilbert?"

"Oh, Roger surely knew what was happening—he and Alan have been thick for years—but I rather think he's just along for the ride. I doubt he knows much more."

"Hmm." Hornbuckle picked a blade of grass and twisted it around his finger. So far Singer's remarks fitted the consensus of police interrogators in Zurich. "All right, John," he said finally, "tell us what more you know."

"Well . . ." Singer squirmed. "I have heard—I can't say this for fact, but I think it may be straight—about a bundle of the stuff being stashed in a certain place."

"You mean more of the American twenties?"

"Yes. Well, counterfeits, anyway."

"Where?"

Singer drew a long, shuddering breath. "What I heard . . . a place, a freight storeroom at Ferrari's. In Elwood, down by St. Kilda."

"Where'd you hear this?"

"Just around. One always picks up bits of gossip."

"Who's supposed to have stashed it?"

"That I didn't hear."

"What's the quantity?"

"I can't say. But the word I got is there's two suitcases."

"Okay. Anything else?" Hornbuckle peered at him. "Think carefully, John. You hold out on me, and—" The detective jerked a hand across his throat.

"It's all I have! If I hear anything more, I'll pass it on. I just want to keep you off my neck. Isn't that enough?"

"We'll see," said Hornbuckle. "If this doesn't play out, your neck mightn't be worth much."

FERRARI'S TRANSPORT SERVICE occupied a two-story office building located in a shopping center on Glenhuntly Road. After looking over the area outside, Hornbuckle, accompanied by two senior constables—detectives David Smith and Gary Ayres—marched in. Hornbuckle told the owner, Peter Ferrari, that they were searching for two suitcases thought to have been stored here recently, perhaps within the past month.

Perplexed, Ferrari began thumbing a book of invoices. Then he paused and looked up. "Two suitcases? Are they gray? Quite heavy?"

"Could be."

"I think I know the ones." He riffled through the invoices and stopped at one. "They were sent here for storage by a friend of mine. Here—the twenty-first of January. Could this be what you want?"

The invoice read, "5 pm, 21/1/74; 2 stcs, fr St. Kilda sta; cnsgnee Ray Groves."

"Ray Groves—that's your friend?" one of the officers asked.

"No," said Ferrari. "An employee, I believe. My friend is Harry Charalambeas."

"Who is . . . ?"

"I've known him for years," Ferrari said. "He has a hairdressing salon in Melbourne."

"And does he frequently place items in storage with you?"

"No, actually not. He asked me to store these for another friend of his."

"Who?"

"He didn't say."

"What *did* he say about these cases?"

"As I recall, Harry said they contained schoolbooks belonging to a student—the son of his friend, I imagine—who was off touring somewhere. Said it would be for two or three weeks."

"Let's go see."

The suitcases were found in an office, one case being used to hold open the office door to admit a breeze. They were dusty, evidently unopened since having been deposited ten days earlier. The detectives hefted them to a table—they *were* heavy, perhaps seventy pounds apiece—and gingerly snapped the locks. Fitted snugly inside each case were six gray cardboard cartons, like shoeboxes, each sealed with tape. They tore open one of the cartons. It was crammed with crisp new American twenty-dollar bills, probably numbering thousands! The other eleven cartons were examined in turn and each was like the first.

The detectives brought their catch back to headquarters, where Hornbuckle rang up Chief Superintendent L. N. Patterson, commander of the CIB, at his home. On hearing the news, the chief, just returned from leave, said he would come in at once for a staff review and strategy meeting.

Officers were dispatched to follow up the find. A unit was posted at Ferrari's to watch for anyone showing up to claim the cases. Other detectives went to the St. Kilda railway station, where the cases had been picked up by Ferrari's. There, records showed that they had come in by train on Monday, January 21, from Hawksburn.

At Hawksburn, the stationmaster, Fred Maddock, looked up the consignment and recollected the circumstances. On Saturday, January 19, the cases had been brought in by a nervous young man. Told that there would be no parcel delivery to St. Kilda until Monday, he said that was all right, and he signed the shipment order "Ray Groves." What made the incident stand out in his mind, Maddock said, was that two evenings earlier he'd been visited at the parcel counter by two other men inquiring about how to consign a couple of pieces of luggage containing books to another station, farther north. Maddock described the pair as dark complexioned ("Latin they looked—Italian, or maybe Greek"), trim, of average height, thirtyish.

A third team of detectives looked up Harry Charalambeas. His salon, called Just Hair, was located in the Tivoli Arcade in central Melbourne, and he resided in South Yarra. He had no record of any criminal activity or ties. Charalambeas said he'd personally telephoned his old friend Peter Ferrari on Monday, the twenty-first, to arrange collection of the suitcases from the St. Kilda station. That was after having sent one of his stylists, Barry Groves, to deliver the bags to Hawksburn on Saturday, as instructed.

"Whose instructions?" a detective asked.

Charalambeas looked discomfited. But after a moment he said, "Another acquaintance of mine. Chap named John Singer."

The hairdresser said that Singer had come to the salon two or three days earlier to ask his advice about a safe way to store some luggage containing valuable books and prints. Charalambeas had suggested Ferrari's. "A day or so later," he went on, "John returned and asked if I could have the cases picked up and delivered to Hawksburn for shipment to St. Kilda, where Ferrari's could then collect them. So I sent young Groves. Poor fellow said he fair broke his back toting them, they were that heavy."

"Where did Groves pick them up?"

"They were at a house in Hawthorn—his brother-in-law's place, John said. He said he was afraid the children would get at them. He gave me a key to a storeroom there. I gave it to Groves."

"Why couldn't Singer have done all this himself?"

"He didn't say, actually. My impression was that he was tied up in something and couldn't take the time. I didn't mind helping out. I did suggest Ferrari's, after all, and John is not known there, while of course I am."

"Did you or Singer instruct Groves to falsify his name in signing for these cases?" asked a detective.

Charalambeas expressed surprise. "Goodness, no! Did he?"

Barry Groves was a slim, boyish-looking man in his early twenties. When told the nature of the present inquiry, his eyes widened and he exclaimed, "I *knew* there was something funny going on with those cases! They weighed a ton. When I dragged them out of my car at Hawksburn one fell open, and inside weren't books, as I'd been told, but a number of cardboard boxes, all sealed tight. I closed the suitcase up and left the pair of them at the parcel counter and got away from there right quick."

"Signing yourself Ray Groves?"

He smiled lamely. "Silly. But of a sudden it just didn't smell right to me, you know, and I thought— I didn't want to use a complete alias, lest Mr. Charalambeas check on it and wonder about it. So I compromised—clumsily, I suppose."

CHAPTER 4

THE SUITCASES MEANWHILE had been transferred under guard to the Reserve Bank of Australia, where a hastily conscripted senior bank officer, Richard A. S. Bywater, general manager of the note issue department, set at the arduous task of itemizing the contraband. Formal evaluation would be issued later, but Bywater's immediate judgment of the twenty-dollar notes affirmed that they were indeed counterfeit. Each cardboard carton was found to contain on average some eight thousand notes, give or take a few per box. It took Bywater well into the night to complete his count. The total in the twelve cartons came to 94,374 twenties, the equivalent of $1,887,480! They appeared all to be of the same series as those picked up in Switzerland.

The suddenly realized magnitude of the affair was staggering; to reap such a harvest in a single swoop was almost beyond probability! And yet—the conception hardly dared grope for recognition—was this all of it, *was* it finished?

The meeting late that night in the Victoria Breaking Squad office was alternately heady and businesslike. Superintendent Patterson congratulated his men but put a firm lid on any triumphant public announcements just yet. They had to proceed on the conjecture, however unthinkable, that some part of the iceberg might yet lurk beneath the surface—at least until all soundings failed to discover any more depth to it. The CIB was put on tight security footing until further notice.

An advisory on the Ferrari find was transmitted to Interpol Bern and Paris, along with the urgent request that ranking Australian investigators be permitted to confront the suspects Wray and Gilbert in Zurich—the hope being that, under the crunch of these developments, direct pressure from Australian police might compel at least one of the men to contribute something to ease his own way before matters got beyond redemption.

Word was quickly returned, from Interpol headquarters at St. Cloud, that the Swiss police would welcome Australian officers. On Saturday morning Detective Inspector Donald Plant of the Victoria CIB and Commonwealth police Inspector Ray McCabe were preparing to leave Melbourne for Zurich.

Interpol's worldwide transmission of the Australian police coup had stirred satisfaction among law-enforcement agencies. But there was also, particularly on the American side, increased concern. How many more of the fraudulent U.S. twenty-dollar bills might yet be loosed, or were even now being sneaked into the world's currency markets? Who was behind the conspiracy and how widespread was the network of distribution? Most important, the actual printing mechanism, including the vital plates capable of turning out additional forged notes, had to be discovered and deactivated before there could be any final indulgence in jubilation.

As a result of a series of urgent Interpol cables, Australian authorities granted direct American liaison with the investigation. The U.S. Secret Service office at Honolulu was to assign a special agent to proceed at once to Melbourne.

To THE VICTORIA Breaking Squad, the key to the conspiracy lay more than ever with John Singer. He'd said he himself had had no part in any counterfeiting plot, but he'd heard of a cache of the fake money. But then the police discovered that it was Singer himself who'd arranged to cache it!

Officially Charalambeas and Groves could not be dismissed as suspected accomplices, and perhaps Peter Ferrari as well. Privately, however, the detectives considered them as probable tools, honestly unaware of having been so used.

Detective Sergeant Rex Hornbuckle, upon recovery of the two suitcases, had had a torrent of new thoughts about his informer,

Singer. *The gall of the man!* was the most spontaneous. But anger soon gave way to reason and hope. If Singer was, as now appeared certain, an actual participant in the scheme, or at least had far more knowledge about its workings than he'd let on, and still had been willing to forfeit so large an amount of contraband for the purpose of covering his tracks, then it was logical to assume that he calculated his loss as affordable because there was a good deal more of the counterfeit money available.

Moreover, as Singer had helped place the fake money at Ferrari's, the likelihood was great that he would know where to lay hands on a lot more of it. Hornbuckle also guessed that Singer had been one of the two dark strangers who'd earlier inquired at the Hawksburn railway station about consignment of luggage. If so, Singer had at least one other accomplice, apart from Alan Wray and Roger Gilbert. Uncovering the identity of that individual could further the investigation.

So, on the Saturday afternoon after the episode at Ferrari's, Hornbuckle got in touch with Singer for another confrontation. Again he allowed Singer to choose the place—this time another park, the King's Domain, off St. Kilda Road in the South Yarra section. This was dominated by the Shrine of Remembrance, a formidable, step pyramid memorial to Australia's war dead.

Singer was waiting near a statue of a heroic general when the unmarked car drove up. Hornbuckle opened the door on the passenger side and beckoned to Singer, who got in. They drove slowly through the park in thick silence for several minutes. Finally Singer asked, as if to break the ice, "Well, how'd it go?"

Hornbuckle turned narrow eyes on him. "Not bad. The stuff was where you'd said, right enough. Quite a lot of funny money. Know how much?"

"No idea."

"Close to two million, face value."

Singer arched his brows and whistled.

"You didn't know that?" asked Hornbuckle, reading the other's well-chiseled, swarthy features.

"How should I know? I mean, if there were two suitcases full, I supposed it must be quite a bundle, but I didn't—"

"You mean you didn't count it before you deposited it?"

Singer froze, staring at the detective. "Before *I* deposited it?"

"John Singer," Hornbuckle said with exaggerated patience, "do you really take us for such dullards that we wouldn't find out in about five minutes flat it was *you* who'd had those bags put in storage at Ferrari's?"

"No, I—I— Of course not. I just . . ." For once Singer's glibness had fled him; he was speechless.

"Ferrari, Charalambeas, Singer," Hornbuckle ticked off. "We scarcely worked up a sweat. But it does cause us to wonder, Just what sort of game is our friend John Singer playing? Especially when we find that the objects in question were transferred from previous storage at your own sister's place!"

Singer sat rigid. "My sister and her family know nothing of this," he said. "Leave them out of it, please!"

"Possibly. Right now it's you we're concerned over, John. You never hinted that the suitcases you'd heard about at Ferrari's were in fact your own. Explain that little oversight to me, John."

"I— They're not mine. . . ."

"They're not? Well, appearances certainly can be misleading, then, can't they? Why, the way you cared for those bags, one could only think . . . Then it must be you were tending them for someone else—favoring a friend, is that it? Perhaps you even *believed* they were filled with schoolbooks?"

"Yes—no. I mean— They do belong to a friend. I was only . . ." He groped for words.

"Doing another good turn," Hornbuckle finished for him. "Good sort, aren't you, John? This would be the same friend you'd first made inquiries for, months back?"

Singer stared off bleakly.

"Why didn't you tell us straight out, John?"

"Naturally, I didn't want to seem involved," said Singer. "And my sister's family . . ."

"You did know all along what was in the suitcases, then."

"Not until after I— Look, a while back, after Christmas, someone comes to me and asks if I can take a couple of bulky items off his hands for a bit, he's got no room. Later I find out what I'm holding for him." He spread his hands. "What could I do then?"

"You could have told this party to retrieve his bloody bags and leave you out of it. Better yet, you could have reported it, once you knew. But obviously you didn't let us know right away. Why did you decide to tell us about the bags at all?"

"Well . . . I got scared, thinking you were trying to tie me directly into this counterfeiting business. I thought that if I helped you this much—you know, to intercept the stuff before any real harm's done—you'd be satisfied and let it, well, blow over."

"You know better," chided Hornbuckle. "This is no sporting contest. A serious crime's the stake here, printing illegal currency— whether distributed or not—and someone's got to pay for it." He curled an eyebrow. "You may have helped us some, John, but I'm afraid you've done far less for yourself."

"What do you mean?"

"Need I put it in block letters?" Hornbuckle asked. "So far we've rounded up nearly two million dollars in counterfeit American twenties, and the only one we can connect with it is you. And, of course, your chums in Switzerland. I might add that while our grounds for linking you to all this may actually have been somewhat weak before, now—thanks to you—I'd say the case is beginning to look quite solid indeed."

"But I tell you," Singer protested, "I'm not— I just—"

"Either it is you," Hornbuckle pressed on, "or you're standing up for someone else. I'd call that just plain stupid. Would they do the same for you?"

"One doesn't so lightly turn in a friend," muttered Singer.

"Oh, admirable, John!" replied Hornbuckle tartly. "But then, you know what they say, 'With friends like these . . .' "

Singer's expression had darkened; he seemed to withdraw inside himself. He gazed beyond the car window at the verdant park drifting past in dappled sunlight, and then cleared his throat and murmured, "I didn't want any part of it. I knew it was trouble the minute he—I heard of it. I've got coppers spying on me all the time as is. But he— Finally I said, 'Okay, I'll help you bury the stuff, and good riddance. Just leave me out now.' "

"The bloke with you at Hawksburn," inserted Sergeant Hornbuckle quickly, while the man seemed vulnerable, "the night you inquired—he's the one?"

Singer looked up in surprise.

"Italian, isn't he?" The detective gambled. "Or maybe Greek?"
The other's silence showed Hornbuckle had made a perfect hit.
Singer nodded dumbly.

"Tell me about him."

Singer exhaled slowly. "Petros his name is. Lyberakis." He spelled
it for Hornbuckle.

"What's your relationship?"

"Just friends, now. We were in business together once. Sheepskins
and . . . printing."

"Printing! You and he. Do you still . . . ?"

"He managed a small printshop that I had a financial interest in,"
Singer answered. "We lost it in a fire."

"Is that the shop where these twenty-dollar notes were printed—
unbeknownst to yourself, perhaps?"

"No! The fire was long before."

"How long?"

"Oh, a year or more."

"Have you and this Petros remained associated since?"

"Not in business. Socially."

"What does he do now?"

"He has a job at the Greek consulate—welfare officer."

"He's a Greek national?"

"No. An immigrant, as a kid."

"How old now?"

"Middle twenties, I'd say."

"What else about him?"

"I know he's studying architecture and design. And he travels the
art circles."

"He's an artist?"

"No . . . I don't think he paints, himself. But he knows a lot
about art."

Hornbuckle mused aloud, "Sometime printer, would-be designer,
into artwork . . . Where does he do up the notes?"

"I—I don't really know. I can't even say that he's printed them—
himself, I mean."

"What about associates, backers?"

Singer shook his head. "No, I—"

"But he did try to bring *you* in?"

"Yes."

"Why you?"

"I don't know. I suppose because of my . . . contacts. And he kept after me. Petros is a hard one to put off."

"No doubt. Has he any more of these notes about?"

"I—" Singer hesitated, on a brink. Then softly he said, "Yes."

"Circulating? Stored? What?"

"I don't know of any in circulation. But I—I believe I do know where some are."

"Where?"

"At his parents' place."

"His parents! Is this a family operation?"

"No, not that I'm aware. They're straight, I think."

"Then how . . . ?"

"Their garage. Petros laid up a trunk. They needn't know."

"And how do *you* know?"

"Petros—he mentioned it."

"Where is this place?"

"In Caulfield." He gave the south suburban address to Sergeant Hornbuckle.

There was a thoughtful pause. "What we need to figure," Hornbuckle said at last, "is how to collect Petros and the money at the same time and place." He looked with raised eyebrows at Singer.

"Oh no," Singer blurted. "You're not going to make me finger Petros direct."

"Like Judas?" Hornbuckle smiled thinly. "Have you any suggestions, then?"

"Well . . ." Singer paused in thought. "Yes, I think so," he said. "Tomorrow's Sunday? Most Sundays, Petros goes down to Caulfield for lunch. It's a regular family thing."

"What hour?"

"Oh . . . one, two. Stays the afternoon, as a rule."

"And you believe tomorrow he—"

"I'm just telling you what he usually does. I can't say if this Sunday will be different."

Hornbuckle regarded him. "Okay. It sounds worth a go. You stay clear of it. Just keep your ears open. Should you hear anything between now and then that indicates a change of plans, I want to know it directly. Meanwhile"—he began to pull the car over—"keep your mouth shut."

Singer nodded, frowning. The car stopped, and he got out without speaking. Hornbuckle left him in the park, his back to the Shrine of Remembrance.

A SMATTERING OF background had been dug up on Petros Lyberakis by early Sunday. Twenty-six, born in Athens; in Australia from childhood. Fourth-year student at a Melbourne architectural college. Part-time position at Greek consulate as welfare officer, or financial counselor, for recent immigrants. No police record.

Overnight, stakeouts had been set up both at Lyberakis' in-town apartment on King William Street, Fitzroy, and at his parents' residence in Caulfield, while the CIB applied for search warrants covering both premises. By midday Sunday the police were primed.

A little past one o'clock the Fitzroy surveillance team reported that Lyberakis had left his apartment alone and driven off. A short while later he was sighted entering the Caulfield house. Hornbuckle, with constables David Smith and Gary Ayres, arrived there just after two. It was a neat cottage in a well-kept residential street. The door was opened to them by a wiry, olive-skinned, graying man of about fifty, who, shown their credentials, identified himself in a marked accent as Michalis Lyberakis, owner of the house.

"You have a son, Petros?" asked Hornbuckle.

"Yes." The man looked apprehensive.

"Is he here now?"

"Yes. We are eating." He hesitated, then stepped back. "You want come in, please?"

"Thank you."

The detectives stepped inside, and Mr. Lyberakis led them into a small sitting room furnished in dark wood and fringed upholstered chairs. Light voices and a clatter of dinnerware could be heard from an adjoining room. He said, "Please," indicating the chairs, and left the room. There were gilt-framed icons on the walls and lacy curtains at the windows. After a moment a sharp-featured young man with longish jet-black hair entered, followed tentatively by the elder Lyberakis.

"Petros Lyberakis?"

"Yes. You are police?" His accent was slight.

Hornbuckle, displaying his shield and ID, identified himself, Smith and Ayres. "We regret interrupting your meal. But there are questions we must ask of you. It is my duty to advise you, however, that you are not obliged to answer unless you choose to do so. Should you so choose, anything you say here may be used as evidence in a court of law. Do you understand what I—"

"What is this? Am I a criminal?" the younger Lyberakis demanded. His father shot him a startled, fearful look, but Petros raised a quieting hand without taking his eyes off the policemen.

"It could be rather serious, I assure you," said Hornbuckle tonelessly. "Now, I must also warn you that whether you choose to cooperate or not"—he took a folded document from a pocket and held it out—"we have a warrant authorizing a search of these premises. So it will be less troublesome all round if you cooperate."

The young man glanced warily from the sergeant to the other detectives but set his mouth and said nothing.

"What do you look for?" asked his father anxiously.

"We'll get right to that, sir," replied Hornbuckle. Then, addressing the son, "I ask you if you have recently brought or caused to have delivered to this house any sort of large, bulky container—like a trunk, say?"

There was a guarded exchange of glances between father and son before Petros Lyberakis muttered, "I . . . believe so."

"You believe so. Well, *was* it a trunk?"

"Yes."

"And is it still here?"

"Yes."

"Where?"

The young man drew a breath. "In the garage," he said, with another defensive look toward his father.

"Show us, please."

Petros led them out to a garage shed beside the house. Inside was a typical clutter of discarded household furnishings, boxed refuse, garden and workshop tools and automotive accessories. At the rear were stacks of old magazines and newspapers; clearing some of these away, Petros revealed a sturdy black trunk with brass fastenings. He stood aside to let the officers approach.

"This is it, then?" inquired Hornbuckle.

He got a spare nod in answer.

"Right. Let's do a bo-peep, eh?"

Petros unlatched the lid. The trunk appeared to be packed with magazines. He looked blandly at Hornbuckle. The detective waggled a hand at the trunk. Petros bent and withdrew a handful of the magazines. Now, underneath, could be seen a number of gray cardboard boxes stacked snugly on end.

The three officers exchanged triumphant looks. "Let's see what you have in the cartons," Hornbuckle ordered.

Petros reached in and tugged out one box and handed it over. The top was unattached and came off easily. The box was filled with green plastic book covers. The detectives looked at him quizzically.

"A friend of mine manufactures them," Petros Lyberakis said, as though this fully explained their being in the garage.

"Mmm. Let's see another," said Hornbuckle.

Petros fished out a second carton. It, too, contained book covers. His father, looking more at ease, laid a hand on Petros' shoulder.

Hornbuckle, however, motioned to Dave Smith, who came forward and squatted before the trunk; digging under the top row of cartons, he worked another gray box from beneath. It was plain at once that this one, unlike the two Lyberakis had produced, was sealed carefully with tape.

"What's in here?" Smith, still in a crouch, looked up at Petros.

The young man wet his lips before replying, "More of the same, likely."

Smith slit the tape all around and removed the top. He whistled. The carton was stuffed with money—U.S. twenty-dollar bills.

"Petros!" The father choked, recoiling.

Hornbuckle hefted the carton as Ayres joined Smith in emptying the trunk. "Do you care to explain this?" he asked, the question aimed primarily at Petros but taking in the older man as well.

Petros stared from the carton to Hornbuckle. "I never saw that before," he said, his voice raspy.

"You're saying you did not know these notes were in this trunk? But you yourself brought this trunk here. You admit that?"

"Yes."

"Then how do you account for it?"

The young man set his teeth and stared away.

Hornbuckle measured him. "All right," he said patiently. "Where did you bring the trunk here from?"

Petros bit his lip, then muttered, "A friend's. He had no place. I said I would lay it up for him."

"Nicky," the father breathed out audibly.

Petros' eyes snapped at him.

"Nicky, you say," Hornbuckle prodded. "Who is Nicky?"

Petros, still glaring at his father, shook his head.

The older man's expression was pleading. "No," he managed at last, "I do not let you to get blame." He addressed Hornbuckle. "He tell me trunk comes from Nicky's."

"Nicky who?"

"Kypraios. Nicky Kypraios. Petros and him—"

"He's just a friend, an artist," his son cut in. "We do some work together."

"Petros do *everything* for him," Mr. Lyberakis insisted. "Watch out for him like brother. Help start up shop for him . . . everything. And now—"

"Papa, get off it!" his son broke in again. Then, to Hornbuckle, "Nick said a customer left the trunk at his place. He has little spare room, so he asks me—" His words dropped off before the sharply incredulous expression on the detective's face.

"First the trunk was yours, next it was your chum Nick's, now it's some unknown third party's—" Hornbuckle cut off as his partners straightened from their inventory of the trunk. It was empty now, its contents stacked on the floor around it. "What's the tally there?" he asked.

Gary Ayres read from his note pad. "Three cartons of plastic covers. Fourteen cartons of currency—at a glance, all American twenties. Look to be the same gravure as the last."

"Fourteen! Must come to another two million, then—or more!" Hornbuckle turned back to Petros Lyberakis and spied a tic of uncertainty fluttering in the taut, brooding features. "Two million in counterfeits," the detective repeated at last. "That's *very* serious. And in your possession, so I'm afraid you're in for it. Unless, of course, you can help us find some reasonable explanation. About this Nick Kypraios?"

"*Sure* you got to ask Nicky!" cried Mr. Lyberakis. "The trunk comes from him, don't it?"

"Where might we find this Nicky?" asked Hornbuckle.

Petros wavered. Perspiration dampened his forehead.

"I tell them if you don't!" his father appealed.

With a final look of exasperation at the older man, Petros muttered, "His place is in Abbotsford."

"Residence or place of business—the shop you spoke of?"

"Both. But," Petros added quickly, "he'll be shut on a Sunday."

"Yes. What *is* his business?"

"I told you, he's an artist."

"It's a studio, then?"

Petros frowned. He started at a sudden movement by his father alongside, who seemed about to speak out. Shaking his head, he said hoarsely, "No, it's sort of . . . a small printing plant."

Nick Kypraios, artist and *printer!* The three detectives beamed at one another. "Beauty!" said Rex Hornbuckle.

CHAPTER 5

THE CIB WAS INFORMED of developments via police radio, using a special security channel. Detective Sergeant Hornbuckle would stand by at the Caulfield residence garage until a backup unit came to collect the trunkful of counterfeits, while detectives Smith and Ayres proceeded with Petros Lyberakis, first to a search of his apartment in the inner suburb of Fitzroy, then to locate the printer Nick Kypraios in adjacent Abbotsford.

Hornbuckle also called Trewhitt at headquarters and learned that Superintendent Patterson was off at a barbecue in the hills north of Melbourne. The two policemen agreed that their chief would certainly want to be in on this possible kill, and a car ought to be sent to hustle him back to town. As it happened, the only vehicle available just then was a riot van. It amused them to imagine its clanging arrival and the impression it would make on the chief's friends. Trewhitt said he would rendezvous with Smith and Ayres at Petros Lyberakis' apartment.

While waiting at the garage, Hornbuckle got some background

from the elder Lyberakis. Nick Kypraios, who was several years older than Petros, had come from Greece only within the past few years. More than a printer, he was regarded as a painter of considerable promise and already had had at least one exhibition in Melbourne. Petros, who through his consulate post had wide contacts with the Greek community, had been quite taken with the newcomer and had done much to ease his way in the strange land. Having himself a great interest in art, Petros had helped Nick sell a number of his paintings.

Together they'd conceived publishing a special magazine for Greek Australians. Because Nick understood little English, Petros had handled everything—leasing a building, procuring the printing equipment and so forth. It had taken them until about the past October to pull it all together. But then, somehow, nothing much had ever come of it.

Mr. Lyberakis didn't really know why, but the magazine had never appeared; all he'd ever seen printed—the firm was called Icono Graphics—were some religious calendars and a few handbills. Petros seemed disinclined to talk of whatever had disrupted their plans, even of Nick Kypraios lately, for that matter. Mr. Lyberakis had no idea where they'd secured their original financing. Detective Sergeant Hornbuckle passed along these details to his associates via the special police channel.

At four thirty p.m. Dave Smith and Gary Ayres were going through Petros Lyberakis' rooms on King William Street, Fitzroy. The apartment was orderly, sparely but tastefully furnished, and they uncovered nothing incriminating. In the small kitchen, however, Smith did come upon an address book containing some interesting names: Charalambeas, H. . . . Gilbert, Roger . . . Singer (no other identification). Smith slipped the book into a pocket. Detective Senior Sergeant Trewhitt arrived as they were finishing up, and Lyberakis was directed to lead them next to Nick Kypraios' shop.

Abbotsford, one of the inner suburbs girding Melbourne, is a gray area some two miles northeast of the central city, inward of the meandering Yarra River. Mainly a gritty cluster of light industry and working-class housing, its one undisputed claim to recognition is as the breeding ground of many of Victoria's toughest soccer players.

The printshop was located at 14 Greenwood Street—a short, narrow, one-way lane between banks of small factories and warehouses, the solid facing walls broken only by a random freight enclosure or junkyard and, here and there, a cramped private house. Number 14 was huddled midway in the block, below the noisy elevated tracks of the Melbourne Suburban Rail Network's main north-south line. It was a shabby brick structure, smaller than most on the street, only about twenty-five feet square plus an ell to the rear that left space for a few vehicles to park off the street. A sign over a recessed entrance read ICONO GRAPHICS.

The street, it being a Sunday, was all but deserted. The detectives parked in front of the building, and Trewhitt remained in his car with Petros. Ayres and Smith got out and tried the front door. It was shielded by an iron grille, which was padlocked. A wider, corrugated roller door to the left was also secured. Ayres went around to the right and up an alleyway, where he found another door; it, too, was fast. There were two small windows on that side: one looked into a tiny, bare office; the other was opaque.

Ayres rejoined the others, and Trewhitt said to Lyberakis, "Where's your friend, the printer?"

Lyberakis shrugged. "Who knows? I already said he'd be shut on Sunday."

"Where's he live?" Trewhitt asked.

The other frowned. Truculently he said, "He keeps a flat a street or two over. It's on Park Street, number seventy-seven."

Trewhitt continued to stay with Lyberakis while Smith and Ayres drove to Nick Kypraios' home, a narrow brick dwelling among a string of similarly drab row houses. The door was opened to their knock by a slight, dark man of about thirty. He appeared apprehensive when Smith and Ayres identified themselves as police officers, and nodded mutely when asked if he were the Nick Kypraios who operated the printshop on Greenwood Street. He stepped aside to let them enter. The apartment was small and clean, spartanly furnished, with framed Greek scrollwork on the walls and some austere religious statuary the only decorative notes.

"You are familiar with Petros Lyberakis?" asked Ayres.

The man's eyes widened. "Petros . . . yes."

"He is associated with you in your printing business?" Kypraios gaped at the question as though uncomprehending. "Icono Graphics," Dave Smith added.

Kypraios paled at the name. "Icono Graphics . . . yes, yes." His pronunciation was thickly foreign.

"Your friend Petros is in custody," said Ayres. "He—Petros is waiting for *you*." He pointed directly at Kypraios. "He is waiting at the printshop—at Icono Graphics. You come with us." Now he gestured toward the door.

Bewildered—but evidently having grasped the officer's meaning, Kypraios started outside.

"Wait," called Smith. "You have the keys?" He made a twisting motion with his hand and a sweep of the arm, as if opening a door. "Keys—to Icono Graphics?"

Kypraios nodded in understanding and took a ring of keys from a sideboard near the door.

"Okay, let's go," Smith said curtly.

They joined Trewhitt and Lyberakis in front of the printshop and waited for a forensic scientific team, which Trewhitt had summoned. Kypraios and Lyberakis confronted each other without speaking, Nick gazing uncertainly, Petros staring back narrowly. "His English is mighty skimpy," murmured Dave Smith to Sergeant Trewhitt. "We'll need an interpreter."

"Soon as the lab boys get here," said Trewhitt, "and we can get these two downtown, we'll find somebody."

After about twenty minutes, the team arrived with black satchels and assorted mechanical gear. Then Nick Kypraios was escorted to the entrance and told to open up. He unlatched the grille; then with another key he unlocked the heavy wooden door. Just inside, a hanging canvas screened the interior from view. At a nod from Trewhitt, Nick pulled the canvas back. The police officers stood in the doorway, peering in.

The place was not quite in darkness; there was a translucent skylight in the ceiling. A sharp musty odor reached their nostrils—a miasma of chemicals, ink and moldy paper and the dank staleness of vacancy. As vision adjusted to the half-light, an unadorned box-like room could be made out; the floor was littered with scraps of paper, used cans of varying sizes, soiled rags, lengths of electrical wiring and . . . Against one wall were stacked familiar gray cardboard cartons. Trewhitt stepped back, motioning to Smith and Ayres to stay with him.

As the forensic team swarmed inside, switching on lights, Trewhitt turned to Nick Kypraios. "Where is your printing equipment?"

The printer blinked at him, then looked to Lyberakis. They spoke rapidly in Greek. Lyberakis said, "The machinery has been taken back."

"Where to? When?"

Lyberakis glanced at Kypraios. "Only yesterday—Saturday. By the owners."

"Who're they?"

"Seligson and Clare, in Bouverie Street, Carlton."

"You're saying the equipment has been repossessed?"

Lyberakis shrugged ruefully. "We—Nick couldn't keep up payments," he said.

The policemen had to suppress their smiles. The rascals had printed millions of dollars, and here they'd forfeited their machinery for failure to pay bills!

Lyberakis and Kypraios were then taken downtown for thorough interviews and statements for the record.

AT RUSSELL STREET headquarters, while Hornbuckle, Trewhitt and Superintendent Patterson discussed events to date and sketched out provisional strategies, detectives Dave Smith and Gary Ayres first took on Petros Lyberakis in one of the Breaking Squad interrogation rooms. There had been some delay in securing a reliable interpreter for Kypraios, though one was now on his way.

Ayres manned a typewriter, and at seven fifteen Smith began the interview. It was past ten thirty when it was over, and though Petros Lyberakis had not exactly cracked, detectives Smith and Ayres felt he'd said enough to affirm definite incrimination in the counterfeit operation. Lyberakis was formally charged and taken to the City Watchhouse.

If the crime had not warranted full status of eminence before, it certainly did now. The report had come in from the Reserve Bank of Australia, whose note issue manager, Richard Bywater, had for the second time this weekend been rousted from his home to undertake the drudging tally of thousands of confiscated bank notes. This time the catch was greater; in the boxes removed from the Lyberakis garage was a total of 112,373 counterfeit U.S. twenties, having a face value of $2,247,460. That added up to $4,134,940 recovered in Melbourne alone; with the seizure in Zurich, a grand total so far of $4,235,020.

Stupendous! In perhaps as little as a month's time, two at most, that shabby little printing plant evidently had turned out well over two hundred thousand bogus U.S. notes of generally passable quality. Figuring a five-day workweek, which was reasonable, since unceasing activity over weekends could have risked unwanted curiosity, they may have been producing as many as eight thousand counterfeit bills a day!

But a question lodged in police minds about this apparent prolific output. Several questions, rather. Was it, in fact, the only source of this illicit currency? Had they now recovered *all* the fake bills? How many more could there be?

And one other essential item still eluded them: the actual plates from which the twenty-dollar bills were printed. The managing director of Seligson and Clare, the company from which Icono Graphics had purchased its machinery, confirmed repossession of the equipment on Saturday; it had not yet been cleaned, and the police could send in a lab team to examine it anytime after the plant opened on Monday. That might solve the question of the missing plates. For the moment, then, that left them to deal with Nick Kypraios.

When Kypraios was brought into the interrogation cubicle, along with an interpreter recommended by the Greek consulate, it was after midnight, already Monday, February 4. This time Dave Smith and Gary Ayres reversed roles—Ayres asked the questions and Smith typed.

Kypraios' manner was of one entering a confessional: respectful, uneasy, intent upon conveying the sincerity of his remorse. Ayres started him off gently, always addressing him sympathetically. After eliciting the routine personal data, the detective asked the man to describe his background as printer and artist.

Born on the Greek island of Samos, Nikos ("Nick") Kypraios had gone to Athens in his teens to study art. While there he'd also learned the printing trade as a means of livelihood. By 1968, at the age of twenty-four, he had his own small printing business. At the same time he was gaining some recognition as a painter, and his work had been included in a number of exhibitions in Athens and elsewhere in Greece. In 1971, paintings of his were being admired as far abroad as the United States.

However, by then a steadily worsening political climate had had a stifling effect upon his chief livelihood, printing; and having heard from visiting Greek émigrés of the untapped opportunities open to one of talent in burgeoning Australia, early in 1972 Nick and his young wife, with their infant son, decided to forsake their homeland for the distant horizon.

Kypraios and his family arrived in Melbourne on March 30. Nick soon got a job with a printing firm, which helped support them while he also pursued his painting.

When and how, Ayres asked, had he come together with Petros Lyberakis?

Kypraios thought it was toward the end of 1972. They had met through another Greek Australian, who had suggested that Petros might be of help in selling some of Nick's art. He remembered Petros first coming to his apartment with two other men—one an Italian sculptor; the other an Australian, John Singer—where he showed them some sixty of his paintings. Petros seemed impressed, and he promised Nick not only that he would find buyers (he would take a twenty-five percent commission on any sales) but that he would see about arranging a major exhibition for him in the area. Petros did stimulate a certain amount of interest in his work, Nick said—one memorable sale was to the Greek consul in Melbourne, who bought his painting *Paul the Apostle* for five hundred dollars—and by early 1973 he was encouraged enough to leave his salaried employment and work full time at home.

"How, then," interjected Ayres, "did you end up in a printshop of your own?"

"Well, I had been thinking for some time," Nick said (through the interpreter), "of designing a quality magazine, with much fine art and other cultural features, that would especially appeal to the Greek community here."

"And so you set up Icono Graphics."

"Yes . . . with Petros." Kypraios appeared to pale.

The interview continued.

AYRES: When did you lease the premises at 14 Greenwood Street, Abbotsford?

KYPRAIOS: I don't remember, but I think it was the first of October, 1973.

AYRES: Who did you rent the premises from?

KYPRAIOS: I don't know. Petros did that.

AYRES: What part did Petros play in this—that is, the setting up of a printing business?

Nick started to answer, then suddenly appeared very flustered. He paled and swayed as if close to a faint.

"What's wrong? Are you sick?" asked Ayres.

Kypraios swallowed hard and gripped the arms of his chair. He uttered something, almost gagging, in Greek.

"What?" Ayres turned anxiously to the interpreter.

"He says can he please go to the toilet."

Dave Smith and the interpreter escorted Kypraios down the corridor to a lavatory. As the others waited uncomfortably, Kypraios lowered the toilet seat and slumped on it, head in his hands. He began to weep, softly at first, then with increasing spasms of misery. Smith, feeling awkward, went and laid a calming hand on his shoulder; almost as abruptly as they'd come on, the man's racking sobs began to subside, and in a minute Kypraios just sat sniffling.

At last Smith spoke gently. "Any better now?"

Kypraios nodded. Then he looked up at Smith, his eyes red and cheeks damp and streaked, and murmured hoarsely. The interpreter said, "He wonders if you might permit him to rest for a while, so that he may compose himself."

"That'll be all right. Tell him we'll leave him alone till he's come round."

Smith and Ayres went to the chief's office to report the suspect's breakdown. They honestly were sorry for the man's wretched turmoil. He seemed at bottom an open, uncalloused individual—not a common type in such circumstances.

Kypraios appeared drained and tired when they all returned to the interrogation room, but calm and in control of himself. He apologized for his behavior. Smith, Ayres and Kypraios, the interpreter alongside, resumed their places around the table desk, Smith again at the typewriter.

Ayres said, "You're sure you're up to it now?"

"Yes," said Nick, a slight quaver in his voice. "I want to—to say what is the—what is truth." He spoke with difficulty in English. He paused, as though grasping for words, then went on in Greek, with the interpreter translating. "But it is that I am frightened for my life!"

"What—or who—are you frightened of?" asked Ayres.

"The people with the money. They will kill me!"

"Which people?"

Nick's expression pleaded as he turned to Ayres and then looked around at the other policeman. He wiped a trembling hand across his face and looked on the verge of tears again. But, drawing a long breath, he seemed to collect himself. "I would like to be deported, sent back to Greece. I blame myself for doing what those people wanted."

Ayres continued. "Will you tell us in your own words how you became involved in the printing of forged currency?"

"Yes. . . . Last summer, 1973, we were having a difficult time of it, my wife and I. Work, commissions, were not so easy as I had hoped . . . as Petros had promised. He had told me to prepare my paintings for an exhibition, but months went by and nothing happened, and finally he told me he was unable to complete arrangements because I was an immigrant and not yet a citizen of Australia. So now I was selling only a few paintings, and we were spending our savings. My wife and I, we had thought one day of a home of our own. In August we decided that my wife and our child should return to Greece for a while. I would stay here a bit longer, to the end of the year, to make one final try to establish myself. If I succeeded, I would send for her. If I failed, I, too, would return home."

He paused, frowning. "At that time I was doing a small job for a man who was thinking of publishing a Greek newspaper, designing sample layouts—but suddenly he went off somewhere, and he owed me eighty dollars. I was depending on that fee, and I tried everywhere to locate him, but he kept dodging me. I was furious, but I did not know what to do about it, until Petros suggested I bring the matter to court and sue. He took me to his own solicitor, a man called Rubinstein—this would have been about the middle of August. This Rubinstein did not seem enthusiastic about my chances of collecting, but he said he would make some inquiries. I have yet to see that eighty dollars, by the way.

"Anyway, as Petros and I were leaving the solicitor's that day—please excuse so long a prelude, but this is how it started—since we had just been discussing the proposed Greek newspaper, you know, I said to Petros, 'I don't know why you and I couldn't make a success out of publishing something good like that. Maybe not a newspaper,' I said, 'but something with more style.' And I told him of my idea for a magazine. I said, 'Between us, I'll wager we could put it out ourselves and make a profit.' Petros said it might have possibilities at that. He wanted to think more on it.

"The very next day Petros came round to my place and he seemed excited. 'About that magazine,' he said to me. 'I believe you have a good idea there! With your talent and my contacts, we can do it! I've already got some people interested in financing us!' When I asked who, he did not give any names, but he indicated there was a successful clothing manufacturer he was friendly with, and someone else who managed a number of companies, and of course I knew that he did have good contacts through his consulate position—so I didn't pursue it, I was too excited myself. Straightaway we began looking about for machinery—"

Ayres now said, "But Petros told us *you* put up the money for the machinery and paid the lease on the factory out of your own bank account."

Kypraios shook his head vigorously. "This is not true!"

"You realize we can check your bank statements?"

"Of course. And you will see. I had little money left then."

"All right," said Ayres. "Go on."

Nick reflected a moment. "Wait. I see how it is true, but in a different way. Petros was getting this money, and as we needed it we would deposit some funds in the bank, and then, yes, with that I would pay for things—but I never thought of it as my money but ours, the business's, the support of our patrons."

"I see. All right. . . ."

"I signed for everything. I chose the equipment, Petros arranged the terms and I signed the papers. Petros located the plant and organized everything, and all I had to do was sign the lease. Petros told me that the people putting up the money wanted to remain anonymous because of something to do with taxation. That was fine with me; I was happy to sign the contracts myself, because I thought it would help build security for me.

"By October we were set. We had all the necessary machinery in, Petros had obtained the paper and ink I wanted, we had a darkroom set up for photographic processing. It was all on a modest scale, but it would work, and I was happy. Then Petros made a suggestion to me about finding some clever way to advertise the business, to attract attention and customers right away. He had an idea to run off a number of fliers in the form of money, with only one side imprinted like a real note and an announcement of our services on the other. I thought that sounded like a good idea—it would certainly catch one's fancy, say, to pick up what looked like cash lying about and then find our advertisement. But I only meant to do one side—I knew it was wrong and against the law to print money, but I thought just one side would be all right.

"Petros said it would not do to duplicate Australian dollars, however, as that might lead to complications. He said he would find another currency, something foreign that no one here could mistake to use illegally and get us into trouble. I agreed, and I had him order two thousand sheets of special paper.

"A day or so later, at lunchtime, Petros came to the plant with that friend of his, John Singer. I had met him before—the first time when he came to the flat to look at my paintings, and then several other times out socially with Petros. . . . They seemed quite good friends. This day, Singer showed us five or six new-looking American twenty-dollar notes—the first I'd ever seen. Petros said this would be a good note to copy; they weren't so common in Australia yet, but being American currency they would have high recognition value. They asked me if I thought I could simulate the twenties. I was sure I could, with a little time for experimentation.

"It took me three days, and I used up a lot of paper, but finally I thought I had it right—the side of the twenty with the White House on it; the other side was blank, where our advertisement was to go. I made several copies, and when I showed them to Petros—I believe that evening—he was delighted.

"The next noon, Petros came to the plant again, with John Singer and also a third man I didn't know, a huge, grossly fat man who was expensively dressed. Petros introduced him to me as Charlie. They examined a note I'd done, comparing it closely with a real American twenty, and they all three showed amazement at it and became very excited—jubilant, you might even say. They congratulated me and left together in high spirits.

"Petros and Singer returned the next day. They took me aside and Petros said, 'Nick, we are on to something bigger than you and I even dreamed of. We're not going to make just one-sided notes. We are going to print both sides—to make full reproductions of twenty-dollar bills!'

"I was shocked! 'Print false money?' I said. 'We can't do that. It is a serious crime. In my country, if you're caught at this, they take you out and shoot you!' But Petros was very consoling. 'There is nothing to worry about,' he told me. 'The notes you make are not Australian, but more than that, they will not even be seen in Australia. The moment they are printed, they will be taken out of the country. There will be no crime *here*, so you need have no fear of the law here!'

"I was totally confused. Despite what Petros said, printing those twenty-dollar bills *had* to be wrong—a crime. It couldn't be so easy as he was making out. But Petros insisted they had powerful friends in the Greek consulate who would look out for us, and Singer told me not to worry, because he had a relative who was a judge in Hong Kong. I thought, Fine protection that is, a judge in Hong Kong! I told them I had to think about it. They did not like it, but they let me go home to think.

"I had a terrible night . . . my nerves, I couldn't sleep. Petros came alone to the flat to persuade me further, and I argued, pleaded with him to leave me out of it. But he said that if I didn't go along with them, Singer might kill me!

"The next day, they were there at the plant again. I was in an awful state. Petros gave me some pills to calm me. Then he said, 'Do it, Nick, and there'll be a special bonus for you. No more payments on the machines—they'll be yours, free and clear. You can print that magazine you want.' Singer was looking at me as though prepared to strangle me on the spot if I continued to resist. I couldn't see any way out of it!

"I had trouble making the plates for the other side of the twenty-dollar note—with the President's picture. Maybe it was my nervousness. Anyway, I ruined a lot of plates before I got it right, and even then I could not quite get the serial numbers right, and Petros had to come in and do that. They wanted many different plates, with twenty-eight different serial numbers on each plate. It was difficult, and there was a lot of wastage.

"I can't say exactly how many notes I printed all told—we threw away a lot, burned them—but I know how many boxes were filled with them, and I know there were seven to eight thousand notes in each box filled. There was a time when these boxes were stacked almost to the ceiling, and one day when I was alone I had a chance to count them. I counted seventy-four boxes. Calculating roughly, that came to something like twelve million dollars I'd printed."

As Kypraios paused and reflected, there was total silence in the room. The police officers sat frozen. *Twelve million?* So far they'd picked up barely a third of that amount, and they'd been smugly speculating that maybe they had it all!

"There is another reason this incident stays with me," continued Kypraios. "It is because that was also the last time I saw those boxes full of notes. I remember it was a Friday, late in November, and I counted the boxes as I was closing up the plant for the weekend. When I came back on Monday morning, they were gone—every last box. Somebody had come in during the weekend and taken all the money away. I didn't know anything about it, and I still do not know for sure who did it—but the only one I know of who had a key to the plant besides myself was Petros. And the place was locked when I left on Friday and still locked when I returned on Monday—and it had not been broken into. So—" His voice caught as he tried to swallow a painful memory.

"Who supplied the boxes?" Ayres asked.

"Petros got them. I don't know where."

"And you and he had packed them with the finished notes?"

"Yes. And John Singer, he helped. It took us three or four days."

"When would this packing have been done?"

"About the middle of November."

"And to your knowledge, before that weekend late in November none of the filled boxes had been removed from the plant—Petros hadn't taken any out, or Singer?"

"I'm sure not."

"Has there been any further discussion about printing additional twenty-dollar notes?"

"No. I haven't even seen John Singer since. I suppose they've got all they wanted. That was the end of it. I was sick inside afterward. I couldn't bear even to go near the plant again. I've printed nothing else there. The only times I've gone there have been every so often to use the telephone—to talk with my poor wife in Greece. . . ." Nick's voice died off in melancholy.

"So that's why the machinery finally was repossessed?" asked Ayres.

"Well, of course we have not been producing anything. But even before this, after the notes were all printed, the money we were getting to operate—that Petros was getting—dried up. From that fellow Charlie, I imagine, and whoever else had supported us. So we could no longer afford the installments. Petros showed me the letter from Seligson and Clare saying they were taking back their equipment. He said there would be a rebate due, part of the deposit put down, and I should go to Seligson's and collect it—twenty-five hundred dollars. Petros told me I could take out from that the cost of my air fare back to Greece, if I wished, and return the rest to him."

"And did you pick up the refund?"

"No. I'd planned to go there tomorrow," Kypraios said. "That's today now, Monday."

"Tell us," said Ayres, "about this man Charlie, your backer."

"I know little about him," answered Nick. "He came to the plant only a couple of times. He is very fat, as I have said. Around forty years old. And he drives a big green car." He stopped, seeming to pick at his memory. "Something about that car. I watched them drive off one day—he and Petros and Singer—and I remember noticing the license plate: the letters were LBJ, the same as the initials of the former American President."

"You don't know Charlie's surname?"

"Zukas, or something like that."

Dave Smith, at the typewriter, asked the interpreter to have Nick spell the name. After an exchange in Greek, the interpreter said, "He can only guess. He never saw it written, you understand. He spells it Z-u-k-a-s."

Ayres continued. "In addition to this Charlie fellow, earlier you mentioned a clothing manufacturer Petros had said might also be a backer. Can you tell us anything more about him?"

Through the interpreter Nick answered, "Not much. I myself do not know the person, but I think he was a friend of Petros' family." Nick added, "A countryman, a Greek named Pappas, I believe."

"All right," said Ayres. "One last thing, and most important. What of the plates you made to print the notes? Are they still on the press?"

"No. Petros took them."

"He did! Where to? When?"

"Some time ago. I assumed he'd destroyed them."

The policemen looked at each other blearily. Rotten luck. Now they were compelled not only to keep on searching for the plates but, failing recovery, to verify their destruction satisfactorily—*if* they'd been destroyed.

Ayres glanced over his notes and said to Nick, "Is there anything further you wish to say on this matter?"

Nick gazed off, then lowered his eyes, blinking. He murmured something. The interpreter said, "He wishes only to apologize to this country, to the Australian people, who treated him so well. He cannot forgive himself for doing this wrong, bad thing to them, to you."

The interview was concluded at four twenty a.m. Like his friend Petros Lyberakis, Nick was formally charged and taken to the City Watchhouse.

CHAPTER 6

NICK KYPRAIOS HAD dispelled many shadows. But the new illumination also had revealed a dismaying breadth to the affair. Seventy-four cartons filled with counterfeit U.S. twenty-dollar bills, with a probable total face value of some twelve million dollars, had been moved out of Icono Graphics. To date the Australian police had recovered, from two locations, twenty-six such cartons—each sealed, thus presumably intact—containing something over four million dollars. If Kypraios' tally was accurate, that left forty-eight cartons unaccounted for—up to eight million dollars more in forgeries still at large. Just over one hundred thousand dollars had been picked up in Zurich, which could account for a good part of one carton, but where were the others? Were they still in Melbourne? Still in Australia? Or had they already been shipped abroad, broadcast into world markets, polluting the international currency streams? Equally unsettling was the disappearance of the vital printing plates. If they had not been destroyed, would they be used again? Perhaps they were in use at the very moment—running off limitless thousands more twenties on some other clandestine press!

The police were already at work on Kypraios' alleged backer, Charlie Zukas . . . and now found an individual who seemed to be the man: Charles *Zuker* of Martin Court, Toorak—a well-to-do residential area southeast of Melbourne proper. Owner-operator of a green sedan—its license plate indeed including the letters LBJ. Business executive. No criminal record. Age forty-five. Weight, three hundred and sixty-five pounds. *Big* Charlie Zuker!

Dave Smith remembered the address book he'd picked up at Petros Lyberakis' apartment. Sure enough, under Z, there it was: "Zuker, C." Alongside, a telephone number only, but it was not the number listed in the Toorak directory as Zuker's residence phone. Smith turned back a few pages in the address book. Nick Kypraios had said he thought another possible backer was a friend of Petros' family named Pappas. . . . "Pappas, K." and again a telephone number, but also the notation "Brunswick St." There were Brunswick streets in several localities, one in Fitzroy near Petros Lyberakis' apartment, and thus practically next door to Abbotsford and the printing plant. A canvass of local directories, however, failed to turn up a Pappas with a Brunswick Street address.

Smith brought the discoveries to his superiors. It was by now well past dawn on Monday. Rex Hornbuckle telephoned Michalis Lyberakis in Caulfield. He advised the worried father of the gravity of his son's position and explained that Petros' present adamant refusal to be cooperative could be most damaging later to his defense. "Perhaps you can help," concluded Hornbuckle.

"Anything," said Mr. Lyberakis anxiously. "But how? Yesterday is first I know of this terrible thing. I still don't hardly believe it!"

"It is most urgent," the detective said, "that certain associates of Petros' be located. A major part of the counterfeit notes may be in the possession of these individuals. If we can recover the notes, it could make things a bit easier on your son. Do you understand?"

"Yes, yes, I see. But what can I . . . ?"

"Can you tell me of any persons—perhaps businessmen, or people with access to ready cash—with whom Petros may have had some association in, say, the past six months?"

The man thought. "No," he said at length. "I mean, I don't know. Petros never— There *is* one fellow. Singer, John Singer." He said the name with unmistakable distaste. "Petros and him was in a business one time—bad, big fire, lose everything. He still comes around. To me, that one is fish—slippery, I think. But . . . I don't remember others."

Hornbuckle thought, Yes, indeed, good old John Singer. But he asked, "Does the name Charles Zuker mean anything to you?"

"No . . . no, I don't know that."

"How about a Pappas?"

"Jack Pappas? Sure, he's old friend to me, to family— Hey! I remember. Last year, when Petros starts up printing business, he goes to Jack for help—you know, for money to invest—I can give only little. Jack is good. I think he does help Petros, for him and Nicky to start. But not—"

"Jack Pappas. Right." The notation in Petros' book had it as K. Pappas. "And what is his business?"

"He makes things for ladies. Pajamas."

A garment manufacturer; so far, so good. "Do you know where?"

"Some place in city. Fitzroy, maybe. But, Sergeant—"

"On Brunswick Street, possibly?" Hornbuckle kept on. He didn't want to lose the thread.

"I think, maybe," mused Lyberakis.

"And is this business listed under Pappas?"

"No, I don't think— No, he calls it something, some name cute, for the women, you know. I don't remember it. But anyhow, it would not go by Pappas."

"Oh? Why not?"

"Because he only takes that name—is easy to say for English people. His real name—in the Greek, you know—is difficult."

"What is that?"

"Papadimitropoulos. Kyriakos Papadimitropoulos—a good Greek name, but hard for the English. So he makes it Jack Pappas. But,

Sergeant, you must tell me—you think Jack, my friend, helps my son do wrong?" It was an implication he could not reckon with.

"I don't know, sir," replied Hornbuckle with sincerity. "His name has come up, and we're checking everyone. It may prove to be nothing at all. Thanks for your help. We'll keep you informed."

Charles Zuker, and now the Greek garment maker Pappas—it seemed to be coming together. While the latter's name was run through records, the investigators reviewed what had been compiled by now on the former.

Charles Izzak Zuker, not quite forty-six, a millionaire probably many times over; direct interests in a number of business enterprises, notably a Melbourne construction firm and a leather-goods factory; and directorships in many other companies. Known widely for generous philanthropy; for patronage of the arts—he owned a gallery in South Yarra (the Bartoni International Gallery—B.I.G.) and a theater on the beach at St. Kilda; and for a stamp collection estimated to be worth well over a quarter of a million dollars. Devoted wife and three children; fine home in Toorak.

Shortly, a digest was received on Papadimitropoulos as well:

Kyriakos Papadimitropoulos (Pappas, K.), forty-three; prosperous clothing manufacturer. Immigrant from Greece at age twenty-five. Over the years he has built his garment business from storefront to thriving factory. The plant—whose product, mostly sleepwear, is labeled Heart's Content—is situated on Brunswick Street, Fitzroy. Lives comfortably, with wife and four children, in the outer northeast suburb of Doncaster.

Were these, then, the moneymen who'd sponsored the illicit scheme and no doubt stood to gain the most from its successful execution? The police knew they had to find out quickly. Should any word have seeped out of the arrests over this past weekend, the quarry might already be scurrying to make themselves scarce, perhaps taking the remaining notes as well.

First, though, it would be wise to seek corroboration, if not indeed additional helpful insights, from their primary informer. Trewhitt ordered that John Singer be questioned.

Since Hornbuckle's last meeting with Singer on Saturday afternoon, the man had been kept under careful watch. The surveillance reports noted that he'd indulged in more than his normal quota of carousing on Saturday and Sunday nights, without any appearance of furtiveness. Now, when Hornbuckle met him a little before nine a.m. on Monday, Singer did look much the worse for wear: wrinkled, bleary, the brittle early sunlight magnifying his every whisker and puff of flesh.

"Morning, John," Hornbuckle greeted Singer.

"Morning, hell! Are you out to do me in?" he rasped. "Talking to me in broad bloody daylight! I get spotted with you, and I'm—" He stared at Hornbuckle in sudden suspicion. "Is this a pinch?"

"Calm yourself, John," said Hornbuckle evenly. "Of course, I could make it a pinch."

Singer eyed him. "What are you getting at?"

"It's this counterfeit business. You've put us into something of a quandary, John."

"I don't follow. How— What happened yesterday?"

"It turned out rather well," Hornbuckle responded. "I might even say the results have exceeded our expectations. That's our difficulty, you see; your information has been good—as far as it's gone. But we keep finding out things you *haven't* told us, and with each new incident, the impression grows more and more distinct that you're playing both sides of the street, John. And this dismays us."

"I don't get what you mean," said Singer warily.

"I'm sure you know very well," Hornbuckle insisted. "Shall we go over the litany once more? First, you're reported touting new counterfeit American twenties. Next, two friends of yours are picked up in Switzerland with a load of them. You tell us that in the first instance you were only acting as intermediary for another friend, unnamed, and an alleged third party, unknown—you know nothing more about the forgeries.

"Then you admit to having heard on the grapevine of a cache of such notes down in Elwood. So we haul that in, and it soon becomes evident that *you* helped bury it—you and another. So you tell us yes, you did know about it, this fellow had *tried* to bring you into it, but, of course, you'd resisted, and you'd only helped him in a few minor ways because he was so persistent and he was, after all, a friend. Whereupon you baldly proceed to identify this friend—and more, lead us to another cache that he himself has buried. Am I accurate so far?"

Singer just looked across at him dourly.

"All right, so now it becomes even more interesting," Hornbuckle went on. "On your information, we nab your friend, Petros Lyberakis, and his pile of notes, and he in turn leads us to an associate of his—a printer, Nick Kypraios, *the* printer, to all appearances. And what do we learn from them? That you, in fact, were rather more than a disinterested bystander to this operation—that you were in on the beginnings of it, abetted it, helped persuade the printer into undertaking it, even participated in stuffing the finished notes into their bloody cartons. Why, man, altogether this marks you as nothing less than a co-conspirator."

"If you believe what a couple of crooks tell you!" protested Singer. "It's their word against mine. Where's the proof? You've never found *me* with any of that stuff."

"Who knows what hard evidence we'll turn up before we're through digging?" remarked Hornbuckle. "Frankly, we think the weight of suspicion alone is great enough right now to cave you in. Enough, certainly, for us to make your life a misery for a long time to come. Think about it. Thanks to you, we have collected over four million dollars' worth of these counterfeit twenties. But that's not all of it, is it?"

"I— Look, I—"

"Come on, man!"

Singer cleared his throat and sighed, frowning. "No."

"How much more?"

"I never actually counted it, you understand. I helped pack some in cartons, yes—anything to close out this business, get rid of it. But I think I know how much they *could* have printed. I believe they'd stocked enough paper and ink to have turned out about fifteen million dollars in twenties. In the end they might have junked as much as three millions' worth, for imperfections and such, you know."

Hornbuckle could not help being awed again by the audacity of it . . . and somewhat daunted anew by the reaffirmation of how much farther the detectives might yet have to go before resolving the affair. But he was encouraged by Singer's apparent candor; his estimate closely matched the numbers given them by the printer him-self, Kypraios.

"Around eight million still missing, then," calculated Hornbuckle. "Where? Has any of it got out? Or is it all being held somewhere? Who has it?"

"I honestly don't know for certain how Petros has distributed it. He is the one, you know. Petros conceived it, and he ran it. I really never handled the stuff—I mean, I never took any, never passed any and I don't have any."

"We were led to understand from Petros," said Hornbuckle, "that you had notes in your possession as recently as January. That would have been as long as two months *after* the packed cartons had been cleared out of the plant."

Singer flushed. "I— Well, yes, I guess that's true. But not the way it sounds. I thought it was all over, the notes were long gone, wherever, and let me tell you I was relieved. And then Petros came back to me and again insisted I try to find some new distribution outlets for him. He gave me some notes—I don't recall how many, just a hand-ful, a couple of hundred dollars' worth—and he wouldn't take no for an answer."

"Were you also to arrange financing for him?" asked Hornbuckle.

"No— Well, not directly. When he first approached me—"

"Which would have been when?" Hornbuckle cut in.

"About the middle of last year, I think. He asked if I wanted to get in the printing business with him, and I said, 'No, thanks.' Not only was I not interested, I had no ready cash. He asked me where he might scrape together some money, and I"—he paused as though catching himself; after a beat, continuing—"I suggested Alan Wray. Petros knew Alan, and he said, 'Where would Wray get any money?' I said, 'Perhaps he would sell, or pawn, that big diamond ring he brought back from South Africa.' Which he did—"

"So Wray has been in it all the way also?"

"No, not at that point. I spoke to him—we'd known one another for some time, and Petros had met him through me—about an opportunity to invest in some bonds that promised a ten-to-one re-turn. It sounded like a killing to Alan. He sold his ring for some-thing like seventy-five hundred or eight thousand dollars, and he gave me fifty-five hundred, which I turned over to Petros."

"Eventually Wray did learn the true nature of his investment?" asked Hornbuckle.

"Yes, of course. He didn't object."

"And Roger Gilbert?"

"Roger knew nothing. . . . Not until it was too late, anyhow. Alan brought him in. I didn't think Roger was cut out for this sort of thing, but—"

"Who's Robert, or Bob?" Hornbuckle asked abruptly.

"Robert who?"

"Wray's connection here—an American, or Canadian."

Singer looked puzzled. "I don't know of anyone. . . ."

"And what's the significance of Leeds, England?"

"Leeds?" He shook his head. "No idea."

"Who else did you recruit?"

"I don't recruit," Singer complained.

"Didn't you bring in Charlie Zuker?"

Singer glared at Hornbuckle. "Absolutely not," he said. "I'd introduced Petros to Charlie, but in this he went to Charlie himself."

"Went to Charlie for what?"

"Money." Singer spat it out.

"And Charlie threw in with him?"

"I think, at first, Charlie thought it was a legitimate investment—the Greek magazine. He pledged a few thousand. Petros is a strong salesman."

"But Charlie soon found out differently, didn't he?"

"Yes."

"And what did he do then?"

"He—he put in more."

"How much more?"

"Maybe seventy-five hundred."

"So Charlie Zuker was a major backer," Hornbuckle declared. "Do you know if he is now in possession of the major share, if not all, of these notes?"

Singer, face drawn, pulled at his chin. "I don't *know*, but I shouldn't be surprised. He said once he'd like to come out of this with about five million clear and resettle in Switzerland."

"Where," asked Hornbuckle, "would a Charlie Zuker be apt to keep the notes, if he were still sitting on them?"

"Lord, I don't know. He's into so many things—businesses, investments, banks. I doubt anywhere about his home, though. Charlie's right proper in his private life."

"Banks . . ." Hornbuckle pondered aloud. "A safe-deposit vault?" He sat a moment in silent contemplation, then asked, "Where does Jack Pappas fit in?"

Singer visibly stiffened. "You *have* been digging deep, haven't you!" he exclaimed. "Pappas— Petros told me about him, a friend of the family, a Greek, in the garment business, I believe. Petros said he'd hit him up for the Greek magazine."

"Like Zuker?"

"Not so much, I don't think. Perhaps five thousand. I don't know a lot about him. Really."

They fell silent again. "Anything else?" Hornbuckle asked.

"You asked me to level with you, and I've leveled," he grumbled. "But you'll never be satisfied, will you?"

"Perhaps not. I know you too well, John."

Singer sighed wearily. It was almost ten o'clock. "Can I go now?" he asked.

"Of course, John."

CHAPTER 7

A TEAM FROM THE forensic lab was waiting at Seligson and Clare, on Bouverie Street in Carlton, when the plant opened. Examining the equipment repossessed from Icono Graphics, they found the press to be a well-used Heidelberg offset machine, standard but for slight modifications made since its leasing to Kypraios. One of the press rollers clearly bore the impression of a U.S. twenty-dollar bill. But the plates themselves were missing.

Meanwhile, following the interview with John Singer, Hornbuckle had ordered a check of confidential interbank files to fill out the profile of Charles Zuker. It was found that Zuker kept accounts of varying size in several Melbourne banks. In only one, however, did he rent a large personal safe-deposit vault: the Australia and New Zealand Bank Corporation (ANZ) on Collins Street, in the financial district.

Rex Hornbuckle was still pondering this new information, surmising that Zuker's vault in the ANZ bank just might contain a few surprises, when he received a telephone call from Michalis Lyberakis. Petros' father apologized for disturbing the sergeant, who must be very busy, but he'd learned something interesting, which he thought Hornbuckle should know. He sounded relieved.

"I talk with my friend, Jack," Lyberakis said.

"You what? Pappas? How?"

"Is great worry to me, maybe Jack help my Petros do bad. You see? Would be terrible thing—Jack is my old friend. I must find out."

"What happened?"

"I ring up Jack at factory. I don't sound like I think anything funny. I say only—like father, you know, just talking about son—what good friend Jack is to help Petros with money for printing business. He say is nothing, he don't like putting money in printing business, but he decide for Petros. Then he say, By the way, what happens to Petros' business? He don't hear from Petros in long time, ever since Petros leave two cases at factory about Christmas—"

"Two cases?" the detective interrupted. "Cases of *what?*"

"Is what I call to tell you!" exclaimed Lyberakis, his voice brightening. "I ask Jack this, and he say, Oh, some printing things—papers, magazines maybe, things like so. He say, Ask Petros when he is coming to collect them, Jack needs the space. So you see, Sergeant, Jack is okay. And maybe Petros is not so bad like you think. Maybe is mistake, someplace?"

Hornbuckle considered. Then he said kindly, "I would like to hope that, sir. I'll be the first to apologize if we find it to be so. Thank you for calling."

But as he rang off, Hornbuckle, his pulse increasing in tempo, was thinking. Two suitcases stored in Pappas' garment factory, and a large bank vault in Zuker's name—large enough, perhaps, to hold several cases. Were these the final links that would draw it all together? Briskly he summoned the others of the Breaking Squad, and they clicked off a strike plan. It would be a simultaneous thrust, or as nearly so as they could manage, descending upon Zuker and Pappas independently so as not to provide either with the opportunity of forewarning the other.

By Monday afternoon all was in readiness. Telephone inquiries had been made to several of Zuker's Melbourne offices. A confidential secretary, assured that it was an official matter of special delicacy, had said that Mr. Zuker was spending the day at home in Toorak. (Why *this* day? Had he got on to something—was he preparing to cut and run?)

Surveillance at Pappas' garment factory confirmed that the boss was on the premises, attending to business as usual. At four o'clock two groups moved out of the Russell Street headquarters: Hornbuckle, Dave Smith and a Commonwealth counterpart proceeding south to Toorak; Gary Ayres and Detective Sergeant John McIver leading the raiding party to Fitzroy.

The Zuker home, in a landscape of tall trees and richly manicured lawns, was white and quietly elegant. A maid opened the door to the three business-suited visitors. She did not appear surprised when they identified themselves as police officers; without hesitation she led them through a tasteful living room, with thick carpeting and sunlit French doors that overlooked an expanse of green, and finally into a paneled study. Rising ponderously to receive them from behind a great polished desk was one of the largest figures they had ever seen. Neither short nor tall, his girth almost obscured the window behind him. He wore a dressing gown over an open-necked shirt and chino trousers.

"Good afternoon, gentlemen," Charles Zuker greeted them. "How can I be of service to you?" His manner was jovial, but Hornbuckle perceived no warmth in it.

They identified themselves again, and he nodded as though accepting unnecessary formalities. "You were expecting us, it seems," said Hornbuckle.

Zuker smiled. "My office was good enough to advise me of your inquiries. I was biding time going over my stamp collection," he said, indicating a large album open on the desk. "Stamps are an incurable vice with me—have been since I was a lad. I've accumulated quite a few. Perhaps you've heard? It's been written up, you know. Come, have a look. Are any of you interested in stamps? They fascinate me." He bade them join him around the desk and proceeded to instruct them on his collection. His enthusiasm seemed unfeigned, but it struck Hornbuckle as a smoke screen of verbiage to put off what he must have surmised was inevitable.

After five minutes of his exuberant lecturing on his collection, and their polite but strained acknowledgments, Hornbuckle spoke out bluntly. "Mr. Zuker, we've come on an official inquiry, which I'm afraid is rather serious. If you don't mind . . ."

"Of course, of course. I'm so sorry." He closed the album. "Now. Yes . . . ?"

"Sir, you have come under suspicion as a participant in a major counterfeiting conspiracy. It's my duty to inform you that—"

"Counterfeiting! *Me?* And you've come to arrest me?"

"Perhaps. If we find certain evidence we believe to be in your possession."

"Well, I can assure you there are no counterfeits in *this* house." He gestured about him, taking in the whole house. "Surely you can't think, in the fortunate circumstances I've managed to sustain, that I should have required dabbling with play money?"

"We don't think you have any of it here," said Hornbuckle, unabashed. "We want to look in your bank—specifically, in your vault at the ANZ. So, if you'll kindly accompany us, sir . . ."

"I see." Zuker's face clouded for an instant, but he resumed his air of good-natured tolerance. "Then please excuse me briefly, gentlemen, while I go to dress."

Leaving the house a few minutes later, Zuker noticed the time and remarked pleasantly to Hornbuckle, "This may be a wasted trip after all, Sergeant. The bank should have shut for the day before we can get there."

Hornbuckle replied quietly, "No problem, Mr. Zuker. It'll be open to us."

The bank manager was prepared, ushering them in anxiously and with evident deference to his valued depositor. In the vault, oblong metal boxes were laid out on a table; the manager at his shoulder, Zuker opened each. They contained only private documents.

"You see," chided Zuker brightly, "nothing at all here of interest to you chaps."

Hornbuckle said, "How about that luggage?"

A pair of gray vinyl suitcases stood in a corner. Dave Smith got them and hefted them onto the table. Each bore the monogram CZ. They were locked.

"Open them," instructed Hornbuckle.

Zuker fumbled with a key ring, found a small key and released the locks on both bags, then stood back.

"Go on, please," said Hornbuckle. "Open them."

Zuker's fingers trembled, and the humor had fled his face as he unsnapped the latches. Inside one suitcase were five familiar cardboard cartons; in the other, four. Each carton was tied with cord, sealed at the knot with wax.

"Let it be noted that we open the contents of these cases in the presence of yourself and Mr. Zuker," Hornbuckle said to the manager.

The cartons all were filled with U.S. twenty-dollar bills.

"Must be well over a million here," breathed Smith.

They all turned to Zuker. His face was an ashen sculpture of shocked dismay. Color flooded back into his features under their accusing gaze, and he stammered, "I don't— I was merely storing them for—a friend."

Hornbuckle smiled. "Whose initials also just happen to be CZ?" He shook his head. "I'd have to say it looks more as though you have been, after all—how did you put it, Mr. Zucker?—dabbling. . . ."

THE SQUAD LED by Ayres and McIver entered the Heart's Content factory on Brunswick Street at about the time Zuker was being escorted from his home. The garment manufacturing layout was small, in a typically unadorned loftlike room dominated by several long tables, at which sat half a dozen women solemnly huddled over patterns and bolts and lengths of fabric. To one side were the various machines for cutting, stitching, pressing. There was a glassed-in office beyond the work area, and a set of stairs led to a floor above.

The workers looked up in wonderment and some alarm at the sudden entrance of four burly and purposeful-looking strangers. The proprietor hurried out of his office to confront them. Kyriakos Papadimitropoulos—Pappas—was a trim little man in his forties, neatly dressed in shirt and tie, even rather dapper in appearance, with his thin, carefully groomed mustache and graying sideburns. With arched eyebrows and tentative smile he asked the visitors if he could help them. His English was thickly accented.

Sergeant McIver showed him the search warrant, which he seemed to understand well enough; as he scanned it, his brow furrowed and then he looked up at the sergeant and about at the others with obvious concern. Pappas quickly bestirred himself, however. "Please, gentlemen," he said. "Help yourself."

The detectives fanned out and inspected the factory area, under the sometimes resentful stares of the women, who chattered back and forth in a rapid foreign tongue—they all were Greek immigrants, their employer volunteered after a time. The search produced nothing.

"What's upstairs?" Ayres asked Pappas.

The natty little man shrugged. "Only spare rooms. My children come to play after school."

"Let's have a look," Ayres said, with a nod to one of his colleagues to stay below.

There were two doors on the upper floor. One was open, revealing a small room, bare but for a number of children's playthings scattered about. The other door was closed and locked. "What's in here?" asked McIver.

Pappas said, "Like other room. It has bed."

"Well, open it up," ordered McIver.

"I don't have key."

"Why do you keep it locked?"

But now Pappas' English failed him. He simply shook his head disconcertedly.

McIver took a ring of jangling keys and other small implements from a pocket and picked at the door's lock. Nothing clicked. The sergeant turned to the other two detectives. "Seems there's only one way." The three of them stepped to the door and in a single coordinated thrust kicked it open.

There was a cot in the room, unmade, and beneath it two large steamer trunks. The officers hauled these out and set both onto the cot. They were heavy. "Let's see inside." Ayres gestured to Pappas.

Hesitantly the man unlatched one of the trunks. It was filled with sealed gray cardboard cartons. The detectives raised the lid of the other trunk. Gray cartons, to the brim. One carton was removed from each trunk and opened. American twenty-dollar bills.

"Petros, that—" Pappas sputtered.

They counted thirty-nine cartons, all but two packed full with twenties. The haul of hauls—a bobby-dazzler!

U.S. SECRET SERVICE AGENT Thomas Collins would arrive from Honolulu in time for the final tally of the counterfeit American dollars that had been confiscated in the Melbourne area within approximately seventy-two hours. Charlie Zuker's nine cartons yielded 72,849 notes, for $1,456,980 face value. The cache of thirty-nine cartons from Kyriakos Papadimitropoulos' garment factory was counted by employees of the Reserve Bank, supervised by the indefatigable Mr. Bywater. The final total: 303,792 notes—$6,075,840! Two of the cartons had been previously unsealed and were less than half full, indicating that some of the forgeries had been taken out—at best guess $200,000 worth or more. The $100,000-odd with Wray and Gilbert in Switzerland could have been part of what had been removed from the two opened cartons.

The grand total recovered in Melbourne, then: the equivalent of $11,667,760. Close indeed, adding on the estimated amount missing, to the twelve million dollars suggested by Nick Kypraios. He'd said that seventy-four boxes of notes had been removed from the printing plant; and the police now had seventy-four boxes, all but two intact. If Nick was truthful—and the investigators were inclined to believe that he was—it would seem that they had succeeded to a remarkable degree in aborting what had to be the most ambitious single counterfeiting scheme on record!

In the separate interrogations of Zuker and Papadimitropoulos at the Russell Street offices, each had blamed Petros Lyberakis for his plight—the millionaire more in a sadness of disillusionment, the Greek in the blistering vindictiveness of one betrayed.

Zuker readily admitted having been persuaded to invest in what Lyberakis had described to him as an innovative publishing venture; he put in about seventy-five hundred dollars for starters, Zuker estimated. He said Lyberakis had come to him independently after they'd met earlier through a mutual friend.

Was that friend John Singer?

Zuker said yes, showing some discomfiture. Zuker had looked in on the printshop once, he continued, and met Kypraios briefly only that time. After that, he'd had no direct contact with the operation, leaving it to Petros, whom he found a clever, enterprising young fellow, to handle affairs. Then, sometime before Christmas, Zuker said, Petros had come to him with the two monogrammed bags,

and to his amazement they were filled with these realistic U.S. twenty-dollar bills! He'd never dreamed—

The police interrupted to advise him sternly that they possessed convincing evidence that indeed he had dreamed of a wholesale output of counterfeit notes, that he'd been in on the birth of the scheme and had eagerly agreed to subsidize its development.

At that, Zuker broke down and confessed he had allowed unnatural greed to overcome his normally shrewd business judgment. He did insist that at the outset he'd really thought that he was helping to finance the two earnest young men, Lyberakis and Kypraios, in a legitimate and worthy enterprise, which also offered some promise of at least a modest profit on his investment. It was when they showed him the sample one-sided twenty-dollar notes and Lyberakis outlined all the well-conceived plans for distributing them outside Australia that he could not resist the challenge and lure of windfall profits.

In a matter of minutes the great bulk of a man had lost whatever grace he'd formerly managed. He sagged in remorse and shame.

Kyriakos Papadimitropoulos was not remorseful. He was outraged, and his marginal English all but fled him; the interrogators had to bring in their Greek interpreter once again. He denied ever having knowingly contributed support—money or encouragement—to *any* illegal undertaking. Not once in his life, he declared, in his native Greece or in Australia, had he had the least experience with breaking the law.

Yes, Petros Lyberakis had approached Papadimitropoulos months before for financial help on some publishing business. He was leery of investing in anything he himself was not part of, but Petros persisted, and out of sympathy and friendship for Petros' family he gave him a small sum. He had not expected to see that money again.

Then, he went on bitterly, just before Christmas, Petros came to see him at his factory in Fitzroy to ask a favor. Petros said that his little printing operation in Abbotsford was coming along nicely, but that he and his partners were becoming concerned that their shop was insecure; there had been several recent thefts, and they feared that their insurance might be revoked if break-ins continued. Would Papadimitropoulos allow him to leave a couple of boxes of printed material for safekeeping in the garment factory? Papadimitropoulos thought it an unusual request, but he couldn't think why it shouldn't be all right.

The "couple of boxes" turned out to be two rather large trunks— but no matter. Papadimitropoulos suggested one of the rooms above his work space. These rooms were used regularly as a play area by two of his children, who attended school in Fitzroy and came to the factory every afternoon after classes to wait for their mother to pick them up and drive them home. Petros objected, saying that he knew kids, and he didn't want them scampering about and perhaps upsetting his materials, which he said he hoped to ship within a matter of weeks. Until then, would Kyriakos mind if he, Petros, installed a lock on the door? Papadimitropoulos agreed to it.

And so the room with Petros' trunks had been sealed off around Christmastime. As far as Papadimitropoulos knew, it had not been reopened until the present afternoon. He himself had no duplicate of Petros' key, and Petros had not returned for the trunks.

The man's indignation seemed genuine. In truth, investigation of Papadimitropoulos had brought to light no other link between himself and this illicit business or any other. Yet he did concede to having put development cash into the operation and to storing Lyberakis' trunks. Having found a man with some six million counterfeit dollars hidden on his premises, the police could scarcely accept his protestations of ignorance, pat him on the shoulder understandingly and send him on his way. Only the court could judge Papadimitropoulos' complicity or credibility. He had to be booked as a principal conspirator.

That Monday evening the news media had been summoned to Russell Street for a briefing by the Victoria and Commonwealth police. The official news had been cabled to Interpol Paris; in a matter of hours it would reverberate around the world.

Interpol Canberra received an exultant wire from Frank Leyva, the U.S. Secret Service chief in Paris.

MY CONGRATULATIONS AND THAT OF MY COLLEAGUES TO THE AUS-TRALIAN POLICE ON A JOB WELL DONE. YOURS WAS AN EXCEPTIONAL PERFORMANCE WITH EXCEPTIONAL RESULTS.

HAVE BEEN IN TELEPHONE CONTACT WITH MCCABE AND PLANT. THEY ARE QUESTIONING WRAY AND GILBERT TODAY.

CHAPTER 8

As THE SENSATIONAL announcements were being issued on Monday evening in Melbourne, Detective Inspector Donald Plant, of the Victoria CIB, and Commonwealth police Inspector Ray McCabe were arriving in Zurich, where it was still Monday morning. They'd had no way of knowing, of course, the outcome of the CIB's planned raid on Sunday of the Lyberakis home, much less of the dramatic developments on the day following. The news that greeted them in Zurich, then, was elating and yet, in a way, deflating. Their particular mission somehow seemed of less moment, now that back home the counterfeit plot appeared to have been smashed and its ringleaders rounded up. Their hope had been, in light of the first important breakthrough at Ferrari's Transport, to persuade Roger Gilbert or Alan Wray into revealing some hidden key to it all. But it was just conceivable that the two couriers might disclose some new, unsuspected clues—to other, still unknown parties to the scheme or to the existence of yet more forged currency.

After checking into their hotel, Plant and McCabe spent the rest of Monday at Zurich police headquarters reviewing the case with the local authorities. Wray still was conceding no guilt about possession of the $100,080 in counterfeit twenties. He continued to insist that his only wrong had been in transporting illegally out of Australia what he'd thought to be legitimate currency at the behest of the man he knew only as Bob or Robert.

Gilbert, on the other hand, had gone so far as to declare that Wray had known the notes were forgeries and had disclosed this to him upon their arrival in Zurich. He conceded, for his own part, that he was guilty of having knowingly cashed several of the counterfeits in violation of Swiss law. But Gilbert still swore that he'd had no idea when leaving Australia what they were up to and would have had none of it if he *had* known.

Both men acknowledged friendship with John Singer; but Wray flatly denied having conspired with Singer, and Gilbert expressed what impressed the Swiss officials as honest surprise at the intimation that his onetime roommate was part of any conspiracy.

Inspectors Plant and McCabe were hopeful that, armed with the climactic late developments in Melbourne, they could wring more out of the pair than that. On Tuesday morning, then, following consultation with the district attorney, they were escorted to the prison at Regensdorf.

Gilbert, interviewed first, proved an easy mark. Unhappy, fidgety, sapped by consuming anxiety about what was to become of him, he collapsed as the Australian policemen impressively described to him the complete rout of the counterfeiting ring. They told him of John Singer's integral complicity and that Singer had directly implicated him—on record. Tears brimmed in Gilbert's eyes, and he was unable to speak for a few moments. Then, sounding almost relieved, he confessed having known of the counterfeits prior to departing for Zurich. "Only a day or two before we left, Alan showed me a few of the notes, but he wouldn't tell me anything of the plan until we arrived here. I never had any idea how much was involved, until—"

"But still you went ahead," Plant said, "knowing you were engaged in a criminal act."

Gilbert looked at them with mingled shame and supplication. "I was scared witless. But Alan told me—assured me—it was not dangerous. No one could be hurt, really. It was just an easy way to make some money fast." He sagged, then with an effort braced himself. "I was broke, so much in debt, creditors hounding me. I imagined this as my one chance, even if there *was* some risk, of bailing out."

"How did Alan come by the notes?"

Gilbert's brow wrinkled. "I really don't know. He mentioned someone named Robert, but I don't know. . . ."

"Can you think of a Robert he might possibly have meant?"

"No. I've thought and thought, and I can't."

"How about John Singer? He was not mentioned as the source?"

"No, never. He—" Gilbert paused, newly thoughtful. "You know, that day at the airport—when John saw us off—there were things he and Alan talked about that I didn't connect. . . . Not *what* they said, especially, so much as, I don't know, *how* they were talking, or behaving. It did make me wonder. But I decided it was all in my mind, you know, nerves—seeing spooks under one's bed, rather. All I actually recall John saying before we boarded was something like

'Keep in touch,' and that he might come over to Europe himself shortly for some skiing. Anyway, I asked Alan about it later, on the plane, to find out if John knew anything, and he said no, so I forgot about it."

"And Petros Lyberakis?" Plant asked.

"I met him only socially, with Alan . . . and, I think, John. I don't—didn't know him well at all."

They asked him if he was acquainted with, or had ever heard mentioned in this affair, Nick Kypraios, Charles Zuker, Kyriakos Papadimitropoulos or Jack Pappas. He thought he might have heard of Zuker—in the newspaper, perhaps—but did not know him or any of the others.

The inspectors were persuaded that Gilbert now had really told all he was able to tell.

Confronting Alan Wray next, they found him cut from stiffer cloth than was Gilbert. Though soft of speech and even-mannered with them, Wray was resistant to interrogation. Without batting an eye, he received the advice that the ring in Australia had been smashed, and that not only his friend Singer but the plotter Lyberakis and the printer Kypraios had dragged him into the net. "I'm sure all that seems of great significance to you," he said, "but it means nothing to me. I know of no conspiracy or ring."

"Your friends mean nothing to you?" Plant chided him.

"I am surprised about John. He should know better."

"He does—now. And what of Petros Lyberakis and poor Nick Kypraios?"

"I hardly know them. I may have met them here or there. Too bad for them."

"Yet you are charged with possession of one hundred thousand American dollars of the same type of forgeries as these men have printed. How do you account for this?"

"I have accounted—I was unaware they were counterfeit. I was led to believe they were genuine by the man who asked me to take them out of the country. That is my only crime, and I have admitted to it."

"The man you call Robert but barely know," said McCabe.

"Yes. Find him, and—"

"There is no Robert," McCabe fired back. "We know *all* the

principals involved now, and there is no Robert. There never was, was there?"

Wray shrugged. "I say there was and is. You'll have to prove otherwise."

"You and Roger Gilbert were employed as advance couriers by this group to test the waters abroad," stated Plant. "But when you foundered, they were perfectly willing to let you both sink, along with the one hundred thousand. Do you want to know why?"

Wray folded his arms and assumed an expression of thin patience.

"I think this may surprise even you," Plant said. "Your hundred thousand was a throwaway. What they ultimately had at stake—what we've *recovered*—was almost twelve million!"

Wray blanched. "Twelve million!"

McCabe pulled from his pocket a folded page of newspaper. "You might be interested in this," he said, handing it to Wray.

It was the front page of a Zurich morning edition. The language was German, but the headlines and enough of the prominently featured story below were plain to anyone familiar with the case.

Wray stared, absorbed, at the creased sheet of newsprint, shaking his head. At length he looked up at the waiting Australian policemen, and across at the Swiss officers also watching him silently, and then his eyes crinkled wryly. "Bloody good show, what?" he said to McCabe and Plant.

At last Wray let it all out. What it amounted to, however, was disappointing—little more than certification of his own involvement, minor compared with most of the others, and of the relative ingenuousness of his cat's-paw, Roger Gilbert. The pair's accounts jibed on most points, and Plant and McCabe were satisfied that now they'd gotten the truth, so far as it went. But how much more could Wray add?

"You mention certain parties, the mysterious backers," said Plant. "Did you know, or ever manage to find out, who they were?"

"The only ones I really knew to be in it," Wray said, "were Singer and Petros Lyberakis—and, of course, the printer. They never did say in so many words who the others were. But I had some hints, and heard a few things around, on the outside. And I got an idea Big Charlie Zuker might have a slice of it."

"And the Greek—Jack Pappas?"

"I knew of him as a family friend of Petros'. But I don't think his name ever came up in this connection—not that *I* heard, leastways."

"All right." Plant scanned his notes. "Now, you received the quantity of forgeries from whom? Precisely."

"From Singer. He brought them to my flat one night."

"Right. And you were to spend your way, so to speak, across the Continent. Then what? If it had all come off without a hitch, were you really to rendezvous with anyone at Leeds, in England?"

Wray smiled wanly. "I thought that a quaint touch. Oh, we were to finish up in London, and I might have looked in on Leeds—had my boyhood there, you know, old times and all that."

"Then what *were* you to do with the proceeds?"

"We were to fly back to Switzerland and put it in a special bank account—all of it but Roger's and my ten percent—then return to Melbourne. If we'd gotten that far with it, I guess they'd have turned us round with another consignment."

"What bank?" asked McCabe.

"We'd have been instructed somewhere along the route, I expect."

"So it was Lyberakis who instructed you, and Singer who actually supplied you the notes. Then this Robert person you've mentioned so often . . . ?"

Wray shook his head with a sigh. "Just a cover. There's no Robert."

The inspectors leaned back and looked at their Swiss counterparts, inviting final questions. The others shook their heads, seemingly content to have Wray's confession at last. The prisoner sat reflecting on the newspaper page still in his hands.

"That's about all, then," said Plant as he and McCabe rose.

Plant and McCabe sent detailed reports on the interviews to the Interpol central headquarters. From St. Cloud a separate advisory went to London, informing Scotland Yard that the Leeds angle could be forgotten; a query was sent to Canberra, asking further instructions. The reply from home was informal but brief: CHEERS FOR MISSION ACCOMPLISHED. SUGGEST RETURN EARLIEST CONVENIENCE.

To the veteran inspectors, whatever they'd accomplished seemed minuscule and drab alongside what had happened in their absence. They'd traveled almost halfway around the world, only to miss out on most of the fun.

YET THE JUBILATION OF THE police in Melbourne was tempered during the ensuing week by some consternation. First, against vigorous protests by government prosecutors, a city court saw fit to grant bail to each of the four accused in the conspiracy. And surprisingly low bail at that—only two thousand dollars, for instance, for Charles Zuker. The lawmen were seriously concerned that any or all of the men could disappear prior even to the first hearing, set for April 23. Checks could be made regularly on their whereabouts, but manpower was too strained to allow for steady surveillance of four men already properly arrested and facing indictment.

Then, on the heels of Zuker's release, rumors began filtering in to the police from various informers, suggesting that the millionaire might be planning to flee the country. It was learned at the government passport office that Charles Zuker had renewed his passport as recently as January.

A legal appeal was made at once for an injunction debarring the defendant from traveling outside the country. Given the circumstances, the court approved, and on February 11, one week after his arrest, Charles Zuker was required to surrender his passport. He also was ordered to report his whereabouts, personally, to the police every day.

Another source of aggravation to the otherwise triumphant investigators was their continuing lack of success in tracing the missing printing plates—a matter of particular concern to U.S. Secret Service agent Thomas Collins, who naturally wanted assurance that production of these fake twenty-dollar bills was closed off once and for all. Nick Kypraios had said that Petros Lyberakis had removed the plates. Lyberakis, however, steadfastly refused to say what he had done with them. Nor would he concede that he had in fact removed them from the press. Charlie Zuker and Kyriakos Papadimitropoulos each professed no knowledge of the matter; and the police agreed that it was probably safe to assume neither had been involved in the mechanics of the actual printing operation.

That left, once again, the only other individual besides Nick and Petros who'd had frequent access to the printshop and its components: John Singer. Rex Hornbuckle had kept after Singer about the plates since the arrests, but all he'd gotten from him were repeated assurances that he was as much in the dark as Hornbuckle.

The detective had not lost sight of Singer's powerful instinct for preserving some hoard of self-interest at any cost, and he was not entirely persuaded to accept the man's earnest protestations of ignorance about this essential missing piece in the case.

So Hornbuckle confronted Singer once more, and came squarely to the point. Alan Wray's confession, added to all else known of Singer's part in this counterfeiting operation, now virtually made Singer a bona fide codefendant. Only his unequivocal cooperation, which meant full disclosure, offered him any hope.

"What more do you want?" complained Singer. "I've given you the whole case on a silver platter!"

"The plates, John," Hornbuckle said flatly. "The plates that printed the twenties. It's not complete till we can place them."

The man's face clouded. Before he could mouth a reply, Hornbuckle resumed. "You see, without those plates this investigation must remain open; we shan't be able to rest it. And of course that means *nobody* involved will have any rest either. It'll be a terrible bother all round, but . . ." Hornbuckle folded his arms in resignation, brows furrowing.

"Why don't you ask Petros?" argued Singer. "He planned it all. He'd—" He cut off at a snort from Hornbuckle.

"That's funny," Hornbuckle bluffed. "Petros said to ask you!"

Singer examined his manicured fingernails, his face going through a succession of changes reflecting inner debate. At last he heaved a deep sigh and looked up, breaking into a small, rueful, ironic smile. "Well, you can't blame a chap for trying, can you?"

As Singer put it, characteristically downgrading his own culpability, he had helped Petros Lyberakis dispose of the plates in the Yarra River. On a Saturday in late December, Petros had inserted the plates into two mixtures of concrete, and when the blocks were hardened they transported them from the plant by car to the river bridge nearby and dropped them in. They hoped—that is, Petros did—that perhaps one day the blocks could be dug out, and if the plates were still usable . . .

On Wednesday, February 13, a party of police went to the site in Abbotsford, a scant mile from the printshop, where a footbridge spans the narrow Yarra, only some sixty feet wide at that point. They walked out to the center of the bridge—Hornbuckle, Breaking Squad detectives Dave Smith and Gary Ayres, and the American agent Thomas Collins. The contrasting views from the bridge, some twenty-five feet over the water, were impressive. On the Abbotsford side, to the west, dingy factories cluttered the ridge of the escarpment; opposite, toward suburban Kew, the setting was parklike and serene, lush with trees and grassy hillocks—a vivid demarcation between toil and leisure. Appropriate place this, thought Hornbuckle, to have buried those things that meant so much to a few persons who yearned for leisure's pleasures without the obligatory rigors of ordinary toil.

A team of divers from the Victoria police Search and Rescue Squad was directed to plumb the river directly below the footbridge. It was quite shallow there but thick with mud. Their efforts reduced virtually to slow motion by the viscosity of the riverbed, the divers searched carefully. More than half an hour later they looked up triumphantly at the men on the bridge. Lodged snugly in the muck, the concrete blocks had been found. With the aid of a pulley set up on the bridge itself, two rough blocks—each about two feet in length, a foot wide and six inches thick—were brought up, dripping filthy water, and dumped on the bridge. A detective wiped away some of the muddy residue, and the blocks were rushed to the Victoria police Forensic Science Laboratory. Carefully they were chipped apart. Embedded within them were forty-eight printing plates, which experts from the Reserve Bank judged to match the U.S. twenty-dollar notes confiscated. Each plate was tested for possible fingerprints, but only one of the forty-eight yielded an identifiable set of prints—those of Nick Kypraios.

CHAPTER 9

THE HURLY-BURLY OF the sensational case quieted, as all high-urgency police investigations do, in the weeks following its one great concentration of thrust and climax. The officers concerned had, as always, no time to linger over their laurels, however well earned, nor would such professionals as they have wanted to. They turned their attention to other problems, most of them mundane but each in its way as demanding, if not as far-reaching and intriguing, as the counter-

feiting case. There was still much to do for that one, though; they had to collate and put into order all the accumulated evidence to be presented to the crown's prosecutors for use at trial. Whenever engaged in such routine but all-important chores, the principal investigators could, of course, indulge themselves a little in reflecting over the superior results achieved. One source of special gratification and pride to the Victoria police was a handsome plaque received from the U.S. Secret Service, warmly commending and thanking the department for its exceptional role in breaking the case. This lasting gift of recognition—a gesture not common among the world's law-enforcement agencies—was placed in a position of honor in the lobby of the Russell Street headquarters.

One short end still dangled untied, however, and it continued to prick the curiosity of Detective Sergeant Rex Hornbuckle. Two of the seventy-four cartons recovered had been found to be more than half empty. The forgeries seized in Zurich accounted for only some of the notes presumably removed. But there were thousands of dollars' worth still afloat. Hornbuckle took it personally as a taunt to keep the case open.

Which of the conspirators were likely culprits? Hornbuckle went back over his reports. Kypraios had sworn that when last he'd seen the boxes of notes—just prior to their being spirited from the printing plant—all seventy-four were intact. Hornbuckle thought the printer too scared and too honest to have pilfered from his confederates. On that assumption, then, someone else had dipped into the till between the boxes' removal from Icono Graphics and their discovery by the police at their respective depositories. And the only two less than full boxes were among those found at the garment factory. Papadimitropoulos maintained that those had been left by Petros Lyberakis. That would narrow it down to either or both of those two. Yet the garment maker insisted that the second-floor room had remained locked and unentered from the time the trunks were stored there, which could mean that the missing forgeries were extracted *before* storage—thus pointing directly to Lyberakis as the dipper—along with, possibly, accomplices unknown.

But not necessarily unknown, the detective corrected himself. There was always John Singer to consider.

Although expecting full well that chances of anything instructive coming of it were practically nil, Hornbuckle went through the elementary motions of returning to talk to each of the principals— all, to his disgruntlement, still at liberty pending court action—and inquiring of them about the unaccounted-for twenties. He suggested that prosecution could go easier for the one who, now the game was irretrievably up, volunteered to help solve this final nagging detail. Nick Kypraios repeated that all the cartons were sealed when last he'd seen them. Charles Zuker brusquely said he knew nothing of the matter and dismissed further discussion unless counsel were present. Papadimitropoulos bristled, reiterating his vigorous protestation of ignorance of the entire affair, to say nothing of such petty connivance.

Petros Lyberakis—whom the detective encountered, surly and hostile, in a coffeehouse sparsely attended by glum Bohemian types— disdained to speak of it at all. As Hornbuckle made his way from the place, however, Lyberakis called after him, "Tell your mate John I've been thinking of him—constantly!"

Lastly, Hornbuckle did put the question to John Singer. He refrained from mentioning Lyberakis' remark, lest it arouse in his informer new anxieties that could inhibit him. Singer professed to know nothing of any missing notes. He'd never really handled them anyway, he insisted again; it was always Petros who—

"John, you are simply too much!" interrupted Hornbuckle in irritation. "I do believe you've lost all idea of where lies end and truth begins! We know, now, that you personally delivered those notes to Wray and Gilbert. Why keep trying to weasel? You're going to get us doubting you again!"

Singer looked nonplussed. But only for a second. "Well—what I mean is, that wasn't *handling* the stuff, really. Petros put it together in a suitcase and told me to hand that over to Alan. I was just a delivery boy, you see."

"No way, of course, that you would have pocketed a few for your own use?"

"No way. Alan knew how much he was to have for transport— from Petros."

"And how much did you understand it to be?"

"Well, good Lord, *you* know! A hundred thousand or so, right?"

"Hmm. . . . But about this other?"

"I never took any for myself," Singer declared again, "and I—I can't even say that Petros did."

No further warnings or cajoling could budge Singer. Or any of them, evidently—just yet. For the moment, at least, it was a mystery.

SUMMER OF 1974 HAD passed into autumn, the weather growing cooler each day as the Australian winter approached. Then, in mid-May, the police got the break that would disclose the final secret of the great counterfeiting case: they learned that a number of forged U.S. twenty-dollar bills had turned up in Bangkok, Thailand.

The report came from Interpol, the result of a separate investigation in quite another area. Undercover police agents in Bangkok, acting upon information channeled by Interpol, had been probing an international narcotics ring assertedly operating from the Thai capital, when they'd run across the fake American currency. Routinely, samples had been sent on to Interpol's central counterfeit section at St. Cloud, and analysis there had identified the Bangkok notes as similar to those recovered in Zurich and Melbourne. Agents in Bangkok could give no positive indication of the notes' source. However, Interpol did pass along other information of particular interest.

A prime suspect in the Bangkok narcotics investigation happened to be one Arthur Ford, an Australian national. There was no evidence to date linking Ford directly with the counterfeits, but there was something. Thought to be a close contact of Ford's was a Thai named Veera Thong Thang, who held a responsible position with a transport company in Bangkok that regularly handled international freight shipments. In January 1974 Veera had personally received a parcel, of some bulk, by air from Melbourne. Air-freight invoices at Bangkok airport showed the parcel had been consigned to an S. Parks. That meant either Veera had picked it up for someone else, or he was S. Parks.

The Interpol advisory concluded by noting that the narcotics agents were reluctant to approach either Veera or Ford on the counterfeit matter lest they compromise their own investigation. It was hoped that the present information might enable the Australian police to follow up independently.

When this report reached the Victoria CIB, Detective Sergeant

Rex Hornbuckle felt a surge of excitement. The name Arthur Ford was not a new one to him. No indeed, for Arthur Ford was a frequent chum of none other than their own John Singer! And Singer was known to have visited Bangkok on a number of occasions. Add Veera Thong Thang, collaborator of Ford's—and thus quite possibly of Singer's—and recipient of a large parcel from Melbourne in January, at the virtual peak of the counterfeit investigation. And now, American twenties surfacing in Thailand! This could be the wrap-up.

Hornbuckle checked air-freight records at the Melbourne airport. He found a shipment on January 5 to S. Parks, Bangkok, via Trans-Australia Airlines from I. McKenzie, Melbourne. Who was this I. McKenzie? Hornbuckle contacted John Singer for a meeting.

As usual, the policeman let Singer pick the place. This time, instead of some out-of-the-way spot, Singer suggested the cocktail lounge of the Windsor Hotel—Melbourne's most prestigious, in the heart of the city. When they'd been seated at a quiet corner table and had ordered drinks, Hornbuckle smiled quizzically at Singer, whose jeans and suede jacket seemed to flout their stately, old-world surroundings. "Feeling rather chipper these days, eh, John?" he said.

Singer dismissed any concern he might have felt with a flip of a hand. "Well," he replied, "I'm glad it's over and done."

"I'm afraid it isn't quite over, John," Hornbuckle said.

The other searched his face. "What's *that* mean?"

The detective pondered for a beat. "Well, it's those missing notes. It's really been quite annoying, this one snag knotting up our whole smooth skein. Only a pittance, you might say, against all the rest—a hundred thousand, two hundred thousand. Still, it *is* out there somewhere, and we can't very well shut our eyes to that, can we?" He sighed heavily. "Nor shut the case, either, until we pin it down."

"What can *I* do about it?" urged Singer. "Haven't I given you—"

Hornbuckle shushed him as the drinks arrived. Then he hunched across the table conspiratorially. "We think now we have traced the stuff. But it's a long way off, and out of our jurisdiction. We need certain guidance." He paused to appraise Singer. "You've done a fair bit of travel abroad, haven't you, John?"

"Here and there."

"Thailand . . . Bangkok?"

"I've been there." There was the slightest note of defensiveness now in Singer's tone.

"Done some business out there, have you?" continued Hornbuckle in the same easy manner.

"Now and again. Nothing very big."

"But you still have some contacts there—in business?"

"In Bangkok? I suppose I— Look, what's this about?"

"In fact," Hornbuckle chatted on, "one of your old chums has been there a long time, hasn't he—Arthur Ford?"

Singer stared at the detective. Then he said, "Now I see. This is a setup! You want Ford, so— Listen," he spat, "I've nothing on with him!"

"Perhaps," Hornbuckle conceded. "But you do have business, on occasion, with a certain associate of his"—he savored drawing it out—"a Mr. Veera Thong Thang?" Hornbuckle sipped his drink, eyes riveting the other over the glass rim. "Sometimes uses the name Parks, I believe. Odd name for a Thai. Now, this Veera—or Parks— also has dealings here in Melbourne, it seems. With one chap we know of, at least. Perhaps you've run across him? McKenzie?"

Singer sat frozen, but he uttered nothing. Hornbuckle knew he'd scored a bull's-eye.

He pulled out his note pad and read, more crisply to the point. " 'On the fifth of January last, our Mr. McKenzie air-shipped a heavy parcel to S. Parks in Bangkok—entered three forty-five p.m., Trans-Australia Airlines. The parcel was received, signed for, in Bangkok by Mr. Parks—Veera Thong Thang. Not long after' "—he glanced at Singer, who had closed his eyes as though in pain—" 'counterfeit American twenty-dollar notes began appearing around Bangkok.' "

At this last, Singer looked up sharply. But the flash dimmed almost at once and he slumped back, only shaking his head. "One just can't trust anyone today, can one?" he muttered.

Hornbuckle regarded him a moment. Then he said softly, "Let's have it all out, John."

Singer studied his glass for a while. Then, with a sigh, falteringly at first but flattening out into a weary monotone, he related the little there remained to know.

At the start, Petros had wondered if any of Singer's contacts in the Far East could distribute the fake notes. Singer asked Arthur Ford if he was interested, but Ford said no. Later, however, when Petros was parceling out the stuff around Melbourne, he suggested Singer ship a quantity of the twenties to Ford in Bangkok anyway, on the chance Ford might change his mind. Singer couldn't send the fake money directly to Ford, whom he knew to be under police surveillance, so he chose Veera Thong Thang, whom he'd met sometime earlier through Ford and who was reliable.

In January Singer took one hundred and fifty thousand dollars' worth of the forged twenties given him by Lyberakis and packed them into a suitcase. Ironically, it was a blue suitcase of Alan Wray's, containing some of his clothing, which Wray had discarded before departing for Europe because with the addition of the case full of currency he would have gone over his Qantas weight allowance. Locked and wrapped securely, the case was then sent off to Veera Thong Thang. Veera's instructions were simply to hold it, to turn it over to no one but Arthur Ford—unless otherwise specifically authorized by Singer himself.

"And has Ford ever changed his mind, taken it over?" asked Hornbuckle.

"Not that I was ever told," grumbled Singer.

"Veera's still got it, then."

"So I'd thought. But now you tell me the notes got out."

"Only a fraction, we understand, so far." Hornbuckle looked at Singer with curiosity. "Why didn't *you* hop over and retrieve it, John?"

"I don't want it, man! I keep telling you, to me it's poison."

"Well, somebody will have to go after it now. I suspect I'll be elected."

Singer was slowly shaking his head. "That might not be so simple as it seems. I know Veera. He won't give it up."

"He'd give it over to you."

"To me—or Art Ford—yes. But—" He turned suddenly wide eyes upon the detective.

Hornbuckle beamed. "Why, then, we'll have to go together!"

Singer gawked at him, stunned. "Now hold on!"

"If it's the only way, John . . ."

"Marvelous. We traipse arm in arm around Bangkok, and I take you up to my friends and say, 'Meet my traveling companion, Detective Sergeant Hornbuckle. He and I are here to do you all in.' No, thank you!"

Hornbuckle grinned. "Oh, it needn't be so obvious as all that. We'll work out a way."

Singer's eyes were hot with resentment. "You bastards!"

HORNBUCKLE AND SINGER, under tight security, took a flight out of Melbourne on Thursday, May 30, and arrived in Bangkok early the next morning. Waiting for them was U.S. Secret Service agent Thomas Collins. He had returned to his post in Honolulu in February, but had boarded a plane as soon as word had been relayed through Interpol of Hornbuckle's mission. He had arrived only a couple of hours earlier.

At a downtown hotel, Hornbuckle and Collins had Singer telephone Veera to announce his arrival and arrange a meeting, but Singer was to give no indication that he was other than alone. An appointment was set for eleven that same morning, Friday, May 31. The strategy was well thought out. It was paramount not only that Singer meet Veera alone but that he seem able to move about freely. At the same time, it was equally imperative that Singer be watched every minute; an undercover unit would attend to that.

Singer, under close but detached surveillance, went by taxi to the airport, where Veera's transport company had an office in a cargo terminal. After some thirty-five minutes, Singer and Veera, a stocky, middle-aged man with slicked-back hair and hooded eyes, emerged. Singer carried a blue suitcase and a khaki knapsack. They hailed a taxi and rode back to Bangkok. The cab stopped at a hospital, where Veera got out and, waving amiably to his companion, went inside. Singer then drove on. It was later ascertained that Veera had gone to the hospital to see his father, a patient.

Singer brought the luggage to the room where Hornbuckle and Collins waited, and dumped it on a bed. The suitcase contained only some clothing. "Veera switched the stuff," Singer noted.

"No problems?" asked Hornbuckle.

"Not really. He was a little surprised . . . and disappointed."

"How did you explain your sudden visit?"

"I just said it's all blown up at home, and I decided I'd better take out what little I could before the coppers learned of this lot."

"Did he offer any explanation of how some of it's got out around Bangkok?"

"Well . . ." Singer drawled, with just a hint of his old evasiveness, it seemed to Hornbuckle. "I couldn't very well let on I *knew* that, could I?"

"Bingo!" exclaimed Collins. He was pulling bound packets of twenty-dollar bills from the knapsack and spreading them over the bed. He grinned up at his colleague. "I believe we've hit the jackpot!"

"Yes," mused Hornbuckle.

The two spent the next several hours counting the notes, Singer sitting by, disconsolate and restless. The final tally came to 6587 notes—face value $131,740.

Hornbuckle said to Singer, "We appear short by almost twenty thousand dollars. You did say you'd packaged up a hundred and fifty thousand to ship out here?"

"About that, give or take a few dollars."

The detective peered across at Singer. Could he have pocketed those notes himself, or privately made a deal with Veera, or with Arthur Ford? There really wasn't much Hornbuckle could do about it, after all. He doubted any more value could be squeezed out of Singer. Nor could he properly go after Veera—the Thai was out of his jurisdiction. In all, now, something in excess of 590,000 bogus twenties had been recovered, he figured—a total face value near the estimated twelve million dollars' worth printed. And that estimate probably was not precise. No investigation ever wound up without some loose end, and that should go double for one of such scope as this had been. For all practical purposes, the case was wrapped up now. It was time to quit it and go home.

EPILOGUE

ALAN WRAY AND Roger Gilbert were first to be tried—in September 1974 in the district court, Zurich. Wray's left arm was in a cast and sling, fractured in a fall during exercises in the Regensdorf prison courtyard. A wall seemed to have risen between him and Gilbert; they spoke only when necessary and otherwise stayed apart. In an opening statement, when asked by the judge what plans he contemplated when and if released, Gilbert said he hoped at first to go to England to work and reorient himself, and then added gratuitously that one thing he had promised himself—and his parents—was never to have anything more to do with Alan Wray. The other, asked the same question, said he, too, planned to return to England eventually; and he agreed with Gilbert, though in a sadder and less dogmatic way, that it was best that they not associate in future.

Both men straightforwardly admitted their respective guilt without hedging. The prosecutor asked them incredulously if they hadn't realized that disposing successfully of their more than five thousand twenties would have required spending no less than fourteen of them each day for a full year. Gilbert disparaged himself as "probably one of the stupidest men in the world"; and Wray, who acknowledged himself as the dominant of the two, said, "We just did not know what we were doing—we were two complete idiots!" Wray no longer had any qualms about citing his friend John Singer as the one who had seduced him into the undertaking.

Their court-appointed attorneys, while not disputing the guilt of either confessed defendant, separately made similar appeals for light punishment. Aside from the established facts that neither was a habitual or hardened criminal, and that indeed they had been extraordinarily naïve and amateurish in attempting to execute their illicit intent, counsel argued that the crime perpetrated was, in the final analysis, minimal: only four illegal notes had been passed by them, in face value eighty U.S. dollars (about 260 Swiss francs). The accused had already been held in custody for almost nine months.

The court in essence agreed with the defense. Gilbert and Wray both were found guilty of having introduced forged currency, in violation of the Swiss penal code, and were acquitted of the charge of professional fraud. Gilbert was sentenced to fourteen months in prison and Wray to eighteen months, such penalties to be suspended under three years' probation for each. They were to be jointly responsible both for court costs and for reimbursement in francs to the shopkeepers bilked by the counterfeit notes. Finally, both were ordered expelled from Switzerland forthwith and prohibited reentry for a period of ten years.

Roger Gilbert was escorted to the Zurich airport and put aboard a plane to London. Alan Wray was permitted to depart by train to West Germany.

In the time since, the Australian police have heard that Gilbert may have remained in his homeland, but he has given them no cause to verify that. As for Wray, at last report he was traveling widely, apparently having not yet found a spot to light and sink new roots. Officially, his whereabouts are unknown—evidently a self-sentenced expatriate.

AFTER THE INITIAL court hearing in April 1974, the trial of the four accused in Melbourne had been postponed time and again by one excuse or motion after another. Finally, fourteen months following their arrests, Charles Zuker, Kyriakos Papadimitropoulos, Nick Kypraios and Petros Lyberakis were ordered to appear together on April 7, 1975. When the court convened that day, however, one of them was absent: Petros Lyberakis. Marshals sent to search him out found only frustration: the last trace of him in Melbourne that could be verified had been two weeks earlier, shortly after the judicial order had set April 7 as the trial date. Lyberakis had skipped.

Interpol sections were alerted around the world; the consensus was that Europe would have been Lyberakis' most likely destination, but of course he might have fled anywhere, even to America. There was a report he'd been spotted briefly in Rome, then a confirmation that he was in Paris. But in each instance, if indeed the sightings were reliable, he melted away.

In Melbourne, millionaire Charles Zuker, furious over having been left, as he saw it, holding the bag, sent two lawyers abroad on a whirlwind private investigation. When the pair pestered authorities in Athens to step up efforts, they were advised tersely to get on the next plane out of Greece and not return soon.

The trial began at the end of April without Lyberakis, regarded by the prosecution as the key conspirator. The central figure remaining was Zuker—not only because of his local prominence and his wealth but also because an aura of mystery had crept over the case, with rumors of his involvement in some international political intrigue. There was much talk outside the courtroom that Big Charlie was a dedicated supporter of a secret political organization, for which the anticipated counterfeiting profits, if not the fake notes themselves, had really been destined. He would go to jail, people said, before betraying the identity or aims of that operation.

Until just before the trial opened, John Maxwell Singer had been treated—as much for his own protection as for legal advantage—as one of those indicted. Meanwhile, however, he'd been giving exhaustive depositions to the authorities about all he knew of the conspiracy and of its other participants. Finally, at a strategic moment, the state's attorney general withdrew Singer from among the codefendants and he was granted immunity from prosecution in this case—designated thenceforth only a co-conspirator. While the trial was in session, it was difficult to gauge exactly how the jury was responding to the glib Singer's damning recitation. But it could hardly fail to influence the panel's judgment of Zuker, and of the absent Petros Lyberakis in particular.

Nick Kypraios had no functional defense. The sensitive printer-artist was no doubt naïve, impressionable and too easily manipulated, and he'd been frightened. But he did not gainsay that, so far as the charges against him went, he was guilty. He could only put himself at the mercy of the court.

Kyriakos Papadimitropoulos, who pleaded not guilty, put his entire defense in the assertion that he was an unknowing victim of the duplicity of Petros Lyberakis—whom he had trusted as a family friend and who had treacherously deceived him. The bulk of evidence against Papadimitropoulos was the discovery of the greatest quantity of the forged notes on the premises of his factory. But his counsel produced witnesses who testified that they had seen Lyberakis alone deliver the trunks in which the notes were later found, and that Papadimitropoulos had not shown any secretiveness about the trunks, indicating his lack of concern or awareness of their volatile contents—even after Lyberakis personally had installed a lock on the upstairs room. No one had ever seen the accused enter that room until the police came. And there was indeed no evidence whatever that Papadimitropoulos had touched any of the forged notes. He was a hardworking businessman, a devoted husband and father, and he'd never before had the slightest brush with the law.

Charles Zuker pleaded guilty to conspiring to print and distribute counterfeit notes with intent to defraud.

Nick Kypraios was found guilty of having forged the illicit notes with similar intent to defraud. The panel included a strong recommendation of clemency for Kypraios.

Kyriakos Papadimitropoulos was acquitted of all charges and released.

Petros Lyberakis, the real culprit, all seemed to agree, had escaped his just deserts.

On June 4 Mr. Justice Murphy pronounced sentence on Kypraios and Zuker. Kypraios was given three years on each of two counts and ordered imprisoned for a minimum of two years before being eligible for parole.

As for Zuker, the judge first heard a plea from his counsel that due to gross overweight his client had serious medical problems, including diabetes, that would make imprisonment difficult for him. Mr. Justice Murphy said he had considered that, and before determining sentence had consulted with both state health and penal officials, who assured him that prison medical facilities were entirely adequate to attend to Zuker's condition.

Murphy looked down severely upon the prisoner: Charles Zuker was a millionaire in his own right, the judge said, rebuking him, yet it was in the end his greed and a latent dishonesty that were responsible for furtherance of this base enterprise, in particular for the exceedingly great number of notes forged. The judge had no doubt that the "archcriminal in this conspiracy" was the absent Petros Lyberakis; and he accepted that in the beginning Zuker really may have thought he was financing a legitimate business. But there was nothing to contradict the evidence that when Zuker became aware of the true intent of the business, he had encouraged and abetted the other conspirators to proceed on an even larger scale. Nor, Murphy continued, was there any evident contradiction of the persuasive accounts of John Singer—"that traitorous informer," the judge characterized the crown's star witness—in detailing Zuker's self-interest.

Therefore, the forty-seven-year-old capitalist would receive the maximum sentence allowable in the instance: imprisonment for five years, to serve no less than four before becoming eligible for parole.

As LATE AS November 1981, Petros Lyberakis had yet to be run down. All charges were still open against him in Australia. Interpol keeps him in its active fugitive file.

Considerable sympathy had been generated at the trial for the hapless printer Nick Kypraios—and, coincidentally, a flush of unaccustomed interest in him as an expressionist painter. Once late in 1975 and twice the following year, artworks of Kypraios' were featured in shows honoring Greek-Australian artists. More than a year later Melbourne's Lito Gallery opened a month-long exhibition of Kypraios' paintings.

In an opinion written for the exhibition brochure, artist Georg Mihelakakis delivered high praise of Kypraios, particularly for his newer works, in which were detected a "poetic-dreamlike quality" reminiscent of the great Marc Chagall. The critic interpreted Kypraios as preoccupied with those "human situations . . . those difficulties and mainly those disappointments with which we meet in everyday life. . . . In his work he has faced the truth and has refused to take the easy way out, which would be to cover up reality." But the critic also saw conflicting forces in Kypraios' work: this raw, unselfconscious portrayal of the ugliness of the society in which he lived; and yet a softer, more hopeful vision of beauty influenced by religious mythology. "Regardless of whether the subject of the painting is religious, or a vase of flowers, or a grotesque human being, the same feelings of loneliness, the same sadness, the same mystery are experienced by the painter and are reflected in his work. . . . He paints human faces so that they reflect the tragic truth of his life, which is consumed in a passion of artistic creativity. In the words of a French philosopher 'a life is slowly eaten away by outward duty and inward necessity.' "

The location of the Lito Gallery, with its sober celebration of the art of Nick Kypraios, was ironically appropriate: on Victoria Street in Abbotsford, around a corner from his former Icono Graphics printing plant.

ILLUSTRATION CREDITS